Excel 2003 Bible

Excel 2003 Bible

John Walkenbach

WILEY

Wiley Publishing, Inc.

Excel 2003 Bible

Published by
Wiley Publishing, Inc.
10475 Crosspoint Boulevard
Indianapolis, IN 46256
www.wiley.com

ISBN: 0-7645-3967-1

Manufactured in the United States of America

10 9 8 7 6

1B/RY/QZ/QT/IN

For general information on our other products and services or to obtain technical support, please contact our Customer Care Department within the U.S. at (800) 762-2974, outside the U.S. at (317) 572-3993 or fax (317) 572-4002.

Wiley also publishes its books in a variety of electronic formats. Some content that appears in print may not be available in electronic books.

Library of Congress Control Number: 2003101915

About the Author

John Walkenbach is the author of approximately three dozen spreadsheet books. Visit his Web site at http://.j-walk.com.

Credits

Acquisitions Manager
Gregory S. Croy

Project Editor
Linda Morris

Technical Editor
Bill Manville

Senior Copy Editor
Diana R. Conover

Editorial Manager
Kevin Kirschner

Vice President & Executive Group Publisher
Richard Swadley

Vice President and Publisher
Andy Cummings

Editorial Director
Mary C. Corder

Project Coordinator
Erin Smith

Graphics and Production Specialists
Carrie Foster
LeAndra Hosier
Michael Kruzil
Lynsey Osborn
Heather Pope
Mary Gillot Virgin

Quality Control Technicians
Laura Albert
Susan Moritz
Carl William Pierce
Brian H. Walls

Senior Permissions Editor
Carmen Krikorian

Media Development Specialist
Greg Stafford

Proofreading and Indexing
TECHBOOKS Production Services

Preface

Thanks for purchasing the *Excel 2003 Bible.* My goal in writing this book is to share with you some of what I know about Excel, and in the process, make you more efficient on the job.

The book contains everything that you need to know to learn the basics of Excel and then move on to more advanced topics at your own pace. You'll find many useful examples and lots of tips and tricks that I've accumulated over the years.

Is This Book for You?

The *Bible* series from Wiley Publishing, Inc. is designed for beginning, intermediate, and advanced users. This book covers all the essential components of Excel and provides clear and practical examples that you can adapt to your own needs.

In this book, I've tried to maintain a good balance between the basics that every Excel user needs to know and the more complex topics that will appeal to power users. I've used Excel for many years, and I realize that almost everyone still has something to learn (including myself). My goal is to make that learning an enjoyable process.

Software Versions

This book was written for Excel 2003 for Windows. However, Excel hasn't really changed much lately, so most of the information also applies to earlier versions and also to the Macintosh version. If you use a version prior to Excel 97, you'll find that a significant portion of this book does not apply.

Conventions This Book Uses

Take a minute to scan this section to learn some of the typographical and organizational conventions that this book uses.

Excel commands

In Excel, as in all Windows programs, you select commands from the pull-down menu system. In this book, such commands appear in normal typeface. An option available under a particular menu is indicated after an ➪ symbol, as in "Choose File ➪ Print to print your document."

Filenames, named ranges, and your input

Input that you make from the keyboard appears in bold. Named ranges may appear in a `code font`. Lengthy input usually appears on a separate line. For instance, I may instruct you to enter a formula such as the following:

```
="Part Name: " &VLOOKUP(PartNumber,PartList,2)
```

Key names

Names of the keys on your keyboard appear in normal type. When two keys should be pressed simultaneously, they are connected with a plus sign, like this: "Press Alt+E to select the Edit menu." Here are the key names as I refer to them throughout the book:

Alt	down arrow	Num Lock	right arrow
Backspace	End	Pause	Scroll Lock
Caps Lock	Home	PgDn	Shift
Ctrl	Insert	PgUp	Tab
Delete	left arrow	Print Screen	up arrow

Functions

Excel's built-in worksheet functions appear in uppercase, like this: "Enter a SUM formula in cell C20."

Mouse conventions

You'll come across some of the following mouse-related terms, all standard fare:

✦ **Mouse pointer:** The small graphic figure that moves onscreen when you move your mouse. The mouse pointer is usually an arrow, but it changes shape when you move to certain areas of the screen or when you're performing certain actions.

✦ **Point:** Move the mouse so that the mouse pointer is on a specific item: for example, "Point to the Save button on the toolbar."

✦ **Press:** Press the left mouse button once and keep it pressed. Normally, this is used when dragging.

✦ **Click:** Press the left mouse button once and release it immediately.

✦ **Right-click:** Press the right mouse button once and release it immediately. The right mouse button is used in Excel to pop up shortcut menus that are appropriate for whatever is currently selected.

✦ **Double-click:** Press the left mouse button twice in rapid succession. If your double-clicking doesn't seem to be working, you can adjust the double-click sensitivity by using the Windows Control Panel icon.

✦ **Drag:** Press the left mouse button and keep it pressed while you move the mouse. Dragging is often used to select a range of cells or to change the size of an object.

What the Icons Mean

Throughout the book, you'll see special graphic symbols, or icons, in the left margin. These call your attention to points that are particularly important or relevant to a specific group of readers. The icons in this book are as follows:

This icon signals the fact that something is important or worth noting. Notes may alert you to a concept that helps you master the task at hand, or they may denote something that is fundamental to understanding subsequent material.

This icon marks a more efficient way of doing something that may not be obvious.

I use this symbol when a possibility exists that the operation we're describing could cause problems if you're not careful.

This icon indicates that a related topic is discussed elsewhere in the book.

This icon indicates that a related example or file is available on the companion CD-ROM.

This icon indicates a feature that is new to Excel 2003.

How This Book Is Organized

Notice that the book is divided into six main parts, followed by five appendixes.

Part I: Getting Started With Excel: This part consists of seven chapters that provide background about Excel. These chapters are considered required reading for Excel newcomers, but even experienced users will probably find some new information here.

Part II: Working with Formulas and Functions: The chapters in Part II cover everything that you need to know to become proficient with performing calculations in Excel.

Part III: Creating Charts and Graphics: The chapters in Part III describe how to create effective charts as well as use graphics in your workbooks.

Part IV: Analyzing Data with Excel: Data analysis is the focus of the chapters in Part IV. Users of all levels will find some of these chapters of interest.

Part V: Using Advanced Excel Features: This part consists of nine chapters dealing with topics that are sometimes considered advanced. However, many beginning and intermediate users may find this information useful as well.

Part VI: Programming Excel with VBA: Part VI is for those who want to customize Excel for their own use or who are designing workbooks or add-ins that are to be used by others. It starts with an introduction to VBA programming and then provides coverage of UserForms, add-ins, toolbars, menus, and events.

Part VII: Appendixes: Part VII contains a wide variety of appendixes that cover everything from Excel worksheet functions, to the contents of the book's CD-ROM, to some fun games and diversions created using Excel.

How to Use This Book

This book is not intended to be read cover to cover. Rather, it's a reference book that you can consult when:

✦ You're stuck while trying to do something.

✦ You need to do something that you've never done before.

✦ You have some time on your hands, and you're interested in learning something new.

The index is comprehensive, and each chapter typically focuses on a single broad topic. If you're just starting out with Excel, I recommend that you read the first few chapters to gain a basic understanding of the product and then do some experimenting on your own. After you become familiar with Excel's environment, you can refer to the chapters that interest you most. Some users, however, may prefer to follow the chapters in order.

Don't be discouraged if some of the material is over your head. Most users get by just fine by using only a small subset of Excel's total capabilities. In fact, the 80/20 rule applies here: 80 percent of Excel users use only 20 percent of its features. However, using only 20 percent of Excel's features still gives you lots of power at your fingertips.

New Features in Excel 2003

This section briefly describes the new features in Excel 2003, relative to Excel 2002. Where applicable, I provide additional details later in this book. You'll notice that the list is surprisingly short.

XML support

Excel 2003 has improved support for XML (eXtensible Markup Language). This means that you can import XML data and assign the data elements to specific cells in a worksheet.

List ranges

You can define a portion of a workbook as a list range. This may make it a bit easier to work with the list—for example, add new items and summary formulas. You can also export the list range to SharePoint Team Services to share it with others. The list on a Web site based on SharePoint Team Services can be linked to the original range of cells.

Research Pane

A new feature, Research Pane, lets you search standard reference books and Web sites by using Excel's Task Pane.

Smart tag improvements

In the past, smart tags could either be turned on or off. It's now possible to enable smart tags only for a specified range of cells.

Statistical functions

Advanced users often complain about the inaccuracy of some of Excel's statistical functions. Microsoft claims to have corrected these long-standing problems.

What's on the Companion CD and Web Site

Wiley has provided so much add-on value to this book that we couldn't fit it all on one CD! With the purchase of this book, you not only get access to over 200 bonus software programs and demos, but you also get an entire eBook—free!

Please take a few minutes to explore the bonus material included on the CD:

+ **Author-created materials:** Demonstration and sample files from the book.

+ **Bonus software materials:** Over 200 programs (shareware, freeware, GNU software, trials, demos, and evaluation software) that work with Office. A ReadMe file on the CD includes complete descriptions of each software item.

+ *Office 2003 Super Bible* **eBook:** Wiley created this special eBook, consisting of over 500 pages of content about how Microsoft Office components work together and with other products. The content has been pulled from select chapters of the individual Office *Bible* titles. In addition, some original content has been created just for this *Super Bible*.

+ **PDF version of this title:** As always, if you prefer your text in electronic format, the CD offers a completely searchable, PDF version of the book that you hold in your hands.

After you familiarize yourself with all that we have packed onto the CD, be sure to visit the companion Web site at `www.wiley.com/compbooks/officebibles2003/`. Here's what you'll find on the Web site:

+ Links to all the software that wouldn't fit onto the CD

+ Links to all the software found on the CD

+ Complete, detailed tables of contents for all the Wiley Office 2003 *Bibles: Access 2003 Bible, Excel 2003 Bible, FrontPage 2003 Bible, Office 2003 Bible, Outlook 2003 Bible, PowerPoint Bible,* and *Word 2003 Bible*

+ Links to other Wiley Office titles

Contents at a Glance

Contents

Part II: Working with Formulas and Functions   139

Part III: Creating Charts and Graphics 337

Part IV: Analyzing Data with Excel 435

Chapter 19: Working with Lists 437

Part VII: Appendixes   785

Getting Started with Excel

The chapters in this part are intended to provide essential background information for working with Excel. Here you'll see how to make use of the basic features that are required for every Excel user. If you've used Excel (or even a different spreadsheet program) in the past, much of this information may seem like review. Even so, it's possible that you'll find quite a few tricks and techniques.

Introducing Excel

This chapter serves as an introductory overview of Excel. It is intended primarily for those who have no experience with this product. But even if you're already familiar with Excel, you may find a few new wrinkles here. If you're moving up from Excel 2002, you'll also find a quick summary of the new features in Excel 2003.

What Is It Good For?

Excel, as you probably know, is a spreadsheet program and is part of the Microsoft Office suite. Several other spreadsheet programs are available, but Excel is by far the most popular.

Much of the appeal of Excel is due to the fact that it's so versatile. Excel's forte, of course, is performing numerical calculations, but Excel is also very useful for non-numerical applications. Here are just a few of the uses for Excel:

✦ **Number crunching:** Create budgets, analyze survey results, and perform just about any type of financial analysis you can think of.

✦ **Creating charts:** Create a wide variety of highly customizable charts.

✦ **Organizing lists:** Use the row-and-column layout to store lists efficiently.

✦ **Accessing other data:** Import data from a wide variety of sources.

✦ **Creating graphics and diagrams:** Use Excel AutoShapes to create simple (and not-so-simple) diagrams.

✦ **Automating complex tasks:** Perform a tedious task with a single mouse click with Excel's macro capabilities.

Understanding Workbooks and Worksheets

The work you do in Excel is performed in a workbook file, which appears in its own window. You can have as many workbooks open as you need. By default, workbooks use an XLS file extension.

Each *workbook* is comprised of one or more worksheets, and each *worksheet* is made up of individual *cells*. Each cell contains a value, a formula, or text. Each worksheet is accessible by clicking the *tab* at the bottom of the workbook. In addition, workbooks can store chart sheets. A *chart sheet* displays a single chart and is also accessible by clicking a tab.

Newcomers to Excel are often intimidated by all of the different elements that appear within Excel's window. You'll soon see that the Excel screen really isn't all that difficult to understand after you learn what the various pieces do.

Figure 1-1 shows you the more important bits and pieces of Excel. As you look at the figure, refer to Table 1-1 for a brief explanation of the items shown in the figure.

Table 1-1
Parts of the Excel Screen That You Need to Know

Name	Description
Active cell indicator	This dark outline indicates the currently active cell (one of the 16,777,216 cells on each worksheet).
Application close button	Clicking this button closes Excel.
Window close button	Clicking this button closes the active workbook window.
Column headings	Letters range from A to IV—one for each of the 256 columns in the worksheet. After column Z comes column AA, which is followed by AB, AC, and so on. After column AZ comes BA, BB, and so on until you get to the last column, labeled IV. You can click a column heading to select an entire column of cells.
Formula bar	When you enter information or formulas into Excel, they appear in this line.
Horizontal scrollbar	Enables you to scroll the sheet horizontally.

Name	*Description*
Maximize/Restore button	Clicking this button increases the workbook window's size to fill Excel's complete workspace. If the window is already maximized, clicking this button "unmaximizes" Excel's window so that it no longer fills the entire screen.
Menu bar	This is Excel's main menu. Clicking a word on the menu drops down a list of menu items, which is one way for you to issue a command to Excel.
Minimize application button	Clicking this button minimizes Excel's window.
Minimize window button	Clicking this button minimizes the workbook window.
Name box	Displays the active cell address or the name of the selected cell, range, or object.
Row headings	Numbers range from 1 to 65,536—one for each row in the worksheet. You can click a row heading to select an entire row of cells.
Sheet tabs	Each of these notebook-like tabs represents a different sheet in the workbook. A workbook can have any number of sheets, and each sheet has its name displayed in a sheet tab. By default, each new workbook that you create contains three sheets.
Tab scroll buttons	These buttons let you scroll the sheet tabs to display tabs that aren't visible.
Status bar	This bar displays various messages as well as the status of the Num Lock, Caps Lock, and Scroll Lock keys on your keyboard.
Task pane	This pane displays options that are relevant to the task you are performing.
Task pane selector	Clicking here enables you to select from different task panes so you can open workbooks, use the Office Clipboard, or work with XML data.
Title bar	All Windows programs have a title bar, which displays the name of the program and holds some control buttons that you can use to modify the window.
Toolbars	The toolbars hold buttons that you click to issue commands to Excel. Some of the buttons expand to show additional buttons or commands.
Vertical scrollbar	Lets you scroll the sheet vertically.

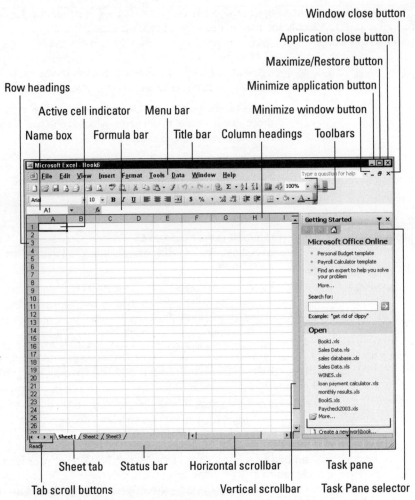

Figure 1-1: The Excel screen has many useful elements that you will use often.

Moving Around a Worksheet

This section describes various ways to navigate through the cells in a worksheet. Every worksheet consists of rows (numbered 1 through 65,536) and columns (labeled A through IV). After column Z comes column AA; after column AZ comes column BA, and so on. The intersection of a row and a column is a single cell. At any given time, one cell is the *active cell*. You can identify the active cell by its darker border, as shown in Figure 1-2. Its address (its column letter and row number) appears in the Name box. Depending on the technique that you use to navigate through a workbook, you may or may not change the active cell when you navigate.

Tip   The row and column headings of the active cell are displayed in different colors to make it easier to identify the row and column of the active cell.

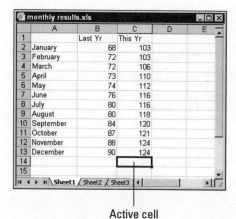

Figure 1-2: The active cell is the cell with the dark border — in this case, cell C14.

Active cell

Navigating with your keyboard

As you probably already know, you can use the standard navigational keys on your keyboard to move around a worksheet. These keys work just as you would expect: The down arrow moves the active cell down one row, the right arrow moves it one column to the right, and so on. PgUp and PgDn move the active cell up or down one full window. (The actual number of rows moved depends on the number of rows displayed in the window.)

Tip   You can scroll through the worksheet without changing the active cell by turning on Scroll Lock. This can be useful if you need to view another area of your worksheet and then quickly return to your original location. Just press Scroll Lock and use the direction keys to scroll through the worksheet. When you want to return to the original position (the active cell), press Ctrl+Backspace. Then, press Scroll Lock again to turn it off. When Scroll Lock is turned on, Excel displays SCRL in the status bar at the bottom of the window.

The Num Lock key on your keyboard controls how the keys on the numeric keypad behave. When Num Lock is on, Excel displays NUM in the status bar, and the keys on your numeric keypad generate numbers. Most keyboards have a separate set of navigational (arrow) keys located to the left of the numeric keypad. These keys are not affected by the state of the Num Lock key.

Table 1-2 summarizes all the worksheet movement keys available in Excel.

Table 1-2
Excel's Worksheet Movement Keys

Key	Action
Up arrow	Moves the active cell up one row
Down arrow	Moves the active cell down one row
Left arrow	Moves the active cell one column to the left
Right arrow	Moves the active cell one column to the right
PgUp	Moves the active cell up one screen
PgDn	Moves the active cell down one screen
Alt+PgDn	Moves the active cell right one screen
Alt+PgUp	Moves the active cell left one screen
Ctrl+Backspace	Scrolls to display the active cell
Up arrow*	Scrolls the screen up one row (active cell does not change)
Down arrow*	Scrolls the screen down one row (active cell does not change)
Left arrow*	Scrolls the screen left one column (active cell does not change)
Right arrow*	Scrolls the screen right one column (active cell does not change)

* With Scroll Lock on

Navigating with your mouse

To change the active cell by using the mouse, click another cell; it becomes the active cell. If the cell that you want to activate is not visible in the workbook window, you can use the scrollbars to scroll the window in any direction. To scroll one cell, click either of the arrows on the scrollbar. To scroll by a complete screen, click either side of the scrollbar's scroll box. You also can drag the scroll box for faster scrolling.

Tip   If your mouse has a wheel on it, you can use the mouse wheel to scroll vertically. Also, if you click the wheel and move the mouse in any direction, the worksheet scrolls automatically in that direction. The more you move the mouse, the faster the scrolling. If you prefer to use the mouse wheel to zoom the worksheet, select Tools ⇨ Options, click the General tab, and then select the Zoom on Roll with IntelliMouse check box.

Using the scrollbars or scrolling with your mouse doesn't change the active cell. It simply scrolls the worksheet. To change the active cell, you must click a new cell after scrolling.

Using the Excel Menus and Toolbars

If you've used other software, you will have no problem adapting to Excel. Its user interface (that is, the menus and toolbars) offers few surprises, and they work just like the other programs you've used.

In many cases, you can issue a particular command in several different ways. For example, if you want to save your workbook, you can use the menu (the File ➪ Save command), a shortcut menu (right-click the workbook's title bar and click Save), a toolbar button (the Save button on the Standard toolbar), or a shortcut key combination (Ctrl+S). The particular method you use is up to you.

Using menus

Excel, like most other Windows programs, has a menu bar located directly below the title bar (see Figure 1-3). This menu bar is always available and ready for your command. The Excel menus change, depending on what you're doing. For example, if you're working with a chart, the menus change to give you options that are appropriate for a chart. This all happens automatically, so you don't even have to think about it.

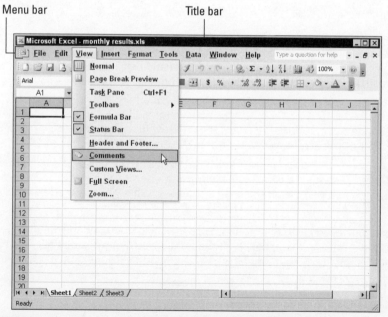

Figure 1-3: When you click an Excel menu, you gain access to the commands that tell the program what you want to do.

Using the menu is quite straightforward. Click the menu that you want to open, and it drops down to display menu items. Click the menu item to issue the command.

Tip   To issue a menu command from the keyboard, press Alt and then the menu's hot key. (The *hot key* is the underlined letter in the menu.) You can then press the appropriate hot key for a command on the menu. For example, to issue the Print command on the File menu, press Alt+F, followed by P.

Some menu items lead to an additional submenu; when you click the menu item, the submenu appears to its right. Menu items that have a submenu display a small triangle. For example, the View ➪ Toolbars command has a submenu, as shown earlier in Figure 1-3. Excel's designers incorporated submenus primarily to keep the menus from becoming too lengthy and overwhelming to users.

Sometimes, you'll notice that a menu item appears grayed out. This simply means that the menu item isn't appropriate for what you're doing. Nothing happens if you try to select such a menu item.

Menu items that are followed by an ellipsis (three dots) always display a dialog box. Menu commands that don't have an ellipsis are executed immediately. For example, the File ➪ Open command results in a dialog box because Excel needs more information about the command. Excel doesn't need any more information to execute the File ➪ Print Preview command, so Excel performs this command immediately, without displaying a dialog box.

Tip   The Excel menu bar is actually a toolbar in disguise. Consequently, you can move it to a new location if you prefer. To move the menu bar, just click the set of vertical gray dashes at the left side of the menu bar and drag it to its new location. You can drag the menu bar to any of the window borders or leave it free-floating.

Changing Your Mind

Just about every command in Excel can be reversed by using the Edit ➪ Undo command. Select Edit ➪ Undo after issuing a command in error, and it's as if you never issued the command. You can reverse the effects of the last 16 commands that you executed by selecting Edit ➪ Undo more than once.

Rather than use Edit ➪ Undo, you may prefer to use the Undo button on the Standard toolbar. If you click the arrow on the right side of the button, you can see a description of the commands that can be reversed. In addition, you can press Ctrl+Z to undo the last action.

The Redo button performs in the opposite direction of the Undo button: Redo repeats commands that have been undone.

Tip When you click a menu, you may find that not all of the menu items are displayed. If this is the case, the *adaptive menu option* is in effect. I highly recommend that you turn off this option. To do so, choose View ⇨ Toolbars ⇨ Customize. In the Customize dialog box, click the Options tab and make sure that a check mark is next to Always Show Full Menus. Note to Microsoft: This is, without a doubt, the dumbest option you guys have ever come up with!

Using shortcut menus

Besides the omnipresent menu bar, Excel features a slew of shortcut menus, which you access by right-clicking just about anything within Excel. Shortcut menus don't contain every relevant command, just those that are most commonly used for whatever is selected.

As an example, Figure 1-4 shows the shortcut menu that appears when you right-click a cell. The shortcut menu appears at the mouse-pointer position, which makes selecting a command fast and efficient. The shortcut menu that appears depends on what you're doing at the time. For example, if you're working with a chart, the right-click shortcut menu contains commands that are pertinent to what is selected.

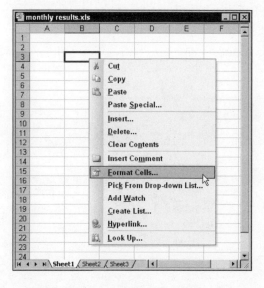

Figure 1-4: Click the right mouse button to display a shortcut menu with the commands that you are most likely to use.

Using shortcut keys

Some menu items also have shortcut keys associated with them. For example, the File ⇨ Save command's shortcut key combination is Ctrl+S. As you use Excel, you'll find that learning the shortcut keys for commands you use often can save you a lot of time.

The best way to learn the shortcut keys is to watch for them on the Excel menus. The most useful ones display next to the menu item when you open the menus.

Using toolbars

Excel includes convenient toolbars that provide another way of issuing commands. In many cases, a toolbar button is simply a substitute for a menu command. For example, the Copy button is a substitute for Edit ⇨ Copy. Some toolbar buttons, however, don't have a menu equivalent. One example is the AutoSum button, which automatically inserts a formula to calculate the sum of a range of cells.

To learn what the toolbar buttons do, you can hold the mouse pointer over a toolbar button (but don't click it). A small box that tells you the name of the button appears. Often, this provides enough information for you to determine whether the button is what you want. If these toolbar tips do not display, choose Tools ⇨ Customize to display the Customize dialog box. Click the Options tab, and place a check mark next to Show ScreenTips on Toolbars.

Table 1-3 lists some of Excel's more useful built-in toolbars.

Table 1-3 Excel's Most Useful Built-In Toolbars	
Toolbar	*Use*
Standard	Issues commonly used commands
Formatting	Changes how your worksheet or chart looks
Borders	Adds borders around selected areas
Chart	Manipulates charts
Drawing	Inserts or edits drawings on a worksheet
Control Toolbox	Adds controls (buttons, spinners, and so on) to a worksheet
Formula Auditing	Identifies errors in your worksheet
Picture	Inserts or edits graphic images
PivotTable	Works with pivot tables

Toolbar	Use
Protection	Controls what types of changes can be made in your worksheet
Reviewing	Provides tools to use workbooks in groups
Text to Speech	Provides tools to read aloud cell contents
Web	Provides tools to access the Internet from Excel
WordArt	Inserts or edits a picture composed of words

Hiding or showing toolbars

By default, Excel displays two toolbars (named Standard and Formatting). You have complete control over which toolbars are displayed and where they are located. In addition, you can create custom toolbars, made up of buttons that you find most useful.

To hide or display a particular toolbar, choose View ➪ Toolbars or right-click any toolbar. Either of these actions displays a list of common toolbars (but not all toolbars). The toolbars that have a check mark next to them are currently visible. To hide a toolbar, click it to remove the check mark. To display a toolbar, click it to add a check mark.

For control over *all* toolbars, select Tools ➪ Customize. In the Customize dialog box, click the Toolbars tab to display a list of all available toolbars. Place a check mark next to the toolbars that you want to be displayed.

Moving toolbars

Toolbars can be moved to any of the four sides of the Excel window, or they can be free-floating. A free-floating toolbar can be dragged on-screen anywhere that you want. You also can change a toolbar's size simply by dragging any of its borders. To hide a free-floating toolbar, click its Close button.

Note When a toolbar isn't free-floating, it's said to be docked. A *docked toolbar* is stuck to the edge of the Excel window and doesn't have a title bar. Therefore, a docked toolbar can't be resized.

To move a docked toolbar, click the toolbar's vertical gray dashes and drag. To move a free-floating toolbar, click and drag the toolbar's title bar. When you drag a toolbar toward the window's edge, it automatically docks itself there. When a toolbar is docked, its shape changes to a single row or single column.

Working with Dialog Boxes

Many Excel commands display dialog boxes. In fact, all menu items that end with an ellipsis (three dots) display a dialog box. A dialog box is simply the Excel way of getting more information from you. For example, if you choose View ➪ Zoom (which changes the magnification of the worksheet), Excel can't carry out the command until it finds out from you what magnification level you want.

The Excel dialog boxes vary in how they work. A few of them can remain on-screen as you work (for example, the Find dialog box, which appears when you select Edit ➪ Find). But most of Excel's dialog boxes must be dismissed before you can do anything. If the dialog box obscures an area of your worksheet that you need to see, simply click the dialog box's title bar and drag the box to another location.

When a dialog box appears, you make your choices by manipulating the controls. When you're finished, click the OK button (or press Enter) to continue. If you change your mind, click the Cancel button (or press Esc), and nothing further happens — it's as if the dialog box never appeared.

Understanding dialog box controls

Most people find working with dialog boxes to be quite straightforward and natural. If you've used other programs, you'll feel right at home. The controls can be manipulated either with your mouse or directly from the keyboard.

Figure 1-5 shows the Print dialog box, which contains most of the common dialog box controls you'll encounter. Table 1-4 describes these controls and a few others you may encounter.

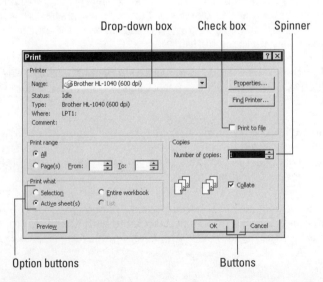

Figure 1-5: Use the dialog box controls to enter information and control the dialog box.

Table 1-4
Common Dialog Box Controls

Name	Description
Buttons	A button control is about as simple as it gets. Just click it, and it does its thing. Pressing the Alt key and the button's underlined letter is equivalent to clicking the button.
Option buttons	Option buttons are sometimes known as *radio* buttons because they work like the preset station buttons on an old-fashioned car radio. Like those car radios, only one option button at a time can be "pressed." When you click an option button, the previously selected option button is unselected. Option buttons usually are enclosed in a group box, and a single dialog box can have several sets of option buttons.
Check boxes	A check box control is used to indicate whether an option is on or off. Unlike option buttons, each check box is independent of the others. Clicking a check box toggles it on and off.
Range selection boxes	A range selection box enables you to specify a worksheet range by dragging inside the worksheet. A range selection box has a small button that, when clicked, collapses the dialog box to make it easier for you to select the range by dragging in the worksheet.
Spinners	A spinner control makes specifying a number easy. You can click the arrows to increment or decrement the displayed value. A spinner is almost always paired with an edit box. You can either enter the value directly into the edit box or use the spinner to change it to the desired value.
List boxes	A list box control contains a list of options from which you choose. If the list is longer than will fit in the list box, you can use its vertical scrollbar to scroll through the list.
Drop-down boxes	Drop-down boxes are similar to list boxes, but they show only a single option at a time. When you click the arrow on a drop-down box, the list drops down to display additional choices.

Navigating dialog boxes

Navigating dialog boxes is generally very easy—you simply click the control you wish to activate.

Although dialog boxes were designed with mouse users in mind, you can also use the keyboard. Every dialog box control has text associated with it, and this text always has one underlined letter (a *hot key* or *accelerator key*). You can access the control from the keyboard by pressing the Alt key and then the underlined letter. You also can use Tab to cycle through all the controls on a dialog box. Shift+Tab cycles through the controls in reverse order.

Tip When a control is selected, it appears with a darker outline. You can use the space-bar to activate a selected control.

Using tabbed dialog boxes

Many of Excel's dialog boxes are "tabbed" dialog boxes. A *tabbed dialog box* includes notebook-like tabs, each of which is associated with a different panel. When you click a tab, the dialog box changes to display a new panel containing a new set of controls. The Options dialog box, which appears in response to the Tools ➪ Options command, is a good example. This dialog box is shown in Figure 1-6; it has 13 tabs, which makes it functionally equivalent to 13 different dialog boxes.

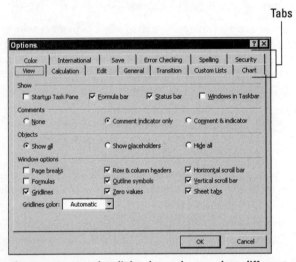

Figure 1-6: Use the dialog box tabs to select different functional areas in the dialog box.

Tabbed dialog boxes are quite convenient because you can make several changes in a single dialog box. After you make all of your setting changes, click OK or press Enter.

Tip To select a tab by using the keyboard, use Ctrl+PgUp or Ctrl+PgDn, or simply press the first letter of the tab that you want to activate.

Specifying Options in Excel: More Confusing Than It Should Be

Excel is a very flexible program, and it provides you with many options to control how it looks and works. But the problem is *finding* those options.

The Options dialog box is essentially Excel's junk drawer. With every new upgrade, the developers cram more options into this dialog box. This dialog box is a prime candidate for the cover of the *Journal of Bad User Interface Design*.

I've been using Excel for more than a decade, and when I bring up the Options dialog box, I still can't remember which tab to use. Typically, it will take two or three tab clicks to locate the desired option. But the main problem with the Options dialog box is inconsistency. Some of the options affect only the active sheet, and others affect Excel as a whole — and they are scattered all over the place, with no clear indication as to which is which.

To make matters worse, the Options dialog box contains a number of buttons that, when clicked, display other dialog boxes that contain even more options. Dig around in Excel's Options dialog box, and you'll find buttons that display a half dozen other dialog boxes.

But wait! There's more. Don't forget about the Customize dialog box (Tools ⇨ Customize). Here you'll find still more options, which are not accessible from the Options dialog box. I'm not done yet. When you save a workbook, the Save As dialog box leads to even more options, accessible via the Tools menu in the dialog box. I'm sure most Excel users could never find this dialog box even if they knew what they were looking for.

We old-timers have grown accustomed to this user-interface nightmare, and we tend to take it in stride. But I have deep and sincere pity for the new user who simply wants to change a few things — and ends up on an unexpected adventure that may or may not be successful.

Every new release of Excel provides Microsoft with an opportunity to clean up this confusing mess, and they most certainly have the resources to do so. But, for some reason, Microsoft just keeps cramming more stuff into the junk drawer.

Creating Your First Excel Worksheet

This section presents an introductory hands-on session with Excel. If you haven't used Excel, you may want to follow along on your computer to get a feel for how this program works.

In this example, you'll create a simple monthly sales projection table along with a chart.

Getting started on your worksheet

To begin, launch Excel by using the Windows Start button. You'll be greeted with an empty workbook.

The sales projection will consist of two columns of information. Column A will contain the month names, and column B will store the projected sales numbers. You begin by entering some descriptive titles into the worksheet. Here's how to begin:

1. Move the cell pointer to cell A1 by using the direction keys. The Name box displays the cell's address.

2. Enter **Month** into cell A1. Just type the text and then press Enter. Depending on your setup, Excel either moves the cell pointer to a different cell, or the pointer remains in cell A1.

3. Move the cell pointer to B1, type **Projected Sales**, and press Enter.

Filling in the month names

In this step, you enter the month names in column A.

1. Move the cell pointer to A2 and type **Jan** (an abbreviation for January).

   At this point, you could enter the other month name abbreviations manually, but we'll let Excel do some of the work by taking advantage of the AutoFill feature.

2. Make sure that cell A2 is selected. Notice that the active cell is displayed with a heavy outline. At the bottom-right corner of the outline, you'll see a small square known as the *fill handle*. Move your mouse pointer over the fill handle, click, and drag down until you've highlighted from A2 down to A13. Release the mouse button, and Excel will automatically fill in the month names.

Your worksheet should resemble the one shown in Figure 1-7.

Figure 1-7: Your worksheet, after entering the column headings and month names.

Entering the sales data

Assume that January's sales are projected to be $50,000 and that sales will increase by 2.5 percent in each of the subsequent months.

1. Move the cell pointer to B2 and type **$50,000**, the projected sales for January. If your currency symbol is not a dollar sign, substitute the appropriate currency symbol.

2. To enter a formula to calculate the projected sales for February, move to cell B3 and enter the following: **=B2*102.5%**. When you press Enter, the cell will display $51,250.0. The formula returns the contents of cell B2, multiplied by 102.5%. In other words, February sales are projected to be 2.5% greater than January sales.

3. The projected sales for subsequent months will use a similar formula. But rather than retype the formula for each cell in column B, once again take advantage of the AutoFill feature. Make sure that cell B3 is selected. Click the cell's fill handle, drag down to cell B13, and release the mouse button.

At this point, your worksheet should resemble the one shown in Figure 1-8. Keep in mind that, except for cell B2, the values in column B are calculated with formulas. To demonstrate, try changing the projected sales value for the initial month, January (in cell B2). You'll find that the formulas recalculate and return different values. But these formulas all depend on the initial value in cell B2.

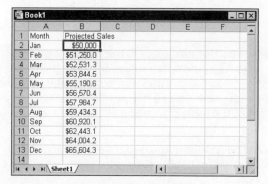

Figure 1-8: Your worksheet, after creating the formulas.

Summing the values

The worksheet displays the monthly projected sales, but what about the total sales for the year? To display the yearly total, another formula is required.

1. Move to cell A14 and type **Total**.

2. Move to cell B14, which is the first empty cell below the sales data.

3. Locate the AutoSum button, which is on the Standard toolbar. The AutoSum button contains the Greek letter sigma.

4. Click the AutoSum button and press Enter.

You'll find that Excel added this formula to cell B14: =SUM(B2:B13)

This formula calculates the sum of the cells beginning with B2 and ending with B13 and displays the result. You could have typed that formula yourself, but using the AutoSum button is faster.

Making your worksheet look a bit fancier

At this point, you have a functional worksheet — but it could use some help in the appearance department.

1. Start by adding a title above the table. You'll need to insert some new rows, so select cell A1 and choose Insert ➪ Rows to insert one new row. An additional blank row would be even better, so issue this command again.

Notice that the existing information is "pushed down" to make room for the new rows. If you examine the formulas, you'll find that they still work — Excel adjusted the cell references just as you may have expected.

2. Move to cell A1 and type **Sales Projections**.

3. To make this title stand out, select cell A1 and click the Bold button on the Formatting toolbar. (That button has a *B* on it.) Then change the font size to something larger, say 14 points. The font size control is directly to the left of the Bold button.

4. You could apply other formatting to the actual table, but let Excel do the work. Start by selecting any cell within the data table — for example, cell B3. The exact cell doesn't matter because Excel will figure out the table's boundaries. Just make sure that you don't select a cell in rows 1 or 2, which are outside of the table. (Remember that the table now begins in row 3 because of the rows inserted in Step 1.)

5. Click the Format menu and choose AutoFormat. Two things happen: Excel determines the table boundaries and highlights the entire table, and it displays the AutoFormat dialog box.

6. The AutoFormat dialog box offers 16 canned formats to choose from (plus one called None that removes all formatting). Click the table format that you want to apply.

7. Click the OK button. Excel applies the formats to your table.

8. If you don't like the result, choose Edit ➪ Undo to return to the original formatting. Or use the Format ➪ AutoFormat command again and try a different option. Because the table contains currency values, you may want to choose an AutoFormat that displays either two decimal places or no decimal places.

Creating a chart

Next, you create a chart that shows the projected sales for each month.

1. Start by selecting the data that will appear in the chart. In this case, click cell A3, and then drag down and to the right to include cell B15. Notice that the total row (row 16) is not included in the selection.

2. Click the Chart Wizard button, in the Standard toolbar (it has a picture of a column chart).

3. You'll see the Chart Wizard dialog box, which is shown in Figure 1-9.

4. In the Chart Type list, click Column. You'll see seven subtypes listed.

5. The default subtype will be fine, so click Finish to create your chart.

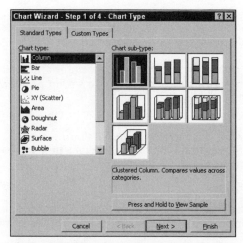

Figure 1-9: The Chart Wizard dialog box.

Excel puts the chart in the middle of the screen. You can drag the chart to a new location, and even change the size and proportions by clicking and dragging on the chart's border. You can make many other changes to the chart. For example, you may want to remove the legend. To do so, click the legend and press Del.

Figure 1-10 shows the chart after it was moved adjacent to the data table.

This workbook is available on the companion CD-ROM.

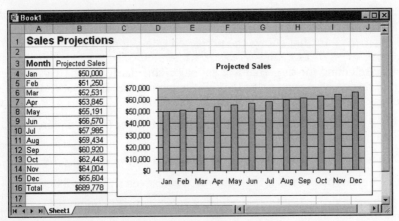

Figure 1-10: Your worksheet, after creating a chart.

Printing your worksheet

Printing your worksheet is very easy (assuming that you have a printer attached and that it works properly). Before printing, it's a good idea to do a print preview.

1. First, make sure that the chart is not selected. Just press Esc or click any cell to deselect the chart.

2. Click the Preview button on the Standard toolbar. Excel opens a new window and displays a preview of the printed output.

3. Click Close to return to your worksheet.

4. If the preview was acceptable, click the Print button on the Standard toolbar. (This button has an image of a printer on it.) The worksheet is printed using the default settings.

Note   You may need to adjust the size or position of the chart so it is not split across two pages.

Saving your workbook

Until now, everything that you've done has occurred in your computer's memory. If the power should fail, all may be lost — unless Excel's AutoRecover feature happened to kick in. It's time to save your work to a file on your hard drive.

1. Click the Save button on the Standard toolbar. (This button looks like a floppy disk.) Excel responds with the Save As dialog box.

2. In the box labeled File Name, enter **Monthly Sales Projection**, and then click Save or press Enter.

Excel saves the workbook as a file. The workbook remains open so that you can work with it some more.

 Note   By default, Excel saves a copy of your work automatically every ten minutes. To adjust this setting (or turn if off), use the Options dialog box. (Select Tools ⇨ Options and click the Save tab.)

But, of course, you've barely scratched the surface. The remainder of this book will cover these tasks (and many, many more) in much greater detail.

Entering and Editing Worksheet Data

✦ ✦ ✦ ✦

In This Chapter

Understanding the types of data you can use

Entering text and values into your worksheets

Entering dates and times into your worksheets

Modifying and editing information

Using built-in number formats

✦ ✦ ✦ ✦

This chapter describes what you need to know about entering, using, and modifying data in your worksheets. As you'll see, Excel doesn't treat all data equally. Therefore, it's important to understand the various types of data that you can use in an Excel worksheet.

Understanding the Types of Data You Can Use

An Excel workbook can hold any number of worksheets, and each worksheet is made up of a large number of cells. A cell can hold any of three basic types of data:

- ✦ Numerical values
- ✦ Text
- ✦ Formulas

A worksheet also can hold charts, drawings, pictures, buttons, and other objects. These objects are not contained in cells. Rather, they reside on the worksheet's *draw layer,* which is an invisible layer on top of each worksheet.

 Cross-Reference The draw layer is discussed in Chapter 18.

Understanding numerical values

Numerical values represent a quantity of some type: sales amounts, number of employees, atomic weights, test scores, and so on. Values also can be dates (such as 26-Feb-2004) or times (such as 3:24 a.m.).

Cross-Reference Excel can display values in many different formats. Later in this chapter, you'll see how different format options can affect the display of numerical values.

Understanding text entries

Most worksheets also include text in some of their cells. You can insert text to serve as labels for values, headings for columns, or instructions about the worksheet. Text is often used to clarify what the values in a worksheet mean. In most cases, the text is more important to someone viewing the worksheet than it is to Excel because the text makes it easier for the viewer to determine which numerical values are which—Excel knows what the values represent from the way that they are used in formulas.

Excel's Numerical Limitations

You may be curious about the types of values that Excel can handle. In other words, how large can numbers be? And how accurate are large numbers?

Excel's numbers are precise up to 15 digits. For example, if you enter a large value, such as 123,123,123,123,123,123 (18 digits), Excel actually stores it with only 15 digits of precision: 123,123,123,123,123,000. This may seem quite limiting, but in practice, it rarely causes any problems.

One situation in which the 15-digit accuracy can cause a problem is when entering credit card numbers. Most credit card numbers are 16 digits long. As noted earlier, Excel can't handle this, and it will substitute a zero for the last credit-card digit. The solution? Enter the credit card numbers as text. The easiest way to do this is to preformat the cell as Text (use the Number tab of the Format Cells dialog box, and choose Text from the Category list). Or you can precede the credit card number with an apostrophe. Either of these methods prevents Excel from interpreting the entry as a number.

Here are some of Excel's other numerical limits:

Largest positive number: 9.9E+307

Smallest negative number: −9.9E+307

Smallest positive number: 1E−307

Largest negative number: −1E−307

These numbers are expressed in scientific notation. For example, the largest positive number is "9.9 times 10 to the 307th power." (In other words, 99 followed by 306 zeros.) But keep in mind that this number only has 15 digits of accuracy.

Text that begins with a number is still considered text. For example, if you type **12 Apples** into a cell, Excel considers this to be text rather than a value. Consequently, you can't use this cell for numeric calculations.

Understanding formulas

Formulas are what make a spreadsheet a spreadsheet. Excel enables you to enter powerful formulas that use the values (or even text) in cells to calculate a result. When you enter a formula into a cell, the formula's result appears in the cell. If you change any of the values used by a formula, the formula recalculates and shows the new result.

Formulas can be simple mathematical expressions, or they can use some of the powerful functions that are built into Excel. Figure 2-1 shows an Excel worksheet set up to calculate monthly loan payments. The worksheet contains values, text, and formulas. The cells in column A contain text. Column B contains four values and two formulas. The formulas are in cells B6 and B10. Column C, for reference, shows the actual contents of the cells in column B.

On the CD-ROM This workbook is available on the companion CD-ROM.

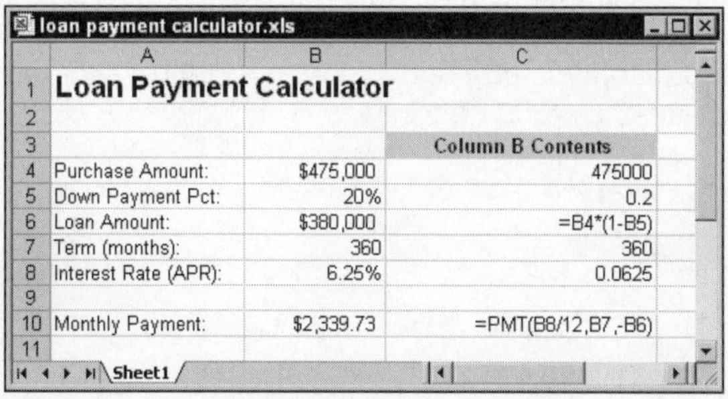

	A	B	C
	Loan Payment Calculator.xls		
	A	B	C
1	**Loan Payment Calculator**		
2			
3			Column B Contents
4	Purchase Amount:	$475,000	475000
5	Down Payment Pct:	20%	0.2
6	Loan Amount:	$380,000	=B4*(1-B5)
7	Term (months):	360	360
8	Interest Rate (APR):	6.25%	0.0625
9			
10	Monthly Payment:	$2,339.73	=PMT(B8/12,B7,-B6)
11			

Figure 2-1: You can use values, text, and formulas to create useful Excel worksheets.

Cross-Reference You'll learn much more about formulas in the chapters in Part II.

Entering Text and Values into Your Worksheets

To enter a numerical value into a cell, move the cell pointer to the appropriate cell, type the value, and then press Enter. The value is displayed in the cell and also appears in Excel's Formula bar when the cell is active. You can include decimal points and currency symbols when entering values, along with plus signs, minus signs, and commas. If you precede a value with a minus sign or enclose it in parentheses, Excel considers it to be a negative number.

Note Sometimes, a value won't be displayed exactly as you entered it. For example, if you enter a very large number (one with a large number of digits), it may be converted to scientific notation. Notice, however, that the Formula bar displays the value that you entered originally. Excel simply reformats the value so that it fits into the cell. If you make the column wider, the number is displayed as you entered it. To increase the width of a column, drag the border next to the column header.

Entering text into a cell is just as easy as entering a value: Activate the cell, type the text, and then press Enter. A cell can contain a maximum of about 32,000 characters—more than enough to hold a typical chapter in this book. Even though a cell can hold a huge number of characters, you'll find that it's not possible to actually display all of these characters.

Tip If you type an exceptionally long text entry into a cell, the characters appear to wrap around when they reach the right edge of the window, and the Formula bar expands so that the text wraps around.

What happens when you enter text that's longer than its column's current width? If the cells to the immediate right are blank, Excel displays the text in its entirety, appearing to spill the entry into adjacent cells. If an adjacent cell is not blank, Excel displays as much of the text as possible. (The full text is contained in the cell; it's just not displayed.) If you need to display a long text string in a cell that's adjacent to a nonblank cell, you can take one of several actions:

✦ Edit your text to make it shorter

✦ Increase the width of the column

✦ Use a smaller font

✦ Wrap the text within the cell so that it occupies more than one line

✦ Use Excel's "shrink to fit" option (see Chapter 5 for details)

Entering Dates and Times into Your Worksheets

Excel treats dates and times as special types of numeric values. Typically, these values are formatted so that they appear as dates or times because humans find it far easier to understand these values when they appear in the correct format.

Entering date values

If you work with dates and times, you need to understand Excel's date and time system. Excel handles dates by using a serial number system. The earliest date that Excel understands is January 1, 1900. This date has a serial number of 1. January 2, 1900, has a serial number of 2, and so on. This system makes it easy to deal with dates in formulas. For example, you can enter a formula to calculate the number of days between two dates.

Note   Excel 97 and later versions support dates from January 1, 1900, through December 31, 9999 (serial number = 2,958,465). Previous versions of Excel support a much smaller range of dates: from January 1, 1900, through December 31, 2078 (serial number = 65,380).

Most of the time, you don't have to be concerned with Excel's serial number date system. You can simply enter a date in a familiar date format, and Excel takes care of the details behind the scenes.

For example, if you need to enter June 1, 2004, you can simply enter the date by typing **June 1, 2004** (or use any of several different date formats). Excel interprets your entry and stores the value 38139 — which is the date serial number for that date.

Note   The date examples in this book use the U.S. English system. Depending on your regional settings, entering a date in a format (such as **June 1, 2004**) may be interpreted as text rather than a date. In such a case, you would need to enter the date in a format that corresponds to your regional date settings — for example, **1 June, 2004**.

Cross-Reference   For more information about working with dates and times, refer to Chapter 10.

Entering time values

When you work with times, you simply extend Excel's date serial number system to include decimals. In other words, Excel works with times by using fractional days. For example, the date serial number for June 1, 2004, is 38139. Noon on June 1, 2004 (halfway through the day), is represented internally as 38139.5 because the time fraction is simply added to the date serial number to get the full date/time serial number.

Again, you normally don't have to be concerned with these serial numbers (or fractional serial numbers, for times). Just enter the time into a cell in a recognized format.

Cross-Reference   Refer to Chapter 10 for more information about working with time values.

Modifying Cell Contents

After you enter a value or text into a cell, you can modify it in several ways:

✦ Erase the cell's contents

✦ Replace the cell's contents with something else

✦ Edit the cell's contents

Erasing the contents of a cell

To erase the contents of a cell, just click the cell and press Delete. To erase more than one cell, select all the cells that you want to erase and then press Delete. Pressing Delete removes the cell's contents but doesn't remove any formatting (such as bold, italic, or a different number format) that you may have applied to the cell.

> **Tip**   You can also erase a range of cells by using the fill handle — the small square that appears at the bottom right of the selected range. Just click the fill handle and drag back across the selected cells.

For more control over what gets deleted, you can use the Edit ➪ Clear command. This menu item has a submenu with four additional choices:

✦ **All:** Clears everything from the cell

✦ **Formats:** Clears only the formatting and leaves the value, text, or formula

✦ **Contents:** Clears only the cell's contents and leaves the formatting

✦ **Comments:** Clears the comment (if one exists) attached to the cell

Replacing the contents of a cell

To replace the contents of a cell with something else, just click the cell and type your new entry, which replaces the previous contents. Any formatting that you previously applied to the cell remains in place and is applied to the new content.

> **Tip**   You can also replace cell contents by dragging and dropping or by pasting data from the Clipboard. In both cases, the cell formatting will be replaced by the format of the new data (unless you use the Edit ➪ Paste Special command or the Paste Options button to choose to paste the data without altering the destination format).

Editing the contents of a cell

If the cell contains only a few characters, replacing its contents by typing new data usually is easiest. But if the cell contains lengthy text or a complex formula and you need to make only a slight modification, you probably want to edit the cell rather than re-enter information.

When you want to edit the contents of a cell, you can use one of the following ways to enter cell-edit mode:

✦ Double-click the cell. This enables you to edit the cell contents directly in the cell.

✦ Activate the cell and press F2. This enables you to edit the cell contents directly in the cell.

✦ Activate the cell that you want to edit and then click inside the Formula bar. This enables you to edit the cell contents in the Formula bar.

You can use whichever method you prefer. Some people find it easier to edit directly in the cell; others prefer to use the Formula bar to edit a cell.

Note   The Edit tab of the Options dialog box contains several settings that affect how editing works. (To access this dialog box, choose Tools⇨Options.) If the Edit Directly in Cell option is not enabled, you will not be able to edit a cell by double-clicking. In addition, pressing F2 will allow you to edit the cell in the Formula bar (not directly in the cell).

All of these methods cause Excel to go into *edit mode*. (The word EDIT appears at the left side of the status bar at the bottom of the screen.) When Excel is in edit mode, the Formula bar displays two new icons: the X and Check Mark (see Figure 2-2). Clicking the X icon cancels editing, without changing the cell's contents. (Pressing Esc has the same effect.) Clicking the Check Mark icon completes the editing and enters the modified contents into the cell. (Pressing Enter has the same effect.)

The X icon   The Check Mark icon

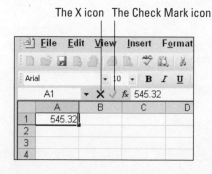

Figure 2-2: While editing a cell, the Formula bar displays two new icons.

When you begin editing a cell, the insertion point appears as a vertical bar, and you can move the insertion point by using the direction keys. Use Home to move the insertion point to the beginning of the cell, and use End to move the insertion point to the end. You can add new characters at the location of the insertion point. To select multiple characters, press Shift while you use the arrow keys. You also can use the mouse to select characters while you're editing a cell. Just click and drag the mouse pointer over the characters that you want to select.

Learning some handy data-entry techniques

You can simplify the process of entering information into your Excel worksheets and make your work go quite a bit faster by using a number of useful tricks, described in the sections that follow.

Automatically moving the cell pointer after entering data

By default, Excel automatically moves the cell pointer to the next cell down when you press the Enter key after entering data into a cell. To change this setting, choose Tools ➪ Options and click the Edit tab (see Figure 2-3). The check box that controls this behavior is labeled Move Selection After Enter. You can also specify the direction in which the cell pointer moves (down, left, up, or right).

Your choice is completely a matter of personal preference. I prefer to keep this option turned off. When entering data, I use the arrow keys rather than the Enter key (see the next section).

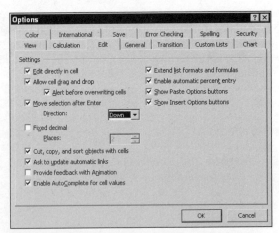

Figure 2-3: You can use the Options dialog box Edit tab to select a number of very helpful input option settings.

Using arrow keys instead of pressing Enter

Instead of pressing the Enter key when you're finished making a cell entry, you also can use any of the direction keys to complete the entry. Not surprisingly, these direction keys send you in the direction that you indicate. For example, if you're entering data in a row, press the right-arrow ($\rightarrow$) key rather than Enter. The other arrow keys work as expected, and you can even use PgUp and PgDn.

Selecting a range of input cells before entering data

Here's a tip that most Excel users don't know about: When a range of cells is selected, Excel automatically moves the cell pointer to the next cell in the range when you press Enter. If the selection consists of multiple rows, Excel moves down the column; when it reaches the end of the selection in the column, it moves to the first selected cell in the next column. To skip a cell, just press Enter without entering anything. To go backward, press Shift+Enter. If you prefer to enter the data by rows rather than by columns, press Tab rather than Enter.

Using Ctrl+Enter to place information into multiple cells simultaneously

If you need to enter the same data into multiple cells, Excel offers a handy shortcut. Select all the cells that you want to contain the data, enter the value, text, or formula, and then press Ctrl+Enter. The same information will be inserted into each cell in the selection.

Entering decimal points automatically

If you need to enter lots of numbers with a fixed number of decimal places, Excel has a useful tool that works like some adding machines. Select Tools ➪ Options and click the Edit tab. Select the check box labeled Fixed Decimal and make sure that the Places box is set for the correct number of decimal places for the data you need to enter.

When the Fixed Decimal option is set, Excel supplies the decimal points for you automatically. For example, if you enter **12345** into a cell, Excel interprets it as 123.45. (It adds the decimal point.) To restore things to normal, just uncheck the Fixed Decimal check box in the Options dialog box. Changing this setting doesn't affect any values that you have already entered.

Caution

The fixed-decimal-places option is a global setting and applies to all workbooks (not just the active workbook). If you forget that this option is turned on, you can easily end up entering incorrect values.

Using AutoFill to enter a series of values

Excel's AutoFill feature makes it easy to insert a series of values or text items in a range of cells. It uses the AutoFill handle (the small box at the lower right of the active cell). You can drag the AutoFill handle to copy the cell or automatically complete a series.

If you drag the AutoFill handle while you press the right mouse button, Excel will display a shortcut menu with additional fill options.

Using AutoComplete to automate data entry

Excel's AutoComplete feature makes it very easy to enter the same text into multiple cells. With AutoComplete, you type the first few letters of a text entry into a cell, and Excel automatically completes the entry, based on other entries that you've already made in the column. Besides reducing typing, this feature also ensures that your entries are spelled correctly and are consistent.

Here's how it works. Suppose that you're entering product information in a column. One of your products is named Widgets. The first time that you enter **Widgets** into a cell, Excel remembers it. Later, when you start typing **Widgets** in that same column, Excel recognizes it by the first few letters and finishes typing it for you. Just press Enter and you're done. It also changes the case of letters for you automatically. If you start entering **widget** (with a lowercase *w*) in the second entry, Excel makes the *w* uppercase to be consistent with the previous entry in the column.

Tip   You also can access a mouse-oriented version of AutoComplete by right-clicking the cell and selecting Pick from List from the shortcut menu. Excel then displays a drop-down box that has all the entries in the current column, and you just click the one that you want.

Keep in mind that AutoComplete works only within a contiguous column of cells. If you have a blank row, for example, AutoComplete will only identify the cell contents below the blank row.

If you find the AutoComplete feature distracting, you can turn it off on the Edit tab of the Options dialog box. Remove the check mark from the check box labeled Enable AutoComplete for cell values.

Forcing text to appear on a new line within a cell

If you have lengthy text in a cell, you can force Excel to display it in multiple lines within the cell. Use Alt+Enter to start a new line in a cell.

Note   When you add a line break, Excel automatically changes the cell's format to Wrap Text. But unlike normal text wrap, your manual line break forces Excel to break the text at a specific place within the text. This gives you more precise control over the appearance of the text than if you rely on automatic text wrapping.

Tip

To remove a manual line break, open the text in the cell for editing and press Delete when the insertion point is located at the end of the line that contains the manual line break. You won't see any symbol to indicate the position of the manual line break, but the text that follows it will move up when the line break is deleted.

Using AutoCorrect for shorthand data entry

You can use Excel's AutoCorrect feature to create shortcuts for commonly used words or phrases. For example, if you work for a company named Consolidated Data Processing Corporation, you can create an AutoCorrect entry for an abbreviation, such as cdp. Then, whenever you type **cdp**, Excel automatically changes it to Consolidated Data Processing Corporation.

Excel includes quite a few built-in AutoCorrect terms (mostly common misspellings), and you can add your own. To set up your custom AutoCorrect entries, use the Tools ➪ AutoCorrect Options command. Click the AutoCorrect tab, check the option labeled Replace Text As You Type, and then enter your custom entries. (Figure 2-4 shows an example.) You can set up as many custom entries as you like. Just be careful not to use an abbreviation that might appear normally in your text.

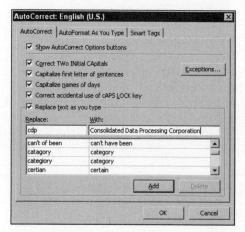

Figure 2-4: AutoCorrect allows you to create shorthand abbreviations for text you enter often.

Tip

Excel shares your AutoCorrect list with other Office applications. Any AutoCorrect entries you created in Word will also work in Excel.

Entering numbers with fractions

To enter a fraction into a cell, leave a space between the whole number and the fraction. For example, to enter 6⅞, enter **6 7/8**, and then press Enter. When you select the cell, 6.875 appears in the Formula bar, and the cell entry appears as a fraction. If you have a fraction only (for example, ⅛), you must enter a zero first, like this: **0 1/8**—otherwise Excel will likely assume that you are entering a date. When you select the cell and look at the Formula bar, you see 0.125. In the cell, you see ⅛.

Simplifying data entry by using a form

Many people use Excel to manage simple spreadsheet lists in which the information is arranged in rows. Excel offers a simple way to work with this type of data through the use of a data entry form that Excel can create automatically. Figure 2-5 shows an example of this.

Figure 2-5: Excel's built-in data form can simplify many data-entry tasks.

To use a data entry form, you must arrange your data so that Excel can recognize it as a list. Start by entering headings for the columns in the first row of your data entry range. Select any cell in the table and choose Data ⇨ Form. Excel then displays a dialog box similar to the one shown in Figure 2-5. You can use Tab to move between the text boxes and supply information. When you complete the data form, click the New button. Excel enters the data into a row in the worksheet and clears the dialog box for the next row of data.

Cross-Reference To learn more about using data forms, see Chapter 19.

Entering the current date or time into a cell

If you need to date-stamp or time-stamp your worksheet, Excel provides two short-cut keys that do this for you:

✦ **Current date:** Ctrl+; (semicolon)

✦ **Current time:** Ctrl+Shift+; (semicolon)

Caution When you use either of these shortcuts to enter a date or time into your worksheet, Excel enters a static value into the worksheet. In other words, the date or time that is entered does not change when the worksheet is recalculated. In most cases, this is probably what you want, but you should be aware of this limitation.

Applying Number Formatting

Number formatting refers to the process of changing the appearance of values contained in cells. As you'll see, Excel provides a wide variety of number formatting options. In the following sections, you'll see how to use many of Excel's formatting options to quickly improve the appearance of your worksheets.

Tip Remember that the formatting you apply works with the selected cell or cells. Therefore, you need to select the cell (or range of cells) before applying the formatting.

Improving readability by formatting numbers

Values that you enter into cells normally are unformatted. In other words, they simply consist of a string of numerals. Typically, you want to format the numbers so that they are easier to read or are more consistent in terms of the number of decimal places shown.

Figure 2-6 shows a worksheet that has two columns of values. The first column consists of unformatted values. The cells in the second column have been formatted to make the values easier to read.

On the CD-ROM This workbook is available on the companion CD-ROM.

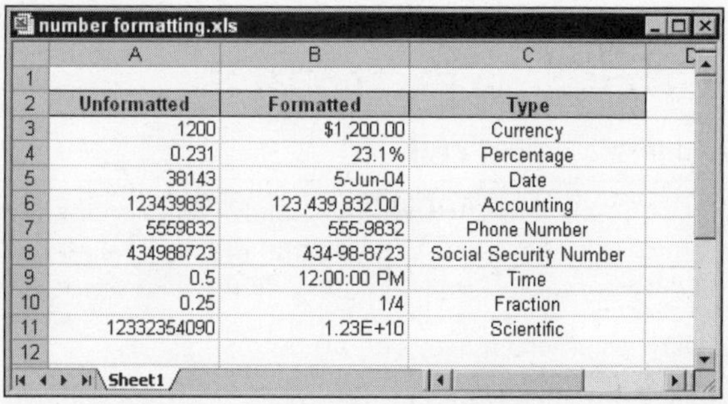

	A	B	C	
1				
2	Unformatted	Formatted	Type	
3	1200	$1,200.00	Currency	
4	0.231	23.1%	Percentage	
5	38143	5-Jun-04	Date	
6	123439832	123,439,832.00	Accounting	
7	5559832	555-9832	Phone Number	
8	434988723	434-98-8723	Social Security Number	
9	0.5	12:00:00 PM	Time	
10	0.25	1/4	Fraction	
11	12332354090	1.23E+10	Scientific	
12				

number formatting.xls — Sheet1

Figure 2-6: Use numeric formatting to make it easier to understand what the values in the worksheet represent.

Tip   If you move the cell pointer to a cell that has a formatted value, you find that the Formula bar displays the value in its unformatted state. This is because the formatting affects only how the value is displayed in the cell—not the actual value contained in the cell.

Using automatic number formatting

Excel is smart enough to perform some formatting for you automatically. For example, if you enter **12.2%** into a cell, Excel knows that you want to use a percentage format and applies it for you automatically. If you use commas to separate thousands (such as 123,456), Excel applies comma formatting for you. And, if you precede your value with a dollar sign, the cell will be formatted for currency (assuming that the dollar sign is your system currency symbol).

Tip   A handy feature in Excel makes it easier to enter percentage values into cells. Select Tools ➪ Options, and click the Edit tab in the Options dialog box. If the check box labeled Enable Automatic Percent Entry is checked, you can simply enter a normal value into a cell formatted as a percent (for example, **12.5** for 12.5%). If this check box is not checked, you must enter the value as a decimal (for example, **.125** for 12.5%).

Cross-Reference   See "Entering Dates and Times into Your Worksheets," earlier in this chapter, for information on formats that Excel automatically recognizes as date entries.

Formatting numbers by using the toolbar

The Formatting toolbar contains several buttons that let you quickly apply common number formats. When you click one of these buttons, the active cell takes on the specified number format. You also can select a range of cells (or even an entire row or column) before clicking these buttons. If you select more than one cell, Excel applies the number format to all the selected cells. Table 2-1 summarizes the formats that these Formatting toolbar buttons perform.

Table 2-1
Number-Formatting Buttons on the Formatting Toolbar

Button Name	Formatting Applied
Currency Style	Adds a dollar sign to the left, separates thousands with a comma, and displays the value with two digits to the right of the decimal point. The result may be different for systems that use a different currency symbol.
Percent Style	Displays the value as a percentage, with no decimal places
Comma Style	Separates thousands with a comma and displays the value with two digits to the right of the decimal place
Increase Decimal	Increases the number of digits to the right of the decimal point by one
Decrease Decimal	Decreases the number of digits to the right of the decimal point by one

These five toolbar buttons actually apply predefined "styles" to the selected cells. These styles are similar to those used in word-processing programs.

 Cross-Reference Chapter 5 describes how to modify existing styles and create new styles.

Using shortcut keys to format numbers

Another way to apply number formatting is to use shortcut keys. Table 2-2 summarizes the shortcut-key combinations that you can use to apply common number formatting to the selected cells or range.

	Table 2-2
	Number-Formatting Keyboard Shortcuts

Key Combination	Formatting Applied
Ctrl+Shift+~	General number format (that is, unformatted values)
Ctrl+Shift+$	Currency format with two decimal places (negative numbers appear in parentheses)
Ctrl+Shift+%	Percentage format, with no decimal places
Ctrl+Shift+^	Scientific notation number format, with two decimal places
Ctrl+Shift+#	Date format with the day, month, and year
Ctrl+Shift+@	Time format with the hour, minute, and AM or PM
Ctrl+Shift+!	Two decimal places, thousands separator, and a hyphen for negative values

Formatting numbers using the Format Cells dialog box

In some cases, the number formats that are accessible from the Formatting toolbar are just fine. More often, however, you want more control over how your values appear. Excel offers a great deal of control over number formats through the use of the Format Cells dialog box. Figure 2-7 shows this dialog box. For formatting numbers, you need to use the Number tab.

There are three ways to bring up the Format Cells dialog box. Start by selecting the cell or cells that you want to format and then do the following:

✦ Select the Format ➪ Cells command.

✦ Right-click and choose Format Cells from the shortcut menu.

✦ Press the Ctrl+1 shortcut key.

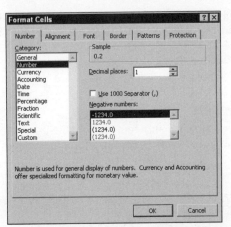

Figure 2-7: When you need more control over number formats, use the Format Cells dialog box.

The Number tab of the Format Cells dialog box displays 12 categories of number formats from which to choose. When you select a category from the list box, the right side of the tab changes to display appropriate options.

The Number category has three options that you can control: the number of decimal places displayed, whether to use a thousand separator, and how you want negative numbers displayed. Notice that the Negative Numbers list box has four choices (two of which display negative values in red) and the choices change depending on the number of decimal places and whether you choose to separate thousands. Also, notice that the top of the tab displays a sample of how the active cell will appear with the selected number format. After you make your choices, click OK to apply the number format to all the selected cells.

When Numbers Appear to Add Up Incorrectly

Applying a number format to a cell doesn't change the value — only how the value appears in the worksheet. For example, if a cell contains .874543, you might format it to appear as 87%. If that cell is used in a formula, the formula uses the full value (.874543), not the displayed value (.87).

In some situations, formatting may cause Excel to display calculation results that appear incorrect, such as when totaling numbers with decimal places. For example, if values are formatted to display two decimal places, you may not see the actual numbers that are used in calculations. But because Excel uses the full precision of the values in its formula, the sum of two values may appear to be incorrect.

Several solutions to this problem are available. You can format the cells to display more decimal places. You can use the ROUND function on individual numbers and specify the number of decimal places Excel should round to. Or you can instruct Excel to change the worksheet values to match their displayed format. To do this, choose Tools ➪ Options, select the Calculation tab, and then check the Precision as Displayed check box.

Caution Selecting the Precision as Displayed option changes the numbers in your worksheets to permanently match their appearance onscreen. This setting applies to all sheets in the active workbook.

Cross-Reference ROUND and other built-in functions are discussed in Chapter 8.

The following are the number-format categories, along with some general comments:

✦ **General:** The default format; it displays numbers as integers, as decimals, or in scientific notation if the value is too wide to fit in the cell.

✦ **Number:** Enables you to specify the number of decimal places, whether to use a comma to separate thousands, and how to display negative numbers (with a minus sign, in red, in parentheses, or in red and in parentheses).

✦ **Currency:** Enables you to specify the number of decimal places, whether to use a currency symbol, and how to display negative numbers (with a minus sign, in red, in parentheses, or in red and in parentheses). This format always uses a comma to separate thousands.

✦ **Accounting:** Differs from the Currency format in that the currency symbols always line up vertically.

✦ **Date:** Enables you to choose from several different date formats.

✦ **Time:** Enables you to choose from several different time formats.

✦ **Percentage:** Enables you to choose the number of decimal places and always displays a percent sign.

✦ **Fraction:** Enables you to choose from among nine fraction formats.

✦ **Scientific:** Displays numbers in exponential notation (with an E): 2.00E+05 = 200,000; 2.05E+05 = 205,000. You can choose the number of decimal places to display to the left of E.

✦ **Text:** When applied to a value, causes Excel to treat the value as text (even if it looks like a number). This feature is useful for such items as part numbers.

✦ **Special:** Contains four additional number formats (Zip Code, Zip Code +4, Phone Number, and Social Security Number).

✦ **Custom:** Enables you to define custom number formats that aren't included in any of the other categories. Custom number formats are described in the next section.

Tip If a cell displays a series of hash marks (such as ##########), it usually means that the column is not wide enough to display the value in the number format that you selected. Either make the column wider or change the number format.

Adding your own custom number formats

Sometimes you may want to display numerical values in a format that simply isn't included in any of the other categories. If so, the answer is to create your own custom format. Excel provides you with a great deal of flexibility — so much so that I've devoted an entire chapter (Chapter 25) to custom number formatting.

✦　　✦　　✦

Essential Worksheet Operations

This chapter covers some essential information regarding
worksheets. You'll learn how to take control of your worksheets so that you will be more efficient using the program.

Learning the Fundamentals of Excel Worksheets

In Excel, each file is called a workbook, and each workbook
can contain one or more worksheets. You may find it helpful
to think of an Excel workbook as a notebook and worksheets
as pages in the notebook. As with a notebook, you can activate a particular sheet, add new sheets, remove sheets, copy
sheets, and so on.

The following sections describe the operations that you can
perform with worksheets.

Working with Excel's windows

The files that Excel uses are known as *workbooks*. A workbook
can hold any number of sheets, and these sheets can be either
worksheets (sheets consisting of rows and columns) or chart
sheets (sheets that hold a single chart). A worksheet is what
people usually think of when they think of a spreadsheet. You
can open as many Excel workbooks as necessary at the same
time.

Figure 3-1 shows Excel with four workbooks open, each in a separate window. One of the windows is minimized and appears near the lower-left corner of the screen. (When a workbook is minimized, only its title bar is visible.) Worksheet windows can overlap, and the title bar of one window is a different color. That's the window that contains the active workbook.

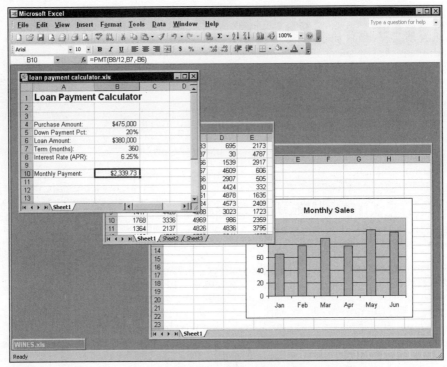

Figure 3-1: You can open several Excel workbooks at the same time.

The workbook windows that Excel uses work much like the windows in any other Windows program. Each window has three buttons at the right side of its title bar. From left to right, they are Minimize, Maximize (or Restore), and Close. When a workbook window is maximized, the three buttons appear directly below Excel's title bar.

Excel's windows can be in one of the following states:

✦ **Maximized:** Fills Excel's entire workspace. A maximized window does not have a title bar, and the workbook's name appears in Excel's title bar. To maximize a window, click its Maximize button.

✦ **Minimized:** Appears as a small window with only a title bar. To minimize a window, click its Minimize button.

✦ **Restored:** A nonmaximized size. To restore a maximized or minimized window, click its Restore button.

If you work with more than one workbook simultaneously (which is quite common), you have to learn how to move, resize, and switch among the workbook windows.

Moving and resizing windows

To move a window, make sure that it's not maximized. Then click and drag its title bar with your mouse.

To resize a window, click and drag any of its borders until it's the size that you want it to be. When you position the mouse pointer on a window's border, the mouse pointer changes to a double-sided arrow, which lets you know that you can now click and drag to resize the window. To resize a window horizontally and vertically at the same time, click and drag any of its corners.

Note You cannot move or resize a workbook window if it is maximized. You can move a minimized window, but doing so has no effect on its position when it is subsequently restored.

If you want all of your workbook windows to be visible (that is, not obscured by another window), you can move and resize the windows manually, or you can let Excel do it for you. The Window ➪ Arrange command displays the Arrange Windows dialog box, as shown in Figure 3-2. This dialog box has four window-arrangement options. Just select the one that you want and click OK.

Figure 3-2: Use the Arrange Windows dialog box to quickly arrange all open workbook windows.

Switching among windows

At any given time, one (and only one) workbook window is the active window. This is the window that accepts your input, and it is the window on which your commands work. The active window's title bar is a different color, and the window appears at the top of the stack of windows. To work in a different window, you need to make that window active. There are several ways to make a different window the active workbook:

✦ Click another window, if it's visible. The window you click moves to the top and becomes the active window.

✦ Press Ctrl+Tab (or Ctrl+F6) to cycle through all open windows until the window that you want to work with appears on top as the active window. Shift+Ctrl+Tab (or Shift+Ctrl+F6) cycles through the windows in the opposite direction.

✦ Click the workbook icon in the Windows Taskbar. If you don't see workbook icons in your Windows Taskbar, activate the Options dialog box, select the View tab, and put a check mark next to Windows in Taskbar.

✦ Click the Window menu and select the window that you want from the bottom part of the pull-down menu (the active window has a check mark next to it). This menu can display up to nine windows. If you have more than nine workbook windows open, choose More Windows (which appears below the nine window names).

Tip   Most people prefer to do most of their work with maximized workbook windows. This enables you to see more cells and eliminates the distraction of other workbook windows getting in the way.

When you maximize one window, all the other windows are maximized, too (even though you don't see them). Therefore, if the active window is maximized and you activate a different window, the new active window is also maximized. If the active workbook window is maximized, you can't select another window by clicking it (because other windows aren't visible). You must use either Ctrl+Tab, the Windows taskbar, or the Window menu to activate another window.

Tip   You also can display a single workbook in more than one window. For example, if you have a workbook with two worksheets, you may want to display each worksheet in a separate window. All the window-manipulation procedures described previously still apply. You use the Window ➪ New Window command to open a new window in the active workbook.

Closing windows

If you have multiple windows open, you may want to close those windows that you no longer need. To close a window, select File ➪ Close or simply click the Close button (the *X* icon) on the worksheet window's title bar. If the workbook window is maximized, its title bar is not visible, so its Close button appears directly below Excel's Close button.

When you close a workbook window, Excel checks whether you have made any changes since the last time you saved the file. If not, the window closes without a prompt from Excel. If you've made any changes, Excel prompts you to save the file before it closes the window.

Making a worksheet the active sheet

At any given time, one workbook is the active workbook, and one sheet is the active sheet in the active workbook. To activate a different sheet, just click its sheet tab, located at the bottom of the workbook window. You also can use the following shortcut keys to activate a different sheet:

✦ **Ctrl+PgUp:** Activates the previous sheet, if one exists

✦ **Ctrl+PgDn:** Activates the next sheet, if one exists

If your workbook has many sheets, all of its tabs may not be visible. You can use the tab-scrolling buttons (see Figure 3-3) to scroll the sheet tabs. The sheet tabs share space with the worksheet's horizontal scroll bar. You also can drag the tab split box to display more or fewer tabs. Dragging the tab split box simultaneously changes the number of tabs and the size of the horizontal scroll bar.

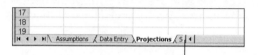

Figure 3-3: Use the tab controls to activate a different worksheet or to see additional worksheet tabs.

Drag the tab split box to change the number of tabs.

Tip   When you right-click any of the tab-scrolling buttons to the left of the worksheet tabs, Excel displays a list of all sheets in the workbook. You can quickly activate a sheet by selecting it from the list.

Adding a new worksheet to your workbook

Worksheets can be an excellent organizational tool. Instead of placing everything on a single worksheet, you can use additional worksheets in a workbook to separate various workbook elements logically. For example, if you have several products whose sales you track individually, you might want to assign each product to its own worksheet and then use another worksheet to consolidate your results.

The following are three ways to add a new worksheet to a workbook:

✦ Select the Insert ➪ Worksheet command.

✦ Press Shift+F11.

✦ Right-click a sheet tab, choose the Insert command from the shortcut menu, select Worksheet from the Insert dialog box, and then click OK.

When you add a new worksheet to the workbook, Excel inserts the new worksheet before the active worksheet, and the new worksheet becomes the active worksheet.

Tip   To insert more than one worksheet at a time, hold down the Shift key and click a range of worksheet tabs. When you issue the command to insert a worksheet, Excel will add as many worksheets as the number of worksheet tabs you selected before issuing the command.

Deleting a worksheet you no longer need

If you no longer need a worksheet, or if you want to get rid of an empty worksheet in a workbook, you can delete it in either of two ways:

✦ Select the Edit ➪ Delete Sheet command.

✦ Right-click the sheet tab and choose the Delete command from the shortcut menu.

If the worksheet contains any data, Excel asks you to confirm that you want to delete the sheet. If you have never used the worksheet, Excel deletes it immediately without asking for confirmation.

Tip   You can delete multiple sheets with a single command by selecting the sheets that you want to delete. To select multiple sheets, press Ctrl while you click the sheet tabs that you want to delete. To select a group of contiguous sheets, click the first sheet tab, press Shift, and then click the last sheet tab. Then use either method to delete the selected sheets.

Caution   When you delete a worksheet, it's gone for good. This is one of the few operations in Excel that can't be undone.

Changing the name of a worksheet

The default names Excel uses for worksheets — Sheet1, Sheet2, and so on — aren't very descriptive. If you don't change the worksheet names, it can be a bit hard to remember where to find things in multiple-sheet workbooks. That's why providing more-meaningful names for your worksheets is often a good idea.

Changing the Number of Sheets in Your Workbooks

By default, Excel automatically creates three worksheets in each new workbook. You can change this default behavior. For example, I prefer to start each new workbook with a single worksheet. After all, it's easy enough to add new sheets if and when they are needed. To change the default number of worksheets:

1. Select Tools ➪ Options.

2. In the Options dialog box, click the General tab.

3. Change the value for the Sheets in New Workbook Setting and click OK.

Making this change will affect all new workbooks but will have no effect on existing workbooks.

To change a sheet's name, use any of the following methods to begin:

✦ Choose Format ➪ Sheet ➪ Rename.

✦ Double-click the sheet tab.

✦ Right-click the sheet tab and choose the Rename command from the shortcut menu.

After you have done one of the above actions, Excel highlights the name on the sheet tab so that you can edit the name or replace it with a new name.

Tip   To edit the worksheet name rather than replace it completely, it's usually easiest to double-click the sheet tab and then click within the name where you want to make a change.

Sheet names can be up to 31 characters, and spaces are allowed. However, you can't use the following characters in sheet names:

:	colon
/	slash
\	backslash
?	question mark
*	asterisk

Keep in mind that a longer worksheet name results in a wider tab, which takes up more space on-screen. Therefore, if you use lengthy sheet names, you won't be able to see very many sheet tabs without having to scroll the tab list.

Changing a sheet tab's color

Excel allows you to change the color of one or more of your worksheet tabs. For example, you may prefer to color-code the sheet tabs to make it easier to identify the worksheet's contents.

To change the color of a sheet tab, right-click the tab and choose Tab Color. Then select the color in the Format Tab Color dialog box.

Rearranging your worksheets

You may want to rearrange the order of worksheets in a workbook. If you have a separate worksheet for each sales region, for example, arranging the worksheets in alphabetical order or by total sales might be helpful. You may want to move a worksheet from one workbook to another. (To move a worksheet to a different workbook, both workbooks must be open.) You can also create copies of worksheets.

You can move or copy a worksheet in the following ways:

✦ Select the Edit ➪ Move or Copy Sheet command to display the Move or Copy dialog box.

✦ Right-click the sheet tab and select the Move or Copy command. (This also displays the same Move or Copy dialog box.)

✦ To move a worksheet, click the worksheet tab and drag it to its desired location (either in the same workbook or in a different workbook) to move the worksheet. When you drag, the mouse pointer changes to a small sheet, and a small arrow guides you.

✦ To copy a worksheet, click the worksheet tab, press Ctrl, and drag the tab to its desired location (either in the same workbook or in a different workbook). When you drag, the mouse pointer changes to a small sheet with a plus sign on it.

Tip   You can move or copy multiple sheets simultaneously. First select the sheets by clicking their sheet tabs while holding down the Ctrl key. Then you can move or copy the set of sheets by using the methods just described.

Dragging is usually the easiest method, but if the workbook has many sheets, you may prefer to use the Move or Copy dialog box. This dialog box is shown in Figure 3-4, and it enables you to select the workbook and the new location.

Figure 3-4: Use the Move or Copy dialog box to move or copy worksheets in the same or another workbook.

If you move or copy a worksheet to a workbook that already has a sheet with the same name, Excel changes the name to make it unique. For example, Sheet1 becomes Sheet1 (2).

Note   When you move or copy a worksheet to a different workbook, any defined names and custom formats also get copied to the new workbook.

Hiding and unhiding a worksheet

In some situations, you may want to hide one or more worksheets. Hiding a sheet may be useful if you don't want others to see it, or if you just want to get it out of the way. When a sheet is hidden, its sheet tab is also hidden. At least one sheet must remain visible. (You can't hide all the sheets in a workbook.)

To hide a worksheet, choose Format ⇨ Sheet ⇨ Hide. The active worksheet (or selected worksheets) will be hidden from view.

Making a Sheet Very Hidden

It's also possible to make a sheet "very hidden." A sheet that is very hidden does not appear in the Unhide dialog box. To make a sheet very hidden:

1. Activate the worksheet.

2. Select View ⇨ Toolbars ⇨ Control Toolbox. This displays the Control Toolbox toolbar.

3. Click the Properties button on the Control Toolbox toolbar. This displays the Properties box, shown in the following figure.

4. In the Properties box, select the Visible option, and choose 2 - xlSheetVeryHidden.

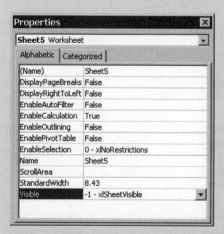

After performing these steps, the worksheet will be hidden, and it will not appear in the Unhide dialog box.

Be careful. After you make a sheet very hidden, you can't use the Properties box to unhide it because you won't be able to select the sheet! In fact, the only way to unhide such a sheet is to use a VBA macro. (See Part VI for more information about VBA.) This VBA statement will unhide Sheet1 in the active workbook:

```
ActiveWorkbook.Worksheets("Sheet1").Visible = True
```

To unhide a hidden worksheet, choose Format ⇨ Sheet ⇨ Unhide. Excel opens its Unhide dialog box that lists all hidden sheets. Choose the sheet that you want to redisplay and click OK. You can't select multiple sheets from this dialog box, so you need to repeat the command for each sheet that you want to redisplay.

Tip   To more fully protect a workbook from unauthorized changes, use the Tools ⇨ Protection menu commands. These commands give you several options in deciding how much access other users will have to the worksheets in your workbooks. Be aware that this is a very weak security measure. It is relatively easy to crack Excel's protection features.

Controlling the Worksheet View

As you add more information to a worksheet, you may find that it gets more difficult to navigate and locate what you want. Excel includes a few options that enable you to view your sheet, and sometimes multiple sheets, more efficiently. This section discusses a few additional worksheet options at your disposal.

Viewing a worksheet in multiple windows

Sometimes, you may want to view two different parts of a worksheet simultaneously — perhaps to make it easier to reference a distant cell in a formula. Or you may want to examine more than one sheet in the same workbook simultaneously. You can accomplish either of these actions by opening a new view to the workbook, using one or more additional windows.

To create and display a new view of the active workbook, choose Window ⇨ New Window.

Tip   If the workbook is maximized when you create a new window, you may not even notice that Excel has created the new window; but if you look at the Excel title bar, you'll see that the workbook title now has :2 appended to the name. Select Window ⇨ Arrange and choose one of the options in the Arrange Windows dialog box to display the open windows.

Excel displays a new window for the active workbook, similar to the one shown in Figure 3-5. In this case, each window shows a different worksheet in the workbook. Notice the text in the windows' title bars: climate data.xls:1 and climate data.xls:2. To help you keep track of the windows, Excel appends a colon and a number to each window.

A single workbook can have as many views (that is, separate windows) as you want. Each window is independent of the others. In other words, scrolling to a new location in one window doesn't cause scrolling in the other window(s).

climate data.xls:1

	A	B	C	D	E	F
45	REDDING, CA	6.5	5.49	5.15	2.4	1.6E
46	SACRAMENTO, CA	3.84	3.54	2.8	1.02	0.53
47	SAN DIEGO, CA	2.28	2.04	2.26	0.75	0.:
48	SAN FRANCISCO AP, C.					
49	SAN FRANCISCO C.O.,					
50	SANTA BARBARA, CA					
51	SANTA MARIA, CA					
52	STOCKTON, CA					
53	ALAMOSA, CO					
54	COLORADO SPRINGS, (					
55	DENVER, CO					
56	GRAND JUNCTION, CO					
57	PUEBLO, CO					
58	BRIDGEPORT, CT					
59	HARTFORD, CT					
60	WILMINGTON, DE					

Sheet1 / Sheet2 /

climate data.xls:2

	A	B	C	D	E	F
316	HARTFORD, CT	53	56	57	55	57
317	WASHINGTON NAT'L AP, D.C.	46	50	55	57	58
318	APALACHICOLA, FL	58	61	65	74	77
319	JACKSONVILLE, FL	58	62	68	73	70
320	KEY WEST, FL	74	77	82	84	8:
321	MIAMI, FL	66	68	74	76	72
322	PENSACOLA, FL	48	53	61	63	67
323	TAMPA, FL	63	65	71	75	75
324	ATLANTA, GA	49	54	58	66	68
325	MACON, GA	56	61	65	73	71
326	SAVANNAH, GA	54	57	62	71	68
327	HILO, HI	46	46	42	37	37
328	HONOLULU,HI	65	68	72	70	72
329	KAHULUI, HI	64	64	64	63	68
330	LIHUE, HI	55	57	56	55	61

Sheet1 \ **Sheet2** /

Figure 3-5: Use multiple windows to view different sections of the workbook at the same time.

You can close these additional windows when you no longer need them. For example, clicking the Close button on the active window's title bar closes the active window but doesn't close the other windows.

Tip

> Multiple windows make it easier to copy information from one worksheet to another. You can use Excel's drag-and-drop procedures to do this. In addition, multiple windows are useful when examining formulas.

Comparing sheets side by side

New Feature

> The Compare Side by Side feature is new to Excel 2003.

In some situations, you may want to compare two worksheets that are in different windows. A new feature in Excel 2003 makes this task a bit easier. The sheets can be in the same workbook or in different workbooks.

First, make sure that the two sheets are displayed in separate windows. If you want to compare two sheets in the same workbook, use the Window ➪ New Window command to create a new window for the active workbook. Activate the first window; then choose Window ➪ Compare Side by Side With. If more than two windows are open, you'll see a dialog box that lets you select the window for the comparison.

The two windows will be tiled horizontally, not really "side by side." If you prefer a true side-by-side arrangement, select Window ➪ Arrange and select Vertical in the Arrange Windows dialog box.

When using the Compare Side by Side feature, you'll find that scrolling in one of the windows also scrolls the other window. When you use this command, the Compare Side by Side toolbar is displayed. This toolbar contains the following buttons:

✦ **Synchronous Scrolling:** Toggles automatic windows scrolling on and off.

✦ **Reset Window Position:** If you have rearranged or moved the windows, clicking this button puts them back in the initial horizontal arrangement.

✦ **Close Side by Side:** Breaks out of side-by-side mode and returns to the previous window positions. You can also use the Window ➪ Break Side by Side command for this.

Keep in mind that this feature is for manual comparison only. Unfortunately, Excel does not provide a way to show you the differences between two sheets.

Splitting the worksheet window into panes

If you prefer not to clutter your screen with additional windows, Excel provides another option for viewing multiple parts of the same worksheet. The Window ➪ Split command splits the active worksheet into two or four separate panes. The split occurs at the location of the cell pointer. You can use the mouse to drag the individual panes to resize them.

Figure 3-6 shows a worksheet split into two panes. Notice that row numbers aren't continuous. In other words, splitting panes enables you to display in a single window widely separated areas of a worksheet. To remove the split panes, choose Window ➪ Remove Split.

Another way to split and unsplit panes is to drag either the vertical or horizontal split bar. These bars are the small rectangles that normally appear just above the top of the vertical scroll bar and just to the right of the horizontal scroll bar. When you move the mouse pointer over a split bar, the mouse pointer changes to a pair of parallel lines with arrows pointing outward from each line. To remove split panes by using the mouse, drag the pane separator all the way to the edge of the window or just double-click it.

Keeping the titles in view by freezing panes

If you set up a worksheet with row or column headings, it's easy to lose track of just where you are when you scroll to a different location in the worksheet. Excel provides a handy solution to this problem: freezing panes. This keeps the headings visible while you are scrolling through the worksheet.

	A	B	C	D	E	F	G	H
45	REDDING, CA	6.5	5.49	5.15	2.4	1.66	0.69	
46	SACRAMENTO, CA	3.84	3.54	2.8	1.02	0.53	0.2	
47	SAN DIEGO, CA	2.28	2.04	2.26	0.75	0.2	0.09	
48	SAN FRANCISCO AP, CA	4.45	4.01	3.26	1.17	0.38	0.11	
49	SAN FRANCISCO C.O., CA	4.72	4.15	3.4	1.25	0.54	0.13	
50	SANTA BARBARA, CA	3.57	4.28	3.51	0.63	0.23	0.05	
51	SANTA MARIA, CA	2.64	3.23	2.94	0.91	0.32	0.05	
522	DENVER, CO	29.2	33.2	39.6	47.6	57.2	67.6	
523	GRAND JUNCTION, CO	26.1	34.1	43.4	50.9	60.5	71.1	
524	PUEBLO, CO	29.3	34.6	41.8	49.9	59.7	69.8	
525	BRIDGEPORT, CT	29.9	31.9	39.5	48.9	59	68	
526	HARTFORD, CT	25.7	28.8	38	48.9	59.9	68.5	
527	WILMINGTON, DE	31.5	34.2	42.7	52.4	62.5	71.5	
528	WASHINGTON DULLES AP, D.	31.7	34.8	43.4	53.1	62.3	70.9	
529	WASHINGTON NAT'L AP, D.C.	34.9	38.1	46.5	56.1	65.6	74.5	
530	APALACHICOLA, FL	52.7	55.3	60.7	66.8	74.1	80	
531	DAYTONA BEACH, FL	58.4	60	64.7	68.9	74.8	79.7	
532	FORT MYERS, FL	64.9	66	69.9	73.6	78.8	82.2	
533	GAINESVILLE, FL	54.3	57	62.5	67.6	74.3	79.2	

Figure 3-6: You can also split the worksheet window to view different areas of the worksheet at the same time.

To freeze panes, start by moving the cell pointer to the cell below the row that you want to remain visible as you scroll and to the right of the column that you want to remain visible as you scroll. Then, select Window ⇨ Freeze Panes. Excel inserts dark lines to indicate the frozen rows and columns. You'll find that the frozen row and column remain visible as you scroll throughout the worksheet. To remove the frozen panes, select Window ⇨ Unfreeze Panes.

Figure 3-7 shows a worksheet with frozen panes. In this case, rows 1:3 and column A are frozen in place. This allows you to scroll down and to the right to locate some information while keeping the column titles and the column A entries visible.

Tip If you press Ctrl+Home while the worksheet has frozen panes, the cell selector moves to the top-left unfrozen cell. You can move into the frozen rows or columns by using the direction keys or your mouse.

Zooming in or out for a better view

Excel enables you to zoom in or out to scale the size of your worksheets. Normally, everything you see on-screen is displayed at 100 percent. You can change the *zoom percentage* from 10 percent (very tiny) to 400 percent (huge). Using a small zoom percentage can help you to get a bird's-eye view of your worksheet to see how it's laid out. Zooming in is useful if your eyesight isn't quite what it used to be and you have trouble deciphering tiny type. Figure 3-8 shows a window zoomed to 10 percent and a window zoomed to 400 percent.

climate data.xls							_ □ ×
A	F	G	H	I	J	K	N
1 Normal Monthly Precipitation							
2 NORMALS 1971-2000							
3	MAY	JUN	JUL	AUG	SEP	OCT	N
58 BRIDGEPORT, CT	4.03	3.57	3.77	3.75	3.58	3.54	
59 HARTFORD, CT	4.39	3.85	3.67	3.98	4.13	3.94	
60 WILMINGTON, DE	4.15	3.59	4.28	3.51	4.01	3.08	
61 WASHINGTON DULLES AP, D.	4.22	4.07	3.57	3.78	3.82	3.37	
62 WASHINGTON NAT'L AP, D.C.	3.82	3.13	3.66	3.44	3.79	3.22	
63 APALACHICOLA, FL	2.62	4.3	7.31	7.29	7.1	4.18	
64 DAYTONA BEACH, FL	3.26	5.69	5.17	6.09	6.61	4.48	
65 FORT MYERS, FL	3.42	9.77	8.98	9.54	7.86	2.59	
66 GAINESVILLE, FL	3.23	6.78	6.1	6.63	4.37	2.5	
67 JACKSONVILLE, FL	3.48	5.37	5.97	6.87	7.9	3.86	
68 KEY WEST, FL	3.48	4.57	3.27	5.4	5.45	4.34	
69 MIAMI, FL	5.52	8.54	5.79	8.63	8.38	6.19	
70 ORLANDO, FL	3.74	7.35	7.15	6.25	5.76	2.73	
71 PENSACOLA, FL	4.4	6.39	8.02	6.85	5.75	4.13	
72 TALLAHASSEE, FL	4.95	6.92	8.04	7.03	5.01	3.25	
73 TAMPA, FL	2.85	5.5	6.49	7.6	6.54	2.29	
74 VERO BEACH, FL	3.8	6.03	6.53	6.04	6.84	5.04	

Figure 3-7: By freezing certain columns and rows, they remain visible while you scroll the worksheet.

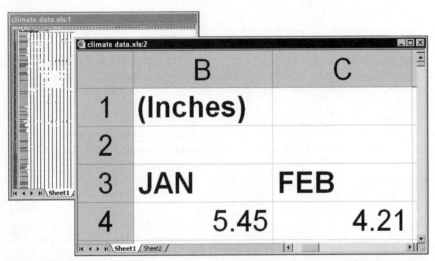

Figure 3-8: You can zoom in or out for a better view of your worksheets.

You can easily change the zoom factor of the active worksheet by using the Zoom tool on the Standard toolbar. Just click the arrow and select the desired zoom factor. Your screen transforms immediately. You can also type a zoom percentage directly into the Zoom tool. If you choose Selection from the drop-down list, Excel zooms the worksheet to display only the selected cells (useful if you want to view only a particular range).

Tip

Zooming affects only the active worksheet, so you can use different zoom factors for different worksheets. Also, if you have a worksheet displayed in two different windows, you can set a different zoom factor for each of the windows.

Cross-Reference

If your worksheet uses named ranges (see Chapter 4), you'll find that zooming your worksheet to 39 percent or less displays the name of the range overlaid on the cells. This is useful for getting an overview of how a worksheet is laid out.

You can also set the zoom percentage by using the View ➪ Zoom command. This command displays the Zoom dialog box, where you can select an option or enter a value between 10 and 400.

Cross-Reference

Excel contains separate options for changing the size of your printed output. (Use the File ➪ Page Setup command.) See Chapter 7 for details.

Caution

In some situations, using a zoom factor other than 100 may cause some strange display problems with Excel, especially if charts and graphics are used. If you experience any odd display problems, setting the zoom factor to 100 may fix it.

Saving your view settings

If you create a number of different worksheet views for different purposes, you may want to save those view settings so that you can easily recall them without going through all of the necessary setup steps each time you want to use the same view. To save your view settings, create a *named* view.

A named view includes settings for window size and position, frozen panes or titles, outlining, zoom factor, the active cell, print area, and many of the settings in the Options dialog box. A named view can also include hidden print settings and hidden rows and columns. If you find that you're constantly fiddling with these settings and then changing them back, using named views can save you lots of effort.

To create a named view, begin by setting up the view settings the way you want them (for example, hide some columns). Then select View ➪ Custom Views to display the Custom Views dialog box. Click the Add button and provide a name in the Add View dialog box that appears (see Figure 3-9). You can also specify what to include in the view by using the two check boxes. Click OK to save the named view.

The Custom Views dialog box displays a list of all named views. To select a particular view, just select it from the list and click the Show button. To delete a named view from the list, click the Delete button.

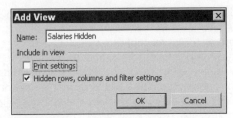

Figure 3-9: Use the Add View dialog box to create a named view.

Monitoring cells with a Watch Window

In some situations, you may want to keep track of the value in a particular cell. As you scroll throughout the worksheet, that cell may disappear from view. Using a Watch Window can help.

The Watch Window is actually a special type of toolbar. To display the Watch Window toolbar, choose View ➪ Toolbars ➪ Watch Window. Then click Add Watch and specify the cell that you want to watch. The Watch Window will display the value in that cell. You can add any number of cells to the Watch Window, and you can move the toolbar to a convenient location. Figure 3-10 shows the Watch Window monitoring two cells.

Book	Sheet	Name	Cell	Value	Formula	
Sales Data.xls	Sheet1		I18	8582.077192	=SUM(I1:I17)	
Sales Data.xls	Sheet2		F23	18	=COUNTA(C:C)	

Figure 3-10: Use the Watch Window toolbar to monitor the value in one or more cells.

Working with Rows and Columns

This section discusses some worksheet operations that involve rows and columns. Rows and columns make up an Excel worksheet. Every worksheet has exactly 65,536 rows and 256 columns.

Note
One of the most commonly asked questions about Excel is *How can I increase the number of rows and columns?* Unfortunately, there is no way to do it. The number of rows and columns is fixed, and you can't change them. One would think that a company with seemingly unlimited resources could design a more flexible spreadsheet, but apparently Microsoft chooses to focus its development efforts in other areas.

Inserting rows and columns

Although the number of rows and columns in a worksheet is fixed, you can still insert and delete rows and columns if you need to make room for additional information — perhaps to include additional items in a calculation, for example. These operations don't change the number of rows or columns. Rather, inserting a new row moves down the other rows to accommodate the new row. The last row is simply removed from the worksheet if it is empty. Inserting a new column shifts the columns to the right, and the last column is removed if it's empty.

Note

If the last row (row 65,536) is not empty, you can't insert a new row. Similarly, if the last column (column IV) contains information, Excel won't let you insert a new column. Attempting to add a row or column displays the dialog box shown in Figure 3-11.

Figure 3-11: You can't add a new row or column if doing so would move nonblank cells off the worksheet.

To insert a new row or rows, you can use any of the following techniques:

✦ Select an entire row or multiple rows by clicking the row numbers in the worksheet border. Select the Insert ⇨ Rows command.

✦ Select an entire row or multiple rows by clicking the row numbers in the worksheet border. Right-click and choose Insert from the shortcut menu.

✦ Move the cell pointer to the row that you want to insert and then select Insert ⇨ Rows. If you select multiple cells in the column, Excel inserts additional rows that correspond to the number of cells selected in the column and moves the rows below the insertion down.

The procedure for inserting a new column or columns is similar, but you use the Insert ⇨ Column command.

You also can insert cells, rather than just rows or columns. Select the range into which you want to add new cells and then select Insert ⇨ Cells (or right-click the selection and choose Insert). To insert cells, the other cells must be shifted to the right or shifted down. Therefore, Excel displays the Insert dialog box shown in Figure 3-12 to learn the direction in which you want to shift the cells.

Figure 3-12: You can insert partial rows or columns by using the Insert dialog box.

Deleting rows and columns

You may also find that it's necessary to delete rows or columns in a worksheet. For example, your sheet may contain old data that is no longer needed.

To delete a row or rows, use any of the following methods:

✦ Select an entire row or multiple rows by clicking the row numbers in the worksheet border and then select Edit ➪ Delete.

✦ Select an entire row or multiple rows by clicking the row numbers in the worksheet border. Right-click and choose Delete from the shortcut menu.

✦ Move the cell pointer to the row that you want to delete and then select Edit ➪ Delete. In the dialog box that appears, choose the Entire row option. If you select multiple cells in the column, Excel deletes all selected rows.

Deleting columns works in a similar way. If you discover that you accidentally deleted a row or column, select Edit ➪ Undo (or Ctrl+Z) to undo the action.

Hiding rows and columns

If necessary, you can hide rows and columns. This may be useful if you don't want users to see particular information or if you need to print a report that summarizes the information in the worksheet without showing all the details.

Cross-Reference   Chapter 28 discusses another way to summarize worksheet data without showing all the details — outlining.

To hide rows or columns in your worksheet, select the row or rows that you want to hide and then choose Format ➪ Row ➪ Hide. Or select the column or columns that you want to hide and then choose Format ➪ Column ➪ Hide.

Tip   You also can drag the row or column's border to hide the row or column. You must drag the border in the row or column heading. Drag the bottom border of a row upward or the border of a column to the left.

A hidden row is actually a row with its height set to zero. Similarly, a hidden column has a column width of zero. When you use the arrow keys to move the cell pointer, cells in hidden rows or columns are skipped. In other words, you can't use the arrow keys to move to a cell in a hidden row or column.

Unhiding a hidden row or column can be a bit tricky because selecting a row or column that's hidden is difficult. The solution is to select the columns or rows that are adjacent to the hidden column or row. (Select at least one column or row on either side.) Then select Format ➪ Row ➪ Unhide or Format ➪ Column ➪ Unhide. Another method is to select Edit ➪ Go To (or its F5 equivalent) to select a cell in a hidden row or column. For example, if column A is hidden, you can press F5 and specify cell A1 (or any other cell in column A) to move the cell pointer to the hidden column. Then you can use the appropriate command to unhide the column.

Changing column widths and row heights

Often, you'll want to change the width of a column or the height of a row. For example, you can make columns narrower to accommodate more information on a printed page. Or you may want to increase row height to create a "double spaced" effect.

Excel provides several different ways to change the widths of columns and the height of rows.

Changing column widths

Column width is measured in terms of the number of characters of a *fixed pitch font* that will fit into the cell's width. By default, each column's width is 8.43 characters. This is actually a rather meaningless measurement because most of the fonts you will use are *proportional fonts* — the width of individual characters varies; for example, the letter *i* is much narrower than the letter *W*.

Tip   If hash symbols (#) fill a cell that contains a numerical value, the column isn't wide enough to accommodate the information in the cell. Widen the column to solve the problem.

Before you change the width, you can select multiple columns, so that the width will be the same for all selected columns. To select multiple columns, either click and drag in the column border or press Ctrl while you select individual columns. To select all columns, click the Select All button in the upper-left corner of the worksheet border (or press Ctrl+A). You can change columns widths by using any of the following techniques.

✦ Drag the right-column border with the mouse until the column is the desired width.

✦ Choose Format ➪ Column ➪ Width and enter a value in the Column Width dialog box.

✦ Choose Format ➪ Column ➪ AutoFit Selection. This adjusts the width of the selected column so that the widest entry in the column fits. If you want, you can just select cells in the column, and the column is adjusted based on the widest entry in your selection.

✦ Double-click the right border of a column header to set the column width automatically to the widest entry in the column.

Tip

To change the default width of all columns, use the Format ➪ Column ➪ Standard Width command. This displays a dialog box into which you enter the new default column width. All columns that haven't been previously adjusted take on the new column width.

Caution

After you manually adjust a column's width, Excel will no longer automatically adjust the column to accommodate longer numerical entries.

Changing row heights

Row height is measured in points (a standard unit of measurement in the printing trade — 72 points is equal to 1 inch). The default row height depends on the font defined in the Normal style. Excel adjusts row heights automatically to accommodate the tallest font in the row. So, if you change the font size of a cell to 20 points, for example, Excel makes the column taller so that the entire text is visible.

You can set the row height manually, however, by using any of the following techniques. As with columns, you can select multiple rows.

✦ Drag the lower row border with the mouse until the row is the desired height.

✦ Choose Format ➪ Row ➪ Height and enter a value (in points) in the Row Height dialog box.

✦ Double-click the bottom border of a row to set the row height automatically to the tallest entry in the row. You also can use the Format ➪ Row ➪ AutoFit command for this.

Changing the row height is useful for spacing out rows and is almost always preferable to inserting empty rows between lines of data.

✦   ✦   ✦

Working with Cells and Ranges

Much of the work you do in Excel involves cells and ranges. Understanding how best to manipulate cells and ranges will save you time and effort. This chapter discusses a variety of techniques that you can use to work with cells and ranges.

Understanding Cells and Ranges

A *cell* is a single element in a worksheet that can hold a value, some text, or a formula. A cell is identified by its *address,* which consists of its column letter and row number. For example, cell D12 is the cell in the fourth column and the twelfth row.

A group of cells is called a *range.* You designate a range address by specifying its upper-left cell address and its lower-right cell address, separated by a colon.

Here are some examples of range addresses:

C24	A range that consists of a single cell.
A1:B1	Two cells that occupy one row and two columns.
A1:A100	100 cells in column A.
A1:D4	16 cells (four rows by four columns).
C1:C65536	An entire column of cells; this range also can be expressed as C:C.
A6:IV6	An entire row of cells; this range also can be expressed as 6:6.
A1:IV65536	All cells in a worksheet.

Selecting ranges

To perform an operation on a range of cells in a worksheet, you must first select the range. For example, if you want to make the text bold for a range of cells, you must select the range and then click the Bold button on the Formatting toolbar.

When you select a range, the cells appear highlighted in light gray. The exception is the active cell, which remains its normal color. Figure 4-1 shows an example of a selected range (B4:C11) in a worksheet. Cell B4, the active cell, is selected but not highlighted.

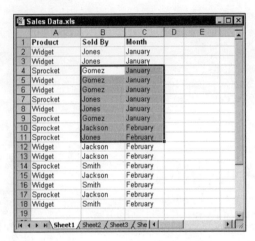

Figure 4-1: When you select a range, it appears highlighted, but the active cell within the range is not highlighted.

You can select a range in several ways:

✦ Use the mouse to drag, highlighting the range. If you drag to the end of the screen, the worksheet will scroll.

✦ Press the Shift key while you use the direction keys to select a range.

✦ Press F8 and then move the cell pointer with the direction keys to highlight the range. Press F8 again to return the direction keys to normal movement.

✦ Type the cell or range address into the Name box and press Enter. Excel selects the cell or range that you specified.

✦ Use the Edit ➪ Go To command (or press F5) and enter a range's address manually into the Go To dialog box. When you click OK, Excel selects the cells in the range that you specified.

Tip

As you're selecting a range, Excel displays the number of rows and columns in your selection in the Name box (located on the left side of the formula bar). As soon as you finish the selection, the Name box reverts to showing the address of the active cell.

Selecting complete rows and columns

Often, you'll need to select an entire row or column. For example, you may want to apply the same numeric format or the same alignment options to an entire row or column. You can select entire rows and columns in much the same manner as you select ranges, as follows:

✦ Click the row or column border to select a single row or column.

✦ To select multiple adjacent rows or columns, click a row or column border and drag to highlight additional rows or columns.

✦ To select multiple (nonadjacent) rows or columns, press Ctrl while you click the row or column borders that you want.

✦ Press Ctrl+spacebar to select a column. The column of the active cell (or columns of the selected cells) is highlighted.

✦ Press Shift+spacebar to select a row. The row of the active cell (or rows of the selected cells) is highlighted.

Tip Press Ctrl+A to select all cells in the worksheet, which is the same as selecting all rows and all columns.

Selecting noncontiguous ranges

Most of the time, the ranges that you select are contiguous — a single rectangle of cells. Excel also enables you to work with noncontiguous ranges, which consist of two or more ranges (or single cells) that are not next to each other. This is also known as a *multiple selection*. If you want to apply the same formatting to cells in different areas of your worksheet, one approach is to make a multiple selection. When the appropriate cells or ranges are selected, the formatting that you select is applied to them all. Figure 4-2 shows a noncontiguous range selected in a worksheet. (Three ranges are selected.)

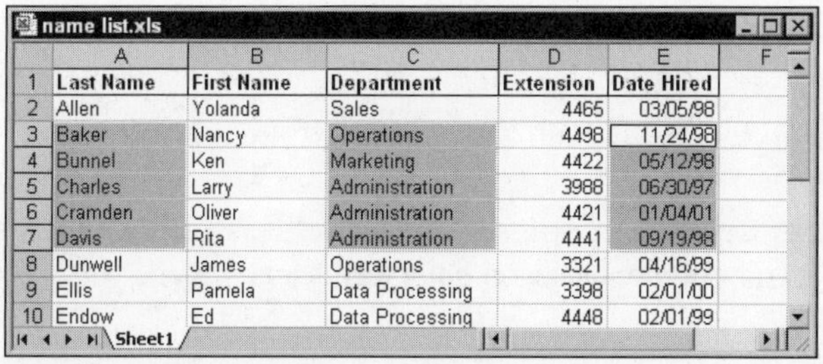

	A	B	C	D	E	F
1	Last Name	First Name	Department	Extension	Date Hired	
2	Allen	Yolanda	Sales	4465	03/05/98	
3	Baker	Nancy	Operations	4498	11/24/98	
4	Bunnel	Ken	Marketing	4422	05/12/98	
5	Charles	Larry	Administration	3988	06/30/97	
6	Cramden	Oliver	Administration	4421	01/04/01	
7	Davis	Rita	Administration	4441	09/19/98	
8	Dunwell	James	Operations	3321	04/16/99	
9	Ellis	Pamela	Data Processing	3398	02/01/00	
10	Endow	Ed	Data Processing	4448	02/01/99	

Figure 4-2: Excel enables you to select noncontiguous ranges, as shown here.

You can select a noncontiguous range in several ways:

✦ Press Ctrl as you click and drag the mouse to highlight the individual cells or ranges.

✦ From the keyboard, select a range as described previously (using F8 or the Shift key). Then press Shift+F8 to select another range without canceling the previous range selections.

✦ Select Edit ➪ Go To and then enter a range's address manually into the Go To dialog box. Separate the different ranges with commas. When you click OK, Excel selects the cells in the ranges that you specified.

Note   Noncontiguous ranges differ from contiguous ranges in several important ways. One obvious difference is that you cannot use drag-and-drop methods to move or copy noncontiguous ranges.

Selecting multisheet ranges

In addition to two-dimensional ranges on a single worksheet, ranges can extend across multiple worksheets to be three-dimensional ranges.

Suppose that you have a workbook set up to track budgets. A common approach is to use a separate worksheet for each department, making it easy to organize the data. You can click a sheet tab to view the information for a particular department.

Figure 4-3 shows a simplified example. The workbook has four sheets, named Totals, Marketing, Operations, and Manufacturing. The sheets are laid out identically. The only difference is the values. The Totals sheet contains formulas that compute the sum of the corresponding items in the three departmental worksheets.

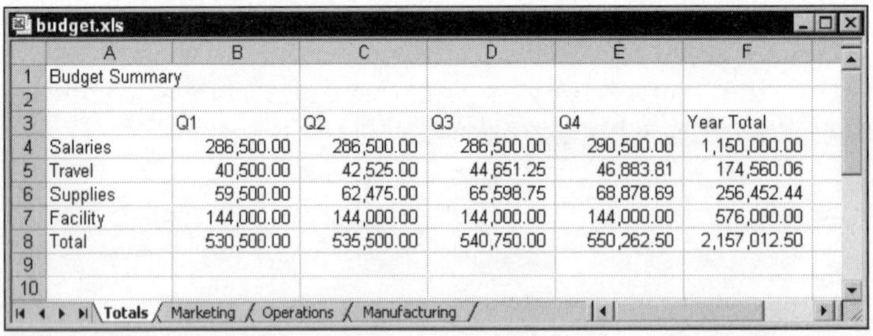

	A	B	C	D	E	F
1	Budget Summary					
2						
3		Q1	Q2	Q3	Q4	Year Total
4	Salaries	286,500.00	286,500.00	286,500.00	290,500.00	1,150,000.00
5	Travel	40,500.00	42,525.00	44,651.25	46,883.81	174,560.06
6	Supplies	59,500.00	62,475.00	65,598.75	68,878.69	256,452.44
7	Facility	144,000.00	144,000.00	144,000.00	144,000.00	576,000.00
8	Total	530,500.00	535,500.00	540,750.00	550,262.50	2,157,012.50
9						
10						

budget.xls — Totals / Marketing / Operations / Manufacturing /

Figure 4-3: This workbook is laid out identically on each worksheet.

On the CD-ROM   This workbook is available on the companion CD-ROM.

Assume that you want to apply formatting to the sheets — for example, make the column headings bold with background shading. One (not so efficient) approach is simply to format the cells in each worksheet separately. A better technique is to select a multisheet range and format the cells in all the sheets simultaneously. The following is a step-by-step example of multisheet formatting, using the workbook shown in Figure 4-3.

1. Activate the Totals worksheet by clicking its tab.

2. Select the range B3:F3.

3. Press Shift and click the sheet tab labeled Manufacturing. This selects all worksheets between the active worksheet (Totals) and the sheet tab that you click — in essence, a three-dimensional range of cells (see Figure 4-4). Notice that the workbook window's title bar displays [Group]. This is a reminder that you've selected a group of sheets and that you're in Group edit mode.

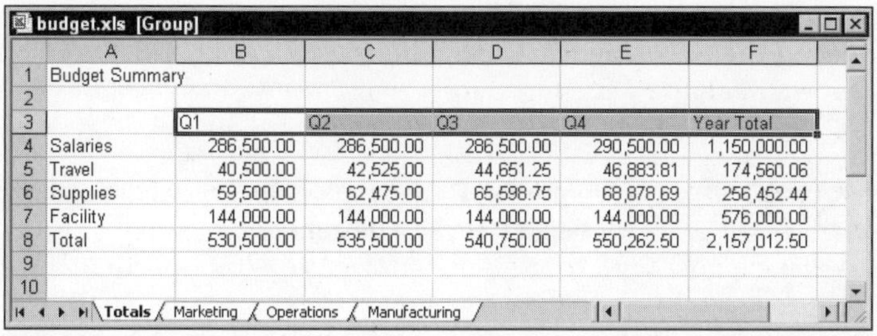

Figure 4-4: Place Excel in Group mode with a three-dimensional range of cells selected to apply the same formatting to the entire range at once.

4. Click the Bold button on the Formatting toolbar, and then use the Fill Color control to apply a colored background.

5. Click one of the other sheet tabs. This selects the sheet and also cancels Group mode; [Group] is no longer displayed in the title bar.

You'll see that Excel applied the formatting to the selected range across the selected sheets.

Tip   When a workbook is in Group mode, any changes that you make to cells in one worksheet also apply to all of the other grouped worksheets. You can use this to your advantage when you want to set up a group of identical worksheets because any labels, data, formatting, or formulas you enter will automatically be added to the same cells in all of the grouped worksheets.

In general, selecting a multisheet range is a simple two-step process: Select the range in one sheet and then select the worksheets to include in the range. To select a group of contiguous worksheets, you can press Shift and click the sheet tab of the last worksheet that you want to include in the selection. To select individual work-sheets, press Ctrl and click the sheet tab of each worksheet that you want to select. If all the worksheets in a workbook aren't laid out the same, you can skip the sheets that you don't want to format. When you make the selection, the sheet tabs of the selected sheets appear as black text on a white background, and Excel displays [Group] in the title bar.

Tip   To select all sheets in a workbook, right-click any sheet tab and choose Select All Sheets from the shortcut menu.

Selecting special types of cells

As you use Excel, you'll probably find yourself wondering how you can locate specific types of cells in your worksheets. For example, wouldn't it be handy to be able to locate every cell that contains a formula—or perhaps all of the cells whose value depends on the current cell? Excel provides an easy way to locate these and many other special types of cells. You do this by choosing Edit ➪ Go To to display the Go To dialog box and then clicking the Special button to display the Go To Special dialog box, as shown in Figure 4-5.

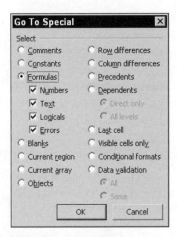

Figure 4-5: Use the Go To Special dialog box to select specific types of cells.

After you make your choice in the dialog box, Excel selects the qualifying subset of cells in the current selection. Usually, this results in a multiple selection. If no cells qualify, Excel lets you know with the message No cells were found.

Tip   If you bring up the Go To Special dialog box with only one cell selected, Excel bases its selection on the entire active area of the worksheet. Otherwise, the selection is based on the selected range.

Table 4-1 offers a description of the options available in the Go To Special dialog box. Some of the options are very useful.

Table 4-1
Go To Special Options

Option	What It Does
Comments	Selects only the cells that contain cell comments.
Constants	Selects all nonempty cells that don't contain formulas. This option is useful if you have a model set up and want to clear out all input cells and enter new values. The formulas remain intact. Use the check boxes under the Formulas option to choose which cells to include.
Formulas	Selects cells that contain formulas. Qualify this by selecting the type of result: numbers, text, logical values (TRUE or FALSE), or errors.
Blanks	Selects all empty cells.
Current Region	Selects a rectangular range of cells around the active cell. This range is determined by surrounding blank rows and columns. You can also the use Ctrl+Shift+* shortcut key combination.
Current Array	Selects the entire array. See Chapter 14 for more information about arrays.
Objects	Selects all graphic objects on the worksheet.
Row Differences	Analyzes the selection and selects cells that are different from other cells in each row.
Column Differences	Analyzes the selection and selects the cells that are different from other cells in each column.
Precedents	Selects cells that are referred to in the formulas in the active cell or selection (limited to the active sheet). You can select either direct precedents or precedents at any level.
Dependents	Selects cells with formulas that refer to the active cell or selection (limited to the active sheet). You can select either direct dependents or dependents at any level.
Last Cell	Selects the bottom-right cell in the worksheet that contains data or formatting.
Visible Cells Only	Selects only visible cells in the selection. This option is useful when dealing with outlines or a filtered list.
Conditional Formats	Selects cells that have a conditional format applied (using the Format ⇨ Conditional Formatting command).
Data Validation	Selects cells that are set up for data-entry validation (using the Data ⇨ Validation command). The All option selects all such cells. The Same option selects only the cells that have the same validation rules as the active cell.

Selecting Cells by Searching

Another way to select cells is to use Excel's Edit ➪ Find command (or press Ctrl+F). This allows you to select cells by their contents. The Find and Replace dialog box is shown below. This figure shows additional options that are available when you click the Options ➪ button.

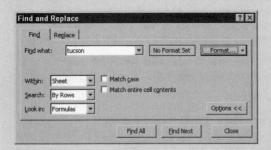

Enter the text that you're looking for; then click Find All. The dialog box will expand to display all of the cells that match your search criteria. For example, the figure below shows the dialog box after Excel has located all cells that contain the text Tucson. You can click on an item in the list, and the screen will scroll so you can view the cell in context. To select all of the cells in the list, first select any single item in the list. Then press Ctrl+A to select them all.

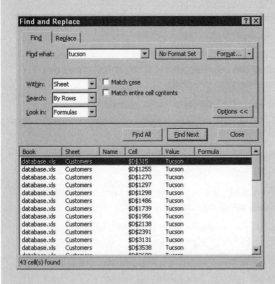

Note that the Find and Replace dialog box allows you to return to the worksheet without dismissing the dialog box.

Tip   When you select an option in the Go To Special dialog box, be sure to note which suboptions become available. For example, when you select Constants, the suboptions under Formulas become available to help you further refine the results. Likewise, the suboptions under Dependents also apply to Precedents, and those under Data Validation also apply to Conditional formats.

Copying or Moving Ranges

As you create a worksheet, you may find it necessary to copy or move information from one place to another. Fortunately, Excel makes copying or moving ranges of cells very easy. Here are some common things you might do:

✦ Copy a cell to another cell.

✦ Copy a cell to a range of cells. The source cell is copied to every cell in the destination range.

✦ Copy a range to another range. Both ranges must be the same size.

✦ Move a range to another range.

Tip   The primary difference between copying and moving a range is the effect of the operation on the source range. When you copy a range, the source range is unaffected. When you move a range, the contents are removed from the source range.

Note   Copying a cell normally copies the cell's contents, any formatting that is applied to the original cell (including conditional formatting and data validation), and the cell comment (if it has one). When you copy a cell that contains a formula, the cell references in the copied formulas are changed automatically to be relative to their new destination.

Copying or moving consists of two steps (although shortcut methods exist, as you'll see later):

1. Select the cell or range to copy (the source range) and copy it to the Clipboard. To move the range instead of copying it, cut the range rather than copying it.

2. Move the cell pointer to the range that will hold the copy (the destination range) and paste the Clipboard contents.

Caution   When you paste information, Excel overwrites any cells that get in the way without warning you. If you find that pasting overwrote some essential cells, choose Edit ➪ Undo (or press Ctrl+Z).

Because copying (or moving) is used so often, Excel provides many different methods. I discuss each method in the following sections. Because copying and moving are such similar operations, I'll only point out any important differences between the two.

Copying by using toolbar buttons

Clicking the Copy button transfers a copy of the selected cell or range to the Windows Clipboard and the Office Clipboard. After performing the copy part of this operation, select the cell that will hold the copy and click the Paste button.

Tip   If you click the Copy button more than once before you click the Paste button, Excel automatically displays the Office Clipboard toolbar.

If you're copying a range, you don't need to select an entire range before clicking the Paste button. You need only activate the upper-left cell in the destination range.

If you want to fill a range with the copied values, Excel uses the following methods to determine what to do:

✦ If you select a single cell as the destination, Excel will paste a complete copy of the range you copied into as many cells as you originally copied.

✦ If you select a destination range of more than one cell, but with fewer cells than the source range, Excel will still paste the entire range of cells you copied — even though this will extend beyond the selected destination range.

✦ If the selected destination range matches the size of the source range, it will be completely filled by the copy.

Understanding the Office Clipboard

Whenever you cut or copy information from a Windows program, Windows stores the information on the Windows Clipboard, which is an area of memory. Each time that you cut or copy information, Windows replaces the information previously stored on the Clipboard with the new information that you cut or copied. The Windows Clipboard can store data in a variety of formats. Because Windows manages information on the Clipboard, it can be pasted to other Windows applications, regardless of where it originated.

Office has its own Clipboard, the Office Clipboard, which is available only in Office programs. Whenever you cut or copy information in an Office program, such as Excel, the program places the information on both the Windows Clipboard and the Office Clipboard. However, the program treats information on the Office Clipboard differently than it treats information on the Windows Clipboard. Instead of replacing information on the Office Clipboard, the program appends the information to the Office Clipboard. With multiple items stored on the Clipboard, you can then paste the items either individually or as a group. You'll learn how the Office Clipboard works later in this chapter.

Copying by using menu commands

If you prefer, you can use the following menu commands for copying and pasting:

✦ Edit ⇨ Copy copies the selected cells to the Clipboard. (Use Edit ⇨ Cut to move.)

✦ Edit ⇨ Paste pastes the Clipboard contents to the selected cell or range.

✦ Right-click the range and select Copy (or Cut) from the shortcut menu to copy the selected cells to the Clipboard.

✦ Right-click and select Paste from the shortcut menu that appears to paste the Clipboard contents to the selected cell or range.

Copying by using shortcut keys

The copy and paste operations also have shortcut keys associated with them:

✦ Ctrl+C copies the selected cells to both the Windows and Office Clipboards.

✦ Ctrl+X cuts the selected cells to both the Windows and Office Clipboards.

✦ Ctrl+V pastes the Windows Clipboard contents to the selected cell or range.

Tip   These shortcut keys also are used by most other Windows applications.

Copying by using drag-and-drop

Excel also enables you to copy or move a cell or range by dragging. Be aware, however, that dragging and dropping does not place any information on either the Windows Clipboard or the Office Clipboard.

Tip   The drag-and-drop method of moving or copying does offer one big advantage over the copy and paste method—Excel warns you if a drag-and-drop operation will overwrite existing cell contents.

To copy using drag-and-drop, select the cell or range that you want to copy and then move the mouse pointer to one of its four borders. When the mouse pointer turns into an arrow pointing up and to the left, press Ctrl; the mouse pointer is augmented with a small plus sign. Then, simply drag the selection to its new location while you continue to press the Ctrl key. The original selection remains behind, and Excel makes a new copy when you release the mouse button. To move using drag-and-drop, don't press Ctrl while dragging.

Tip   If the mouse pointer doesn't turn into an arrow when you point to the border of a cell or range, you need to make a change to your settings. Select Tools ⇨ Options, click the Edit tab, and place a check mark on the option labeled Allow Cell Drag and Drop.

Using Smart Tags When Inserting and Pasting

Some cell and range operations—specifically inserting, pasting, and filling cells by dragging—result in the display of a Smart Tag. A *Smart Tag* is a small square that, when clicked, presents you with some options. For example, if you copy a range and then paste it to a different location, a Smart Tag will appear at the lower right of the pasted range. Click the Smart Tag and you'll see the options shown in the following figure. These options enable you to specify how the data should be pasted. In this case, using the Smart Tag is an alternative to using some of the options in the Paste Special dialog box.

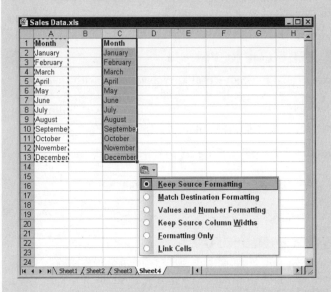

Some users find these Smart Tags helpful, while others think that they are annoying. (Count me in the latter group.) To turn off these Smart Tags, select Tools ➪ Options and choose the Edit tab. Remove the check mark from the Show Paste Options buttons and Show Insert Options buttons.

Copying to adjacent cells

Often, you'll find that you need to copy a cell to an adjacent cell or range. This type of copying is quite common when working with formulas. For example, if you're working on a budget, you might create a formula to add the values in column B. You can use the same formula to add the values in the other columns. Rather than re-enter the formula, you can copy it to the adjacent cells.

Excel provides some additional options on its Edit menu for copying to adjacent cells. To use these commands, select the cell that you're copying and the cells that you are copying to. Then issue the appropriate command from the following list for one-step copying:

✦ Edit ⇨ Fill ⇨ Down (or Ctrl+D) copies the cell to the selected range below.

✦ Edit ⇨ Fill ⇨ Right (or Ctrl+R) copies the cell to the selected range to the right.

✦ Edit ⇨ Fill ⇨ Up copies the cell to the selected range above.

✦ Edit ⇨ Fill ⇨ Left copies the cell to the selected range to the left.

✦ Edit ⇨ Fill ⇨ Series displays the Series dialog box, as shown in Figure 4-6.

None of these commands places information on either the Windows Clipboard or the Office Clipboard.

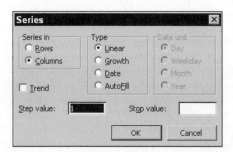

Figure 4-6: The Series dialog box enables you to fill a series of cells.

Tip   You also can use AutoFill to copy to adjacent cells by dragging the selection's fill handle (the small square in the bottom-right corner of the selected cell or range). Excel copies the original selection to the cells that you highlight while dragging. For more control over the AutoFill operation, drag the fill handle with the right mouse button, and you'll get a shortcut menu with additional options. AutoFill doesn't place any information on either the Windows Clipboard or the Office Clipboard.

Copying a range to other sheets

You can use the copy procedures described previously to copy a cell or range to another worksheet, even if the worksheet is in a different workbook. You must, of course, activate the other worksheet before you select the location to which you want to copy.

Excel offers a quicker way to copy a cell or range and paste it to other worksheets in the same workbook. Start by selecting the range to copy. Then, press Ctrl and click the sheet tabs for the worksheets to which you want to copy the information. (Excel displays [Group] in the workbook's title bar.) Select Edit ⇨ Fill ⇨ Across Worksheets, and a dialog box appears that asks what you want to copy (All, Contents, or Formats). Make your choice and then click OK. Excel copies the selected range to the selected worksheets; the new copy will occupy the same cells in the selected worksheets as the original occupies in the initial worksheet.

Caution   Be careful with the Edit ⇨ Fill ⇨ Across Worksheets command because Excel doesn't warn you if the destination cells contain information. You can quickly overwrite lots of cells with this command and not even realize it.

Using the Office Clipboard to paste

As mentioned earlier, whenever you cut or copy information in an Office program, such as Excel, you can place the data on both the Windows Clipboard and the Office Clipboard. When you copy information to the Office Clipboard, you append the information to the Office Clipboard instead of replacing what is already there. With multiple items stored on the Office Clipboard, you can then paste the items either individually or as a group.

To use the Office Clipboard, you first need to open it. Select View ⇨ Task Pane to open the task pane. Then use the task pane selector to view the Clipboard task pane.

Tip   To make the Office Clipboard task pane open automatically, click the Options button near the bottom of the task pane and choose the Show Office Clipboard Automatically option.

After you have opened the Clipboard task pane, select the first cell or range that you want to copy to the Office Clipboard and copy it by using any of the techniques described earlier. Repeat this process, selecting the next cell or range that you want to copy. As soon as you copy the information, the Office Clipboard task pane shows you the number of items that you've copied and a brief description (it will hold up to 24 items). Figure 4-7 shows the Office Clipboard with three copied items.

When you're ready to paste information, select the cell into which you want to paste information. To paste an individual item, click it in the Clipboard task pane. To paste all the items that you've copied, click the Paste All button.

You can clear the contents of the Office Clipboard by clicking the Clear All button.

The following items about the Office Clipboard and its functioning are worth noting:

✦ Excel pastes the contents of the Windows Clipboard when you paste either by clicking the Paste tool on the Standard toolbar, by choosing Edit ⇨ Paste, by pressing Ctrl+V, or by right-clicking to choose Paste from the shortcut menu.

✦ The last item that you cut or copied appears on both the Office Clipboard and the Windows Clipboard.

✦ Pasting from the Office Clipboard places that item on the Windows Clipboard. If you choose Paste All from the Office Clipboard toolbar, you paste all items stored on the Office Clipboard onto the Windows Clipboard as a single item.

✦ Clearing the Office Clipboard also clears the Windows Clipboard.

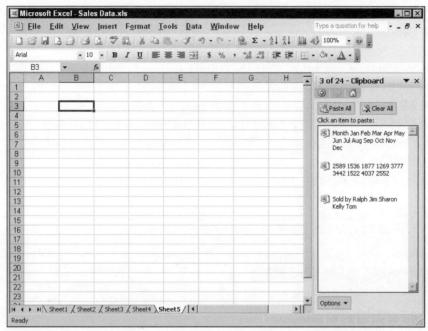

Figure 4-7: Use the Clipboard task pane to copy and paste multiple items.

Pasting in special ways

You may not always want to copy everything from the source range to the destination range. For example, you may want to copy only the current values of formulas rather than the formulas themselves. Or you may want to copy the number formats from one range to another without overwriting any existing data or formulas. To control what is copied into the destination range, you use the Edit ➪ Paste Special command — a much more versatile version of the Edit ➪ Paste command. Figure 4-8 shows the Paste Special dialog box that appears when you select this command. This dialog box has several options, which are explained in the following list. (You can also right-click and select Paste Special to display this dialog box.)

Tip   For the Paste Special command to be available, you need to copy a cell or range. (Using Edit ➪ Cut won't work.)

✦ **All:** Equivalent to using the Edit ➪ Paste command. It copies the cell's contents, formats, and data validation from the Windows Clipboard.

✦ **Formulas:** Only formulas contained in the source range are copied.

✦ **Values:** Copies the results of formulas. The destination for the copy can be a new range or the original range. In the latter case, Excel replaces the original formulas with their current values.

✦ **Formats:** Copies only the formatting.

✦ **Comments:** Copies only the cell comments from a cell or range. This option doesn't copy cell contents or formatting.

✦ **Validation:** Copies the validation criteria so the same data validation will apply.

✦ **All except borders:** Copies everything except any borders that appear in the source range.

✦ **Column widths:** Copies column width information from one column to another.

✦ **Formulas and number formats:** Copies all formulas and numeric formats, but no values.

✦ **Values and number formats:** Copies all current values and numeric formats, but not the formulas themselves.

Figure 4-8: Use the Paste Special dialog box to control what is copied from the source to the destination range.

Performing mathematical operations without formulas

The option buttons in the Operation section of the Paste Special dialog box let you perform an arithmetic operation. For example, you can copy a range to another range and select the Multiply operation. Excel multiplies the corresponding values in the source range and the destination range and replaces the destination range with the new values.

Skipping blanks when pasting

The Skip Blanks option in the Paste Special dialog box prevents Excel from overwriting cell contents in your paste area with blank cells from the copied range. This option is useful if you're copying a range to another area but don't want the blank cells in the copied range to overwrite existing data.

Transposing a range

The Transpose option in the Paste Special dialog box changes the orientation of the copied range. Rows become columns, and columns become rows. Any formulas in the copied range are adjusted so that they work properly when transposed. Note that this check box can be used with the other options in the Paste Special dialog box. Figure 4-9 shows an example of a horizontal range (A1:F1) that was transposed to a vertical range (A3:A8).

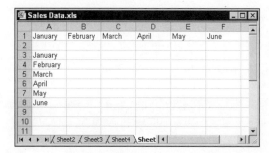

Figure 4-9: Transposing a range changes the orientation as the information is pasted into the worksheet.

Tip   If you click the Paste Link button in the Paste Special dialog box, you create an active link to the source range. This means that the destination range will automatically reflect changes in the source.

Using Names to Work with Ranges

Dealing with cryptic cell and range addresses can sometimes be confusing. (This becomes even more apparent when you deal with formulas, which are discussed in Chapter 8.) Fortunately, Excel allows you to assign descriptive names to cells and ranges. For example, you can give a cell a name such as Interest_Rate, or you can name a range JulySales. Working with these names (rather than cell or range addresses) has several advantages:

✦ A meaningful range name (such as Total_Income) is much easier to remember than a cell address (such as AC21).

✦ Entering a name is less error-prone than entering a cell or range address.

✦ You can quickly move to areas of your worksheet either by using the Name box, located at the left side of the formula bar (click the arrow to drop down a list of defined names) or by choosing Edit ⇨ Go To (or F5) and specifying the range name.

◆ Creating formulas is easier. You can paste a cell or range name into a formula by using the Insert ➪ Name ➪ Paste command, by selecting a name from the Name box, or simply by typing the name.

◆ Names make your formulas more understandable and easier to use. A formula such as =Income-Taxes is more intuitive than =D20-D40.

Creating range names in your workbooks

Excel provides several different methods that you can use to create range names. Before you begin, however, you should be aware of some important rules about what is acceptable:

◆ Names can't contain any spaces. You might want to use an underscore character to simulate a space (such as Annual_Total).

◆ You can use any combination of letters and numbers, but the name must begin with a letter. A name can't begin with a number (such as 3rdQuarter) or look like a cell reference (such as Q3).

◆ Symbols, except for underscores and periods, aren't allowed.

◆ Names are limited to 255 characters, but it's a good practice to keep names as short as possible yet still be meaningful and understandable.

Excel also uses a few names internally for its own use. Although you can create names that override Excel's internal names, you should avoid doing so. To be on the safe side, avoid using the following for names: Print_Area, Print_Titles, Consolidate_Area, and Sheet_Title.

To create a range name, start by selecting the cell or range that you want to name. Then, select Insert ➪ Name ➪ Define (or press Ctrl+F3). Excel displays the Define Name dialog box, which is shown in Figure 4-10.

Type a name in the box labeled Names in Workbook (or use the name that Excel proposes, if any). The active or selected cell or range address appears in the box labeled Refers To. Verify that the address listed is correct and then click OK to add the name to your worksheet and close the dialog box. Or you can click the Add button to continue adding names to your worksheet. If you do this, you must specify the Refers To range either by typing an address (make sure to begin with an equal sign) or by pointing to it in the worksheet. Each name appears in the list box.

Tip   A faster way to create a name is to use the Name box (to the left of the formula bar). Select the cell or range to name and then click the Name box and type the name. Press Enter to create the name. (You must press Enter to actually record the name; if you type a name and then click in the worksheet, Excel won't create the name.) If a name already exists, you can't use the Name box to change the range to which that name refers. Attempting to do so simply selects the range.

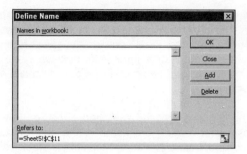

Figure 4-10: Create names for cells or ranges by using the Define Name dialog box.

The Name box is a drop-down list and shows all names in the workbook. To choose a named cell or range, click the Name box and choose the name. The name appears in the Name box, and Excel selects the named cell or range in the worksheet.

You may have a worksheet that contains text that you want to use for names for adjacent cells or ranges. For example, you might want to use the text in column A to create names for the corresponding values in column B. Excel makes this very easy to do.

To create names by using adjacent text, start by selecting the name text and the cells that you want to name. (These can be individual cells or ranges of cells.) The names must be adjacent to the cells that you're naming. (A multiple selection is allowed.) Then, choose Insert ➪ Name ➪ Create. Excel displays the Create Names dialog box, as shown in Figure 4-11. The check marks in this dialog box are based on Excel's analysis of the selected range. For example, if Excel finds text in the first row of the selection, it proposes that you create names based on the top row. If Excel didn't guess correctly, you can change the check boxes. Click OK, and Excel creates the names.

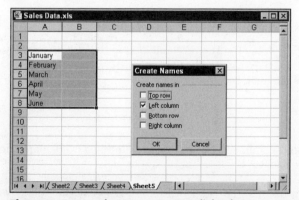

Figure 4-11: Use the Create Names dialog box to name cells using labels that appear in the worksheet.

Note If the text contained in a cell would result in an invalid name, Excel modifies the name to make it valid. For example, if a cell contains the text Net Income (which is invalid for a name because it contains a space), Excel converts the space to an underscore character. If Excel encounters a value or a numeric formula where text should be, however, it doesn't convert it to a valid name. It simply doesn't create a name—and does not inform you of that fact.

Caution If the upper-left cell of the selection contains text and you choose the Top Row and Left Column options, Excel uses that text for the name of the entire data excluding the top row and left column. So, before you accept the names that Excel creates, take a minute to make sure that they refer to the correct ranges.

Creating a table of range names

After you create a large number of range names, you may need to know the ranges that each name defines, particularly if you're trying to track down errors or document your work. Excel lets you create a list of all names in the workbook and their corresponding addresses. To create a table of names, first move the cell pointer to an empty area of your worksheet—the table is created at the active cell position and will overwrite any information at that location. Use the Insert ⇨ Name ⇨ Paste command (or press F3). Excel displays the Paste Name dialog box, which lists all the defined names. To paste a list of names, click the Paste List button.

Modifying existing range names

You may discover that the range names you have created don't completely fill your needs. For example, you may have created a range name that refers to a single cell but should actually refer to a group of cells. Or perhaps you have a large number of range names in the workbook that you no longer need.

Redefining names

If you want to change the cell or range to which a range name refers, start by selecting Insert ⇨ Name ⇨ Define to display the Define Name dialog box. Click the name that you want to change and then edit the cell or range address in the Refers To edit box. If you want to, you can click the edit box and select a new cell or range by pointing in the worksheet.

Deleting names

If you no longer need a defined name, you can delete it. Deleting a range name does not delete information in the range.

To remove a range name, choose Insert ⇨ Name ⇨ Define to display the Define Name dialog box. Choose the name that you want to delete from the list and then click the Delete button.

Caution   Be extra careful when deleting names. If the name is used in a formula, deleting the name causes the formula to become invalid. (It will display #NAME?.) However, deleting a name can be undone, so if you find that formulas return #NAME? after you delete a name, select Edit ⇨ Undo to get the name back.

If you delete the rows or columns that contain named cells or ranges, the names contain an invalid reference. For example, if cell A1 on Sheet1 is named Interest and you delete row 1 or column A, Interest then refers to =Sheet1!#REF! (that is, to an erroneous reference). If you use Interest in a formula, the formula displays #REF.

Adding Comments to Cells

Having some documentation that explains certain elements in the worksheet can often be helpful. One way to do so is to add comments to cells. This feature is useful when you need to document a particular value or explain how a formula works.

To add a comment to a cell, select the cell and then choose Insert ⇨ Comment (or press Shift+F2). Excel inserts a comment that points to the active cell, as shown in Figure 4-12. Initially, the comment consists of your name. Enter the text for the cell comment and then click anywhere in the worksheet to hide the comment. You can change the size of the comment by clicking and dragging any of its borders.

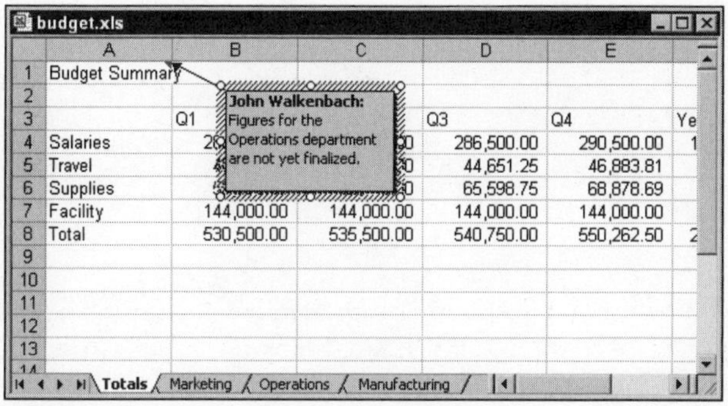

	A	B	C	D	E	
1	Budget Summary					
2						
3		Q1	John Walkenbach: Figures for the	Q3	Q4	Ye
4	Salaries	26	Operations department	286,500.00	290,500.00	1
5	Travel		are not yet finalized.	44,651.25	46,883.81	
6	Supplies			65,598.75	68,878.69	
7	Facility	144,000.00	144,000.00	144,000.00	144,000.00	
8	Total	530,500.00	535,500.00	540,750.00	550,262.50	2

budget.xls

Totals / Marketing / Operations / Manufacturing /

Figure 4-12: You can add comments to cells to help clarify important items in your worksheets.

Cells that have a comment attached display a small red triangle in the upper-right corner. When you move the mouse pointer over a cell that contains a comment, the comment becomes visible.

Tip   Select Tools ⇨ Options and click the View tab to control how cell comment indicators are displayed. You can turn off these indicators if you like.

If you want all cell comments to be visible (regardless of the location of the cell pointer), select View ⇨ Comments. This command is a toggle; select it again to hide all cell comments. To edit a comment, activate the cell, right-click, and then choose Edit Comment from the shortcut menu.

Tip   You can use the Reviewing toolbar to navigate between the comments in the worksheet.

To delete a cell comment, activate the cell that contains the comment, right-click, and then choose Delete Comment from the shortcut menu.

✦   ✦   ✦

Worksheet Formatting

Formatting is like the icing on a cake—it may not be absolutely necessary, but it can make the end product a lot more attractive. In an Excel worksheet, formatting can also make it easier for others to understand the worksheet's purpose.

Stylistic formatting isn't essential for every workbook that you develop—especially if it is for your own use only. On the other hand, it only takes a few moments to apply some simple formatting, and, once applied, the formatting will remain in place without further effort on your part.

In this chapter, I show you how to work with the Excel formatting tools: fonts, colors, and styles such as bold and italic. I even cover custom styles that you can create to make formatting large amounts of material in a similar way easier.

Figure 5-1 shows how even simple formatting can significantly improve a worksheet's readability.

Getting to Know the Formatting Tools

When you want to apply formatting to your worksheets, you can use either of Excel's formatting tools—the Formatting toolbar or the Format Cells dialog box. Generally, using the toolbar is faster, but the dialog box offers more options.

Cross-Reference Excel provides another way to format cells that is based on the cell's contents. Conditional formatting is discussed in Chapter 27.

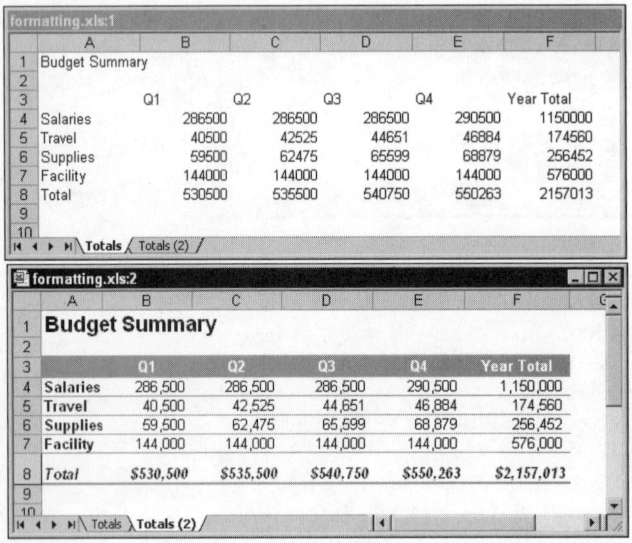

	A	B	C	D	E	F
1	Budget Summary					
2						
3		Q1	Q2	Q3	Q4	Year Total
4	Salaries	286500	286500	286500	290500	1150000
5	Travel	40500	42525	44651	46884	174560
6	Supplies	59500	62475	65599	68879	256452
7	Facility	144000	144000	144000	144000	576000
8	Total	530500	535500	540750	550263	2157013
9						
10						

	A	B	C	D	E	F
1	**Budget Summary**					
2						
3		**Q1**	**Q2**	**Q3**	**Q4**	**Year Total**
4	**Salaries**	286,500	286,500	286,500	290,500	1,150,000
5	**Travel**	40,500	42,525	44,651	46,884	174,560
6	**Supplies**	59,500	62,475	65,599	68,879	256,452
7	**Facility**	144,000	144,000	144,000	144,000	576,000
8	*Total*	*$530,500*	*$535,500*	*$540,750*	*$550,263*	*$2,157,013*
9						
10						

Figure 5-1: In just a few minutes, some simple formatting can greatly improve the appearance of your worksheets.

Using the Formatting toolbar

The Formatting toolbar provides quick access to the most commonly used formatting options. Start by selecting the cell or range; then use the appropriate tool on the Formatting toolbar. This process is very intuitive, and the best way to familiarize yourself with these tools is to experiment. Enter some data, select some cells, and then click the buttons to change the appearance. Note that three of these toolbar buttons (Borders, Fill Color, and Font Color) are actually drop-down controls. Click the small arrow on the button, and the button expands to display your choices.

The Formatting toolbar has many options, but some types of formatting require that you use the Format Cells dialog box.

Using the Format Cells dialog box

Throughout this chapter, you'll use the Format Cells dialog box to apply different formatting options. This is a tabbed dialog box from which you can apply nearly any type of stylistic formatting (as well as number formatting). The formats that you choose in the Format Cells dialog box apply to the cells that you have selected at the time.

After selecting the cell or range to format, you can display the Format Cells dialog box by using any of the following methods:

✦ Choose the Format ➪ Cells command.

✦ Press Ctrl+1.

✦ Right-click the selected cell or range and choose Format Cells from the short-cut menu.

The Format Cells dialog box contains six tabs: Number, Alignment, Font, Border, Patterns, and Protection. The sections that follow contain more information about the formatting options available in this dialog box.

Using Formatting in Your Worksheets

Applying stylistic formatting to Excel worksheets is not an exact science. People have varying opinions about what constitutes a good-looking worksheet. Therefore, the following sections focus on the mechanics. It's up to you to choose the formatting options that are most appropriate.

Using different fonts

You can use different fonts, sizes, or text attributes in your worksheets to make various parts, such as the headers for a table, stand out. You also can adjust the font size. For example, using a smaller font will allow more information on a single page.

Cross-Reference

Reducing the font size so that your report fits on a certain number of pages isn't always necessary. Excel has a handy "fit to" option that automatically scales your printed output to fit on a specified number of pages; I discuss this option in Chapter 7.

By default, Excel uses the 10-point Arial font. A font is described by its typeface (Arial, Times New Roman, Courier New, and so on) as well as by its size, measured in points. (Seventy-two points equal one inch.) Excel's row height, by default, is 12.75 points. Therefore, 10-point type entered into 12.75-point rows leaves a small amount of blank space between the characters in adjacent rows.

Tip

If you have not manually changed a row's height, Excel automatically adjusts the row height based on the tallest text that you enter into the row.

If you plan to distribute a workbook to other users, you should stick with the standard fonts that are included with any version of Windows. If you open a workbook and your system doesn't have the font with which the workbook was created,

Windows attempts to use a similar font. Sometimes this works, and sometimes it doesn't. To be on the safe side and make your fonts as compatible as possible, use only the following fonts if you plan to share your workbook with others:

✦ Arial

✦ Courier New

✦ Symbol

✦ Times New Roman

✦ Wingdings

Use the Font and Font Size tools on the Formatting toolbar to change the font or size for selected cells. Just select the cells, click the appropriate tool, and then choose the font or size from the drop-down list.

If you would like the font list to display a sample of each font, choose Tools ⇨ Customize to display the Customize dialog box. Select the Options tab, and choose the option labeled List Font Names in Their Font. Figure 5-2 shows the Font tool when this option is in effect.

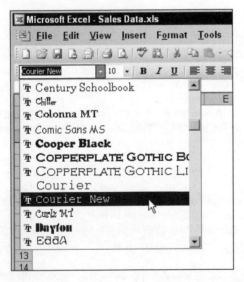

Figure 5-2: Excel can display samples of each font to make it easier for you to select the font you want.

You also can use the Font tab in the Format Cells dialog box to choose fonts, as shown in Figure 5-3. This tab enables you to control several other font attributes that aren't available on the Formatting toolbar. Besides choosing the font, you can change the font style (bold, italic), underlining, color, and effects (strikethrough, superscript, or subscript). If you click the check box labeled Normal Font, Excel displays the selections for the font defined for the Normal style. I discuss styles later in this chapter.

Figure 5-4 shows several different examples of font formatting. In this figure, the gridlines were turned off to make seeing the underlining easier. Notice, in the figure, that Excel provides four different underlining styles. In the two non-accounting underline styles, only the cell contents are underlined. In the two accounting under-line styles, the entire width of the cells is always underlined.

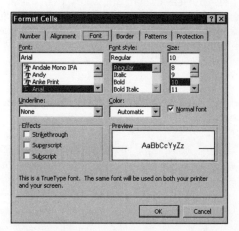

Figure 5-3: The Font tab of the Format Cells dialog box gives you many additional font attribute options to choose.

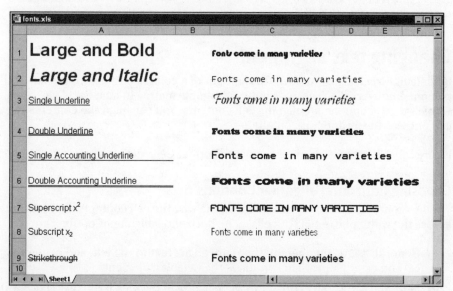

Figure 5-4: You can choose many different font-formatting options for your Excel worksheets.

Using Multiple Formatting Styles in a Single Cell

If a cell contains text that you've entered, Excel also enables you to format individual characters in the cell. To do so, switch to Edit mode (double-click the cell) and then select the characters that you want to format. You can select characters either by dragging the mouse over them or by pressing the Shift key as you press the left- or right-arrow key. Then use any of the standard formatting techniques (for example, toolbar buttons or the Format Cells dialog box). The changes apply to only the selected characters in the cell. This technique doesn't work with cells that contain values or formulas.

If you prefer to keep your hands on the keyboard, you can use the following shortcut keys to format a selected range quickly:

✦ **Ctrl+B:** Bold

✦ **Ctrl+I:** Italic

✦ **Ctrl+U:** Underline

✦ **Ctrl+5:** Strikethrough

These shortcut keys act as toggles. For example, you can turn bold on and off by repeatedly pressing Ctrl+B.

Changing text alignment

By default, Excel aligns numbers to the right of a column and text to the left of the column. But overriding these defaults is a simple matter. In fact, Excel gives you a whole range of options for aligning cell contents. You can align the contents of a cell both vertically and horizontally.

Figure 5-5 shows the Alignment tab of the Format Cells dialog box.

Choosing horizontal alignment options

The horizontal alignment options control the way the cell contents are distributed across the width of the cell (or cells). The horizontal alignment options are

✦ **General:** Aligns numbers to the right, aligns text to the left, and centers logical and error values. This option is the default alignment.

✦ **Left:** Aligns the cell contents to the left side of the cell. If the text is wider than the cell, the text spills over to the cell to the right. If the cell to the right is not empty, the text is truncated and not completely visible. If you choose Left (Indent), you can also specify the amount to indent the text.

✦ **Center:** Centers the cell contents in the cell. If the text is wider than the cell, the text spills over to cells on either side if they are empty. If the adjacent cells aren't empty, the text is truncated and not completely visible.

✦ **Right:** Aligns the cell contents to the right side of the cell. If the text is wider than the cell, the text spills over to the cell to the left. If the cell to the left isn't empty, the text is truncated and not completely visible. If you choose Right (Indent), you can also specify the amount to indent the text.

✦ **Fill:** Repeats the contents of the cell until the cell's width is filled. If cells to the right also are formatted with Fill alignment, they also are filled.

✦ **Justify:** Justifies the text to the left and right of the cell. This option is applicable only if the cell is formatted as wrapped text and uses more than one line.

✦ **Center across selection:** Centers the text over the selected columns. This option is useful for precisely centering a heading over a number of columns.

✦ **Distributed:** Distributes the text evenly across the selected column.

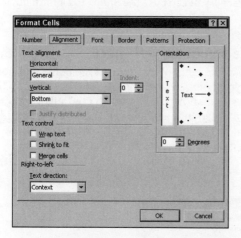

Figure 5-5: Use the Alignment tab to choose text alignment options for your Excel worksheets.

Choosing vertical alignment options

The vertical alignment options typically aren't used as often as the horizontal alignment options. In fact, these settings are useful only if you've adjusted row heights so they are considerably taller than normal.

The vertical alignment options are

✦ **Top:** Aligns the cell contents to the top of the cell.

✦ **Center:** Centers the cell contents vertically in the cell.

✦ **Bottom:** Aligns the cell contents to the bottom of the cell.

✦ **Justify:** Justifies the text vertically in the cell; this option is applicable only if the cell is formatted as wrapped text and uses more than one line.

✦ **Distributed:** Distributes the text evenly vertically in the cell.

Wrapping or shrinking text to fit the cell

If you have text that is too wide to fit the column width but don't want that text to spill over into adjacent cells, you can use either the Wrap Text option or the Shrink to Fit option to accommodate that text.

The Wrap Text option displays the text on multiple lines in the cell if necessary. Use this option to display lengthy headings without having to make the columns too wide, and without reducing the size of the text.

The Shrink to Fit option reduces the size of the text so that it fits into the cell without spilling over to the next cell.

Tip   If you apply Wrap Text formatting to a cell, you can't use the Shrink to Fit formatting.

Merging worksheet cells to create additional text space

Excel also enables you to merge two or more cells. When you merge cells, you don't combine the contents of cells. Rather, you combine a group of cells that occupy the same space into a single cell. The worksheet shown in Figure 5-6 contains two sets of merged cells. Range C1:H1 has been merged into a single cell that holds the table's title. Range B3:B7 has also been merged to hold a title for the table's rows. In the latter case, the text direction has been changed (see "Controlling the text direction," later in this chapter).

merged.xls							
				Quarterly Sales by Region			
		Q1	Q2	Q3	Q4	Year Total	
	North	155,643	156,938	160,782	162,685	1,150,000	
Region	South	160,340	163,352	162,394	156,196	174,560	
	West	156,033	158,005	157,771	157,206	256,452	
	East	154,944	154,503	159,514	159,476	576,000	
	Total	$530,500	$535,500	$540,750	$550,263	$2,157,013	

Figure 5-6: Merge worksheet cells to make them act as if they were a single cell.

You can merge any number of cells occupying any number of rows and columns. However, the range that you intend to merge should be empty except for the upper-left cell. If any of the other cells that you intend to merge are not empty, Excel displays a warning. If you continue, all of the data (except in the upper-left cell) will be deleted. To avoid deleting data, click Cancel in response to the warning.

You can use the Alignment tab in the Format Cells dialog box to merge cells, but using the Merge and Center button on the Formatting toolbar is simpler. (The Merge and Center button is the one with the letter *a* and two arrows centered inside a small box.) To merge cells, select the cells that you want to merge and then click the Merge and Center button. This button acts as a toggle. To "unmerge" cells, select the merged cells and click the Merge and Center button again.

Displaying text at an angle

Another way to create more visual impact is to display text at an angle within a cell. You can display text horizontally, vertically, or at an angle between 90 degrees up and 90 degrees down.

To change the orientation, select the cell or range, open the Format Cells dialog box, and select the Alignment tab. Use the Degrees spinner control—or just drag the pointer in the gauge. You can specify a text angle between –90 and +90 degrees. Figure 5-7 shows an example of text displayed at a 45-degree angle.

Note Often, rotated text may look a bit distorted on-screen, but the printed output is usually of much better quality.

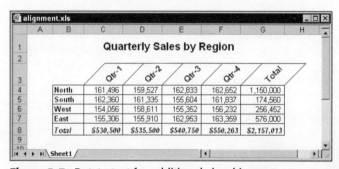

Figure 5-7: Rotate text for additional visual impact.

Controlling the text direction

Not all languages use the same character direction. Although most Western languages run left to right, some other languages are read right to left. You can use the Text Direction option to select the appropriate setting for the language you use.

Don't confuse the Text Direction setting with the Orientation setting (discussed in the previous section). Changing the text orientation is common. Changing the text direction is used only in very specific situations.

Note Just changing the Text Direction setting won't have any effect unless you have the proper language drivers installed on your system. For example, you must install Japanese language support from the Office CD-ROM to use right-to-left text direction Japanese characters.

Using colors and shading

Excel provides the tools to create some very colorful worksheets. You can change the color of the text or add colors to the backgrounds of the worksheet cells. In most cases, color is most effective when used sparingly.

You control the color of the cell's text in the Font tab of the Format Cells dialog box, and you control the cell's background color in the Patterns tab. You can also use tools on the Formatting toolbar (Font Color and Fill Color) to change the color of the font and the cell backgrounds.

A cell's background can be solid (one color) or consist of a pattern that uses two colors. Using a background pattern usually makes the text much more difficult to read. Consequently, patterns are best suited for empty cells.

To select a pattern, click the Pattern drop-down list from the Patterns tab in the Format Cells dialog box. The drop-down list expands, as shown in Figure 5-8. Choose a pattern from the top part of the box and a second color from the bottom part. The Sample box to the right shows how the colors and pattern will look. If you plan to print the worksheet, you need to experiment to determine how the color patterns translate to your printer.

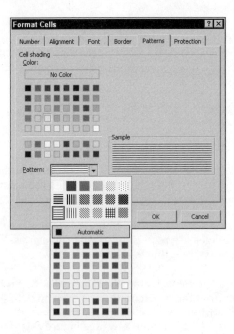

Figure 5-8: Choose a fill pattern and color to add a colored background to worksheet cells.

About Excel Colors

You may be surprised to learn that Excel is very limited when it comes to colors. Each workbook stores a color palette that consists of 56 colors. Therefore, your workbook must use colors that are contained in this palette. However, it is possible to change any or all of the palette colors. To do so, follow these steps:

1. Select Tools ⇨ Options.

2. In the Options dialog box, click the Color tab.

3. Click a color that you want to change; then click Modify.

This displays the Colors dialog box.

4. Select a new color and click OK to return to the Options dialog box.

5. Continue modifying colors, or click OK to quit.

Keep in mind that modifying a color will affect all cells that use the color. For example, if you change the red color to yellow, all instances of red will display yellow.

You can also use the Color tab of the Options dialog box to copy the color palette from a different workbook to the active workbook.

You may want to use a background color to make a large table of data easier to read. You probably are familiar with computer printer paper that has alternating green-and-white horizontal shading (often referred to as "green bar"). You can use background colors to simulate this effect in Excel.

Cross-Reference Refer to Chapter 27 for a much better way to apply alternate row shading, using conditional formatting.

Tip To quickly hide the contents of a cell, make the background color the same as the font text color. The cell contents are still visible in the formula bar when you select the cell. Keep in mind, however, that some printers may override this, and the text may be visible when printed.

Adding borders and lines

Borders (and lines within the borders) are another visual enhancement that you can add around groups of cells. Borders are often used to group a range of similar cells or to delineate rows or columns. Excel offers 13 different styles of borders, as you can see on the Border tab in the Format Cells dialog box (see Figure 5-9). This dialog box works with the selected cell or range and enables you to specify which, if any, border style to use for each border of the selection.

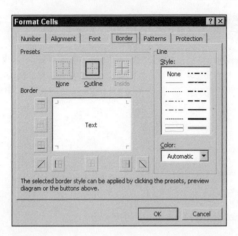

Figure 5-9: Use the Border tab to add lines around and through worksheet cells.

Before you open the Border tab of the Format Cells dialog box, select the cell or range to which you want to add borders. First, choose a line style and then choose the border position for the line style by clicking one of the Border icons.

Notice that the Border tab has three preset icons, which can save you some clicking. If you want to remove all borders from the selection, click None. To put an outline around the selection, click Outline. To put borders inside the selection, click Inside.

Excel displays the selected border style in the dialog box. You can choose different styles for different border positions; you can also choose a color for the border. Using this dialog box may require some experimentation, but you'll get the hang of it.

When you apply diagonal lines to a cell or range, the selection looks like it has been crossed out.

Tip   If you use border formatting in your worksheet, you might want to turn off the grid display in order to make the borders more pronounced. Select Tools ⇨ Options, choose the View tab, and select the Gridlines check box to do this.

Adding a background image to a worksheet

Excel also enables you to choose a graphics file to serve as a background for a worksheet similar to the wallpaper that you may display on your Windows desktop. The image that you choose is repeated so that it fills the entire worksheet.

To add a background to a worksheet, choose Format ⇨ Sheet ⇨ Background. Excel displays a dialog box that enables you to choose a graphics file. When you locate a file, click OK. Excel tiles the graphic across your worksheet. You also want to turn off the gridline display because the gridlines show through the graphic. Figure 5-10 shows a worksheet that uses an image of a brick wall as a background.

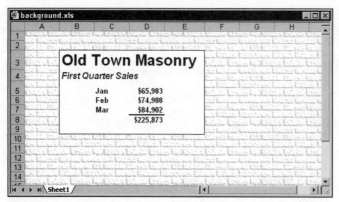

Figure 5-10: You can add almost any image file as a worksheet background image.

Caution   Some backgrounds make viewing text difficult, so you may want to use a solid background color for cells that contain text.

Note   The graphic background on a worksheet is for on-screen display only—it isn't printed when you print the worksheet.

Using AutoFormat for quick and easy worksheet formatting

So far, I've described the individual formatting commands and tools at your disposal. Excel also has an AutoFormat feature that is designed to save you time when formatting lists and tables of data.

To apply an AutoFormat, move the cell pointer anywhere within the table that you want to format; Excel determines the table's boundaries automatically. Then choose Format ⇨ AutoFormat. Excel responds with the AutoFormat dialog box, as shown in Figure 5-11. Choose one of the 16 AutoFormats from the list and click OK. Excel formats the table for you.

Excel applies AutoFormat rather intelligently. For example, it analyzes the data contained in the table and then formats the table to handle such items as subtotals.

Although you can't define your own AutoFormats, you can control the type of formatting that is applied. When you click the Options button in the AutoFormat dialog box, the dialog box expands to show six options that appear at the bottom of Figure 5-11.

Copying Formats by Painting

Perhaps the quickest way to copy the formats from one cell to another cell or range is to use the Format Painter button (the button with the paintbrush image) on the Standard toolbar.

Start by selecting the cell or range that has the formatting attributes you want to copy. Then click the Format Painter button. Notice that the mouse pointer changes to include a paint-brush. Next, select the cells to which you want to apply the formats. Release the mouse button, and Excel applies the same set of formatting options that were in the original range.

If you double-click the Format Painter button, you can paint multiple areas of the worksheet with the same formats. Excel applies the formats that you copy to each cell or range that you select. To get out of Paint mode, click the Format Painter button again (or press Esc).

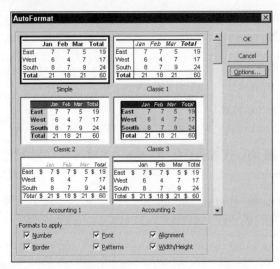

Figure 5-11: Use the AutoFormat dialog box to quickly apply a preset selection of formatting options to a range of cells.

Initially, the six check boxes are all checked—which means that Excel will apply formatting from all six categories. If you want it to skip one or more categories, just deselect the appropriate box before you click OK. For example, if you've already formatted the numbers, you may want to turn off the Number option.

Using Named Styles for Easier Formatting

One of the most underutilized features in Excel is named styles. Named styles make it very easy to apply a set of predefined formatting options to a cell or range. In addition to saving time, using named styles helps to ensure a consistent look.

A style can consist of settings for up to six different attributes:

✦ Number format

✦ Font (type, size, and color)

✦ Alignment (vertical and horizontal)

✦ Borders

✦ Pattern

✦ Protection (locked and hidden)

The real power of styles is apparent when you change a component of a style. All cells that use that named style automatically incorporate the change. Suppose that you apply a particular style to a dozen cells scattered throughout your worksheet. Later, you realize that these cells should have a font size of 14 points rather than 12 points. Rather than change each cell, simply edit the style. All cells with that particular style change automatically.

You work with styles in the Style dialog box, which appears after you choose the Format ⇨ Style command. By default, all cells have the Normal style. Figure 5-12 shows the Style dialog box, and it displays the formatting attributes for the Normal style. By default, all cells are assigned the Normal style.

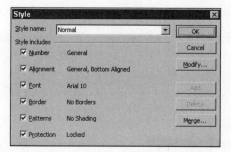

Figure 5-12: Use the Style dialog box to work with named styles.

Here's a quick example of how you can use styles to change the default font used throughout your workbook.

1. Choose the Format ⇨ Style command.

   Excels displays the Style dialog box.

2. Make sure that Normal appears in the Style Name drop-down box and click the Modify button.

   Excel displays the Format Cells dialog box.

3. Click the Font tab and choose the font and size that you want as the default.

4. Click OK to return to the Style dialog box.

5. Click OK again to close the Style dialog box.

The font for all cells that use the Normal style changes to the font that you specified. You can change the formatting attributes for the Normal style at any time.

In addition, Excel provides five other built-in styles that control only the cell's number format. The styles that are available in every workbook are listed in Table 5-1. If these styles don't meet your needs (and they probably don't), you can easily create new styles.

Table 5-1
Excel's Built-In Styles

Style Name	Description	Number Format Example
Normal	Excel's default style	1234
Comma*	Comma with two decimal places	1,234.00
Comma[0]	Comma with no decimal places	1,234
Currency*	Left-aligned currency symbol with two decimal places	$ 1,234.00
Currency[0]	Left-aligned currency symbol with no decimal places	$ 1,234
Percent*	Percent with no decimal places	12%

*This style can be applied by clicking a button on the Standard toolbar.

Applying styles to your worksheets

You can use several different methods to apply one of the named styles to cells or ranges.

✦ You can use the Currency Style, Percent Style, or Comma Style buttons on the Standard toolbar to attach a particular style to a cell or range. You need to understand that when you use these buttons to format a value, you're really changing the cell's style. Consequently, if you later want to change the Normal style, cells formatted with any of these buttons won't be affected by the change.

✦ You also can apply a style by using the Format ➪ Style command, which prompts Excel to display its Style dialog box. Just choose the style that you want to apply from the Style Name drop-down list, and click OK.

If you plan to work with named styles, you may want to make an addition to one of your toolbars. Excel has a handy Style tool available that does not normally appear on any of the built-in toolbars. To add the Style tool to a toolbar (the Formatting toolbar is a good choice), follow these steps:

1. Right-click any toolbar and choose Customize from the shortcut menu.

   Excel displays its Customize dialog box.

2. Click the Commands tab.

3. In the Categories list box on the Commands tab, click Format.

   The Buttons box displays all available tools in the Formatting category.

4. Click the Style tool (it's a drop-down box labeled Style) and drag it to your Formatting toolbar.

   If you drag the Style tool to the middle of the toolbar, the other tools move over to make room for it.

5. Click the Close button in the Customize dialog box.

To apply a style by using the Style tool, select the cell or range, open the Style drop-down box, and then choose the style that you want to apply.

Creating new styles

In addition to using the Excel program's built-in styles, you can create your own styles. This can be quite handy because it enables you to apply your favorite formatting options very quickly and consistently.

You have two ways to create a new style: You can use the Format ➪ Style command, or you can use the Style tool. To create a new style, follow these steps:

1. First select a cell and apply all the formatting that you want to include in the new style.

   You can use any of the formatting that is available in the Format Cells dialog box.

2. After you format the cell to your liking, choose Format ➪ Style.

   Excel displays its Style dialog box. Excel displays the name of the current style of the cell (probably Normal) in the Style Name drop-down list box. This box is highlighted so that you can simply enter a new style name by typing it.

3. Enter a new style name in the Style Name drop-down list box.

   When you do so, Excel displays the words By Example to indicate that it's basing the style on the current cell. (Note that the Add button is not available unless you type a new style name.)

   The check boxes display the current formats for the cell. By default, all check boxes are checked.

4. If you don't want the style to include one or more format categories, remove the check(s) from the appropriate box(es).

5. Click Add to create the style and click OK to close the dialog box.

You also can create a style from scratch in the Style dialog box. Just enter a style name and then click the Modify button to select the formatting.

If you added the Style tool to one of your toolbars, you can create a new style without using the Style dialog box. Just format a cell, click inside the Style tool list box, and then type the name. By using this method, you can't specify which formatting categories to omit from the style; but, as you learn next, you can easily modify an existing style.

Note   The Protection option in the Styles dialog box controls whether users will be able to modify cells for the selected style. This option is effective only if you've also turned on worksheet protection, using the Tools ➪ Protection ➪ Protect Sheet command.

Modifying a style to meet your needs

To change an existing style, select Format ➪ Style to open the Style dialog box. From the Style Name drop-down box, choose the style that you want to modify. You can make changes to the check boxes to include or exclude any of the format categories, or you can click the Modify button to display the Format Cells dialog box. Make the changes that you want and click OK. Click OK again to close the Style dialog box. Excel modifies all the cells formatted with the selected style by applying the new formatting.

Tip   You also can use the Style tool to change a style. Start by modifying the formatting of a cell that uses the style. Then, click inside the Style tool list box, select the style name, and press Enter. Confirm that you want to redefine the style and to change all of the cells that use the style.

After you apply a style to a cell, you can apply additional formatting to it by using any formatting method discussed in this chapter. Formatting modifications that you make to the cell don't affect other cells that use the same style.

Merging styles from other workbooks

If you use styles quite often, you probably don't want to go through all of the work to create copies of those styles in each new Excel workbook. A better approach is to merge the styles from a workbook in which you previously created them.

To merge styles from another workbook, open both the workbook that contains the styles that you want to merge and the workbook into which you want to merge styles. From the workbook into which you want to merge styles, choose Format ➪ Style and click the Merge button. Excel displays the Merge Styles dialog box with a list of all open workbooks. Select the workbook that contains the styles you want to merge and click OK. Excel copies styles from the workbook that you selected into the active workbook.

When you're merging styles, colors are based on the palette stored with the workbook in which you use the style. Therefore, if the two workbooks involved in the merge use different color palettes, the colors used in the styles may not look the same in each workbook.

Tip   You may want to create a master workbook that contains all of your custom styles so that you always know which workbook to merge styles from.

Controlling styles with templates

When you start Excel, it loads with several default settings, including the settings for stylistic formatting. If you spend a lot of time changing the default elements, you should know about templates.

Here's an example. You may prefer to use 12-point Arial rather than 10-point Arial as the default font. And maybe you prefer Wrap Text to be the default setting for alignment. Templates provide an easy way to change defaults.

The trick is to create a workbook with the Normal style modified to the way that you want it. Then, save the workbook as a template in your XLStart folder. After doing so, you can select File ➪ New to display a dialog box from which you can choose the template for the new workbook. Template files also can store other named styles, providing you with an excellent way to give your workbooks a consistent look.

Cross-Reference   Chapter 6 discusses templates in detail.

✦   ✦   ✦

Understanding Files and Templates

Excel, of course, uses files to store its workbooks. This
chapter discusses how Excel uses files — including a special type of file called a *template*. Template files can be used
for a variety of purposes, ranging from custom "fill-in-the-
blanks" workbooks to a way to change Excel's defaults for
new workbooks or new worksheets.

Even if you create Excel worksheets only for your own use,
you'll find templates quite useful. By making your own template files, you save a lot of time in the future when you want
to make use of the same settings, formulas, or even such
things as custom number formats you've developed.

Understanding Excel Files

This section describes the operations that you perform with
workbook files: opening, saving, closing, deleting, and so on.
As you read through this section, remember that you can
have any number of workbooks open simultaneously, and that
at any given time, only one workbook is the active workbook.
The workbook's name is displayed in its title bar (or in the
Excel title bar if the workbook is maximized).

Creating a new workbook

When you start Excel, it automatically creates a new (empty)
workbook called Book1. This workbook exists only in memory
and has not been saved to disk. By default, this workbook
consists of three worksheets named Sheet1, Sheet2, and
Sheet3. If you're starting a new project from scratch, you can
use this blank workbook.

Excel provides several ways to create a new workbook:

✦ Use the File ➪ New command (which opens the New Workbook task pane) and click one of the selections in the New Workbook task pane (as shown in Figure 6-1).

✦ Click the New Workbook button on the Standard toolbar. (This button has an image of a sheet of paper.)

✦ Press the Ctrl+N shortcut key combination.

Tip　Pressing Ctrl+N or clicking the New button on the Standard toolbar bypasses the New Workbook Task Pane and creates a new default workbook immediately. If you want to create a new workbook based on a template, you can use one of the template options on the New Workbook task pane.

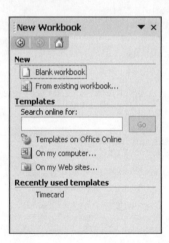

Figure 6-1: The New Workbook task pane enables you to create a new workbook.

Templates can come from several sources: Microsoft's Web site, your computer, or your own Web site (if you have one). If you select On My Computer from the New Workbook task pane, Excel displays the Templates dialog box. This is a tabbed dialog box that enables you to choose a template for the new workbook. If you don't have any custom templates defined, the General tab displays only one option: Workbook. Clicking this gives you a plain workbook. Templates that are included with Excel are listed in the Spreadsheet Solutions tab. If you choose one of these templates, your new workbook is based on the selected template file.

Starting Excel Without an Empty Workbook

If you prefer to avoid the empty workbook displayed when Excel starts up, you can do so by editing the command line that is used to start Excel. For example, if you normally launch Excel by clicking a shortcut on your desktop, you can modify the shortcut as follows:

1. Right-click the shortcut icon and choose Properties.

2. In the Properties dialog box, click the Shortcut tab.

3. Edit the Target field by adding a space, followed by **/e**, to the end. For example:

```
"C:\Program Files\Microsoft Office\OFFICE11\EXCEL.EXE" /e
```

4. Click OK.

After making that change, Excel will not display an empty workbook when it is started by clicking that shortcut icon.

Opening an existing workbook

Following are some of the ways to open a workbook that has been saved on your hard drive:

✦ Select the file you want from the list at the top of the New Workbook task pane. Only the most recently used files are listed there.

✦ Select the workbook you want from the list at the bottom of the File menu. Again, only recently used files are listed.

✦ Use the File ⇨ Open command.

✦ Click the Open button on the Standard toolbar. (The Open button has an image of a file folder opening.)

✦ Press the Ctrl+O shortcut key combination.

The last three of these methods display the Open dialog box, as shown in Figure 6-2. Note that this is a resizable dialog box. To make it larger or smaller, click the lower-right corner and drag.

To open a workbook from the Open dialog box, you must provide two pieces of information: the name of the workbook file (specified in the File Name field) and its folder (specified in the Look In field). Click Open, and the file opens. You also can just double-click the filename to open it.

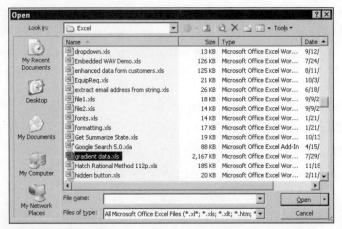

Figure 6-2: Use the Open dialog box to open any of your Excel workbook files.

The Open button is actually a drop-down list. Click the arrow, and you see the additional options:

✦ **Open:** Opens the file normally.

✦ **Open Read-Only:** Opens the selected file in read-only mode. When a file is opened in this mode, changes cannot be saved to the original filename.

✦ **Open as Copy:** Opens a copy of the selected file. If the file is named `budget.xls`, the workbook that opens is named `Copy of budget.xls`.

✦ **Open in Browser:** Opens the file in your default Web browser.

✦ **Open and Repair:** Opens the file after a crash and recovers from any damage that may have resulted from the crash.

Tip   You can hold down the Ctrl key and select multiple workbooks. When you click OK, all the selected workbook files will open.

Right-clicking a filename in the Open dialog box displays a shortcut menu with many extra choices. For example, you can copy the file, delete it, modify its properties, and so on.

Tip   You can also open an Excel workbook directly from a Windows Explorer file list. Just double-click the filename (or icon), and the workbook opens in Excel. If Excel is not running, Windows automatically starts Excel and loads the workbook file.

Selecting a different location

The Look In field is actually a drop-down box. Click the arrow, and the box expands to show your folders. You can select a different drive or directory from this list. The Up One Level icon (a file folder with an upward arrow) moves up one level in the folder hierarchy.

Choosing to open a different type of file

At the bottom of the Open dialog box is a drop-down list labeled Files of Type. When this dialog box is displayed, it shows All Microsoft Excel Files (and a long list of file extensions). This means that the files displayed are filtered, and you see only files of that type. In other words, you see only standard Excel files.

If you want to open a file of a different type, click the arrow in the drop-down list and select the file type that you want to open. This changes the filtering and displays only files of the type that you specify.

Choosing your file display preferences

The Open dialog box can display your workbook filenames in several different styles. You control the style by clicking the View icon and then selecting from the drop-down list. The View icon is located in the upper-right section of the Open dialog box just to the left of the Tools button. The style that you choose is entirely up to you.

Using the Tools menu

Clicking the Tools menu, listed last in the upper-right section of the Open dialog box, displays a shortcut menu. The following are the menu items displayed and what they do:

- ✦ **Search:** Opens a new dialog box that enables you to search for a particular file.
- ✦ **Delete:** Deletes the selected file(s).
- ✦ **Rename:** Enables you to rename the selected file.
- ✦ **Print:** Opens the selected file, prints it, and then closes it.
- ✦ **Add to My Places:** Adds a shortcut to the selected file to your My Network Places folder.
- ✦ **Map Network Drive:** Displays a dialog box that enables you to map a network directory to a drive designator.
- ✦ **Properties:** Displays the Properties dialog box for the selected file. This enables you to examine or modify the file's properties without actually opening it.

Opening Workbooks Automatically

Many people work on the same workbooks each day. If this describes you, you'll be happy to know that you can have Excel open specific workbook files automatically whenever you start Excel.

The XLStart folder is located within your Excel document folder. For example, the path may be:

```
C:\Documents and Settings\<username>\Application
Data\Microsoft\Excel\XLStart
```

Another XLStart folder may be located here:

```
C:\Program Files\Microsoft Office\Office11\XLStart
```

Any workbook files (excluding template files) that are stored in an XLStart folder open automatically when Excel starts. If one or more files open automatically from an XLStart folder, Excel won't start up with a blank workbook.

You can specify an alternate startup folder in addition to the XLStart folder. Choose Tools ➪ Options and select the General tab. Enter a new folder name in the field labeled At Startup, Open All Files In. After you do that, when you start Excel, it automatically opens all workbook files in both the XLStart folder and the alternate folder that you specified.

Saving and closing your workbooks

When you're working on a workbook, it's vulnerable to day-ruining events, such as power failures and system crashes. Therefore, you should save your work often. Saving a file takes only a few seconds, but re-creating hours of lost work takes many hours.

Excel provides four ways to save your workbook:

✦ Use the File ➪ Save command.

✦ Click the Save button on the Standard toolbar.

✦ Press the Ctrl+S shortcut key combination.

✦ Press the Shift+F12 shortcut key combination.

If your workbook has already been saved, it's saved again using the same filename. If you want to save the workbook to a new file, use the File ➪ Save As command (or press F12).

Tip

If your workbook has never been saved, its title bar displays a default name, such as Book1 or Book2. Although Excel allows you to use these generic workbook names for filenames, you'll be better off using more descriptive filenames. Therefore, the first time that you save a new workbook, Excel displays the Save As dialog box to let you provide a more meaningful name.

The Save As dialog box is similar to the Open dialog box. Again, you need to specify two pieces of information: the workbook's name and the folder in which to store it. If you want to save the file to a different folder, select the desired folder in the Save In field. If you want to create a new folder, click the Create New Folder icon in the Save As dialog box. The new folder is created within the folder that's displayed in the Save In field.

After you select the folder, enter the filename in the File Name field. You don't need to specify a file extension — Excel adds it automatically, based on the file type specified in the Save As Type field. By default, files are saved in the standard Excel file format, which uses an `.xls` file extension.

If a file with the same name already exists in the folder that you specify, Excel asks whether you want to overwrite that file with the new file. Be careful: You can't recover the previous file after you overwrite it.

Caution

Remember that saving a file overwrites the previous version of the file on your hard drive. If you open a workbook and then completely mess it up, don't save the file! Instead, close the workbook without saving it, and then reopen the good copy on your hard drive.

Using AutoRecover

The Excel AutoRecover feature automatically saves a backup copy of your work at a predetermined time interval. In addition, the feature may be able to save your work when Excel crashes. You can turn this feature on and off (and also specify the save time interval) in the Save tab of the Options dialog box.

Keep in mind that AutoRecover does not overwrite your actual file. Rather, it saves a *copy* of the file. Therefore, you should continue to save your work at frequent intervals, even if AutoRecover is turned on.

When you restart Excel after it crashes, you see a list of documents that were open at the time of the crash. You can then choose to open the original version, or the AutoRecovered version.

After you're finished with a workbook, you should close it to free the memory that it uses. You can close a workbook by using any of the following methods:

✦ Use the File ➪ Close command.

✦ Click the Close button in the workbook's title bar.

✦ Double-click the icon on the left side of the workbook's title bar.

✦ Press the Ctrl+F4 shortcut key.

✦ Press the Ctrl+W shortcut key.

If you've made any changes to your workbook since it was last saved, Excel asks whether you want to save the changes to the workbook before closing it.

File-Naming Rules

The Excel workbook files are subject to the same rules that apply to other Windows files. A filename can be up to 255 characters, including spaces. This enables you to give meaningful names to your files. You can't, however, use any of the following characters in your filenames:

\ (slash)

? (question mark)

: (colon)

* (asterisk)

" (quote)

< (less than)

> (greater than)

| (vertical bar)

You can use uppercase and lowercase letters in your names to improve readability. The filenames aren't case sensitive — My 2004 Budget and MY 2004 BUDGET are equivalent names.

Tip   To close all open workbooks, press the Shift key and choose File ⇨ Close All. This command appears only when you hold down the Shift key while you click the File menu. Excel closes each workbook, prompting you for each unsaved workbook.

Setting the file-saving options

The Save As dialog box has a drop-down menu labeled Tools. When you click this menu, one of the options displayed is labeled General Options. Selecting this item displays the Save Options dialog box, as shown in Figure 6-3. This dialog box enables you to set the following options:

✦ **Always Create Backup:** If this option is checked, the existing version of the workbook is renamed before the workbook is saved. The new filename will be named "Backup of *xxx*.xlk," where *xxx* represents the original filename. Creating a backup enables you to go back to the previously saved version of your workbook.

✦ **Password to Open:** If you enter a password in this box, the password is required before anyone can open the workbook. Passwords can be up to 15 characters long and are case sensitive. Be careful with this option because it is impossible to open the workbook (using normal methods) if you forget the password.

✦ **Password to Modify:** This option enables you to specify a password that will be required before changes to the workbook can be saved under the same file-name. Use this option if you want to make sure that changes aren't made to the original version of the workbook.

✦ **Read-Only Recommended:** If this option is checked, Excel presents a dialog box suggesting that the file be opened as read-only. The person opening the file can override this suggestion if he or she likes.

✦ **Advanced:** Clicking this button enables you to select the type of encryption that is used to protect your workbook. Depending on your security needs, dif-ferent encryption methods may provide superior protection.

Figure 6-3: Use the Save Options dialog box to protect your Excel workbook files with passwords or backup copies.

Setting the workbook summary information

When you save a file, Excel saves some additional information about the file, too. This information includes such items as the title, author, and statistics about the file. You can view this information and modify some of it by using the workbook's Properties dialog box. You can access the Properties dialog box for the active work-book at any time by selecting File ➪ Properties (as shown in Figure 6-4).

Figure 6-4: Use the Properties dialog box to store additional information about your workbook.

The Properties dialog box has five tabs:

✦ **General:** Displays general information about the file — its name, size, location, date created, and so on. You can't change any of the information in this panel.

✦ **Summary:** Contains nine fields of information that you can enter and modify. You can use the information in this panel to quickly locate workbooks that meet certain criteria. If you would like to be prompted to enter this summary information when you first save a file, use the General tab of the Options dialog box, and place a check mark next to Prompt for Workbook Properties.

✦ **Statistics:** Shows additional information about the file and can't be changed.

✦ **Contents:** Displays the names of the sheets in the workbook, and the named ranges.

✦ **Custom:** Can be quite useful if you use it consistently. Basically, it enables you to store, in a sort of database, a variety of information about the file. For example, if the workbook deals with a client named Smith and Jones Corp., you can keep track of this bit of information and use it to help locate the file later.

Safeguarding your work

Nothing is worse than spending hours creating a complicated Excel workbook only to have it destroyed by a power failure, a hard-drive crash, or even by human error. Fortunately, protecting yourself from these disasters is not a difficult task.

Earlier in the chapter, you learned how to make Excel create a backup copy of your workbook when you save the file. That's a good idea, but it certainly isn't the only backup protection you should use. If a file is truly important, you need to take extra steps to ensure its safety. The following are several backup options for ensuring the safety of individual files:

✦ **Keep a backup copy of the file on the same drive:** This is essentially what happens when you select the Always Create a Backup option when you save a workbook file. Although this offers some protection if you make a mess of the worksheet, it won't do you any good if the entire hard drive crashes.

✦ **Keep a backup copy on a different hard drive:** This assumes, of course, that your system has more than one hard drive. This offers more protection than the preceding method, because the likelihood that both hard drives will fail is remote. If the entire system is destroyed or stolen, however, you're out of luck.

✦ **Keep a backup copy on a network server:** This assumes that your system is connected to a server on which you can write files. This method is fairly safe. If the network server is located in the same building, however, you're at risk if the entire building burns down or is otherwise destroyed.

✦ **Keep a backup copy on a removable medium:** This is the safest method. Using a removable medium, such as a CD-ROM, enables you physically to take the backup to another location. So, if your system (or the entire building) is damaged, your backup copy remains intact.

Tip   Excel, like all of the applications in Microsoft Office, has the capability to recover the workbook that was in use at the time of a crash. When you reopen Excel after a crash, the program presents you with a list of workbooks that were recovered so that you can choose which copies to save. This feature is not, however, a substitute for keeping a backup copy of important workbook files.

Understanding Excel Templates

A *template* is essentially a model that serves as the basis for something else. An Excel template is a workbook that's used to create other workbooks. Creating a template takes some time; but in the long run, doing so may save you a lot of work.

For example, you may always like to use a particular header or footer on your printouts. Consequently, the first time that you print a worksheet, you need to select File ➪ Page Setup to add your page header. Although this isn't a lot of work, wouldn't it be easier if Excel simply remembered your favorite page settings and used them automatically?

The solution is to modify the template that Excel uses to create new workbooks. In this case, you modify the template file by inserting your header into the template. Save the template file, and then every new workbook that you create has your customized page settings.

Excel supports three types of templates:

✦ **The default workbook template:** Used as the basis for new workbooks.

✦ **The default worksheet template:** Used as the basis for new worksheets that are inserted into a workbook.

✦ **Custom workbook templates:** Usually, these are ready-to-run workbooks that include formulas, but they can be as simple or as complex as you like. Typically, these templates are set up so that a user can simply plug in values and get immediate results. The Spreadsheet Solutions templates (included with Excel) are examples of this type of template.

Each template type is discussed in the following sections.

Working with the default templates

The term *default template* may be a little misleading. In reality, Excel uses its own internal settings — not an actual template file — if you haven't created your own template files to control the default settings. That is, Excel uses your template files to set the defaults for new workbooks or worksheets, but if you haven't created these files, Excel is perfectly happy to use its own settings.

Using the workbook template to change workbook defaults

Every new workbook that you create starts out with some default settings. For example, the workbook's worksheets have gridlines, text appears in Arial 10-point font, values that are entered display in the General number format, and so on. If you're not happy with any of the default workbook settings, you can change them.

Making changes to Excel's default workbook is fairly easy to do, and it can save you lots of time in the long run. Here's how you change Excel's workbook defaults:

1. Open a new workbook.

2. Add or delete sheets to give the workbook the number of worksheets that you want.

3. Make any other changes that you want to make, which can include column widths, named styles, page setup options, and many of the settings that are available in the Options dialog box.

   To change the default formatting for cells, choose Format ➪ Style, and then modify the settings for the Normal style. For example, you can change the default font, size, or number format.

4. When your workbook is set up to your liking, select File ➪ Save As.

5. In the Save As dialog box, select Template (*.xlt) from the box labeled Save As Type.

6. Enter **book.xlt** for the filename.

Caution   Excel will offer the name `Book1.xlt`. You must change this name to `book.xlt` if you want Excel to use your template to set the workbook defaults.

7. Save the file in your \XLStart folder.

Tip   The \XLStart folder may be located within your `C:\Program Files\Microsoft Office\Office` folder, in the `C:\Windows\Application Data\Microsoft\Excel` folder, or in your `C:\Windows\Profiles\`*user_name*`\Application Data\Microsoft\Excel` folder (where *user_name* is your user name). The exact location depends on the version of Windows you are using.

8. Close the file.

9. Close and then restart Excel. (If you skip this step, Excel won't use your new template until the next time you do restart Excel.)

> **Tip** You can also save your `book.xlt` template file in the folder that is specified on the General tab of the Options dialog box in the box labeled At Startup, Open All Files In.

After you perform the preceding steps, the new default workbook is based on the `book.xlt` workbook template. You can create a workbook based on your template by using any of these methods:

✦ Click the New button on the Standard toolbar.

✦ Press Ctrl+N.

✦ Open Excel without first selecting a workbook to open.

Using the worksheet template to change worksheet defaults

When you insert a new worksheet into a workbook, Excel uses its built-in worksheet defaults for the worksheet. This includes items such as column width, row height, and so on.

If you don't like the default settings for a new worksheet, you can change them by following these steps:

1. Start with a new workbook, deleting all the sheets except one.

2. Make any changes that you want to make, which can include column widths, named styles, page setup options, and many of the settings that are available in the Options dialog box.

3. When your workbook is set up to your liking, select File ➪ Save As.

4. In the Save As dialog box, select Template (*.xlt) from the Save As Type box.

5. Enter **sheet.xlt** for the filename.

6. Save the file in your \XLStart folder (or in the folder that is specified on the General tab of the Options dialog box in the box labeled At Startup, Open All Files In).

7. Close the file.

8. Close and restart Excel.

After performing this procedure, all new sheets that you insert with the Insert ➪ Worksheet command will be formatted like your `sheet.xlt` template.

When you right-click a sheet tab and choose Insert from the shortcut menu, Excel displays its Insert dialog box (which looks just like the New dialog box). If you've created a template named `sheet.xlt`, you can select it by clicking the icon labeled Worksheet.

Editing your templates

After you create your `book.xlt` or `sheet.xlt` templates, you may discover that you need to change them. You can open the template files and edit them just like any other workbook. After you make your changes, save the file and close it.

Resetting the default workbook and worksheet settings

If you create a `book.xlt` or `sheet.xlt` file and then decide that you would rather use the standard default settings, simply delete the `book.xlt` or `sheet.xlt` template file—depending on whether you want to use the standard workbook or worksheet defaults—from the XLStart folder. Excel then goes back to its built-in default settings for new workbooks or worksheets.

Tip   You can also rename or move the template files if you'd like to keep them for future use.

Creating custom templates

The `book.xlt` and `sheet.xlt` templates discussed in the preceding section are two special types of templates that determine default settings for new workbooks and new worksheets. This section discusses other types of templates, referred to as *workbook templates,* which are simply workbooks that you set up as the basis for new workbooks or worksheets.

Why use a workbook template? The simple answer is that it saves you from repeating work. Assume that you create a monthly sales report that consists of your company's sales by region, plus several summary calculations and charts. You can create a template file that consists of everything except the input values. Then, when it's time to create your report, you can open a workbook based on the template, fill in the blanks, and be finished.

You could, of course, just use the previous month's workbook and save it with a different name. This is prone to errors, however, because you easily can forget to use the Save As command and accidentally overwrite the previous month's file.

When you create a workbook that is based on a template, the default workbook name is the template name with a number appended. For example, if you create a new workbook based on a template named `Sales Report.xlt`, the workbook's default name is `Sales Report1.xls`. The first time that you save a workbook that is created from a template, Excel displays its Save As dialog box so that you can give the template a new name if you want to.

A *custom template* is essentially a normal workbook, and it can use any Excel feature, such as charts, formulas, and macros. Usually, a template is set up so that the user can enter values and get immediate results. In other words, most templates include everything but the data, which is entered by the user.

Tip If novices use the template, you might consider locking all the cells except the input cells. (On the Protection panel of the Format Cells dialog box, check the Locked check box.) Then protect the worksheet by choosing Tools ➪ Protection commands.

Saving your custom templates

To save the workbook as a template, choose File ➪ Save As and select Template (*.xlt) from the drop-down list labeled Save As Type. Save the template in your Templates folder — which Excel automatically suggests — or a folder within that Templates folder.

If you later discover that you want to modify the template, choose File ➪ Open to open and edit the template.

Tip Before you save the template, you may want to specify that the file be saved with a preview image. Select File ➪ Properties and, in the Summary tab, check the box labeled Save Preview Picture. That way, the New dialog box displays the preview when the template's icon is selected.

Ideas for creating templates

This section provides a few ideas that may spark your imagination for creating templates. The following is a partial list of the settings that you can adjust and use in your custom templates:

✦ **Multiple formatted worksheets:** You can, for example, create a workbook template that has two worksheets — one formatted to print in landscape mode and one formatted to print in portrait mode.

✦ **Several settings in the View panel of the Options dialog box:** For example, you may not like to see sheet tabs, so you can turn off this setting.

✦ **Color palette:** Use the Color panel of the Options dialog box to create a custom color palette for a workbook.

✦ **Style:** The best approach is to choose Format ➪ Style and modify the attributes of the Normal style. For example, you can change the font or size, the alignment, and so on.

✦ **Custom number formats:** If you create number formats that you use frequently, these can be stored in a template.

✦ **Column widths and row heights:** You may prefer that columns be wider or narrower, or you may want the rows to be taller.

✦ **Print settings:** Change these settings in the Page Setup dialog box. You can adjust the page orientation, paper size, margins, header and footer, and several other attributes.

✦ **Sheet settings:** These are options in the Options dialog box. They include gridlines, automatic page break display, and row and column headers.

You can, of course, also create complete workbooks and save them as templates. For example, if you frequently need to produce a specific report, you might want to create a template that has everything for the report except for the data you need to enter. By saving your master copy as a template, you are less likely to overwrite the original file when you save the file after entering your data.

✦   ✦   ✦

Printing Your Work

Despite predications of the "paperless office," reports printed on paper remain commonplace, and they will be around for a long time. Many of the worksheets that you develop with Excel can easily serve as printed reports. You'll find that printing from Excel is quite easy and that you can generate attractive, well-formatted reports with minimal effort. In addition, Excel has many options that provide you with a great deal of control over the printed page so that you can make your printed reports even better. These options are explained in this chapter.

Printing with One Click

If you simply want to print a copy of a worksheet with no fuss and bother, use the Print button on the Standard toolbar. Clicking this button prints the current worksheet, using the default settings. If you've changed any of the default print settings, Excel uses the new settings; otherwise, it uses the following default settings:

- ✦ Prints the active worksheet (or all selected worksheets), including any embedded charts or drawing objects.

- ✦ Prints one copy.

- ✦ Prints the entire worksheet.

- ✦ Prints in portrait mode.

- ✦ Doesn't scale the printed output.

- ✦ Uses 1-inch margins for the top and bottom, and 75-inch margins for the left and right margins (for the U.S. version).

- ✦ Prints with no headers or footers.

- ✦ For wide worksheets that span multiple pages, it prints down and then across.

When you print a worksheet, Excel prints only the active area of the worksheet. In other words, it won't print all sixteen million cells — just those that have data in them. If the worksheet contains any embedded charts or drawing objects, they also are printed (unless you have modified the Print Object property of the object).

Tip

To quickly determine the active area of the worksheet, press Ctrl+End to move to the last active cell in the worksheet. The active area is the area between cell A1 and the last active cell. You may notice that Ctrl+End isn't always accurate. For example, if you've deleted some rows, Ctrl+End will take you to the last row that you deleted. However, when the sheet is printed, the active area is reset, so the empty rows are not printed.

Adjusting Your Print Settings for Better Results

Although simply clicking the Print button may produce acceptable results in many cases, you'll probably find that a little tweaking of the print settings will improve your printed reports.

You adjust Excel's various print settings in two different dialog boxes:

✦ The Print dialog box (accessed either by the File ➪ Print command or by pressing Ctrl+P).

✦ The Page Setup dialog box (accessed by the File ➪ Page Setup command). This is a tabbed dialog box with four tabs.

Both of these dialog boxes have a Preview button that previews the printed output on-screen.

Cross-Reference

See "Using Print Preview," later in this chapter, for more information on using the Print Preview feature.

Adjusting the settings in the Print dialog box

You use the Print dialog box to select which printer you wish to use, to choose what part of the worksheet you want to print, to specify the number of copies you want, and to access the properties settings for your printer. After you select your print settings, click OK in the Print dialog box to print your work.

Tip

Clicking OK in the Print dialog box without adjusting any settings is the equivalent of clicking Excel's Print button.

Figure 7-1 shows the Print dialog box; the following sections describe the settings in this dialog box.

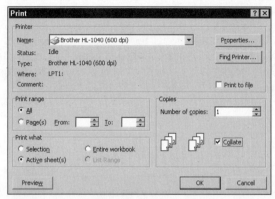

Figure 7-1: Use the Print dialog box to select a printer or choose what will print.

Choosing your printer

The Printer section of the Print dialog box enables you to choose which printer you want to use as well as to access the settings that are specific to the selected printer.

Before printing, it's a good idea to make sure that you have selected the correct printer (applicable only if you have access to more than one printer). You can select the printer from the Name drop-down list. This section of the dialog box also lists information about the selected printer, such as its status and where it's connected.

Note   If you want to adjust the printer's settings, click the Properties button to display a property box for the selected printer. The exact dialog box that you see depends on the printer. The Properties dialog box lets you adjust printer-specific settings, such as the print quality and the paper source. In most cases, you won't have to change any of these settings, but you should be familiar with the settings that you can change.

After you print a worksheet, Excel displays dashed lines to indicate where the page breaks occur. This is a useful feature because the display adjusts dynamically. For example, if you find that your printed output is too wide to fit on a single page, you can adjust the column widths (keeping an eye on the page-break display) until they are narrow enough to print on one page.

Tip   If you don't want to see the page breaks displayed in your worksheet, use Tools ➪ Options to open the Options dialog box; then click the View tab and remove the check mark from the Page Breaks check box. If you use macros, displaying page breaks can often cause your macros to run more slowly.

Crash When Printing?

If Excel crashes when you print or preview your work, it's possible that the problem is with your printer drivers or video card drivers. It's a good idea to make sure that you have the most recent drivers installed on your system. Find out the exact model number of your printer, and then visit the manufacturer's Web site. Look around, and you'll find a section to download the drivers. Make sure that you get the correct drivers, and then follow the installation instructions. If that doesn't solve your problem, the culprit may be your video drivers. Find out the make and model of your video display card and then download and install the drivers.

Specifying what you want to print

Sometimes you may want to print only a part of the worksheet rather than the entire active area. Or you may want to reprint selected pages of a report without printing all of the pages. You can make both of these types of selections in the Print dialog box, too (refer to Figure 7-1).

The Print What section of the Print dialog box lets you specify what to print. You have three options:

✦ **Selection:** Prints only the range that you selected before issuing the File ➪ Print command.

✦ **Active Sheet(s):** Prints the active sheet or sheets that you selected. (This is the default.) You can select multiple sheets by pressing Ctrl and clicking the sheet tabs. If you select multiple sheets, Excel begins printing each sheet on a new page.

✦ **Entire Workbook:** Prints the entire workbook, including chart sheets.

Tip   You can also select File ➪ Print Area ➪ Set Print Area to specify the range or ranges to print. Before you choose this command, select the range or ranges that you want to print. To clear the print area, select File ➪ Print Area ➪ Clear Print Area.

If your printed output uses multiple pages, you can select which pages to print by indicating the number of the first and last pages to print in the Print Range section of the Print dialog box. You can either use the spinner controls or type the page numbers in the edit boxes.

Printing multiple copies of a report

If you need to print multiple copies of a report, it's far easier to issue the print command one time and let your PC make certain you get the correct number of copies.

To select the number of copies to print, use the Number of Copies spin control. Simply enter the number of copies you want and then click OK to print them.

Tip   If you are printing multiple copies of a report, make certain that the Collate check box is selected. If you choose this option, Excel prints the pages in order for each set of output. If you're printing only one page, Excel ignores the Collate setting.

Note   Many printers — especially laser printers — enable your PC to specify the number of copies to print rather than requiring your PC to send the same print job multiple times. Needless to say, this is far more efficient and enables you to do other things with your PC while the printer is managing the print job.

Adjusting the Page Setup settings

For more control over how your reports print, you may need to adjust the settings that are found in the Page Setup dialog box. Using the Page Setup dialog box, you can control page layout settings, adjust the margins, create headers and footers, and adjust several worksheet appearance settings. Choose File ➪ Page Setup to open the Page Setup dialog box; Figure 7-2 shows the Page tab of the Page Setup dialog box.

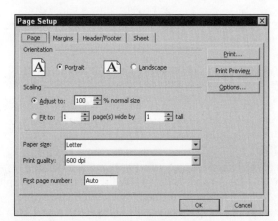

Figure 7-2: Use the Page Setup dialog box to choose a number of important appearance options.

Selecting your page appearance settings

You use the Page tab of the Page Setup dialog box to control several options that can greatly affect the appearance of your printed report. The Page tab options enable you to control these settings:

✦ **Orientation:** Choose either Portrait (tall pages) or Landscape (wide pages). Landscape orientation is useful when you have a wide range that doesn't fit on a vertically oriented page.

✦ **Scaling:** You can set a scaling factor manually or let Excel scale the output automatically to fit on the number of pages that you specify. Scaling can range from 10 percent to 400 percent of normal size. If you want to return to normal scaling, enter 100 in the box labeled Adjust to % Normal Size.

Tip

If your report is just a little too large and spills over onto extra pages, you can shrink the printout just enough to fit the desired number of pages by using the option labeled Fit To.

✦ **Paper Size:** This setting enables you to select the paper size that you're using. Click the box and see the choices. Remember, though, that you must also load the selected size of paper into your printer.

✦ **Print Quality:** If the installed printer supports it, you can change the printer's resolution, which is expressed in dots per inch (dpi). Higher numbers (resolutions) represent better print quality, but higher resolutions may take longer to print.

✦ **First Page Number:** You can specify a page number for the first page. This is useful if the pages that you're printing will be part of a larger document and you want the page numbering to be consecutive. Use Auto if you want the beginning page number to be 1 or to correspond to the pages that you selected in the Print dialog box. If you're not printing page numbers in your header or footer, this setting is irrelevant.

Tip

The Options button opens the Properties dialog box for your printer so that you can adjust the printer settings. If you selected a nonstandard paper size, you may be able to use this dialog box to specify an alternate paper tray if your printer supports this feature.

Adjusting the report margins

Margins are the unprinted areas along the sides, top, and bottom of a printed page. You can control all four page margins from the Margins tab of the Page Setup dialog box, as shown in Figure 7-3. (See the "Changing print settings while previewing" section, later in this chapter, where I discuss how to view and edit page breaks in Print Preview.)

To change a margin, click the appropriate spinner (or you can enter a value directly).

Note

The Preview box in the center of the dialog box is a bit deceiving because it doesn't really show you how your changes look in relation to the page; rather, it displays a darker line to let you know which margin you're adjusting.

Caution

Most printers cannot print to the very edge of the paper. If you specify a print margin that is too small for your printer, it's likely that some of the text in your report will simply not appear in the printout.

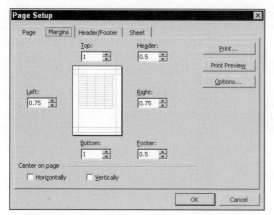

Figure 7-3: Use the Margins tab to control the amount of unprinted area around your report.

In addition to the page margins, you can adjust the distance of the header from the top of the page and the distance of the footer from the bottom of the page. These settings should be less than the corresponding margin; otherwise, the header or footer may overlap with the printed output.

Normally, Excel aligns the printed page at the top and left margins. If you would like the output to be centered vertically or horizontally, check the appropriate check box in the section of this tab labeled Center on Page.

Cross-Reference
You also can change the margins while you're previewing your output — ideal for last-minute adjustments before printing. Previewing is explained in "Using Print Preview," later in this chapter.

Adding a header or footer to your reports

A *header* is a line of information that appears at the top of each printed page. A *footer* is a line of information that appears at the bottom of each printed page. You can align information in headers and footers at the left margin, in the center of the header or footer, or at the right margin. For example, you can create a header that prints your name at the left margin, the worksheet name centered in the header, and the page number at the right margin. By default, new workbooks do not have any headers or footers.

The Header/Footer tab of the Page Setup dialog box appears in Figure 7-4. This dialog box displays the current header and footer and gives you other header and footer options in the drop-down lists labeled Header and Footer.

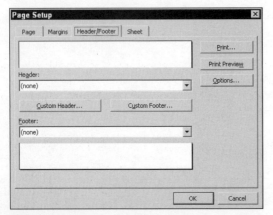

Figure 7-4: Use the Header/Footer tab to add headers or footers to your report.

When you click the Header (or Footer) drop-down list, Excel displays a list of prede-fined headers (or footers). If you see one that you like, select it. You then can see how it looks in the sample header or footer area. If you don't want a header or footer, choose the option labeled (none) for both the Header and Footer drop-down list boxes.

If you don't find a predefined header or footer that is exactly what you want, you can define a custom header or footer. Click the Custom Header or Custom Footer button, and Excel displays a dialog box like the one shown in Figure 7-5.

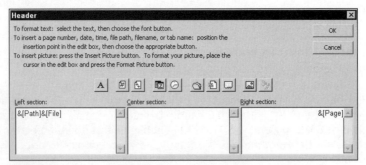

Figure 7-5: If none of the predefined headers or footers is satisfactory, you can define a custom header or custom footer.

This dialog box enables you to enter text or codes in each of the three sections. To enter text, just click in the section and enter the text. To enter variable information, such as the current date or the page number, you can click one of the buttons.

Clicking the button inserts a special code. The buttons and their functions are listed in Table 7-1.

Table 7-1
Custom Header/Footer Buttons and Their Functions

Button	Code	Function
Font	Not applicable	Lets you choose a font for the selected text
Page Number	&[Page]	Inserts the page number
Total Pages	&[Pages]	Inserts the total number of pages to be printed
Date	&[Date]	Inserts the current date
Time	&[Time]	Inserts the current time
Path and filename	&[Path]&[File]	Inserts the workbook's complete path and filename
File	&[File]	Inserts the workbook name
Sheet	&[Tab]	Inserts the sheet's name
Insert Picture	Not applicable	Enables you to add a picture
Format Picture	Not applicable	Enables you to change the picture's settings

You can combine text and codes and insert as many codes as you like into each section. If the text that you enter uses an ampersand (&), you must enter the ampersand twice (because Excel uses an ampersand to signal a code). For example, to enter the text *Research & Development* into a section of a header or footer, enter **Research && Development**.

You also can use different fonts and sizes in your headers and footers. Just select the text that you want to change and then click the Font button. Excel displays its Fonts dialog box so that you can make your choice. If you don't change the font, Excel uses the font defined for the Normal style.

Tip   You can use as many lines as you like. Use Alt+Enter to force a line break for multiline headers or footers.

After you define a custom header or footer, it appears at the bottom of the appropriate drop-down list on the Header/Footer tab of the Page Setup dialog box. You can have only one custom header and one custom footer in a workbook. So, if you edit a custom header, for example, it replaces the existing custom header in the drop-down list.

Unfortunately, you can't print the contents of a specific cell in a header or footer. For example, you might want Excel to use the contents of cell A1 as part of a header. To do so, you need to enter the cell's contents manually—or write a macro to perform this operation.

Note Two header/footer-related printing features were introduced in Excel 2002: the capability to specify a file's path and the capability to insert a picture. If you use either of these features and then print the file using Excel 2000 or earlier, the new features will not appear on printed output.

Setting the sheet printing options

The Sheet tab of the Page Setup dialog box (as shown in Figure 7-6) contains several additional options. Each option is described in the sections that follow.

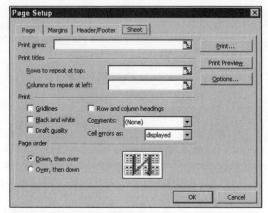

Figure 7-6: Use the Sheet tab to select the final page setup options.

Choosing the print area

The Print Area box lists the range defined as the print area. If you select a range of cells and choose the Selection option in the Print dialog box, the selected range address appears in this box. Excel also defines this as the reference for the Print_Area name.

If the Print Area box is blank, Excel prints the entire worksheet. You can activate this box and select a range (Excel will modify its definition of Print_Area), or you can enter a previously defined range name into the box.

Printing row and column titles

If your worksheet is set up with titles in the first row and descriptive names in the first column, it can be difficult to understand data that appears on printed pages where those titles do not appear. To resolve this problem, you can choose to print selected rows or columns as titles on each page of the printout.

Cross-Reference Row and column titles serve pretty much the same purpose on a printout as frozen panes do in navigating within a worksheet. See Chapter 3 for more information on freezing panes. Keep in mind, however, that these features are independent of each other. In other words, freezing panes does not affect the printed output.

Caution Don't confuse print titles with headers; these are two different concepts. *Headers* appear at the top of each page and contain information, such as the worksheet name, date, or page number. *Print titles* describe the data being printed, such as field names in a database table or list.

You can specify particular rows to repeat at the top of every printed page or particular columns to repeat at the left of every printed page. To do so, just activate the appropriate box and select the rows or columns in the worksheet. Or you can enter these references manually. For example, to specify rows 1 and 2 as repeating rows, enter **1:2**.

Tip You can specify different print titles for each worksheet in the workbook. Excel remembers print titles by creating sheet-level names (Print_Titles).

Choosing optional elements in the printout

The section labeled Print contains several options:

✦ **Gridlines:** If checked, Excel prints the gridlines to delineate cells.

✦ **Black and White:** If checked, Excel ignores any colors in the worksheet and prints everything in black and white. By taking advantage of this option, you can format your worksheet for viewing on your monitor and still get readable print output.

✦ **Draft Quality:** If checked, Excel prints in draft mode. In draft mode, Excel doesn't print embedded charts or drawing objects, cell gridlines, or borders, which reduces the printing time.

✦ **Row and Column Headings:** If checked, Excel prints the row and column headings on the printout, enabling you to easily identify specific cells from a printout.

✦ **Comments:** Excel prints cell notes by using the option that you specify: None, At the End of the Sheet, or As Displayed on Sheet.

✦ **Cell Errors As:** This option lets you choose how to print cell error values. For example, you may choose to print the error values (the default setting) or choose another option, such as Blank (which hides error values).

Selecting the page printing order

The final section on the Sheet tab, Page order, specifies how Excel should print the pages if the printout uses more than one page. You can choose to print the pages top to bottom or side to side.

Controlling where pages break in your printouts

If you print lengthy reports, controlling where pages break is often important. For example, you normally wouldn't want a row to print on a page by itself. Fortunately, Excel allows you to control page breaks.

As you may have discovered, Excel handles page breaks automatically. After you print or preview your worksheet, it even displays dashed lines to indicate where page breaks occur. Sometimes, however, you want to force a page break — either a vertical or a horizontal one — so that the report prints the way you want it to. For example, if your worksheet consists of several distinct sections, you may want to print each section on a separate sheet of paper.

Forcing a page break to appear where you want it

To insert a horizontal page-break line, move the cell pointer to the cell that will begin the new page, but make sure that you place the pointer in column A; otherwise, you'll insert a vertical page break *and* a horizontal page break. For example, if you want row 14 to be the first row of a new page, select cell A14. Then choose Insert ➪ Page Break. Excel displays a dashed line to indicate the page break.

To insert a vertical page-break line, move the cell pointer to the cell that will begin the new page, but in this case, make sure that you place the pointer in row 1. Select Insert ➪ Page Break to create the page break.

Removing page breaks you've added

To remove a manual page break, move the cell pointer to the first row beneath (or the first column to the right) of the manual page break and then select Insert ➪ Remove Page Break. (This command appears only when you place the cell pointer adjacent to a manual page break.)

Tip   To remove all manual page breaks in the worksheet, click the Select All button (or press Ctrl+A) and then choose Insert ➪ Remove Page Break.

Cross-Reference   See "Using Print Preview," later in this chapter, to see how to get an overview of the page breaks in the worksheet.

Preventing certain cells from being printed

If you have a worksheet that contains confidential information, you may want to print the worksheet but not the confidential parts. You can use several techniques to prevent certain parts of a worksheet from printing:

✦ When you hide rows or columns, the hidden rows aren't printed. To hide rows, use Format ➪ Row ➪ Hide. To hide columns, use Format ➪ Column ➪ Hide.

✦ You can hide cells or ranges by making the text color the same color as the background color. Be aware, however, that this may not work for all printers.

✦ You can hide cells by using a custom number format that consists of three semicolons (;;;). See Chapter 27 for more information about using custom number formats.

✦ You can mask off a confidential area of a worksheet by covering it with a rectangle object. Click the Rectangle tool on the Drawing toolbar and drag the rectangle to the proper size. For best results, you can make the rectangle white with no border.

Cross-Reference

If you find that you must regularly hide data before you print certain reports, consider using the Custom Views feature to create a named view that doesn't show the confidential information. See "Creating custom views of your worksheet," later in this chapter, for more information.

Using Print Preview

When you're creating a report, it's not necessary to waste a lot of time and printing supplies to fine-tune all of the print settings. It's more efficient to use Excel's Print Preview feature to display an image of the printed output on your screen.

Viewing the print preview

Excel offers several ways to preview your document:

✦ Select the File ➪ Print Preview command.

✦ Click the Print Preview button on the Standard toolbar. Or, you can press Shift and click the Print button on the Standard toolbar. (The Print button serves a dual purpose.)

✦ Click the Preview button in the Print dialog box.

✦ Click the Print Preview button in the Page Setup dialog box.

Any one of these methods changes Excel's window to a preview window, similar to that shown in Figure 7-7.

The preview window has several buttons along the top that you can use to control the process:

✦ **Next:** Displays an image of the next page.

✦ **Previous:** Displays an image of the previous page.

✦ **Zoom:** Zooms the display in or out. This button toggles between the two levels of zooming that are available. You also can simply click the preview image to toggle between zoom modes.

✦ **Print:** Sends the job to the printer.

✦ **Setup:** Displays the Page Setup dialog box, so that you can adjust some settings. When you close the dialog box, you return to the preview screen, so that you can see the effects of your changes.

✦ **Margins:** Displays adjustable columns and margins, which are described in the next section.

✦ **Page Break Preview:** Displays the worksheet in Page Break Preview mode.

✦ **Close:** Closes the preview window.

✦ **Help:** Displays help for the preview window.

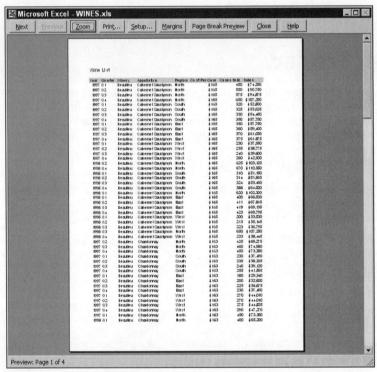

Figure 7-7: Use the Print Preview command to save paper by previewing the printed output.

Changing print settings while previewing

If you discover a problem while previewing, you can make some changes directly in the Print Preview window and see the effect of those changes immediately.

When you click the Margins button in the preview window, Excel adds markers to the preview that indicate column borders and margins, as shown in Figure 7-8.

(The window is zoomed in to better show the markers.) You can drag the column or margin markers to make changes that appear on-screen.

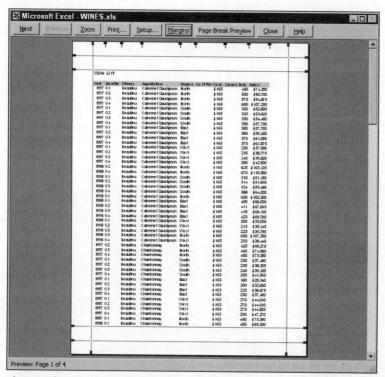

Figure 7-8: You can adjust column widths or margins directly from the Print Preview window.

For example, if you print a worksheet and discover that Excel is printing the last column on a second page, you can adjust the column widths or margins in the preview window to force all the columns to print on a single page. After you drag one of these markers, Excel updates the display so that you can see what effect it had.

When you make changes to the column widths in the preview window, these changes also are made in your worksheet. Similarly, changing the margins in the preview window changes the settings that appear in the Margins tab of the Page Setup dialog box.

Using Page Break Preview mode

The Print Preview window shows you how the individual pages of the report will appear, but it can be a little difficult to visualize just how the overall print job will break down into pages. For this overview, you might want to view your worksheets in Page Break Preview mode.

To enter Page Break Preview mode, choose the View ➪ Page Break Preview command or click the Page Break Preview button in the Print Preview window. The worksheet display changes, and you can see exactly what will be printed and where the page breaks occur, as shown in Figure 7-9.

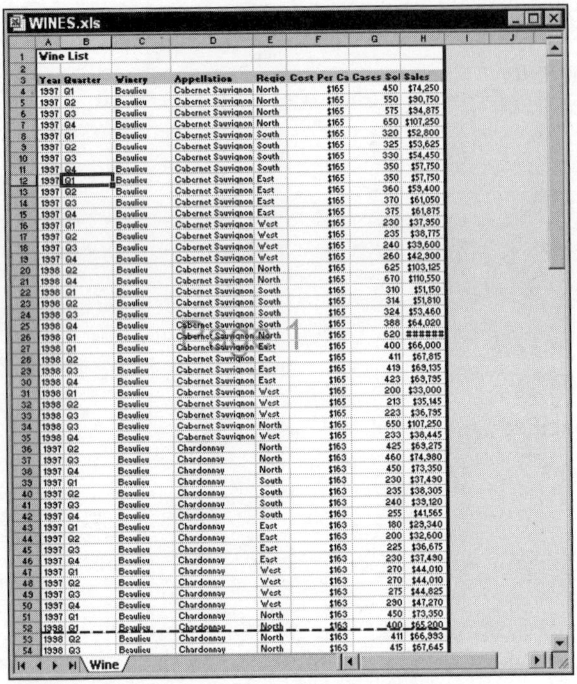

Figure 7-9: Page Break Preview mode gives you a bird's-eye view of your worksheet and shows exactly where the page breaks occur.

When you enter Page Break Preview mode, Excel

✦ Changes the zoom factor so that you can see more of the worksheet.

✦ Displays the page numbers overlaid on the pages.

✦ Displays the current print range with a white background; nonprinting data appears with a gray background.

✦ Displays all page breaks.

When you're in Page Break Preview mode, you can drag the borders to change the print range or the page breaks. When you change the page breaks, Excel automatically adjusts the scaling so that the information fits on the pages, per your specifications.

Tip   In Page Break Preview mode, you still have access to all of Excel's commands. You can change the zoom factor if you find the text to be too small.

To return to normal viewing, select the View ⇨ Normal command.

Creating custom views of your worksheet

If you need to create several different reports from the same Excel workbook, you may find that setting up the specific settings for a report can be a tedious project. An excellent way to simplify the process is to create custom-named views of your worksheets that include the proper settings for each report.

The Custom Views feature enables you to give names to various views of your worksheet, and you can quickly switch among these named views. A view includes settings for the following:

✦ Print settings, as specified in the Page Setup dialog box (optional)

✦ Hidden rows and columns (optional)

✦ Display settings, as specified in the Options Display dialog box

✦ Selected cells and ranges

✦ The active cell

✦ Window sizes and positions

✦ Frozen panes

For example, you might define a view that hides a few columns of numbers, another view with a print range defined as a summary range only, another view with the page setup set to landscape, and so on.

Cross-Reference   To learn more about creating custom views, see Chapter 3.

✦   ✦   ✦

Working with Formulas and Functions

Formulas and worksheet functions are essential to manipulating data and obtaining useful information from your Excel workbooks. The chapters in this part present a wide variety of formula examples that use many of Excel's functions. Two of the chapters are devoted to array formulas. These are intended primarily for advanced users who need to perform calculations that might otherwise be impossible.

Introducing Formulas and Functions

Formulas are what make a spreadsheet so useful. You use formulas in your Excel worksheets to calculate results from the data stored in the worksheet. When data changes, those formulas produce updated results without extra effort on your part. This chapter introduces formulas and functions and helps you get up to speed with this important element.

Understanding Formula Basics

A formula is entered into a cell. It performs a calculation and returns a result. Formulas use arithmetic operators to work with values, text, worksheet functions, and other formulas to calculate a value in the cell. Values and text can be located in other cells, which makes changing data easy and gives worksheets their dynamic nature. In essence, you can see multiple scenarios quickly by changing the data in a worksheet and letting formulas do the work.

A formula can consist of any of these elements:

✦ Mathematical operators, such as + (for addition) and × (for multiplication)

✦ Cell references (including named cells and ranges)

✦ Values or text

✦ Worksheet functions (such as SUM or AVERAGE)

After you enter a formula, the cell displays the calculated result of the formula. The formula itself appears in the formula bar when you select the cell, however.

Following are a few examples of formulas:

`=150*.05`	Multiplies 150 times 0.05. This formula uses only values and isn't all that useful.
`=A1+A2`	Adds the values in cells A1 and A2.
`=Income-Expenses`	Subtracts the cell named Expenses from the cell named Income.
`=SUM(A1:A12)`	Adds the values in the range A1:A12.
`=A1=C12`	Compares cell A1 with cell C12. If they are identical, the formula returns TRUE; otherwise, it returns FALSE.

Note   Formulas always begin with an equal sign so that Excel can distinguish formulas from text.

Using operators in formulas

Excel lets you use a variety of *operators* in your formulas. Operators are symbols that tell Excel what type of mathematical operation you want the formula to perform. Table 8-1 lists the operators that Excel recognizes. In addition to these, Excel has many built-in functions that enable you to perform additional calculations.

Table 8-1
Operators Used in Formulas

Operator	Name
+	Addition
–	Subtraction
*	Multiplication
/	Division
^	Exponentiation
&	Concatenation
=	Logical comparison (equal to)
>	Logical comparison (greater than)
<	Logical comparison (less than)
>=	Logical comparison (greater than or equal to)
<=	Logical comparison (less than or equal to)
<>	Logical comparison (not equal to)

You can, of course, use as many operators as you need. (Formulas can be quite complex.)

Following are some examples of formulas that use various operators.

Formula	What It Does
`="Part-"&"23A"`	Joins (concatenates) the two text strings to produce Part-23A.
`=A1&A2`	Concatenates the contents of cell A1 with cell A2. Concatenation works with values as well as text. If cell A1 contains 123 and cell A2 contains 456, this formula would return the value 123456.
`=6^3`	Raises 6 to the third power (216).
`=216^(1/3)`	Returns the cube root of 216 (6).
`=A1<A2`	Returns TRUE if the value in cell A1 is less than the value in cell A2. Otherwise, it returns FALSE. Logical comparison operators also work with text. If A1 contained Bill and A2 contained Julia, the formula would return TRUE, because Bill comes before Julia in alphabetical order.
`=A1<=A2`	Returns TRUE if the value in cell A1 is less than or equal to the value in cell A2. Otherwise, it returns FALSE.
`=A1<>A2`	Returns TRUE if the value in cell A1 isn't equal to the value in cell A2. Otherwise, it returns FALSE.

Understanding operator precedence in formulas

When Excel calculates the value of a formula, it uses certain rules to determine the order in which the various parts of the formula are resolved. You need to understand these rules if you want your formulas to produce the desired results.

Table 8-2 lists the Excel operator precedence. This table shows that exponentiation has the highest precedence (that is, it's performed first) and logical comparisons have the lowest precedence.

You use parentheses to override the Excel program's built-in order of precedence. Expressions within parentheses are always evaluated first.

In the following formula, parentheses are used to control the order in which the calculations occur. In this case, cell B3 is subtracted from cell B2 and the result is multiplied by cell B4.

```
=(B2-B3)*B4
```

	Table 8-2	
	Operator Precedence in Excel Formulas	
Symbol	**Operator**	**Precedence**
^	Exponentiation	1
*	Multiplication	2
/	Division	2
+	Addition	3
–	Subtraction	3
&	Concatenation	4
=	Equal to	5
<	Less than	5
>	Greater than	5

If you enter the formula without the parentheses, Excel computes a different answer. Because multiplication has a higher precedence, the cell B3 is multiplied by cell B4. Then this result is subtracted from cell B2. This isn't what was intended.

The formula without parentheses looks like this:

```
=B2-B3*B4
```

You can also *nest parentheses* in formulas, which means putting parentheses inside of parentheses. If you do so, Excel evaluates the most deeply nested expressions first and works its way out. Here is an example of a formula that uses nested parentheses.

```
=((B2*C2)+(B3*C3)+(B4*C4))*B6
```

This formula has four sets of parentheses — three sets are nested inside the fourth set. Excel evaluates each nested set of parentheses and then adds up the three results. This sum is then multiplied by the value in B6.

Although the preceding formula uses four sets of parentheses, only the outer set is really necessary. If you understand operator precedence, it should be clear that the formula above could be rewritten as

```
=(B2*C2+B3*C3+B4*C4)*B6
```

However, using the extra parentheses makes the calculation much clearer.

Every left parenthesis, of course, must have a matching right parenthesis. If you have many levels of nested parentheses, keeping them straight can sometimes be difficult. If the parentheses don't match, Excel displays a message explaining the problem and won't let you enter the formula.

In some cases, if your formula contains mismatched parentheses, Excel may propose a correction to your formula. Figure 8-1 shows an example of the Formula AutoCorrect feature. You may be tempted simply to accept the proposed correction, but be careful — in many cases, the proposed formula, although syntactically correct, isn't the formula that you want.

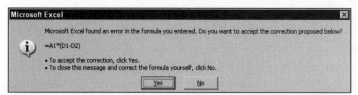

Figure 8-1: Excel's Formula AutoCorrect feature often suggests a correction to an erroneous formula.

Tip Excel lends a hand in helping you match parentheses. When the insertion point moves over a parenthesis while editing a cell, Excel momentarily bolds it and its matching parenthesis.

Using functions in your formulas

Most of the formulas that you create will use worksheet functions. Functions enable you to greatly enhance the power of your formulas and perform calculations that are not possible by using the operators discussed previously. For example, you can use the TAN function to calculate the tangent of an angle. This calculation would be impossible when using only the mathematical operators.

Examples of formulas that use functions

A built-in function can simplify a formula significantly. To calculate the average of the values in 10 cells (A1:A10) without using a function, you need to construct a formula like this:

    =(A1+A2+A3+A4+A5+A6+A7+A8+A9+A10)/10

Not very pretty, is it? Even worse, you would need to edit this formula if you added another cell to the range. You can replace this formula with a much simpler one that uses one of Excel's built-in worksheet functions:

    =AVERAGE(A1:A10)

The following formula demonstrates how using a function can enable you to perform calculations that would not be possible otherwise. What if you need to determine the largest value in a range? A formula can't tell you the answer without using a function. Here's a simple formula that returns the largest value in the range A1:D100:

```
=MAX(A1:D100)
```

Functions also can sometimes eliminate manual editing. Assume that you have a worksheet that contains 1,000 names in cells A1:A1000 and all the names appear in all capital letters. Your boss sees the listing and informs you that the names will be mail-merged with a form letter and that all uppercase is not acceptable; for example, JOHN F. CRANE must appear as John F. Crane. You could spend the next several hours re-entering the list — or you could use a formula like the following, which uses a function to convert the text in cell A1 to proper case:

```
=PROPER(A1)
```

Enter this formula once in cell B1, and then copy it down to the next 999 rows. Then select B1:B1000 and use the Edit ➪ Copy command to copy the range. Next, with B1:B1000 still selected, use the Edit ➪ Paste Special command (selecting the Values option) to convert the formulas to values. Delete the original column, and you've just accomplished several hours of work in less than a minute.

One last example should convince you of the power of functions. Suppose that you have a worksheet that calculates sales commissions. If the salesperson sold more than $100,000 of product, the commission rate is 7.5 percent; otherwise, the commission rate is 5.0 percent. Without using a function, you would have to create two different formulas and make sure that you use the correct formula for each sales amount. Here's a formula that uses the IF function to ensure that you calculate the correct commission, regardless of the sales amount:

```
=IF(A1<100000,A1*5%,A1*7.5%)
```

This formula accomplishes some simple decision-making. The formula checks the value of cell A1. If this value is less than 100,000, the formula returns cell A1 multiplied by 5 percent. Otherwise, it returns cell A1 multiplied by 7.5 percent.

Function arguments

In the preceding examples, you may have noticed that all the functions used parentheses. The information inside the parentheses is called the *list of arguments*.

Functions vary in how they use arguments. Depending on the function, a function may use

✦ No arguments

✦ One argument

✦ A fixed number of arguments

✦ An indeterminate number of arguments

✦ Optional arguments

The NOW function, which returns the current date and time, doesn't use an argument. Even if a function doesn't use an argument, however, you must still provide a set of empty parentheses, like this:

```
=NOW()
```

If a function uses more than one argument, you must separate each argument by a comma. The examples at the beginning of the chapter used cell references for arguments. Excel is quite flexible when it comes to function arguments, however. An argument can consist of a cell reference, literal values, literal text strings, expressions, and even other functions.

Note   A comma is the list-separator character for the U.S. version of Excel. Some versions may use a semicolon. This is a Windows setting, which can be adjusted in the Windows Control Panel (the Regional and Language Options dialog box).

More about functions

All told, Excel includes more than 300 functions. And if that's not enough, you can purchase additional specialized functions from third-party suppliers and even create your own custom functions (by using VBA) if you're so inclined.

You can easily be overwhelmed by the sheer number of functions, but you'll probably find that you use only a dozen or so of the functions on a regular basis. And as you'll see, Excel's Insert Function dialog box (described later in this chapter) makes it easy to locate and insert a function, even if it's not one that you use frequently.

Cross-Reference   You'll find many examples of Excel's built-in functions in Chapters 9 through 13. Appendix A contains a complete listing of Excel's worksheet functions, with a brief description of each. Chapter 35 covers the basics of creating custom functions with VBA.

Entering Formulas into Your Worksheets

As mentioned earlier, a formula must begin with an equal sign to inform Excel that the cell contains a formula rather than text. Basically, two ways exist to enter a formula into a cell: Enter it manually, or enter it by pointing to cell references. Each method is discussed in the following sections.

Entering formulas manually

Entering a formula manually involves, well, entering a formula manually. In a selected cell, you simply type an equal sign (=) followed by the formula. As you type, the characters appear in the cell and in the formula bar. You can, of course, use all the normal editing keys when entering a formula.

Entering formulas by pointing

Even though you can enter formulas by typing in the entire formula, Excel provides another method of entering formulas that is generally easier, faster, and less error prone. This other method of entering a formula still involves some manual typing, but you can simply point to the cell references instead of entering them manually. For example, to enter the formula =A1+A2 into cell A3, follow these steps:

1. Move the cell pointer to cell A3.

2. Type an equal sign (=) to begin the formula. Notice that Excel displays Enter in the status bar (bottom left of your screen).

3. Press the up arrow twice. As you press this key, Excel displays a faint moving border around the cell, and the cell reference appears in cell A3 and in the Formula bar. In addition, Excel displays Point in the status bar.

4. Type a plus sign (+). A solid color border replaces the faint border, and Enter reappears in the status bar.

5. Press the up arrow again. A2 is added to the formula.

6. Press Enter to end the formula.

Tip You can also point to the data cells by using your mouse.

Pasting range names into formulas

If your formula uses named cells or ranges, you can either type the name in place of the address or choose the name from a list and have Excel insert the name for you automatically. Two ways to insert a name into a formula are available:

✦ **Select Insert ➪ Name ➪ Paste:** Excel displays its Paste Name dialog box with all the names listed. Select the name and click OK. Or you can double-click the name, which inserts the name and closes the dialog box.

✦ **Press F3:** This also displays the Paste Name dialog box.

Figure 8-2 shows an example. The worksheet contains two defined names: Expenses and Sales. The Paste Name dialog box is being used to insert a name (Sales) into the formula being entered in cell B11.

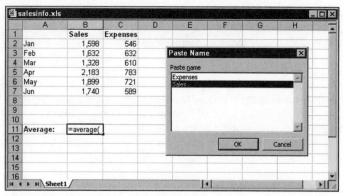

Figure 8-2: You can use the Paste Name dialog box to quickly enter a defined name into a formula.

Inserting functions into formulas

The easiest way to enter a function into a formula is to use the Excel program's Insert Function dialog box. Doing so ensures that the function is spelled correctly and has the proper number of arguments in the correct order.

To insert a function, start by selecting the function from the Insert Function dialog box, as shown in Figure 8-3. You can open this dialog box by using any of the following methods:

✦ Choose the Insert ➪ Function command from the menu bar.

✦ Click the Function icon, directly to the left of the Formula bar. (This icon displays f×.)

✦ Press Shift+F3.

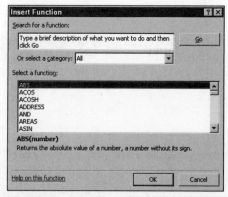

Figure 8-3: The Insert Function dialog box.

The Insert Function dialog box shows a drop-down list of function categories. Select a category, and the functions in that category are displayed in the list box. To access a function that you've used recently, select Most Recently Used from the Or Select a Category drop-down list.

If you're not sure which function you need, you can search for the appropriate function by using the Search for a Function box at the top of the dialog box. Enter your search terms, click Go, and you'll get a list of relevant functions. When you select a function in the Select a Function list box, notice that Excel displays the function (and its argument names) in the dialog box along with a brief description of what the function does.

When you locate the function that you want to use, highlight it and click OK. Excel then displays its Function Arguments dialog box, as shown in Figure 8-4. Use this dialog box to specify the arguments for the function. The dialog box will vary, depending on the function you're inserting, and it will show one text box for each of the function's arguments. To use a cell or range reference as an argument, you can enter the address manually or click inside the argument box and select the cell or range in the sheet (that is, point to it). After you've specified all of the function arguments, click OK.

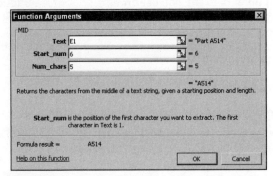

Figure 8-4: The Function Arguments dialog box.

Tip   Another way to insert a function is to use the Function List to the left of the Formula bar. When you are entering or editing a formula, the space normally occupied by the Name box displays a list of the functions you've used most recently. After you select a function from this list, Excel displays the Function Arguments dialog box.

Function entry tips

The following are some additional tips to keep in mind when you use the Insert Function dialog box to enter functions:

✦ When the Insert Function dialog box is displayed, you can find out more about the selected function by clicking Help on this function.

✦ You can use the Insert Function dialog box to insert a function into an existing formula. Just edit the formula and move the insertion point to the location where you want to insert the function. Then open the Insert Function dialog box and select the function.

✦ You can also use the Function Arguments dialog box to modify the arguments for a function in an existing cell. Click on the function in the Formula bar and then click the Insert Function button (the fx button, to the left of the Formula bar).

✦ If you change your mind about entering a function, click the Cancel button.

✦ The number of boxes that you see in the Function Arguments dialog box is determined by the number of arguments used by the function that you selected. If a function uses no arguments, you won't see any boxes. If the function uses a variable number of arguments (such as the AVERAGE function), Excel adds a new box every time that you enter an optional argument.

✦ As you provide arguments in the Function Argument dialog box, the value of each argument is displayed to the right of each box.

✦ A few functions, such as INDEX, have more than one form. If you choose such a function, Excel displays another dialog box that lets you choose which form you want to use.

✦ As you become familiar with the functions, you can bypass the Insert Function dialog box and enter the function directly. Excel prompts you with argument names as you enter the function.

Editing Formulas

You can edit your formulas just like you can edit any other cell. You may need to edit a formula if you make some changes to your worksheet and need to adjust the formula to accommodate the changes. Or the formula may return an error value, and you need to edit the formula to correct the error.

The following are some of the ways to get into Cell-Edit mode:

✦ Double-click the cell, which enables you to edit the cell contents directly in the cell.

✦ Press F2, which enables you to edit the cell contents directly in the cell.

✦ Select the cell that you want to edit, and then click in the Formula bar. This enables you to edit the cell contents in the Formula bar.

✦ If the cell contains a formula that returns an error, Excel will display a small triangle in the upper-left corner of the cell. Activate the cell, and you'll see a Smart Tag. Click the Smart Tag, and you can choose one of the options for correcting the error. (The options will vary according to the type of error in the cell.) You can control whether Excel displays these Smart Tags in the Error Checking tab of the Options dialog box.

While you're editing a formula, you can select multiple characters either by dragging the mouse cursor over them or by pressing Shift while you use the direction keys.

Tip   If you have a formula that you can't seem to edit correctly, you can convert the formula to text and tackle it again later. To convert a formula to text, just remove the initial equal sign (=). When you're ready to try again, insert the initial equal sign to convert the cell contents back to a formula.

Using Cell References in Formulas

Nearly all formulas include references to cells or ranges. These references enable your formulas to work with the data contained in those cells or ranges rather than simply with fixed values. For example, if your formula refers to cell A1 and you change the value contained in A1, the formula result changes to reflect the new value. If you didn't use references in your formulas, you would need to edit the formulas themselves in order to change the values used in the formulas.

Using relative, absolute, and mixed references

When you use a cell (or range) reference in a formula, you can use three types of references:

✦ **Relative:** The row and column references can change when you copy the formula to another cell because the references are actually offsets from the current row and column.

✦ **Absolute:** The row and column references do not change when you copy the formula because the reference is to an actual cell address.

✦ **Mixed:** Either the row or column reference is relative, and the other is absolute.

An absolute reference uses two dollar signs in its address: one for the column letter and one for the row number (for example, $A$5). Excel also allows mixed references in which only one of the address parts is absolute (for example, $A4 or A$4).

By default, Excel creates relative cell references in formulas except when the formula includes cells in different worksheets or workbooks. The distinction becomes apparent when you copy a formula to another cell.

Figure 8-5 shows a simple worksheet. The formula in cell D2, which multiplies the quantity by the price, is

```
=B2*C2
```

This formula uses relative cell references. Therefore, when the formula is copied to the cells below, the references will adjust in a relative manner. For example, the formula in cell D3 is

```
=B3*C3
```

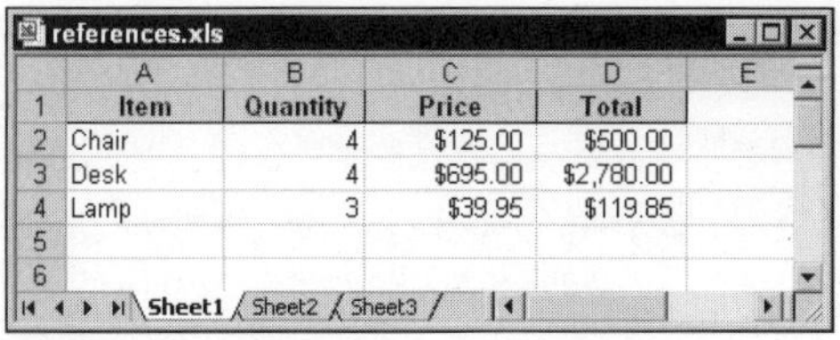

references.xls

	A	B	C	D	E
1	Item	Quantity	Price	Total	
2	Chair	4	$125.00	$500.00	
3	Desk	4	$695.00	$2,780.00	
4	Lamp	3	$39.95	$119.85	
5					
6					

Sheet1 Sheet2 Sheet3

Figure 8-5: Copying a formula that contains relative references.

What if the cell references in D2 contained absolute references, like this?

```
=$B$2*$C$2
```

In this case, copying the formula to the cells below would produce incorrect results. The formula in cell D3 would be exactly the same as the formula in cell D2.

Now, I'll extend the example to calculate sales tax, which is stored in cell B7 (see Figure 8-6). In this situation, the formula in cell D2 is

```
=B2*C2*$B$7
```

The quantity is multiplied by the price, and the result is multiplied by the sales tax rate stored in cell B7. Notice that the reference to B7 is an absolute reference. When the formula in D2 is copied to the cells below, cell D3 will contain this formula:

```
=B3*C3*$B$7
```

The references to cells B2 and C2 were adjusted, but the reference to cell B7 was not — which is exactly what I want.

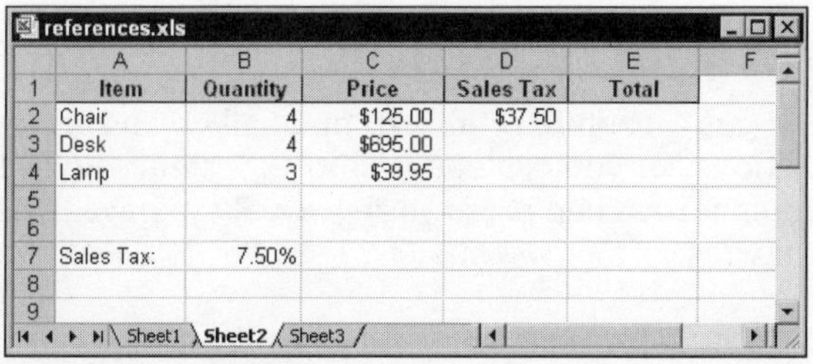

references.xls

	A	B	C	D	E	F
1	Item	Quantity	Price	Sales Tax	Total	
2	Chair	4	$125.00	$37.50		
3	Desk	4	$695.00			
4	Lamp	3	$39.95			
5						
6						
7	Sales Tax:	7.50%				
8						
9						

Sheet1 Sheet2 Sheet3

Figure 8-6: Formula references to the sales tax cell should be absolute.

Figure 8-7 demonstrates the use of mixed references. The formulas in the table calculate the area for various lengths and widths. The formula in cell C3 is

```
=$B3*C$2
```

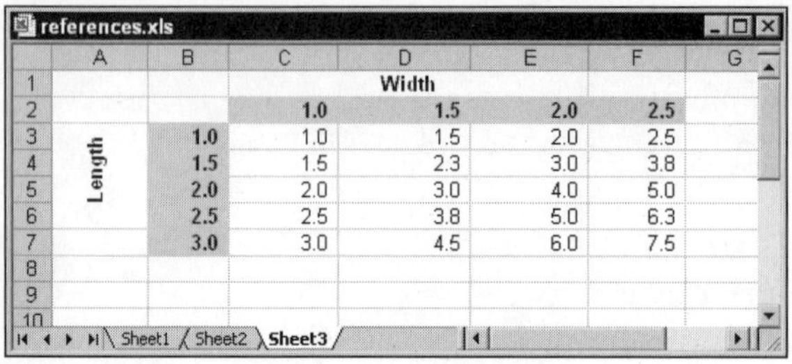

	A	B	C	D	E	F	G
1				Width			
2			1.0	1.5	2.0	2.5	
3		1.0	1.0	1.5	2.0	2.5	
4		1.5	1.5	2.3	3.0	3.8	
5		2.0	2.0	3.0	4.0	5.0	
6		2.5	2.5	3.8	5.0	6.3	
7		3.0	3.0	4.5	6.0	7.5	
8							
9							
10							

(Column A labeled "Length" vertically. references.xls. Sheets: Sheet1, Sheet2, **Sheet3**)

Figure 8-7: Using mixed cell references.

Notice that both cell references are mixed. The reference to cell B3 uses an absolute reference for the column ($B), and the reference to cell C2 uses an absolute reference for the row ($2). As a result, this formula can be copied down and across, and the calculations will be correct. For example, the formula in cell F7 is

    =$B7*F$2

If C3 used either absolute or relative references, copying the formula would produce incorrect results.

On the CD-ROM

The workbook that demonstrates the various types of references is available on the companion CD-ROM.

Note

When you cut and paste a formula (move it to another location), the cell references in the formula aren't adjusted. Again, this is what you usually want to happen. When you move a formula, you generally want it to continue to refer to the original cells.

Changing the types of your references

You can enter nonrelative references (absolute or mixed) manually by inserting dollar signs in the appropriate positions. Or you can use a handy shortcut: the F4 key. When you've entered a cell reference, you can press F4 repeatedly to have Excel cycle through all four reference types.

For example, if you enter **=A1** to start a formula, pressing F4 converts the cell reference to =$A$1. Pressing F4 again converts it to =A$1. Pressing it again displays =$A1. Pressing it one more time returns to the original =A1. Keep pressing F4 until Excel displays the type of reference that you want.

Note

When you name a cell or range, Excel (by default) uses an absolute reference for the name. For example, if you give the name SalesForecast to A1:A12, the Refers To box in the Define Name dialog box lists the reference as $A$1:$A$12. This is almost always what you want. If you copy a cell that has a named reference in its formula, the copied formula contains a reference to the original name.

Referencing cells outside the worksheet

Formulas can also refer to cells in other worksheets — and the worksheets don't even have to be in the same workbook. Excel uses a special type of notation to handle these types of references.

Referencing cells in other worksheets

To use a reference to a cell in another worksheet in the same workbook, use this format:

```
SheetName!CellAddress
```

In other words, precede the cell address with the worksheet name followed by an exclamation point. Here's an example of a formula that uses a cell on the Sheet2 worksheet:

```
=A1*Sheet2!A1
```

This formula multiplies the value in cell A1 on the current worksheet by the value in cell A1 on Sheet2.

Tip If the worksheet name in the reference includes one or more spaces, you must enclose it in single quotation marks. (Excel will do this automatically if you use the point-and-click method.) For example, here's a formula that refers to a cell on a sheet named All Depts:

```
=A1*'All Depts'! A1
```

Referencing cells in other workbooks

To refer to a cell in a different workbook, use this format:

```
=[WorkbookName]SheetName!CellAddress
```

In this case, the workbook name (in square brackets), the worksheet name, and an exclamation point precede the cell address. The following is an example of a formula that uses a cell reference in the Sheet1 worksheet in a workbook named Budget:

```
=[Budget.xls]Sheet1!A1
```

If the workbook name in the reference includes one or more spaces, you must enclose it (and the sheet name) in single quotation marks. For example, here's a formula that refers to a cell on Sheet1 in a workbook named Budget For 2004:

```
=A1*'[Budget For 2004.xls]Sheet1'!A1
```

When a formula refers to cells in a different workbook, the other workbook doesn't need to be open. If the workbook is closed, however, you must add the complete path to the reference. Here's an example:

```
=A1*'C:\My Documents\[Budget For 2004.xls]Sheet1'!A1
```

A linked file can also reside on another system that's accessible on your corporate network. The formula below, for example, refers to a cell in a workbook in the files directory of a computer named DataServer.

```
='\\DataServer\files\[budget.xls]Sheet1'!$D$7
```

Cross-Reference

Refer to Chapter 29 for more information about linking workbooks.

Tip

To create formulas that refer to cells not in the current worksheet, point to the cells rather than entering the references manually. Excel takes care of the details regarding the workbook and worksheet references. The workbook that you're using in your formula must be open to use the pointing method.

Note

If you point to a different worksheet or workbook when creating a formula, you'll notice that Excel always inserts absolute cell references. Therefore, if you plan to copy the formula to other cells, make sure that you change the cell references to relative.

Correcting Common Formula Errors

Sometimes when you enter a formula, Excel displays a value that begins with a hash mark (#). This is a signal that the formula is returning an error value. You have to correct the formula (or correct a cell that the formula references) to get rid of the error display.

Tip

If the entire cell is filled with hash mark characters, this means that the column isn't wide enough to display the value. You can either widen the column or change the number format of the cell.

In some cases, Excel won't even let you enter an erroneous formula. For example, the following formula is missing the closing parenthesis:

```
=A1*(B1\I2
```

If you attempt to enter this formula, Excel will inform you of the error and propose a correction.

Table 8-3 lists the types of error values that may appear in a cell that has a formula. Formulas may return an error value if a cell to which they refer has an error value. This is known as the *ripple effect*—a single error value can make its way into lots of other cells that contain formulas that depend on the cell.

Table 8-3
Excel Error Values

Error Value	Explanation
#DIV/0!	The formula is trying to divide by zero. This also occurs when the formula attempts to divide by a cell that is empty.
#NAME?	The formula uses a name that Excel doesn't recognize. This can happen if you delete a name that's used in the formula or if you have unmatched quotes when using text.
#N/A	The formula is referring (directly or indirectly) to a cell that uses the NA function to signal that data is not available. Some functions (for example, VLOOKUP) can also return #N/A.
#NULL!	The formula uses an intersection of two ranges that don't intersect. (This concept is described later in the chapter.)
#NUM!	A problem with a value exists; for example, you specified a negative number where a positive number is expected.
#REF!	The formula refers to a cell that isn't valid. This can happen if the cell has been deleted from the worksheet.
#VALUE!	The formula includes an argument or operand of the wrong type. An *operand* is a value or cell reference that a formula uses to calculate a result.

Handling circular references

When you're entering formulas, you may occasionally see a message from Excel similar to the one shown in Figure 8-8, indicating that the formula you just entered will result in a *circular reference*. A circular reference occurs when a formula refers to its own value — either directly or indirectly. For example, you create a circular reference if you enter =A1+A2+A3 into cell A3 because the formula in cell A3 refers to cell A3. Every time the formula in A3 is calculated, it must be calculated again because A3 has changed. The calculation would go on forever.

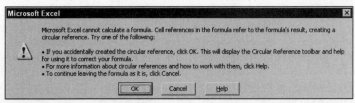

Figure 8-8: If you attempt to create a circular reference, Excel warns you about the potential error.

When you get the circular reference message after entering a formula, Excel gives you three options:

✦ Click OK to attempt to locate the circular reference.

✦ Click Cancel to enter the formula as is.

✦ Click Help for more information about circular references.

Usually, you want to correct any circular references, so you should choose OK. When you do so, Excel displays the Help topic on circular references and the Circular Reference toolbar (which is shown in Figure 8-9). On the Circular Reference toolbar, click the first cell in the Navigate Circular Reference drop-down list box and then examine the cell's formula. If you cannot determine whether the cell is the cause of the circular reference, click the next cell in the Navigate Circular Reference box. Continue to review the formulas until the status bar no longer displays `Circular`.

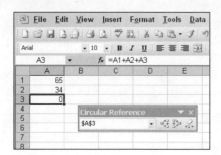

Figure 8-9: You can use the Circular Reference toolbar to investigate the cause of a circular reference.

Tip   If Excel does not automatically display the Circular Reference toolbar, select View ➪ Toolbars ➪ Circular Reference.

If you ignore the circular reference message (by clicking Cancel), Excel lets you enter the formula and displays a message in the status bar to remind you that a circular reference exists.

Note   Excel won't tell you about a circular reference if the Iteration setting is on. You can check this in the Options dialog box (in the Calculation tab). If Iteration is on, Excel performs the circular calculation the number of times specified in the Maximum Iterations field (or until the value changes by less than 0.001 or whatever value is in the Maximum Change field). In a few situations, you may use a circular reference intentionally. In these cases, the Iteration setting must be on. However, keeping the Iteration setting turned off is best, so that you are warned of circular references. Most of the time, a circular reference indicates an error that you must correct.

Usually, a circular reference is quite obvious and, therefore, easy to identify and correct. Sometimes, however, circular references are indirect. In other words, a formula may refer to a formula that refers to a formula that refers back to the original formula. In some cases, it may require a bit of detective work to get to the problem.

Intentional Circular References

You can sometimes use a circular reference to your advantage. For example, a company has a policy of contributing 5 percent of its net profit to charity. The contribution itself, however, is considered an expense and is therefore subtracted from the net profit figure. This produces a circular reference.

The Contributions cell contains the following formula:

```
=5%*Net_Profit
```

The Net Profit cell contains the following formula:

```
=Gross_Income-Expenses-Contributions
```

These formulas produce a resolvable circular reference. If the Iteration setting is on, Excel keeps calculating until the Contributions value is, indeed, 5 percent of Net Profit. In other words, the result becomes increasingly more accurate until it converges on the final solution.

On the CD-ROM

The companion CD-ROM contains a workbook that demonstrates an intentional circular reference.

Changing when formulas are calculated

You've probably noticed that Excel calculates the formulas in your worksheet immediately. If you change any cells that the formula uses, Excel displays the formula's new result with no effort on your part. All this happens when Excel's Calculation mode is set to Automatic. In Automatic Calculation mode (which is the default mode), Excel follows these rules when calculating your worksheet:

✦ When you make a change—enter or edit data or formulas, for example— Excel calculates immediately those formulas that depend on new or edited data.

✦ If Excel is in the middle of a lengthy calculation, it temporarily suspends the calculation when you need to perform other worksheet tasks; it resumes calculating when you're finished with your other worksheet tasks.

✦ Formulas are evaluated in a natural sequence. In other words, if a formula in cell D12 depends on the result of a formula in cell D11, Excel calculates cell D11 before calculating D12.

Sometimes, however, you may want to control when Excel calculates formulas. For example, if you create a worksheet with thousands of complex formulas, you'll find that things can slow to a snail's pace while Excel does its thing. In such a case, set Excel's calculation mode to Manual, which you can do in the Calculation tab of the Options dialog box (as shown in Figure 8-10).

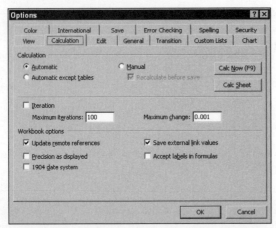

Figure 8-10: You can control when Excel calculates formulas by selecting the Manual option button on the Calculation tab.

To select Manual Calculation mode, click the Manual option button. When you switch to Manual Calculation mode, Excel automatically places a check in the box labeled Recalculate Before Save. You can remove the check if you want to speed up file-saving operations.

Tip

If your worksheet uses any data tables (described in Chapter 22), you may want to select the option labeled Automatic Except Tables. Large data tables calculate notoriously slowly.

When you're working in Manual Calculation mode, Excel displays Calculate in the status bar when you have any uncalculated formulas. You can use the following shortcut keys to recalculate the formulas:

✦ **F9:** Calculates the formulas in all open workbooks.

✦ **Shift+F9:** Calculates only the formulas in the active worksheet. Other worksheets in the same workbook aren't calculated.

Note

Excel's Calculation mode isn't specific to a particular worksheet. When you change Excel's Calculation mode, it affects all open workbooks, not just the active workbook.

Using Advanced Naming Techniques

Using range names certainly makes your formulas easier to understand. Excel offers a number of advanced techniques that make using names even more useful. For example, consider the following formula:

```
=(B30-B45)*C12
```

If the worksheet had names defined for these cells, the formula would be a lot more readable. Here's the same formula after naming the cells:

`=(Income-Expenses)*TaxRate`

Are you beginning to understand the importance of naming ranges?

Using names for constants

Even many advanced Excel users don't realize that you can give a name to an item that doesn't appear in a cell. For example, if formulas in your worksheet use a sales tax rate, you would probably insert the tax rate value into a cell and use this cell reference in your formulas. To make things easier, you would probably also name this cell something similar to *SalesTax*.

Here's how to provide a name for a value that doesn't appear in a cell:

1. Choose Insert ➪ Name ➪ Define (or press Ctrl+F3) to bring up the Define Name dialog box.

2. Enter the name (in this case, **SalesTax**) into the field labeled Names in Workbook.

3. Then, click the Refers To box, delete its contents, and replace it with a value, such as .075. Don't precede the constant with an equal sign.

4. Click OK to close the dialog box.

You just created a name that refers to a constant rather than a cell or range. If you type =**SalesTax** into a cell, this simple formula returns `0.075` — the constant that you defined. You also can use this constant in a formula, such as `=A1*SalesTax`.

Tip   A constant also can be text. For example, you can define a constant for your company's name.

Note   Named constants don't appear in the Name box or in the Go To dialog box — which makes sense because these constants don't reside anywhere tangible. They do appear in the Paste Names dialog box, however, which does make sense because you use these names in formulas.

Using names for formulas

Just as you can create a named constant, you can also create named formulas. Like named constants, named formulas don't appear in the worksheet.

You create named formulas the same way you create named constants — by using the Define Name dialog box. For example, you might create a named formula that calculates the monthly interest rate from an annual rate. Figure 8-11 shows an example of this. In this case, the name MonthlyRate refers to the following formula:

```
=Sheet1!$B$1/12
```

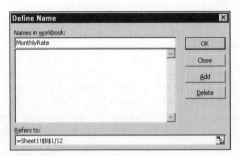

Figure 8-11: Excel lets you give a name to a formula that doesn't exist in a worksheet cell.

When you use the name MonthlyRate in a formula, it uses the value in B1 divided by 12. Notice that the cell reference is an absolute reference.

Naming formulas gets more interesting when you use relative references rather than absolute references. When you use the pointing technique to create a formula in the Refers To box of the Define Name dialog box, Excel always uses absolute cell references, which is unlike its behavior when you create a formula in a cell.

For example, create the name Cubed for the following formula:

```
=Sheet1!A1^3
```

In this example, the relative reference points to the cell to the left of the cell in which the name is used. Therefore, make certain that cell B1 is the active cell before opening the Define Name dialog box—this is very important. The formula contains a relative reference, so when you use this named formula in a worksheet, the cell reference is always relative to the cell that contains the formula. For example, if you enter =**Cubed** into cell D12, cell D12 displays the result of C12 raised to the third power. C12 is the cell directly to the left of D12.

Using range intersections

This section describes an interesting concept that is unique to Excel: range intersections. A *range intersection* refers to cells that two ranges have in common. Excel uses an intersection operator—a space—to determine the overlapping references in two ranges. Figure 8-12 shows a simple example.

The formula in cell B9 is

```
=B1:B6 A3:D3
```

This formula returns 10, the value in cell B3 — that is, the value at the intersection of the two ranges.

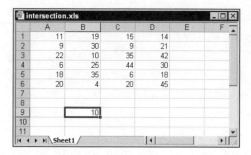

Figure 8-12: You can use a range intersection formula to determine values.

The intersection operator is one of three reference operators for ranges. Table 8-4 lists these operators.

<table>
<tr><td colspan="2">Table 8-4
Reference Operators for Ranges</td></tr>
<tr><td>**Operator**</td><td>**What It Does**</td></tr>
<tr><td>: (colon)</td><td>Specifies a range.</td></tr>
<tr><td>, (comma)</td><td>Specifies the union of two ranges. This operator combines multiple range references into a single reference.</td></tr>
<tr><td>(space)</td><td>Specifies the intersection of two ranges. This operator produces cells that are common to two ranges.</td></tr>
</table>

The real value of knowing about range intersections is apparent when you use names. Examine Figure 8-13, which shows a table of values. I selected the entire table and then used the Insert ➪ Name ➪ Create command to create names automatically by using the top row and left column.

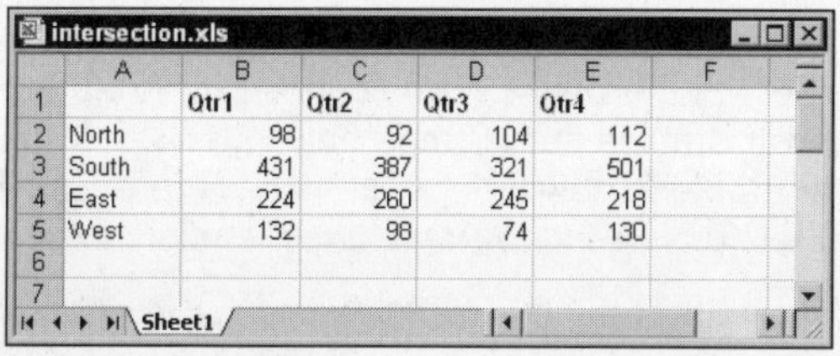

Figure 8-13: When you use names, using a range intersection formula to determine values is even more useful.

Excel created the following names:

North	=Sheet1!$B$2:$E$2	Qtr1	=Sheet1!$B$2:$B$5
South	=Sheet1!$B$3:$E$3	Qtr2	=Sheet1!$C$2:$C$5
West	=Sheet1!$B$4:$E$4	Qtr3	=Sheet1!$D$2:$D$5
East	=Sheet1!$B$5:$E$5	Qtr4	=Sheet1!$E$2:$E$5

With these names defined, you can create formulas that are very easy to read. For example, to calculate the total for Quarter 4, just use this formula:

```
=SUM(Qtr4)
```

But things really get interesting when you use the intersection operator. Move to any blank cell and enter the following formula:

```
=Qtr1 West
```

This formula returns the value for the first quarter for the West region. In other words, it returns the value where the Qtr1 range intersects with the West range. Naming ranges in this manner can help you create very readable formulas.

Applying names to existing references

When you create a new name for a cell or a range, Excel doesn't automatically use the name in place of existing references in your formulas. For example, assume that you have the following formula in cell F10:

```
=A1-A2
```

Using Row and Column Headings as "Names"

You can also use names without actually defining them. Excel lets you use the row and column headers as names in your formulas without first defining the names. For example, in Figure 8-13, you could use the formula

```
=Qtr 2 North
```

without first defining the range names. This technique has several limitations, however. The labels are not *real* names—they don't appear in the Define Name dialog box, nor do they appear in the Name box. For this reason, you can use this method only when the formula refers to cells on the same sheet. The real problem, however, is the inability to document the names. In other words, you can never tell for sure exactly what a name refers to.

In addition, there are some known problems with using this technique. In some situations, these types of names can return incorrect results.

For these reasons, it's usually better to take a few extra seconds and create a *real* range name.

If you define a name *Income* for A1 and *Expenses* for A2, Excel won't automatically change your formula to =Income-Expenses. Replacing cell or range references with their corresponding names is fairly easy, however.

To apply names to cell references in formulas after the fact, start by selecting the range that you want to modify. Then, choose Insert ➪ Name ➪ Apply. Excel displays the Apply Names dialog box, as shown in Figure 8-14. Select the names that you want to apply by clicking them and then click OK. Excel replaces the range references with the names in the selected cells.

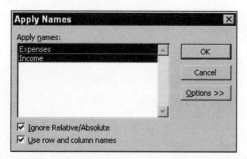

Figure 8-14: You can use the Apply Names dialog box to replace cell or range references with names.

Tips for Working with Formulas

In this section, I offer a few additional tips and pointers relevant to formulas.

Don't hard-code values

When you create a formula, think twice before using a value in the formula. For example, if your formula calculates sales tax (which is 6.5 percent), you may be tempted to enter a formula, such as the following:

```
=A1*.065
```

A better approach is to insert the sales tax rate in a cell and use the cell reference. Or you can define the tax rate as a named constant by using the technique presented earlier in this chapter. Doing so makes modifying and maintaining your worksheet easier. For example, if the sales tax rate changed to 6.75 percent, you would have to modify every formula that uses the old value. If the tax rate is stored in a cell, however, you simply change that one cell, and Excel updates all the formulas.

Using the formula bar as a calculator

If you simply need to perform a calculation, you can use the Formula bar as a calculator. For example, enter the following formula — but don't press Enter:

```
=(145*1.05)/12
```

If you press Enter, Excel enters the formula into the cell. But because this formula always returns the same result, you may prefer to store the formula's result rather than the formula. To do so, press F9. The result now appears in the Formula bar. Press Enter to store the result in the active cell. This also works if the formula uses cell references.

Making an exact copy of a formula

When you copy a formula, Excel adjusts its cell references when you paste the formula to a different location. Sometimes, you may want to make an exact copy of the formula. One way to do this is to convert the cell references to absolute values, but this isn't always desirable. A better approach is to select the formula in Edit mode and then copy it to the Clipboard as text. You can do this in several ways. Here's a step-by-step example of how to make an exact copy of the formula in A1 and to copy it to A2:

1. Double-click A1 (or press F2) to get into Edit mode.

2. Drag the mouse to select the entire formula. You can drag from left to right or from right to left.

3. Click the Copy button on the Standard toolbar. This copies the selected text to the Clipboard.

4. Press Enter to end Edit mode.

5. Select cell A2.

6. Click the Paste button to paste the text into cell A2.

You also can use this technique to copy just part of a formula, to use that part in another formula. Just select the part of the formula that you want to copy by dragging the mouse; then use any of the available techniques to copy the selection to the Clipboard. You can then paste the text to another cell.

Formulas (or parts of formulas) copied in this manner won't have their cell references adjusted when they are pasted to a new cell because the formulas are being copied as text, not as actual formulas.

Tip   You can also convert a formula to text by adding an apostrophe (') in front of the equal sign.

Converting formulas to values

If you have a range of formulas that will always produce the same result (that is, *dead formulas*), you may want to convert them to values. You can use the Edit ➪ Paste Special command to do this. Assume that range A1:A20 contains formulas that have calculated results that will never change or that you don't want to change. For example, if you use the @RAND function to create a set of random numbers and you don't want Excel to recalculate the random numbers each time that you press Enter, convert the formulas to values. To convert these formulas to values:

1. Select A1:A20.

2. Click the Copy button.

3. Select Edit ➪ Paste Special. Excel displays its Paste Special dialog box.

4. Click the Values radio button and then click OK.

5. Press Enter or Esc to cancel Paste mode.

✦   ✦   ✦

Creating Formulas That Manipulate Text

◆   ◆   ◆   ◆

In This Chapter

How Excel handles
text entered into cells

Excel's worksheet
functions that handle
text

Examples of
advanced text
formulas

◆   ◆   ◆   ◆

Excel, of course, is best known for its ability to crunch numbers. However, it is also quite versatile when it comes to handling text. As you know, Excel enables you to enter text for such things as row and column headings, customer names and addresses, part numbers, and just about anything else. And, as you may expect, you can use formulas to manipulate the text contained in cells.

This chapter contains many examples of formulas that use a variety of functions to manipulate text. Some of these formulas perform feats that you may not have thought possible.

A Few Words about Text

When you enter data into a cell, Excel immediately goes to work and determines whether you're entering a formula, a number (including a date or time), or anything else. Anything else is considered text.

Note   You may hear the term *string* used instead of *text.* You can use these terms interchangeably. Sometimes, they even appear together, as in *text string.*

How many characters in a cell?

A single cell can hold up to 32,000 characters. To put things into perspective, this chapter contains about 30,000 characters. I certainly don't recommend using a cell in lieu of a word processor, but you really don't have to lose much sleep worrying about filling up a cell with text.

When a Number Isn't Treated as a Number

If you import data into Excel, you may be aware of a common problem: Sometimes, the imported values are treated as text. Here's a quick way to convert these non-numbers to actual values. Activate any empty cell and choose Edit ⇨ Copy. Then select the range that contains the values you need to fix. Choose Edit ⇨ Paste Special. In the Paste Special dialog box, select the Add option and then click OK. This procedure essentially adds zero to each cell and, in the process, forces Excel to treat the non-numbers as actual values.

Caution   Although a cell can hold up to 32,000 characters, there is a limit on the number of characters that can actually display.

Numbers as text

As I mentioned, Excel distinguishes between numbers and text. If you want to *force* a number to be considered as text, you can do one of the following:

✦ Apply the Text Number format to the cell. Use Format ⇨ Cells, click the Number tab, and select Text from the category list. If you haven't applied other horizontal alignment formatting, the value will appear left-aligned in the cell (like normal text).

✦ Precede the number with an apostrophe. The apostrophe isn't displayed, but the cell entry will be treated as if it were text.

Even though a cell is formatted as Text (or uses an apostrophe), you can still perform *some* mathematical operations on the cell if the entry *looks* like a number. For example, assume cell A1 contains a value preceded by an apostrophe. The formula that follows will display the value in A1, incremented by 1:

```
=A1+1
```

The formula that follows, however, will treat the contents of cell A1 as 0:

```
=SUM(A1:A10)
```

If you're switching from Lotus 1-2-3, you'll find this to be a significant change. Lotus 1-2-3 never treats text as values. In some cases, treating text as a number can be useful. In other cases, it can cause problems. Bottom line? Just be aware of Excel's inconsistency in how it treats a number formatted as text.

Text Functions

Excel has an excellent assortment of worksheet functions that can handle text. For your convenience, Excel's Insert Function dialog box places most of these functions in the Text category. A few other functions that are relevant to text manipulation appear in other function categories. For example, the ISTEXT function is in the Information category in the Insert Function dialog box.

 Cross-Reference Refer to Appendix A for a listing of the functions in the Text category. Or choose Insert ⇨ Function to access the Insert Function dialog box and scroll through the functions in the Text category.

Most of the text functions are not limited for use with text. In other words, these functions can also operate with cells that contain values. You'll find that Excel is very accommodating when it comes to treating numbers as text and text as numbers.

The examples discussed in this section demonstrate some common (and useful) things you can do with text. You may need to adapt some of these examples for your own use.

Determining whether a cell contains text

In some situations, you may need a formula that determines the type of data contained in a particular cell. For example, you may use an IF function to return a result only if a cell contains text. The easiest way to make this determination is to use the ISTEXT function.

The ISTEXT function takes a single argument and returns TRUE if the argument contains text and FALSE if it doesn't contain text. The formula that follows returns TRUE if A1 contains a string:

```
=ISTEXT(A1)
```

Working with character codes

Every character that you see on your screen has an associated code number. For Windows systems, Excel uses the standard ANSI character set. The ANSI character set consists of 255 characters, numbered from 1 to 255.

Figure 9-1 shows a portion of an Excel worksheet that displays all of the 255 characters. This example uses the Arial font. (Other fonts may have different characters.)

 On the CD-ROM The companion CD-ROM includes a copy of this workbook. It contains some simple macros that enable you to display the character set for any font installed on your system.

Two functions come into play when dealing with character codes: CODE and CHAR. These functions aren't very useful by themselves. However, they can prove quite useful in conjunction with other functions. I discuss these functions in the following sections.

character set.xls													
Font: Arial						Size:	10						
1	□	39	'	77	M	115	s	153	™	191	¿	229	å
2	□	40	(	78	N	116	t	154	š	192	À	230	æ
3	□	41	)	79	O	117	u	155	›	193	Á	231	ç
4	□	42	*	80	P	118	v	156	œ	194	Â	232	è
5	□	43	+	81	Q	119	w	157	□	195	Ã	233	é
6	□	44	,	82	R	120	x	158	ž	196	Ä	234	ê
7	□	45	-	83	S	121	y	159	Ÿ	197	Å	235	ë
8	□	46	.	84	T	122	z	160		198	Æ	236	ì
9	□	47	/	85	U	123	{	161	¡	199	Ç	237	í
10	□	48	0	86	V	124			162	¢	200	È	238	î
11	□	49	1	87	W	125	}	163	£	201	É	239	ï
12	□	50	2	88	X	126	~	164	¤	202	Ê	240	ð
13	□	51	3	89	Y	127	□	165	¥	203	Ë	241	ñ
14	□	52	4	90	Z	128	€	166	¦	204	Ì	242	ò
15	□	53	5	91	[	129	□	167	§	205	Í	243	ó
16	□	54	6	92	\	130	‚	168	¨	206	Î	244	ô
17	□	55	7	93	]	131	ƒ	169	©	207	Ï	245	õ

Figure 9-1: The ANSI character set (for the Arial font).

The CODE function

Excel's CODE function returns the character code for its argument. The formula that follows returns 65, the character code for uppercase *A*:

```
=CODE("A")
```

If the argument for CODE consists of more than one character, the function uses only the first character. Therefore, this formula also returns 65:

```
=CODE("Abbey Road")
```

The CHAR function

The CHAR function is essentially the opposite of the CODE function. Its argument should be a value between 1 and 255, and the function should return the corresponding character. The following formula, for example, returns the letter *A*:

```
=CHAR(65)
```

To demonstrate the opposing nature of the CODE and CHAR functions, try entering this formula:

```
=CHAR(CODE("A"))
```

This formula (illustrative rather than useful) returns the letter *A*. First, it converts the character to its code value (65), and then it converts this code back to the corresponding character.

Assume cell A1 contains the letter *A* (uppercase). The following formula returns the letter *a* (lowercase):

```
=CHAR(CODE(A1)+32)
```

This formula takes advantage of the fact that the alphabetic characters all appear in alphabetical order within the character set, and the lowercase letters follow the uppercase letters (with a few other characters tossed in between). Each lowercase letter lies exactly 32 character positions higher than its corresponding uppercase letter.

Determining whether two strings are identical

You can set up a simple logical formula to determine whether two cells contain the same entry. For example, use this formula to determine whether cell A1 has the same contents as cell A2:

```
=A1=A2
```

This formula will return either TRUE of FALSE. However, Excel is a bit lax in its comparisons when text is involved. Consider the case in which A1 contains the word *January* (initial capitalization), and A2 contains *JANUARY* (all uppercase). You'll find that the previous formula returns TRUE, even though the contents of the two cells are not really the same. In other words, the comparison is not case sensitive.

In many cases, you don't need to worry about the case of the text. But if you need to make an exact, case-sensitive comparison, you can use the Excel EXACT function. The formula that follows returns TRUE only if cells A1 and A2 contain *exactly* the same entry:

```
=EXACT(A1,A2)
```

The following formula returns FALSE because the first string contains a trailing space:

```
=EXACT("zero ","zero")
```

Joining two or more cells

Excel uses an ampersand as its concatenation operator. *Concatenation* is simply a fancy term that describes what happens when you join the contents of two or more cells. For example, if cell A1 contains the text *San Diego* and cell A2 contains the text *California,* the following formula will return *San DiegoCalifornia*:

```
=A1&A2
```

Inserting Special Characters

If you need to insert special characters not found on your keyboard, you can use the Symbol dialog box (which appears when you select Insert ➪ Symbol). This dialog box makes inserting special characters (including Unicode characters) into cells easy. For example, you may want to display the Greek letter pi in your spreadsheet. Access Excel's Symbol dialog box and select the Symbol font (see the accompanying figure). Examine the characters, locate the pi character, and click Insert. You'll see (in the Character Code area of the Symbol dialog box) that this character has a code of 80.

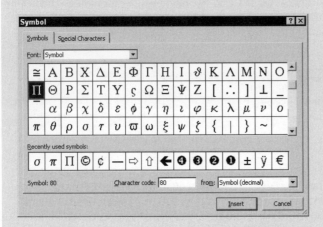

In addition, Excel has several built-in AutoCorrect symbols. For example, if you type **(c)**, Excel converts it to a copyright symbol. To see the other symbols that you can enter like this, select Tools ➪ AutoCorrect Options to access the AutoCorrect dialog box. Then click the AutoCorrect tab.

If you find that Excel makes an autocorrection that you don't want, press Ctrl+Z to undo the autocorrection.

Notice that the two strings are joined together without an intervening space. To add a space between the two entries (to get *San Diego California*), use a formula like this one:

    =A1&" "&A2

Or, even better, use a comma and a space to produce *San Diego, California*:

    =A1&", "&A2

If you'd like to force a word wrap, concatenate the strings using CHAR (10) — which inserts a line-break character. Also, make sure that you apply the wrap text format to the cell. The following example joins the text in cell A1 and the text in cell B1, with a line break in between:

```
=A1&CHAR(10)&B1
```

Here's another example of the CHAR function. The following formula returns the string *Stop* by concatenating four characters returned by the CHAR function:

```
=CHAR(83)&CHAR(116)&CHAR(111)&CHAR(112)
```

Here's a final example of using the & operator. In this case, the formula combines text with the result of an expression that returns the maximum value in column C:

```
="The largest value in Column C is " &MAX(C:C)
```

Note   Excel also has a CONCATENATE function, which takes up to 30 arguments. This function simply combines the arguments into a single string. You can use this function if you like, but using the & operator results in shorter formulas.

Displaying formatted values as text

The Excel TEXT function enables you to display a value in a specific number format. Although this function may appear to have dubious value, it *does* serve some useful purposes, as the examples in this section demonstrate. Figure 9-2 shows a simple worksheet. The formula in cell D3 is

```
="The net profit is " & B3
```

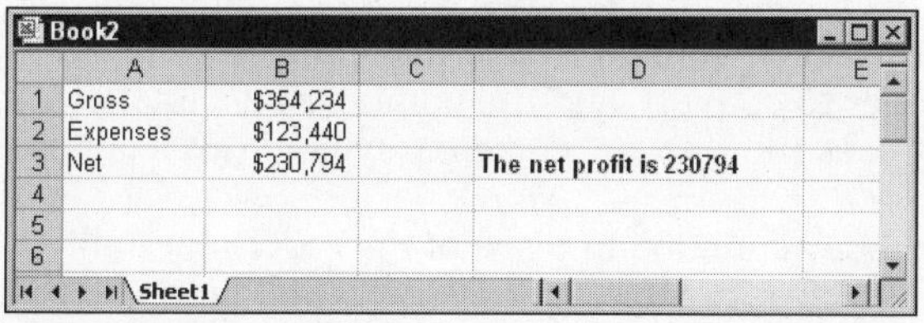

	A	B	C	D	E
1	Gross	$354,234			
2	Expenses	$123,440			
3	Net	$230,794		The net profit is 230794	
4					
5					
6					

Figure 9-2: The formula in D3 doesn't display the formatted number.

This formula essentially combines a text string with the contents of cell B3 and displays the result. Note, however, that the contents of B3 are not formatted in any way. You might want to display the contents of B3 using a currency number format.

Note   Contrary to what you might expect, applying a number format to the cell that contains the formula has no effect. This is because the formula returns a string, not a value.

Here's a revised formula that uses the TEXT function to apply formatting to the value in B3:

```
="The net profit is " & TEXT(B3," $#,##0")
```

This formula displays the text along with a nicely formatted value: *The net profit is $230,794.*

The second argument for the TEXT function consists of a standard Excel number format string. You can enter any valid number format string for this argument.

The preceding example uses a simple cell reference (B3). You can, of course, use an expression instead. Here's an example that combines text with a number resulting from a computation:

```
="Average Expenditure: "& TEXT(AVERAGE(A:A),"$#,##0.00")
```

This formula might return a string, such as *Average Expenditure: $7,794.57.*

Here's another example that uses the NOW function (which returns the current date and time). The TEXT function displays the date and time, nicely formatted.

```
="Report printed on "&TEXT(NOW(),"mmmm d, yyyy at h:mm AM/PM")
```

The formula might display the following: *Report printed on July 22, 2003 at 3:23 PM.*

Cross-Reference   Refer to Chapter 25 for details on Excel number formats.

Displaying formatted currency values as text

The Excel DOLLAR function converts a number to text using the currency format. It takes two arguments: the number to convert, and the number of decimal places to display. The DOLLAR function uses the regional currency symbol (for example, a $).

You can sometimes use the DOLLAR function in place of the TEXT function. The TEXT function, however, is much more flexible because it doesn't limit you to a specific number format.

The following formula returns *Total: $1,287.37.* The second argument for the DOLLAR function specifies the number of decimal places.

```
="Total: "&DOLLAR(1287.367, 2)
```

Repeating a character or string

The REPT function repeats a text string (first argument) any number of times you specify (second argument). For example, this formula returns *HoHoHo*:

```
=REPT("Ho",3)
```

You can also use this function to create crude vertical dividers between cells. This example displays a squiggly line, 20 characters in length:

```
=REPT("~",20)
```

Creating a text histogram

A clever use for the REPT function is to create a simple *histogram* (or frequency distribution chart) directly in a worksheet. Figure 9-3 shows an example of such a histogram. You'll find this type of graphical display especially useful when you need to visually summarize many values. In such a case, a standard chart may be unwieldy.

	A	B	C	D	E	F	G
1							
2		Budget	Actual	Pct. Diff	Under Budget		Exceeded Budget
3	Jan	300	311	3.7%		Jan	▪▪▪▪
4	Feb	300	298	-0.7%	▪	Feb	
5	Mar	300	305	1.7%		Mar	▪▪
6	Apr	350	351	0.3%		Apr	
7	May	350	402	14.9%		May	▪▪▪▪▪▪▪▪▪▪▪▪▪▪▪
8	Jun	350	409	16.9%		Jun	▪▪▪▪▪▪▪▪▪▪▪▪▪▪▪▪▪
9	Jul	500	421	-15.8%	▪▪▪▪▪▪▪▪▪▪▪▪▪▪▪▪	Jul	
10	Aug	500	454	-9.2%	▪▪▪▪▪▪▪▪▪	Aug	
11	Sep	500	474	-5.2%	▪▪▪▪▪	Sep	
12	Oct	500	521	4.2%		Oct	▪▪▪▪
13	Nov	500	476	-4.8%	▪▪▪▪▪	Nov	
14	Dec	500	487	-2.6%	▪▪▪	Dec	
15							

Sheet1

Figure 9-3: Using the REPT function to create a histogram in a worksheet range.

The formulas in columns E and G graphically depict monthly budget variances by displaying a series of characters in the Wingdings font. This example uses the character *n*, which displays as a small square in the Wingdings font. A formula using the REPT function determines the number of characters displayed. Key formulas include

```
E3: =IF(D3<0,REPT("n",-ROUND(D3*100,0)),"")
F3: =A3
G3: =IF(D3>0,REPT("n",ROUND(D3*100,0)),"")
```

Assign the Wingdings font to cells E3 and G3, and then copy the formulas down the columns to accommodate all the data. Right-align the text in column E, and adjust any other formatting. Depending on the numerical range of your data, you may need to change the scaling. Experiment by replacing the 100 value in the formulas. You can substitute any character you like for the *n* in the formulas to produce a different character in the chart.

On the CD-ROM   The workbook shown in Figure 9-3 also appears on the companion CD-ROM.

Padding a number

You're probably familiar with a common security measure (frequently used on printed checks) in which numbers are padded with asterisks on the right. The following formula displays the value in cell A1, along with enough asterisks to make 24 characters total:

```
=(A1 & REPT("*",24-LEN(A1)))
```

Or, if you'd prefer to pad the number with asterisks on the left, use this formula:

```
=REPT("*",24-LEN(A1))&A1
```

The formula below displays asterisk padding on both sides of the number. It returns 24 characters when the number in cell A1 contains an even number of characters; otherwise, it returns 23 characters.

```
=REPT("*",12-LEN(A1)/2)&A1&REPT("*",12-LEN(A1)/2)
```

The preceding formulas are a bit deficient because they don't show any number formatting. Note this revised version that displays the value in A1 (formatted), along with the asterisk padding on the right:

```
=(TEXT(A1,"$#,##0.00")&REPT("*",24-LEN(TEXT(A1,"$#,##0.00"))))
```

Figure 9-4 shows this formula in action.

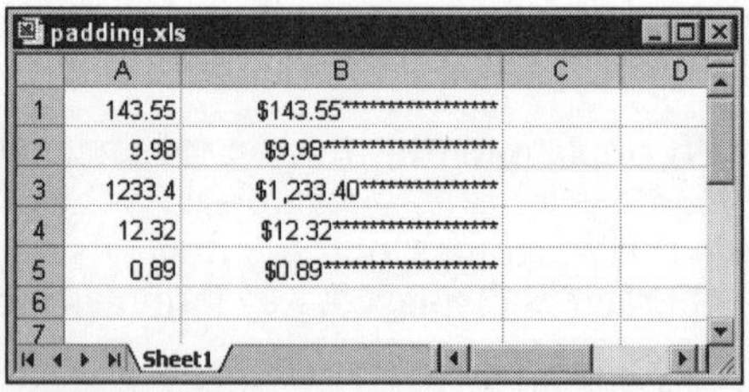

Figure 9-4: Using a formula to pad a number with asterisks.

You can also pad a number by using a custom number format. To repeat the next character in the format to fill the column width, include an asterisk (*) in the custom number format code. For example, use this number format to pad the number with dashes:

```
$#,##0.00*-
```

To pad the number with asterisks, use two asterisks, like this:

```
$#,##0.00**
```

Refer to Chapter 25 for more information about custom number formats, including additional examples using the asterisk format code.

Removing excess spaces and nonprinting characters

Often, data imported into an Excel worksheet contains excess spaces or strange (often unprintable) characters. Excel provides you with two functions to help whip your data into shape: TRIM and CLEAN.

✦ **TRIM** removes all leading and trailing spaces and replaces internal strings of multiple spaces by a single space.

✦ **CLEAN** removes all nonprinting characters from a string. These "garbage" characters often appear when you import certain types of data.

This example uses the TRIM function. The formula returns *Fourth Quarter Earnings* (with no excess spaces):

```
=TRIM("   Fourth   Quarter   Earnings   ")
```

Counting characters in a string

Excel's LEN function takes one argument and returns the number of characters in the argument. For example, assume the string *September Sales* is contained in cell A1. The following formula will return 15:

```
=LEN(A1)
```

Notice that space characters are included in the character count.

The following formula returns the total number of characters in the range A1:A3:

```
=LEN(A1)+LEN(A2)+LEN(A3)
```

You see example formulas that demonstrate how to count the number of specific characters within a string later in this chapter. Chapter 11 covers counting techniques further, and Chapter 15 deals with array formulas.

Changing the case of text

Excel provides three handy functions to change the case of text:

✦ **UPPER** converts the text to ALL UPPERCASE.

✦ **LOWER** converts the text to all lowercase.

✦ **PROPER** converts the text to Proper Case (The First Letter In Each Word Is Capitalized).

Transforming Data with Formulas

Many of the examples in this chapter describe how to use functions to transform data in some way. For example, you can use the UPPER function to transform text into uppercase. Often, you'll want to replace the original data with the transformed data. To do so, use the Paste Special dialog box. Specifically:

1. Create your formulas to transform the original data.

2. Select the formula cells.

3. Choose Edit ⇨ Copy.

4. Select the original data cells.

5. Choose Edit ⇨ Paste Special to display the Paste Special dialog box.

6. Select the Values option, and click OK. This replaces the original data with the transformed data.

After performing these steps, you can delete the formulas.

These functions are quite straightforward. The formula that follows, for example, converts the text in cell A1 to proper case. If cell A1 contained the text *MR. JOHN Q. PUBLIC*, the formula would return *Mr. John Q. Public*.

```
=PROPER(A1)
```

These functions operate only on alphabetic characters; they simply ignore all other characters and return them unchanged.

Extracting characters from a string

Excel users often need to extract characters from a string. For example, you may have a list of employee names (first and last names) and need to extract the last name from each cell. Excel provides several useful functions for extracting characters:

✦ **LEFT** returns a specified number of characters from the beginning of a string.

✦ **RIGHT** returns a specified number of characters from the end of a string.

✦ **MID** returns a specified number of characters beginning at any position within a string.

The formula that follows returns the last 10 characters from cell A1. If A1 contains fewer than 10 characters, the formula returns all of the text in the cell.

```
=RIGHT(A1,10)
```

This next formula uses the MID function to return five characters from cell A1, beginning at character position 2. In other words, it returns characters 2–6.

```
=MID(A1,2,5)
```

The following example returns the text in cell A1 with only the first letter in uppercase. It uses the LEFT function to extract the first character and convert it to uppercase. This then concatenates to another string that uses the RIGHT function to extract all but the first character (converted to lowercase).

```
=UPPER(LEFT(A1))&RIGHT(LOWER(A1),LEN(A1)-1)
```

If cell A1 contained the text *FIRST QUARTER*, the formula would return *First quarter*.

Replacing text with other text

In some situations, you may need to replace a part of a text string with some other text. For example, you may import data that contains asterisks, and you need to convert the asterisks to some other character. You could use the Edit ➪ Replace command to make the replacement. If you prefer a formula-based solution, you can take advantage of either of two functions:

✦ **SUBSTITUTE** replaces specific text in a string. Use this function when you know the character(s) to be replaced but not the position.

✦ **REPLACE** replaces text that occurs in a specific location within a string. Use this function when you know the position of the text to be replaced but not the actual text.

The following formula uses the SUBSTITUTE function to replace 2003 with 2004 in the string *2003 Budget*. The formula returns *2004 Budget*.

```
=SUBSTITUTE("2003 Budget","2003","2004")
```

The following formula uses the SUBSTITUTE function to remove all spaces from a string. In other words, it replaces all space characters with an empty string. The formula returns the title of an excellent Liz Phair CD: *Whitechocolatespaceegg*.

```
=SUBSTITUTE("White chocolate space egg"," ","")
```

The following formula uses the REPLACE function to replace one character beginning at position 5 with nothing. In other words, it removes the fifth character (a hyphen) and returns *Part544*.

```
=REPLACE("Part-544",5,1,"")
```

Finding and searching within a string

Excel's FIND and SEARCH functions enable you to locate the starting position of a particular substring within a string:

✦ **FIND** finds a substring within another text string and returns the starting position of the substring. You can specify the character position at which to begin searching. Use this function for case-sensitive text comparisons. Wildcard comparisons are not supported.

✦ **SEARCH** finds a substring within another text string and returns the starting position of the substring. You can specify the character position at which to begin searching. Use this function for non-case-sensitive text or when you need to use wildcard characters.

The following formula uses the FIND function and returns 7, the position of the first *m* in the string. Notice that this formula is case sensitive.

```
=FIND("m","Big Mama Thornton",1)
```

The formula that follows, which uses the SEARCH function, returns 5, the position of the first *m* (either uppercase or lowercase):

```
=SEARCH("m","Big Mama Thornton",1)
```

You can use the following wildcard characters within the first argument for the SEARCH function:

✦ Question mark (?) matches any single character.

✦ Asterisk (*) matches any sequence of characters.

Tip   If you want to find an actual question mark or asterisk character, type a tilde (~) before the question mark or asterisk.

The next formula examines the text in cell A1 and returns the position of the first three-character sequence that has a hyphen in the middle of it. In other words, it looks for any character followed by a hyphen and any other character. If cell A1 contains the text *Part-A90*, the formula returns 4.

```
=SEARCH("?-?",A1,1)
```

Searching and replacing within a string

You can use the REPLACE function in conjunction with the SEARCH function to replace part of a text string with another string. In effect, you use the SEARCH function to find the starting location used by the REPLACE function.

For example, assume that cell A1 contains the text *Annual Profit Figures*. The following formula searches for the word *Profit* and replaces it with the word *Loss*:

```
=REPLACE(A1,SEARCH("Profit",A1),6,"Loss")
```

This next formula uses the SUBSTITUTE function to accomplish the same effect in a more efficient manner:

```
=SUBSTITUTE(A1,"Profit","Loss")
```

Advanced Text Formulas

The examples in this section appear more complex than the examples in the preceding section. But, as you see, these examples can perform some very useful text manipulations. Space limitations prevent a detailed explanation of how these formulas work.

 You can access all of the examples in this section on the companion CD-ROM.

Counting specific characters in a cell

This formula counts the number of *Bs* (uppercase only) in the string in cell A1:

```
=LEN(A1)-LEN(SUBSTITUTE(A1,"B",""))
```

This formula works by using the SUBSTITUTE function to create a new string (in memory) that has all of the *B*'s removed. Then the length of this string is subtracted from the length of the original string. The result reveals the number of *B*'s in the original string.

The following formula is a bit more versatile. It counts the number of *B*'s (both uppercase and lowercase) in the string in cell A1.

```
=LEN(A1)-LEN(SUBSTITUTE(UPPER(A1),"B",""))
```

Counting the occurrences of a substring in a cell

The formulas in the preceding section count the number of occurrences of a particular character in a string. The following formula works with more than one character. It returns the number of occurrences of a particular substring (contained in cell B1) within a string (contained in cell A1). The substring can consist of any number of characters.

```
=(LEN(A1)-LEN(SUBSTITUTE(A1,B1,"")))/LEN(B1)
```

For example, if cell A1 contains the text *Blonde On Blonde* and B1 contains the text *Blonde*, the formula returns 2.

The comparison is case sensitive, so if B1 contains the text *blonde*, the formula returns 0. The following formula is a modified version that performs a case-insensitive comparison:

```
=(LEN(A1)-LEN(SUBSTITUTE(UPPER(A1),UPPER(B1),"")))/LEN(B1)
```

Extracting a filename from a path specification

The following formula returns the filename from a full path specification. For example, if cell A1 contains *c:\windows\desktop\myfile.xls*, the formula returns *myfile.xls*.

```
=MID(A1,FIND("*",SUBSTITUTE(A1,"\","*",LEN(A1)-
LEN(SUBSTITUTE(A1,"\",""))))+1,LEN(A1))
```

This formula assumes that the system path separator is a backslash (\). It essentially returns all of the text following the last backslash character. If cell A1 doesn't contain a backslash character, the formula returns an error.

Extracting the first word of a string

To extract the first word of a string, a formula must locate the position of the first space character and then use this information as an argument for the LEFT function. The following formula does just that:

```
=LEFT(A1,FIND(" ",A1)-1)
```

This formula returns all of the text prior to the first space in cell A1. However, the formula has a slight problem: It returns an error if cell A1 consists of a single word. A slightly more complex formula that checks for the error with an IF function solves that problem:

```
=IF(ISERR(FIND(" ",A1)),A1,LEFT(A1,FIND(" ",A1)-1))
```

Extracting the last word of a string

Extracting the last word of a string is more complicated because the FIND function only works from left to right. Therefore, the problem rests with locating the *last* space character. The formula that follows, however, solves this problem. It returns the last word of a string (all of the text following the last space character):

```
=RIGHT(A1,LEN(A1)-FIND("*",SUBSTITUTE(A1," ","*",LEN(A1)-
LEN(SUBSTITUTE(A1," ","")))))
```

This formula, however, has the same problem as the first formula in the preceding section: It fails if the string does not contain at least one space character. The following modified formula uses an IF function to count the number of spaces in cell A1. If it contains no spaces, the entire contents of cell A1 are returned. Otherwise, the previous formula kicks in.

```
=IF(ISERR(FIND(" ",A1)),A1,RIGHT(A1,LEN(A1)-
FIND("*",SUBSTITUTE(A1," ","*",LEN(A1)-LEN(SUBSTITUTE(A1,"
",""))))))
```

Extracting all but the first word of a string

The following formula returns the contents of cell A1, except for the first word:

```
=RIGHT(A1,LEN(A1)-FIND(" ",A1,1))
```

If cell A1 contains *2002 Operating Budget*, the formula returns *Operating Budget*.

Extracting first names, middle names, and last names

Suppose you have a list consisting of people's names in a single column. You have to separate these names into three columns: one for the first name, one for the middle name or initial, and one for the last name. This task is more complicated than you may think because not every name has a middle initial. However, you can still do it.

Note

The task becomes a *lot* more complicated if the list contains names with titles (such as *Mr.* or *Dr.*) or names followed by additional details (such as *Jr.* or *III*). In fact, the following formulas will *not* handle these complex cases. However, they still give you a significant head start if you're willing to do a bit of manual editing to handle the special cases.

The formulas that follow all assume that the name appears in cell A1.

You can easily construct a formula to return the first name:

```
=LEFT(A1,FIND(" ",A1)-1)
```

This formula returns the last name:

```
=RIGHT(A1,LEN(A1)-FIND("*",SUBSTITUTE(A1," ","*",LEN(A1)-
LEN(SUBSTITUTE(A1," ","")))))
```

The formula that follows extracts the middle name and requires that you use the other formulas to extract the first name and the last name. It assumes that the first name is in B1 and the last name is in C1.

```
=IF(LEN(B1&C1)+2>=LEN(A1),"",MID(A1,LEN(B1)+2,LEN(A1)-
LEN(B1&C1)-2))
```

Splitting Text Strings without Using Formulas

In many cases, you can eliminate the use of formulas and use Excel's Data➪Text to Columns command to parse strings into their component parts. Selecting this command displays the Excel Convert Text to Columns Wizard, which consists of a series of dialog boxes that walk you through the steps to convert a single column of data into multiple columns. Generally, you want to select the Delimited option (in Step 1) and use Space as the delimiter (in Step 2), as shown in the following figure.

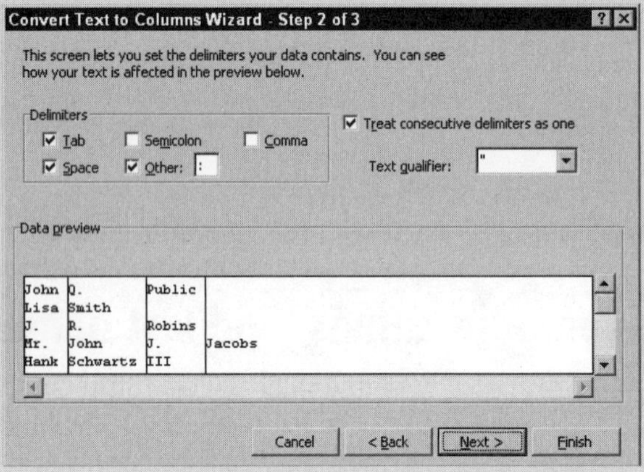

As you can see in Figure 9-5, the formulas work fairly well. There are a few problems, however, notably names that contain four "words." But, as I mentioned earlier, you can clean these cases up manually.

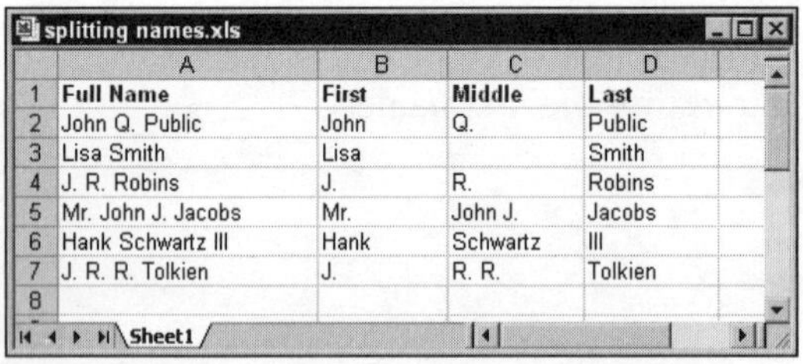

splitting names.xls

	A	B	C	D
1	Full Name	First	Middle	Last
2	John Q. Public	John	Q.	Public
3	Lisa Smith	Lisa		Smith
4	J. R. Robins	J.	R.	Robins
5	Mr. John J. Jacobs	Mr.	John J.	Jacobs
6	Hank Schwartz III	Hank	Schwartz	III
7	J. R. R. Tolkien	J.	R. R.	Tolkien
8				

Sheet1

Figure 9-5: This worksheet uses formulas to extract the first name, last name, and middle name (or initial), and from a list of names in column A.

Removing titles from names

You can use the formula that follows to remove three common titles (*Mr., Ms.,* and *Mrs.*) from a name. For example, if cell A1 contains *Mr. Fred Munster*, the formula would return *Fred Munster*.

```
=IF(OR(LEFT(A1,2)="Mr",LEFT(A1,3)="Mrs",LEFT(A1,2)="Ms"),
RIGHT(A1,LEN(A1)-FIND(" ",A1)),A1)
```

Counting the number of words in a cell

The following formula returns the number of words in cell A1:

```
=LEN(TRIM(A1))-LEN(SUBSTITUTE( (A1)," ",""))+1
```

The formula uses the TRIM function to remove excess spaces. It then uses the SUBSTITUTE function to create a new string (in memory) that has all of the space characters removed. The length of this string is subtracted from the length of the original (trimmed) string to get the number of spaces. This value is then incremented by 1 to get the number of words.

Note that this formula will return 1 if the cell is empty. The following modification solves that problem.

```
=IF(LEN(A1)=0,0,LEN(TRIM(A1))-LEN(SUBSTITUTE(TRIM(A1)," 
",""))+1)
```

✦ ✦ ✦

Working with Dates and Times

◆   ◆   ◆   ◆

In This Chapter

An overview of using dates and times in Excel

Excel's date-related functions

Excel's time-related functions

◆   ◆   ◆   ◆

Beginners often find that working with dates and times in Excel can be frustrating. To eliminate this frustration, you need a good understanding of how Excel handles time-based information. This chapter provides the information you need to create powerful formulas that manipulate dates and times.

Note   The dates in this chapter correspond to the United States English date format: month/day/year. For example, the date 3/1/1952 refers to March 1, 1952, not January 3, 1952. I realize that this is very illogical, but that's the way we Americans have been trained. I trust that the non-American readers of this book can make the adjustment.

How Excel Handles Dates and Times

This section presents a quick overview of how Excel deals with dates and times. It includes coverage of the Excel program's date and time serial number system, and it offers tips for entering and formatting dates and times.

Understanding date serial numbers

To Excel, a date is simply a number. More precisely, a date is a *serial number* that represents the number of days since January 0, 1900. A serial number of 1 corresponds to January 1, 1900; a serial number of 2 corresponds to January 2, 1900, and so on. This system makes it possible to deal with dates in formulas. For example, you can create a formula to calculate the number of days between two dates.

Choose Your Date System: 1900 or 1904

Excel actually supports two date systems: the 1900 date system and the 1904 date system. Which system you use in a workbook determines what date serves as the basis for dates. The 1900 date system uses January 1, 1900, as the day assigned to date serial number 1. The 1904 date system uses January 1, 1904, as the base date. By default, Excel for Windows uses the 1900 date system, and Excel for Macintosh uses the 1904 date system. Excel for Windows supports the 1904 date system for compatibility with Macintosh files. You can choose the date system from the Options dialog box (which you can visit by selecting Tools ➪ Options and selecting the Calculation tab). You cannot change the date system if you use Excel for Macintosh.

Generally, you should use the default 1900 date system. And you should exercise caution if you use two different date systems in workbooks that are linked together. For example, assume that Book1 uses the 1904 date system and contains the date 1/15/1999 in cell A1. Assume that Book2 uses the 1900 date system and contains a link to cell A1 in Book1. Book2 will display the date as 1/14/1995. Both workbooks will use the same date serial number (34713), but they will be interpreted differently.

One advantage to using the 1904 date system is that it enables you to display negative time values. With the 1900 date system, a calculation that results in a negative time (for example, 4:00 PM–5:30 PM) cannot be displayed. When using the 1904 date system, the negative time displays as –1:30 (that is, a difference of 1 hour and 30 minutes).

You may wonder about January 0, 1900. This *non-date* (which corresponds to date serial number 0) is actually used to represent times that are not associated with a particular day. This non-date business becomes clear later in this chapter.

To view a date serial number as a date, you must format the cell as a date. Select Format ➪ Cells to bring up the Format Cells dialog box, click the Number tab, and choose Date from the Category list. Then choose a date format from the Type list.

Note   Excel 97 and later versions support dates from January 1, 1900, through December 31, 9999 (serial number = 2,958,465). Previous versions of Excel support a much smaller range of dates: from January 1, 1900, through December 31, 2078 (serial number = 65,380).

Entering dates

You can enter a date directly as a serial number (if you know it), but more often you enter a date using any of several recognized date formats. Excel automatically converts your entry into the corresponding date serial number (which it uses for calculations), and it also applies the default date format to the cell so it displays as an actual date rather than a cryptic serial number.

For example, if you need to enter June 18, 2004, you can simply enter the date by typing **June 18, 2004** (or use any of several different date formats). Excel interprets your entry and stores the value 38156, the date serial number for that date. It also applies the default date format, so the cell contents may not appear exactly as you typed them.

Note Depending on your regional settings, entering a date in a format, such as June 18, 2004, may be interpreted as a text string. In such a case, you would need to enter the date in a format that corresponds to your regional settings, such as 18 June, 2004.

When you activate a cell that contains a date, the formula bar shows the cell contents formatted by using the default date format — which corresponds to your system's *short date format*. The formula bar does not display the date's serial number. If you need to find out the serial number for a particular date, format the cell using a non-date number format.

Tip To change the default date format, you need to change a system-wide setting. Access the Windows Control Panel and select Regional and Language Options. Then click the Customize button to display the Customize Regional Options dialog box. Select the Date tab. The item selected in the Short Date Format drop-down list box determines the default date format used by Excel.

Table 10-1 shows a sampling of the date formats that Excel recognizes (using the U.S. settings). Results will vary if you use a different regional setting.

Table 10-1	
Date Entry Formats Recognized by Excel	
Entry	**Excel's Interpretation (U.S. Settings)**
6-18-04	June 18, 2004
6-18-2004	June 18, 2004
6/18/04	June 18, 2004
6/18/2004	June 18, 2004
6-18/04	June 18, 2004
June 18, 2004	June 18, 2004
Jun 18	June 18 of the current year
June 18	June 18 of the current year
6/18	June 18 of the current year

Continued

Table 10-1 *(continued)*	
Entry	*Excel's Interpretation (U.S. Settings)*
6-18	June 18 of the current year
18-Jun-2004	June 18, 2004
2004/6/18	June 18, 2004

As you can see in Table 10-1, Excel is rather intelligent when it comes to recognizing dates entered into a cell. It's not perfect, however. For example, Excel does *not* recognize any of the following entries as dates:

✦ June 18 2004

✦ Jun-18 2004

✦ Jun-18/2004

Rather, it interprets these entries as text. If you plan to use dates in formulas, make sure that Excel can recognize the date you enter as a date; otherwise, the formulas that refer to these dates will produce incorrect results.

If you attempt to enter a date that lies outside of the supported date range, Excel interprets it as text. If you attempt to format a serial number that lies outside of the supported range as a date, the value displays as a series of hash marks (###########).

Understanding time serial numbers

When you need to work with time values, you simply extend the Excel date serial number system to include decimals. In other words, Excel works with times by using fractional days. For example, the date serial number for June 1, 2004, is 38139. Noon (halfway through the day) is represented internally as 38139.5.

The serial number equivalent of one minute is approximately 0.00069444. The formula that follows calculates this number by multiplying 24 hours by 60 minutes, and dividing the result into 1. The denominator consists of the number of minutes in a day (1,440).

```
=1/(24*60)
```

Similarly, the serial number equivalent of one second is approximately 0.00001157, obtained by the following formula: 1 divided by 24 hours times 60 minutes times 60 seconds. In this case, the denominator represents the number of seconds in a day (86,400).

```
=1/(24*60*60)
```

Searching for Dates

If your worksheet uses many dates, you may need to search for a particular date by using the Excel Find dialog box (which you can access with the Edit ➪ Find command or Ctrl+F). You'll find that Excel is rather picky when it comes to finding dates. You must enter a full four-digit year into the Find What field in the Find dialog box. The format must correspond to the way dates are displayed in the formula bar.

In Excel, the smallest unit of time is one one-thousandth of a second. The time serial number shown here represents 23:59:59.999 (or one one-thousandth of a second before midnight):

0.99999999

Table 10-2 shows various times of day along with each associated time serial numbers.

Table 10-2
Times of Day and Their Corresponding Serial Numbers

Time of Day	Time Serial Number
12:00:00 AM (midnight)	0.00000000
1:30:00 AM	0.06250000
3:00:00 AM	0.12500000
4:30:00 AM	0.18750000
6:00:00 AM	0.25000000
7:30:00 AM	0.31250000
9:00:00 AM	0.37500000
10:30:00 AM	0.43750000
12:00:00 PM (noon)	0.50000000
1:30:00 PM	0.56250000
3:00:00 PM	0.62500000
4:30:00 PM	0.68750000
6:00:00 PM	0.75000000

Continued

Table 10-2 *(continued)*

Time of Day	Time Serial Number
7:30:00 PM	0.81250000
9:00:00 PM	0.87500000
10:30:00 PM	0.93750000

Entering times

As with entering dates, you normally don't have to worry about the actual time serial numbers. Just enter the time into a cell using a recognized format. Table 10-3 shows some examples of time formats that Excel recognizes:

Table 10-3
Time Entry Formats Recognized by Excel

Entry	Excel's Interpretation
11:30:00 am	11:30 AM
11:30:00 AM	11:30 AM
11:30 pm	11:30 PM
11:30	11:30 AM
13:30	1:30 PM

Because the preceding samples don't have a specific day associated with them, Excel (by default) uses a date serial number of 0, which corresponds to the non-day January 0, 1900. Often, you'll want to combine a date and time. Do so by using a recognized date-entry format, followed by a space, and then a recognized time-entry format. For example, if you enter **6/18/2004 11:30** in a cell, Excel interprets it as 11:30 a.m. on June 18, 2004. Its date/time serial number is 38156.4791666667.

When you enter a time that exceeds 24 hours, the associated date for the time increments accordingly. For example, if you enter **25:00:00** into a cell, it is interpreted as 1:00 AM on January 1, 1900. The day part of the entry increments because the time exceeds 24 hours. Keep in mind that a time value without a date uses January 0, 1900 as the date.

Similarly, if you enter a date *and* a time (and the time exceeds 24 hours), the date that you entered is adjusted. If you enter **9/18/2004 25:00:00**, for example, it is interpreted as 9/19/2004 1:00:00 AM.

If you enter a time only (without an associated date), you'll find that the maximum time that you can enter into a cell is 9999:59:59 (just under 10,000 hours). Excel adds the appropriate number of days. In this case, 9999:59:59 is interpreted as 3:59:59 PM on 02/19/1901. If you enter a time that exceeds 10,000 hours, the time appears as a text string.

Formatting dates and times

You have a great deal of flexibility in formatting cells that contain dates and times. For example, you can format the cell to display the date part only, the time part only, or both the date and time parts.

You format dates and times by selecting the cells and then using the Number tab of the Format Cells dialog box, as shown in Figure 10-1. The Date category shows built-in date formats, and the Time category shows built-in time formats. Some of the formats include both date and time displays. Just select the desired format from the Type list and click OK.

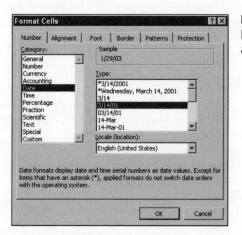

Figure 10-1: Use the Number tab in the Format Cells dialog box to change the appearance of dates and times.

Tip   When you create a formula that refers to a cell containing a date or a time, Excel automatically formats the formula cell as a date or a time. Sometimes, this is very helpful; other times, it's completely inappropriate and downright annoying. Unfortunately, you cannot turn off this automatic date formatting. You can, however, use a shortcut-key combination to remove all number formatting from the cell and return to the default General format. Just select the cell and press Ctrl+Shift+~.

If none of the built-in formats meets your needs, you can create a custom number format. Select the Custom category and then type the custom format codes into the Type box. (See Chapter 25 for information on creating custom number formats.)

Tip   A particularly useful custom number format for displaying times is:

`[h]:mm:ss`

Using square brackets around the hour part of the format string causes Excel to display hours beyond 24 hours. You will find this useful when adding times, especially if the total exceeds 24 hours. For an example, see "Summing times that exceed 24 hours," later in this chapter.

Problems with dates

Excel has some problems when it comes to dates. Many of these problems stem from the fact that Excel was designed many years ago, before the acronym *Y2K* became a household term. And as I describe, the Excel designers basically emulated the Lotus 1-2-3 program's limited date and time features, which contain a nasty bug duplicated intentionally in Excel. In addition, versions of Excel show inconsistency in how they interpret a cell entry that has a two-digit year. And finally, how Excel interprets a date entry depends on your regional date settings.

If Excel were being designed from scratch today, I'm sure it would be much more versatile in dealing with dates. Unfortunately, we're currently stuck with a product that leaves much to be desired in the area of dates.

Excel's leap year bug

A leap year, which occurs every four years, contains an additional day (February 29). Although the year 1900 was not a leap year, Excel treats it as such. In other words, when you type **2/29/1900** into a cell, Excel does not complain. It interprets this as a valid date and assigns a serial number of 60.

If you type **2/29/1901**, however, Excel correctly interprets it as a mistake and doesn't convert it to a date. Rather, it simply makes the cell entry a text string.

How can a product used daily by millions of people contain such an obvious bug? The answer is historical. The original version of Lotus 1-2-3 contained a bug that caused it to consider 1900 as a leap year. When Excel was released some time later, the designers knew of this bug and chose to reproduce it in Excel to maintain compatibility with Lotus worksheet files.

Why does this bug still exist in later versions of Excel? Microsoft asserts that the disadvantages of correcting this bug outweigh the advantages. If the bug were eliminated, it would mess up hundreds of thousands of existing workbooks. In addition, correcting this problem would affect compatibility between Excel and other programs that use dates. As it stands, this bug really causes very few problems because most users do not use dates before March 1, 1900.

Pre-1900 dates

The world, of course, didn't begin on January 1, 1900. People who work with historical information using Excel often need to work with dates before January 1, 1900. Unfortunately, the only way to work with pre-1900 dates is to enter the date into a cell as text. For example, you can enter **July 4, 1776** into a cell, and Excel won't complain.

You can't, however, perform any manipulation on dates that are entered as text. For example, you can't change its numeric formatting, you can't determine which day of the week this date occurred on, and you can't calculate the date that occurs seven days later.

 On the CD-ROM The companion CD-ROM contains an add-in called Extended Date Functions that I developed. When you install this add-in, you'll have access to eight new worksheet functions that enable you to work with any date in the years 0100 through 9999. Figure 10-2 shows a worksheet that uses these functions in column D to perform calculations that involve pre-1900 dates.

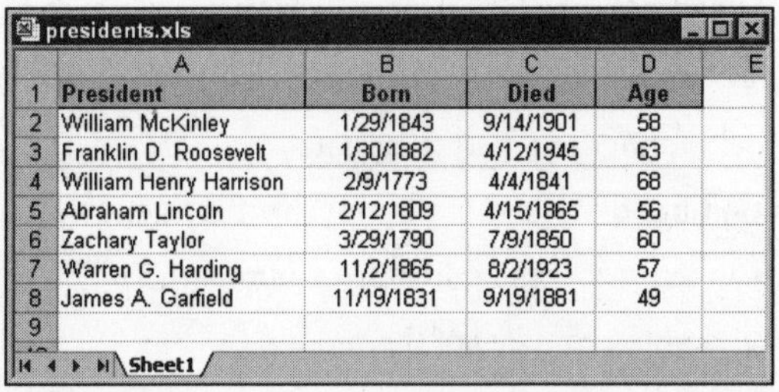

	A	B	C	D	E
1	President	Born	Died	Age	
2	William McKinley	1/29/1843	9/14/1901	58	
3	Franklin D. Roosevelt	1/30/1882	4/12/1945	63	
4	William Henry Harrison	2/9/1773	4/4/1841	68	
5	Abraham Lincoln	2/12/1809	4/15/1865	56	
6	Zachary Taylor	3/29/1790	7/9/1850	60	
7	Warren G. Harding	11/2/1865	8/2/1923	57	
8	James A. Garfield	11/19/1831	9/19/1881	49	
9					

presidents.xls — Sheet1

Figure 10-2: The Extended Date Functions add-in enables you to work with pre-1900 dates.

Inconsistent date entries

You need to exercise caution when entering dates by using two digits for the year. When you do so, Excel has some rules that kick in to determine which century to use. And those rules vary, depending on the version of Excel that you use.

Two-digit years between 00 and 29 are interpreted as twenty-first century dates, and two-digit years between 30 and 99 are interpreted as twentieth century dates. For example, if you enter 12/15/28, Excel interprets your entry as December 15, 2028. But if you enter 12/15/30, Excel sees it as December 15, 1930. This is because Windows uses a default boundary year of 2029. You can keep the default as is, or change it by using the Windows Control Panel (use the spinner in the Calendar area of the Date tab of the Regional and Language Settings Properties dialog box).

Tip   The best way to avoid any surprises is to simply enter *all* years using all four digits for the year.

Date-Related Functions

Excel has quite a few functions that work with dates. When you use Insert ⇨ Function to access the Insert Function dialog box, these functions appear in the Date & Time function category.

Table 10-4 summarizes the date-related functions available in Excel. Some of Excel's date functions require that you install the Analysis ToolPak.

Cross-Reference   See Chapter 24 for more information about the Analysis ToolPak.

Table 10-4
Date-Related Functions

Function	Description
DATE	Returns the serial number of a particular date
DATEDIF	Calculates the number of days, months, or years between two dates
DATEVALUE	Converts a date in the form of text to a serial number
DAY	Converts a serial number to a day of the month
DAYS360	Calculates the number of days between two dates based on a 360-day year
EDATE*	Returns the serial number of the date that represents the indicated number of months before or after the start date
EOMONTH*	Returns the serial number of the last day of the month before or after a specified number of months
MONTH	Converts a serial number to a month
NETWORKDAYS*	Returns the number of whole workdays between two dates
NOW	Returns the serial number of the current date and time
TODAY	Returns the serial number of today's date
WEEKDAY	Converts a serial number to a day of the week
WEEKNUM*	Returns the week number in the year

Function	Description
WORKDAY*	Returns the serial number of the date before or after a specified number of workdays
YEAR	Converts a serial number to a year
YEARFRAC*	Returns the year fraction representing the number of whole days between start_date and end_date

* Function is available only when the Analysis ToolPak add-in is installed.

Displaying the current date

The following function displays the current date in a cell:

```
=TODAY()
```

You can also display the date combined with text. The formula that follows, for example, displays text, such as *Today is Monday, April 9, 2003*.

```
="Today is "&TEXT(TODAY(),"dddd, mmmm d, yyyy")
```

It's important to understand that the TODAY function is updated whenever the worksheet is calculated. For example, if you enter either of the preceding formulas into a worksheet, the formulas will display the current date. But when you open the workbook tomorrow, they will display the current date (not the date when you entered the formula).

Tip   To enter a "date stamp" into a cell, press Ctrl+; (semicolon). This enters the date directly into the cell and does not use a formula. Therefore, the date will not change.

Displaying any date

As explained earlier in this chapter, you can easily enter a date into a cell by simply typing it while using any of the date formats that Excel recognizes. You can also create a date by using the DATE function, which takes three arguments: the year, the month, and the day. The following formula, for example, returns a date comprised of the year in cell A1, the month in cell B1, and the day in cell C1:

```
=DATE(A1,B1,C1)
```

Note   The DATE function accepts invalid arguments and adjusts the result accordingly. For example, the following formula uses 13 as the month argument and returns January 1, 2004. The month argument is automatically translated as month 1 of the following year.

    =DATE(2003,13,1)

Often, you'll use the DATE function with other functions as arguments. For example, the formula that follows uses the YEAR and TODAY functions to return the date for Independence Day (July 4th) of the current year:

    =DATE(YEAR(TODAY()),7,4)

The DATEVALUE function converts a text string that looks like a date into a date serial number. The following formula returns 37855, the date serial number for August 22, 2003:

    =DATEVALUE("8/22/2003")

To view the result of this formula as a date, you need to apply a date number format to the cell.

Caution   Be careful when using the DATEVALUE function. A text string that looks like a date in your country may not look like a date in another country. The preceding example works fine if your system is set for U.S. date formats, but it returns an error for other regional date formats because Excel is looking for the eighth day of the 22nd month!

Generating a series of dates

Often, you want to insert a series of dates into a worksheet. For example, in tracking weekly sales, you may want to enter a series of dates, each separated by seven days. These dates will serve to identify the sales figures.

The most efficient way to enter a series of dates doesn't require any formulas. Use the Excel AutoFill feature to insert a series of dates. Enter the first date and drag the cell's fill handle while pressing the right mouse button. Release the mouse button, and select an option from the shortcut menu (see Figure 10-3).

The advantage of using formulas (instead of the AutoFill feature) to create a series of dates is that you can change the first date, and the others update automatically. You need to enter the starting date into a cell and then use formulas (copied down the column) to generate the additional dates.

The following examples assume that you entered the first date of the series into cell A1 and the formula into cell A2. You can then copy this formula down the column as many times as needed.

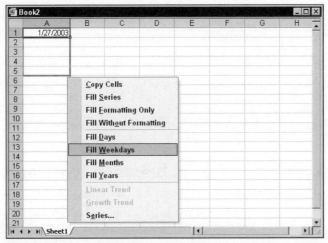

Figure 10-3: Using Excel's AutoFill feature to create a series
of dates.

To generate a series of dates separated by seven days, use this formula:

```
=A1+7
```

To generate a series of dates separated by one month, use this formula:

```
=DATE(YEAR(A1),MONTH(A1)+1,DAY(A1))
```

To generate a series of dates separated by one year, use this formula:

```
=DATE(YEAR(A1)+1,MONTH(A1),DAY(A1))
```

To generate a series of weekdays only (no Saturdays or Sundays), use the formula
that follows. This formula assumes that the date in cell A1 is not a weekend day.

```
=IF(WEEKDAY(A1)=6,A1+3,A1+1)
```

Converting a non-date string to a date

You may import data that contains dates coded as text strings. For example, the following text represents August 21, 2001 (a four-digit year followed by a two-digit
month, followed by a two-digit day):

```
20010821
```

To convert this string to an actual date, you can use a formula, such as this one. (It assumes that the coded data is in cell A1.)

```
=DATE(LEFT(A1,4),MID(A1,5,2),RIGHT(A1,2))
```

This formula uses text functions (LEFT, MID, and RIGHT) to extract the digits, and then it uses these extracted digits as arguments for the DATE function.

Cross-Reference   Refer to Chapter 9 for more information about using formulas to manipulate text.

Calculating the number of days between two dates

A common type of date calculation determines the number of days between two dates. For example, you may have a financial worksheet that calculates interest earned on a deposit account. The interest earned depends on the number of days the account is open. If your sheet contains the open date and the close date for the account, you can calculate the number of days the account was open.

Because dates store as consecutive serial numbers, you can use simple subtraction to calculate the number of days between two dates. For example, if cells A1 and B1 both contain a date, the following formula returns the number of days between these dates:

```
=A1-B1
```

Excel automatically formats this formula cell as a date rather than as a numeric value. Therefore, you will need to change the number format so the result is displayed as a non-date. If cell B1 contains a more recent date than the date in cell A1, the result will be negative.

Note   If this formula does not display the correct value, make sure that A1 and B1 both contain actual dates — not text that *looks* like a date.

Sometimes, calculating the difference between two days is more difficult. To demonstrate, consider the common *fence-post analogy*. If somebody asks you how many units make up a fence, you can respond with either of two answers: the number of fence posts, or the number of gaps between the fence posts. The number of fence posts is always one more than the number of gaps between the posts.

To bring this analogy into the realm of dates, suppose you start a sales promotion on February 1 and end the promotion on February 9. How many days was the promotion in effect? Subtracting February 1 from February 9 produces an answer of eight days. Actually, the promotion lasted nine days. In this case, the correct answer involves counting the fence posts, not the gaps. The formula to calculate the length of the promotion (assuming that you have appropriately named cells) appears like this:

```
=EndDay-StartDay+1
```

Calculating the number of workdays between two dates

When calculating the difference between two dates, you may want to exclude weekends and holidays. For example, you may need to know how many business days fall in the month of November. This calculation should exclude Saturdays, Sundays, and holidays. The NETWORKDAYS function can help out. (You can access this function only when you install the Analysis ToolPak.)

Note   The NETWORKDAYS function has a very misleading name. This function has nothing to do with networks or networking. Rather, it calculates the net number of workdays between two dates.

The NETWORKDAYS function calculates the difference between two dates, excluding weekend days (Saturdays and Sundays). As an option, you can specify a range of cells that contain the dates of holidays, which are also excluded. Excel has absolutely no way of determining which days are holidays, so you must provide this information in a range.

Figure 10-4 shows a worksheet that calculates the workdays between two dates. The range A2:A11 contains a list of holiday dates. The formulas in column C calculate the workdays between the dates in column A and column B. For example, the formula in cell C15 is:

```
=NETWORKDAYS(A15,B15,A2:A11)
```

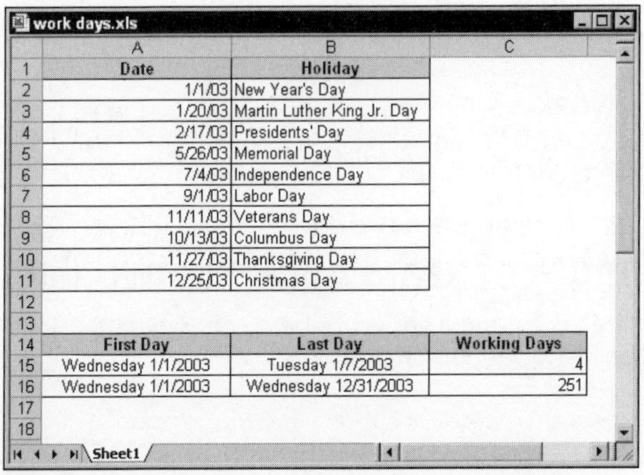

	A	B	C
	work days.xls		
	Date	Holiday	
1	**Date**	**Holiday**	
2	1/1/03	New Year's Day	
3	1/20/03	Martin Luther King Jr. Day	
4	2/17/03	Presidents' Day	
5	5/26/03	Memorial Day	
6	7/4/03	Independence Day	
7	9/1/03	Labor Day	
8	11/11/03	Veterans Day	
9	10/13/03	Columbus Day	
10	11/27/03	Thanksgiving Day	
11	12/25/03	Christmas Day	
12			
13			
14	**First Day**	**Last Day**	**Working Days**
15	Wednesday 1/1/2003	Tuesday 1/7/2003	4
16	Wednesday 1/1/2003	Wednesday 12/31/2003	251
17			
18			

Sheet1

Figure 10-4: Using the NETWORKDAYS function to calculate the number of working days between two dates.

This formula returns 4, which means that the seven-day period beginning with January 1 contains four workdays. In other words, the calculation excludes one holiday, one Saturday, and one Sunday. The formula in cell C16 calculates the total number of workdays in the year.

On the CD-ROM   This workbook is available on the companion CD-ROM.

Offsetting a date using only workdays

The WORKDAY function, which is available only when you install the Analysis ToolPak, is the opposite of the NETWORKDAYS function. For example, if you start a project on January 4, and the project requires 10 working days to complete, the WORKDAY function can calculate the date you will finish the project.

The following formula uses the WORKDAY function to determine the date 10 working days from January 4, 2001. A working day consists of a weekday (Monday through Friday).

```
=WORKDAY("1/4/2001",10)
```

The formula returns January 18, 2001 (four weekend dates fall between January 4 and January 18).

Caution   The preceding formula may return a different result, depending on your regional date setting. (The hard-coded date may be interpreted as April 1, 2001.) A better formula is

```
=WORKDAY(DATE(2001,1,4),10)
```

The second argument for the WORKDAY function can be negative. And as with the NETWORKDAYS function, the WORKDAY function accepts an optional third argument (a reference to a range that contains a list of holiday dates).

Calculating the number of years between two dates

The following formula calculates the number of years between two dates. This formula assumes that cells A1 and B1 both contain dates:

```
=YEAR(A1)-YEAR(B1)
```

This formula uses the YEAR function to extract the year from each date and then subtracts one year from the other. If cell B1 contains a more recent date than the date in cell A1, the result will be negative.

Where's the DATEDIF Function?

In several places throughout this chapter, I refer to the DATEDIF function. You may notice that this function does not appear in the Paste Function dialog box. Therefore, when you use this function, you must always enter it manually.

The DATEDIF function has its origins in Lotus 1-2-3, and apparently Excel provides it for compatibility purposes. For some reason, Microsoft wants to keep this function a secret. Versions prior to Excel 2000 failed to even mention the DATEDIF function in the online help. Interestingly, references to this function were removed from the online help for Excel 2002 and Excel 2003 (although the function is still available).

DATEDIF is a handy function that calculates the number of days, months, or years between two dates. The function takes three arguments: start_date, end_date, and a code that represents the time unit of interest. The following table displays valid codes for the third argument. (You must enclose the codes in quotation marks.)

Unit Code	Returns
"y"	The number of complete years in the period.
"m"	The number of complete months in the period.
"d"	The number of days in the period.
"md"	The difference between the days in start_date and end_date. The months and years of the dates are ignored.
"ym"	The difference between the months in start_date and end_date. The days and years of the dates are ignored.
"yd"	The difference between the days of start_date and end_date. The years of the dates are ignored.

The start_date argument must be earlier than the end_date argument, or the function returns an error.

Note that this function doesn't calculate *full* years. For example, if cell A1 contains 12/31/2001 and cell B1 contains 01/01/2002, the formula returns a difference of one year, even though the dates differ by only one day.

Calculating a person's age

A person's age indicates the number of full years that the person has been alive. The formula in the previous section (for calculating the number of years between two dates) won't calculate this value correctly. You can use two other formulas, however, to calculate a person's age.

The following formula returns the age of the person whose date of birth you enter into cell A1. This formula uses the YEARFRAC function, which is available only when you install the Analysis ToolPak add-in.

```
=INT(YEARFRAC(TODAY(),A1,1))
```

The following formula, which doesn't rely on an Analysis ToolPak function, uses the DATEDIF function to calculate an age. (See the nearby sidebar, "Where's the DATE-DIF Function?")

```
=DATEDIF(A1,TODAY(),"Y")
```

Determining the day of the year

January 1 is the first day of the year, and December 31 is the last day. But what about all of those days in between? The following formula returns the day of the year for a date stored in cell A1:

```
=A1-DATE(YEAR(A1),1,0)
```

The day of the year is sometimes referred to as a *Julian date*.

The following formula returns the number of days remaining in the year after a particular date (assumed to be in cell A1):

```
=DATE(YEAR(A1),12,31)-A1
```

When you enter either of these formulas, Excel applies date formatting to the cell. You need to apply a non-date number format to view the result as a number.

To convert a particular day of the year (for example, the 90th day of the year) to an actual date in a specified year, use the formula that follows. This formula assumes that the year is stored in cell A1 and the day of the year is stored in cell B1.

```
=DATE(A1,1,B1)
```

Determining the day of the week

The WEEKDAY function accepts a date argument and returns an integer between 1 and 7 that corresponds to the day of the week. The following formula, for example, returns 5 because the first day of the year 2004 falls on a Thursday:

```
=WEEKDAY(DATE(2002,1,1))
```

The WEEKDAY function uses an optional second argument that specifies the day numbering system for the result. If you specify 2 as the second argument, the function returns 1 for Monday, 2 for Tuesday, and so on. If you specify 3 as the second argument, the function returns 0 for Monday, 1 for Tuesday, and so on.

Tip　　You can also determine the day of the week for a cell that contains a date by applying a custom number format. A cell that uses the following custom number format displays the day of the week, spelled out:

```
dddd
```

Determining the date of the most recent Sunday

You can use the following formula to return the date for the previous Sunday. If the current day is a Sunday, the formula returns the current date:

```
=TODAY()-MOD(TODAY()-1,7)
```

To modify this formula to find the date of a day other than Sunday, change the 1 to a different number between 2 (for Monday) and 7 (for Saturday).

Determining the first day of the week after a date

This next formula returns the specified day of the week that occurs after a particular date. For example, use this formula to determine the date of the first Monday after June 1, 2004. The formula assumes that cell A1 contains a date and cell A2 contains a number between 1 and 7 (1 for Sunday, 2 for Monday, and so on).

```
=A1+A2-WEEKDAY(A1)+(A2<WEEKDAY(A1))*7
```

If cell A1 contains June 1, 2004, and cell A2 contains 2 (for Monday), the formula returns June 7, 2004. This is the first Monday after June 1, 2004 (which is a Tuesday).

Determining the nth occurrence of a day of the week in a month

You may need a formula to determine the date for a particular occurrence of a weekday. For example, suppose your company payday falls on the second Friday of each month, and you need to determine the paydays for each month of the year. The following formula will make this type of calculation:

```
=DATE(A1,A2,1)+A3-WEEKDAY(DATE(A1,A2,1))+
(A4-(A3>=WEEKDAY(DATE(A1,A2,1))))*7
```

The formula in this section assumes that

- ✦ Cell A1 contains a year.

- ✦ Cell A2 contains a month.

- ✦ Cell A3 contains a day number (1 for Sunday, 2 for Monday, and so on).

- ✦ Cell A4 contains the occurrence number (for example, 2 to select the second occurrence of the weekday specified in cell A3).

If you use this formula to determine the date of the first Friday in June 2004, it returns June 4, 2004.

Note   If the value in cell A4 exceeds the number of the specified day in the month, the formula returns a date from a subsequent month. For example, if you attempt to determine the date of the fifth Friday in June 2004 (there is no such date), the formula returns the first Friday in July.

Calculating dates of holidays

Determining the date for a particular holiday can be tricky. Some, such as New Year's Day and U.S. Independence Day are no-brainers because they always occur on the same date. For these kinds of holidays, you can simply use the DATE function, which I covered earlier in this chapter. To enter New Year's Day (which always falls on January 1) for a specific year in cell A1, you can enter this function:

```
=DATE(A1,1,1)
```

Other holidays are defined in terms of a particular occurrence of a particular weekday in a particular month. For example, Labor Day falls on the first Monday in September.

Figure 10-5 shows a workbook with formulas that calculate the date for 10 U.S. holidays. The formulas, which reference the year in cell A1, are listed in the sections that follow.

On the CD-ROM   The workbook shown in Figure 10-5 also appears on the companion CD-ROM.

New Year's Day

This holiday always falls on January 1:

```
=DATE(A1,1,1)
```

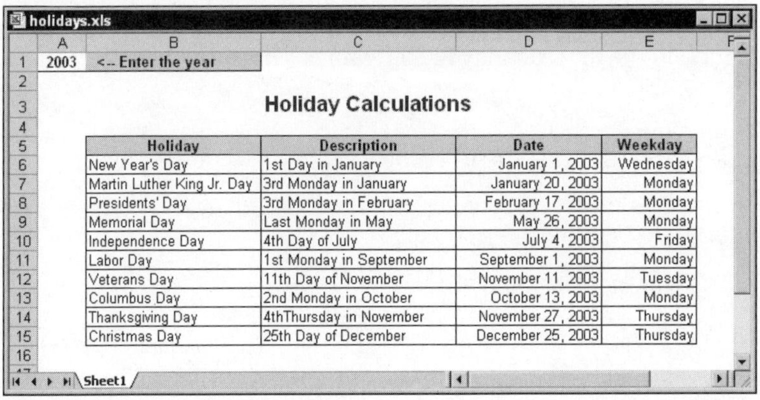

holidays.xls

2003 <-- Enter the year

Holiday Calculations

Holiday	Description	Date	Weekday
New Year's Day	1st Day in January	January 1, 2003	Wednesday
Martin Luther King Jr. Day	3rd Monday in January	January 20, 2003	Monday
Presidents' Day	3rd Monday in February	February 17, 2003	Monday
Memorial Day	Last Monday in May	May 26, 2003	Monday
Independence Day	4th Day of July	July 4, 2003	Friday
Labor Day	1st Monday in September	September 1, 2003	Monday
Veterans Day	11th Day of November	November 11, 2003	Tuesday
Columbus Day	2nd Monday in October	October 13, 2003	Monday
Thanksgiving Day	4thThursday in November	November 27, 2003	Thursday
Christmas Day	25th Day of December	December 25, 2003	Thursday

Sheet1

Figure 10-5: Using formulas to determine the date for various holidays.

Martin Luther King Jr. Day

This holiday occurs on the third Monday in January. This formula calculates Martin Luther King Jr. Day for the year in cell A1:

```
=DATE(A1,1,1)+IF(2<WEEKDAY(DATE(A1,1,1)),7-WEEKDAY
(DATE(A1,1,1))+2,2-WEEKDAY(DATE(A1,1,1)))+((3-1)*7)
```

Presidents' Day

Presidents' Day occurs on the third Monday in February. This formula calculates Presidents' Day for the year in cell A1:

```
=DATE(A1,2,1)+IF(2<WEEKDAY(DATE(A1,2,1)),7-WEEKDAY
(DATE(A1,2,1))+2,2-WEEKDAY(DATE(A1,2,1)))+((3-1)*7)
```

Memorial Day

The last Monday in May is Memorial Day. This formula calculates Memorial Day for the year in cell A1:

```
=DATE(A1,6,1)+IF(2<WEEKDAY(DATE(A1,6,1)),7-WEEKDAY
(DATE(A1,6,1))+2,2-WEEKDAY(DATE(A1,6,1)))+((1-1)*7)-7
```

Notice that this formula actually calculates the first Monday in June, and then subtracts 7 from the result to return the last Monday in May.

Independence Day

This holiday always falls on July 4:

```
=DATE(A1,7,4)
```

Labor Day

Labor Day occurs on the first Monday in September. This formula calculates Labor Day for the year in cell A1:

```
=DATE(A1,9,1)+IF(2<WEEKDAY(DATE(A1,9,1)),7-WEEKDAY
(DATE(A1,9,1))+2,2-WEEKDAY(DATE(A1,9,1)))+((1-1)*7)
```

Veterans Day

This holiday always falls on November 11:

```
=DATE(A1,11,11)
```

Columbus Day

This holiday occurs on the second Monday in October. This formula calculates Columbus Day for the year in cell A1:

```
=DATE(A1,10,1)+IF(2<WEEKDAY(DATE(A1,10,1)),7-WEEKDAY
(DATE(A1,10,1))+2,2-WEEKDAY(DATE(A1,10,1)))+((2-1)*7)
```

Thanksgiving Day

Thanksgiving Day is celebrated on the fourth Thursday in November. This formula calculates Thanksgiving Day for the year in cell A1:

```
=DATE(A1,11,1)+IF(5<WEEKDAY(DATE(A1,11,1)),7-WEEKDAY
(DATE(A1,11,1))+5,5-WEEKDAY(DATE(A1,11,1)))+((4-1)*7)
```

Christmas Day

This holiday always falls on December 25:

```
=DATE(A1,12,25)
```

Determining the last day of a month

To determine the date that corresponds to the last day of a month, you can use the DATE function. However, you need to increment the month by 1 and use a day value of 0. In other words, the "0th" day of the next month is the last day of the current month.

The following formula assumes that a date is stored in cell A1. The formula returns the date that corresponds to the last day of the month.

```
=DATE(YEAR(A1),MONTH(A1)+1,0)
```

You can use a variation of this formula to determine how many days comprise a specified month. The formula that follows returns an integer that corresponds to the number of days in the month for the date in cell A1:

```
=DAY(DATE(YEAR(A1),MONTH(A1)+1,0))
```

Determining whether a year is a leap year

To determine whether a particular year is a leap year, you can write a formula that determines whether the 29th day of February occurs in February or March. You can take advantage of the fact that Excel's DATE function adjusts the result when you supply an invalid argument — for example, a day of 29 when February contains only 28 days.

The following formula returns TRUE if the year of the date in cell A1 is a leap year. Otherwise, it returns FALSE.

```
=IF(MONTH(DATE(YEAR(A1),2,29))=2,TRUE,FALSE)
```

Caution   This function returns the wrong result (TRUE) if the year is 1900. See "Excel's leap year bug," earlier in this chapter.

Determining a date's quarter

For financial reports, you may find it useful to present information in terms of quarters. The following formula returns an integer between 1 and 4 that corresponds to the calendar quarter for the date in cell A1:

```
=ROUNDUP(MONTH(A1)/3,0)
```

This formula divides the month number by 3 and then rounds up the result.

Time-Related Functions

Excel, as you may expect, also includes a number of functions that enable you to work with time values in your formulas. This section contains examples that demonstrate the use of these functions.

Table 10-5 summarizes the time-related functions available in Excel. When you use the Paste Function dialog box, these functions appear in the Date & Time function category.

Table 10-5
Time-Related Functions

Function	Description
HOUR	Converts a serial number to an hour
MINUTE	Converts a serial number to a minute
MONTH	Converts a serial number to a month
NOW	Returns the serial number of the current date and time
SECOND	Converts a serial number to a second
TIME	Returns the serial number of a particular time
TIMEVALUE	Converts a time in the form of text to a serial number

Displaying the current time

This formula displays the current time as a time serial number (or as a serial number without an associated date):

```
=NOW()-TODAY()
```

Tip   To enter a time stamp into a cell, press Ctrl+Shift+: (colon).

You need to format the cell with a time format to view the result as a recognizable time. For example, you can apply the following number format:

```
hh:mm AM/PM
```

You can also display the time, combined with text. The formula that follows displays the text "The current time is 6:28 PM".

```
="The current time is "&TEXT(NOW(),"h:mm AM/PM")
```

Note   These formulas are updated only when the worksheet is calculated.

Displaying any time

Earlier in this chapter, I described how to enter a time value into a cell: Just type it into a cell, making sure that you include at least one colon (:). You can also create a time by using the TIME function. For example, the following formula returns a time comprised of the hour in cell A1, the minute in cell B1, and the second in cell C1:

```
=TIME(A1,B1,C1)
```

Like the DATE function, the TIME function accepts invalid arguments and adjusts the result accordingly. For example, the following formula uses 80 as the minute argument and returns 10:20:15 AM. The 80 minutes are simply added to the hour, with 20 minutes remaining.

```
=TIME(9,80,15)
```

Caution If you enter a value greater than 24 as the first argument for the TIME function, the result may not be what you expect. Logically, a formula such as the one that follows should produce a date/time serial number of 1.041667 (that is, one day and one hour).

```
=TIME(25,0,0)
```

In fact, this formula is equivalent to the following:

```
=TIME(1,0,0)
```

You can also use the DATE function along with the TIME function in a single cell. The formula that follows generates 37959.7708333333, the serial number that represents 6:30 PM on December 4, 2003:

```
=DATE(2003,12,4)+TIME(18,30,0)
```

The TIMEVALUE function converts a text string that looks like a time into a time serial number. This formula returns 0.2395833333, the time serial number for 5:45 AM:

```
=TIMEVALUE("5:45 am")
```

To view the result of this formula as a time, you need to apply number formatting to the cell. The TIMEVALUE function doesn't recognize all common time formats. For example, the following formula returns an error because Excel doesn't like the periods in "a.m."

```
=TIMEVALUE("5:45 a.m.")
```

Calculating the difference between two times

Because times are represented as serial numbers, you can subtract the earlier time from the later time to get the difference. For example, if cell A2 contains 5:30:00 and cell B2 contains 14:00:00, the following formula returns 08:30:00 (a difference of eight hours and 30 minutes):

```
=B2-A2
```

If the subtraction results in a negative value, however, it becomes an invalid time; Excel displays a series of hash marks (########) because a time without a date has a date serial number of 0. A negative time results in a negative serial number, which is not permitted.

If the direction of the time difference doesn't matter, you can use the ABS function to return the absolute value of the difference:

```
=ABS(B2-A2)
```

This "negative time" problem often occurs when calculating an elapsed time — for example, calculating the number of hours worked given a start time and an end time. This presents no problem if the two times fall in the same day. But if the work shift spans midnight, the result is an invalid negative time. For example, you may start work at 10:00 PM and end work at 6:00 AM the next day. Figure 10-6 shows a worksheet that calculates the hours worked. As you can see, the shift that spans midnight presents a problem (cell C3).

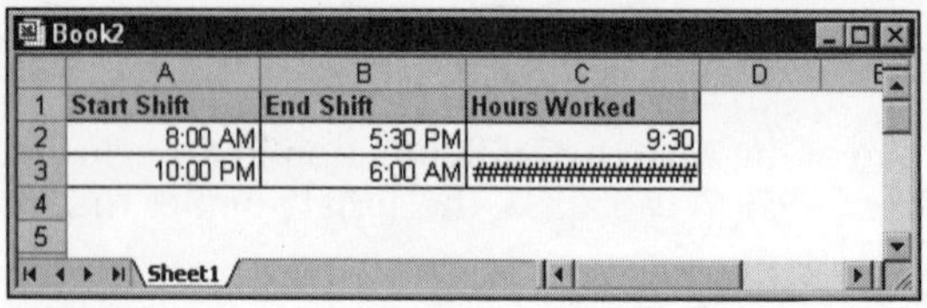

Figure 10-6: Calculating the number of hours worked returns an error if the shift spans midnight.

Using the ABS function (to calculate the absolute value) isn't an option in this case because it returns the wrong result (16 hours). The following formula, however, *does* work:

```
=IF(B2<A2,B2+1,B2)-A2
```

Tip   Negative times *are* permitted if the workbook uses the 1904 date system. To switch to the 1904 date system, select Tools ➪ Options and click the Calculation tab. Place a check mark next to the 1904 Date System option. But beware! When changing the workbook's date system, if the workbook uses dates, the dates will be off by four years.

Summing times that exceed 24 hours

Many people are surprised to discover that when you sum a series of times that exceed 24 hours Excel doesn't display the correct total. Figure 10-7 shows an example. The range B2:B8 contains times that represent the hours and minutes worked each day. The formula in cell B9 is

```
=SUM(B2:B8)
```

As you can see, the formula returns a seemingly incorrect total (17 hours, 45 minutes). The total should read 41 hours, 45 minutes. The problem is that the formula is displaying the total as a date/time serial number of 1.7395833, but the cell formatting is not displaying the *date* part of the date/time. The answer is incorrect because cell B9 has the wrong number format.

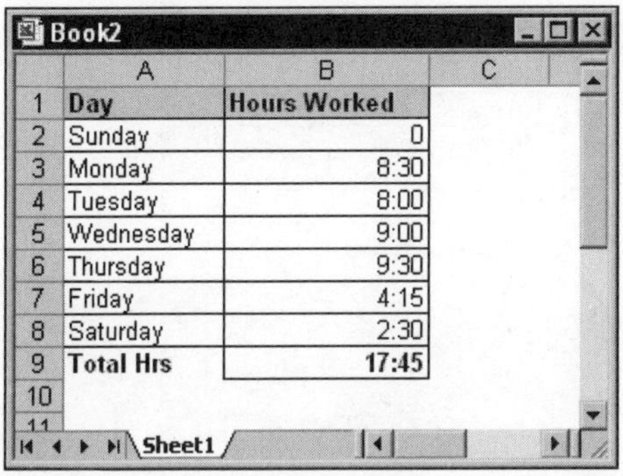

	A	B	C
1	Day	Hours Worked	
2	Sunday	0	
3	Monday	8:30	
4	Tuesday	8:00	
5	Wednesday	9:00	
6	Thursday	9:30	
7	Friday	4:15	
8	Saturday	2:30	
9	Total Hrs	17:45	
10			

Figure 10-7: Incorrect cell formatting makes the total appear incorrectly.

To view a time that exceeds 24 hours, you need to change the number format for the cell so square brackets surround the *hour* part of the format string. Applying the number format here to cell B9 displays the sum correctly:

```
[h]:mm
```

Figure 10-8 shows another example of a worksheet that manipulates times. This worksheet keeps track of hours worked during a week (regular hours and overtime hours).

On the CD-ROM This workbook is available on the companion CD-ROM.

The week's starting date appears in cell D5, and the formulas in column B fill in the dates for the days of the week. Times appear in the range D8:G14, and formulas in column H calculate the number of hours worked each day. For example, the formula in cell H8 is

```
=IF(E8<D8,E8+1-D8,E8-D8)+IF(G8<F8,G8+1-G8,G8-F8)
```

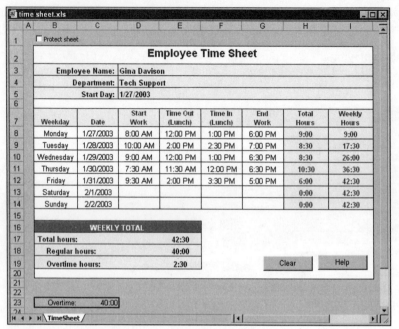

Figure 10-8: An employee timesheet workbook.

The first part of this formula subtracts the time in column D from the time in column E to get the total hours worked before lunch. The second part subtracts the time in column F from the time in column G to get the total hours worked after lunch. I use IF functions to accommodate graveyard shift cases that span midnight — for example, an employee may start work at 10:00 PM and begin lunch at 2:00 AM. Without the IF function, the formula returns a negative result.

The following formula in cell E17 calculates the weekly total by summing the daily totals in column H:

```
=SUM(H8:H14)
```

This worksheet assumes that hours that exceed 40 hours in a week are considered overtime hours. The worksheet contains a cell named *Overtime*, in cell C23. This cell contains 40:00. If your standard workweek consists of something other than 40 hours, you can change this formula.

The following formula (in cell E18) calculates regular (nonovertime) hours. This formula returns the smaller of two values: the total hours, or the overtime hours.

```
=MIN(E17,Overtime)
```

The final formula, in cell E19, simply subtracts the regular hours from the total hours to yield the overtime hours.

```
=E17-E18
```

The times in E17:E19 may display time values that exceed 24 hours, so these cells use a custom number format:

```
[h]:mm
```

Converting from military time

Military time is expressed as a four-digit number from 0000 to 2359. For example, 1:00 AM is expressed as 0100 hours, and 3:30 PM is expressed as 1530 hours. The following formula converts such a number (assumed to appear in cell A1) to a standard time:

```
=TIMEVALUE(LEFT(A1,2)&":"&RIGHT(A1,2))
```

The formula returns an incorrect result if the contents of cell A1 do not contain four digits. The following formula corrects the problem, and it returns a valid time for any military time value from 0 to 2359:

```
=TIMEVALUE(LEFT(TEXT(A1,"0000"),2)&":"&RIGHT(A1,2))
```

Following is a simpler formula that uses the TEXT function to return a formatted string, and then it uses the TIMEVALUE function to express the result in terms of a time.

```
=TIMEVALUE(TEXT(A1,"00\:00"))
```

Converting decimal hours, minutes, or seconds to a time

To convert decimal hours to a time, divide the decimal hours by 24. For example, if cell A1 contains 9.25 (representing hours), this formula returns 09:15:00 (nine hours, 15 minutes):

```
=A1/24
```

To convert decimal minutes to a time, divide the decimal hours by 1,440 (the number of minutes in a day). For example, if cell A1 contains 500 (representing minutes), the following formula returns 08:20:00 (eight hours, 20 minutes):

```
=A1/1440
```

To convert decimal seconds to a time, divide the decimal hours by 86,400 (the number of seconds in a day). For example, if cell A1 contains 65,000 (representing seconds), the following formula returns 18:03:20 (18 hours, three minutes, and 20 seconds):

```
=A1/86400
```

Adding hours, minutes, or seconds to a time

You can use the TIME function to add any number of hours, minutes, or seconds to a time. For example, assume that cell A1 contains a time. The following formula adds 2 hours and 30 minutes to that time and displays the result:

```
=A1+TIME(2,30,0)
```

You can use the TIME function to fill a range of cells with incremental times. Figure 10-9 shows a worksheet with a series of times in 10-minute increments. Cell A1 contains a time that was entered directly. Cell A2 contains the following formula, which copied down the column:

```
=A1+TIME(0,10,0)
```

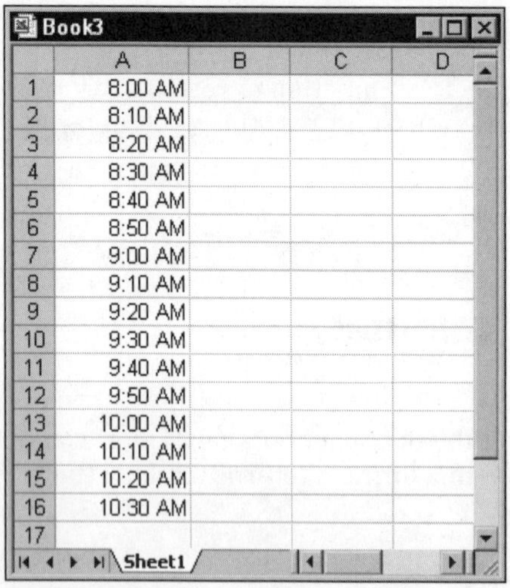

	A	B	C	D
1	8:00 AM			
2	8:10 AM			
3	8:20 AM			
4	8:30 AM			
5	8:40 AM			
6	8:50 AM			
7	9:00 AM			
8	9:10 AM			
9	9:20 AM			
10	9:30 AM			
11	9:40 AM			
12	9:50 AM			
13	10:00 AM			
14	10:10 AM			
15	10:20 AM			
16	10:30 AM			
17				

Figure 10-9: Using a formula to create a series of incremental times.

Rounding time values

You may need to create a formula that rounds a time to a particular value. For example, you may need to enter your company's time records rounded to the nearest 15 minutes. This section presents examples of various ways to round a time value.

The following formula rounds the time in cell A1 to the nearest minute:

```
=ROUND(A1*1440,0)/1440
```

The formula works by multiplying the time by 1440 (to get total minutes). This value is passed to the ROUND function, and the result is divided by 1440. For example, if cell A1 contains 11:52:34, the formula returns 11:53:00.

The following formula resembles this example, except that it rounds the time in cell A1 to the nearest hour:

```
=ROUND(A1*24,0)/24
```

If cell A1 contains 5:21:31, the formula returns 5:00:00.

The following formula rounds the time in cell A1 to the nearest 15 minutes (a quarter of an hour):

```
=ROUND(A1*24/0.25,0)*(0.25/24)
```

In this formula, 0.25 represents the fractional hour. To round a time to the nearest 30 minutes, change 0.25 to 0.5, as in the following formula:

```
=ROUND(A1*24/0.5,0)*(0.5/24)
```

Working with non-time-of-day values

Sometimes, you may want to work with time values that don't represent an actual time of day. For example, you may want to create a list of the finish times for a race or record the time you spend jogging each day. Such times don't represent a time of day. Rather, a value represents the time for an event (in hours, minutes, and seconds). The time to complete a test, for instance, might be 35 minutes and 45 seconds. You can enter that value into a cell as:

```
00:35:45
```

Excel interprets such an entry as 12:35:45 AM, which works fine. (Just make sure that you format the cell so it appears as you like.) When you enter such times that do not have an hour component, you must include at least one zero for the hour. If you omit a leading zero for a missing hour, Excel interprets your entry as 35 hours and 45 minutes.

Figure 10-10 shows an example of a worksheet set up to keep track of someone's jogging activity. Column A contains simple dates. Column B contains the distance in miles. Column C contains the time it took to run the distance. Column D contains formulas to calculate the speed in miles per hour. For example, the formula in cell D2 is

```
=B2/(C2*24)
```

	A	B	C	D	E	F	G	H
	Date	Distance	Time	Speed (mph)	Pace (min/mile)	YTD Distance	Cumulative Time	
1								
2	1/1/2003	1.50	00:18:45	4.80	12.50	1.50	00:18:45	
3	1/2/2003	1.50	00:17:40	5.09	11.78	3.00	00:36:25	
4	1/3/2003	2.00	00:21:30	5.58	10.75	5.00	00:57:55	
5	1/4/2003	1.50	00:15:20	5.87	10.22	6.50	01:13:15	
6	1/5/2003	2.40	00:25:05	5.74	10.45	8.90	01:38:20	
7	1/6/2003	3.00	00:31:06	5.79	10.37	11.90	02:09:26	
8	1/7/2003	3.80	00:41:06	5.55	10.82	15.70	02:50:32	
9	1/8/2003	5.00	01:09:00	4.35	13.80	20.70	03:59:32	
10	1/9/2003	4.00	00:45:10	5.31	11.29	24.70	04:44:42	
11	1/10/2003	3.00	00:29:06	6.19	9.70	27.70	05:13:48	
12	1/11/2003	5.50	01:08:30	4.82	12.45	33.20	06:22:18	
13								
14								

Figure 10-10: This worksheet uses times not associated with a time of day.

Column E contains formulas to calculate the pace, in minutes per mile. For example, the formula in cell E2 is

```
=(C2*60*24)/B2
```

Columns F and G contain formulas that calculate the year-to-date distance (using column B) and the cumulative time (using column C). The cells in column G are formatted using the following number format (which permits time displays that exceed 24 hours):

```
[hh]:mm:ss
```

On the CD-ROM You can also access the workbook shown in Figure 10-10 on the companion CD-ROM.

✦   ✦   ✦

Creating Formulas That Count and Sum

✦　✦　✦　✦

In This Chapter

Information on counting and summing cells

Basic counting formulas

Advanced counting formulas

Formulas for performing common summing tasks

Conditional summing formulas using a single criterion

Conditional summing formulas using multiple criteria

✦　✦　✦　✦

Many of the most frequently asked spreadsheet questions involve counting and summing values and other worksheet elements. It seems that people are always looking for formulas to count or to sum various items in a worksheet. If I've done my job, this chapter answers the vast majority of such questions. It contains many examples that you can easily adapt to your own situation.

Counting and Summing Worksheet Cells

Generally, a *counting formula* returns the number of cells in a specified range that meet certain criteria. A *summing formula* returns the sum of the values of the cells in a range that meet certain criteria. The range you want counted or summed may or may not consist of a worksheet database.

Table 11-1 lists the Excel worksheet functions that come into play when creating counting and summing formulas. Not all of these functions are covered in this chapter. If none of the functions in Table 11-1 can solve your problem, it's likely that an array formula can come to the rescue.

Cross-Reference　See Chapters 14 and 15 for detailed information and examples of array formulas used for counting and summing. In addition, see Chapter 19 for information about summing and counting data in a list.

Table 11-1
Excel's Counting and Summing Functions

Function	Description
COUNT	Returns the number of cells in a range that contain a numeric value
COUNTA	Returns the number of nonblank cells in a range
COUNTBLANK	Returns the number of blank cells in a range
COUNTIF	Returns the number of cells that meet a specified criterion in a range
DCOUNT	Counts the number of records that meet specified criteria in a worksheet database
DCOUNTA	Counts the number of nonblank records that meet specified criteria in a worksheet database
DEVSQ	Returns the sum of squares of deviations of data points from the sample mean; used primarily in statistical formulas
DSUM	Returns the sum of a column of values that meet specified criteria in a worksheet database
FREQUENCY	Calculates how often values occur within a range of values and returns a vertical array of numbers; used only in a multicell array formula
SUBTOTAL	When used with a first argument of 2 or 3, returns *a count* of cells that comprise a subtotal; when used with a first argument of 9, returns *the sum* of cells that comprise a subtotal
SUM	Returns the sum of its arguments
SUMIF	Returns the sum of cells that meet a specified criterion in a range
SUMPRODUCT	Multiplies corresponding cells in two or more ranges and returns the sum of those products
SUMSQ	Returns the sum of the squares of its arguments; used primarily in statistical formulas
SUMX2PY2	Returns the sum of the sum of squares of corresponding values in two ranges; used primarily in statistical formulas
SUMXMY2	Returns the sum of squares of the differences of corresponding values in two ranges; used primarily in statistical formulas
SUMX2MY2	Returns the sum of the differences of squares of corresponding values in two ranges; used primarily in statistical formulas

Getting a Quick Count or Sum

In Excel 97, Microsoft introduced a feature known as AutoCalculate. This feature displays, in the status bar, information about the selected range. Normally, the status bar displays the sum of the values in the selected range. You can, however, right-click the AutoCalculate display to bring up a menu with some other options.

20	26	4	72	53
99	70	62	96	62
49	22	50	45	92
73	35	57	28	23
89	37	16	44	68
75	99	3	62	97
28	42	28	40	
61	60	3	56	
85	57	88	9	
43	57	19	26	
40	57	34	12	
28	54	22	0	
79	74	3	93	
83	25	1	9	

None
Average
Count
Count Nums
Max
Min
✓ Sum

Sum=1481

Right-click to bring up an AutoCalculate menu.

If you select Count, the status bar displays the number of nonempty cells in the selected range. If you select Count Nums, the status bar displays the number of numeric cells in the selected range.

Basic Counting Formulas

The basic counting formulas presented here are all straightforward and relatively simple. They demonstrate the capability of the Excel counting functions to count the number of cells in a range that meet specific criteria. Figure 11-1 shows a worksheet that uses formulas (in column E) to summarize the contents of range A1:B10 — a 20-cell range named *Data*.

On the CD-ROM   You can access the workbook shown in Figure 11-1 on the companion CD-ROM.

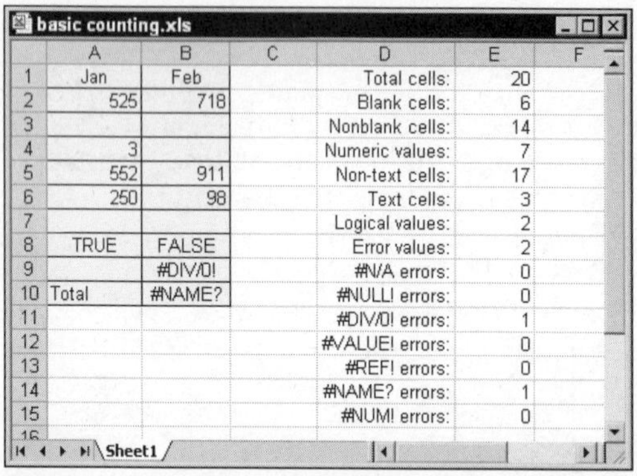

basic counting.xls

	A	B	C	D	E	F
1	Jan	Feb		Total cells:	20	
2	525	718		Blank cells:	6	
3				Nonblank cells:	14	
4	3			Numeric values:	7	
5	552	911		Non-text cells:	17	
6	250	98		Text cells:	3	
7				Logical values:	2	
8	TRUE	FALSE		Error values:	2	
9		#DIV/0!		#N/A errors:	0	
10	Total	#NAME?		#NULL! errors:	0	
11				#DIV/0! errors:	1	
12				#VALUE! errors:	0	
13				#REF! errors:	0	
14				#NAME? errors:	1	
15				#NUM! errors:	0	

Sheet1

Figure 11-1: Formulas provide various counts of the data in A1:B10.

Counting the total number of cells

To get a count of the total number of cells in a range, use the following formula. This formula returns the number of cells in a range named *Data*. It simply multiplies the number of rows (returned by the ROWS function) by the number of columns (returned by the COLUMNS function).

```
=ROWS(Data)*COLUMNS(Data)
```

About This Chapter's Examples

Most of the examples in this chapter use named ranges for function arguments. When you adapt these formulas for your own use, you'll need to substitute either the actual range address or a range name defined in your workbook.

Also, some of the examples consist of array formulas. An *array formula* is a special type of formula that enables you to perform calculations that would not otherwise be possible. You can spot an array formula because it is enclosed in curly brackets when it is displayed in the formula bar. In addition, I use this syntax for the array formula examples presented in this book. For example:

```
{=Data*2}
```

When you enter an array formula, press Ctrl+Shift+Enter (not just Enter) and don't type the brackets. (Excel inserts the brackets for you.) If you need to edit an array formula, don't forget to use Ctrl+Shift+Enter when you've finished editing (otherwise, the array formula will revert to a normal formula and it will return an incorrect result). Refer to Chapter 14 for an introduction to array formulas.

Counting blank cells

The following formula returns the number of blank (empty) cells in a range named *Data*:

```
=COUNTBLANK(Data)
```

The COUNTBLANK function also counts cells containing a formula that returns an empty string. For example, the formula that follows returns an empty string if the value in cell A1 is greater than 5. If the cell meets this condition, the COUNTBLANK function counts that cell.

```
=IF(A1>5,"",A1)
```

 Note The COUNTBLANK function does not count cells that contain a zero value, even if you uncheck the Zero values option in the Options dialog box (select Tools⇨ Options, and then click the View tab).

You can use the COUNTBLANK function with an argument that consists of entire rows or columns. For example, this next formula returns the number of blank cells in column A:

```
=COUNTBLANK(A:A)
```

The following formula returns the number of empty cells on the entire worksheet named Sheet1. You must enter this formula on a sheet other than Sheet1 or it will create a circular reference.

```
=COUNTBLANK(Sheet1!1:65536)
```

Counting nonblank cells

The following formula uses the COUNTA function to return the number of nonblank cells in a range named *Data*:

```
=COUNTA(Data)
```

The COUNTA function counts cells that contain values, text, or logical values (TRUE or FALSE).

 Note If a cell contains a formula that returns an empty string, that cell is included in the count returned by COUNTA, even though the cell appears to be blank.

Counting numeric cells

To count only the numeric cells in a range, use the following formula (which assumes the range is named *Data*):

```
=COUNT(Data)
```

Cells that contain a date or a time are considered to be numeric cells. Cells that contain a logical value (TRUE or FALSE) are not considered to be numeric cells.

Counting nontext cells

The following array formula uses Excel's ISNONTEXT function, which returns TRUE if its argument refers to any nontext cell (including a blank cell). This formula returns the count of the number of cells not containing text (including blank cells):

```
{=SUM(IF(ISNONTEXT(Data),1))}
```

Counting text cells

To count the number of text cells in a range, you need to use an array formula. The array formula that follows returns the number of text cells in a range named *Data*:

```
{=SUM(IF(ISTEXT(Data),1))}
```

Counting logical values

The following array formula returns the number of logical values (TRUE or FALSE) in a range named *Data*:

```
{=SUM(IF(ISLOGICAL(Data),1))}
```

Counting error values in a range

Excel has three functions that help you determine if a cell contains an error value:

✦ **ISERROR:** Returns TRUE if the cell contains any error value (#N/A, #VALUE!, #REF!, #DIV/0!, #NUM!, #NAME?, or #NULL!)

✦ **ISERR:** Returns TRUE if the cell contains any error value except #N/A

✦ **ISNA:** Returns TRUE if the cell contains the #N/A error value

You can use these functions in an array formula to count the number of error values in a range. The following array formula, for example, returns the total number of error values in a range named *Data*:

```
{=SUM(IF(ISERROR(data),1))}
```

Depending on your needs, you can use the ISERR or ISNA function in place of ISERROR.

If you would like to count specific types of errors, you can use the COUNTIF function. The following formula, for example, returns the number of #DIV/0! error values in the range named *Data*:

```
=COUNTIF(Data,"#DIV/0!")
```

Advanced Counting Formulas

Most of the basic examples I presented previously use functions or formulas that perform conditional counting. The advanced counting formulas that I present here represent more-complex examples for counting worksheet cells, based on various types of criteria.

Cross-Reference   Some of these examples are array formulas. Refer to Chapters 14 and 15 for more information about array formulas.

Counting cells by using the COUNTIF function

Excel's COUNTIF function is useful for single-criterion counting formulas. The COUNTIF function takes two arguments:

✦ *range*: The range that contains the values that determine whether to include a particular cell in the count

✦ *criteria*: The logical criteria that determine whether to include a particular cell in the count

Several examples of formulas that use the COUNTIF function are listed in Table 11-2. These formulas all work with a range named *Data*. As you can see, the *criteria* argument proves quite flexible. You can use constants, expressions, functions, cell references, and even wildcard characters (* and ?).

Table 11-2
Examples of Formulas Using the COUNTIF Function

Formula	Description
=COUNTIF(Data,12)	Returns the number of cells containing the value 12
=COUNTIF(Data,"<0")	Returns the number of cells containing a negative value
=COUNTIF(Data,"<>0")	Returns the number of cells not equal to 0
=COUNTIF(Data,">5")	Returns the number of cells greater than 5
=COUNTIF(Data,A1)	Returns the number of cells equal to the contents of cell A1
=COUNTIF(Data,">"&A1)	Returns the number of cells greater than the value in cell A1
=COUNTIF(Data,"*")	Returns the number of cells containing text
=COUNTIF(Data,"???")	Returns the number of text cells containing exactly three characters
=COUNTIF(Data,"budget")	Returns the number of cells containing the single word *budget* (not case sensitive)
=COUNTIF(Data,"*budget*")	Returns the number of cells containing the text *budget* anywhere within the text
=COUNTIF(Data,"A*")	Returns the number of cells containing text that begins with the letter *A* (not case sensitive)
=COUNTIF(Data,TODAY())	Returns the number of cells containing the current date
=COUNTIF(Data,">"& AVERAGE(Data))	Returns the number of cells with a value greater than the average
=COUNTIF(Data,">"& AVERAGE(Data)+STDEV (Data)*3)	Returns the number of values exceeding three standard deviations above the mean
=COUNTIF(Data,3)+ COUNTIF(Data,-3)	Returns the number of cells containing the value 3 or –3
=COUNTIF(Data,TRUE)	Returns the number of cells containing logical TRUE
=COUNTIF(Data,TRUE)+ COUNTIF(Data,FALSE)	Returns the number of cells containing a logical value (TRUE or FALSE)
=COUNTIF(Data,"#N/A")	Returns the number of cells containing the #N/A error value

Counting cells by using multiple criteria

In many cases, your counting formula will need to count cells only if two or more criteria are met. These criteria can be based on the cells that are being counted or based on a range of corresponding cells.

Figure 11-2 shows a simple worksheet that I use for the examples in this section. This sheet shows sales data categorized by Month, SalesRep, and Type. The worksheet contains named ranges that correspond to the labels in row 1.

On the CD-ROM   This workbook is available on the companion CD-ROM.

	A	B	C	D	E
	Month	SalesRep	Type	Amount	
1	Month	SalesRep	Type	Amount	
2	January	Albert	New	85	
3	January	Albert	New	675	
4	January	Brooks	New	130	
5	January	Cook	New	1350	
6	January	Cook	Existing	685	
7	January	Brooks	New	1350	
8	January	Cook	New	475	
9	January	Brooks	New	1205	
10	February	Brooks	Existing	450	
11	February	Albert	New	495	
12	February	Cook	New	210	
13	February	Cook	Existing	1050	
14	February	Albert	New	140	
15	February	Brooks	New	900	
16	February	Brooks	New	900	
17	February	Cook	New	95	
18	February	Cook	New	780	
19	March	Brooks	New	900	
20	March	Albert	Existing	875	
21	March	Brooks	New	50	
22	March	Brooks	New	875	
23	March	Cook	Existing	225	
24	March	Cook	New	175	
25	March	Brooks	Existing	400	
26	March	Albert	New	840	
27	March	Cook	New	132	

Figure 11-2: This worksheet demonstrates various counting techniques that use multiple criteria.

Using And criteria

An And criterion counts cells if all specified conditions are met. A common example is a formula that counts the number of values that fall within a numerical range. For example, you may want to count cells that contain a value greater than 0 *and* less than or equal to 12. Any cell that has a positive value less than or equal to 12 will be included in the count. For this example, the COUNTIF function will do the job:

```
=COUNTIF(Data,">0")-COUNTIF(Data,">12")
```

This formula uses a range named Data. The formula counts the number of values that are greater than 0 and then subtracts the number of values that are greater than 12. The result is the number of cells that contain a value greater than 0 and less than or equal to 12.

Creating this type of formula can be confusing because the formula refers to a condition ">12" even though the goal is to count values that are less than or equal to 12. An alternate technique is to use an array formula, like the one that follows. You may find it easier to create this type of formula.

```
{=SUM((Data>0)*(Data<=12))}
```

Note   When you enter an array formula, remember to use Ctrl+Shift+Enter.

Sometimes, the counting criteria will be based on cells other than the cells being counted. You may, for example, want to count the number of sales that meet the following criteria:

✦ Month is January, *and*

✦ SalesRep is Brooks, *and*

✦ Amount is greater than 1000

The following array formula returns the number of items that meets all three criteria:

```
{=SUM((Month="January")*(SalesRep="Brooks")*(Amount>1000))}
```

When using And criteria, you can avoid using an array formula by using the SUMPRODUCT function. The formula below returns the same result as the previous formula.

```
=SUMPRODUCT((Month="January")*(SalesRep="Brooks")*(Amount>1000))
```

Using Or criteria

To count cells by using an Or criterion, you can sometimes use multiple COUNTIF functions. The following formula, for example, counts the number of 1s, 3s, and 5s in the range named *Data*:

```
=COUNTIF(Data,1)+COUNTIF(Data,3)+COUNTIF(Data,5)
```

You can also use the COUNTIF function in an array formula. The following array formula, for example, returns the same result as the previous formula:

```
{=SUM(COUNTIF(Data,{1,3,5}))}
```

But if you base your Or criteria on cells other than the cells being counted, the COUNTIF function won't work. Refer to Figure 11-2. Suppose you want to count the number of sales that meet the following criteria:

✦ Month is January, *or*

✦ SalesRep is Brooks, *or*

✦ Amount is greater than 1000

The following array formula returns the correct count:

```
{=SUM(IF((Month="January")+(SalesRep="Brooks")+(Amount>1000),1))}
```

Combining And and Or criteria

In some cases, you may need to combine And and Or criteria when counting. For example, perhaps you want to count sales that meet the following criteria:

✦ Month is January, *and*

✦ SalesRep is Brooks, *or*

✦ SalesRep is Cook

This array formula returns the number of sales that meet the criteria:

```
{=SUM((Month="January")*IF((SalesRep="Brooks")+
(SalesRep="Cook"),1))}
```

Counting the most frequently occurring entry

The Excel MODE function returns the most frequently occurring value in a range. Figure 11-3 shows a worksheet with values in range A1:A10 (named *Data*). The formula that follows returns 10 because that value appears most frequently in the *Data* range:

```
=MODE(Data)
```

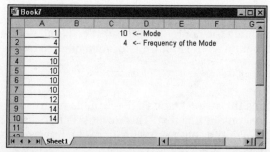

Figure 11-3: The MODE function returns the most frequently occurring value in a range.

To count the number of times the most frequently occurring value appears in the range (in other words, the frequency of the mode), use the following formula:

```
=COUNTIF(Data,MODE(Data))
```

This formula returns 4, because the modal value (10) appears four times in the *Data* range.

The MODE function works only for numeric values. It simply ignores cells that contain text. To find the most frequently occurring text entry in a range, you need to use an array formula.

To count the number of times the most frequently occurring item (text or values) appears in a range named *Data*, use the following array formula:

```
{=MAX(COUNTIF(Data,Data))}
```

This next array formula operates like the MODE function, except that it works with both text and values:

```
{=INDEX(Data,MATCH(MAX(COUNTIF(Data,Data)),COUNTIF(Data,Data),0
))}
```

Counting the occurrences of specific text

The examples in this section demonstrate various ways to count the occurrences of a character or text string in a range of cells. Figure 11-4 shows a worksheet used for these examples. Various text appears in the range A1:A10 (named *Data*); cell B1 is named *Text*.

On the CD-ROM The companion CD-ROM contains a workbook that demonstrates the formulas in this section.

Entire cell contents

To count the number of cells containing the contents of the *Text* cell (and nothing else), you can use the COUNTIF function as the following formula demonstrates:

```
=COUNTIF(Data,Text)
```

For example, if the *Text* cell contains the string "Alpha", the formula returns 2 because two cells in the *Data* range contain this text. This formula is not case sensitive, so it counts both "Alpha" (cell A2) and "alpha" (cell A10). Note, however, that it does not count the cell that contains "Alpha Beta" (cell A8).

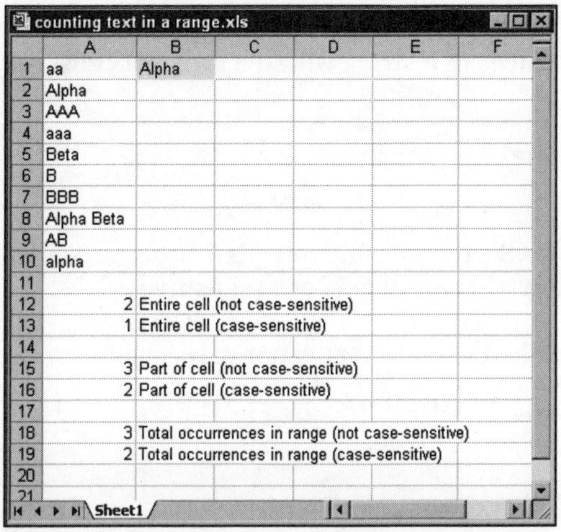

Figure 11-4: This worksheet demonstrates various ways to count characters in a range.

The following array formula is similar to the preceding formula, but this one is case sensitive:

```
{=SUM(IF(EXACT(Data,Text),1))}
```

Partial cell contents

To count the number of cells that contain a string that includes the contents of the *Text* cell, use this formula:

```
=COUNTIF(Data,"*"&Text&"*")
```

For example, if the *Text* cell contains the text "Alpha", the formula returns 3 because three cells in the *Data* range contain the text "alpha" (cells A2, A8, and A10). Note that the comparison is not case sensitive.

If you need a case-sensitive count, you can use the following array formula:

```
{=SUM(IF(LEN(Data)-LEN(SUBSTITUTE(Data,Text,""))>0,1))}
```

If the *Text* cells contain the text "Alpha", the preceding formula returns 2 because the string appears in two cells (A2 and A8).

Total occurrences in a range

To count the total number of occurrences of a string within a range of cells, use the following array formula:

```
{=(SUM(LEN(Data))-SUM(LEN(SUBSTITUTE(Data,Text,""))))/
LEN(Text)}
```

If the *Text* cell contains the character "B", the formula returns 7 because the range contains seven instances of the string. This formula is case sensitive.

The following array formula is a modified version that is not case sensitive:

```
{=(SUM(LEN(Data))-SUM(LEN(SUBSTITUTE(UPPER(Data),
UPPER(Text),""))))/LEN(Text)}
```

Counting the number of unique values

The following array formula returns the number of unique values in a range named *Data*:

```
{=SUM(1/COUNTIF(Data,Data))}
```

To understand how this formula works, you need a basic understanding of array formulas. (See Chapter 14 for an introduction to this topic.) In Figure 11-5, range A1:A12 is named *Data*. Range C1:C12 contains the following multicell array formula (a single formula was entered into all 12 cells in the range):

```
{=COUNTIF(Data,Data)}
```

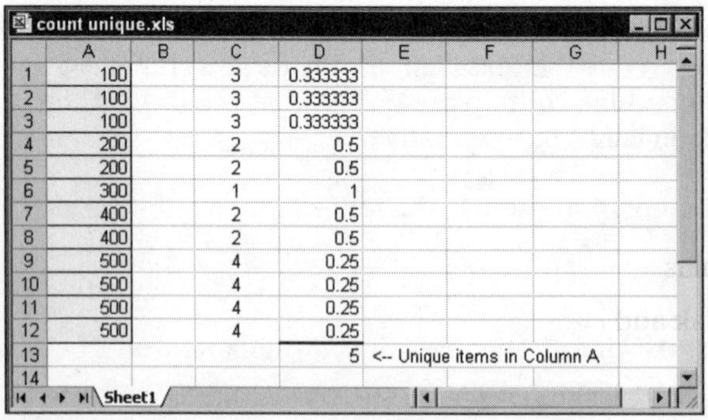

	A	B	C	D	E	F	G	H
1	100		3	0.333333				
2	100		3	0.333333				
3	100		3	0.333333				
4	200		2	0.5				
5	200		2	0.5				
6	300		1	1				
7	400		2	0.5				
8	400		2	0.5				
9	500		4	0.25				
10	500		4	0.25				
11	500		4	0.25				
12	500		4	0.25				
13				5	<-- Unique items in Column A			
14								

Figure 11-5: Using an array formula to count the number of unique values in a range.

You can access the workbook shown in Figure 11-5 on the companion CD-ROM.

The array in range C1:C12 consists of the count of each value in *Data*. For example, the number 100 appears three times, so each array element that corresponds to a value of 100 in the *Data* range has a value of 3.

Range D1:D12 contains the following array formula:

```
{=1/C1:C12}
```

This array consists of each value in the array in range C1:C12, divided into 1. For example, each cell in the original *Data* range that contains a 200 has a value of 0.5 in the corresponding cell in D1:D12.

Summing the range D1:D12 gives the number of unique items in *Data*. The array formula presented at the beginning of this section essentially creates the array that occupies D1:D12 and sums the values.

This formula has a serious limitation: If the range contains any blank cells, it returns an error. The following array formula solves this problem:

```
{=SUM(IF(COUNTIF(Data,Data)=0,"",1/COUNTIF(Data,Data)))}
```

To find out how to create an array formula that returns a list of unique items in a range, refer to Chapter 15.

Creating a frequency distribution

A frequency distribution basically comprises a summary table that shows the frequency of each value in a range. For example, an instructor may create a frequency distribution of test scores. The table would show the count of A's, B's, C's, and so on. Excel provides a number of ways to create frequency distributions. You can

✦ Use the FREQUENCY function

✦ Create your own formulas

✦ Use the Analysis ToolPak add-in

A workbook that demonstrates these three techniques appears on the companion CD-ROM.

Note   If your data is in the form of a database, you can also use a pivot table to create a frequency distribution. See Chapter 21 for more information on pivot tables.

The FREQUENCY function

Using Excel's FREQUENCY function presents the easiest way to create a frequency distribution. This function always returns an array, so you must use it in an array formula entered into a multicell range.

Figure 11-6 shows some data in range A1:E20 (named *Data*). These values range from 1 to 500. The range G2:G11 contains the bins used for the frequency distribution. Each cell in this bin range contains the upper limit for the bin. In this case, the bins consist of 1–50, 51–100, 101–150, and so on.

	A	B	C	D	E	F	G	H
1	55	316	223	185	124		**Bins**	
2	124	93	163	213	314		50	
3	211	41	231	241	212		100	
4	118	113	400	205	254		150	
5	262	1	201	172	101		200	
6	167	479	205	337	118		250	
7	489	15	89	362	148		300	
8	179	248	125	197	177		350	
9	456	153	269	49	127		400	
10	289	500	198	317	300		450	
11	126	114	303	314	270		500	
12	151	279	347	314	170			
13	250	175	93	209	61			
14	166	113	356	124	242			
15	152	384	157	233	99			
16	277	195	436	6	240			
17	147	80	173	211	244			
18	386	93	330	400	141			
19	332	173	129	323	188			
20	338	263	444	84	220			
21								

Figure 11-6: Creating a frequency distribution for the data in A1:E20.

To create the frequency distribution, select a range of cells that corresponds to the number of cells in the bin range. Then enter the following array formula:

```
{=FREQUENCY(Data,G2:G11)}
```

The array formula enters the count of values in the *Data* range that fall into each bin. To create a frequency distribution that consists of percentages, use the following array formula:

```
{=FREQUENCY(Data,G2:G11)/COUNT(Data)}
```

Figure 11-7 shows two frequency distributions — one in terms of counts and one in terms of percentages. The figure also shows a chart (histogram) created from the frequency distribution.

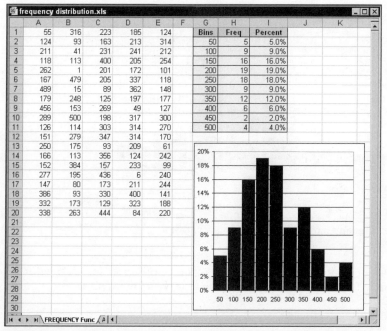

Figure 11-7: Frequency distributions created by using the FREQUENCY function

Using formulas to create a frequency distribution

Figure 11-8 shows a worksheet that contains test scores for 50 students in column B (the range is named *Grades*). Formulas in columns G and H calculate a frequency distribution for letter grades. The minimum and maximum values for each letter grade appear in columns D and E. For example, a test score between 80 and 89 (inclusive) qualifies for a B.

The formula in cell G2 that follows is an array formula that counts the number of scores that qualify for an A:

```
{=SUM((Grades>=D2)*(Grades<=E2))}
```

You may recognize this formula from a previous section in this chapter (see "Counting cells by using multiple criteria"). This formula was copied to the four cells below G2.

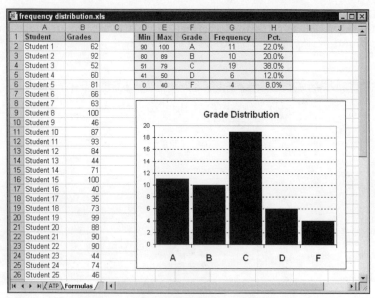

Figure 11-8: Creating a frequency distribution of test scores.

The formulas in column H calculate the percentage of scores for each letter grade. The formula in H2, which was copied to the four cells below H2, is

```
=G2/SUM($G$2:$G$6)
```

Using the Analysis ToolPak to create a frequency distribution

After you install the Analysis ToolPak add-in, you can use the Histogram option to create a frequency distribution. Start by entering your bin values in a range. Then select Tools ⇨ Data Analysis to display the Data Analysis dialog box. Next, select Histogram and click OK. You should see the Histogram dialog box shown in Figure 11-9.

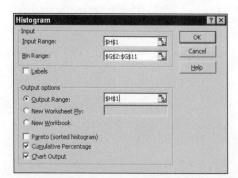

Figure 11-9: The Analysis ToolPak's Histogram dialog box.

Specify the ranges for your data (Input Range), bins (Bin Range), and results (Output Range), and then select any options. Figure 11-10 shows a frequency distribution (and chart) created with the Histogram option.

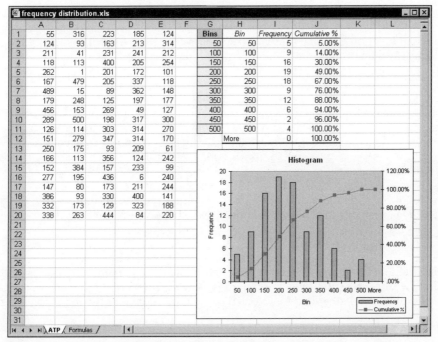

Figure 11-10: A frequency distribution and chart generated by the Analysis ToolPak's Histogram option.

Caution Note that the frequency distribution consists of values, not formulas. Therefore, if you make any changes to your input data, you need to rerun the Histogram procedure to update the results.

Summing Formulas

The examples in this section demonstrate how to perform common summing tasks by using formulas. The formulas range from very simple to relatively complex array formulas that compute sums by using multiple criteria.

Summing all cells in a range

It doesn't get much simpler than this. The following formula returns the sum of all values in a range named *Data*:

```
=SUM(Data)
```

The SUM function can take up to 30 arguments. The following formula, for example, returns the sum of the values in five noncontiguous ranges:

```
=SUM(A1:A9,C1:C9,E1:E9,G1:G9,I1:I9)
```

You can use complete rows or columns as an argument for the SUM function. The formula that follows, for example, returns the sum of all values in column A. If this formula appears in a cell in column A, it generates a circular reference error.

```
=SUM(A:A)
```

The following formula returns the sum of all values on Sheet1. To avoid a circular reference error, this formula must appear on a sheet other than Sheet1.

```
=SUM(Sheet1!1:65536)
```

The SUM function is very versatile. The arguments can be numerical values, cells, ranges, text representations of numbers (which are interpreted as values), logical values, and even embedded functions. For example, consider the following formula:

```
=SUM(B1,5,"6",,SQRT(4),A1:A5,TRUE)
```

This formula, which is a perfectly valid formula, contains all of the following types of arguments, listed here in the order of their presentation:

✦ A single cell reference

✦ A literal value

✦ A string that looks like a value

✦ A missing argument

✦ An expression that uses another function

✦ A range reference

✦ A logical TRUE value

Caution   The SUM function is versatile, but it's also inconsistent when you use logical values (TRUE or FALSE). Logical values stored in cells are always treated as 0. But logical TRUE, when used as an argument in the SUM function, is treated as 1.

Computing a cumulative sum

You may want to display a cumulative sum of values in a range — sometimes known as a "running total." Figure 11-11 illustrates a cumulative sum. Column B shows the monthly amounts, and column C displays the cumulative (year-to-date) totals.

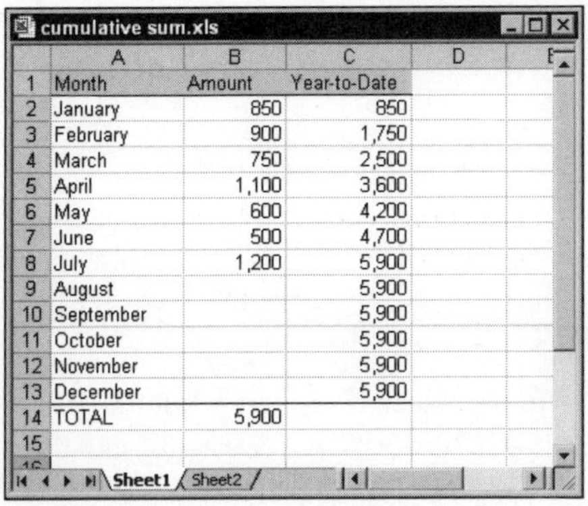

	A	B	C	D	E
1	Month	Amount	Year-to-Date		
2	January	850	850		
3	February	900	1,750		
4	March	750	2,500		
5	April	1,100	3,600		
6	May	600	4,200		
7	June	500	4,700		
8	July	1,200	5,900		
9	August		5,900		
10	September		5,900		
11	October		5,900		
12	November		5,900		
13	December		5,900		
14	TOTAL	5,900			

cumulative sum.xls — Sheet1 / Sheet2

Figure 11-11: Simple formulas in column C display a cumulative sum of the values in column B.

The formula in cell C2 is

```
=SUM(B$2:B2)
```

Notice that this formula uses a *mixed reference;* that is, the first cell in the range reference always refers to the same row (in this case, row 2). When this formula is copied down the column, the range argument adjusts such that the sum always starts with row 2 and ends with the current row. For example, after copying this formula down column C, the formula in cell C8 is

```
=SUM(B$2:B8)
```

You can use an IF function to hide the cumulative sums for rows in which data hasn't been entered. The following formula, entered in cell C2 and copied down the column, is

```
=IF(B2<>"",SUM(B$2:B2),"")
```

Figure 11-12 shows this formula at work.

On the CD-ROM This workbook is available on the companion CD-ROM.

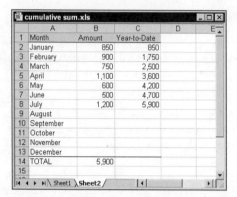

Figure 11-12: Using an IF function to hide cumulative sums for missing data.

Summing the "top *n*" values

In some situations, you may need to sum the *n* largest values in a range — for example, the top ten values. One approach is to sort the range in descending order and then use the SUM function with an argument consisting of the first *n* values in the sorted range. An array formula, such as this one, accomplishes the task without sorting:

```
{=SUM(LARGE(Data,{1,2,3,4,5,6,7,8,9,10}))}
```

This formula sums the ten largest values in a range named *Data*. To sum the ten smallest values, use the SMALL function instead of the LARGE function:

```
{=SUM(SMALL(Data,{1,2,3,4,5,6,7,8,9,10}))}
```

These formulas use an array constant comprised of the arguments for the LARGE or SMALL function. If the value of *n* for your top *n* calculation is large, you may prefer to use the following variation. This formula returns the sum of the top 30 values in the *Data* range. You can, of course, substitute a different value for 30.

```
{=SUM(LARGE(Data,ROW(INDIRECT("1:30"))))}
```

Cross-Reference   See Chapter 14 for more information about array constants.

Conditional Sums Using a Single Criterion

Often, you need to calculate a *conditional sum*. With a conditional sum, values in a range that meet one or more conditions are included in the sum. This section presents examples of conditional summing by using a single criterion.

The SUMIF function is very useful for single-criterion sum formulas. The SUMIF function takes three arguments:

✦ *range*: The range containing the values that determine whether to include a particular cell in the sum.

✦ *criteria*: An expression that determines whether to include a particular cell in the sum.

✦ *sum_range*: Optional. The range that contains the cells you want to sum. If you omit this argument, the function uses the range specified in the first argument.

The examples that follow demonstrate the use of the SUMIF function. These formulas are based on the worksheet shown in Figure 11-13, set up to track invoices. Column F contains a formula that subtracts the date in column E from the date in column D. A negative number in column F indicates a past-due payment. The worksheet uses named ranges that correspond to the labels in row 1.

	A	B	C	D	E	F
1	InvoiceNum	Office	Amount	DateDue	Today	Difference
2	AG-0145	Oregon	$5,000.00	2-Apr	6-May	-34
3	AG-0189	California	$450.00	20-Apr	6-May	-16
4	AG-0220	Washington	$3,211.56	29-Apr	6-May	-7
5	AG-0310	Oregon	$250.00	1-May	6-May	-5
6	AG-0355	Washington	$125.50	5-May	6-May	-1
7	AG-0409	Washington	$3,000.00	11-May	6-May	5
8	AG-0581	Oregon	$2,100.00	24-May	6-May	18
9	AG-0600	Oregon	$335.39	24-May	6-May	18
10	AG-0602	Washington	$65.00	29-May	6-May	23
11	AG-0633	California	$250.00	31-May	6-May	25
12	TOTAL		$14,787.45			26

Figure 11-13: A negative value in column F indicates a past-due payment.

All of the examples in this section also appear on the companion CD-ROM.

Summing only negative values

The following formula returns the sum of the negative values in column F. In other words, it returns the total number of past-due days for all invoices. For this worksheet, the formula returns –58.

```
=SUMIF(Difference,"<0")
```

Let a Wizard Create Your Formula

Excel ships with an add-in called Conditional Sum Wizard. After you install this add-in, you can invoke the wizard by selecting Tools ⇨ Conditional Sum.

You can specify various conditions for your summing, and the add-in creates the formula for you (always an array formula). The Conditional Sum Wizard add-in, although a handy tool, is not all that versatile. For example, you can combine multiple criteria by using an And condition but not an Or condition.

Because you omit the third argument, the second argument ("<0") applies to the values in the *Difference* range.

Note   You can also use the following array formula to sum the negative values in the *Difference* range:

```
{=SUM(IF(Difference<0,Difference))}
```

You do not need to hard-code the arguments for the SUMIF function into your formula. For example, you can create a formula, such as the following, which gets the criteria argument from the contents of cell G2:

```
=SUMIF(Difference,G2)
```

This formula returns a new result if you change the criteria in cell G2.

Summing values based on a different range

The following formula returns the sum of the past-due invoice amounts (in column C):

```
=SUMIF(Difference,"<0",Amount)
```

This formula uses the values in the *Difference* range to determine if the corresponding values in the *Amount* range contribute to the sum.

Note   You can also use the following array formula to return the sum of the values in the *Amount* range, where the corresponding value in the *Difference* range is negative:

```
{=SUM(IF(Difference<0,Amount))}
```

Summing values based on a text comparison

The following formula returns the total invoice amounts for the Oregon office:

```
=SUMIF(Office,"=Oregon",Amount)
```

Using the equal sign is optional. The following formula has the same result:

```
=SUMIF(Office,"Oregon",Amount)
```

To sum the invoice amounts for all offices *except* Oregon, use this formula:

```
=SUMIF(Office,"<>Oregon",Amount)
```

Summing values based on a date comparison

The following formula returns the total invoice amounts that have a due date after June 1, 1999:

```
=SUMIF(DateDue,">="&DATE(1999,6,1),Amount)
```

Notice that the second argument for the SUMIF function is an expression. The expression uses the DATE function, which returns a date. Also, the comparison operator, enclosed in quotes, is concatenated (using the & operator) with the result of the DATE function.

The formula that follows returns the total invoice amounts that have a future due date (including today):

```
=SUMIF(DateDue,">="&TODAY(),Amount)
```

Conditional Sums Using Multiple Criteria

The examples in the preceding section all used a single comparison criterion. The examples in this section involve summing cells based on multiple criteria. Because the SUMIF function does not work with multiple criteria, you need to resort to using an array formula. Figure 11-14 shows the sample worksheet again, for your reference. The worksheet also shows several formulas that demonstrate summing by using multiple criteria.

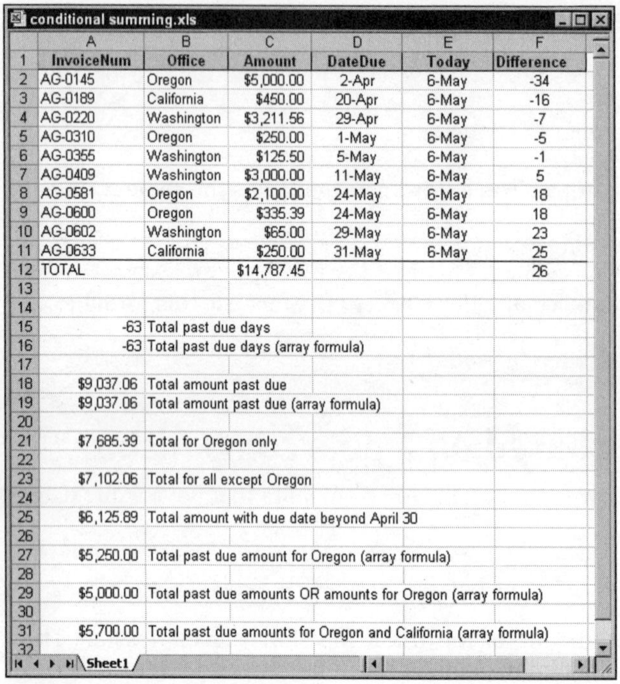

conditional summing.xls

	A	B	C	D	E	F
1	InvoiceNum	Office	Amount	DateDue	Today	Difference
2	AG-0145	Oregon	$5,000.00	2-Apr	6-May	-34
3	AG-0189	California	$450.00	20-Apr	6-May	-16
4	AG-0220	Washington	$3,211.56	29-Apr	6-May	-7
5	AG-0310	Oregon	$250.00	1-May	6-May	-5
6	AG-0355	Washington	$125.50	5-May	6-May	-1
7	AG-0409	Washington	$3,000.00	11-May	6-May	5
8	AG-0581	Oregon	$2,100.00	24-May	6-May	18
9	AG-0600	Oregon	$335.39	24-May	6-May	18
10	AG-0602	Washington	$65.00	29-May	6-May	23
11	AG-0633	California	$250.00	31-May	6-May	25
12	TOTAL		$14,787.45			26
13						
14						
15	-63	Total past due days				
16	-63	Total past due days (array formula)				
17						
18	$9,037.06	Total amount past due				
19	$9,037.06	Total amount past due (array formula)				
20						
21	$7,685.39	Total for Oregon only				
22						
23	$7,102.06	Total for all except Oregon				
24						
25	$6,125.89	Total amount with due date beyond April 30				
26						
27	$5,250.00	Total past due amount for Oregon (array formula)				
28						
29	$5,000.00	Total past due amounts OR amounts for Oregon (array formula)				
30						
31	$5,700.00	Total past due amounts for Oregon and California (array formula)				

Sheet1

Figure 11-14: This worksheet demonstrates summing based on multiple criteria.

Using And criteria

Suppose you want to get a sum of the invoice amounts that are past due *and* associated with the Oregon office. In other words, the value in the *Amount* range will be summed only if both of the following criteria are met:

- ✦ The corresponding value in the *Difference* range is negative.
- ✦ The corresponding text in the *Office* range is "Oregon."

The following array formula does the job:

```
{=SUM((Difference<0)*(Office="Oregon")*Amount)}
```

This formula creates two new arrays (in memory):

- ✦ A Boolean array that consists of TRUE if the corresponding *Difference* value is less than zero; FALSE otherwise.
- ✦ A Boolean array that consists of TRUE if the corresponding *Office* value equals "Oregon"; FALSE otherwise.

Multiplying Boolean values results in the following:

```
TRUE * TRUE = 1

TRUE * FALSE = 0

FALSE * FALSE = 0
```

Therefore, the corresponding *Amount* value returns non-zero only if the corresponding values in the memory arrays are both TRUE. The result produces a sum of the *Amount* values that meet the specified criteria.

Using Or criteria

Suppose that you want to get a sum of past-due invoice amounts *or* ones associated with the Oregon office. In other words, the value in the *Amount* range will be summed if either of the following criteria is met:

✦ The corresponding value in the *Difference* range is negative.

✦ The corresponding text in the *Office* range is "Oregon."

The following array formula does the job:

```
{=SUM(IF((Office="Oregon")+(Difference<0),1,0)*Amount)}
```

A plus sign (+) joins the conditions; you can include more than two conditions.

Using And and Or criteria

As you may expect, things get a bit tricky when your criteria consists of both And and Or operations. For example, you may want to sum the values in the *Amount* range when both of the following conditions are met:

✦ The corresponding value in the *Difference* range is negative.

✦ The corresponding text in the Office range is "Oregon" or "California."

Notice that the second condition actually consists of two conditions joined with Or. The following array formula does the trick:

```
{=SUM((Difference<0)*IF((Office="Oregon")+
(Office="California"),1)*Amount)}
```

✦   ✦   ✦

Creating Formulas That Look Up Values

This chapter discusses various techniques that you can use to look up a value in a table. Excel has three functions (LOOKUP, VLOOKUP, and HLOOKUP) designed for this task, but you may find that these functions don't quite cut it.

This chapter provides many lookup examples, including alternative techniques that go well beyond the Excel program's normal lookup capabilities.

Introducing Lookup Formulas

A *lookup formula* essentially returns a value from a table (in a range) by looking up another value. A common telephone directory provides a good analogy. If you want to find a person's telephone number, you first locate the name (look it up) and then retrieve the corresponding number.

Figure 12-1 shows a simple worksheet that uses several lookup formulas. This worksheet contains a table of employee data, beginning in row 7. This range is named *EmpData*. When you enter a name into cell C2, lookup formulas in D2:G2 retrieve the matching information from the table. The following lookup formulas use the VLOOKUP function:

```
D2  =VLOOKUP(C2,EmpData,2,FALSE)
E2  =VLOOKUP(C2,EmpData,3,FALSE)
F2  =VLOOKUP(C2,EmpData,4,FALSE)
G2  =VLOOKUP(C2,EmpData,5,FALSE)
```

This particular example uses four formulas to return information from the *EmpData* range. In many cases, you only want a single value from the table, so use only one formula.

About This Chapter's Examples

Most of the examples in this chapter use named ranges for function arguments. When you adapt these formulas for your own use, you need to substitute the actual range address or a range name defined in your workbook.

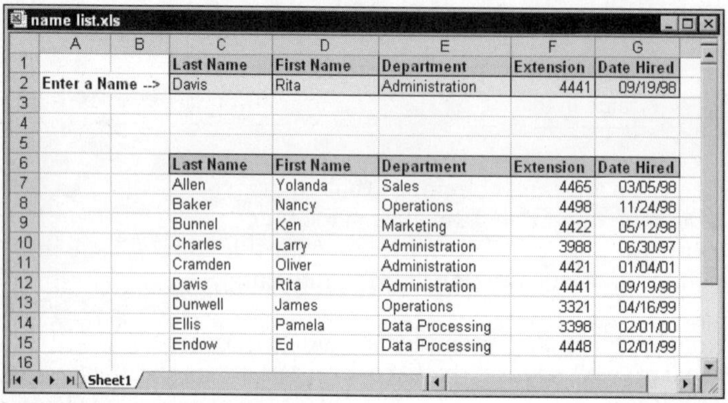

name list.xls

	A	B	C	D	E	F	G
1			Last Name	First Name	Department	Extension	Date Hired
2	Enter a Name -->		Davis	Rita	Administration	4441	09/19/98
3							
4							
5							
6			Last Name	First Name	Department	Extension	Date Hired
7			Allen	Yolanda	Sales	4465	03/05/98
8			Baker	Nancy	Operations	4498	11/24/98
9			Bunnel	Ken	Marketing	4422	05/12/98
10			Charles	Larry	Administration	3988	06/30/97
11			Cramden	Oliver	Administration	4421	01/04/01
12			Davis	Rita	Administration	4441	09/19/98
13			Dunwell	James	Operations	3321	04/16/99
14			Ellis	Pamela	Data Processing	3398	02/01/00
15			Endow	Ed	Data Processing	4448	02/01/99
16							

Sheet1

Figure 12-1: Lookup formulas in row 2 look up the information for the employee name in cell C2.

Functions Relevant to Lookups

Several Excel functions are useful when writing formulas to look up information in a table. Table 12-1 lists and describes these functions.

Table 12-1
Functions Used in Lookup Formulas

Function	*Description*
CHOOSE	Returns a specific value from a list of values (up to 29) supplied as arguments.
HLOOKUP	Horizontal lookup. Searches for a value in the top row of a table and returns a value in the same column from a row you specify in the table.
IF	Returns one value if a condition you specify is TRUE, and returns another value if the condition is FALSE.
INDEX	Returns a value (or the reference to a value) from within a table or range.

Function	Description
LOOKUP	Returns a value either from a one-row or one-column range. Another form of the LOOKUP function works like VLOOKUP but is restricted to returning a value from the last column of a range.
MATCH	Returns the relative position of an item in a range that matches a specified value.
OFFSET	Returns a reference to a range that is a specified number of rows and columns from a cell or range of cells.
VLOOKUP	Vertical lookup. Searches for a value in the first column of a table and returns a value in the same row from a column you specify in the table.

The examples in this chapter use the functions listed in Table 12-1.

Using the IF Function for Simple Lookups

The Excel IF function is very versatile and is often suitable for simple decision-making problems. The accompanying figure shows a worksheet with student grades in column B. Formulas in column C use the IF function to return text: either Pass (a score of 65 or higher) or Fail (a score below 65). For example, the formula in cell C2 is

```
=IF(B2>=65,"Pass","Fail")
```

	A	B	C	D
1	Student	Score	Grade	
2	Andy	82	Pass	
3	Barbara	57	Fail	
4	Chuck	73	Pass	
5	Dave	54	Fail	
6	Ella	82	Pass	
7	Frank	72	Pass	
8				

You can "nest" IF functions to provide even more decision-making ability. The formula below, for example, returns one of four strings: Excellent, Very Good, Fair, or Poor.

```
=IF(B2>=90,"Excellent",IF(B2>=70,"Very
Good",IF(B2>=50,"Fair","Poor")))
```

Excel does not allow more than seven levels of nesting for IF functions. And besides, nesting more than a few levels will make your formula confusing and unwieldy. In such a case, you want to use one of the lookup techniques described in this chapter.

Basic Lookup Formulas

You can use the Excel basic lookup functions to search a column or row for a lookup value to return another value as a result. Excel provides three basic lookup functions: HLOOKUP, VLOOKUP, and LOOKUP. The MATCH and INDEX functions are often used together to return a cell or relative cell reference for a lookup value.

The VLOOKUP function

The VLOOKUP function looks up the value in the first column of the lookup table and returns the corresponding value in a specified table column. The lookup table is arranged vertically. The syntax for the VLOOKUP function is

```
VLOOKUP(lookup_value,table_array,col_index_num,range_lookup)
```

The VLOOKUP function's arguments are as follows:

+ ***lookup_value***: The value to be looked up in the first column of the lookup table.

+ ***table_array***: The range that contains the lookup table.

+ ***col_index_num***: The column number within the table from which the matching value is returned.

+ ***range_lookup***: Optional. If TRUE or omitted, an approximate match is returned. (If an exact match is not found, the next largest value that is less than *lookup_value* is returned.) If FALSE, VLOOKUP will search for an exact match. If VLOOKUP cannot find an exact match, the function returns #N/A.

Note   If the *range_lookup* argument is TRUE or omitted, the first column of the lookup table must be in ascending order. If *lookup_value* is smaller than the smallest value in the first column of *table_array*, VLOOKUP returns #N/A. If the *range_lookup* argument is FALSE, the first column of the lookup table need not be in ascending order. If an exact match is not found, the function returns #N/A.

Tip   Although not indicated in the online help, if the *lookup_value* argument is text, it can include wildcard characters * and ?.

A very common use for a lookup formula involves an income tax rate schedule (see Figure 12-2). The tax rate schedule shows the income tax rates for various income levels. The following formula (in cell B3) returns the tax rate for the income in cell B2:

```
=VLOOKUP(B2,D2:F7,3)
```

On the CD-ROM   You can access the workbook shown in Figure 12-2 on the companion CD-ROM.

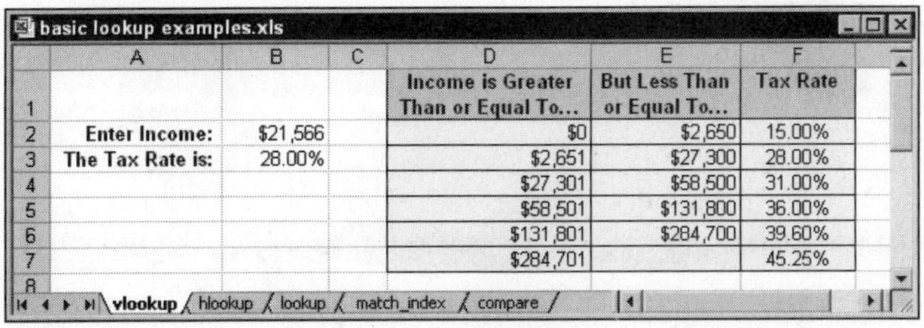

	A	B	C	D	E	F
1				Income is Greater Than or Equal To...	But Less Than or Equal To...	Tax Rate
2	Enter Income:	$21,566		$0	$2,650	15.00%
3	The Tax Rate is:	28.00%		$2,651	$27,300	28.00%
4				$27,301	$58,500	31.00%
5				$58,501	$131,800	36.00%
6				$131,801	$284,700	39.60%
7				$284,701		45.25%
8						

Figure 12-2: Using VLOOKUP to look up a tax rate.

The lookup table resides in a range that consists of three columns (D2:F7). Because the last argument for the VLOOKUP function is 3, the formula returns the corresponding value in the third column of the lookup table.

Note that an exact match is not required. If an exact match is not found in the first column of the lookup table, the VLOOKUP function uses the next largest value that is less than the lookup value. In other words, the function uses the row in which the value you want to look up is greater than or equal to the row value but less than the value in the next row. In the case of a tax table, this is exactly what you want to happen.

The HLOOKUP function

The HLOOKUP function works just like the VLOOKUP function except that the lookup table is arranged horizontally instead of vertically. The HLOOKUP function looks up the value in the first row of the lookup table and returns the corresponding value in a specified table row.

The syntax for the HLOOKUP function is

```
HLOOKUP(lookup_value,table_array,row_index_num,range_lookup)
```

The HLOOKUP function's arguments are as follows

✦ *lookup_value*: The value to be looked up in the first row of the lookup table.

✦ *table_array*: The range that contains the lookup table.

✦ *row_index_num*: The row number within the table from which the matching value is returned.

✦ *range_lookup*: Optional. If TRUE or omitted, an approximate match is returned. (If an exact match is not found, the next largest value less than *lookup_value* is returned.) If FALSE, VLOOKUP will search for an exact match. If VLOOKUP cannot find an exact match, the function returns #N/A.

Tip   Although not indicated in the online help, if the *lookup_value* argument is text, it can include wildcard characters * and ?.

Figure 12-3 shows the tax rate example with a horizontal lookup table (in the range E1:J3). The formula in cell B3 is

```
=HLOOKUP(B2,E1:J3,3)
```

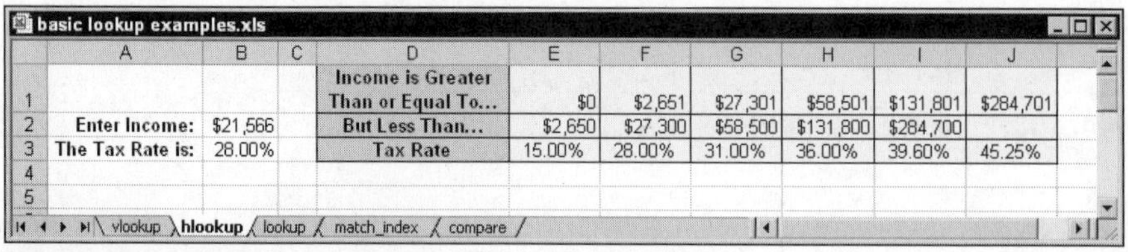

	A	B	C	D	E	F	G	H	I	J
1				Income is Greater Than or Equal To...	$0	$2,651	$27,301	$58,501	$131,801	$284,701
2	Enter Income:	$21,566		But Less Than...	$2,650	$27,300	$58,500	$131,800	$284,700	
3	The Tax Rate is:	28.00%		Tax Rate	15.00%	28.00%	31.00%	36.00%	39.60%	45.25%
4										
5										

basic lookup examples.xls

vlookup \ **hlookup** / lookup / match_index / compare /

Figure 12-3: Using HLOOKUP to look up a tax rate.

The LOOKUP function

The LOOKUP function has the following syntax:

```
LOOKUP(lookup_value,lookup_vector,result_vector)
```

The function's arguments are as follows:

✦ **lookup_value**: The value to be looked up in the *lookup_vector*.

✦ **lookup_vector**: A single-column or single-row range that contains the values to be looked up. These values must be in ascending order.

✦ **result_vector**: The single-column or single-row range that contains the values to be returned. It must be the same size as the *lookup_vector*.

The LOOKUP function looks in a one-row or one-column range (*lookup_vector*) for a value (*lookup_value*) and returns a value from the same position in a second one-row or one-column range (*result_vector*).

Caution   Values in the *lookup_vector* must be in ascending order. If *lookup_value* is smaller than the smallest value in *lookup_vector*, LOOKUP returns #N/A.

Note   Excel Help also lists an *array syntax* for the LOOKUP function. This alternate syntax is included for compatibility with other spreadsheet products. In general, you can use the VLOOKUP or HLOOKUP functions rather than the array syntax.

Figure 12-4 shows the tax table again. This time, the formula in cell B3 uses the LOOKUP function to return the corresponding tax rate. The formula in cell B3 is

```
=LOOKUP(B2,D2:D7,F2:F7)
```

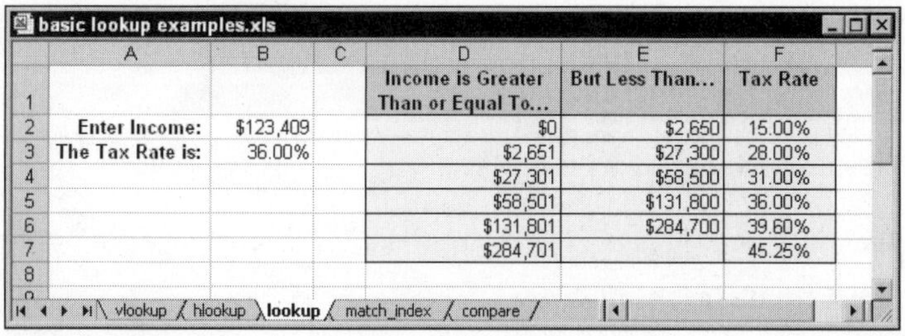

	A	B	C	D	E	F
1				Income is Greater Than or Equal To...	But Less Than...	Tax Rate
2	Enter Income:	$123,409		$0	$2,650	15.00%
3	The Tax Rate is:	36.00%		$2,651	$27,300	28.00%
4				$27,301	$58,500	31.00%
5				$58,501	$131,800	36.00%
6				$131,801	$284,700	39.60%
7				$284,701		45.25%
8						

basic lookup examples.xls

⏮ ◀ ▶ ⏭ \ vlookup ╱ hlookup ╲ **lookup** ╱ match_index ╱ compare ╱

Figure 12-4: Using LOOKUP to look up a tax rate.

Caution   If the values in the first column are not arranged in ascending order, the LOOKUP function may return an incorrect value.

Note that LOOKUP (as opposed to VLOOKUP) requires two range references (a range to be looked in, and a range that contains result values). VLOOKUP, on the other hand, uses a single range for the lookup table, and the third argument determines which column to use for the result. This argument, of course, can consist of a cell reference.

Combining the MATCH and INDEX functions

The MATCH and INDEX functions are often used together to perform lookups. The MATCH function returns the relative position of a cell in a range that matches a specified value. The syntax for MATCH is

```
MATCH(lookup_value,lookup_array,match_type)
```

The MATCH function's arguments are as follows:

✦ **lookup_value**: The value you want to match in *lookup_array*. If *match_type* is 0 and the *lookup_value* is text, this argument can include wildcard characters "*" and "?"

✦ **lookup_array**: The range being searched.

✦ **match_type**: An integer (–1, 0, or 1) that specifies how the match is determined.

Note   If *match_type* is 1, MATCH finds the largest value less than or equal to *lookup_value*. (*lookup_array* must be in ascending order.) If *match_type* is 0, MATCH finds the first value exactly equal to *lookup_value*. If *match_type* is –1, MATCH finds the smallest value greater than or equal to *lookup_value*. (*lookup_array* must be in descending order.) If you omit the *match_type* argument, this argument is assumed to be 1.

The INDEX function returns a cell from a range. The syntax for the INDEX function is

```
INDEX(array,row_num,column_num)
```

The INDEX function's arguments are as follows:

✦ **array**: A range

✦ **row_num**: A row number within *array*

✦ **col_num**: A column number within *array*

Note
If *array* contains only one row or column, the corresponding *row_num* or *column_num* argument is optional.

Figure 12-5 shows a worksheet with dates, day names, and amounts in columns D, E, and F. When you enter a date in cell B1, the following formula (in cell B2) searches the dates in column D and returns the corresponding amount from column F. The formula in cell B2 is

```
=INDEX(F2:F21,MATCH(B1,D2:D21,0))
```

	A	B	C		D	E	F	
1	Date:	1/19/2003			Date	Weekday	Amount	
2	Amount:	114			1/1/2003	Wednesday	23	
3					1/2/2003	Thursday	179	
4					1/3/2003	Friday	149	
5					1/4/2003	Saturday	196	
6					1/5/2003	Sunday	131	
7					1/6/2003	Monday	179	
8					1/7/2003	Tuesday	134	
9					1/8/2003	Wednesday	179	
10					1/9/2003	Thursday	193	
11					1/10/2003	Friday	191	
12					1/11/2003	Saturday	176	
13					1/12/2003	Sunday	189	
14					1/13/2003	Monday	163	
15					1/14/2003	Tuesday	121	
16					1/15/2003	Wednesday	100	
17					1/16/2003	Thursday	109	
18					1/17/2003	Friday	151	
19					1/18/2003	Saturday	138	
20					1/19/2003	Sunday	114	
21					1/20/2003	Monday	156	
22								

Figure 12-5: Using the INDEX and MATCH functions to perform a lookup.

To understand how this works, start with the MATCH function. This function searches the range D2:D21 for the date in cell B1. It returns the relative row number where the date is found. This value is then used as the second argument for the INDEX function. The result is the corresponding value in F2:F21.

When a Blank Is Not a Zero

The Excel lookup functions treat empty cells in the result range as zeros. The worksheet in the accompanying figure contains a two-column lookup table, and this formula looks up the name in cell B1 and returns the corresponding amount:

```
=VLOOKUP(B1,D2:E8,2)
```

Note that the Amount cell for Charlie is blank, but the formula returns a 0.

If you need to distinguish zeros from blank cells, you must modify the lookup formula by adding an IF function to check whether the length of the returned value is 0. When the looked up value is blank, the length of the return value is 0. In all other cases, the length of the returned value is non-zero. The following formula displays an empty string (a blank) whenever the length of the looked-up value is zero and the actual value whenever the length is anything but zero:

```
=IF(LEN(VLOOKUP(B1,D2:E8,2))=0,"",(VLOOKUP(B1,D2:E8,2)))
```

Alternatively, you can specifically check for an empty string, as in the following formula:

```
=IF(VLOOKUP(B1,D2:E8,2)="","",(VLOOKUP(B1,D2:E8,2)))
```

Specialized Lookup Formulas

You can use some additional types of lookup formulas to perform more-specialized lookups. For instance, you can look up an exact value, search in another column besides the first in a lookup table, perform a case-sensitive lookup, return a value from among multiple lookup tables, and perform other specialized and complex lookups.

Looking up an exact value

As demonstrated in the previous examples, VLOOKUP and HLOOKUP don't necessarily require an exact match between the value to be looked up and the values in the lookup table. An example is looking up a tax rate in a tax table. In some cases, you may require a perfect match. For example, when looking up an employee number, you would probably require a perfect match for the number.

To look up an exact value only, use the VLOOKUP (or HLOOKUP) function with the optional fourth argument set to FALSE.

Figure 12-6 shows a worksheet with a lookup table that contains employee numbers (column C) and employee names (column D). The lookup table is named *EmpList*. The formula in cell B2, which follows, looks up the employee number entered in cell B1 and returns the corresponding employee name:

```
=VLOOKUP(B1,EmpList,2,FALSE)
```

	A	B	C	D
	employee list.xls			
1	Employee No.:	999	**Employee Number**	**Employee Name**
2	Employee Name:	#N/A	873	Charles K. Barkley
3			1109	Francis Jenikins
4			1549	James Brackman
5			1334	Linda Harper
6			1643	Louise Victor
7			1101	Melinda Hindquest
8			1873	Michael Orenthal
9			983	Peter Yates
10			972	Sally Rice
11			1398	Walter Franklin
12				
13				

Figure 12-6: This lookup table requires an exact match.

Because the last argument for the VLOOKUP function is FALSE, the function returns a value only if an exact match is found. If the value is not found, the formula returns #N/A. This, of course, is exactly what you want to happen because returning an approximate match for an employee number makes no sense. Also, notice that the employee numbers in column C are not in ascending order. If the last argument for VLOOKUP is FALSE, the values need not be in ascending order.

Tip   If you prefer to see something other than #N/A when the employee number is not found, you can use an IF function to test for the #N/A result (using the ISNA function) and substitute a different string. The following formula displays the text Not Found rather than #N/A:

```
=IF(ISNA(VLOOKUP(B1,EmpList,2,FALSE)),"Not Found",
VLOOKUP(B1,EmpList,2,FALSE))
```

Looking up a value to the left

The VLOOKUP function always looks up a value in the first column of the lookup range. But what if you want to look up a value in a column other than the first column? It would be helpful if you could supply a negative value for the third argument for VLOOKUP — but you can't.

Figure 12-7 illustrates the problem. Suppose you want to look up the batting average (column B, in a range named *Averages*) of a player in column C (in a range named *Players*). The player you want data for appears in a cell named *LookupValue*. The VLOOKUP function won't work because the data is not arranged correctly. One option is to rearrange your data, but sometimes that's not possible.

	A	B	C	D	E	F	G	H	I
	At Bats	Average	Player		Player to lookup:	Darr			
1	**At Bats**	**Average**	**Player**		**Player to lookup:**	Darr			
2	12	0.333	Arias						
3	41	0.390	Darr		Average	0.390	<-- LOOKUP		
4	24	0.333	Davis		At Bats:	41	<-- LOOKUP		
5	25	0.160	Gomez						
6	23	0.217	Gonzolez		Average	0.390	<-- INDEX and MATCH		
7	30	0.300	Gwynn		At Bats:	41	<-- INDEX and MATCH		
8	0	0.000	Henderson						
9	51	0.333	Jackson						
10	43	0.186	Klesko						
11	36	0.139	Kotsay						
12	9	0.333	Magadan						
13	16	0.313	Mendez						
14	44	0.341	Nevin						
15	14	0.286	Perez						
16	28	0.321	Trammell						
17									

Figure 12-7: The VLOOKUP function can't look up a value in column B, based on a value in column C.

One solution is to use the LOOKUP function, which requires two range arguments. The following formula (in cell F3) returns the batting average from column B of the player name contained in the cell named *LookupValue*:

```
=LOOKUP(LookupValue,Players,Averages)
```

Using the VLOOKUP function requires that the lookup range (in this case, the *Players* range) is in ascending order. In addition to this limitation, the formula suffers from a slight problem: If you enter a nonexistent player (in other words, the *LookupValue* cell contains a value not found in the *Players* range), the formula returns an erroneous result.

A better solution uses the INDEX and MATCH functions. The formula that follows works just like the previous one except that it returns #N/A if the player is not found. Another advantage is that the player names need not be sorted.

```
=INDEX(Averages,MATCH(LookupValue,Players,0))
```

On the CD-ROM   You can access a workbook that demonstrates both of the formulas in this section on the companion CD-ROM.

Performing a case-sensitive lookup

The Excel lookup functions (LOOKUP, VLOOKUP, and HLOOKUP) are not case sensitive. For example, if you write a lookup formula to look up the text *budget*, the formula considers any of the following a match: *BUDGET*, *Budget*, or *BuDgEt*.

Figure 12-8 shows a simple example. Range D2:D7 is named *Range1*, and range E2:E7 is named *Range2*. The word to be looked up appears in cell B1 (named *Value*).

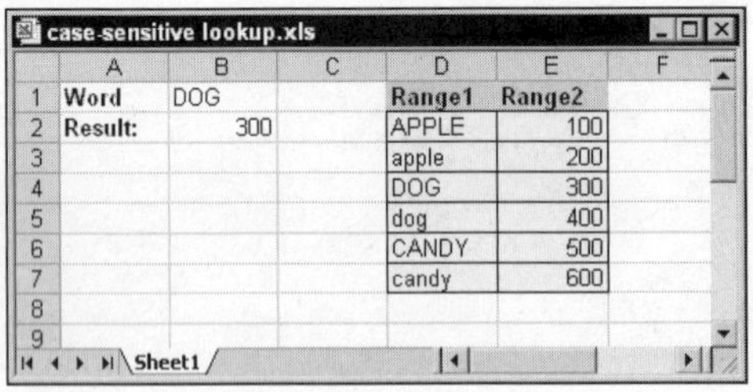

	A	B	C	D	E	F
1	Word	DOG		Range1	Range2	
2	Result:	300		APPLE	100	
3				apple	200	
4				DOG	300	
5				dog	400	
6				CANDY	500	
7				candy	600	
8						
9						

Figure 12-8: Using an array formula to perform a case-sensitive lookup.

On the CD-ROM   You can access the workbook shown in Figure 12-8 on the companion CD-ROM.

The array formula that follows is in cell B2. This formula does a case-sensitive lookup in *Range1* and returns the corresponding value in *Range2*.

```
{=INDEX(Range2,MATCH(TRUE,EXACT(Value,Range1),0))}
```

The formula looks up the word *DOG* (uppercase) and returns 300. The following standard LOOKUP formula (which is not case sensitive) returns 400:

```
=LOOKUP(Value,Range1,Range2)
```

Note   When entering an array formula, remember to use Ctrl+Shift+Enter.

Choosing among multiple lookup tables

You can, of course, have any number of lookup tables in a worksheet. In some cases, your formula may need to decide which lookup table to use. Figure 12-9 shows an example.

	A	B	C	D	E	F	G	H	I	J	K	
				Comm.			<3 Years Tenure			3+ Years Tenure		
1	Sales Rep	Years	Sales	Rate	Commission		Amt Sold	Rate		Amt Sold	Rate	
2	Benson	2	120,000	7.00%	8,400		0	1.50%		0	2.00%	
3	Davidson	1	210,921	7.00%	14,764							
4	Ellison	1	100,000	7.00%	7,000		5,000	3.25%		50,000	6.25%	
5	Gomez	2	87,401	6.00%	5,244		10,000	3.50%		100,000	7.25%	
6	Hernandez	6	310,983	9.25%	28,766		20,000	5.00%		200,000	8.25%	
7	Kelly	3	43,902	2.00%	878		50,000	6.00%		300,000	9.25%	
8	Martin	2	121,021	7.00%	8,471		100,000	7.00%		500,000	10.00%	
9	Oswald	3	908	2.00%	18		250,000	8.00%				
10	Reginald	1	0	1.50%	0							
11	Veras	4	359,832	9.25%	33,284							
12	Wilmington	4	502,983	10.00%	50,298							
13												

Figure 12-9: This worksheet demonstrates the use of multiple lookup tables.

This workbook calculates sales commission and contains two lookup tables: G3:H9 (named *Table1*) and J3:K8 (named *Table2*). The commission rate for a particular sales representative depends on two factors: the sales rep's years of service (column B) and the amount sold (column C). Column D contains formulas that look up the commission rate from the appropriate table. For example, the formula in cell D2 is

```
=VLOOKUP(C2,IF(B2<3,Table1,Table2),2)
```

The second argument for the VLOOKUP function consists of an IF formula that uses the value in column B to determine which lookup table to use.

The formula in column E simply multiplies the sales amount in column C by the commission rate in column D. The formula in cell E2, for example, is

```
=C2*D2
```

You can access the workbook shown in Figure 12-9 on the companion CD-ROM.

Determining letter grades for test scores

A common use of a lookup table is to assign letter grades for test scores. Figure 12-10 shows a worksheet with student test scores. The range E2:F6 (named *GradeList*) displays a lookup table used to assign a letter grade to a test score.

The companion CD-ROM contains a workbook that demonstrates both formulas in this section.

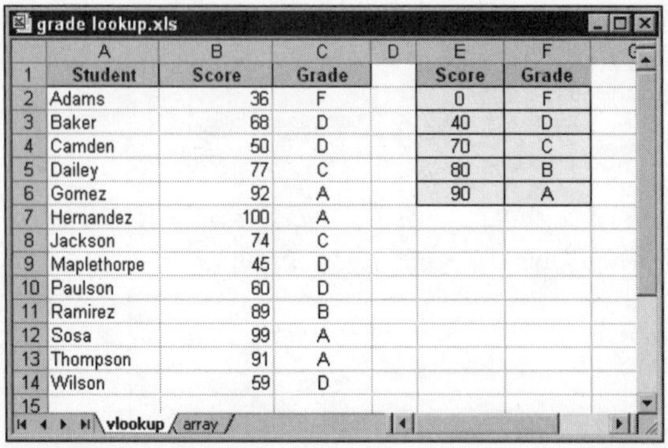

grade lookup.xls

	A	B	C	D	E	F
1	Student	Score	Grade		Score	Grade
2	Adams	36	F		0	F
3	Baker	68	D		40	D
4	Camden	50	D		70	C
5	Dailey	77	C		80	B
6	Gomez	92	A		90	A
7	Hernandez	100	A			
8	Jackson	74	C			
9	Maplethorpe	45	D			
10	Paulson	60	D			
11	Ramirez	89	B			
12	Sosa	99	A			
13	Thompson	91	A			
14	Wilson	59	D			
15						

vlookup / array

Figure 12-10: Looking up letter grades for test scores.

Column C contains formulas that use the VLOOKUP function and the lookup table to assign a grade based on the score in column B. The formula in cell C2, for example, is

```
=VLOOKUP(B2,GradeList,2)
```

When the lookup table is small (as in the example shown earlier in Figure 12-10), you can use a literal array in place of the lookup table. The formula that follows, for example, returns a letter grade without using a lookup table. Rather, the information in the lookup table is hard-coded into an array. See Chapter 14 for more information about arrays.

```
=VLOOKUP(B2,{0,"F";40,"D";70,"C";80,"B";90,"A"},2)
```

Another approach, which uses a more legible formula, is to use the LOOKUP function with two array arguments:

```
=LOOKUP(B2,{0,40,70,80,90},{"F","D","C","B","A"})
```

Calculating a grade-point average

A student's grade-point average (GPA) is a numerical measure of the average grade received for classes taken. This discussion assumes a letter grade system, in which each letter grade is assigned a numeric value (A=4, B=3, C=2, D=1, and F=0). The GPA comprises an average of the numeric grade values weighted by the credit hours of the course. A one-hour course, for example, receives less weight than a three-hour course. The GPA ranges from 0 (all Fs) to 4.00 (all As).

Figure 12-11 shows a worksheet with information for a student. This student took five courses, for a total of 13 credit hours. Range B2:B6 is named *CreditHours*. The grades for each course appear in column C. (Range C2:C6 is named *Grades*.) Column D uses a lookup formula to calculate the grade value for each course. The lookup formula in cell D2, for example, follows. This formula uses the lookup table in G2:H6 (named *GradeTable*).

```
=VLOOKUP(C2,GradeTable,2,FALSE)
```

	A	B	C	D	E	F	G	H
1	Course	Credit Hrs	Grade	Grade Val	Weighted Val		GradeTable	
2	Psych 101	3	A	4	12		A	4
3	PhysEd	2	C	2	4		B	3
4	PoliSci 101	4	B	3	12		C	2
5	IndepStudy	1	A	4	4		D	1
6	IntroMath	3	A	4	12		F	0
7								
8	GPA:	3.38	<-- Requires multiple formulas and lookup table					
9								
10								

Figure 12-11: Using multiple formulas to calculate a GPA.

Formulas in column E calculate the weighted values. The formula in cell E2 is

```
=D2*B2
```

Cell B8 computes the GPA by using the following formula:

```
=SUM(E2:E6)/SUM(B2:B6)
```

The preceding formulas work fine, but you can streamline the GPA calculation quite a bit. In fact, you can use a single array formula to make this calculation and avoid using the lookup table and the formulas in columns D and E. This array formula does the job:

```
{=SUM((MATCH(Grades,{"F","D","C","B","A"},0)-1)*CreditHours)
/SUM(CreditHours)}
```

You can access a workbook that demonstrates both the multiformula and the array formula techniques on the companion CD-ROM.

Performing a two-way lookup

Figure 12-12 shows a worksheet with a table that displays product sales by month. To retrieve sales for a particular month and product, the user enters a month in cell B1 and a product name in cell B2.

The companion CD-ROM contains the workbook shown in Figure 12-12.

	A	B	C	D	E	F	G	H
1	Month:	July			Widgets	Sprockets	Snapholytes	Combined
2	Product:	Sprockets		January	2,892	1,771	4,718	9,381
3				February	3,380	4,711	2,615	10,706
4	Month Offset:	8		March	3,744	3,223	5,312	12,279
5	Product Offset:	3		April	3,221	2,438	1,108	6,767
6	Sales:	3,337		May	4,839	1,999	1,994	8,832
7				June	3,767	5,140	3,830	12,737
8				July	5,467	3,337	3,232	12,036
9	Single-formula -->	3,337		August	3,154	4,895	1,607	9,656
10				September	1,718	2,040	1,563	5,321
11				October	1,548	1,061	2,590	5,199
12				November	5,083	3,558	3,960	12,601
13				December	5,753	2,839	3,013	11,605
14				Total	44,566	37,012	35,542	117,120
15								

Figure 12-12: This table demonstrates a two-way lookup.

To simplify things, the worksheet uses the following named ranges:

Name	Refers To
Month	B1
Product	B2
Table	D1:H14
MonthList	D1:D14
ProductList	D1:H1

The following formula (in cell B4) uses the MATCH function to return the position of the *Month* within the *MonthList* range. For example, if the month is January, the formula returns 2 because January is the second item in the *MonthList* range (the first item is a blank cell, D1).

```
=MATCH(Month,MonthList,0)
```

The formula in cell B5 works similarly but uses the *ProductList* range.

```
=MATCH(Product,ProductList,0)
```

The final formula, in cell B6, returns the corresponding sales amount. It uses the INDEX function with the results from cells B4 and B5.

```
=INDEX(Table,B4,B5)
```

You can, of course, combine these formulas into a single formula, as shown here:

```
=INDEX(Table,MATCH(Month,MonthList,0),MATCH(Product,
ProductList,0))
```

Tip   If you use Excel 97 or later, you can use the Lookup Wizard add-in to create this type of formula. The Lookup Wizard add-in is distributed with Excel.

Tip   Another way to accomplish a two-way lookup is to provide a name for each row and column of the table. A quick way to do this is to select the table and use Insert ⇨ Name ⇨ Create. After creating the names, you can use a simple formula, such as:

```
= Sprockets July
```

This formula, which uses the range intersection operator (a space), returns July sales for Sprockets. See Chapter 8 for details about the range intersection operator.

Performing a two-column lookup

Some situations may require a lookup based on the values in two columns. Figure 12-13 shows an example.

	A	B	C	D	E	F	G
1	Make:	Jeep		**Make**	**Model**	**Code**	
2	Model:	Grand Cherokee		Chevy	Blazer	C-094	
3	Code:	J-701		Chevy	Tahoe	C-823	
4				Ford	Explorer	F-772	
5				Ford	Expedition	F-229	
6				Isuzu	Rodeo	I-897	
7				Isuzu	Trooper	I-900	
8				Jeep	Cherokee	J-983	
9				Jeep	Grand Cherokee	J-701	
10				Nissan	Pathfinder	N-231	
11				Toyota	4Runner	T-871	
12				Toyota	Land Cruiser	T-981	
13							

Figure 12-13: This workbook performs a lookup by using information in two columns (D and E).

On the CD-ROM   The workbook shown in Figure 12-13 also appears on the companion CD-ROM.

The lookup table contains automobile makes and models and a corresponding code for each. The worksheet uses named ranges, as shown here:

F2:F12   *Code*

B1   *Make*

B2   *Model*

D2:D12   *Range1*

E2:E12   *Range2*

The following array formula displays the corresponding code for an automobile make and model:

```
{=INDEX(Code,MATCH(Make&Model,Range1&Range2,0))}
```

This formula works by concatenating the contents of *Make* and *Model* and then searching for this text in an array consisting of the concatenated corresponding text in *Range1* and *Range2*.

Determining the cell address of a value within a range

Most of the time, you want your lookup formula to return a value. You may, however, need to determine the cell address of a particular value within a range. For example, Figure 12-14 shows a worksheet with a range of numbers that occupies a single column (named *Data*). Cell B1, which contains the value to look up, is named *Target*.

The formula in cell B2, which follows, returns the address of the cell in the *Data* range that contains the *Target* value:

```
=ADDRESS(ROW(Data)+MATCH(Target,Data,0)-1,COLUMN(Data))
```

If the *Data* range occupies a single row, use this formula to return the address of the *Target* value:

```
=ADDRESS(ROW(Data),COLUMN(Data)+MATCH(Target,Data,0)-1)
```

 On the CD-ROM   The companion CD-ROM contains the workbook shown in Figure 12-14.

If the *Data* range contains more than one instance of the *Target* value, the address of the first occurrence is returned. If the *Target* value is not found in the *Data* range, the formula returns #N/A.

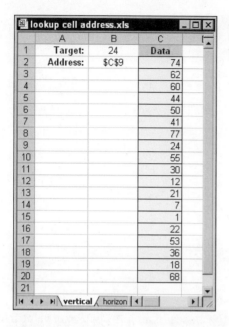

Figure 12-14: The formula in cell B2 returns the address in the *Data* range for the value in cell B1.

Looking up a value by using the closest match

The VLOOKUP and HLOOKUP functions are useful in the following situations:

✦ You need to identify an exact match for a target value. Use FALSE as the function's fourth argument.

✦ You need to locate an approximate match. If the function's fourth argument is TRUE or omitted and an exact match is not found, the next largest value less than the lookup value is returned.

But what if you need to look up a value based on the *closest* match? Neither VLOOKUP nor HLOOKUP can do the job.

Figure 12-15 shows a worksheet with student names in column A and values in column B. Range B2:B20 is named *Data*. Cell E2, named *Target*, contains a value to search for in the *Data* range. Cell E3, named *ColOffset*, contains a value that represents the column offset from the *Data* range.

On the CD-ROM You can access the workbook shown in Figure 12-15 on the companion CD-ROM.

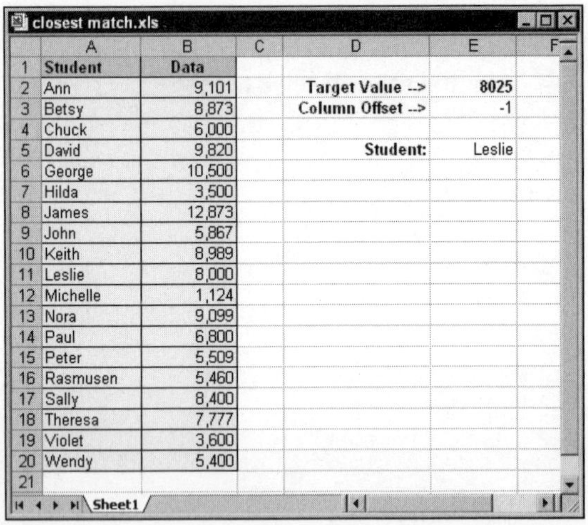
closest match.xls

	A	B	C	D	E
1	Student	Data			
2	Ann	9,101		Target Value -->	8025
3	Betsy	8,873		Column Offset -->	-1
4	Chuck	6,000			
5	David	9,820		Student:	Leslie
6	George	10,500			
7	Hilda	3,500			
8	James	12,873			
9	John	5,867			
10	Keith	8,989			
11	Leslie	8,000			
12	Michelle	1,124			
13	Nora	9,099			
14	Paul	6,800			
15	Peter	5,509			
16	Rasmusen	5,460			
17	Sally	8,400			
18	Theresa	7,777			
19	Violet	3,600			
20	Wendy	5,400			
21					

Sheet1

Figure 12-15: This workbook demonstrates how to perform a lookup by using the closest match.

The array formula that follows identifies the closest match to the *Target* value in the *Data* range and returns the names of the corresponding student in column A (that is, the column with an offset of –1). The formula returns Leslie (with a matching value of 8,000, which is the one closest to the *Target* value of 8,025).

```
{=INDIRECT(ADDRESS(ROW(Data)+MATCH(MIN(ABS(Target-Data)),
ABS(Target-Data),0)-1,COLUMN(Data)+ColOffset))}
```

If two values in the *Data* range are equidistant from the *Target* value, the formula uses the first one in the list.

The value in *ColOffset* can be negative (for a column to the left of *Data*), positive (for a column to the right of *Data*), or 0 (for the actual closest match value in the *Data* range).

To understand how this formula works, you need to understand the INDIRECT function. This function's first argument is a text string in the form of a cell reference (or a reference to a cell that contains a text string). In this example, the text string is created by the ADDRESS function, which accepts a row and column reference and returns a cell address.

✦ ✦ ✦

CHAPTER 13

Creating Formulas for Financial Applications

✦ ✦ ✦ ✦

In This Chapter

A brief overview of the Excel functions that deal with the time value of money

Formulas that perform various types of loan calculations

Formulas that perform various types of investment calculations

An overview of Excel's depreciation functions

✦ ✦ ✦ ✦

It's a safe bet that the most common use of Excel is to perform calculations involving money. Every day, people make hundreds of thousands of financial decisions based on the numbers that are calculated in a spreadsheet. These decisions range from simple (*Can I afford to buy a new car?*) to complex (*Will purchasing XYZ Corporation result in a positive cash flow in the next 18 months?*). This chapter discusses basic financial calculations that you can perform with the assistance of Excel.

The Time Value of Money

Depending on how you look at it, the face value of money may not be what it seems. A key consideration is the time value of money. This concept involves calculating the value of money in the past, present, or future. It is based on the premise that money increases in value over time because of interest earned by the money. In other words, a dollar invested today will be worth more tomorrow.

For example, imagine that your rich uncle decided to give away some money and asked you to choose one of the following options:

- Receive $8,000 today
- Receive $9,500 in one year
- Receive $12,000 in five years
- Receive $150 per month for five years

If your goal is to maximize the amount received, you need to take into account not only the face value of the money but also the *time value* of the money when it arrives in your hands.

The time value of money depends on your perspective. In other words, you're either a lender or a borrower. When you take out a loan to purchase an automobile, you're a borrower, and the institution that provides the funds to you is the lender. When you invest money in a bank savings account, you're a lender; you're lending your money to the bank, and the bank is borrowing it from you.

Several concepts contribute to the time value of money:

✦ **Present Value (PV):** This is the *principal* amount. If you deposit $5,000 in a bank CD (Certificate of Deposit), this amount represents the principal, or present value, of the money you invested. If you borrow $15,000 to purchase a car, this amount represents the principal or present value of the loan. Present Value may be positive or negative.

✦ **Future Value (FV):** This is the principal plus interest. If you invest $5,000 for five years and earn 6 percent annual interest, you receive $6,312.38 at the end of the five-year term. This amount is the future value of your $5,000 investment. If you take out a three-year auto loan for $15,000 and pay 7 percent annual interest, you pay a total of $16,673.16. This amount represents the principal plus the interest you paid. Future Value may be positive or negative, depending on the perspective (lender or borrower).

✦ **Payment (PMT):** This is either principal or principal plus interest. If you deposit $100 per month into a savings account, $100 is the payment. If you have a monthly mortgage payment of $825, the $825 is made up of principal and interest.

✦ **Interest Rate:** Interest is a percentage of the principal, usually expressed on an annual basis. For example, you may earn 5.5 percent annual interest on a bank CD. Or your mortgage loan may have a 7.75 percent interest rate.

✦ **Period:** This represents the point in time when interest is paid or earned (for example, a bank CD that pays interest quarterly or an auto loan that requires monthly payments).

✦ **Term:** This is the amount of time of interest. A 12-month bank CD has a term of one year. A 30-year mortgage loan has a term of 30 years.

Loan Calculations

Now, look at how to calculate various components of a loan. Think of a loan as consisting of the following components:

✦ The loan amount

✦ The interest rate

✦ The number of payment periods

✦ The periodic payment amount

If you know any three of these components, you can create a formula to calculate the unknown component.

Note   The loan calculations in this section all assume a fixed-rate loan with a fixed term.

Worksheet functions for calculating loan information

This section describes five functions: PMT, PPMT, IPMT, RATE, and PV. For information about the arguments used in these functions, see Table 13-1.

Table 13-1
Financial Function Arguments

Argument	Description
rate	The interest rate per period. If the rate is expressed as an annual interest rate, you must divide it by the number of periods.
nper	The total number of payment periods.
per	A particular period. The period must be less than or equal to nper.
pmt	The payment made each period (a constant value that does not change).
fv	The future value after the last payment is made. If you omit fv, it is assumed to be 0. (The future value of a loan, for example, is 0.)
type	Indicates when payments are due — either 0 (due at the end of the period) or 1 (due at the beginning of the period). If you omit type, it is assumed to be 0.

The PMT function

The PMT function returns the loan payment (principal plus interest) per period, assuming constant payment amounts and a fixed interest rate. The syntax for the PMT function is

```
PMT(rate,nper,pv,fv,type)
```

The following formula returns the monthly payment amount for a $5,000 loan with a 6 percent annual percentage rate. The loan has a term of four years (48 months).

```
=PMT(.06/12,48,-5000)
```

This formula returns $117.43, the monthly payment for the loan. Notice that the third argument (*pv*, for present value) is negative, and represents money owed.

The PPMT function

The PPMT function returns the *principal* part of a loan payment for a given period, assuming constant payment amounts and a fixed interest rate. The syntax for the PPMT function is

```
PPMT(rate,per,nper,pv,fv,type)
```

The following formula returns the amount paid to principal for the first month of a $5,000 loan with a 6 percent annual percentage rate. The loan has a term of four years (48 months).

```
=PPMT(.06/12,1,48,-5000)
```

The formula returns $92.43 for the principal, which is about 78.7 percent of the total loan payment. If I change the second argument to 48 (to calculate the principal amount for the last payment), the formula returns $116.84, or about 99.5 percent of the total loan payment.

Note To calculate the cumulative principal paid between any two payment periods, use the CUMPRINC function, which is available only when you install the Analysis ToolPak add-in. This function uses two additional arguments: *start_period* and *end_period*.

The IPMT Function

The IPMT function returns the *interest* part of a loan payment for a given period, assuming constant payment amounts and a fixed interest rate. The syntax for the IPMT function is

```
IPMT(rate,per,nper,pv,fv,type)
```

The following formula returns the amount paid to interest for the first month of a $5,000 loan with a 6 percent annual percentage rate. The loan has a term of four years (48 months).

```
=IPMT(.06/12,1,48,-5000)
```

This formula returns an interest amount of $25.00. By the last payment period for the loan, the interest payment is only $0.58.

Note To calculate the cumulative interest paid between any two payment periods, use the CUMIPMT function, which is available only when you install the Analysis ToolPak add-in. This function uses two additional arguments: *start_period* and *end_period*.

The RATE function

The RATE function returns the periodic interest rate of a loan, given the number of payment periods, the periodic payment amount, and the loan amount. The syntax for the RATE function is

```
RATE(nper,pmt,pv,fv,type,guess)
```

The following formula calculates the annual interest rate for a 48-month loan for $5,000 that has a monthly payment amount of $117.43.

```
=RATE(48,117.43,-5000)*12
```

This formula returns 6.00 percent. Notice that the result of the function multiplies by 12 to get the annual percentage rate.

The NPER function

The NPER function returns the number of payment periods for a loan, given the loan's amount, interest rate, and periodic payment amount. The syntax for the NPER function is

```
NPER(rate, pmt, pv, fv, type)
```

The following formula calculates the number of payment periods for a $5,000 loan that has a monthly payment amount of $117.43. The loan has a 6 percent annual interest rate.

```
=NPER(0.06/12,117.43,-5000)
```

This formula returns 47.997 (that is, 48 months). The monthly payment was rounded to the nearest penny, causing the minor discrepancy.

The PV Function

The PV function returns the present value (that is, the original loan amount) for a loan, given the interest rate, the number of periods, and the periodic payment amount. The syntax for the PV function is

```
PV(rate,nper,pmt,fv,type)
```

The following formula calculates the original loan amount for a 48-month loan that has a monthly payment amount of $117.43. The annual interest rate is 6 percent.

```
=PV(0.06/12,48,-117.43)
```

This formula returns $5,000.21. The monthly payment was rounded to the nearest penny, causing the $0.21 discrepancy.

A loan calculation example

Figure 13-1 shows a worksheet set up to calculate the periodic payment amount for a loan. The loan amount is in cell B1, and the annual interest rate is in cell B2. Cell B3 contains the payment period expressed in months. For example, if cell B3 is 1, the payment is due monthly. If cell B3 is 3, the payment is due every three months, or quarterly. Cell B4 contains the number of periods of the loan. The example shown in this figure calculates the payment for a $10,000 loan at 9.5 percent annual interest with monthly payments for 36 months. The formula in cell B6 is

```
=PMT(B2*(B3/12),B4,-B1)
```

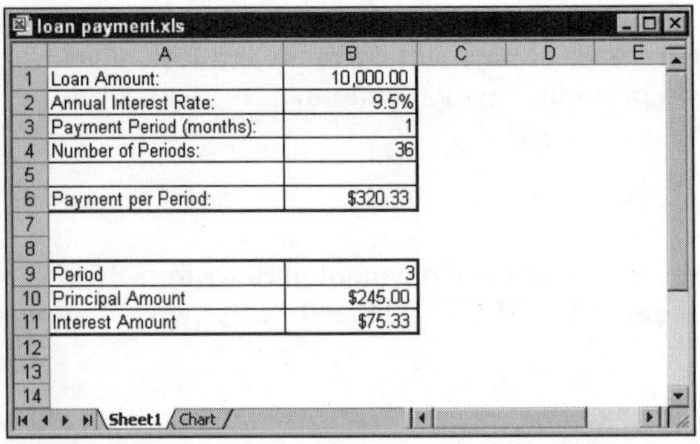
loan payment.xls

	A	B	C	D	E
1	Loan Amount:	10,000.00			
2	Annual Interest Rate:	9.5%			
3	Payment Period (months):	1			
4	Number of Periods:	36			
5					
6	Payment per Period:	$320.33			
7					
8					
9	Period	3			
10	Principal Amount	$245.00			
11	Interest Amount	$75.33			
12					
13					
14					

Sheet1 / Chart

Figure 13-1: Using the PMT function to calculate a periodic loan payment amount.

Notice that the first argument is an expression that calculates the *periodic interest rate* by using the annual interest rate and the payment period. Therefore, if payments are made quarterly on a three-year loan, the payment period is 3, the number of periods is 12, and the periodic interest rate would be calculated as the annual interest rate multiplied by 3/12.

In the worksheet in Figure 13-1, range A9:B11 is set up to calculate the principal and interest amount for a particular payment period. Cell B9 contains the payment period used by the formulas in B10:B11. (The payment period must be less than or equal to the value in cell B4.)

The formula in cell B10, shown here, calculates the amount of the payment that goes toward principal for the payment period in cell B9:

```
=PPMT(B2*(B3/12),B9,B4,-B1)
```

The following formula, in cell B11, calculates the amount of the payment that goes toward interest for the payment period in cell B9:

```
=IPMT(B2*(B3/12),B9,B4,-B1)
```

You should note that the sum of B10 and B11 always remains equal to the total loan payment calculated in cell B6. However, the relative proportion of principal and interest amounts varies with the payment period. (An increasingly larger proportion of the payment is applied toward principal as the loan progresses.) Figure 13-2 shows this graphically.

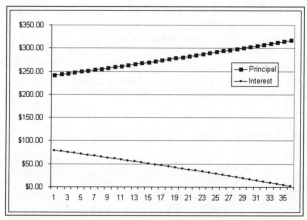

Figure 13-2: This chart shows the relative interest and principal amounts for the payment periods of a loan.

On the CD-ROM The workbook shown in Figure 13-1 and Figure 13-2 is available on the companion CD-ROM.

Credit card payments

Did you ever wonder how long it would take to pay off a credit card balance if you make the minimum payment amount each month? Figure 13-3 shows a worksheet set up to make this type of calculation.

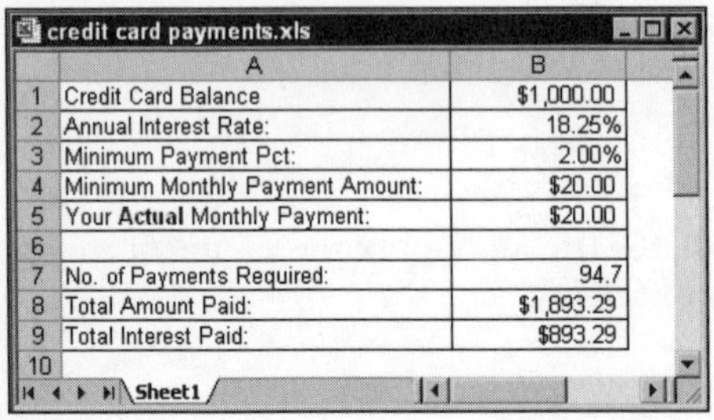

credit card payments.xls		
	A	B
1	Credit Card Balance	$1,000.00
2	Annual Interest Rate:	18.25%
3	Minimum Payment Pct:	2.00%
4	Minimum Monthly Payment Amount:	$20.00
5	Your **Actual** Monthly Payment:	$20.00
6		
7	No. of Payments Required:	94.7
8	Total Amount Paid:	$1,893.29
9	Total Interest Paid:	$893.29
10		

Figure 13-3: This worksheet calculates the number of payments required to pay off a credit card balance by paying the minimum payment amount each month.

On the CD-ROM   The workbook shown in Figure 13-3 is available on the companion CD-ROM.

Range B1:B5 stores input values. In this example, the credit card has a balance of $1,000, and the lender charges 18.25 percent annual percentage rate (APR). The minimum payment is 2.00 percent (typical of many credit card lenders). Therefore, the minimum payment amount for this example is $20. You can enter another value in cell B5. For example, you may choose to pay $50 per month.

Range B7:B9 holds formulas that perform various calculations. The formula in cell B7, which follows, calculates the number of months required to pay off the balance:

```
=NPER(B2/12,B5,-B1,0)
```

The formula in B8 calculates the total amount you will pay. This formula is

```
=B7*B5
```

The formula in cell B9 calculates the total interest paid:

```
=B8-B1
```

In this example, it would take about 95 months (more than seven years) to pay off the credit card balance if you only make the minimum payment amount. This assumes, of course, that you make no additional charges on the account. This example may help explain why you receive so many credit card solicitations in the mail.

Figure 13-4 shows some additional calculations for the credit card example. For example, if you want to pay off the credit card in 12 months, you need to make monthly payments of $91.80. (This results in total payments of $1,101.59 and total interest of $101.59.) The formula in B13 is

```
=PMT($B$2/12,A13,-$B$1)
```

	A	B	C	D
	credit card payments.xls			
1	Credit Card Balance:	$1,000.00		
2	Annual Interest Rate:	18.25%		
3	Minimum Payment Pct:	2.00%		
4	Minimum Monthly Payment Amount:	$20.00		
5	Your **Actual** Monthly Payment:	$20.00		
6				
7	No. of Payments Required:	94.7		
8	Total Amount Paid:	$1,893.29		
9	Total Interest Paid:	$893.29		
10				
11				
12	Other Payoff Periods (months)	Pmt Required	Total Pmts	Total Interest
13	12	$91.80	$1,101.59	$101.59
14	24	$50.04	$1,201.08	$201.08
15	36	$36.28	$1,306.01	$306.01
16	48	$29.51	$1,416.28	$416.28
17	60	$25.53	$1,531.78	$531.78
18	72	$22.95	$1,652.35	$652.35
19	84	$21.16	$1,777.83	$777.83
20	96	$19.88	$1,908.00	$908.00
21	108	$18.91	$2,042.66	$1,042.66
22	120	$18.18	$2,181.57	$1,181.57
23				

Figure 13-4: Column B shows the payment required to pay off the credit card balance for various payoff periods.

Creating a loan amortization schedule

A *loan amortization schedule* is a table of values that depicts various information for each payment period of a loan. Figure 13-5 shows a worksheet that uses formulas to calculate an amortization schedule.

The workbook shown in Figure 13-5 is available on the companion CD-ROM.

The loan parameters are entered into B1:B4, and the formulas beginning in row 9 use these values for the calculations. Table 13-2 shows the formulas in row 9 of the schedule. These formulas were copied down to row 488. Therefore, the worksheet can calculate amortization schedules for a loan with as many as 480 payment periods. The worksheet uses conditional formatting to hide the data in rows that extend beyond the loan term.

See Chapter 27 for more information about conditional formatting.

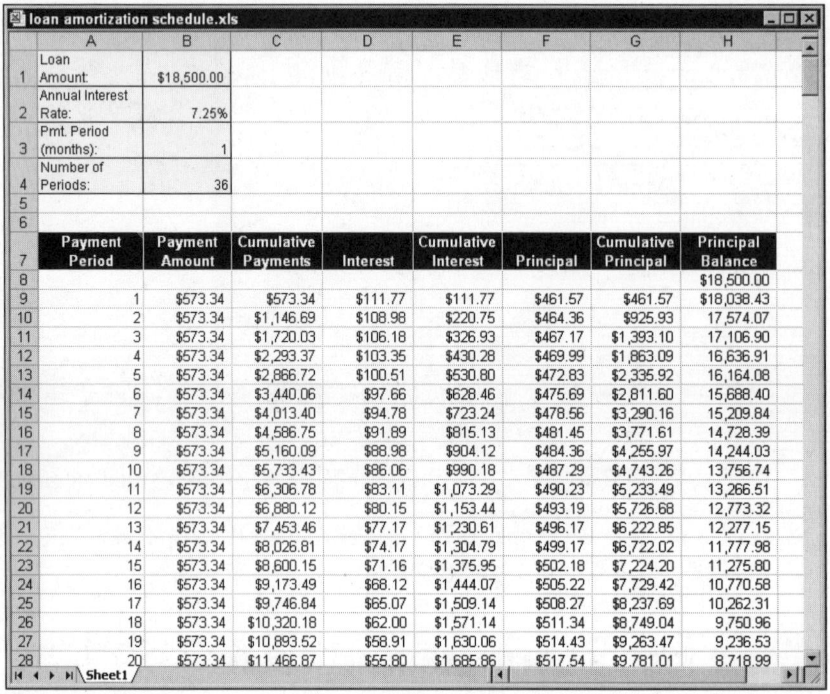

loan amortization schedule.xls

	A	B	C	D	E	F	G	H
1	Loan Amount:	$18,500.00						
2	Annual Interest Rate:	7.25%						
3	Pmt. Period (months):	1						
4	Number of Periods:	36						
5								
6								
7	Payment Period	Payment Amount	Cumulative Payments	Interest	Cumulative Interest	Principal	Cumulative Principal	Principal Balance
8								$18,500.00
9	1	$573.34	$573.34	$111.77	$111.77	$461.57	$461.57	$18,038.43
10	2	$573.34	$1,146.69	$108.98	$220.75	$464.36	$925.93	17,574.07
11	3	$573.34	$1,720.03	$106.18	$326.93	$467.17	$1,393.10	17,106.90
12	4	$573.34	$2,293.37	$103.35	$430.28	$469.99	$1,863.09	16,636.91
13	5	$573.34	$2,866.72	$100.51	$530.80	$472.83	$2,335.92	16,164.08
14	6	$573.34	$3,440.06	$97.66	$628.46	$475.69	$2,811.60	15,688.40
15	7	$573.34	$4,013.40	$94.78	$723.24	$478.56	$3,290.16	15,209.84
16	8	$573.34	$4,586.75	$91.89	$815.13	$481.45	$3,771.61	14,728.39
17	9	$573.34	$5,160.09	$88.98	$904.12	$484.36	$4,255.97	14,244.03
18	10	$573.34	$5,733.43	$86.06	$990.18	$487.29	$4,743.26	13,756.74
19	11	$573.34	$6,306.78	$83.11	$1,073.29	$490.23	$5,233.49	13,266.51
20	12	$573.34	$6,880.12	$80.15	$1,153.44	$493.19	$5,726.68	12,773.32
21	13	$573.34	$7,453.46	$77.17	$1,230.61	$496.17	$6,222.85	12,277.15
22	14	$573.34	$8,026.81	$74.17	$1,304.79	$499.17	$6,722.02	11,777.98
23	15	$573.34	$8,600.15	$71.16	$1,375.95	$502.18	$7,224.20	11,275.80
24	16	$573.34	$9,173.49	$68.12	$1,444.07	$505.22	$7,729.42	10,770.58
25	17	$573.34	$9,746.84	$65.07	$1,509.14	$508.27	$8,237.69	10,262.31
26	18	$573.34	$10,320.18	$62.00	$1,571.14	$511.34	$8,749.04	9,750.96
27	19	$573.34	$10,893.52	$58.91	$1,630.06	$514.43	$9,263.47	9,236.53
28	20	$573.34	$11,466.87	$55.80	$1,685.86	$517.54	$9,781.01	8,718.99

Sheet1

Figure 13-5: A loan amortization schedule.

Table 13-2
Formulas Used to Calculate an Amortization Schedule

Cell	*Formula*	*Description*
A9	=A8+1	Returns the payment number
B9	=PMT($B$2*($B$3/12),$B$4,-$B$1)	Calculates the periodic payment amount
C9	=C8+B9	Calculates the cumulative payment amounts
D9	=IPMT($B$2*($B$3/12),A9,$B$4,-$B$1)	Calculates the interest portion of the periodic payment
E9	=E8+D9	Calculates the cumulative interest paid
F9	=PPMT($B$2*($B$3/12),A9,$B$4,-$B$1)	Calculates the principal portion of the periodic payment
G9	=G8+F9	Calculates the cumulative amount applied toward principal
H9	=H8-F9	Returns the principal balance at the end of the period

Summarizing loan options by using a data table

Excel's Data ⇨ Table command is probably one of the most underutilized tools in Excel. It's a handy way to summarize calculations that depend on one or two "changing" cells. In this case, I use a data table to summarize various loan options. This section describes how to create one-way and two-way data tables.

On the
CD-ROM

A workbook that demonstrates one- and two-way data tables is available on the companion CD-ROM.

Creating a one-way data table

A *one-way data table* shows the results of any number of calculations for different values of a single input cell.

Figure 13-6 shows a one-way data table (in B10:I13) that displays three calculations (payment amount, total payments, and total interest) for a loan, using seven interest rates ranging from 7.00 percent to 8.50 percent. In this example, the input cell is cell B2.

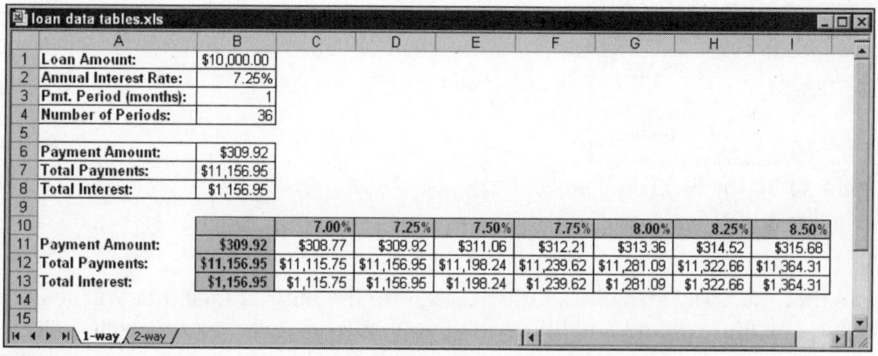

loan data tables.xls	A	B	C	D	E	F	G	H	I
1	Loan Amount:	$10,000.00							
2	Annual Interest Rate:	7.25%							
3	Pmt. Period (months):	1							
4	Number of Periods:	36							
5									
6	Payment Amount:	$309.92							
7	Total Payments:	$11,156.95							
8	Total Interest:	$1,156.95							
9									
10			7.00%	7.25%	7.50%	7.75%	8.00%	8.25%	8.50%
11	Payment Amount:	$309.92	$308.77	$309.92	$311.06	$312.21	$313.36	$314.52	$315.68
12	Total Payments:	$11,156.95	$11,115.75	$11,156.95	$11,198.24	$11,239.62	$11,281.09	$11,322.66	$11,364.31
13	Total Interest:	$1,156.95	$1,115.75	$1,156.95	$1,198.24	$1,239.62	$1,281.09	$1,322.66	$1,364.31
14									
15									

1-way / 2-way

Figure 13-6: Using a one-way data table to display three loan calculations for various interest rates.

To create this one-way data table, follow these steps:

1. Enter the formulas that return the results for use in the data table. In this example, the formulas are in B6:B8.

2. Enter various values for a single input cell in successive columns. In this example, the input value is interest rate, and the values for various interest rates appear in C10:I10.

3. Create a reference to the formula cells in the column to the left of the input values. In this example, the range B11:B13 contains simple formulas that reference other cells. For example, cell B11 contains the following formula:

```
=B6
```

4. Select the rectangular range that contains the entries from the previous steps. In this example, select B10:I13.

5. Select the Data ⇨ Table command. Excel displays the Table dialog box shown in Figure 13-7.

6. For the Row input cell field, specify the cell reference that corresponds to the variable in your Data Table column header row. In this example, the Row input cell is B2.

7. Leave the Column input cell field empty.

8. Click OK. Excel inserts an array formula that uses the TABLE function with a single argument.

9. If you like, you can format the data table. For example, you may want to apply shading to the row and column headers.

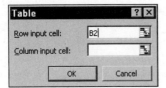

Figure 13-7: The Excel program's Table dialog box.

Note that the array formula is not entered into the entire range that you selected in Step 4. The first column and first row of your selection are not changed.

Tip   When you create a data table, the leftmost column of the data table (the column that contains the references entered in Step 3) contains the calculated values for the input cell. In this example, those values are repeated in column D. You may want to hide the values in column B by making the font color the same color as the background.

Creating a two-way data table

A *two-way data table* shows the results of a single calculation for different values of two input cells. Figure 13-8 shows a two-way data table (in B10:I16) that displays a calculation (payment amount) for a loan, using seven interest rates and six loan amounts.

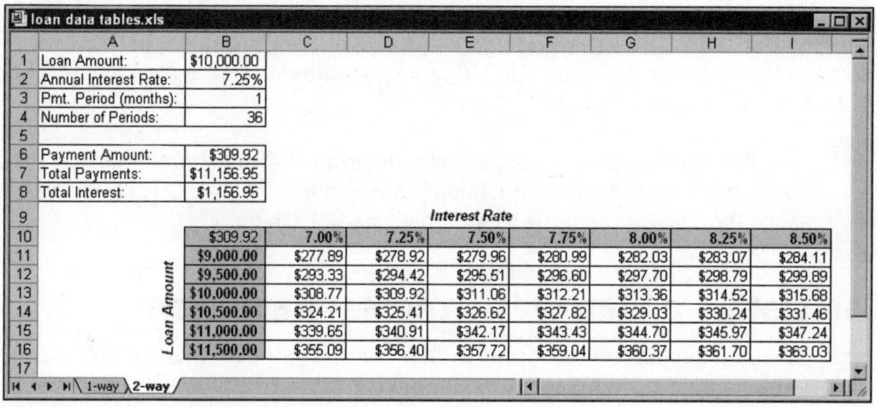

	A	B
1	Loan Amount:	$10,000.00
2	Annual Interest Rate:	7.25%
3	Pmt. Period (months):	1
4	Number of Periods:	36
5		
6	Payment Amount:	$309.92
7	Total Payments:	$11,156.95
8	Total Interest:	$1,156.95

		Interest Rate						
	$309.92	7.00%	7.25%	7.50%	7.75%	8.00%	8.25%	8.50%
Loan Amount	$9,000.00	$277.89	$278.92	$279.96	$280.99	$282.03	$283.07	$284.11
	$9,500.00	$293.33	$294.42	$295.51	$296.60	$297.70	$298.79	$299.89
	$10,000.00	$308.77	$309.92	$311.06	$312.21	$313.36	$314.52	$315.68
	$10,500.00	$324.21	$325.41	$326.62	$327.82	$329.03	$330.24	$331.46
	$11,000.00	$339.65	$340.91	$342.17	$343.43	$344.70	$345.97	$347.24
	$11,500.00	$355.09	$356.40	$357.72	$359.04	$360.37	$361.70	$363.03

Figure 13-8: Using a two-way data table to display payment amounts for various loan amounts and interest rates.

To create this two-way data table, follow these steps:

1. Enter a formula that returns the results that will be used in the data table. In this example, the formula is in cell B6. The formulas in B7:B8 are not used.
2. Enter various values for the first input in successive columns. In this example, the first input value is interest rate, and the values for various interest rates appear in C10:I10.
3. Enter various values for the second input cell in successive rows, to the left and below the input values for the first input. In this example, the second input value is loan amount, and the values for various loan amounts are in B11:B16.
4. Create a reference to the formula that will be calculated in the table. This reference goes in the upper-left corner of the data table range. In this example, cell B10 contains the following formula:

   ```
   =B6
   ```

5. Select the rectangular range that contains the entries from the previous steps. In this example, select B10:I16.
6. Select the Data ⇨ Table command. Excel displays the Table dialog box.
7. For the Row input cell field, specify the cell reference that corresponds to the first input cell. In this example, the Row input cell is B2.
8. For the Column input cell field, specify the cell reference that corresponds to the second input cell. In this example, the Row input cell is B1.
9. Click OK. Excel inserts an array formula that uses the TABLE function with two arguments.

After you create the two-way data table, you can change the calculated cell by changing the cell reference in the upper-left cell of the data table. In this example, you can change the formula in cell B10 to =B8 so the data table displays total interest rather than payment amounts.

Tip   If you find that using data tables slows down the calculation of your workbook, select Tools ➪ Options. In the Options dialog box, click the Calculation tab and change the calculation mode to Automatic Except Tables.

Calculating a loan with irregular payments

So far, the loan calculation examples in this chapter have involved loans with regular periodic payments. In some cases, loan payback is irregular. For example, you may loan some money to friends or family members without formal agreements as to how they will pay the money back.

Figure 13-9 shows a worksheet set up to keep track of such a loan. The annual interest rate for the loan is stored in cell B1 (named *APR*). The original loan amount and loan date are stored in row 5. Formulas, beginning in row 6, track the loan payments and perform calculations.

	Payment Number	Payment Amount	Payment Date	Amount to Interest	Amount to Principal	Cumulative Payments	Cumulative Interest	Loan Balance
1	Interest Rate (APR):	5.50%						
2								
3								
5	Original Loan	($10,000.00)	06/01/98					$10,000.00
6	1	$200.00	07/18/98	$70.82	$129.18	$200.00	$70.82	$9,870.82
7	2	$200.00	08/02/98	$22.31	$177.69	$400.00	$93.13	$9,693.13
8	3	$200.00	09/17/98	$67.19	$132.81	$600.00	$160.32	$9,560.32
9	4	$100.00	12/02/98	$109.49	($9.49)	$700.00	$269.81	$9,569.81
10	5	$250.00	01/12/99	$59.12	$190.88	$950.00	$328.93	$9,378.93
11	Addition to Principal	($500.00)	01/25/99	$0.00	($500.00)	$950.00	$328.93	$9,878.93
12	6	$200.00	02/04/99	$32.51	$167.49	$1,150.00	$361.43	$9,711.43
13	7	$100.00	02/20/99	$23.41	$76.59	$1,250.00	$384.85	$9,634.85
14	8	$200.00	03/01/99	$13.07	$186.93	$1,450.00	$397.91	$9,447.91
15	9	$250.00	03/16/99	$21.35	$228.65	$1,700.00	$419.27	$9,219.27
16	10	$200.00	04/02/99	$23.62	$176.38	$1,900.00	$442.89	$9,042.89
17	11	$200.00	04/19/99	$23.16	$176.84	$2,100.00	$466.05	$8,866.05
18	12	$300.00	05/04/99	$20.04	$279.96	$2,400.00	$486.09	$8,586.09
19	13	$100.00	05/16/99	$15.53	$84.47	$2,500.00	$501.62	$8,501.62
20	14	$200.00	06/02/99	$21.78	$178.22	$2,700.00	$523.39	$8,323.39
21	15	$200.00	06/19/99	$21.32	$178.68	$2,900.00	$544.72	$8,144.72
22	16	$100.00	07/05/99	$19.64	$80.36	$3,000.00	$564.35	$8,064.35
23	17	$100.00	07/15/99	$12.15	$87.85	$3,100.00	$576.50	$7,976.50
24	Addition to Principal	($500.00)	09/01/99	$0.00	($500.00)	$3,100.00	$576.50	$8,476.50
25	18	$100.00	11/02/99	$79.19	$20.81	$3,200.00	$655.70	$8,455.70
26	19	$100.00	11/15/99	$16.56	$83.44	$3,300.00	$672.26	$8,372.26
27	20	$200.00	12/15/99	$37.85	$162.15	$3,500.00	$710.11	$8,210.11

Figure 13-9: This worksheet tracks loan payments that are made on an irregular basis.

Column B stores the payment amount made on the date in column C. Notice that the payments are not made on a regular basis. Also, notice that in two cases (row 11 and row 24) the payment amount is negative. These entries represent additional borrowed money added to the loan balance. Formulas in columns D and E calculate the amount of the payment credited toward interest and principal. Columns F and G keep a running tally of the cumulative payments and interest amounts. Formulas in column H compute the new loan balance after each payment. Table 13-3 lists and describes the formulas in row 6.

Table 13-3
Formulas to Calculate a Loan with Irregular Payments

Cell	Formula	Description
D6	`=IF(B6>0,((((C6-C5)/ 365)*H5)*APR,0)`	If the payment is positive, the formula calculates the interest. If the payment is negative (an addition to the loan), the formula displays 0.
E6	`=B6-D6`	The formula subtracts the interest amount from the payment to calculate the amount credited to principal.
F6	`=IF(B6>0,F5+B6,F5)`	If the payment is positive, the formula adds the payment to the running total. If the payment is negative, the formula displays the running total following the previous payment.
G6	`=IF(B6>0,G5+D6,G5)`	If the payment is positive, the formula adds the interest to the running total. If the payment is negative, the formula displays the running total following the previous payment.
H6	`=H5-E6`	The formula calculates the new loan balance.

The workbook shown in Figure 13-9 is available on the companion CD-ROM.

Investment Calculations

Investment calculations involve calculating interest on fixed-rate investments, such as bank savings accounts, CDs, and annuities. You can make these interest calculations for investments that consist of a single deposit or multiple deposits.

The companion CD-ROM contains a workbook with all of the interest calculation examples in this section.

Future value of a single deposit

Many investments consist of a single deposit that earns interest over the term of the investment. This section describes calculations for simple interest and compound interest.

Calculating simple interest

Simple interest refers to the fact that interest payments are not compounded. The basic formula for computing interest is

```
Interest = Principal * Rate * Term
```

For example, suppose you deposit $1,000 into a bank CD that pays a 5 percent simple annual interest rate. After one year, the CD matures, and you withdraw your money. The bank adds $50, and you walk away with $1,050. In this case, the interest earned is calculated by multiplying the principal ($1,000) by the interest rate (.05) by the term (one year).

If the investment term is less than one year, the simple interest rate is adjusted accordingly, based on the term. For example, $1,000 invested in a six-month CD that pays 5 percent simple annual interest earns $25 when the CD matures. In this case, the annual interest rate multiplies by 6/12.

Figure 13-10 shows a worksheet set up to make simple interest calculations. The formula in cell B7, shown here, calculates the interest due at the end of the term:

```
=B3*B4*B5
```

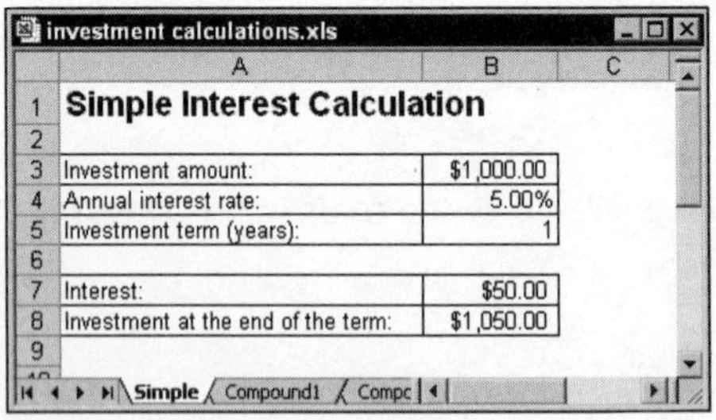

Figure 13-10: This worksheet calculates simple interest payments.

The formula in B8 simply adds the interest to the original investment amount.

Calculating compound interest

Most fixed-term investments pay interest by using some type of compound interest calculation. *Compound interest* refers to the fact that interest is credited to the investment balance, and the investment then earns interest on the interest.

For example, suppose you deposit $1,000 into a bank CD that pays 5 percent annual interest rate, compounded monthly. Each month, the interest is calculated on the balance, and that amount is credited to your account. The next month's interest calculation will be based on a higher amount because it also includes the previous month's interest payment. One way to calculate the final investment amount involves a series of formulas (see Figure 13-11).

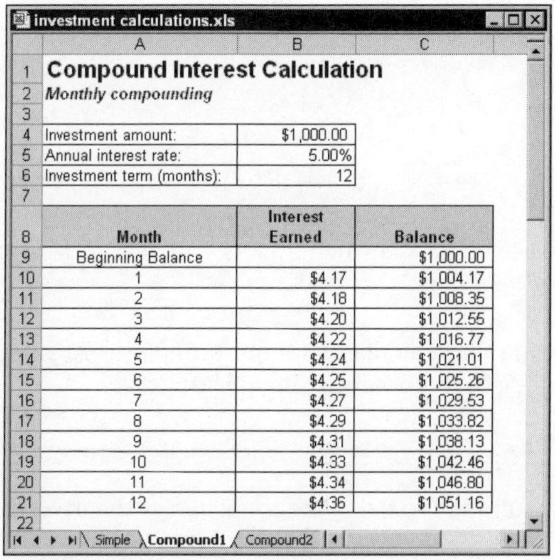
investment calculations.xls

Compound Interest Calculation

Monthly compounding

Investment amount:	$1,000.00
Annual interest rate:	5.00%
Investment term (months):	12

Month	Interest Earned	Balance
Beginning Balance		$1,000.00
1	$4.17	$1,004.17
2	$4.18	$1,008.35
3	$4.20	$1,012.55
4	$4.22	$1,016.77
5	$4.24	$1,021.01
6	$4.25	$1,025.26
7	$4.27	$1,029.53
8	$4.29	$1,033.82
9	$4.31	$1,038.13
10	$4.33	$1,042.46
11	$4.34	$1,046.80
12	$4.36	$1,051.16

Simple | Compound1 | Compound2

Figure 13-11: Using a series of formulas to calculate compound interest.

Column B contains formulas to calculate the interest for one month. For example, the formula in B10 is

```
=C9*($B$5*(1/12))
```

The formulas in column C simply add the monthly interest amount to the balance. For example, the formula in C10 is

```
=C9+B10
```

At the end of the 12-month term, the CD balance is $1,051.16. In other words, monthly compounding results in an additional $1.16 (compared to simple interest).

You can use the Excel FV (Future Value) function to calculate the final investment amount without using a series of formulas. Figure 13-12 shows a worksheet set up to calculate compound interest. Cell B6 is an input cell that holds the number of compounding periods per year. For monthly compounding, the value in B6 would be 12. For quarterly compounding, the value would be 4. For daily compounding, the value would be 365. Cell B7 holds the term of the investment expressed in years.

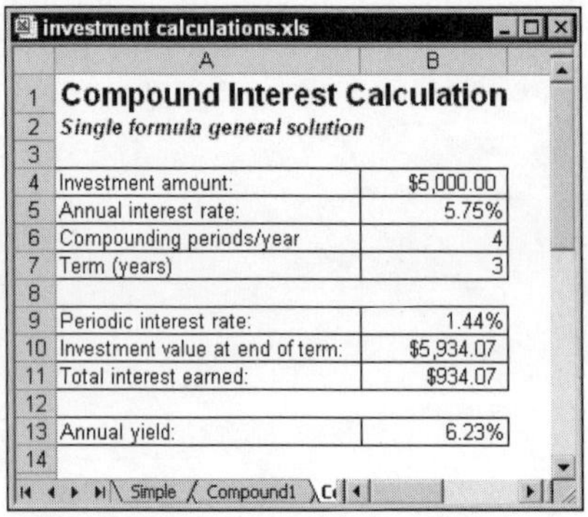

	A	B
	Compound Interest Calculation	
1	**Compound Interest Calculation**	
2	*Single formula general solution*	
3		
4	Investment amount:	$5,000.00
5	Annual interest rate:	5.75%
6	Compounding periods/year	4
7	Term (years)	3
8		
9	Periodic interest rate:	1.44%
10	Investment value at end of term:	$5,934.07
11	Total interest earned:	$934.07
12		
13	Annual yield:	6.23%
14		

Figure 13-12: Using a single formula to calculate compound interest.

Cell B9 contains the following formula that calculates the periodic interest rate. This value is the interest rate used for each compounding period.

```
=B5*(1/B6)
```

The formula in cell B10 uses the FV function to calculate the value of the investment at the end of the term. The formula is

```
=FV(B9,B6*B7,,-B4)
```

The first argument for the FV function is the periodic interest rate, which is calculated in cell B9. The second argument represents the total number of compounding periods. The third argument (pmt) is omitted, and the fourth argument is the original investment amount (expressed as a negative value).

The total interest is calculated with a simple formula in cell B11:

```
=B10-B4
```

Another formula, in cell B13, calculates the annual yield on the investment:

```
=(B11/B4)/B7
```

For example, suppose you deposit $5,000 into a three-year CD with a 5.75 percent annual interest rate compounded quarterly. In this case, the investment has four compounding periods per year, so you enter **4** into cell B6. The term is three years, so you enter **3** into cell B7. The formula in B10 returns $5,934.07.

Perhaps you want to see how this stacks up against a competitor's account that offers daily compounding. Figure 13-13 shows a calculation with daily compounding, using a $5,000 investment (compare this to Figure 13-12). As you can see, the difference is very small ($934.07 versus. $941.28). Over a period of three years, the account with daily compounding earns a total of $7.21 more interest. In terms of annual yield, quarterly compounding earns 6.23%, and daily compounding earns 6.28%.

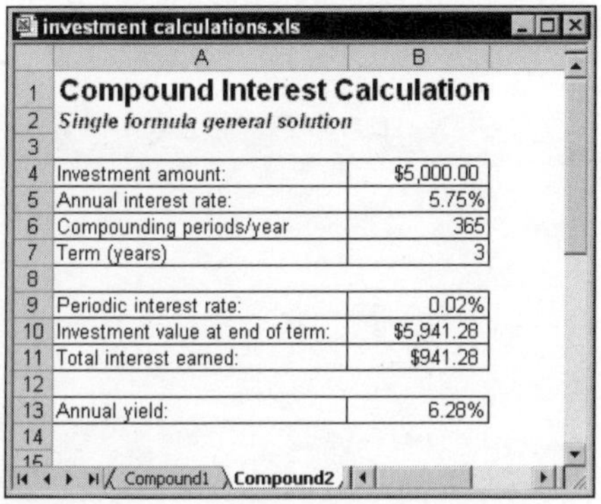

Figure 13-13: Calculating interest by using daily compounding.

Calculating interest with continuous compounding

The term *continuous compounding* refers to interest that is accumulated continuously. In other words, the investment has an infinite number of compounding periods per year. The following formula calculates the future value of a $5,000 investment at 5.75 percent compounded continuously for three years:

```
=5000*EXP(0.0575*3)
```

The formula returns $5,941.36, which is an additional $0.08 compared to daily compounding.

Note   It's possible to calculate compound interest without using the FV function. The general formula to calculate compound interest is

```
Principal * (1 + periodic rate) ^ number of periods
```

For example, consider a five-year, $5,000 investment that earns an annual interest rate of 5 percent compounded monthly. The formula to calculate the future value of this investment is

```
=5000*(1+.05/12)^(12*5)
```

The Rule of 72

Need to make an investment decision, but don't have a computer handy? You can use the "Rule of 72" to determine the number of years required to double your money at a particular interest rate, using annual compounding. Just divide 72 by the interest rate. For example, consider a $10,000 investment at 6 percent interest. How many years will it take to turn that 10 grand into 20 grand? Take 72, divide it by 6, and you get 12 years. What if you can get a 7 percent interest rate? If so, you can double your money in a little over 10 years.

How accurate is the Rule of 72? The table that follows shows Rule of 72 estimated values versus the actual values for various interest rates. As you can see, this simple rule is remarkably accurate. However, for interest rates that exceed 30 percent, the accuracy drops off considerably.

Interest Rate	Rule of 72	Actual
1%	72.00	69.66
2%	36.00	35.00
3%	24.00	23.45
4%	18.00	17.67
5%	14.40	14.21
6%	12.00	11.90
7%	10.29	10.24
8%	9.00	9.01
9%	8.00	8.04
10%	7.20	7.27
15%	4.80	4.96
20%	3.60	3.80
25%	2.88	3.11
30%	2.40	2.64

The Rule of 72 also works in reverse. For example, if you want to double your money in six years, divide 6 into 72; you'll discover that you need to find an investment that pays an annual interest rate of about 12 percent.

Future value of a series of deposits

Now, consider another type of investment, one in which you make a regular series of deposits. This type of investment is known as an *annuity*.

The worksheet functions discussed in the "Loan Calculations" section earlier in this chapter also apply to annuities, but you need to use the perspective of a lender, not a borrower. A simple example of this type of investment is a holiday club savings program offered by some banking institutions. A fixed amount is deducted from each of your paychecks and deposited into an interest-earning account. At the end of the year, you withdraw the money (with accumulated interest) to use for holiday expenses.

Suppose you deposit $200 at the beginning of each month (for 12 months) into an account that pays 4.25 percent annual interest compounded monthly. The following formula calculates the future value of your series of deposits.

```
=FV(0.0425/12,12,-200,,1)
```

This formula returns $2,455.97, which represents the total of your deposits ($2,400) plus the interest ($55.97). The last argument for the FV function is 1, which means that you make payments at the beginning of the month. Figure 13-14 shows a worksheet set up to calculate annuities. Table 13-4 describes the contents of this sheet.

annuity calculator.xls		
Annuity Calculator		
Deposits...		
Initial investment:	$0.00	
Periodic deposit amount:	$200.00	
No. periodic deposits per year :	12	
Deposits made at beginning of period?	TRUE	
Investment Period...		
Length of investment (years):	1	
Interest Rate...		
Annual interest rate:	4.25%	
Calculations		
Initial investment	$0.00	
Additional deposits:	$2,400.00	
Total amount invested:	$2,400.00	
Periodic interest rate:	0.35%	
Value of investment at end of term:	$2,455.97	
Interest earned on investment:	$55.97	

Figure 13-14: This worksheet contains formulas to calculate annuities.

The workbook shown in Figure 13-14 is available on the companion CD-ROM.

Table 13-4
The Annuity Calculator Worksheet

Cell	Formula	Description
B4	None (input cell)	Initial investment (can be 0)
B5	None (input cell)	The amount deposited on a regular basis
B6	None (input cell)	The number of deposits made in 12 months
B7	None (input cell)	TRUE if you make deposits at the beginning of period; FALSE otherwise
B10	None (input cell)	The length of the investment, in years (can be fractional)
B13	None (input cell)	The annual interest rate
B16	=B4	Displays the initial investment amount
B17	=B5*B6*B10	Calculates the total of all regular deposits
B18	=B16+B17	Adds the initial investment to the sum of the deposits
B19	=B13*(1/B6)	Calculates the periodic interest rate
B20	=FV(B19,B6*B10, -B5,-B4,IF(B7,1,0))	Calculates the future value of the investment
B21	=B20-B18	Calculates the interest earned from the investment

Depreciation Calculations

Excel offers five functions to calculate depreciation of an asset over time. Depreciating an asset places a value on the asset at a point in time, based on the original value and its useful life. The *function* that you choose depends on the type of *depreciation method* that you use.

Table 13-5 summarizes the Excel depreciation functions and the arguments used by each. For complete details, consult the Excel online Help system.

Table 13-5
Excel's Depreciation Functions

Function	Depreciation Method	Arguments*
SLN	Straight-line. The asset depreciates by the same amount each year of its life.	Cost, Salvage, Life

Function	Depreciation Method	Arguments*
DB	Declining balance. Computes depreciation at a fixed rate.	Cost, Salvage, Life, Period, [Month]
DDB	Double-declining balance. Computes depreciation at an accelerated rate. Depreciation is highest in the first period and decreases in successive periods.	Cost, Salvage, Life, Period, Month, [Factor]
SYD	Sum of the year's digits. Allocates a large depreciation in the earlier years of an asset's life.	Cost, Salvage, Life, Period
VDB	Variable-declining balance. Computes the depreciation of an asset for any period (including partial periods) using the double-declining balance method or some other method you specify.	Cost, Salvage, Life, Start Period, End Period, [Factor], [No Switch]

* Arguments in brackets are optional.

Here are the arguments for the depreciation functions:

✦ **Cost**: Original cost of the asset.

✦ **Salvage**: Salvage cost of the asset after it has fully depreciated.

✦ **Life**: Number of periods over which the asset will depreciate.

✦ **Period**: Period in the life for which the calculation is being made.

✦ **Month**: Number of months in the first year; if omitted, Excel uses 12.

✦ **Factor**: Rate at which the balance declines; if omitted, it is assumed to be 2 (that is, double-declining).

✦ **Rate**: Interest rate per period. If you make payments monthly, for example, you must divide the annual interest rate by 12.

✦ **No Switch**: True or False. Specifies whether to switch to straight-line depreciation when depreciation is greater than the declining balance calculation.

Figure 13-15 shows depreciation calculations using the SLN, DB, DDB, and SYD functions. The asset's original cost, $10,000, is assumed to have a useful life of 10 years, with a salvage value of $1,000. The range labeled Depreciation Amount shows the annual depreciation of the asset. The range labeled Value of Asset shows the asset's depreciated value over its life.

On the CD-ROM

The workbook shown in Figure 13-14 is available on the companion CD-ROM.

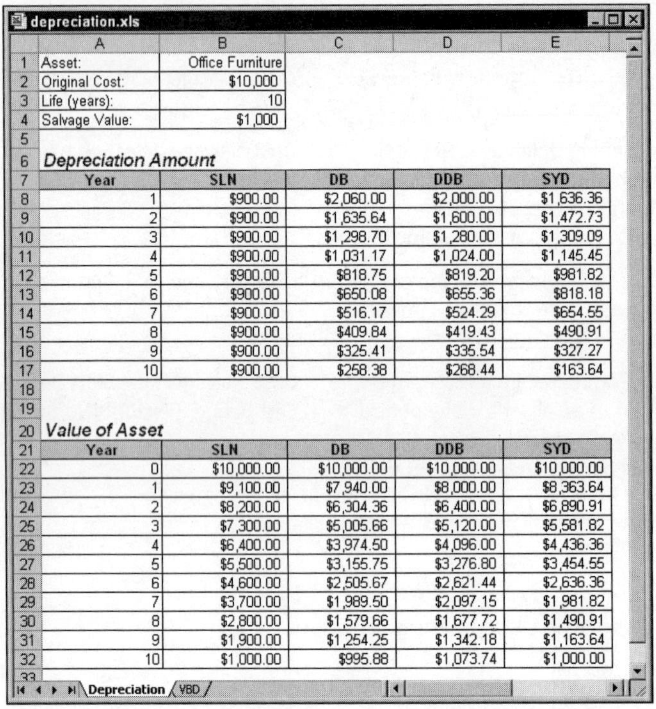

	A	B	C	D	E
	depreciation.xls				
1	Asset:	Office Furniture			
2	Original Cost:	$10,000			
3	Life (years):	10			
4	Salvage Value:	$1,000			
5					
6	**Depreciation Amount**				
7	Year	SLN	DB	DDB	SYD
8	1	$900.00	$2,060.00	$2,000.00	$1,636.36
9	2	$900.00	$1,635.64	$1,600.00	$1,472.73
10	3	$900.00	$1,298.70	$1,280.00	$1,309.09
11	4	$900.00	$1,031.17	$1,024.00	$1,145.45
12	5	$900.00	$818.75	$819.20	$981.82
13	6	$900.00	$650.08	$655.36	$818.18
14	7	$900.00	$516.17	$524.29	$654.55
15	8	$900.00	$409.84	$419.43	$490.91
16	9	$900.00	$325.41	$335.54	$327.27
17	10	$900.00	$258.38	$268.44	$163.64
18					
19					
20	**Value of Asset**				
21	Year	SLN	DB	DDB	SYD
22	0	$10,000.00	$10,000.00	$10,000.00	$10,000.00
23	1	$9,100.00	$7,940.00	$8,000.00	$8,363.64
24	2	$8,200.00	$6,304.36	$6,400.00	$6,890.91
25	3	$7,300.00	$5,005.66	$5,120.00	$5,581.82
26	4	$6,400.00	$3,974.50	$4,096.00	$4,436.36
27	5	$5,500.00	$3,155.75	$3,276.80	$3,454.55
28	6	$4,600.00	$2,505.67	$2,621.44	$2,636.36
29	7	$3,700.00	$1,989.50	$2,097.15	$1,981.82
30	8	$2,800.00	$1,579.66	$1,677.72	$1,490.91
31	9	$1,900.00	$1,254.25	$1,342.18	$1,163.64
32	10	$1,000.00	$995.88	$1,073.74	$1,000.00
33					

Depreciation / VBD /

Figure 13-15: A comparison of four depreciation functions.

Figure 13-16 shows a chart that graphs the asset's value. As you can see, the SLN function produces a straight line; the other functions produce a curved line because the depreciation is greater in the earlier years of the asset's life.

The VBD function is useful if you need to calculate depreciation for multiple periods (for example, years 2 and 3). Figure 13-17 shows a worksheet set up to calculate depreciation using the VBD function. The formula in cell B12 is

```
=VDB(B2,B4,B3,B6,B7,B8,B9)
```

The formula displays the depreciation for the first three years of an asset (starting period of 0 and ending period of 3).

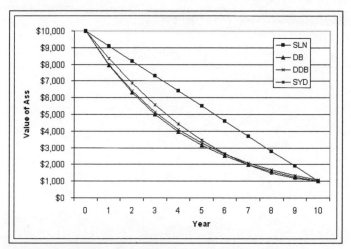

Figure 13-16: This chart shows an asset's value over time, using four depreciation functions.

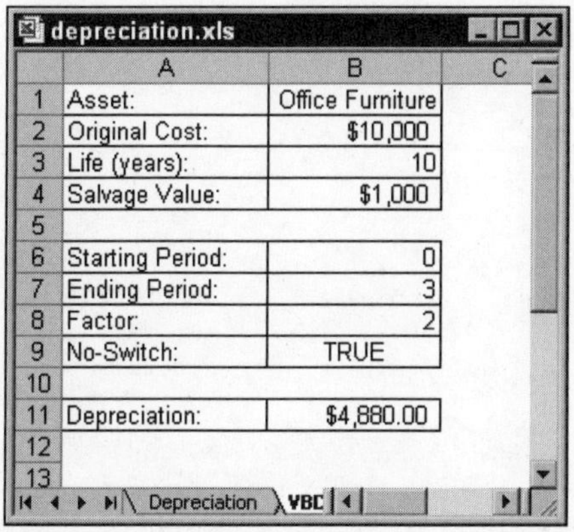

Figure 13-17: Using the VBD function to calculate depreciation for multiple periods.

✦   ✦   ✦

Introducing Array Formulas

One of Excel's most interesting (and most powerful) features is its ability to work with arrays in formulas. When you understand this concept, you'll be able to create elegant formulas that appear to perform magic.

This chapter introduces the concept of arrays and is required reading for anyone who wants to become a master of Excel formulas. Chapter 15 continues with lots of useful examples.

Understanding Array Formulas

If you do any computer programming, you've probably been exposed to the concept of an array. An *array* is simply a collection of items operated on collectively or individually. In Excel, an array can be one dimensional or two dimensional. These dimensions correspond to rows and columns. For example, a *one-dimensional array* can be stored in a range that consists of one row (a horizontal array) or one column (a vertical array). A *two-dimensional array* can be stored in a rectangular range of cells. Excel doesn't support three-dimensional arrays (but its VBA programming language does).

But, as you'll see, arrays need not be stored in cells. You can also work with arrays that exist only in Excel's memory. You can then use an *array formula* to manipulate this information and return a result. An array formula can occupy multiple cells or reside in a single cell.

This section presents two array formula examples: an array formula that occupies multiple cells and another array formula that occupies only one cell.

A multicell array formula

Figure 14-1 shows a simple worksheet set up to calculate product sales. Normally, you would calculate the value in column D (total sales per product) with a formula such as the one that follows, and then you would copy this formula down the column.

```
=B2*C2
```

After copying the formula, the worksheet contains six formulas in column D.

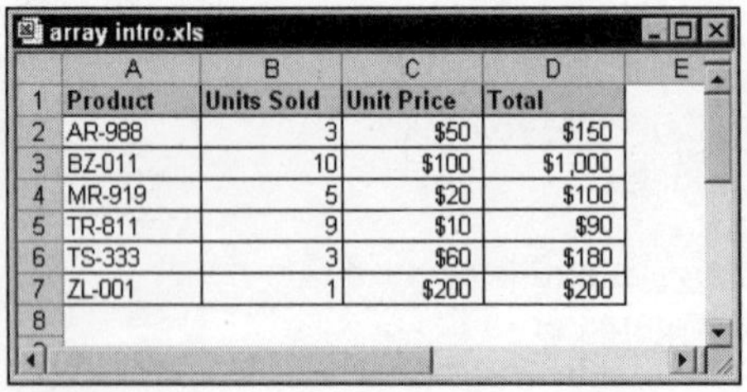

	A	B	C	D	E
1	Product	Units Sold	Unit Price	Total	
2	AR-988	3	$50	$150	
3	BZ-011	10	$100	$1,000	
4	MR-919	5	$20	$100	
5	TR-811	9	$10	$90	
6	TS-333	3	$60	$180	
7	ZL-001	1	$200	$200	
8					

Figure 14-1: Column D contains formulas to calculate the total for each product.

Another alternative uses a *single* formula (an array formula) to calculate all six values in D2:D7. This single formula occupies six cells and returns an array of six values.

To create a single array formula to perform the calculations, follow these steps:

1. Select a range to hold the results. In this case, the range is D2:D7.
2. Enter the following formula:

   ```
   =B2:B7*C2:C7
   ```

3. Normally, you press Enter to enter a formula. Because this is an array formula, however, press Ctrl+Shift+Enter.

The formula is entered into all six of the selected cells. If you examine the formula bar, you see the following:

```
{=B2:B7*C2:C7}
```

Excel places curly brackets around the formula to indicate that it's an array formula.

This formula performs its calculations and returns a six-item array. The array formula actually works with two other arrays, both of which happen to be stored in ranges. The values for the first array are stored in B2:B7, and the values for the second array are stored in C2:C7.

Because it's not possible to display more than one value in a single cell, six cells are required to display the resulting array. That explains why you selected six cells before you entered the array formula.

This array formula, of course, returns exactly the same values as these six normal formulas entered into individual cells in D2:D7:

```
=B2*C2
=B3*C3
=B4*C4
=B5*C5
=B6*C6
=B7*C7
```

Using a single array formula rather than individual formulas does offer a few advantages:

✦ It's a good way of ensuring that all formulas in a range are identical.

✦ Using a multicell array formula makes it less likely you will overwrite a formula accidentally. You cannot change one cell in a multicell array formula. Excel displays an error message if you attempt to do so.

✦ Using a multicell array formula will almost certainly prevent novices from tampering with your formulas.

A single-cell array formula

Now it's time to take a look at a single-cell array formula. Check out Figure 14-2, which is similar to Figure 14-1. Notice, however, that the formulas in column D have been deleted. The goal is to calculate the sum of the total product sales without using the individual calculations that were in column D.

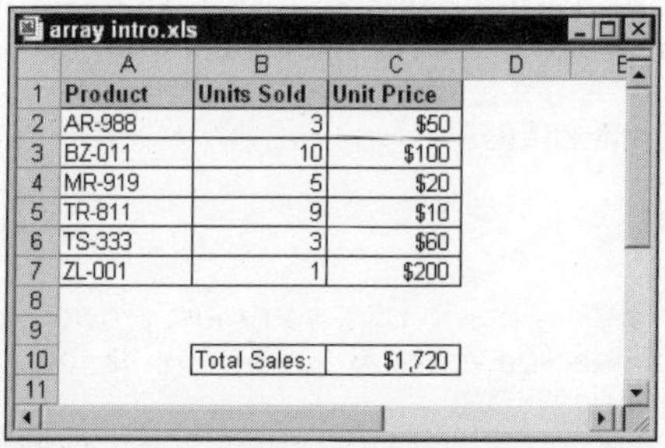

Figure 14-2: The array formula in cell C10 calculates the total sales without using intermediate formulas.

The following array formula is in cell C10:

```
{=SUM(B2:B7*C2:C7)}
```

When you enter this formula, make sure that you use Ctrl+Shift+Enter (and don't type the curly brackets).

This formula works with two arrays, both of which are stored in cells. The first array is stored in B2:B7, and the second array is stored in C2:C7. The formula multiplies the corresponding values in these two arrays and creates a new array (which exists only in memory). The SUM function then operates on this new array and returns the sum of its values.

Note
In this case, you can use Excel's SUMPRODUCT function to obtain the same result without using an array formula:

```
=SUMPRODUCT(B2:B7,C2:C7)
```

As you'll see, however, array formulas allow many other types of calculations that are otherwise not possible.

Creating an array constant

The examples in the preceding section used arrays stored in worksheet ranges. The examples in this section demonstrate an important concept: An array does not have to be stored in a range of cells. This type of array, which is stored in memory, is referred to as an *array constant*.

To create an array constant, list its items and surround them with brackets. Here's an example of a five-item vertical array constant:

```
{1,0,1,0,1}
```

The following formula uses the SUM function, with the preceding array constant as its argument. The formula returns the sum of the values in the array (which is 3). Notice that this formula uses an array, but it is not an array formula. Therefore, you do not use Ctrl+Shift+Enter to enter the formula.

```
=SUM({1,0,1,0,1})
```

Note
When you specify an array directly (as shown previously), you must provide the brackets around the array elements. When you enter an array formula, on the other hand, you do not supply the brackets.

At this point, you probably don't see any advantage to using an array constant. The formula that follows, for example, returns the same result as the previous formula:

```
=SUM(1,0,1,0,1)
```

Keep reading, and the advantages will become apparent.

Following is a formula that uses two array constants:

```
=SUM({1,2,3,4}*{5,6,7,8})
```

This formula creates a new array (in memory) that consists of the product of the corresponding elements in the two arrays. The new array is

```
{5,12,21,32}
```

This new array is then used as an argument for the SUM function, which returns the result (70). The formula is equivalent to the following formula, which doesn't use arrays:

```
=SUM(1*5,2*6,3*7,4*8)
```

A formula can work with both an array constant and an array stored in a range. The following formula, for example, returns the sum of the values in A1:D1, each multiplied by the corresponding element in the array constant:

```
=SUM((A1:D1*{1,2,3,4}))
```

This formula is equivalent to

```
=SUM(A1*1,B1*2,C1*3,D1*4)
```

Array constant elements

An array constant can contain numbers, text, logical values (TRUE or FALSE), and even error values, such as #N/A. Numbers can be in integer, decimal, or scientific format. You must enclose text in double quotation marks (for example, "Tuesday"). You can use different types of values in the same array constant, as in this example:

```
{1,2,3,TRUE,FALSE,TRUE,"Moe","Larry","Curly"}
```

An array constant cannot contain formulas, functions, or other arrays. Numeric values cannot contain dollar signs, commas, parentheses, or percent signs. For example, the following is an invalid array constant:

```
{SQRT(32),$56.32,12.5%}
```

Understanding the Dimensions of an Array

As stated previously, an array can be either one dimensional or two dimensional. A one-dimensional array's orientation can be either vertical or horizontal.

One-dimensional horizontal arrays

The elements in a one-dimensional horizontal array are separated by commas. The following example is a one-dimensional horizontal array constant:

```
{1,2,3,4,5}
```

To display this array in a range requires five consecutive cells in a row. To enter this array into a range, select a range of cells that consists of one row and five columns. Then enter ={1,2,3,4,5} and press Ctrl+Shift+Enter.

If you enter this array into a horizontal range that consists of more than five cells, the extra cells will contain #N/A (which denotes unavailable values). If you enter this array into a *vertical* range of cells, only the first item (1) will appear in each cell.

The following example is another horizontal array; it has seven elements and is made up of text strings:

```
{"Sun","Mon","Tue","Wed","Thu","Fri","Sat"}
```

To enter this array, select seven cells in a row and type the following (followed by Ctrl+Shift+Enter):

```
={"Sun","Mon","Tue","Wed","Thu","Fri","Sat"}
```

One-dimensional vertical arrays

The elements in a one-dimensional vertical array are separated by semicolons. The following is a six-element vertical array constant:

```
{10;20;30;40;50;60}
```

Displaying this array in a range requires six cells in a column. To enter this array into a range, select a range of cells that consists of six rows and one column. Then enter the following formula, followed by Ctrl+Shift+Enter:

```
={10;20;30;40;50;60}
```

The following is another example of a vertical array; this one has four elements:

```
{"Widgets";"Sprockets";"Doodads";"Thingamajigs"}
```

Two-dimensional arrays

A two-dimensional array uses commas to separate its horizontal elements and semicolons to separate its vertical elements. The following example shows a 3×4 array constant:

    {1,2,3,4;5,6,7,8;9,10,11,12}

Displaying this array in a range requires 12 cells. To enter this array into a range, select a range of cells that consists of three rows and four columns. Then type the following formula, followed by Ctrl+Shift+Enter:

    ={1,2,3,4;5,6,7,8;9,10,11,12}

Figure 14-3 shows how this array appears when entered into a range (in this case, B2:E4).

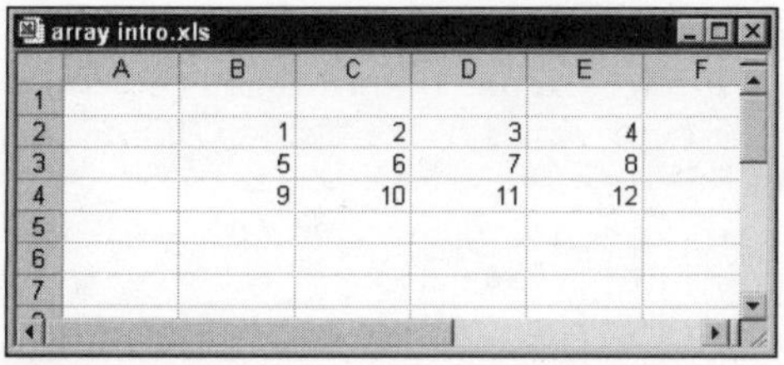

Figure 14-3: A 3×4 array entered into a range of cells.

If you enter an array into a range that has more cells than array elements, Excel displays #N/A in the extra cells. Figure 14-4 shows a 3×4 array entered into a 10×5 cell range.

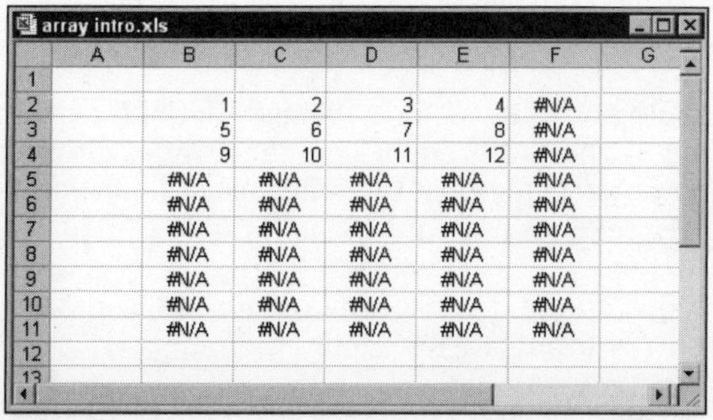

Figure 14-4: A 3×4 array entered into a 10×5 cell range.

Each row of a two-dimensional array must contain the same number of items. The array that follows, for example, is not valid because the third row contains only three items:

```
{1,2,3,4;5,6,7,8;9,10,11}
```

Excel will not allow you to enter a formula that contains an invalid array.

Naming Array Constants

You can create an array constant, give it a name, and then use this named array in a formula. Technically, a named array is a named formula.

 Chapter 4 covers the topic of names and named formulas.

Figure 14-5 shows a named array being created by using the Define Name dialog box. The name of the array is *DayNames*, and it refers to the following array constant:

```
{"Sun","Mon","Tue","Wed","Thu","Fri","Sat"}
```

Figure 14-5: Creating a named array constant.

Notice that, in the Define Name dialog box, the array is defined (in the Refers To box) using a leading equal sign (=). Without this equal sign, the array is interpreted as a text string rather than an array. Also, you must type the curly brackets when defining a named array constant; Excel does not enter them for you.

After creating this named array, you can use it in a formula. Figure 14-6 shows a worksheet that contains a single array formula entered into the range A1:G1. The formula is

```
{=DayNames}
```

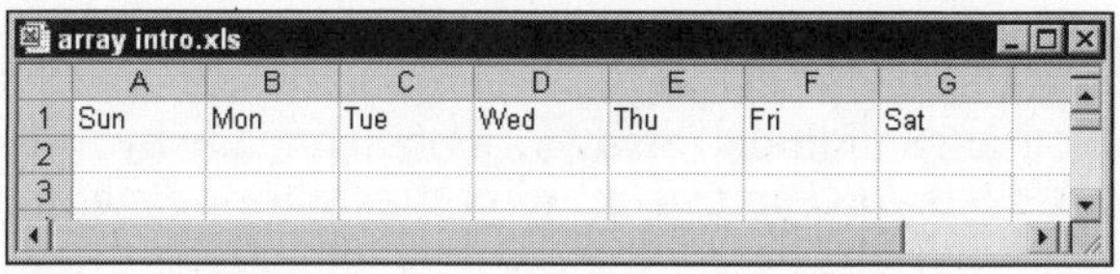

Figure 14-6: Using a named array in an array formula.

Because commas separate the array elements, the array has a horizontal orientation. Use semicolons to create a vertical array. Or you can use the Excel TRANSPOSE function to insert a horizontal array into a vertical range of cells (see "Transposing an array," later in this chapter). The following array formula, which is entered into a seven-cell vertical range, uses the TRANSPOSE function:

```
{=TRANSPOSE(DayNames)}
```

You also can access individual elements from the array by using the Excel INDEX function. The following formula, for example, returns *Wed*, the fourth item in the *DayNames* array:

```
=INDEX(DayNames,4)
```

Working with Array Formulas

This section deals with the mechanics of selecting cells that contain arrays and entering and editing array formulas. These procedures differ a bit from working with ordinary ranges and formulas.

Entering an array formula

When you enter an array formula into a cell or range, you must follow a special procedure so Excel knows that you want an array formula rather than a normal formula. You enter a normal formula into a cell by pressing Enter. You enter an array formula into one or more cells by pressing Ctrl+Shift+Enter.

You can easily identify an array formula, because the formula is enclosed in curly brackets in the formula bar. The following formula, for example, is an array formula:

```
{=SUM(LEN(A1:A5))}
```

Don't enter the curly brackets when you create an array formula; Excel inserts them for you. If the result of an array formula consists of more than one value, you must select all of the cells in the results range *before* you enter the formula. If you fail to do this, only the first element of the result is returned.

Selecting an array formula range

You can select the cells that contain a multicell array formula manually by using the normal cell selection procedures. Or you can use either of the following methods:

✦ Activate any cell in the array formula range. Select Edit ➪ Go To (or press F5), click the Special button, and then choose the Current Array option. Click OK to close the dialog box.

✦ Activate any cell in the array formula range and press Ctrl+/ to select the entire array.

Editing an array formula

If an array formula occupies multiple cells, you must edit the entire range as though it were a single cell. The key point to remember is that you can't change just one element of an array formula. If you attempt to do so, Excel displays the message shown in Figure 14-7.

Figure 14-7: Excel's warning message reminds you that you can't edit just one cell of a multicell array formula.

The following rules apply to multicell array formulas. If you try to do any of these things, Excel lets you know about it:

✦ You can't change the contents of any individual cell that makes up an array formula.

✦ You can't move cells that make up part of an array formula (but you can move an entire array formula).

✦ You can't delete cells that form part of an array formula (but you can delete an entire array).

✦ You can't insert new cells into an array range. This rule includes inserting rows or columns that would add new cells to an array range.

To edit an array formula, select all the cells in the array range and activate the formula bar as usual (click it or press F2). Excel removes the brackets from the formula while you edit it. Edit the formula and then press Ctrl+Shift+Enter to enter the changes. All of the cells in the array now reflect your editing changes.

Caution If you accidentally press Ctrl+Enter (instead of Ctrl+Shift+Enter) after editing an array formula, the formula will be entered into each selected cell, but it will no longer be an array formula.

Although you can't change any individual cell that makes up a multicell array formula, you can apply formatting to the entire array or to only parts of it.

Expanding or contracting a multicell array formula

Often, you may need to expand a multicell array formula (to include more cells) or contract it (to include fewer cells). Doing so requires a few steps:

1. Select the entire range that contains the array formula.
2. Press F2 to enter Edit mode.
3. Press Ctrl+Enter. This step enters an identical (non-array) formula into each selected cell.
4. Change your range selection to include additional or fewer cells.
5. Press F2 to re-enter Edit mode.
6. Press Ctrl+Shift+Enter.

Array Formulas: The Downside

If you've followed along in this chapter, you probably understand some of the advantages of using array formulas. The main advantage, of course, is that an array formula enables you to perform otherwise impossible calculations. As you gain more experience with arrays, however, you undoubtedly will also discover some disadvantages.

Array formulas are one of the least understood features of Excel. Consequently, if you plan to share a workbook with someone who may need to make modifications, you should probably avoid using array formulas. Encountering an array formula when you don't know what it is can be very confusing.

You might also discover that you can easily forget to enter an array formula by pressing Ctrl+Shift+Enter. (And don't forget: If you edit an existing array, you must remember to use this key combination to complete the edits.) Except for logical errors, this is probably the most common problem that users have with array formulas. If you press Enter by mistake after editing an array formula, just press F2 to get back into Edit mode and then press Ctrl+Shift+Enter.

Another potential problem with array formulas is that they can slow your worksheet's recalculations, especially if you use very large arrays. On a faster system, this may not be a problem. But, conversely, using an array formula is almost always faster than using a custom VBA function. See Chapter 35 for more information about creating custom VBA functions.

Using Multicell Array Formulas

This section contains examples that demonstrate additional features of *multicell array formulas* (array formulas that are entered into a range of cells). These features include creating arrays from values, performing operations, using functions, transposing arrays, and generating consecutive integers.

Creating an array from values in a range

The following array formula creates an array from a range of cells. Figure 14-8 shows a workbook with some data entered into A1:C4. The range D8:F11 contains a single array formula:

```
{=A1:C4}
```

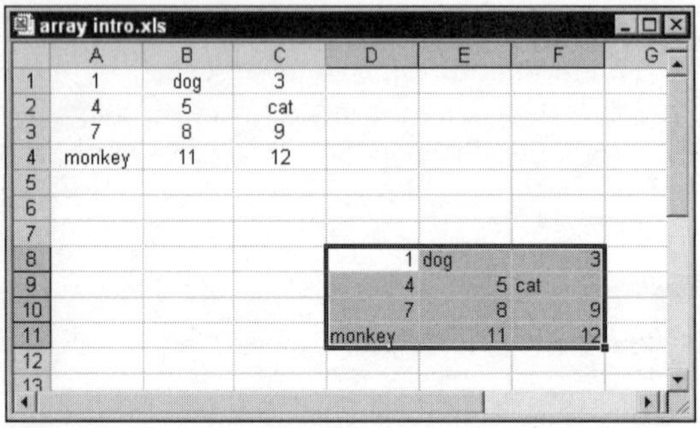

Figure 14-8: Creating an array from a range.

The array in D8:F11 is linked to the range A1:C4. Change any value in A1:C4, and the corresponding cell in D8:F11 reflects that change.

Creating an array constant from values in a range

In the preceding example, the array formula in D8:F11 essentially created a link to the cells in A1:C4. It's possible to "sever" this link and create an array constant made up of the values in A1:C4:

1. To do so, select the cells that contain the array formula (the range D8:F11, in this example).

2. Press F2 to edit the array formula.

3. Press F9 to convert the cell references to values.

4. Press Ctrl+Shift+Enter to re-enter the array formula (which now uses an array constant).

The array constant is

```
{1,"dog",3;4,5,"cat";7,8,9;"monkey",11,12}
```

Figure 14-9 shows how this looks in the formula bar.

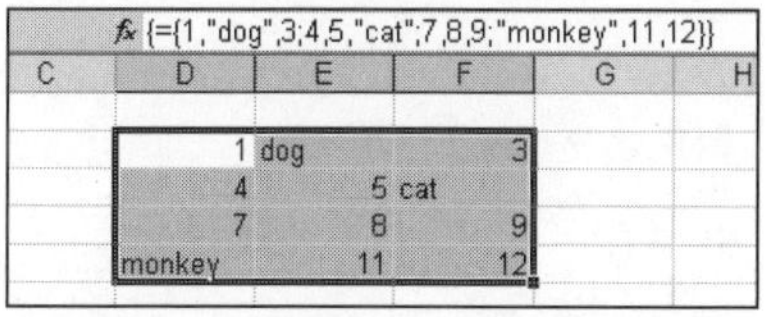

Figure 14-9: After you've pressed F9, the formula bar displays the array constant.

Performing operations on an array

So far, most of the examples in this chapter simply entered arrays into ranges. The following array formula creates a rectangular array and multiplies each array element by 2:

```
{={1,2,3,4;5,6,7,8;9,10,11,12}*2}
```

Figure 14-10 shows the result when you enter this formula into a range:

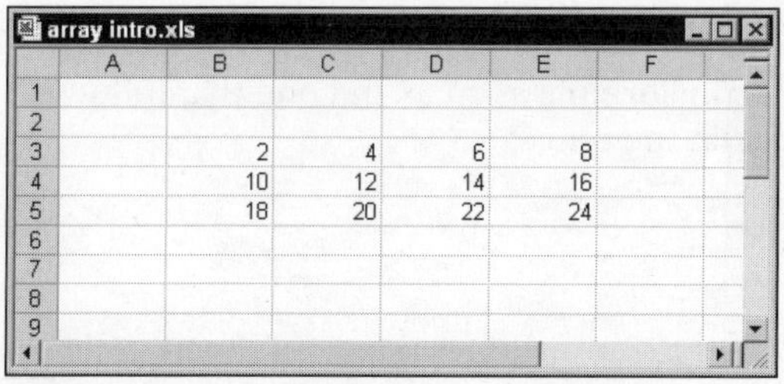

Figure 14-10: Performing a mathematical operation on an array.

The following array formula multiplies each array element by itself. Figure 14-11 shows the result when you enter this formula into a range:

```
{={1,2,3,4;5,6,7,8;9,10,11,12}*{1,2,3,4;5,6,7,8;9,10,11,12}}
```

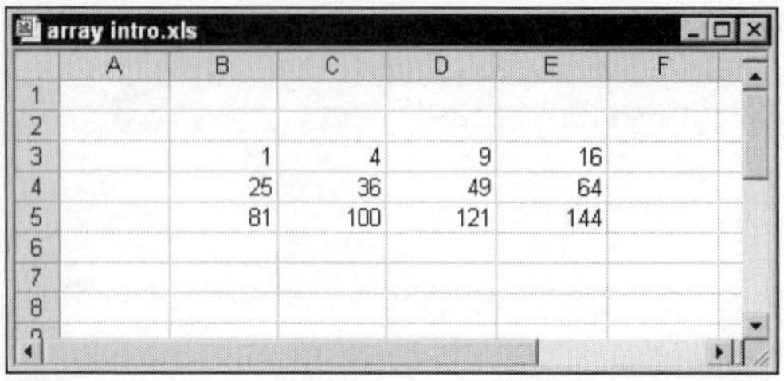

Figure 14-11: Multiplying each array element by itself.

The following array formula is a simpler way of obtaining the same result:

```
{={1,2,3,4;5,6,7,8;9,10,11,12}^2}
```

If the array is stored in a range (such as A1:C4), the array formula returns the square of each value in the range, as follows:

```
{=A1:C4^2}
```

Using functions with an array

As you may expect, you also can use functions with an array. The following array formula, which you can enter into a 10-cell vertical range, calculates the square root of each array element in the array constant:

```
{=SQRT({1;2;3;4;5;6;7;8;9;10})}
```

If the array is stored in a range, an array formula such as the one that follows returns the square root of each value in the range:

```
{=SQRT(A1:A10)}
```

Transposing an array

When you transpose an array, you essentially convert rows to columns and columns to rows. In other words, you can convert a horizontal array to a vertical array (and vice versa). Use the Excel TRANSPOSE function to transpose an array.

Consider the following one-dimensional horizontal array constant:

```
{1,2,3,4,5}
```

You can enter this array into a vertical range of cells by using the TRANSPOSE function. To do so, select a range of five cells that occupy five rows and one column. Then enter the following formula and press Ctrl+Shift+Enter:

```
=TRANSPOSE({1,2,3,4,5})
```

The horizontal array is transposed, and the array elements appear in the vertical range.

Transposing a two-dimensional array works in a similar manner. Figure 14-12 shows a two-dimensional array entered into a range normally and entered into a range by using the TRANSPOSE function. The formula in A1:D3 is

```
{={1,2,3,4;5,6,7,8;9,10,11,12}}
```

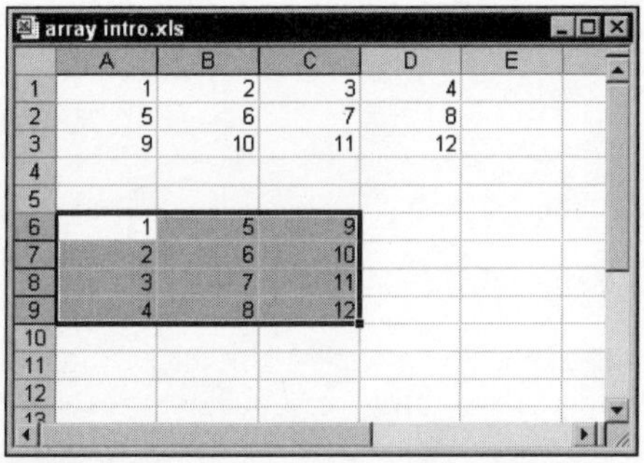

Figure 14-12: Using the TRANSPOSE function to transpose a rectangular array.

The formula in A6:C9 is

```
{=TRANSPOSE({1,2,3,4;5,6,7,8;9,10,11,12})}
```

You can, of course, use the TRANSPOSE function to transpose an array stored in a range. The following formula, for example, uses an array stored in A1:C4 (four rows, three columns). You can enter this array formula into a range that consists of three rows and four columns.

```
{=TRANSPOSE(A1:C4)}
```

Generating an array of consecutive integers

As you will see in Chapter 15, generating an array of consecutive integers for use in an array formula is often useful. The Excel program's ROW function, which returns a row number, is ideal for this. Consider the array formula shown here, entered into a vertical range of 12 cells:

```
{=ROW(1:12)}
```

This formula generates a 12-element array that contains integers from 1 to 12. To demonstrate, select a range that consists of 12 rows and one column and enter the array formula into the range. You'll find that the range is filled with 12 consecutive integers (as shown in Figure 14-13).

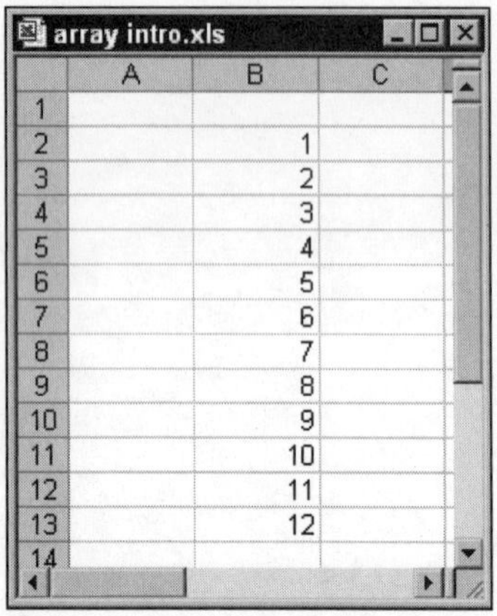

	A	B	C
1			
2		1	
3		2	
4		3	
5		4	
6		5	
7		6	
8		7	
9		8	
10		9	
11		10	
12		11	
13		12	
14			

array intro.xls

Figure 14-13: Using an array formula to generate consecutive integers.

If you want to generate an array of consecutive integers, a formula like the one shown previously is good — but not perfect. To see the problem, insert a new row above the range that contains the array formula. You'll find that Excel adjusts the row references so the array formula now reads:

```
{=ROW(2:13)}
```

The formula that originally generated integers from 1 to 12 now generates integers from 2 to 13.

For a better solution, use this formula:

```
{=ROW(INDIRECT("1:12"))}
```

This formula uses the INDIRECT function, which takes a text string as its argument. Excel does not adjust the references contained in the argument for the INDIRECT function. Therefore, this array formula *always* returns integers from 1 to 12.

 Cross-Reference Chapter 15 contains several examples that use the technique for generating consecutive integers.

Worksheet Functions That Return an Array

Several of the Excel worksheet functions use arrays; you must enter a formula that uses one of these functions into multiple cells as an array formula. These functions are FORECAST, FREQUENCY, GROWTH, LINEST, LOGEST, MINVERSE, MMULT, and TREND. Consult the online help for more information.

Using Single-Cell Array Formulas

The examples in the preceding section all used a multicell array formula — a single array formula entered into a range of cells. The real power of using arrays becomes apparent when you use single-cell array formulas. This section contains examples of array formulas that occupy a single cell.

Counting characters in a range

Suppose you have a range of cells that contains text entries (as shown in Figure 14-14). If you need to get a count of the total number of characters in that range, the "traditional" method involves creating a formula like the one that follows and copying it down the column:

```
=LEN(A1)
```

Figure 14-14: The goal is to count the number of characters in a range of text.

Then you use a SUM formula to calculate the sum of the values returned by the intermediate formulas.

The following array formula does the job without using any intermediate formulas:

```
{=SUM(LEN(A1:A14))}
```

The array formula uses the LEN function to create a new array (in memory) that consists of the number of characters in each cell of the range. In this case, the new array is

```
{10,9,8,5,6,5,5,10,11,14,6,8,8,7}
```

The array formula is then reduced to

```
=SUM({10,9,8,5,6,5,5,10,11,14,6,8,8,7})
```

Summing the three smallest values in a range

The following formula returns the sum of the three smallest values in a range named *Data*:

```
{=SUM(SMALL(Data,{1,2,3}))}
```

The function uses an array constant as the second argument for the SMALL function. This generates a new array, which consists of the three smallest values in the range. This array is then passed to the SUM function, which returns the sum of the values in the new array.

Figure 14-15 shows an example in which the range A1:A10 is named *Data*. The SMALL function is evaluated three times, each time with a different second argument. The first time, the SMALL function has a second argument of 1, and it returns –5. The second time, the second argument for the SMALL function is 2, and it returns 0 (the second smallest value in the range). The third time, the SMALL function has a second argument of 3, and returns the third smallest value of 2.

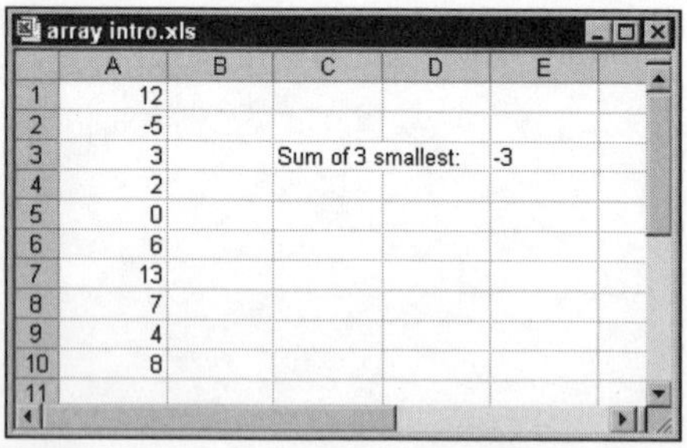

	A	B	C	D	E
1	12				
2	-5				
3	3		Sum of 3 smallest:	-3	
4	2				
5	0				
6	6				
7	13				
8	7				
9	4				
10	8				
11					

Figure 14-15: An array formula returns the sum of the three smallest values in A1:A10.

Therefore, the array that's passed to the SUM function is

```
{-5,0,2}
```

The formula returns the sum of the array (–3).

Counting text cells in a range

The following array formula uses the IF function to examine each cell in a range. It then creates a new array (of the same size and dimensions as the original range) that consists of 1s and 0s, depending on whether the cell contains text. This new array is then passed to the SUM function, which returns the sum of the items in the array. The result is a count of the number of text cells in the range.

```
{=SUM(IF(ISTEXT(A1:D5),1,0))}
```

 Cross-Reference This general array formula type (that is, an IF function nested in a SUM function) is very useful for counting. Refer to Chapter 11 for additional examples.

Figure 14-16 shows an example of the preceding formula in cell C8. The array created by the IF function is

```
{0,1,1,1;1,0,0,0;1,0,0,0;1,0,0,0;1,0,0,0}
```

array intro.xls					
	A	B	C	D	E
1		Jan	Feb	Mar	
2	Region 1	7	4	9	
3	Region 2	8	2	8	
4	Region 3	12	1	9	
5	Region 4	14	6	10	
6					
7					
8	No. of text cells:		7		
9					

Figure 14-16: An array formula returns the number of text cells in the range.

Notice that this array contains four rows of three elements (the same dimensions as the range).

A variation on this formula follows:

```
{=SUM(ISTEXT(A1:D5)*1)}
```

This formula eliminates the need for the IF function and takes advantage of the fact that

```
TRUE * 1 = 1
```

and

```
FALSE * 1 = 0
```

Eliminating intermediate formulas

One of the main benefits of using an array formula is that you can eliminate intermediate formulas in your worksheet. This makes your worksheet more compact and eliminates the need to display irrelevant calculations. Figure 14-17 shows a worksheet that contains pre-test and post-test scores for students. Column D contains formulas that calculate the changes between the pre-test and the post-test scores. Cell D17 contains a formula, shown here, that calculates the average of the values in column D:

```
=AVERAGE(D2:D15)
```

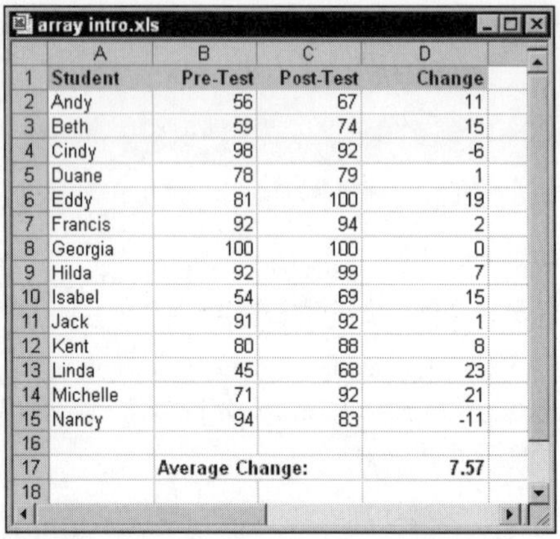

array intro.xls

	A	B	C	D
1	Student	Pre-Test	Post-Test	Change
2	Andy	56	67	11
3	Beth	59	74	15
4	Cindy	98	92	-6
5	Duane	78	79	1
6	Eddy	81	100	19
7	Francis	92	94	2
8	Georgia	100	100	0
9	Hilda	92	99	7
10	Isabel	54	69	15
11	Jack	91	92	1
12	Kent	80	88	8
13	Linda	45	68	23
14	Michelle	71	92	21
15	Nancy	94	83	-11
16				
17		Average Change:		7.57
18				

Figure 14-17: Without an array formula, calculating the average change requires intermediate formulas in column D.

With an array formula, you can eliminate column D. The following array formula calculates the average of the changes but does not require the formulas in column D:

```
{=AVERAGE(C2:C15-B2:B15)}
```

How does it work? The formula uses two arrays, the values of which are stored in two ranges (B2:B15 and C2:C15). The formula creates a *new* array that consists of the differences between each corresponding element in the other arrays. This new array is stored in Excel's memory, not in a range. The AVERAGE function then uses this new array as its argument and returns the result.

The new array consists of the following elements:

    {11,15,-6,1,19,2,0,7,15,1,8,23,21,-11}

The formula, therefore, is reduced to

    =AVERAGE({11,15,-6,1,19,2,0,7,15,1,8,23,21,-11})

You can use additional array formulas to calculate other measures for the data in this example. For instance, the following array formula returns the largest change (that is, the greatest improvement). This formula returns 23, which represents Linda's test scores.

    {=MAX(C2:C15-B2:B15)}

The following array formula returns the smallest change (that is, the least improvement). This formula returns –11, which represents Nancy's test scores.

    {=MIN(C2:C15-B2:B15)}

Using an array in lieu of a range reference

If your formula uses a function that requires a range reference, you may be able to replace that range reference with an array constant. This is useful in situations in which the values in the referenced range do not change.

Note   A notable exception to using an array constant in place of a range reference in a function is with the database functions that use a reference to a criteria range (for example, DSUM). Unfortunately, using an array constant instead of a reference to a criteria range does not work.

Cross-Reference   For information about lookup formulas, refer to Chapter 12. For more about the database functions (including DSUM), see Chapter 19.

Figure 14-18 shows a worksheet that uses a lookup table to display a word that corresponds to an integer. For example, looking up a value of 9 returns *Nine* from the lookup table in D1:E10. The formula in cell C1 is

    =VLOOKUP(B1,D1:E10,2,FALSE)

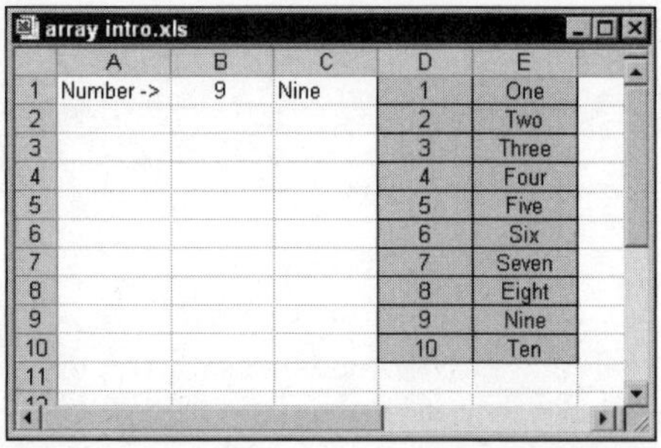

	A	B	C	D	E
1	Number ->	9	Nine	1	One
2				2	Two
3				3	Three
4				4	Four
5				5	Five
6				6	Six
7				7	Seven
8				8	Eight
9				9	Nine
10				10	Ten
11					

Figure 14-18: You can replace the lookup table in D1:E10 with an array constant.

You can use a two-dimensional array in place of the lookup range. The following formula returns the same result as the previous formula, but it does not require the lookup range in D1:E1:

```
=VLOOKUP(B1,{1,"One";2,"Two";3,"Three";4,"Four";5,"Five";
6,"Six";7,"Seven";8,"Eight";9,"Nine";10,"Ten"},2,FALSE)
```

✦ ✦ ✦

Performing Magic with Array Formulas

✦ ✦ ✦ ✦

In This Chapter

More examples of
single-cell array
formulas

More examples of
multicell array
formulas

Returning an array
from a custom VBA
function

✦ ✦ ✦ ✦

The preceding chapter provided an introduction to arrays and array formulas and presented some basic examples to whet your appetite. This chapter continues the saga and provides many useful examples that further demonstrate the power of this feature.

I selected the examples in this chapter to provide a good assortment of the various uses for array formulas. Most can be used as-is. You will, of course, need to adjust the range names or references used. Also, you can modify many of the examples easily to work in a slightly different manner.

On the CD-ROM   Each of the examples in this chapter is demonstrated in a file on the companion CD-ROM. The CD-ROM also contains additional examples not discussed here.

Working with Single-Cell Array Formulas

As I described in the preceding chapter, you enter single-cell array formulas into a single cell (not into a range of cells). These array formulas work with arrays contained in a range or that exist in memory. This section provides some additional examples of such array formulas.

Summing a range that contains errors

You may have discovered that the Excel SUM function doesn't work if you attempt to sum a range that contains one or more error values (such as #DIV/0! or #N/A). Figure 15-1 shows an example. The Sum formula in cell G8 returns an error value because the range that it sums (G1:G7) contains errors.

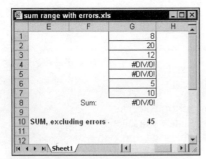

Figure 15-1: An array formula can sum a range of values, even if the range contains errors.

The following array formula, in cell G10, returns a sum of the values, even if the range contains error values:

```
=SUM(IF(ISERROR(G1:G7),"",G1:G7))
```

This formula works by creating a new array that contains the original values but without the errors. The IF function effectively filters out error values by replacing them with an empty string. The SUM function then works on this "filtered" array. This technique also works with other functions, such as MIN and MAX.

Note   You may want to use a function other than ISERROR. The ISERROR function returns TRUE for any error value: #N/A, #VALUE!, #REF!, #DIV/0!, #NUM!, #NAME?, or #NULL!. The ISERR function returns TRUE for any error except #N/A. The ISNA function returns TRUE only if the cell contains #N/A.

Counting the number of error values in a range

The following array formula is similar to the previous example, but it returns a count of the number of error values in a range named *Data*:

```
{=SUM(IF(ISERROR(Data),1,0))}
```

This formula creates an array that consists of 1s (if the corresponding cell contains an error) and 0s (if the corresponding cell does not contain an error value).

You can simplify the formula a bit by removing the third argument for the IF function. If this argument is not specified, the IF function returns FALSE if the condition is not satisfied (that is, the cell does not contain an error value). In this context, Excel treats FALSE as a 0 value. The array formula shown here performs exactly like the previous formula, but it doesn't use the third argument for the IF function:

```
{=SUM(IF(ISERROR(Data),1))}
```

Actually, you can simplify the formula even more:

```
{=SUM(ISERROR(Data)*1)}
```

This version of the formula relies on the fact that

```
TRUE * 1 = 1
```

and

```
FALSE * 1 = 0
```

Summing based on a condition

Often, you need to sum values based on one or more conditions. The array formula that follows, for example, returns the sum of the positive values (it excludes negative values) in a range named *Data*:

```
{=SUM(IF(Data>0,Data))}
```

The IF function creates a new array that consists only of positive values and False values. This array is passed to the SUM function, which ignores the False values and returns the sum of the positive values. The *Data* range can consist of any number of rows and columns.

You can also use the Excel program's SUMIF function for this example. The following formula, which is not an array formula, returns the same result as the preceding array formula:

```
=SUMIF(Data,">0")
```

For multiple conditions, however, using SUMIF gets tricky. For example, if you want to sum only values that are greater than 0 and less than or equal to 5, you can use this non-array formula:

```
SUMIF(data,">0",data)-SUMIF(data,">5",data)
```

This formula sums the values that are greater than zero and then subtracts the sum of the values that are greater than 5. This can be confusing.

Following is an array formula that performs the same calculation:

```
{=SUM((Data>0)*(Data<=5)*Data)}
```

This formula multiplies three arrays together, and calculates the sum. The first two arrays consist of TRUE (1) or FALSE (0) values.

This formula also has a limitation: It will return an error if the *Data* range contains one or more non-numeric cells.

Caution   Contrary to what you may expect, you cannot use the AND function in an array formula. The following array formula, while quite logical, doesn't return the correct result:

```
{=SUM(IF(AND(Data>0,Data<=5),Data))}
```

You can also write an array formula that combines criteria using an OR condition. For example, to sum the values that are less than 0 or greater than 5, use the following array formula:

```
{=SUM(IF((Data<0)+(Data>5),Data))}
```

To understand how this formula works, keep in mind that the argument for the IF function returns TRUE if either Data<0 or Data>5. Otherwise, the argument returns FALSE. If it's FALSE, then the item of the Data range is not included in the sum.

Caution   As with the AND function, you cannot use the OR function in an array formula. The following formula, for example, does not return the correct result:

```
{=SUM(IF(OR(Data<0,Data>5),Data))}
```

Summing the *n* largest values in a range

The following array formula returns the sum of the 10 largest values in a range named *Data*:

```
{=SUM(LARGE(Data,ROW(INDIRECT("1:10"))))}
```

The LARGE function is evaluated 10 times, each time with a different second argument (1, 2, 3, and so on up to 10). The results of these calculations are stored in a new array, and that array is used as the argument for the SUM function.

To sum a different number of values, replace the 10 in the argument for the INDI-RECT function with another value. To sum the *n smallest* values in a range, use the SMALL function instead of the LARGE function.

Computing an average that excludes zeros

Figure 15-2 shows a simple worksheet that calculates average sales. The formula in cell B14 is

```
=AVERAGE(B5:B12)
```

	A	B	C	D	E	F
	single-cell array formulas.xls					
1	Exclude zero from average					
2						
3						
4	Sales Person	Sales				
5	Abner	23,991				
6	Baker	15,092				
7	Charleston	0				
8	Davis	11,893				
9	Ellerman	32,116				
10	Flugelhart	29,089				
11	Gallaway	0				
12	Harrison	33,211				
13						
14		18,174 <-- Average with zeros				
15		24,232 <-- Average without zeros (array formula)				
16						

Figure 15-2: The calculated average includes cells that contain a 0.

This formula, of course, calculates the average of the values in B5:B12. Two of the sales staff had the week off, however, so this average doesn't accurately describe the average sales per representative.

Note   The AVERAGE function ignores blank cells, but it does not ignore cells that contain 0.

The following array formula returns the average of the range but excludes the cells containing 0:

```
{=AVERAGE(IF(B5:B12<>0,B5:B12))}
```

This formula creates a new array that consists only of the non-zero values in the range. The AVERAGE function then uses this new array as its argument. You also can get the same result with a regular (non-array) formula:

```
=SUM(B5:B12)/COUNTIF(B5:B12,"<>0")
```

This formula uses the COUNTIF function to count the number of non-zero values in the range. This value is divided into the sum of the values.

Determining whether a particular value appears in a range

To determine whether a particular value appears in a range of cells, you can choose the Edit ⇨ Find command and do a search of the worksheet. But you also can make this determination by using an array formula.

Figure 15-3 shows a worksheet with a list of names in A5:E24 (named *NameList*). An array formula in cell D3 checks the name entered into cell C3 (named *TheName*). If the name exists in the list of names, the formula displays the text *Found*. Otherwise, it displays *Not Found*.

A	B	C	D	E	F
1 Is a value contained in a range?					
2					
3 Enter a Name -->		Kathy	Found		
4					
5 Al	Daniel	Harold	Lyle	Richard	
6 Allen	Dave	Ian	Maggie	Rick	
7 Andrew	David	Jack	Margaret	Robert	
8 Anthony	Dennis	James	Marilyn	Rod	
9 Arthur	Don	Jan	Mark	Roger	
10 Barbara	Donald	Jeff	Marvin	Ronald	
11 Bernard	Doug	Jeffrey	Mary	Russ	
12 Beth	Douglas	Jerry	Matt	Sandra	
13 Bill	Ed	Jim	Mel	Scott	
14 Bob	Edward	Joe	Merle	Simon	
15 Brian	Eric	John	Michael	Stacy	
16 Bruce	Fran	Joseph	Michelle	Stephen	
17 Cark	Frank	Karl	Mike	Steven	
18 Carl	Fred	Kathy	Norman	Stuart	
19 Charles	Gary	Keith	Patrick	Susan	
20 Chris	George	Kenneth	Paul	Terry	
21 Chuck	Glenn	Kevin	Peter	Thomas	
22 Clark	Gordon	Larry	Phillip	Timothy	
23 Curt	Greg	Leonard	Ray	Vincent	
24 Dan	Gregory	Louise	Rebecca	William	

Figure 15-3: Using an array formula to determine if a range contains a particular value.

The array formula in cell D3 is

```
{=IF(OR(TheName=NameList),"Found","Not Found")}
```

This formula compares *TheName* to each cell in the *NameList* range. It builds a new array that consists of logical TRUE or FALSE values. The OR function returns TRUE if any one of the values in the new array is TRUE. The IF function uses this result to determine which message to display.

A simpler form of this formula follows. This formula displays TRUE if the name is found, and returns FALSE otherwise.

```
{=OR(TheName=NameList)}
```

Counting the number of differences in two ranges

The following array formula compares the corresponding values in two ranges (named *MyData* and *YourData*) and returns the number of differences in the two ranges. If the contents of the two ranges are identical, the formula returns 0.

```
{=SUM(IF(MyData=YourData,0,1))}
```

Tip   The two ranges must be the same size and of the same dimensions.

This formula works by creating a new array of the same size as the ranges being compared. The IF function fills this new array with 0s and 1s. (0 if a difference is found, and 1 if the corresponding cells are the same.) The SUM function then returns the sum of the values in the array.

The following formula, which is simpler, is another way of calculating the same result.

```
{=SUM(1*(MyData<>YourData))}
```

This version of the formula relies on the fact that

```
TRUE * 1 = 1
```

and

```
FALSE * 1 = 0
```

Returning the location of the maximum value in a range

The following array formula returns the row number of the maximum value in a single-column range named *Data*:

```
{=MIN(IF(Data=MAX(Data),ROW(Data), ""))}
```

The IF function creates a new array that corresponds to the *Data* range. If the corresponding cell contains the maximum value in *Data*, the array contains the row number; otherwise, it contains an empty string. The MIN function uses this new array as its second argument, and it returns the smallest value, which corresponds to the row number of the maximum value in *Data*.

If the *Data* range contains more than one cell that has the maximum value, the row of the first maximum cell is returned.

The following array formula is similar to the previous one, but it returns the actual cell address of the maximum value in the *Data* range. It uses the ADDRESS function, which takes two arguments: a row number and a column number.

```
{=ADDRESS(MIN(IF(Data=MAX(Data),ROW(Data), "")),COLUMN(Data))}
```

Finding the row of a value's *n*th occurrence in a range

The following array formula returns the row number within a single-column range named *Data* that contains the *n*th occurrence of the value in a cell named *Value*:

```
{=SMALL(IF(Data=Value,ROW(Data), ""),n)}
```

The IF function creates a new array that consists of the row number of values from the *Data* range that are equal to *Value*. Values from the *Data* range that are not equal to *Value* are replaced with an empty string. The SMALL function works on this new array and returns the *n*th smallest row number.

The formula returns #NUM! if the *Value* is not found or if *n* exceeds the number of the values in the range.

Returning the longest text in a range

The following array formula displays the text string in a range (named *Data*) that has the most characters. If multiple cells contain the longest text string, the first cell is returned.

```
{=INDEX(Data,MATCH(MAX(LEN(Data)),LEN(Data),FALSE),1)}
```

This formula works with two arrays, both of which contain the length of each item in the *Data* range. The MAX function determines the largest value, which corresponds to the longest text item. The MATCH function calculates the offset of the cell that contains the maximum length. The INDEX function returns the contents of the cell containing the most characters. This function works only if the *Data* range consists of a single column.

Determining whether a range contains valid values

You may have a list of items that you need to check against another list. For example, you may import a list of part numbers into a range named *MyList*, and you want to ensure that all of the part numbers are valid. You can do this by comparing the items in the imported list to the items in a master list of part numbers (named *Master*).

The following array formula returns TRUE if every item in the range named *MyList* is found in the range named *Master*. Both of these ranges must consist of a single column, but they don't need to contain the same number of rows.

```
{=ISNA(MATCH(TRUE,ISNA(MATCH(MyList,Master,0)),0))}
```

The array formula that follows returns the number of invalid items. In other words, it returns the number of items in *MyList* that do not appear in *Master*.

```
{=SUM(1*ISNA(MATCH(MyList,Master,0)))}
```

To return the first invalid item in *MyList*, use the following array formula:

```
{=INDEX(MyList,MATCH(TRUE,ISNA(MATCH(MyList,Master,0)),0))}
```

Summing the digits of an integer

The following array formula calculates the sum of the digits in a positive integer, which is stored in cell A1. For example, if cell A1 contains the value 409, the formula returns 13 (the sum of 4, 0, and 9).

```
{=SUM(MID(A1,ROW(INDIRECT("1:"&LEN(A1))),1)*1)}
```

To understand how this formula works, start with the ROW function, as shown here:

```
{=ROW(INDIRECT("1:"&LEN(A1)))}
```

This function returns an array of consecutive integers beginning with 1 and ending with the number of digits in the value in cell A1. For example, if cell A1 contains the value 409, the LEN function returns 3, and the array generated by the ROW functions is

```
{1,2,3}
```

 Cross-Reference For more information about using the INDIRECT function to return this array, see Chapter 14.

This array is then used as the second argument for the MID function. The MID part of the formula, simplified a bit and expressed as values, is the following:

```
{=MID(409,{1,2,3},1)*1}
```

This function generates an array with three elements:

```
{4,0,9}
```

By simplifying again and adding the SUM function, the formula looks like this:

```
{=SUM({4,0,9})}
```

This produces the result of 13.

Note

The values in the array created by the MID function are multiplied by 1 because the MID function returns a string. Multiplying by 1 forces a numeric value result. Alternatively, you can use the VALUE function to force a numeric string to become a numeric value.

Notice that the formula does not work with a negative value because the negative sign is not a numeric value. The following formula solves this problem by using the ABS function to return the absolute value of the number. Figure 15-4 shows a worksheet that uses this formula in cell B2.

```
{=SUM(VALUE(MID(ABS(A2),ROW(INDIRECT("1:"&LEN(ABS(A2)))),1)))}
```

The formula was copied down to calculate the sum of the digits for other values in column A.

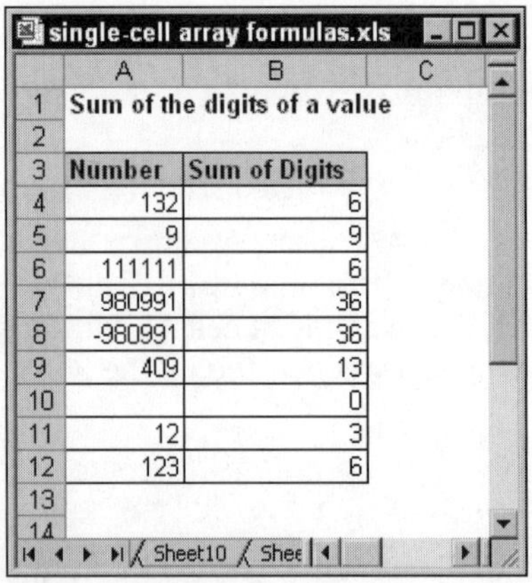

	A	B
1	Sum of the digits of a value	
2		
3	**Number**	**Sum of Digits**
4	132	6
5	9	9
6	111111	6
7	980991	36
8	-980991	36
9	409	13
10		0
11	12	3
12	123	6
13		

Figure 15-4: An array formula calculates the sum of the digits in an integer.

Summing rounded values

Figure 15-5 shows a simple worksheet that demonstrates a common spreadsheet problem: rounding errors. As you can see, the grand total in cell E7 appears to display an incorrect amount. (That is, it's off by a penny.) The values in column E use a number format that displays two decimal places. The actual values, however, consist of additional decimal places that do not display due to rounding (as a result of the number format). The net effect of these rounding errors is a seemingly incorrect total. The total, which is actually $168.320997, displays as $168.32.

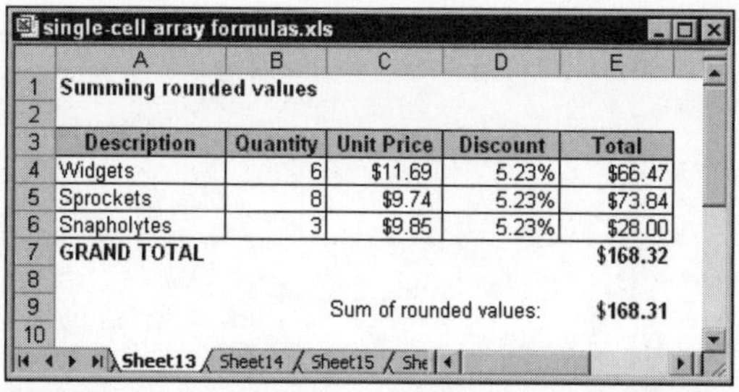
single-cell array formulas.xls

	A	B	C	D	E
1	Summing rounded values				
2					
3	Description	Quantity	Unit Price	Discount	Total
4	Widgets	6	$11.69	5.23%	$66.47
5	Sprockets	8	$9.74	5.23%	$73.84
6	Snapholytes	3	$9.85	5.23%	$28.00
7	GRAND TOTAL				$168.32
8					
9			Sum of rounded values:		$168.31
10					

Sheet13 / Sheet14 / Sheet15 / She

Figure 15-5: Using an array formula to correct rounding errors.

The following array formula creates a new array that consists of values in column E, rounded to two decimal places:

```
{=SUM(ROUND(E4:E6,2))}
```

This formula returns $168.31.

You also can eliminate these types of rounding errors by using the ROUND function in the formula that calculates each row total in column E. This technique does not require an array formula.

Summing every *n*th value in a range

Suppose you have a range of values and you want to compute the sum of every third value in the list — the first, the fourth, the seventh, and so on. One solution is to hard-code the cell addresses in a formula. But a better solution is to use an array formula.

Note to the data in Figure 15-6. The values are stored in a range named *Data*, and the value of *n* is in cell D2 (named *n*).

The following array formula returns the sum of every *n*th value in the range:

```
{SUM(IF(MOD(ROW(INDIRECT("1:"&COUNT(Data)))-1,n)=0,Data,""))}
```

This formula returns 70, which is the sum of every third value in the range.

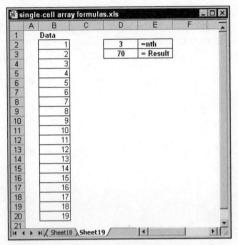

Figure 15-6: An array formula returns the sum of every *n*th value in the range.

This formula generates an array of consecutive integers, and the MOD function uses this array as its first argument. The second argument for the MOD function is the value of *n*. The MOD function creates another array that consists of the remainders when each row number is divided by *n*. When the array item is 0 (that is, the row is evenly divisible by *n*), the corresponding item in the *Data* range will be included in the sum.

You find that this formula fails when *n* is 0 (that is, sums no items). The modified array formula that follows uses an IF function to handle this case:

```
{=IF(n=0,0,SUM(IF(MOD(ROW(INDIRECT("1:"&COUNT(data)))-
1,n)=0,data,"")))}
```

This formula works only when the *Data* range consists of a single column of values. It does not work for a multicolumn range or for a single row of values.

To make the formula work with a horizontal range, you need to transpose the array of integers generated by the ROW function. Excel's TRANPOSE function is just the ticket. The modified array formula that follows works only with a horizontal *Data* range:

```
{=IF(n=0,0,SUM(IF(MOD(TRANSPOSE(ROW(INDIRECT("1:"&COUNT(Data)))
)-1,n)=0,Data,"")))}
```

Using Excel's Formula Evaluator

If you would like to better understand how some of these complex array formulas work, consider using a handy tool: The Formula Evaluator. Select the cell that contains the formula, and then choose Tools ➪ Formula Auditing ➪ Evaluate Formula. You'll see the Evaluate Formula dialog box shown below.

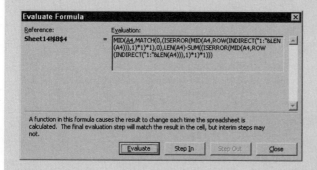

Click the Evaluate button repeatedly to see the intermediate results as the formula is being calculated.

Removing non-numeric characters from a string

The following array formula extracts a number from a string that contains text. For example, consider the string *ABC145Z*. The formula returns the numeric part, 145.

```
{=MID(A1,MATCH(0,(ISERROR(MID(A1,ROW(INDIRECT
("1:"&LEN(A1))),1)*1)*1),0),LEN(A1)-SUM((ISERROR
(MID(A1,ROW(INDIRECT("1:"&LEN(A1))),1)*1)*1))))}
```

This formula works only with a single embedded number. For example, it fails with a string like *X45Z99*.

Determining the closest value in a range

The array formula that follows returns the value in a range named *Data* that is closest to another value (named *Target*):

```
{=INDEX(Data,MATCH(SMALL(ABS(Target-Data),1),ABS(Target-
Data),0)))}
```

If two values in the *Data* range are equidistant from the *Target* value, the formula returns the first one in the list. Figure 15-7 shows an example of this formula. In this case, the *Target* value is 45. The array formula in cell D5 returns 48 — the value closest to 45.

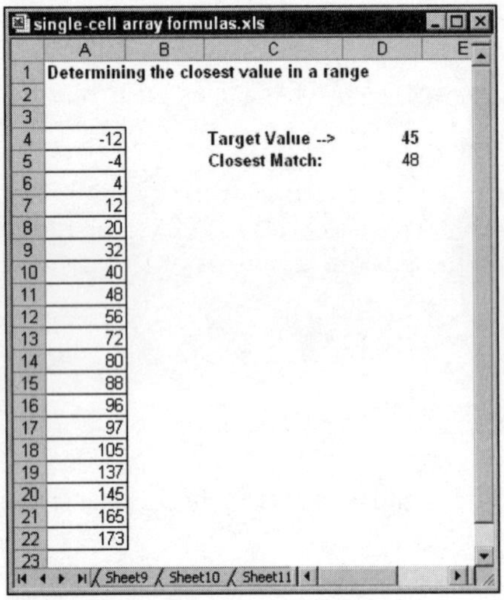

Figure 15-7: An array formula returns the closest match.

Returning the last value in a column

Suppose that you have a worksheet that you update frequently by adding new data to columns. You may need a way to reference the last value in column A (the value most recently entered). If column A contains no empty cells, the solution is relatively simple and doesn't require an array formula:

```
=OFFSET(A1,COUNTA(A:A)-1,0)
```

This formula uses the COUNTA function to count the number of nonempty cells in column A. This value (minus 1) is used as the second argument for the OFFSET function. For example, if the last value is in row 100, COUNTA returns 100. The OFFSET function returns the value in the cell 99 rows down from cell A1 in the same column.

If column A has one or more empty cells interspersed, which is frequently the case, the preceding formula won't work because the COUNTA function doesn't count the empty cells.

The following array formula returns the contents of the last nonempty cell in the first 500 rows of column A:

```
{=INDEX(A1:A500,MAX(ROW(A1:A500)*(A1:A500<>"")))}
```

You can, of course, modify the formula to work with a column other than column A. To use a different column, change the four column references from A to whatever column you need. If the last nonempty cell occurs in a row beyond row 500, you need to change the two instances of 500 to a larger number. The fewer rows referenced in the formula, the faster the calculation speed.

Caution You cannot use this formula, as written, in the same column with which it's working. Attempting to do so generates a circular reference. You can, however, modify it. For example, to use the function in cell A1, change the references so they begin with row 2 instead of row 1.

Returning the last value in a row

The following array formula is similar to the previous formula, but it returns the last nonempty cell in a row (in this case, row 1):

```
{=INDEX(1:1,MAX(COLUMN(1:1)*(1:1<>"")))}
```

To use this formula for a different row, change the 1:1 reference to correspond to the row.

Ranking data with an array formula

Often, computing the rank orders for the values in a range of data is helpful. If you have a worksheet containing the annual sales figures for 20 salespeople, for example, you may want to know how each person ranks, from highest to lowest.

If you've used the Excel program's RANK function, you may have noticed that the ranks produced by this function don't handle ties the way that you may like. For example, if two values are tied for third place, the RANK function gives both of them a rank of 3. You may prefer to assign each an average (or midpoint) of the ranks — in other words, a rank of 3.5 for both values tied for third place.

Figure 15-8 shows a worksheet that uses two methods to rank a column of values (named *Sales*). The first method (column C) uses the Excel RANK function. Column D uses array formulas to compute the ranks.

	A	B	C	D	E	F	G
1	Ranking data with an array formula						
2							
3							
4	Salesperson	Sales	Excel's Rank Function	Ranks With Array Formula			
5	Adams	123,000	6	6			
6	Bigelow	98,000	9	10	Assigned middle rank		
7	Fredericks	98,000	9	10			
8	Georgio	98,000	9	10			
9	Jensen	25,000	12	12			
10	Juarez	101,000	8	8			
11	Klein	305,000	1	1			
12	Lynch	145,000	3	3.5	Assigned average rank		
13	Mayne	145,000	3	3.5			
14	Roberton	121,000	7	7			
15	Slokum	124,000	5	5			
16	Wu	150,000	2	2			
17							

Figure 15-8: Ranking data with the Excel program's RANK function and with array formulas.

The following is the array formula in cell D2:

```
{=SUM(1*(B2<=Sales))-(SUM(1*(B2=Sales))-1)/2}
```

This formula is copied to the cells below it.

> **Note**   Each ranking is computed with a separate array formula, not with an array formula entered into multiple cells.

Each array function works by computing the number of higher values and subtracting one half of the number of equal values minus 1.

Working with Multicell Array Formulas

The preceding chapter introduced array formulas entered into multicell ranges. In this section, I present a few more array multicell formulas. Most of these formulas return some or all of the values in a range, but rearranged in some way.

Returning only positive values from a range

The following array formula works with a single-column vertical range (named *Data*). The array formula is entered into a range that's the same size as *Data* and returns only the positive values in the *Data* range. (Zeroes and negative numbers are ignored.)

```
{=INDEX(Data,SMALL(IF(Data>0,ROW(INDIRECT("1:"&ROWS(Data)))),
ROW(INDIRECT("1:"&ROWS(Data))))))}
```

As you can see in Figure 15-9, this formula works, but not perfectly. The *Data* range is A5:A24, and the array formula is entered into C4:C24. However, the array formula displays `#NUM!` error values for cells that don't contain a value.

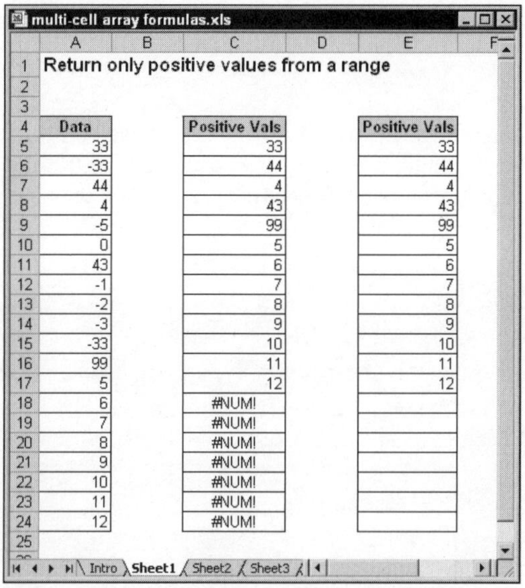

multi-cell array formulas.xls

Return only positive values from a range

Row	A	B	C	D	E
4	Data		Positive Vals		Positive Vals
5	33		33		33
6	-33		44		44
7	44		4		4
8	4		43		43
9	-5		99		99
10	0		5		5
11	43		6		6
12	-1		7		7
13	-2		8		8
14	-3		9		9
15	-33		10		10
16	99		11		11
17	5		12		12
18	6		#NUM!		
19	7		#NUM!		
20	8		#NUM!		
21	9		#NUM!		
22	10		#NUM!		
23	11		#NUM!		
24	12		#NUM!		

Intro / Sheet1 / Sheet2 / Sheet3

Figure 15-9: Using an array formula to return only the positive values in a range.

This more-complex array formula, entered into range E4:E24, avoids the error value display:

```
{=IF(ISERR(SMALL(IF(Data>0,ROW(INDIRECT("1:"&ROWS(Data)))),
ROW(INDIRECT("1:"&ROWS(Data))))),"",INDEX(Data,SMALL(IF
(Data>0,ROW(INDIRECT("1:"&ROWS(Data)))),ROW(INDIRECT
("1:"&ROWS(Data))))))}
```

Returning nonblank cells from a range

The following formula is a variation on the formula in the preceding section. This array formula works with a single-column vertical range named *Data*. The array formula is entered into a range of the same size as *Data* and returns only the nonblank cell in the *Data* range.

```
{=IF(ISERR(SMALL(IF(Data<>"",ROW(INDIRECT("1:"&ROWS(Data)))),
ROW(INDIRECT("1:"&ROWS(Data))))),"",INDEX(Data,SMALL(IF(Data
<>"",ROW(INDIRECT("1:"&ROWS(Data)))),ROW(INDIRECT("1:"&ROWS
(Data))))))}
```

Returning a list of unique items in a range

If you have a single-column range named *Data,* the following array formula returns a list of the unique items in the range:

```
{=INDEX(Data,SMALL(IF(MATCH(Data,Data,0)=ROW(INDIRECT
("1:"&ROWS(Data))),MATCH(Data,Data,0),""),ROW(INDIRECT
("1:"&ROWS(Data)))))}
```

This formula does not work if the *Data* range contains any blank cells. The unfilled cells of the array formula display #NUM!. Figure 15-10 shows an example. Range A5:A23 is named *Data*, and the array formula is entered into range C5:C23.

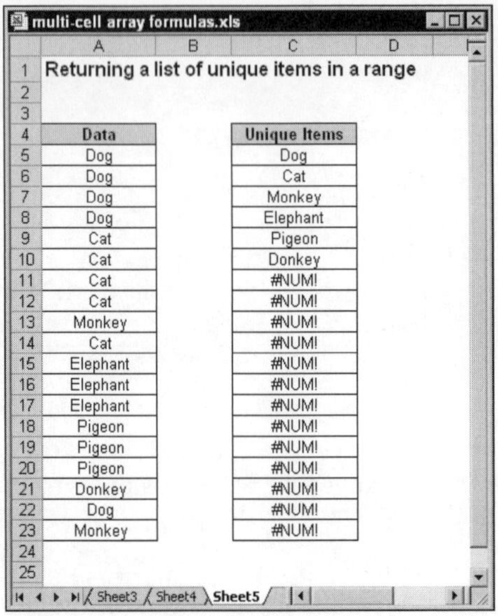

	A	B	C	D
4	Data		Unique Items	
5	Dog		Dog	
6	Dog		Cat	
7	Dog		Monkey	
8	Dog		Elephant	
9	Cat		Pigeon	
10	Cat		Donkey	
11	Cat		#NUM!	
12	Cat		#NUM!	
13	Monkey		#NUM!	
14	Cat		#NUM!	
15	Elephant		#NUM!	
16	Elephant		#NUM!	
17	Elephant		#NUM!	
18	Pigeon		#NUM!	
19	Pigeon		#NUM!	
20	Pigeon		#NUM!	
21	Donkey		#NUM!	
22	Dog		#NUM!	
23	Monkey		#NUM!	

Figure 15-10: Using an array formula to return unique items from a list.

Displaying a calendar in a range

Figure 15-11 shows a calendar displayed in a range of cells. The worksheet has two defined names: *m* (for the month) and *y* (for the year). A single array formula, entered into 42 cells, displays the corresponding calendar. The following array formula is entered into the range B6:H11:

```
{=IF(MONTH(DATE(y,m,1))<>MONTH(DATE(y,m,1)-
(WEEKDAY(DATE(y,m,1))-1)+{0;7;14;21;28;35}+
{0,1,2,3,4,5,6}),"",DATE(y,m,1)-(WEEKDAY
(DATE(y,m,1))-1)+{0;7;14;21;28;35}+{0,1,2,3,4,5,6})}
```

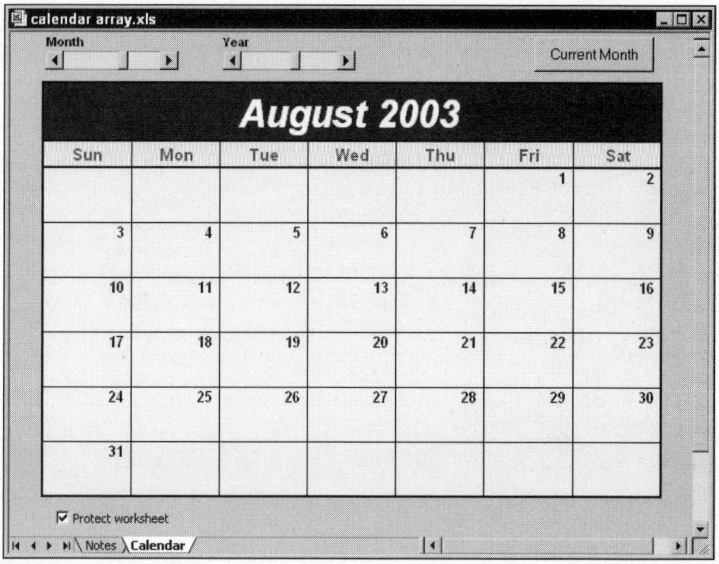

Figure 15-11: Displaying a calendar by using a single array formula.

The array formula actually returns date values, but the cells are formatted to display only the day portion of the date. Also, notice that the array formula uses array constants. You can simplify the array formula quite a bit by removing the IF function.

```
{=DATE(y,m,1)-(WEEKDAY(DATE(y,m,1))-1)+{0;7;14;21;28;35}+
{0,1,2,3,4,5,6}}
```

Cross-Reference   See Chapter 14 for more information about array constants.

This version of the formula displays the days from the preceding month and the next month. The IF function in the original formula checks each date to make sure it's in the current month. If not, the IF function returns an empty string.

✦   ✦   ✦

Creating Charts and Graphics

The three chapters in this section deal with charts and graphics. You'll learn how to use Excel's graphics capabilities to display your data in a chart. In addition, you'll learn to use Excel's other drawing tools to enhance your worksheets.

Getting Started Making Charts

When most people think of Excel, they think of crunching rows and columns of numbers. But as you probably know already, Excel is no slouch when it comes to presenting data visually in the form of a chart. This chapter presents an introductory overview of the Excel program's charting ability.

What Is a Chart?

I start with the basics. A *chart* is a visual representation of numeric values. Charts (also known as *graphs*) have been an integral part of spreadsheets since the early days of Lotus 1-2-3. Charts generated by early spreadsheet products were quite crude but have improved significantly over the years. You'll find that Excel provides you with the tools to create a wide variety of highly customizable charts.

Note   Although Excel can produce some great charts, it certainly doesn't generate the best-looking charts possible. And you'll eventually encounter some limitations with the Excel program's charting features. Not surprisingly, other software products that are devoted exclusively to charting can generate higher-quality charts and provide a great deal more flexibility. Refer to Appendix B for a list of other charting software that's available.

Displaying data in a well-conceived chart can make your numbers more understandable. Because a chart presents a picture, charts are particularly useful for summarizing a series of numbers and their interrelationships. Making a chart can often help you spot trends and patterns that may otherwise go unnoticed.

Figure 16-1 shows a worksheet that contains a simple column chart that depicts a company's sales volume by month.

Viewing the chart makes it very apparent that sales were off in the summer months (June through August), but they increased steadily during the final four months of the year. You could, of course, arrive at this same conclusion simply by studying the numbers. But viewing the chart makes the point much more quickly.

Figure 16-1: A simple column chart depicts the monthly sales volume.

A column chart is just one of many different types of charts that you can create with Excel.

How Excel Handles Charts

Before you can create a chart, you must have some numbers — sometimes known as *data*. The data, of course, is stored in the cells in a worksheet. Normally, the data that a chart uses resides in a single worksheet, but that's not a strict requirement. As you'll see, a chart can use data that's stored in any number of worksheets, and the worksheets can even be in different workbooks.

A chart is essentially an *object* that Excel creates upon request. This object consists of one or more *data series,* displayed graphically. The appearance of the data series depends on the selected *chart type.* For example, if you create a line chart that uses two data series, the chart contains two lines, each representing one data series. The data for each series is stored in a separate row or column. Each point on the line is determined by the value in a single cell and is represented by a marker. You can distinguish each of the lines by its thickness, line style, color, or data markers (squares, circles, and so on).

Figure 16-2 shows a line chart that plots two data series across a 12-year period. I used different data markers (squares versus circles) to identify the two series, as shown in the *legend* at the bottom of the chart.

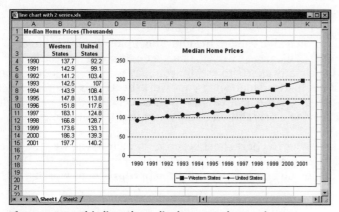

Figure 16-2: This line chart displays two data series.

A key point to keep in mind is that charts are *dynamic*. In other words, a chart series is linked to the data in your worksheet. If the data changes, the chart is updated automatically to reflect those changes.

After you've created a chart, you can always change its type, change the formatting, add new data series to it, or change an existing data series so that it uses data in a different range.

Before you create a chart, you need to determine whether you want it to be an embedded chart or one that resides on a chart sheet. However, you can change your mind later on. It's very easy to convert an embedded chart to a chart sheet (and vice versa).

Embedded charts

An *embedded chart* basically floats on top of a worksheet, on the worksheet's drawing layer. The charts shown previously in this chapter are both embedded charts.

As with other drawing objects (such as a text box or a shape), you can move an embedded chart, resize it, change its proportions, adjust its borders, and perform other operations. Using embedded charts enables you to print the chart next to the data that it uses.

To make any changes to the actual chart in an embedded chart object, you must click it to *activate* the chart. When a chart is activated, Excel's menu changes: The Chart menu replaces the Data menu, and some of the other menus are also changed.

Chart sheets

When you create a chart on a chart sheet, the chart occupies the entire sheet. If you plan to print a chart on a page by itself, using a chart sheet is often your better choice. If you have many charts to create, you may want to create each one on a separate chart sheet to avoid cluttering your worksheet. This technique also makes locating a particular chart easier because you can change the names of the chart sheets' tabs to provide a description of the chart that it contains.

The Excel menus change when a chart sheet is active, similar to the way that they change when you select an embedded chart. The Chart menu replaces the Data menu, and other menus include commands that are appropriate for working with charts.

Excel displays a chart in a chart sheet in WYSIWYG (What You See Is What You Get) mode: The printed chart looks just like the image on the chart sheet. If the chart doesn't fit in the window, you can use the scroll bars to scroll it or adjust the zoom factor.

Tip   You can also size the chart in a chart sheet according to the window size by using the View ➪ Sized with Window command. When this setting is enabled, the chart adjusts itself when you resize the workbook window. (It always fits perfectly in the window.) In this mode, the chart that you're working on may or may not correspond to the way that it looks when printed.

If you create a chart on a chart sheet, you can easily convert it to an embedded chart. Choose Chart ➪ Location and then select the worksheet that holds the embedded chart from the As Object In drop-down box. Excel deletes the chart sheet and moves the chart to the sheet that you specify. This operation also works in the opposite direction: You can select an embedded chart and relocate it to a new chart sheet.

Note   A chart sheet can also contain one or more embedded charts. You can use the Chart ➪ Location command to move embedded charts to an existing chart sheet. The second drop-down box in the Chart Location dialog box includes chart sheets as well as worksheets.

Parts of a Chart

Refer to the chart in Figure 16-3 as you read the following description of the chart's elements.

This particular chart is a *combination chart* that displays two *data series:* Income and Profit Margin. Income is plotted as vertical columns, and the Profit Margin is plotted as a line with square markers. Each bar (or marker on the line) represents a single *data point* (the value in a cell).

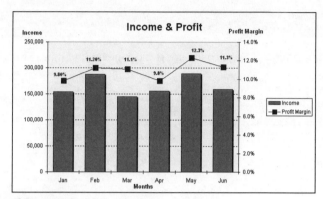

Figure 16-3: Parts of a chart.

The chart has a horizontal axis, known as the *category axis*. This axis represents the category for each data point (January, February, and so on). The label at the bottom, *Months,* is the category axis label.

Notice that this chart has two vertical axes. These are known as *value axes,* and each one has a different scale. The axis on the left is for the columns (Income), and the axis on the right is for the line (Profit Margin).

The value axes also display scale values. The axis on the left displays scale values from 0 to 250,000, in *major unit* increments of 50,000. The value axis on the right uses a different scale: 0 percent to 14 percent in increments of 2 percent.

A chart with two value axes is appropriate because the two data series vary dramatically in scale. If the Profit Margin data were plotted using the left axis, the line would not even be visible.

Most charts provide some method of identifying the data series or data points. A *legend,* for example, is often used to identify the various series in a chart. In this example, the legend appears on the right side of the chart. Some charts also display *data labels* to identify specific data points. The example chart displays data labels for the Profit Margin series, but not for the Income series. In addition, most charts (including the example chart) contain a *chart title* and additional labels to identify the axes or categories.

The example chart also contains horizontal *gridlines* (which correspond to the left value axis). Gridlines are basically extensions of the value axis scale, which makes it easier for the viewer to determine the magnitude of the data points.

In addition, all charts have a *chart area* (the entire background area of the chart) and a *plot area* (the part that shows the actual chart, including the plotted data, the axes, and the axis labels.).

Chart Limitations

The following table lists the limitations of Excel charts. Most users never find these limitations to be a problem.

Item	Limitation
Charts on a worksheet	Limited by available memory
Worksheets referred to by a chart	255
Data series in a chart	255
Data points in a data series	32,000
Data points in a data series (3-D charts)	4,000
Total data points in a chart	256,000

Charts will have additional parts or fewer parts, depending on the chart type. For example, a pie chart has *slices* and no axes. A 3-D chart may have *walls* and a *floor*. Many other types of items can be added to a chart. For example, you can add a *trend line* or display *error bars*.

Creating Charts

This section discusses the various methods available to create a chart. For maximum flexibility, you probably want to use the Chart Wizard for creating most of your charts.

Creating a chart with one keystroke

For a quick demonstration of how easily you can create a chart, follow these steps. This example creates a chart on a separate chart sheet.

1. Enter data to be charted into a worksheet. Figure 16-4 shows an example of data that's appropriate for a chart.

2. Select the range of data that you entered in Step 1, including the row and column titles. For example, if you entered the data shown in Figure 16-4, select A1:C4.

3. Press F11. Excel inserts a new chart sheet (named Chart1) and displays the chart, based on the selected data. Figure 16-5 shows the result.

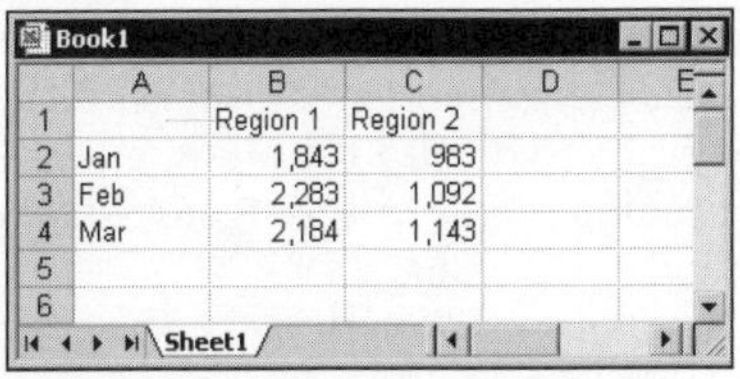

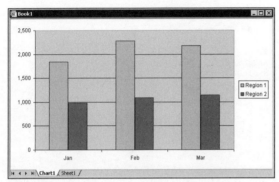

Figure 16-4: This data would make a good chart.

Figure 16-5: This chart was generated with one keystroke.

In this simple example, Excel created its default chart type (which is a two-dimensional column chart), using the default settings. This chart, like all charts, can be further customized in many ways. For example, you would probably want to add a title to the chart, and you may prefer to make other customizations. These operations are all covered later in this chapter.

Creating a chart with a mouse click

To create an embedded chart with a single mouse click:

1. Make sure that the Chart toolbar is displayed. If the toolbar is not displayed, right-click any toolbar and choose Chart.

2. Select the data to be charted.

3. Click the Chart Type tool on the Chart toolbar and select a chart type from the displayed icons.

Excel adds the chart to the worksheet, using the default settings for the chart type you selected.

Note

The Chart Type tool on the Chart toolbar displays an icon for the last selected chart. However, this tool works like a list box; you can expand it to display 18 chart types (as shown in Figure 16-6). Just click the arrow to display the additional chart types. For more information about the Chart toolbar, refer to the nearby sidebar, "The Chart Toolbar."

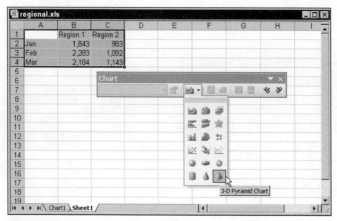

Figure 16-6: The Chart Type tool expands so that you can create the type of chart you want.

Using the Chart Wizard

The preceding sections describe two quick ways to generate a chart. The resulting chart may or may not be what you were expecting. If not, you can always modify the chart or start over and use the Chart Wizard for more control.

The most common — and the most flexible — way to create a chart is to use the Chart Wizard. To use the Chart Wizard:

1. Select the data that you want to chart (optional).

2. Choose Insert ➪ Chart (or click the Chart Wizard tool on the Standard toolbar).

3. Specify various options in Steps 1 through 4 of the Chart Wizard.

4. Click Finish to create the chart.

The next section provides additional information about using the Chart Wizard.

The Chart Toolbar

The Chart toolbar is a context-sensitive toolbar that appears when you click an embedded chart, activate a chart sheet, or choose View ➪ Toolbars ➪ Chart. This toolbar, shown in the accompanying figure, includes nine tools.

You can use these tools to make some common chart changes:

✦ **Chart Objects:** When a chart is activated, the name of the selected chart element is displayed in this control. In addition, you can select a particular chart element by using the drop-down list.

✦ **Format Selected Object:** Displays the Format dialog box for the selected chart element.

✦ **Chart Type:** Expands to display 18 chart types when you click the arrow. After this tool is expanded, you can drag it to a new location — creating, in effect, a miniature floating toolbar.

✦ **Legend:** Toggles the legend display in the active chart.

✦ **Data Table:** Toggles the display of the data table in a chart.

✦ **By Row:** Plots the data by rows.

✦ **By Column:** Plots the data by columns.

✦ **Angle Clockwise:** Displays the selected text at a −45-degree angle.

✦ **Angle Counterclockwise:** Displays the selected text at a +45-degree angle.

The Angle tools are toggles. Click a second time and Excel no longer angles the selected text.

In addition, several tools on the other toolbars work with charts, including the Fill Color, Font Color, Bold, Italic, and Font tools.

Excel includes several other chart-related tools that aren't on the Chart toolbar. You can customize the toolbar to include these additional tools. To customize your Chart toolbar:

1. Make sure the Chart toolbar is displayed.

2. Choose View ➪ Toolbars ➪ Customize to display the Customize dialog box.

3. Select the Commands tab.

4. Choose the Charting from Categories list box.

5. Click an item in the Commands list and drag it to your Chart toolbar.

6. Repeat Step 5 for other commands that you'd like to add.

7. Click Close to close the Customize dialog box.

Hands On: Creating a Chart with the Chart Wizard

The Chart Wizard consists of four sequential dialog boxes that prompt you for various settings for your chart. By the time that you reach the last dialog box, the chart is usually fairly close to what you need. In case you've never created an Excel chart, this section introduces this feature with a hands-on example.

Selecting the data

Before you start the Chart Wizard, select the data that you want to include in the chart. Your selection should include such items as labels and series identifiers (row and column headings). Preselecting the chart data isn't necessary but makes creating the chart easier. If you don't select the data before invoking the Chart Wizard, you can select it in the second Chart Wizard dialog box.

Figure 16-7 shows a worksheet with a range of data set up for a chart. This data consists of the percentage of U.S. citizens who read a daily newspaper, categorized by year and by education level.

 On the CD-ROM   This workbook is available on the companion CD-ROM.

For this example, select the range A3:E9. This range includes the category labels but not the title (which is in A1).

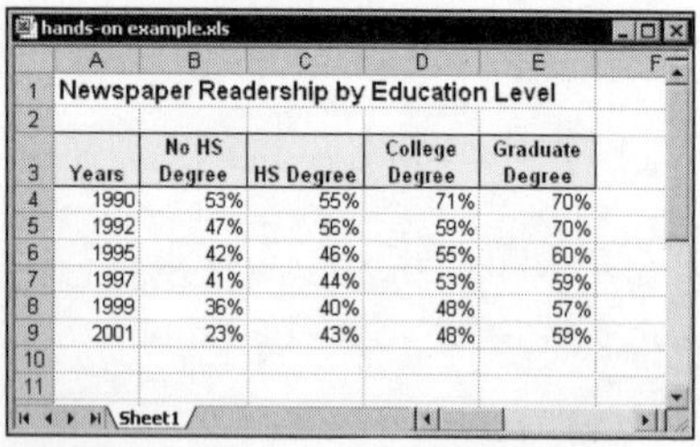

	A	B	C	D	E	F
1	Newspaper Readership by Education Level					
2						
3	Years	No HS Degree	HS Degree	College Degree	Graduate Degree	
4	1990	53%	55%	71%	70%	
5	1992	47%	56%	59%	70%	
6	1995	42%	46%	55%	60%	
7	1997	41%	44%	53%	59%	
8	1999	36%	40%	48%	57%	
9	2001	23%	43%	48%	59%	
10						
11						

Figure 16-7: Data to be charted.

Note   The data that you use in a chart doesn't have to be in contiguous cells. You can press Ctrl and make a multiple selection. The initial data, however, must be on a single worksheet. If you need to plot data that exists on more than one worksheet, you can add more series after the chart is created (or use the Series tab in Step 2 of the Chart Wizard). In all cases, however, data for a single chart series must reside on one sheet. In other words, the data for a chart series cannot extend across multiple worksheets.

After you select the data, start the Chart Wizard, either by clicking the Chart Wizard button on the Standard toolbar or by selecting Insert ➪ Chart. Excel displays the first of four Chart Wizard dialog boxes.

While using the Chart Wizard, you can go back to the preceding step by clicking the Back button. Or you can click Finish to close the Chart Wizard. If you close the Chart Wizard early, Excel creates the chart by using the information that you provided up to that point.

Don't be too concerned about creating the perfect chart. You can always change, at any time, any choice that you make in the Chart Wizard.

Chart Wizard — Step 1 of 4

Figure 16-8 shows the first Chart Wizard dialog box, in which you select the chart type. This dialog box has two tabs: Standard Types and Custom Types. The Standard Types tab displays the 14 basic chart types and the subtypes for each. The Custom Types tab displays some customized charts (including user-defined custom charts).

For this example, a Line chart with markers may be a good choice for this data. Select Line from the Chart Type list box and then click the appropriate icon for the Chart Sub-Type you prefer.

Tip   When you work in the Custom Types tab, the dialog box shows a preview of your data with the selected chart type. In the Standard Types tab, you get a preview by clicking the button labeled Press and Hold to View Sample. When you click this button, keep the mouse button pressed.

When you decide on a chart type and subtype, click the Next button to move to the next step.

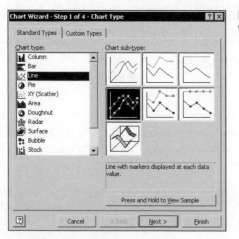

Figure 16-8: The first of four Chart Wizard dialog boxes.

Chart Wizard – Step 2 of 4

In the second step of the Chart Wizard (as shown in Figure 16-9), you

- ✦ Verify the data ranges to be used in the chart — and change them if necessary.
- ✦ Specify the orientation of the data (whether the data series are arranged in rows or in columns).
- ✦ Verify that Excel correctly identified the category data and the series data.

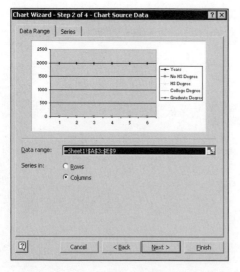

Figure 16-9: Step 2 of the Chart Wizard dialog box.

Verifying the data range

This step of the Chart Wizard dialog box contains two tabs: Data Range and Series. Click the Data Range tab.

The Data range field displays the range address that was selected when you started the Chart Wizard. If you selected only a single cell, this field displays Excel's best guess regarding the range to be plotted.

If the data range is not correct, you can change it by clicking in the Data Range field and then selecting the correct range by dragging in the worksheet. Or you can edit the range address manually.

Tip
    When you activate the Data Range field, you'll discover that this field is in point mode, which means that using the arrow keys on your keyboard selects data in the worksheet. If you would like to edit the actual range address listed in the Data Range, press F2 to get into edit mode.

For this example, the data range that was selected originally is correct.

Changing the data orientation

The orientation of the data has a drastic effect on the look of your chart. Excel has its own rules that it uses to determine the data orientation. If Excel guesses incorrectly, you can change it by selecting either the Rows or Columns radio buttons. This step of the Chart Wizard displays a small preview of your chart so that you can immediately see the effect of changing the chart's orientation.

For this example, Excel guessed correctly: The data is arranged in columns.

Specifying the category data and series data

Look carefully at the preview and you see that the chart is not correct. Excel (incorrectly) identified the years in column A as a data series. In fact, the years are category names and should be treated as text, not plotted as numeric values.

Because the Chart Wizard did not identify the categories, a change is required. This change is made by using the Series tab in Step 2 of the Chart Wizard (see Figure 16-10).

The Series list box shows the names of all the data series for the chart. Select a series in the list box, and the range address for its name and data are shown in the fields to the right. In this example, the Years series has its Name in range A3 and its Values in range A4:A9.

Because the series labeled *Years* is not really a series — it contains the Category (X) Axis Labels — you need to delete it from the Series list box. To do so, select it and click Remove. After removing the incorrect series, the preview updates. Now the chart is looking better — but the years are not displayed along the category (horizontal) axis.

The field for the Category (X) Axis Labels is empty, so you need to specify the range for the category labels. To do so, click in the field and select A4:A9. Now the preview chart looks correct (as shown in Figure 16-11). The years appear as categories on the horizontal axis, and the chart displays the four data series.

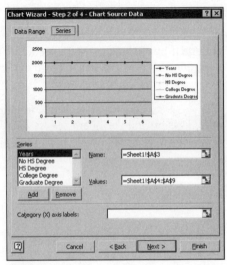

Figure 16-10: The Series tab in Step 2 of the Chart Wizard.

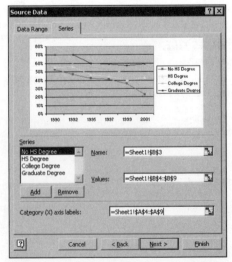

Figure 16-11: The incorrect series has been removed and the Category (X) Axis Labels have been specified.

Note   Excel uses the data type to identify category data. In this example, the years in column A are numeric values, so Excel treats them as data. Also, note that when category data is not specified, Excel uses consecutive integers on the Category axis: 1, 2, 3, and so on. In this example, you may think that formatting the years as text would cause Excel to treat them as categories — but it doesn't work. You can, however, precede each year value with an apostrophe. In such a case, the years are interpreted as text and assigned as the categories. Yet another option is to remove the column heading (Years) from cell A3. After doing so, Excel correctly identifies the data as category labels.

Click the Next button to advance to the next dialog box.

Chart Wizard — Step 3 of 4

In the third Chart Wizard dialog box, as shown in Figure 16-12, you specify most of the options for the chart. This dialog box has six tabs:

✦ **Titles:** Add titles to the chart. Note that these fields are not range selector fields. You must enter text, not a cell address.

✦ **Axes:** Turn on or off axes display and specify the type of axes.

✦ **Gridlines:** Specify gridlines, if any.

✦ **Legend:** Specify whether to include a legend and where to place it.

✦ **Data Labels:** Specify whether to show data labels and what type of labels.

✦ **Data Table:** Specify whether to display a table of the data.

Note   The options available in Step 3 of the Chart Wizard depend on the type of chart that you selected in Step 1.

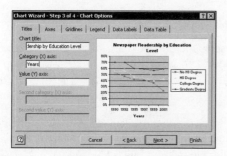

Figure 16-12: You specify the chart options in the third Chart Wizard dialog box.

When you make changes, the changes are reflected in the preview chart.

For this example, just accept the default setting except for the Titles tab. Specify the following titles:

✦ Chart Title: Newspaper Readership by Education Level

✦ Category (X) Axis: Years

After you select the chart options, click Next to move to the final dialog box.

Chart Wizard – Step 4 of 4

Step 4 of the Chart Wizard, as shown in Figure 16-13, is used to specify the location for the chart. Select As New Sheet to create the chart on a chart sheet, or select As Object In to create an embedded chart. Make your choice and click Finish.

Excel creates and displays the chart.

Note   If you create an embedded chart, Excel centers the chart in the workbook window and activates the chart. The proportions of the chart correspond to the proportions of the workbook window.

Changing the Default Chart Type

I mention the default chart type several times in this chapter. The *default chart type* is the chart that is created if you don't specify the type. Excel's default chart type is a 2-D clustered-column chart with a light-gray plot area, a legend on the right, and horizontal gridlines.

If you don't like the looks of this chart or if you typically use a different type of chart, you can easily change the default chart in the following manner:

1. Select your chart to activate it, and then select the Chart ➪ Chart Type command.

2. Choose the chart type that you want to use as the default chart. This can be a chart from either the Standard Types tab or the Custom Types tab.

3. Click the button labeled Set As Default Chart Type. You are asked to verify your choice.

If you have many charts of the same type to create, changing the default chart format to the chart type with which you're working is much more efficient than separately formatting each chart. Then you can create all your charts without having to select the chart type.

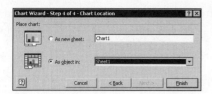

Figure 16-13: Step 4 of the Chart Wizard asks you where to put the chart.

Figure 16-14 shows the complete chart. You may or may not be satisfied with the chart. If not, modifying the chart to your liking is a simple matter.

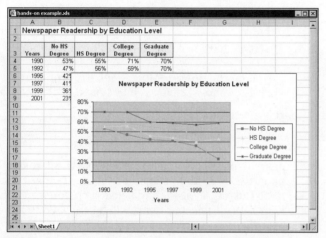

Figure 16-14: The end result of using the Chart Wizard.

Basic Chart Modifications

After you've created a chart, you can modify it in many ways. The modifications you can make to a chart are extensive. This section covers some of the more common chart modifications:

   ✦ Moving and resizing the chart

   ✦ Changing the chart type

   ✦ Moving chart elements

   ✦ Deleting chart elements

   ✦ Formatting the chart elements

Note   Before you can modify a chart, the chart must be activated. To activate an embedded chart, click it. Doing so activates the chart and also selects the element that you click. To activate a chart on a chart sheet, just click its sheet tab.

Moving and resizing a chart

If your chart is an embedded chart, you can freely move and resize it. Click the chart's border and then drag the border to move the chart. Drag any of the eight "handles" to resize the chart. The handles are the black squares that appear on the chart's corners and edges when you click the chart's border.

Changing the chart type

To change the chart type of the active chart, use one of the following methods:

✦ Choose the Chart Type button on the Chart toolbar. Click the drop-down arrow, and this button expands to show 18 basic chart types.

✦ Choose the Chart ➪ Chart Type command.

✦ Right-click and choose Chart Type from the shortcut menu.

The Chart ➪ Chart Type command displays a dialog box much like the first step of the Chart Wizard. Click the Standard Types tab to select one of the standard chart types (and a subtype), or click the Custom Types tab to select a customized chart. After selecting a chart type, click OK. The selected chart will be changed to the type you selected.

Note   If you've customized some aspects of your chart, choosing a new chart type from the Custom Types tab may override some or all of the changes you've made. For example, if you've added gridlines to the chart and then select a custom chart type that doesn't use gridlines, your gridlines disappear. Therefore, it's a good idea to make sure that you're satisfied with the chart before you make too many custom changes to it. However, you can always use Edit ➪ Undo to reverse your actions.

In the Custom Types tab, if you click the User-Defined option, the list box displays the name of any user-defined custom formats.

Copying a chart

To make an exact copy of an embedded chart, press and hold down the Ctrl key. Click the chart and then drag the mouse pointer to a new location. To make a copy of a chart sheet, use the same procedure, but drag the chart sheet's tab.

Deleting a chart

To delete an embedded chart, press Ctrl and click the chart (this selects the chart as an object). Then press Delete. To delete a chart sheet, right-click its sheet tab and choose Delete from the shortcut menu.

Moving and deleting chart elements

Some of the elements within a chart can be moved. The movable chart elements include the titles, the legend, and data labels. To move a chart element, simply click it to select it; then, drag it to the desired location in the chart. To delete a chart element, select it and then press Delete.

Other modifications

When a chart is activated, you can select various parts of the chart to work with. Modifying a chart is similar to everything else you do in Excel. First, you make a selection (in this case, select a chart element). Then you issue a command to do something with the selection. Right-clicking an element in a chart displays a shortcut menu. This menu often (but not always) contains the command you need.

You can use the Fill Color tool (which bears an image of a paint bucket) on the Formatting toolbar to change colors. For example, if you want to change the color of a series, select the series and choose the color you want from the Fill Color tool. You'll find that many other toolbar tools work with charts, too. For example, you can select the chart's legend and then click the Bold button to make the legend text bold.

When you double-click a chart element (or press Ctrl+1 after selecting it), its Formatting dialog box appears. The dialog box that appears varies, depending on the item selected. In most cases, the dialog box is of the tabbed variety. Many modifications are self-evident — for example, changing the font used in a title. Others, however, are a bit more tricky.

 Refer to Chapter 17 for more information about customizing and formatting charts.

In addition, you can right-click a chart element and get a shortcut menu that contains commands related to that element.

Printing Charts

Printing embedded charts is nothing special; you print them the same way that you print a worksheet. As long as you include the embedded chart in the range that you want to print, Excel prints the chart as it appears on-screen. When printing a sheet that contains embedded charts, it's a good idea to preview first to ensure that your charts do not span multiple pages.

Tip   If you select an embedded chart and then choose File ⇨ Print (or click the Print button), Excel prints the chart on a page by itself and does *not* print the worksheet.

If you don't want a particular embedded chart to appear on your printout, right-click a border of the chart and choose Format Chart Area from the shortcut menu. Click the Properties tab in the Format Chart Area dialog box and remove the check mark from the Print Object check box.

If you created the chart on a chart sheet, Excel prints the chart on a page by itself. If you open Excel's Page Setup dialog box when the chart sheet is active, the Sheet tab is replaced with a tab named Chart. Figure 16-15 shows the Chart tab of the Page Setup dialog box, which has several options.

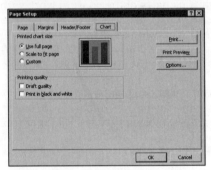

Figure 16-15: The Chart tab of the Page Setup dialog box.

✦ **Use Full Page:** Excel prints the chart to the full width and height of the page margins. This usually isn't a good choice because the chart's relative proportions change and you lose the WYSIWYG advantage.

✦ **Scale to Fit Page:** Expands the chart proportionally in both dimensions until one dimension fills the space between the margins. In other words, the aspect ratio of the chart is maintained. This option usually results in the best printout.

✦ **Custom:** Prints the chart as it appears on your screen. Select View ⇨ Sized with Window to make the chart correspond to the window size and proportions. The chart prints at the current window size and proportions.

The Printing quality options work just like those for worksheet pages. If you choose the Draft quality option for a chart sheet, Excel prints the chart, but its quality may not be high. (The actual effect depends on your printer.) Choosing the Print in Black and White option prints the data series with black-and-white patterns rather than colors. Most noncolor printers handle this fine, even if this option is not set. But you may want to experiment to determine the best output quality for your printer.

Understanding Chart Types

People who create charts usually do so in order to make a point or to communicate a specific message. Often, the message is explicitly stated in the chart's title or in a text box within the chart. The chart itself provides visual support.

Choosing the correct chart type is often a key factor in making the message compelling. Therefore, it's often well worth your time to experiment with various chart types to determine which one is most effective.

In almost every case, the underlying message in a chart is some type of *comparison*. Examples of some general types of comparisons include

✦ **Compare item to other items:** For example, a chart may compare sales in each of a company's sales regions.

✦ **Compare data over time:** For example, a chart may display sales by month and indicate trends over time.

✦ **Make relative comparisons:** An example is a common pie chart that depicts relative values in terms of pie "slices."

✦ **Compare data relationships:** An XY chart is ideal for this. For example, you might show the relationship between marketing expenditures and sales.

✦ **Frequency comparison:** A common histogram, for example, can be used to display the number (or percentage) of students who scored within a particular range.

✦ **Identify "outliers" or unusual situations:** If you have thousands of data points, creating a chart may help identify data that is not representative.

Choosing a chart type

A common question among Excel users is "How do I know which chart type to use for my data?" Unfortunately, there is no cut-and-dried answer to this question. Perhaps the best answer is a vague one: Use the chart type that gets your message across in the simplest way.

Figure 16-16 shows the same set of data plotted by using six different chart types. Although all six charts represent the same information (monthly Web site visitors), they look quite different from one another.

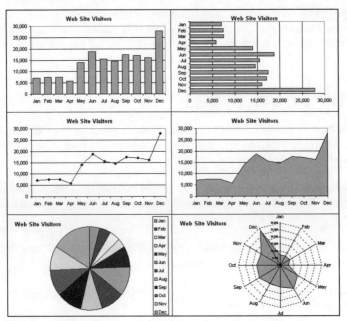

Figure 16-16: The same data, plotted by using six chart types.

The column chart (upper left) is probably the best choice for this particular set of data because it clearly shows the information for each month in discrete units. The bar chart (upper right) is similar to a column chart, but the axes are swapped. Most people are more accustomed to seeing time-based information extend from left to right rather than from top to bottom.

The line chart (middle left) may not be the best choice because it seems to imply that the data is continuous — that points exist in between the 12 actual data points. This same argument could be made against using an area chart (middle right).

The pie chart (lower left) is simply too confusing and does nothing to convey the time-based nature of the data. Pie charts are most appropriate for a data series in which you want to emphasize proportions among a relatively small number of data points. If you have too many data points, a pie chart can be impossible to interpret.

The radar chart (lower right) is clearly inappropriate for this data. People are not accustomed to viewing time-based information in a circular direction!

Fortunately, changing a chart's type is a very easy procedure, so you can experiment with various chart types until you find the one that represents your data accurately and clearly — and as simply as possible.

The remainder of this chapter contains lots of information about Excel's various chart types. The examples and discussion may give you a better handle on determining the most appropriate chart type for your data.

Standard chart types

When you use the Chart Wizard to create a chart, the first step is to select the type of chart. The first step of the Chart Wizard dialog box contains two tabs: Standard Types and Custom Types. Selecting an item in the Chart Type list box displays a number of subtypes for the chart type. For example, a Column chart has seven subtypes.

The remainder of this section discusses each of Excel's standard chart types and shows examples of each.

On the CD-ROM All the subsequent examples are available on this book's companion CD-ROM.

Column charts

Column charts are one of the most common chart types. A *column chart* displays each data point as a vertical column, the height of which corresponds to the value. The value scale is displayed on the vertical axis, which is usually on the left side of the chart. You can specify any number of data series, and the corresponding data points from each series can be stacked on top of each other. Typically, each data series is depicted in a different color or pattern.

Column charts are often used to compare discrete items, and they can depict the differences between items in a series or items across multiple series. Excel offers seven column-chart subtypes.

Figure 16-17 shows an example of a column chart that depicts annual sales for two products. From this chart, it is clear that Sprocket sales have always exceeded Widget sales. In addition, Widget sales have been declining over the years, whereas Sprocket sales are increasing.

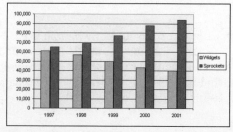

Figure 16-17: This column chart compares sales for two products.

The same data, in the form of a stacked column chart, is shown in Figure 16-18. This chart has the added advantage of depicting the combined sales over time. It shows that total sales have remained relatively steady over the years, but the relative proportions of the two products have changed.

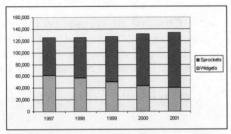

Figure 16-18: This stacked column chart displays sales by product and depicts the total sales.

Figure 16-19 shows the same sales data plotted as a 100% stacked column chart. This chart type shows the relative contribution of each product by year. Notice that the value axis displays percentage values, not sales amounts. This chart provides no information about the actual sales volumes. This type of chart is often a good alternative to using several pie charts. Instead of using a pie to show the relative sales volume in each year, the chart uses a column for each year.

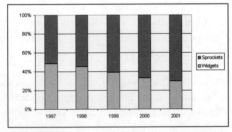

Figure 16-19: This 100% stacked column chart displays annual sales as a percentage.

The data is plotted with a 3-D column chart in Figure 16-20. Many people use this type of chart because it has more visual pizzazz. Although it may be more appealing visually, this type of chart often makes precise comparisons difficult because of the distorted perspective view. Generally speaking, a 3-D column chart is best used when the goal is to show general trends rather than precise comparisons.

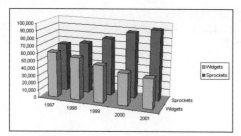

Figure 16-20: A 3-D column chart.

Bar charts

A bar chart is essentially a column chart that has been rotated 90 degrees clockwise. One distinct advantage to using a bar chart is that the category labels may be easier to read. Figure 16-21 shows a bar chart that displays a value for each of 10 survey items. The category labels are lengthy, and displaying them legibly with a column chart would be difficult. Excel offers six bar chart subtypes.

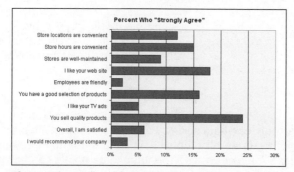

Figure 16-21: If you have lengthy category labels, a bar chart may be a good choice.

Note   Unlike a column chart, there is no subtype that displays multiple series along a third axis. (That is, there is no 3-D Bar Chart subtype type.)

As with a column chart, you can include any number of data series in a bar chart. In addition, the bars can be "stacked" from left to right.

Line charts

Line charts are often used to plot continuous data and are useful for identifying trends. For example, plotting daily sales as a line chart may enable you to identify sales fluctuations over time. Normally, the category axis for a line chart displays equal intervals. Excel supports seven line chart subtypes.

See Figure 16-22 for an example of a line chart that depicts daily sales (200 data points). Although the data varies quite a bit on a daily basis, the chart clearly depicts an upward trend.

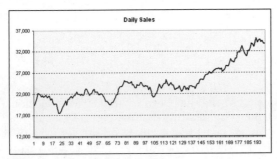

Figure 16-22: A line chart often can help you spot trends in your data.

A line chart can use any number of data series, and you distinguish the lines by using different colors, line styles, or markers.

Pie charts

A pie chart is useful when you want to show relative proportions or contributions to a whole. A pie chart can use only one data series. Pie charts are most effective with a small number of data points. Generally, a pie chart should use no more than five or six data points (or slices). A pie chart with too many data points can be very difficult to interpret.

Note   The values used in a pie chart must all be positive numbers. If you create a pie chart that uses one or more negative values, the negative values will be converted to positive values—which is probably not what you intended!

You can "explode" one or more slices of a pie chart for emphasis (as shown in Figure 16-23). Activate the chart and click any pie slice to select the entire pie. Then click the slice that you want to explode and drag it away from the center.

The pie of pie and bar of pie chart types enables you to display a secondary chart that provides more detail for one of the pie slices. Refer to Figure 16-24 for an example of a bar of pie chart. The pie chart shows the breakdown of four expense categories: Rent, Supplies, Miscellaneous, and Salary. The secondary bar chart provides an additional regional breakdown of the Salary category.

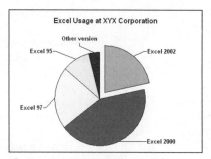

Figure 16-23: A pie chart with one slice exploded.

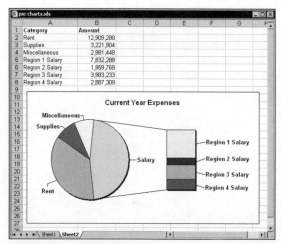

Figure 16-24: A bar of pie chart that shows detail for one of the pie slices.

The data used in the chart resides in A2:B8. When the chart was created, the Chart Wizard used its built-in defaults to make a guess at which categories belong to the secondary chart. In this case, the guess was to use the last three data points for the secondary chart — and the guess was incorrect.

To correct the chart, double-click any of the pie slices to display the Format Data Series dialog box. Click the Options tab and make the changes. In this example, I chose Split Series by Position, and specified that the Second Plot Contains the Last 4 Values in the series.

XY (scatter) charts

Another common chart type is an XY chart (also known as scattergrams or scatter plots). An XY chart differs from most other chart types in that both axes display values. (There is no category axis in an XY chart.)

This type of chart often is used to show the relationship between two variables. Figure 16-25 shows an example of an XY chart that plots the relationship between sales calls (horizontal axis) and actual sales (vertical axis). The chart shows that these two variables are positively related: Months in which more calls were made typically had higher sales volumes.

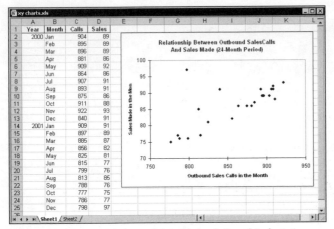

Figure 16-25: An XY chart shows the relationship between two variables.

Note Although these data points correspond to time, the chart does not convey any time-related information. In other words, the data points are plotted based only on their two values.

Area charts

Think of an area chart as a line chart in which the area below the line has been colored in.

Figure 16-26 shows an example of a stacked area chart. Stacking the data series enables you to see clearly the total, plus the contribution by each series.

Figure 16-27 shows the same data, plotted as a 3-D area chart. Although this chart has lots of visual appeal, it has a serious weakness: The data toward the back is often obscured. In this example, the first three quarters for Product C are not even visible.

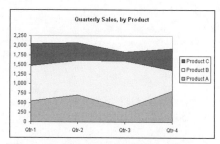

Figure 16-26: A stacked area chart.

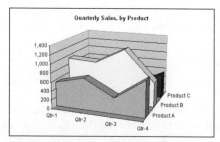

Figure 16-27: The first three quarters for Product C are not visible in this 3-D area chart.

Doughnut charts

A doughnut chart is similar to a pie chart, with two exceptions: It has a hole in the middle, and it can display more than one series of data. Figure 16-28 shows an example of a doughnut chart with two series (1st Half Sales and 2nd Half Sales). The legend identifies the data points. The arrows and series descriptions were added manually. A doughnut chart does not provide a direct way to identify the series.

Notice that Excel displays the data series as concentric rings. As you can see, a doughnut chart with more than one series can be very difficult to interpret. For example, the relatively larger sizes of the slices toward the outer part of the dough-nut can be deceiving. Consequently, doughnut charts should be used sparingly. In many cases, a stacked column chart for such comparisons expresses your meaning better than does a doughnut chart.

Perhaps the best use for a doughnut chart is to plot a single series as a visual alter-native to a pie chart.

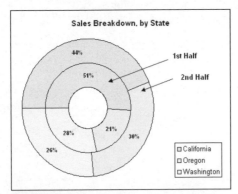

Figure 16-28: A doughnut chart with two data series.

Radar charts

You may not be familiar with radar charts. A radar chart has a separate axis for each category, and the axes extend outward from the center of the chart. The value of each data point is plotted on the corresponding axis.

Figure 16-29 shows an example of a radar chart. This chart plots two data series across 12 categories (months) and shows the seasonal demand for snow skis versus water skis. Note that the water-ski series partially obscures the snow-ski series.

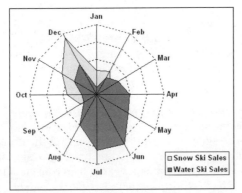

Figure 16-29: A radar chart with 12 categories and 2 series.

Surface charts

Surface charts display two or more data series on a surface. As Figure 16-30 shows, these charts can be quite interesting. Unlike other charts, Excel uses color to distinguish values, not to distinguish the data series. The number of colors used is determined by the major unit scale setting for the value axis. Each color corresponds to one major unit.

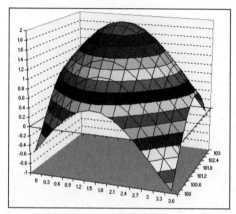

Figure 16-30: A surface chart.

Note   It's important to understand that a surface chart does not plot 3-D data points. The series axis for a surface chart, as with all other 3-D charts, is a category axis — not a value axis. In other words, if you have data that is represented by x, y, and z coordinates, it cannot be plotted accurately on a surface chart unless the x and y values are equally spaced.

Bubble charts

Think of a bubble chart as an XY chart that can display an additional data series, which is represented by the size of the bubbles. As with an XY chart, both axes are value axes — there is no category axis.

Figure 16-31 shows an example of a bubble chart that depicts the results of a weight-loss program. The horizontal value axis represents the original weight, the vertical value axis shows the length of time in the program, and the size of the bubbles represents the amount of weight lost.

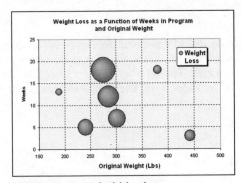

Figure 16-31: A bubble chart.

Stock charts

Stock charts are most useful for displaying stock-market information. These charts require three to five data series, depending on the subtype.

Figure 16-32 shows an example of each of the four stock chart types. The two charts on the bottom display the trade volume and use two value axes. The daily volume, represented by columns, uses the axis on the left. The "up-bars," sometimes referred to as *candlesticks,* are the vertical lines that depict the difference between the opening and closing price. A black up-bar indicates that the closing price was lower than the opening price.

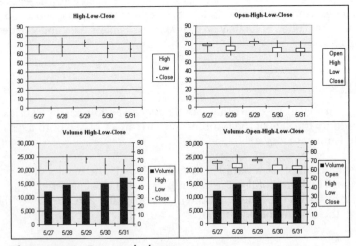

Figure 16-32: Four stock charts.

Cylinder, cone, and pyramid charts

These three chart types are essentially the same — except for the shapes that are used. You can use these charts in place of a 3-D bar or column chart.

Figure 16-33 shows an example of a simple pyramid chart and a cylinder chart.

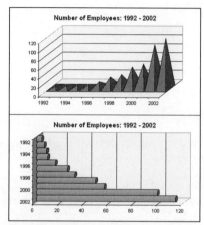

Figure 16-33: A pyramid chart and a cylinder chart.

The preceding sections cover Excel's standard chart types. This section discusses Excel's custom chart types, sometimes known as *user-defined* chart types.

✦ ✦ ✦

Learning Advanced Charting

T he preceding chapter introduced the basics of charting in Excel. This chapter takes the topic to the next level. You learn how to customize your charts to the maximum, so that they look exactly as you want. You also pick up some slick charting tricks that will make your charts even more impressive.

Understanding Chart Customization

Often, the basic chart that Excel creates is sufficient for your needs. If you're using a chart to get a quick visual impression of your data, a chart that's based on one of the standard chart types usually does just fine. But if you want to create the most effective chart possible, you probably want to take advantage of the additional customization techniques available in Excel.

Customizing a chart involves changing its appearance, as well as possibly adding new elements to it. These changes can be purely cosmetic (such as changing colors or modifying line widths) or quite substantial (such as changing the axis scales or rotating a 3-D chart). New elements that you might add include such features as a data table, a trend line, or error bars.

Changing Basic Chart Elements

This section describes how to modify various chart elements.

Selecting chart elements

Modifying a chart is similar to everything else you do in Excel: First you make a selection (in this case, select a chart element); then you issue a command to do something with the selection.

You can select only one chart element at a time. For example, if you want to change the font for two axis labels, you must work on each label separately. The exceptions to the single-selection rule are elements that consist of multiple parts, such as gridlines. Selecting one gridline selects them all.

Excel provides three ways to select a particular chart element:

✦ Use the mouse

✦ Use the keyboard

✦ Use the Chart toolbar

These selection methods are described in the following sections.

Selecting with the mouse

To select a chart element with your mouse, just click it. To ensure that you've selected the chart element that you intended to select, check the Name box (to the left of the Formula bar). The Name box displays the name of the selected element. When a chart is activated, you can't actually access the Name box; it's simply a convenient place for Excel to display the selected chart element's name.

Tip   When you move the mouse over a chart, a small "chart tip" displays the name of the chart element under the mouse pointer. When the mouse pointer is over a data point, the chart tip also displays the value of the data point. If you find these chart tips annoying, you can turn them off. Select Tools ➪ Options and click the Chart tab in the Options dialog box. Remove the check mark from one or both items in the Chart Tips section.

Some chart elements (such as a chart series, a legend, and data labels) consist of multiple items. For example, a chart series is made up of individual data points. To select a particular data point, click twice: First click the series to select it; then click the specific element within the series (for example, a column or a line chart marker). Selecting the element enables you to apply formatting only to a particular data point in a series.

You may find that some chart elements are difficult to select with the mouse. If you rely on the mouse for selecting a chart element, you may have to click it several times before the desired element is actually selected. Fortunately, Excel provides other ways to select a chart element, and it's worth your while to be familiar with them.

Selecting with the keyboard

When a chart is active, you can use the up-arrow and down-arrow keys on your keyboard to cycle among the chart's elements. Again, keep your eye on the Name box (or on the Chart Objects control) to determine which element is selected.

When a chart series is selected, use the left-arrow and right-arrow keys to select an individual data point within the series. Similarly, when a set of data labels is selected, you can select a specific data label by using the left-arrow or right-arrow key. And when a legend is selected, you can select individual elements within the legend by using the left-arrow or right-arrow keys.

Selecting with the Chart toolbar

When you select a chart, the Chart toolbar appears. If this toolbar is not displayed, choose View ➪ Toolbars ➪ Chart.

The Chart Objects control on the Chart toolbar is a drop-down list that lets you select a particular chart element from the active chart (see Figure 17-1). This control lists only the top-level elements in the chart. To select an individual data point within a series, for example, you need to select the series and then use one of the other techniques to select the desired data point.

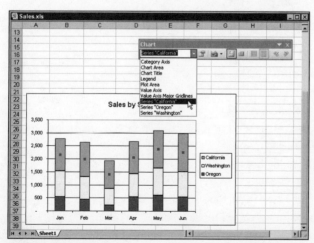

Figure 17-1: You can use the Chart toolbar to select a chart element.

Note   When a single data point is selected, the Chart Objects control *will* display the name of the selected element, even though it's not actually available for selection in the drop-down list.

Modifying properties by using the Format dialog box

When a chart element is selected, you can access the element's Format dialog box to format or set options for the element. Each chart element has a unique Format dialog box. You can access this dialog box by using any of the following methods:

✦ Select the Format ⇨ *selected element* command. (The Format menu adapts according to the element you have selected.)

✦ Double-click a chart element.

✦ Select the chart element and press Ctrl+1.

✦ Right-click the chart element and choose the Format command from the shortcut menu.

Any of these methods displays a tabbed Format dialog box that enables you to make many changes to the selected chart element. For example, Figure 17-2 shows the dialog box that appears when a chart's legend is selected.

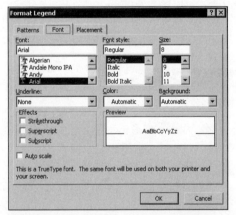

Figure 17-2: Use the Format dialog box to set the properties of a selected chart element — in this case, the chart's legend.

 Tip   When a chart element is selected, you'll find that many of the toolbar buttons that you normally use for worksheet formatting also work with the selected chart element. For example, if you select the chart's Plot Area, you can change its color by using the Fill Color tool on the Formatting toolbar. If you select an element that contains text, you can use the Font Color tool to change the color of the text. Simple formatting using the toolbar buttons is usually more efficient than bringing up the dialog box.

In the following sections, the details of the various types of chart modifications are discussed in depth.

Modifying the Chart Area

The *Chart Area* is an object that contains all other elements in the chart. You can think of it as a chart's master background.

The three tabs of the Format Chart Area dialog box and some key points about each are

✦ **Patterns:** Enables you to change the Chart Area's color and patterns (including fill effects) and add a border if you like.

✦ **Font:** Enables you to change the properties of all fonts used in the chart.

✦ **Properties:** Enables you to specify how the chart is moved and sized with respect to the underlying cells. You also can set the Locked property and specify whether the chart will be printed when the underlying worksheet is printed. This tab is available only for embedded charts.

Modifying the Plot Area

The *Plot Area* is the part of the chart that contains the actual chart. The Format Plot Area dialog box has only one tab: Patterns. This tab enables you to change the color and pattern of the Plot Area and adjust its borders.

Tip If you set the Area option to None, the Plot Area will be transparent. Therefore, the color and patterns applied to the Chart Area will show through.

To reposition the Plot Area, select the Plot Area and then drag a border to move it. To change the size of the Plot Area, drag on one of the corner handles. If you like, you can expand the Plot Area so that it fills the entire Chart Area. The Plot Area of the chart in Figure 17-3 occupies the entire Chart Area. The title and legend have been moved from their default locations and placed over the Plot Area.

Tip To remove all formatting from the Plot Area, select the Plot Area and press Delete. The Plot Area remains, but the Border and Area settings are set to None.

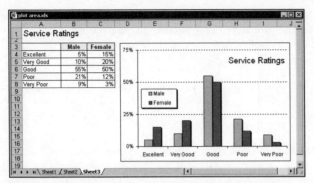

Figure 17-3: The Plot Area for this chart occupies the entire Chart Area.

You'll find that different chart types vary in how they respond to changes in the Plot Area dimensions. For example, you cannot change the relative dimensions of the Plot Area of a pie chart or a radar chart. (The Plot Area of these charts is always square.) But with other chart types, you can change the aspect ratio of the Plot Area by changing either the height or the width.

Also, be aware that the size of the Plot Area can be changed automatically when you adjust other elements of your chart. For example, if you add a legend to a chart, the size of the Plot Area may be reduced to accommodate the legend.

Tip

Changing the size and position of the Plot Area can have a dramatic effect on the overall look of your chart. When you're fine-tuning a chart, you'll probably want to experiment with various sizes and positions for the Plot Area.

Working with chart titles

A chart can have as many as five different titles:

✦ Chart title

✦ Category (X) axis title

✦ Value (Y) axis title

✦ Second category (X) axis title

✦ Second value (Y) axis title

The number of titles that you can use depends on the chart type. For example, a pie chart supports only a chart title because it has no axes.

Adding Free-Floating Text to a Chart

Text in a chart is not limited to titles. In fact, you can add free-floating text anywhere you want. To do so, select any part of the chart except a title or data label. Then type the text in the Formula bar and press Enter. Excel adds a Text Box that contains the text you entered. The Text Box will appear in the center of the chart, but you can move it wherever you want it by dragging a border. Double-click the Text Box to display the Format Text Box dialog box, in which you can apply any formatting you desire.

Many people prefer to use a Text Box in place of a chart's "official" title elements. As noted in the text, Excel's chart titles have some problems. Perhaps the most annoying problem is that text is often cut off in vertical titles. Also, resizing a title is not possible (except by changing its font size). Using a Text Box overcomes both of these problems.

To add titles to a chart, activate the chart and use the Chart ⇨ Chart Options command. Excel displays the Chart Options dialog box. Click the Titles tab and enter text for the title or titles.

Tip   You can drag the chart titles to move them to a different position. However, you cannot change their size by dragging.

To modify a chart title's properties, access its Format dialog box. This dialog box has the following tabs:

✦ **Patterns:** Change the background color and borders.

✦ **Font:** Change the font, size, color, and attributes.

✦ **Alignment:** Adjust the vertical and horizontal alignment and orientation.

Working with the legend

A chart's *legend* consists of text and keys that make it easier to identify the data series. A *key* is a small graphic that corresponds to the chart's series.

To add a legend to your chart, use the Chart ⇨ Chart Options command and then click the Legend tab in the Chart Options dialog box. Place a check mark in the Show Legend check box. You also can specify where to place the legend by using the Placement option buttons.

The quickest way to remove a legend is to select the legend and then press Delete. To move a legend, click and drag it to the desired location. Or you can use the legend's Format dialog box to position the legend (by using the Placement tab).

Tip   The Legend tool in the Chart toolbar acts as a toggle. Use this button to add a leg-end, if one doesn't exist, and to remove a legend, if one exists.

You can select individual text items within a legend and format them separately by using the Format Legend Entry dialog box (which has only a single panel: Font). To access this dialog box, double-click the legend. For example, you may want to make the text bold to draw attention to a particular data series.

Tip   After you move a legend from its default position, you may want to change the size of the Plot Area to fill in the gap left by the legend. Just select the Plot Area and drag a border to make it the desired size.

If you didn't include legend text when you originally selected the cells to create the chart, Excel displays Series 1, Series 2, and so on in the legend. To add series names, choose Chart ➪ Source Data and then select the Series tab in the Source Data dialog box (as shown in Figure 17-4). Select a series from the Series list box, activate the Name box, and then either specify a cell reference that contains the label or directly enter the series name.

Cross-Reference   See "Creating Custom Chart Types," later in this chapter.

Copying Chart Formatting

You created a killer chart and spent hours customizing it. Now you need to create another one just like it. What are your options? You have several choices:

✦ **Copy the formatting.** Create a standard chart with the default formatting. Then select your original chart and choose Edit ➪ Copy. Click your new chart and choose Edit ➪ Paste Special. In the Paste Special dialog box, select Formats. This procedure has an odd side effect: Besides copying the formatting, it also replaces the chart title with the title from the copied chart. This is almost never what you want!

✦ **Copy the chart; change the data sources.** Press Ctrl while you click the original chart and drag. This creates an exact copy of your chart. Then use the Chart ➪ Source Data dialog box to specify the data for the new chart.

✦ **Create a user-defined chart type.** Select your chart and then choose Chart ➪ Chart Type. Click the Custom Types tab and select the User-Defined option. Click the Add button and then provide a name and description. When you create your next chart, use this custom chart type.

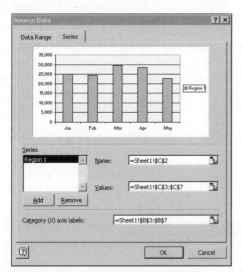

Figure 17-4: Use the Series tab of the Source Data dialog box to change the name of a data series.

Changing the chart gridlines

Gridlines can help you to determine what the chart series represents numerically. Gridlines simply extend the tick marks on the axes. Some charts look better with gridlines; others appear more cluttered. Sometimes, horizontal gridlines alone are enough, although XY charts often benefit from both horizontal and vertical gridlines.

To add or remove gridlines, choose Chart ➪ Chart Options and then select the Gridlines tab. Each axis has two sets of gridlines: major and minor. Major units display a label. Minor units are located between the labels. You can choose which to add or to remove by checking or unchecking the appropriate check boxes. If you're working with a true 3-D chart, the dialog box has options for three sets of gridlines.

To modify the properties of a set of gridlines, double-click on any gridline in the set to access the Format Gridlines dialog box. This dialog box has two tabs:

✦ **Patterns:** Changes the line style, width, and color

✦ **Scale:** Adjusts the scale used on the axis

Modifying the axes

Charts vary in the number of axes that they use. Pie and doughnut charts have no axes. All 2-D charts have two axes (three, if you use a secondary-value axis; four, if you use a secondary-category axis in an XY chart). True 3-D charts have three axes. Excel gives you a lot of control over these axes. To modify any aspect of an axis, double-click the axis to access its Format Axis dialog box, which has five tabs:

✦ **Patterns:** Change the axis line width, tick marks, and placement of tick-mark labels

✦ **Scale:** Adjust the minimum and maximum axis values, units for major and minor gridlines, and other properties

✦ **Font:** Adjust the font used for the axis labels

✦ **Number:** Adjust the number format for the axis labels

✦ **Alignment:** Specify the orientation for the axis labels

Because the axes's properties can dramatically affect the chart's look, the Patterns and Scale dialog-box tabs are discussed separately, in the following sections.

Modifying the axes patterns

The Patterns tab of the Format Axis dialog box enables you to modify various attributes of a chart's axes. This tab has four sections:

✦ **Lines:** Controls the line characteristics of the axis (the style, color, and weight of the line).

✦ **Major Tick Mark Type:** Controls how the major tick marks appear. You can select None (no tick marks), Inside (inside the axis), Outside (outside the axis), or Cross (on both sides of the axis).

✦ **Minor Tick Mark Type:** Controls how the minor tick marks appear. You can select the same options as for the major tick marks.

✦ **Tick Mark Labels:** Controls where the axis labels appear. Normally, the labels appear next to the axis. You can, however, specify that the labels appear High (at the top of the chart), Low (at the bottom of the chart), or not at all (None). These options are useful when the axis doesn't appear in its normal position at the edge of the Plot Area.

Note   Major tick marks are the axis tick marks that normally have labels next to them. Minor tick marks are between the major tick marks.

Modifying the axes scales

Adjusting the scale of a value axis can dramatically affect the chart's appearance. Manipulating the scale, in some cases, can present a false picture of the data. The actual scale that you use depends on the situation. No hard-and-fast rules exist about scale, except that you shouldn't misrepresent data by manipulating the chart to prove a point that doesn't exist.

Tip   If you're preparing several charts that use similarly scaled data, keeping the scales the same is a good idea so that the charts can be compared more easily.

Excel automatically determines the scale for your charts. You can, however, override Excel's choice in the Scale tab of the Format Axis dialog box (as shown in Figure 17-5).

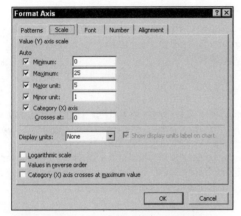

Figure 17-5: Use the Scale tab of the Format Axis dialog box to control the values used on the axis.

Note   The Scale tab varies, depending on which axis is selected.

This dialog box offers the following options:

✦ **Minimum:** Enter a minimum value for the axis. If the check box is checked, Excel determines this value automatically.

✦ **Maximum:** Enter a maximum value for the axis. If the check box is checked, Excel determines this value automatically.

✦ **Major Unit:** Enter the number of units between major tick marks. If the check box is checked, Excel determines this value automatically.

✦ **Minor Unit:** Enter the number of units between minor tick marks. If the check box is checked, Excel determines this value automatically.

✦ **Category (X) Axis Crosses At:** Position the axis at a different location. By default, it's at the edge of the Plot Area.

✦ **Display Units:** Select the unit of measure.

✦ **Show Display Units Label on Chart:** Toggle display of the unit on or off.

✦ **Logarithmic Scale:** Use a logarithmic scale for the axes. A log scale primarily is useful for scientific applications in which the values to plot have an extremely large range. You receive an error message if the scale includes 0 or negative values.

✦ **Values in Reverse Order:** Make the scale values extend in the opposite direction. For a value axis, for example, selecting this option displays the smallest scale value at the top and the largest at the bottom (the opposite of how it normally appears).

✦ **Category (X) Axis Crosses at Maximum Value:** Position the axes at the maximum value of the perpendicular axis. (Normally, the axis is positioned at the minimum value of the perpendicular axis.)

Working with time-based axes

When you create a chart, Excel is smart enough to know whether your category axis contains date or time values. If so, it creates a time-series chart. Figure 17-6 shows a simple example. Column A contains dates, and column B contains the values plotted in the column chart. The data consists of values for only 10 dates, yet Excel created the chart with 31 intervals on the category axis. It recognized that the category axis values were dates and created an equal-interval scale.

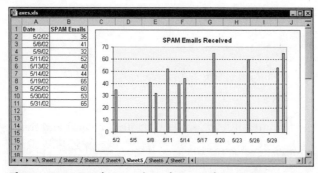

Figure 17-6: Excel recognizes dates and creates a time-based category axis.

If you would like to override Excel's decision to use a time-based category axis, you need to access the Axes tab of the Chart Options dialog box (double-click the axis to display the dialog box). There, you'll discover that the category axis option is Automatic. Change this option to Category, and the chart will resemble that shown in Figure 17-7.

Don't Be Afraid to Experiment — on a Copy

I'll let you in a secret: The key to mastering charts in Excel is experimentation, otherwise known as trial and error. Excel's charting options can be overwhelming, even to experienced users. This book, despite being almost comprehensive, doesn't even pretend to cover all the charting features. Your job, as a potential charting guru, is to dig deep and try new options with your charts.

After you've created a basic chart, you may want to make a copy of the chart for your experimentation. That way, if you mess it up, you can always revert to the original. To make a copy of an embedded chart, press the Ctrl key while you click the chart and drag the mouse pointer to a new location. To make a copy of a chart sheet, press Ctrl while you click the sheet tab and drag it to a new location among the other tabs.

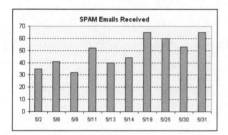

Figure 17-7: The preceding chart, using a standard category axis.

Working with Data Series

Every chart consists of one or more data series. This data translates into chart columns, lines, pie slices, and so on. This section discusses most of the customizations that you can perform with a chart's data series.

To work with a data series, you must first select it. Activate the chart and then click the data series that you want to select. In a Column chart, click a column; in a Line chart, click a line; and so on. Make sure that you select the entire series and not just a single point.

Tip
You may find it easier to select the series by using the Chart Objects tool in the Chart toolbar.

When you select a data series, Excel displays the series name in the Name box (for example, Series 1, or the actual name of the series) and the Series formula in the Formula bar. A selected data series has a small square on each element of the series. In addition, the cells used for the selected series are outlined in color.

Many customizations that you perform with a data series use the Format Data Series dialog box, which is displayed when you double-click a chart series. This dialog box has as many as seven tabs. The number of tabs varies, depending on the type of chart. For example, a pie chart has four tabs, and a 3-D column chart has four tabs. Line and column charts have six tabs, and XY (scatter) charts have seven tabs. The possible tabs in the Format Data Series dialog box are as follows:

✦ **Patterns:** Change the color, pattern, and border style for the data series. For line charts, change the color and style of the data marker in this tab.

✦ **Axis:** Specify which value axis to use for the selected data series.

✦ **Y Error Bars:** Add or modify error bars for the Y axis.

✦ **Data Labels:** Display labels next to each data point.

✦ **Series Order:** Specify the order in which the data series are plotted.

✦ **Options:** Change options specific to the chart type.

✦ **Shape:** Specify the shape of the columns (in 3-D column charts only).

✦ **X Error Bars:** Add or modify error bars for the X axis. This is available only for XY charts.

The sections that follow discuss many of these dialog box options.

Deleting a data series

To delete a data series in a chart, select the data series and press the Delete key. The data series is removed from the chart. The data in the worksheet, of course, remains intact.

 Note   You can delete all data series from a chart. If you do so, the chart appears empty. It retains its settings, however. Therefore, you can add a data series to an empty chart, and it again looks like a chart.

Adding a new data series to a chart

A common need is to add another data series to an existing chart. You could re-create the chart and include the new data series, but adding the data to the existing chart is usually easier. Excel provides several ways to add a new data series to a chart:

✦ Activate the chart and select Chart ➪ Source Data. In the Source Data dialog box, click the Series tab. Click the Add button and then specify the data range in the Values box. (You can enter the range address or point to it.)

✦ Select the range to add and drag it into the chart. When you release the mouse button, Excel updates the chart with the data that you dragged in. This technique works only if the chart is embedded on the worksheet.

✦ Select the range to add and copy it to the Clipboard. Then activate the chart and choose Edit ➪ Paste Special. Excel responds with the Paste Special dialog box shown in Figure 17-8. Complete this dialog box to correspond to the data that you selected.

Figure 17-8: Use the Paste Special dialog box to add a new data series to your chart.

Changing data used by a series

You may find that you need to modify the range that defines a data series. For example, you may need to add new data points or remove old ones from the data set. The following sections describe several ways to change the range used by a data series.

Changing the data range by dragging the range outline

The easiest way to change the data range for a data series is to drag the range outline. This technique works only for embedded charts. When you select a series, Excel outlines the data range used by that series. You can drag the small dot in the lower-right corner of the range outline to extend or contract the data series.

Figure 17-9 shows an example of how this looks. The chart displays five data points, and the series is being extended to include five additional points.

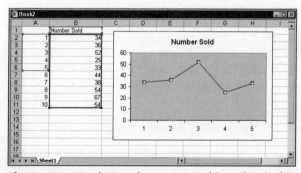

Figure 17-9: To change the range used in a chart's data series, select the data series and drag the small dot at the lower-right corner of the range outline.

Using the Source Data dialog box

Another way to update the chart to reflect a different data range is to activate the chart and select Chart ⇨ Source Data. To display the Source Data dialog box, click the Series tab and then select the series from the Series list box. Adjust the range in the Values box. (You can edit the range reference or point to the new range.)

Editing the Series formula

Every data series in a chart has an associated Series formula, which appears in the Formula bar when you select a data series in a chart (as shown in Figure 17-10). You can edit the range references in the Series formula directly.

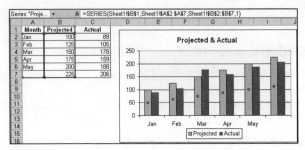

Figure 17-10: When you select a data series, its Series formula appears in the Formula bar.

A Series formula consists of a SERIES function with four arguments. The syntax is as follows:

```
=SERIES(Name_ref,Categories,Values,Plot_order)
```

Excel uses absolute cell references in the SERIES function. To change the data that a series uses, edit the cell references (third argument) in the Formula bar. The first and second arguments are optional and may not appear in the Series formula. If the series doesn't have a name, the *Name_ref* argument is missing, and Excel uses dummy series names in the legend (Series1, Series2, and so on). If no category names exist, the Categories argument is missing, and Excel uses dummy labels (1, 2, 3, and so on).

Caution   If the data series uses category labels, make sure that you adjust the reference for the category labels also. This is the second argument in the Series formula.

Tip
One way to handle data ranges that change over time is to use named ranges. Create names for the data ranges that you use in the chart and then edit the `Series` formula. Replace each range reference with the corresponding range name. After making this change, the chart uses the named ranges. If you add new data to the range, just change the definition for the name, and the chart is updated.

Displaying data labels in a chart

Sometimes, you may want your chart to display the actual data values for each point. You specify data labels in the Data Labels tab of the Chart Options dialog box (see Figure 17-11). This tab has several options. Note that not all options are available for all chart types. If you select the check box labeled Show Legend Key Next to Label, each label displays its legend key next to it.

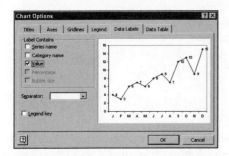

Figure 17-11: Use the Data Labels tab of the Chart Options dialog box to add labels next to the data values.

The data labels are linked to the worksheet, so if your data changes, the labels also change. If you want to override the data label with other text, select the label and enter the new text (or even a cell reference) in the Formula bar.

Tip
Often, you'll find that the data labels aren't positioned properly—for example, a label may be obscured by another data point. If you select an individual label, you can drag the label to a better location.

As you work with data labels, you probably discover that the Excel data-labels feature leaves a bit to be desired. For example, it would be nice to be able to specify a range of text to be used for the data labels. This would be particularly useful in XY charts in which you want to identify each data point with a particular text item. Figure 17-12 shows an XY chart. If you would like to apply data labels to identify each student's score in the chart, you're out of luck.

Despite what must amount to thousands of requests, Microsoft still has not added this feature to Excel! You need to add data labels and then manually edit each label.

On the CD-ROM The Power Utility Pak add-in (available on the companion CD-ROM) overcomes this limitation. It includes a utility that enables you to specify the range that contains the labels.

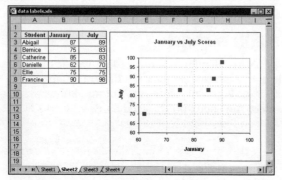

Figure 17-12: Excel provides no direct way to add descriptive data labels to the data points.

Handling missing data

Sometimes, data that you're charting may be missing one or more data points. Excel offers several ways to handle the missing data. You don't control this in the Format Data Series dialog box (as you might expect). Rather, you must select the chart, choose Tools ➪ Options, and then click the Chart tab in the Options dialog box.

The options that you set apply to the entire active chart, and you can't set a different option for different series in the same chart. The following are the options in the Chart panel for the active chart:

✦ **Not Plotted (Leave Gaps):** Missing data is simply ignored, and the data series will have a gap. This is the default.

✦ **Zero:** Missing data is treated as zero.

✦ **Interpolated:** Missing data is calculated by using data on either side of the missing point(s). This option is available only for line charts, area charts, and XY charts.

Controlling a data series by hiding data

Usually, Excel doesn't plot data that is in a hidden row or column. You can sometimes use this to your advantage, because it's an easy way to control what data appears in the chart. If you're working with outlines or data filtering (both of which use hidden rows), however, you may not like the idea that hidden data is removed from your chart. To override this, activate the chart and select the Tools ⇨ Options command. In the Options dialog box, click the Chart tab and remove the check mark from the check box labeled Plot Visible Cells Only.

Cross-Reference See Chapter 28 to learn about worksheet outlining.

Adding error bars

For certain chart types, you can add error bars to your chart. Error bars often are used to indicate "plus or minus" information that reflects uncertainty in the data. Error bars are appropriate only for area, bar, column, line, and XY charts. Click the Y Error Bars tab in the Format Data Series dialog box to display the error bars options.

Tip A data series in an XY chart can have error bars for both the X values and Y values.

Excel enables you to specify several types of error bars:

✦ **Fixed value:** The error bars are fixed by an amount that you specify.

✦ **Percentage:** The error bars are a percentage of each value.

✦ **Standard Deviation(s):** The error bars are in the number of standard-deviation units that you specify. (Excel calculates the standard deviation of the data series.)

✦ **Standard Error:** The error bars are one standard error unit. (Excel calculates the standard error of the data series.)

✦ **Custom:** You set the error bar units for the upper or lower error bars. You can enter either a value or a range reference that holds the error values that you want to plot as error bars.

The chart shown in Figure 17-13 displays error bars.

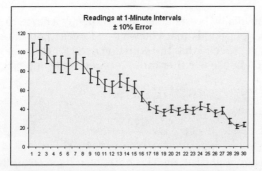

Figure 17-13: This line chart series displays error bars based on percentage.

Adding a trend line

When you're plotting data over time, you may want to plot a trend line that describes the data. A *trend line* points out general trends in your data. In some cases, you can forecast future data with trend lines. A single series can have more than one trend line.

Excel makes adding a trend line to a chart quite simple. Select Chart ➪ Add Trendline to display the Add Trendline dialog box.

The type of trend line that you choose depends on your data. Linear trends are most common, but some data can be described more effectively with another type. One of the options on the Type tab is Moving Average, which is useful for smoothing out data that has a lot of variation (that is, "noisy" data). The Moving Average option enables you to specify the number of data points to include in each average. For example, if you select 5, Excel averages every five data points.

Figure 17-14 shows a chart with a linear trendline.

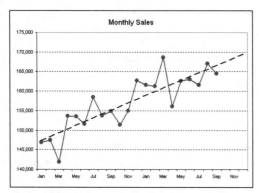

Figure 17-14: This linear trendline forecasts sales for three additional time periods.

The Options tab of the Add Trendline dialog box enables you to specify a name to appear in the legend and the number of periods that you want to forecast. Additional options let you set the intercept value, specify that the equation used for the trend line should appear on the chart, and choose whether the R-squared value appears on the chart.

Modifying 3-D charts

All 3-D charts have a few additional parts that you can customize. For example, most 3-D charts have a floor and walls, and the true 3-D charts also have an additional axis. You can select these chart elements and format them to your liking. Generally, 3-D formatting options work just like the other chart elements.

One area in which 3-D charts differ from Excel's 2-D charts is in the perspective — or viewpoint — from which you see the chart. By changing the view angle, you can see portions of the chart that may otherwise be hidden, thus making the chart easier to understand.

You can rotate a 3-D chart in one of these two ways:

✦ Activate the 3-D chart and choose the Chart ⇨ 3-D View command to display the 3-D View dialog box. You can make your rotations and perspective changes by clicking the appropriate controls. The sample that you see in the dialog box is *not* your actual chart. The displayed sample just gives you an idea of the types of changes that you're making. Make the adjustments and then choose OK to make them permanent (or click Apply to apply them to your chart without closing the dialog box).

✦ Rotate the chart in real time by dragging corners with the mouse. Click one of the corners of the chart. Black handles appear, and the word Corners appears in the Name box. You can drag one of these black handles and rotate the chart's 3-D box to your satisfaction.

Figure 17-15 shows four different views of the same chart.

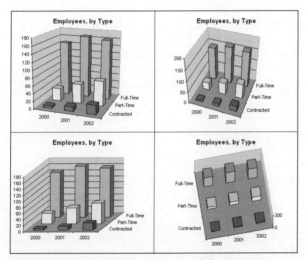

Figure 17-15: Four different views of the same 3-D column chart.

Formatting a surface chart

A surface chart is different from the other chart types because you cannot select any of the series in the chart. Another difference is that the colors in the chart are based on the values.

The number of colored bands used in the chart depends on the major unit setting for the value axis. Figure 17-16 shows two surface charts. In the chart on the left, the value axis major unit is 0.05 (the default). In the chart on the right, the value axis major unit is 0.4 — which covers the entire scale for the chart. Consequently, this chart displays a single color.

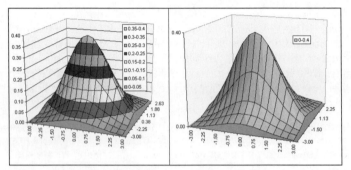

Figure 17-16: Changing the major unit for the value axis controls the number of colors used in a surface chart.

The procedure to adjust the colors used in a surface chart is rather counterintuitive. First, you need to make sure that the chart displays a legend. Next, click the legend to select it and then double-click the color key that you want to change. This displays the Format Legend Key dialog box. Use the Patterns tab to change the color. The Options tab of this dialog box enables you to change the depth of the chart as well as apply 3-D shading to the chart — an option that can make the chart look much better.

Creating combination charts

A *combination chart* is a single chart that consists of series that use different chart types. For example, you may have a chart that shows both columns and lines. A combination chart also can use a single type (all columns, for example) but include a second value axis. A combination chart requires at least two data series.

Creating a combination chart simply involves changing one or more of the data series to a different chart type. Select the data series and then choose Chart ⇨ Chart Type. In the Chart Type dialog box, select the chart type that you want to apply to the selected series.

Note   In some cases, you can't combine chart types. For example, you can't create a combination chart that involves a bubble chart or a 3-D chart. If you choose an incompatible chart type for the series, Excel lets you know.

Tip You can't create combination 3-D charts, but if you use a 3-D column or 3-D bar chart, you can change the shape of the columns or bars. Double-click a series to display the Format Data Series dialog box. Click the Shape tab and then choose the shape for the selected series.

Using secondary axes

If you need to plot data series that have drastically different scales, you probably want to use a secondary scale. For example, assume that you want to create a chart that shows monthly sales along with the average amount sold per customer. These two data series use different scales. (The average sales values are much smaller than the total sales.) Consequently, the average sales data range is virtually invisible in the chart.

The solution is to use a secondary axis for the second data series. Because the two axes can have different scales, you can make both data sets visible on a single chart.

To specify a secondary axis, double-click the data series in the chart to access the Format Data Series dialog box. Click the Axis tab and choose the Secondary axis option.

Displaying a data table

In some cases, you may want to display a *data table,* which displays the chart's data in tabular form, directly in the chart.

To add a data table to a chart, choose Chart ➪ Chart Options and select the Data Table tab in the Chart Options dialog box. Place a check mark next to the option labeled Show Data Table. You also can choose to display the legend keys in the data table. Figure 17-17 shows a chart with a data table.

To adjust the formatting or font used in the data table, double-click the data table to access the Format Data Table dialog box. You'll find that you have very little control over the formatting of a data table. A potential problem with data tables occurs when they are used with embedded charts. If you resize the chart to make it smaller, the data table may not show all the data.

Using a data table is probably best suited for charts on chart sheets. If you need to show the data used in an embedded chart, you can do so using data in cells, which provide you with a lot more flexibility in terms of formatting.

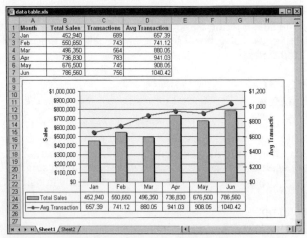

Figure 17-17: This combination chart includes a data table that displays the values of the data points.

Creating Custom Chart Types

The preceding sections cover Excel's standard chart types. This section discusses Excel's custom chart types, sometimes known as *user-defined* chart types.

About custom chart types

It's important to understand that the custom chart *types* are actually standard charts that have been customized in various ways. They are provided as a quick way to generate a customized chart.

Note   Several of the custom chart types are combination charts. A *combination chart* combines two different chart types, such as a column chart and a line chart. In such a case, each series is assigned its own chart type. A combination chart requires that the chart types use the same category axis, but they may use different value axes. Also, 3-D charts cannot be combined with another chart type.

Creating your own custom chart types

The following sections describe how to create your own custom chart type.

Create a chart

The first step is to create a chart that will serve as the basis for your custom chart type. The data you use for this chart is not critical, but for best results, it should be typical of the data that you will eventually be plotting with your custom chart type.

Format the chart

The next step is to provide some formatting and customizations. This will determine how your charts will look.

Add the chart to the custom chart type gallery

When you're satisfied with the look of the chart, add it to the custom chart type gallery. To do so, follow these steps:

1. Select the chart.

2. Choose Chart ➪ Chart Type to display the Chart Type dialog box.

3. Select the Custom Types tab.

4. Choose the User-Defined option.

5. Click the Add button and you'll see the Add Custom Chart Type dialog box.

6. Enter a name and (optionally) a description for the custom chart type (see Figure 17-18).

7. Click OK and you'll see your new custom chart type listed in the Chart Type list box.

8. Click OK again to close the Chart Type dialog box.

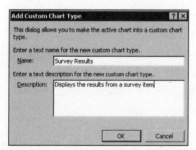

Figure 17-18: The Add Custom Chart Type dialog box.

Test and refine

The final step is to test your creation. You should test the custom chart type with a different data series.

Voilà! The data will be displayed in a highly customized chart that is perfect in every way. Or at least it *should* be. If the chart doesn't look right, you may need to make some additional changes to it. After doing so, you need to go through the previous steps to add the chart to the custom gallery. If you use the same name, Excel asks whether you want to replace the existing user-defined format. Answer in the affirmative.

Learning Some Chart-Making Tricks

This section teaches you some interesting chart-making tricks. Some of these tricks use little-known features, and several tricks enable you to make charts that you may have considered impossible to create.

On the CD-ROM

All of the examples in the following sections are available on the companion CD-ROM.

Creating picture charts

Excel makes it easy to incorporate a pattern, texture, or graphic file for elements in your chart. Figure 17-19 shows an example of a chart that displays a graphic.

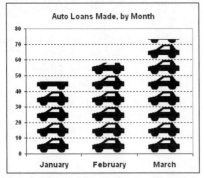

Figure 17-19: You can include graphic images in the columns of a chart.

To convert a data series to pictures, start with a column or bar chart (either standard or 3-D). Then, select the series and choose Format ➪ Selected Data Series to access the chart's Format Data Series dialog box. Select the Patterns tab and click the Fill Effects button to get the Fill Effects dialog box. In the Fill Effects dialog box, click the Picture tab and then click the Select Picture button to locate the graphics file that you want to use. You'll probably find that you need to play around with the settings to make your graphics work out the way you'd like.

Tip

You can also copy any graphic image to the Clipboard. Then, select the chart column or bar series and choose Edit ➪ Paste.

Creating a thermometer chart

You're probably familiar with a "thermometer" type display that shows the percentage of a task that's completed. It's very easy to create such a display in Excel. The trick involves creating a chart that uses a single cell (which holds a percentage value) as a data series.

Figure 17-20 shows a worksheet set up to track daily progress toward a goal: 1,000 new customers in a 15-day period. Cell B18 contains the goal value, and cell B19 contains a simple sum formula:

```
=SUM(B2:B16)
```

Cell B21 contains a formula that calculates the percent of goal:

```
=B19/B18
```

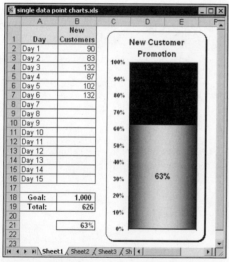

Figure 17-20: This chart displays progress toward a goal.

As you enter new data in column B, the formulas display the current results.

To create the chart, select cell B21, click the Chart Wizard button, and create a column chart. Notice the blank row before cell B21. Without this blank row, Excel uses the entire data block for the chart, not just the single cell. Because B21 is isolated from the other data, the Chart Wizard uses only the single cell. Other changes required:

✦ Select the category (x) axis and press Delete. This removes the category axis from the chart.

✦ Remove the legend.

✦ Add data labels (choose the Value option).

✦ Set the Gap width to 0 (This makes the column occupy the entire width of the plot area.) To do so, double-click the column to display the Format Data Series dialog box. Then select the Options tab, and change the Gap Width setting

✦ Double-click the value axis to access the Format Axis dialog box. In the Format Axis dialog box, select Scale tab; set the Minimum to 0 and the Maximum to 1.

You can then make any other adjustments to get the look you desire.

Creating a gauge chart

Figure 17-21 shows a pie chart set up to resemble a gauge. Although this chart displays a single value (entered in cell B1), it actually uses three data points (in A4:A6).

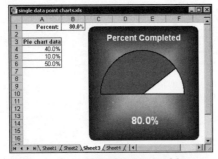

Figure 17-21: This chart resembles a speedometer gauge and displays a value between 0 and 100%.

One slice of the pie — the slice at the bottom — always consists of 50%, and that slice is hidden. (The slice's Area and Border were set to None.) The other two slices are apportioned based on the value in cell B1. The formula in cell B4 is

```
=MIN(B1,100%)/2
```

This formula uses the MIN function to display the smaller of two values: either the value in cell B1 or 100%. It then divides this value by 2 because I'm only dealing with the visible half of the pie chart. Using the MIN function prevents the chart from displaying more than 100%.

The formula in cell A6, shown below, simply calculate the remaining part of the pie — the part to the right of the gauge's "needle."

```
=50%-A5
```

Creating a comparative histogram

With a bit of creativity, you can create charts with Excel that you may have considered impossible. For example, Figure 17-22 shows a comparative histogram chart. Such charts often display population data.

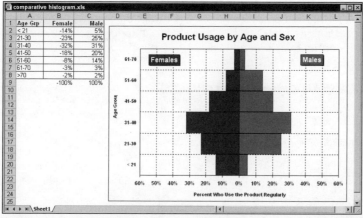

Figure 17-22: With a little ingenuity you can create charts, such as this comparative histogram.

Here's how to create the chart:

1. Enter the data as shown in Figure 17-22. Notice that the values for females are entered as negative values.

2. Select A1:C8 and create a 2-D bar chart. Use the subtype labeled Clustered Bar.

3. Apply the following custom number format to the horizontal axis: 0%;0%;0%. This custom format eliminates the negative signs in the percentages.

4. Double-click the vertical axis to access the Format Axis dialog box. Click the Patterns tab and remove all tick marks. Set the Tick Mark Labels option to Low. This keeps the axis in the center of the chart but displays the axis labels at the left side.

5. Double-click either of the data series to access the Format Data Series dialog box. Click the Options tab and set the Overlap to 100 and the Gap width to 0.

6. Add two text boxes to the chart (**Females** and **Males**) to substitute for the legend. To add a text box, just select the chart's background and start typing your text.

7. Apply other formatting, as desired.

Creating a Gantt chart

A *Gantt chart* is a horizontal bar chart often used in project management applications. Although Excel doesn't support Gantt charts per se, creating a simple Gantt chart is fairly easy. The key is getting your data set up properly.

Figure 17-23 shows a Gantt chart set up to depict the schedule for a project, in range A2:C13. The horizontal axis represents the total time span of the project, and each bar represents a project task. The viewer can quickly see the duration for each task and identify overlapping tasks.

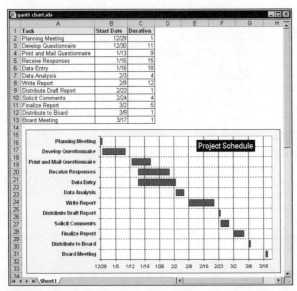

Figure 17-23: You can create a simple Gantt chart from a bar chart.

Column A contains the task name, column B contains the corresponding start date, and column C contains the duration of the task, in days.

Follow these steps to create this chart:

1. Use the Chart Wizard to create a stacked bar chart from the range A2:C13.

2. In Step 2 of the Chart Wizard, select the Columns option. Notice that Excel incorrectly uses the first two columns as the Category axis labels.

3. Also in Step 2 of the Chart Wizard, click the Series tab and add a new data series. Then set the chart's series to the following:

- Series 1: **B2:B13**

- Series 2: **C2:C13**

- Category (x) Axis Labels: **A2:A13**

4. In Step 3 of the Chart Wizard, remove the legend and then click Finish to create an embedded chart.

5. Adjust the height of the chart so that all the axis labels are visible. You can also accomplish this by using a smaller font size for the category axis labels.

6. Double-click the value axis to access the Format Axis dialog box for the value (horizontal) axis. Adjust the horizontal axis Minimum and Maximum scale values to correspond to the earliest and latest dates in the data, (Note that you can enter a date into the Minimum or Maximum box.) You also may want to set the Major unit to 7 to indicate weeks.

7. Access the Format Axis dialog box for the category (vertical) axis. In the Scale tab, select the option labeled Categories in Reverse Order, and also set the option labeled Value (Y) Axis Crosses at Maximum category.

8. Double-click the first data series to access the Format Data Series dialog box. On the Patterns tab, set Border to None and Area to None. This makes the first data series invisible.

9. Apply other formatting as desired.

Creating a chart that updates automatically

If you often need to adjust your data ranges so that your charts plot an updated data range, you may be interested in a trick that forces Excel to update the chart's data range whenever you add new data to your worksheet.

To force Excel to update your chart automatically when you add new data, follow these steps:

1. Create a worksheet similar to the one shown in Figure 17-24.

2. Select Insert ➪ Name ➪ Define to bring up the Define Name dialog box. In the Names in Workbook field, enter **Date**. In the Refers To field, enter this formula:

```
=OFFSET(Sheet1!$A$2,0,0,COUNTA(Sheet1!$A:$A)-1)
```

3. Click Add. Notice that the OFFSET function refers to the first data point (cell A2) and uses the COUNTA function to get the number of data points in the column. Because column A has a heading in row 1, the formula subtracts 1 from the number.

Figure 17-24: This chart is updated automatically whenever you add new data to columns A and B.

4. Type **Sales** in the Names in Workbook field, and in the Refers To field enter

   `=OFFSET(Sheet1!$B$2,0,0,COUNTA(Sheet1!$B:$B)-1)`

5. Click Add and then click OK to close the dialog box.

6. Activate the chart and select the data series. In this example, the formula in the formula bar will read

   `=SERIES(Sheet1!$B$1,Sheet1!$A$2:$A$10,Sheet1!$B$2:$B$10,1)`

7. Replace the range references with the names that you defined in Steps 2 and 4. The formula should read

   `=SERIES(,Sheet1!Date,Sheet1!Sales,1)`

Note   After you edit the formula, Excel may show the workbook name in the formula.

After you perform these steps, when you add data to columns A and B, the chart updates automatically to show the new data.

To use this technique for your own data, make sure that the first argument for the OFFSET function refers to the first data point, and that the argument for COUNTA refers to the entire column of data. Also, if the columns used for the data contain any other entries, COUNTA will return an incorrect value.

Plotting mathematical functions with one variable

An XY chart is useful for plotting various mathematical and trigonometric functions. For example, Figure 17-25 shows a plot of the SIN function. The charts plots y for values of x (expressed in radians) from –5 to +5 in increments of 0.5. Each pair of x and y values appears as a data point in the chart, and the points connect with a line.

The function is expressed as

```
y = SIN(x)
```

The corresponding formula in cell B2 (which is copied to the cells below) is

```
=SIN(A2)
```

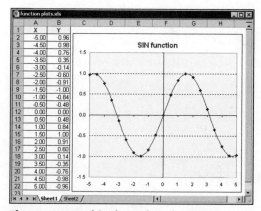

Figure 17-25: This chart plots the SIN(*x*).

The companion CD-ROM also contains a general-purpose single-variable plotting application.

Plotting mathematical functions with two variables

The preceding section described how to plot functions that use a single variable (*x*). You also can plot functions that use two variables. For example, the following function calculates a value of *z* for various values of two variables (*x* and *y*):

```
z = SIN(x)*COS(y)
```

Figure 17-26 shows a surface chart that plots the value of *z* for 21 *x* values ranging from –3 to 0, and for 21 *y* values ranging from 2 to 5. Both *x* and *y* use an increment of 0.15.

The companion CD-ROM also contains a general–purpose, two-variable plotting application.

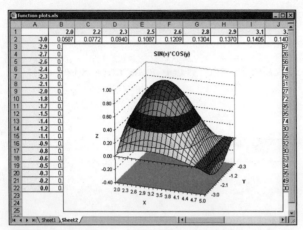

Figure 17-26: Using a surface chart to plot a function with two variables.

Frequently Asked Questions

I wrap up this chapter with answers to common questions that deal with Excel's charting features. Some of these questions are covered in more depth in Chapter 16 or elsewhere in this chapter.

The questions are divided into the following categories:

✦ Chart settings

✦ Chart formatting

✦ Chart series

✦ Chart types

✦ Miscellaneous

Questions about chart settings

What's better: A chart embedded on a worksheet or a chart on a chart sheet?

This question has no answer. Each type of chart serves a purpose. Using chart sheets may make it easier to locate your charts because their tabs can be given descriptive names. Embedded charts, on the other hand, are useful if you'd like to see the chart along with the data that it uses. And, of course, you have more control over the appearance of embedded charts because you can size and position them any way you like. And if you need to print multiple charts on a single sheet, using embedded charts is your only choice.

Can a chart sheet hold more than one chart?

Yes. Create your charts as usual, placing them in a worksheet. Select any blank cell in the worksheet and press F11. This creates an empty chart sheet to hold the embedded charts. Reactivate your worksheet, click an embedded chart, and select Chart ➪ Location to display the Chart Location dialog box. Choose the option labeled As Object In and specify the empty chart sheet. Excel then transfers the embedded chart to your chart sheet.

Select your remaining charts, one at a time, and use Chart ➪ Location to move them to the chart sheet. Now you can arrange and size the charts any way you like. Putting multiple charts on a single chart sheet lets you use the View ➪ Sized with Window command (available when the chart sheet is active) to scale the charts to the window size and dimensions.

I created a line chart, and the empty cells leave a gap in the line. How can I get rid of these gaps?

When you create a line chart in Excel, missing data points (blank cells) won't be plotted, and the line will contain gaps. Excel provides two other ways of handling missing data:

✦ Treat blanks as zeros

✦ Interpolate the data by connecting the line between the nonmissing data points

To set how Excel deals with missing data, select your chart and choose Tools ➪ Options. In the Options dialog box, click the Chart tab and then select the appropriate option. Your choice will apply to all data series in the selected chart.

You can also represent missing data with the formula =NA( ) instead of leaving a cell blank. The chart will use interpolation for data cells that contain this formula, regardless of the setting in the Options dialog box.

Can I link the Min and Max values for an axis to cells?

Unfortunately, it is not possible to do that directly. You can, however, create a VBA macro that is executed whenever a particular range is modified. That macro would then change the appropriate properties of the chart.

I'm using dates for the category axis, and Excel insists on showing dates that don't even appear in my worksheet. How can I fix this?

Activate the chart and choose Chart ➪ Chart Options. In the Chart Options dialog box, click the Axes tab. Make sure that the Category option (not Automatic or Timescale) is selected for the axis.

I hate the default colors that Excel uses for chart series. Can I change them?

Every workbook has a palette of 56 colors, and these colors are stored with the workbook. To change any of these colors select Tools ➪ Options and click the Color tab of the Options dialog box.

This dialog box shows the colors used for chart fills and chart lines. To change a color, select it and click the Modify button. The changes you make will affect all existing charts in the workbook and will also be used for future charts you create in that workbook.

The advice in the previous question works fine. But how can I change the default colors for all new workbooks?

If you would like to make these color changes apply to all new workbooks that you create, you need to create a default workbook template.

1. **Start with a new workbook**

2. **Use Tools ➪ Options, click the Color tab of the Options dialog box, and make the color changes.**

3. **Choose File ➪ Save As to display the Save As dialog box.**

4. **In the Save as type box, select Template. Choose the XlStart folder as the location, and use book.xlt as the filename.**

   The location of the XLStart folder may vary, but it is usually located here:

   ```
   C:\Program Files\Microsoft Office\Office11\XLStart
   ```

5. **Click Save.**

After performing these steps, you can create a new workbook, based on this template, by clicking the New button on the Standard toolbar. The new workbook will be based on your book.xlt template file—and it will have the modified color palette.

Chart formatting questions

How can I select all the embedded charts on my worksheet?

Press Ctrl+G to display the Go To dialog box. Click Special, and then select Objects. This will select all objects on the sheet—not just the charts.

Another option is to select each chart individually. Hold down the Ctrl key and then click all of your charts to select them. This may be easier if you set the Zoom percent to a small number.

I have several embedded charts. How can I make them all the same size?

Select all of the charts. Then choose Format ➪ Object to display the Format Object dialog box. Click the size tab, enter the dimensions for the Height and Width, and click OK. The exact dimensions aren't critical at this point. The charts will be the same size. To fine-tune the size, make sure that all of the charts are still selected, then drag one of the corners. All of the charts will be resized together.

How can I make all of my embedded charts aligned and evenly spaced?

Select all the charts you want to work with. Make sure that the Drawing toolbar is displayed, and use the Draw button to perform various operations on the selected charts.

I created a line chart, and there is a gap between the beginning of the line and the Value axis. How can I get rid of that gap?

Double-click the Category axis to display the Format Axis dialog box. Click the Scale tab, and remove the check mark from the check box labeled Value (Y) Axis Crosses Between Categories.

Can I use superscript or subscript formatting in a chart title?

Yes. Click the title to select it. Then click again to highlight the text that you want to format — in this case, the character that you want to display as superscript or subscript. Choose Format ➪ Selected Chart title and adjust the font setting for the selected text. This technique also works with axis titles.

Can I use superscript or subscript formatting for the values on my axes?

Unfortunately, no.

How can I create a "broken" axis to accommodate data that is much larger than other data points?

Unfortunately, you have no way to do this without resorting to complicated tricks that are not dynamic. One such trick involves creating two charts and superimposing one on top of the other, along with a Shape object to indicate the axis split.

Is it possible to use conditional formatting with a chart? I would like the colors in a column chart to vary, depending on the value.

Excel does not provide any way to do this automatically. However, it is possible to create a VBA macro that applies conditional formatting.

I set the font sizes in my chart, but when I resize the chart, Excel changes them! How do I prevent that?

Select the text item in the chart (a chart title, axis, legend, and so on), and access the Format dialog box for that item. Click the Font tab and specify the font size. Remove the check mark from the Auto Scale check box.

To turn off auto scaling for all text items in the chart, access the Format Chart Area dialog box, choose the Font tab, and remove the check mark from Auto Scale. For best results, do this before making any font formatting changes in the chart — otherwise, all text elements will be formatted identically, and you'll probably need to make additional adjustments.

To turn off auto scaling permanently, you need to make a change to the Windows registry. Use the Windows `regedit.exe` program and navigate to this key (the "11.0" part will vary, depending on the version of Office installed):

```
HKEY_CURRENT_USER\Software\Microsoft\Office\11.0\Excel\Options
```

Use Edit ➪ New — DWORD value to add a new item named AutoChartFontScaling and give it a value of 0.

> **Note**   This change affects only the charts that you create after making the registry change. Previously created charts are not affected. This registry entry simply controls the value of the Auto Scale check box in the Font tab of the Format Chart Area dialog box.

When I create a bar chart, the categories are in reverse order from the way they are arranged in my worksheet. How can I fix that?

The categories for all charts begin at the intersection of the category axis with the value axis. With a bar chart, that position happens to be at the bottom-left corner of the chart. So if your category labels are stored in rows (as opposed to columns), the category labels will be in the opposite order.

The solution is simple: Access the Format Axis dialog box for the category axis, click the Scale tab, and add check marks to the Categories in Reverse Order check box and the Value (Y) Axis Crosses at Maximum Category check box.

The text labels below the category axis are too crowded and are very difficult to read. How I can I correct that?

You can correct this problem in a number of ways. In some cases, you may need to use two or more of these suggestions:

✦ Reduce the font size for the category axis labels.

✦ Increase the width of the Chart Area.

✦ Adjust the options for the category axis scale (using the Scale tab of the Format Axis dialog box).

✦ Adjust the alignment options for the category axis scale (using the Alignment tab of the Format Axis dialog box).

✦ Edit the text used for the category axis labels.

I created a great chart and spent hours customizing it. Now I need to create another one just like it. Is there a quick way to duplicate all of the custom formatting?

You have several options:

✦ **Copy the formatting:** Create a standard chart with the default formatting. Then select your original chart and choose Edit ⇨ Copy. Click your new chart and choose Edit ⇨ Paste Special. In the Paste Special dialog box, select Formats.

✦ **Copy the chart:** Hold down Ctrl while you click the original chart and drag. This creates an exact copy of your chart. Then use the Chart ⇨ Source Data dialog box to specify the data for the new chart.

✦ **Create a user-defined chart type:** Select your chart; then, choose Chart ⇨ Chart Type. Click the Custom Types tab and select the User-Defined option. Click the Add button and then provide a name and description. When you create your next chart, use this custom chart type.

When I hover the mouse pointer over a data point in a chart, I see a small pop-up that displays the value and the name. How can I turn that off?

These are known as chart tips. To turn off chart tips, select Tools ⇨ Options and click the Chart tab in the Options dialog box. There you'll find check boxes that control the display of chart tips.

Is there any way to provide different text in the pop-up chart tips?

No.

Not even with VBA?

No.

Whenever I change the data used by a pivot chart, all of my custom formatting goes away! What's wrong?

The design of the pivot tables is what's wrong. Microsoft has been aware of this problem for a long time, but the problem remains. Two ways around this problem are 1) record a macro that applies the formatting changes and 2) create a user-defined chart type.

Why is there so much empty space around my 3-D column chart?

Good question. I don't know the answer. In some cases, you can experiment with the chart rotation to make better use of the space. To change the rotation of a 3-D chart, use the Chart ➪ 3-D View command.

I created a column chart. How can I change the color of only one column?

Click a column to select the entire series. Then click the specific column you want to change. You can then format this column individually by using the standard formatting techniques.

Chart series questions

My chart has two data series, and one contains much larger values. Because of this, one of the data series is barely visible.

One solution is to use a secondary value axis for the second series. Select the series and choose Format ➪ Data Series. In the Format Data Series dialog box, click the Axis tab and select the Secondary axis option.

When I add new data to my worksheet, why doesn't my chart update itself to display the new data?

That behavior is by design. You can create a self-expanding chart series by creating a named formula. Use the Define Name dialog box to create the following named formula (named Data):

```
=OFFSET(Sheet1!$A$2,0,0,COUNTA(Sheet1!$A:$A)-1,1)
```

This formula assumes that your data begins in cell A2 and that you have a column header in cell A1. Substitute the name Data for the values field in the Series formula. For example:

```
=SERIES(,,Sheet1!Data,1)
```

If you use Excel 2003, you have another option. Create a designated list from your chart data range by using the Date ➪ List ➪ Create List command. After doing so, the chart series adjusts automatically as you add or remove data from the list.

How can I add a straight line to my chart that displays the average of my values?

You need to add a new series to the chart. Generate values for the new series with a formula that calculates the average of your original values. Every data point in the new series will contain this calculated value.

I added a trendline to my chart and selected the option to display the equation. How can I get those numbers into my worksheet?

For a linear trendline you can use the SLOPE, INTERCEPT, and RSQ functions to calculate the values in the trendline equation. For other types of trendlines, you can use the LINEST function.

How can I make a chart using one data point from each of a dozen worksheets?

You'll need to create some simple formulas that reference the other sheets. For example:

```
=Sheet2!A1
=Sheet3!A1
```

Then, create your chart by using the data returned by these formulas.

I have a range of text that I would like to use as data labels in my chart. Is that possible?

Oddly, Excel does not provide this capability. A number of third-party utilities are available, including the Power Utility Pak add-in. (A trial version is available on the companion CD-ROM.) Or you can use this simple VBA macro:

```
Sub PromptForDataLabels()
    Dim RngLabels As Range, Ser As Series, i As Long
    If TypeName(Selection) = "Series" Then
        Set Ser = Selection
        Set RngLabels = Application.InputBox _
            (prompt:="Select the label range:", Type:=8)
        Ser.HasDataLabels = True
        For i = 1 To Ser.Points.Count
            Ser.Points(i).DataLabel.Text = RngLabels(i)
        Next i
    Else
        MsgBox "Select a series in a chart."
    End If
End Sub
```

I have thousands of data points. How can I plot every fifth data point?

The easiest way to do that is to take advantage of autofiltering. Insert a new column next to your chart data and enter a formula, such as

```
=MOD(ROW(),5)
```

This formula divides the row number by 5 and returns the remainder. Then use autofiltering to display only the rows in which this formula returns 0. The result is that every fifth row is hidden. By defaults, charts do not display data in hidden rows.

I added data labels to my chart, but some of them are illegible. Can I reposition them?

Yes, but it's a manual process. Click the data labels to select them all. Then, click on a single data label to select only that label. Drag it to its new position. Repeat this process for other data labels that need to be moved.

Chart type questions

Can I create a Gantt (timeline) chart by using Excel?

Yes, Excel can display a simple Gantt chart. Arrange your data in three columns: Task Name, Start Date, and Duration. Then create a stacked bar chart from this data. Format the first series (Start Date) such that the bar and its border are hidden.

How can I create a histogram?

You have two options:

- ✦ Use the Histogram tool in the Analysis ToolPak. This tool summarizes your data and creates a chart, but it is not dynamic.

- ✦ Create your bins and use the FREQUENCY function to determine the counts for each bin. Then create a chart from the frequency data.

I created a 3-D column chart, but it's difficult to tell which columns are higher than the others. What am I doing wrong?

Excel 3-D column charts may look appealing, but they are not suitable for situations in which precise comparisons need to be made. Use a 2-D column chart instead.

Each of my data points is defined by three variables (x, y, and z). How do I create a 3-D scattergram?

Unfortunately, Excel does not support that type of chart.

I created some user-defined chart types. How can I share them with my co-workers?

You should be able to simply copy your XLUSRGAL.XLS file to the appropriate location on the other system. The XLUSRGAL.XLS file does not exist unless the user has created at least one user-defined chart type. And, if the user has created custom chart types, they will be overwritten when you copy your XLUSRGAL.XLS file.

How can I make a chart that shows lines and columns?

This is known as a combination chart. When you create the chart using the Chart Wizard, you can click Custom Types in Step 1 and then choose the Line ⇨ Column chart type.

Alternatively, you can start with a standard noncombination chart. Then select a series in your chart and choose Chart ⇨ Chart Type. The chart type you choose applies only to the series that is selected.

Can all chart types be used in a combination chart?

No. For example, you can't combine a 3-D chart with any other chart type. If you attempt to create an invalid combination chart, Excel will not allow it.

How can I create a chart that uses a map?

If you use Excel 2000 or earlier, you can use the Data Map feature that's included with Excel. Beginning with Excel 2002, however, that feature is no longer available.

Miscellaneous chart questions

What's the difference between a value axis and a category axis? And what's a series axis?

A *value axis* displays values on a numeric scale. A *category axis* display arbitrary text (which could also be numbers). A *series axis,* relevant only for 3-D charts, is a category axis that extends into the *depth* direction.

A typical column chart has a horizontal category axis and a vertical value axis. An XY chart and a bubble chart have two values axes (and no category axis). A pie chart has no axes.

I created a chart, but Excel seems to treat all my numbers as zero! What's wrong?

Most likely, you imported the data, and Excel does not recognize the data as values. To correct this, follow these steps:

1. **Select any blank cell.**

2. **Choose Edit ⇨ Copy.**

3. **Select your data range.**

4. **Choose Edit ⇨ Paste Special and select the Add option.**

These steps force Excel to treat the values as real values.

How can I keep an embedded chart from expanding in size when I add a new row or column within the chart boundaries?

Press Ctrl and click the chart to select its container. Then choose Format ⇨ Object. In the Format Object dialog box, click the Properties tab. Change the object positioning option to something other than Move and Size With Cells.

How do I save a chart as a GIF file?

One way is to save the workbook as a Web Page (use File ➪ Save As Web Page). This action creates a new directory that contains GIF files for all the charts.

Or you can use a utility (such as my Power Utility Pak add-in) to save a chart as a GIF file.

Yet another option is to use a simple VBA macro. The macro listed below, for example, saves the active chart as a GIF file named `mychart.gif`.

```
Sub ExportToGIF()
    If ActiveChart Is Nothing Then
        MsgBox "Select a chart."
    Else
        ActiveChart.Export "mychart.gif", "GIF"
    End If
End Sub
```

Can I save charts to other graphic file formats?

Yes, as long as the appropriate graphic export filters are installed. To find out which export filters are installed, execute the Windows `regedit.exe` program and navigate to

```
HKEY_LOCAL_MACHINE\SOFTWARE\Microsoft\Shared Tools\Graphics
Filters\Export
```

To install other graphic export filters, rerun the Excel (or Office) Setup program.

I have several embedded charts on a worksheet. How can I prevent these charts from printing?

Press Ctrl and click the chart to select its container. Then choose Format ➪ Object. In the Format Object dialog box, click the Properties tab. Remove the check mark from the Print Object check box.

I need to create a chart, but the data is in nonadjacent columns. Do I need to move all of the data to a single range?

No. You can make a multiple range selection before you create the chart. Select the first range; then press Ctrl and select the other range(s). Or you can create the chart using a single range and then use the Chart ➪ Source Data command to add additional series.

Can I display a chart in a UserForm?

Yes, but you will need to write VBA code to do it. Your code will need to save the chart as a GIF file and then load the GIF file into an Image control placed on the UserForm.

I created a chart, and I would like to keep it as it is. I don't want it to change when I change the data it uses. Is that possible?

Yes, you can unlink a chart from its data ranges and produce a static chart that remains unaffected by later changes in the data. You have two ways to do this:

✦ Copy the chart as a picture. Activate your chart, hold down the Shift key, and choose Edit ➪ Copy Picture. (This option is available only when you hold down Shift as you select Edit.) The Copy Picture dialog box appears. Click OK to accept the defaults. Then click anywhere in your worksheet and choose Edit ➪ Paste.

✦ Convert the range references to arrays. Select a chart series and then click the Formula bar to activate the Series formula. Press F9 to convert the range references into arrays. Repeat this for each series in the chart. Now the chart can still be formatted. (It doesn't become a picture.)

There is a limit to the length of a Series formula, so the second procedure will not work if the chart series contains many data points.

I added an AutoShape to my chart, but it doesn't move with the chart. What's wrong?

Most likely, the chart was not selected when you added the AutoShape, and the AutoShape is on the worksheet, not the chart. To move the AutoShape to your chart, select it and choose Edit ➪ Cut. Then select your chart and choose Edit ➪ Paste. You can then move the AutoShape to the desired position within the chart.

How can I link a chart title to a cell?

First, make sure that the chart has a title. Then click the chart title to select it. Type an equal sign (=) and then click the cell that you want to link to. Press Enter to create the link.

Is it possible to add additional text to a chart, outside of the titles?

Yes. Select your chart and then start typing the text. Press Enter when you are finished. This results in a free-floating text box, which you can move and format to your liking.

Can I make this added text linked to a cell?

Yes. Select your chart, type an equal sign (=), and then click the cell that you want to link to. Press Enter to create the linked text box.

✦   ✦   ✦

Enhancing Your Work with Pictures and Drawings

◆ ◆ ◆ ◆

In This Chapter

Inserting and customizing AutoShapes

Working with other types of graphics

Using diagrams and creating organization charts

◆ ◆ ◆ ◆

When it comes to visual presentation, Excel has a lot more up its sleeve than charts. As you may know, you can insert a wide variety of graphic images into your worksheet to add pizzazz to an otherwise boring report.

This chapter describes the non-chart-related graphic tools available in Excel. These consist of AutoShapes, diagrams, and imported or pasted images.

Using AutoShapes

The Microsoft Office suite of applications, including Excel, provide access to a variety of customizable graphic images known as *AutoShapes*. You can add an AutoShape to a worksheet's drawing layer or to a chart. Access these AutoShapes by using either of two methods:

 ✦ Choose Insert ➪ Picture ➪ AutoShapes to display the AutoShapes toolbar.

 ✦ Use the AutoShapes menu item on the Drawing toolbar.

The AutoShapes toolbar

The AutoShapes toolbar is shown in Figure 18-1.

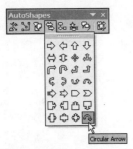

Figure 18-1: The AutoShapes
toolbar.

Drawing objects with the AutoShapes tool is easy and very intuitive. The AutoShapes
toolbar contains several buttons, each of which represents a category of AutoShapes.

Tip   You may find it convenient to "tear off" one or more of the AutoShape categories
and create new toolbars. To do so, click the button for the AutoShape category you
want to work with and then just click and drag the tiny title bar away. The effect will
be a free-floating toolbar that displays the icons for the AutoShapes in the category.

Inserting AutoShapes

As I mentioned earlier, an AutoShape can be added to a worksheet's drawing layer or
added to a chart. To insert an AutoShape on a worksheet, start by selecting any cell.
To insert an AutoShape into a chart, start by activating the chart. Next, click the
AutoShapes button in the AutoShapes toolbar (or in the Drawing toolbar) and click
a category (for example, Basic Shapes). Then click a shape, and drag into the worksheet (or chart) to create the AutoShape. When you release the mouse button, the
object is selected, and its name appears in the Name box (as shown in Figure 18-2).

Note   If a chart is not activated when you insert the AutoShape, you can still insert an
AutoShape on *top* of a chart. The AutoShape may appear to be added to the chart,
but it will actually reside on the worksheet's drawing layer. (This is usually not
what you want.) Consequently, it will not be moved or resized with the chart.

A few of the AutoShapes require a slightly different approach. For example, when
adding a FreeForm AutoShape (from the Lines category), you can click repeatedly
to create lines. Or click and drag to create a nonlinear shape. Double-click to finish
drawing and create the AutoShape. The Curve AutoShape (also in the Lines category) also requires several clicks while drawing.

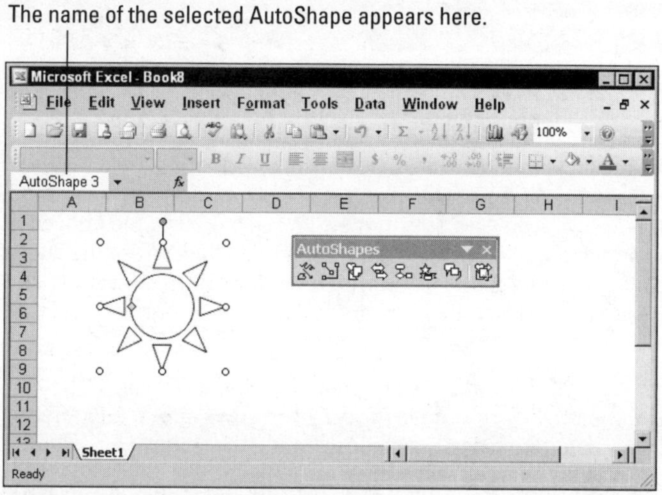

The name of the selected AutoShape appears here.

Figure 18-2: This AutoShape was drawn on the worksheet. Its name (AutoShape 3) appears in the Name box.

Following are a few tips to keep in mind when creating AutoShapes:

✦ Most AutoShapes are given names in the form of *AutoShape 1, AutoShape 2,* and so on. Some, however, are given more-descriptive names. For example, if you create a rectangle AutoShape, it will be named *Rectangle n,* where *n* represents the next AutoShape number. To change the name of an AutoShape, select it, type a new name in the Name box, and press Enter. Oddly, Excel allows multiple AutoShapes to have the same name.

✦ When you create an AutoShape by dragging, you can hold down the Shift key to maintain the object's default proportions. For example, the Rectangle AutoShape will be rendered as a perfect square. To constrain a line or arrow object to angles that are divisible by 15 degrees, press Shift while you draw the object.

✦ You can control how objects appear on-screen on the View tab of the Options dialog box (choose Tools ➪ Options). Normally, the Show All option is selected under Objects. You can hide all objects by choosing Hide All or display objects as placeholders by choosing Show Placeholders. (Hiding objects may speed things up if your worksheet contains complex objects that take a long time to redraw.)

About the Drawing Layer

Every worksheet and chart sheet has what's known as a *drawing layer.* This invisible surface can hold AutoShapes, graphic images, embedded charts, inserted objects, and so on.

Objects placed on the drawing layer can be moved, resized, copied, and deleted — with no effect on any other elements in the worksheet. Objects on the drawing layer have properties that relate to how they are moved and sized when underlying cells are moved and sized. When you right-click on a graphic object and choose Format Object from the shortcut menu, you get a tabbed dialog box (the name will vary, depending on the object). Click the Properties tab to adjust how the object moves or resizes with its underlying cells. Your choices are as follows:

✦ **Move and Size with Cells:** If this option is selected, the object appears to be attached to the cells beneath it. For example, if you insert rows above the object, the object moves down. If you increase the column width, the object gets wider.

✦ **Move But Don't Size with Cells:** If this option is checked, the object moves if rows or columns are inserted, but it never changes its size if you change row heights or column widths.

✦ **Don't Move or Size with Cells:** This option makes the object completely independent of the underlying cells.

The preceding options control how an object is moved or sized with respect to the underlying cells. Excel also lets you *attach* an object to a cell. To do so, choose Tools ➪ Options, click the Edit tab, and place a check mark next to the check box labeled Cut, Copy, and Sort Objects with Cells. After you do so, graphic objects on the drawing layer are attached to the underlying cells.

Adding text to an AutoShape

Many of the AutoShape objects support text. To add text to such an AutoShape, right-click it and then choose Add Text from the shortcut menu that appears, or just select the object and start typing the text. Either of these actions puts the object into Edit mode, which enables you to enter and edit text. When an object is in Edit mode, the word *Edit* appears at the left side of the status bar.

Tip   When an AutoShape contains text, clicking the object will put it into Edit mode. To exit Edit mode and keep the object itself selected, press Escape. Alternatively, you can press Ctrl while you click the AutoShape, or you can click the edge of the AutoShape.

To change the formatting for all of the text in an AutoShape, select the AutoShape object. You can then use the Formatting toolbar buttons, or use the Format AutoShape dialog box. To change the formatting of specific characters within the text, select only those characters, and use the Formatting toolbar buttons or the Format AutoShape dialog box.

Formatting AutoShape objects

You can change the formatting of AutoShapes at any time, which probably comes as no surprise to you. First, you must select the AutoShape object. If the object is filled with a color or pattern, you can click anywhere on the object to select it. If the object is not filled (formatted with "No Fill" to make it transparent), you must click the object's border.

You can make some basic formatting changes by using the buttons on the Formatting or Drawing toolbars. For example, you can change the color by using the Fill Color button. Other modifications require that you use the Format AutoShape dialog box. After selecting one or more objects, you can display this dialog box by using any of the following techniques:

✦ Choose the Format ➪ AutoShape command.

✦ Press Ctrl+1.

✦ Double-click the AutoShape.

✦ Right-click the AutoShape and choose Format AutoShape from the shortcut menu that appears.

The Format AutoShape dialog box has several tabs, the number of which depends on the type of object and whether it contains text. Formatting AutoShapes is fairly intuitive. The best way to master AutoShape formatting is to experiment.

Selecting multiple objects

In many cases, you may want to work with several AutoShapes at one time. Excel provides several methods that enable you to select multiple objects on a worksheet or chart.

✦ Press Ctrl while you click the objects.

✦ Click the Select Objects tool on the Drawing toolbar. The mouse pointer turns into an arrow. Click and "lasso" the objects that you want to select. To return to normal selection mode, press Esc or click the Select Objects tool again.

✦ To select all objects on the worksheet, choose Edit ➪ Go To (or press Ctrl+G) to display the Go To dialog box. Click Special, choose the Objects option button, and click OK.

This method is particularly useful if you want to delete all objects on a worksheet. After the objects are selected, press Delete.

Moving objects

To move an object, select it and drag one of its borders. For more-precise control, use the arrow keys to move the selected object one pixel at a time.

Copying objects

You can use the Excel standard copy and paste operations to copy graphic objects on a worksheet or within a chart. Another alternative is to select one or more objects and then press Ctrl while you drag in the worksheet.

To copy an object from the worksheet's drawing layer into a chart, select the object and choose Edit ➪ Copy. Then activate your chart and choose Edit ➪ Paste.

Rotating AutoShapes

When you select an AutoShape, it displays a small green dot. Click and drag this dot to rotate the AutoShape.

Modifying AutoShapes

Many of the AutoShapes display a small yellow dot when the AutoShape is selected. You can click and drag this dot to change to the AutoShape's outline. The exact behavior varies with the AutoShape, so you should experiment and see what happens.

Changing the stack order of objects

As you add objects to the drawing layer of a worksheet (or to a chart), you find that objects are "stacked" on top of each other in the order in which you add them. New objects are stacked on top of older objects.

In some cases, an object may be partially or completely hidden by an object higher in the stack. You can change the order in this stack. Right-click the object and select Order from the shortcut menu. This command leads to a submenu with the following choices:

- ✦ **Bring to Front:** Brings the object to the top of the stack.
- ✦ **Send to Back:** Sends the object to the bottom of the stack.
- ✦ **Bring Forward:** Brings the object one step higher toward the top of the stack.
- ✦ **Send Backward:** Sends the object one step lower toward the bottom of the stack.

Grouping objects

Excel lets you combine two or more objects into a single object. This feature is known as *grouping*. For example, if you create a design that uses four separate AutoShapes, you can combine them into a group. Then you can manipulate this group as a single object (move it, resize it, and so on).

To group two or more objects, select all the objects and then right-click them. Choose Grouping ⇨ Group from the shortcut menu that appears. Later, if you need to modify one of the objects in the group, you can ungroup them by right-clicking and selecting Grouping ⇨ Ungroup from the shortcut menu. This command breaks the object into its original components.

Using the Drawing Toolbar

To display the Drawing toolbar, click the Drawing button on Excel's Formatting toolbar. This button serves as a toggle, so clicking it again hides the Drawing toolbar. Normally, the Drawing toolbar appears at the bottom of Excel's window, but you can place it anywhere you like.

Figure 18-3 shows the Drawing toolbar. As you can see, there is more to this toolbar than meets the eye.

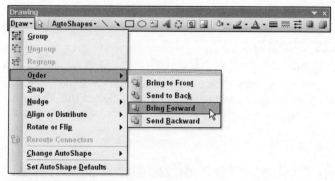

Figure 18-3: The Drawing toolbar.

Aligning objects

When you have several objects on a worksheet, you may want to align these objects with each other, or you may want to align objects with cell borders.

You can drag the objects (which isn't very precise). Or, you can use the keyboard arrow keys to move a selected object one pixel at a time. The fastest way to align objects is to let Excel do it for you.

To align multiple objects, start by selecting them. Then click the Draw tool on the Drawing toolbar. This tool expands to show a menu. Select the Align or Distribute menu option, followed by any of the six alignment options: Align Left, Align Center, Align Right, Align Top, Align Middle, or Align Bottom.

Note   Unfortunately, you cannot specify which object is used as the basis for the alignment. When you're aligning objects to the left (or right), they are always aligned
with the leftmost (or rightmost) object that's selected. When you're aligning
objects to the top (or bottom), they are always aligned with the topmost (or bot-
tommost) object. Aligning the centers (or middles) of objects will align them along
an axis halfway between the left and right (or top and bottom) extremes of the
selected shapes.

To align objects to the cell grid when you create, resize, or move them, you need
to turn on the Snap to Grid option. In the Drawing toolbar, choose Draw ➪ Snap ➪
To Grid. When that option is in effect, all objects that are created or resized will be
aligned with the cell borders. When you move an object, its upper-left corner will
always be at a cell intersection.

You may find it easier to work with objects if you turn off the worksheet grid lines.
The Snap to Grid features work, even if the cell grid lines aren't visible.

Tip   You can override the current Snap to Grid setting by pressing the Alt key while you
move or resize an object.

Spacing objects evenly

You can instruct Excel to distribute three or more objects so that they are equally
spaced horizontally or vertically. Select the objects and then click the Draw tool
on the Drawing toolbar. This tool expands to show a menu. Select the Align or
Distribute menu option, followed by either Distribute Horizontally or Distribute
Vertically.

Changing an AutoShape to a different AutoShape

You can easily change an AutoShape to a different AutoShape. Select it and then
click the Draw tool on the Drawing toolbar. Choose Change AutoShape, select the
category for the new AutoShape, and then select the AutoShape. Any formatting
applied to the AutoShape will remain.

Note   This procedure does not work with AutoShapes from the Lines or Connectors category. AutoShapes in these categories cannot be changed to a different type.

Adding shadows and 3-D effects

You can apply attractive shadows and 3-D effects to AutoShapes (except for those in
the Line and Connectors categories). Use the Shadow and 3-D tools on the Drawing
toolbar to apply these effects. Shadows and 3-D effects are mutually exclusive. In other
words, you can apply either a shadow or a 3-D effect—not both—to an AutoShape.

To apply either of these effects, select an AutoShape that you've drawn on a worksheet or chart and then click either the Shadow or the 3-D tool. The tool expands to show a list of options. Select an option, and it's applied to the selected shape. Figure 18-4 shows some AutoShapes that have been formatted with shadows or 3-D effects.

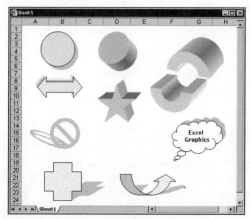

Figure 18-4: AutoShapes with shadows and 3-D effects.

You can adjust the Shadow or 3-D settings by clicking the appropriate tool and then selecting the Shadow Settings or 3-D Settings option. Both these options display a toolbar that lets you fine-tune the effect. You'll find that there are *lots* of options available, and they're all quite straightforward. The best way to become familiar with these effects is to experiment.

Changing the AutoShape defaults

You can change the default settings for the AutoShapes that you draw. For example, if you prefer a particular text color or fill color for your AutoShapes, you can set these as the defaults for all new AutoShapes that you insert.

To change the default settings, create an AutoShape and format it as you like. You can change colors, fill effects, line widths and styles, font settings, and shadow or 3-D effects. Then select the formatted object, right-click, and select Set AutoShape Defaults from the shortcut menu. You can also access this command from the Draw tool on the Drawing toolbar.

Printing objects

By default, objects are printed along with the worksheet. If you don't want the objects to print, access the Sheet panel of the Page Setup dialog box and select the Draft option. Or right-click the object, select Format from the shortcut menu, and uncheck the Print Object check box in the Properties panel.

Working with Other Graphic Types

Excel can import a wide variety of graphics into a worksheet. You have several choices:

✦ Use the Microsoft Clip Organizer to locate and insert an image.

✦ Import a graphic file directly.

✦ Copy and paste an image using the Windows Clipboard.

✦ Obtain the image directly from a digital camera or scanner.

✦ Use any of several special-purpose "applets" provided with Microsoft Office.

About graphics files

Graphics files come in two main categories: *bitmap* and *vector* (picture). Bitmap images are made up of discrete dots. They usually look pretty good at their original size but often lose clarity if you increase or decrease the size. Vector-based images, on the other hand, retain their crispness regardless of their size. Examples of common bitmap file formats include BMP, PCX, DIB, JPG, and GIF. Examples of common vector file formats include CGM, WMF, EPS, and DRW.

Bitmap files vary in the number of colors they use (even black-and-white images use multiple colors because these are usually grayscale images). If you view a high-color bitmap graphic using a video mode that displays only 256 colors, the image usually doesn't look very good.

You can find thousands of graphics files free for the taking on the Internet. Be aware, however, that some files have copyright restrictions.

Note   Using bitmap graphics in a worksheet can dramatically increase the size of your workbook, resulting in more memory usage and longer load and save times. To reduce the file size, you can compress the graphics files. To do so, select an image and choose Compress Pictures from the Picture toolbar.

The most common graphics file formats are GIF, JPG, and BMP, but Excel supports many other formats.

Using the Microsoft Clip Organizer

The Clip Organizer is a shared program that is also accessible from other Microsoft Office applications. In some versions of Office, this is known as the Clip Gallery. Besides providing an easy way to locate and insert images, the Clip Organizer lets you insert sound and video files. This tool also gives you direct access to Microsoft's Design Gallery Live on the Web.

Want a Great Graphics File Viewer?

Many users are content to use the graphics file-viewing capabilities built into Windows. But if you do a lot of work with graphics files, you owe it to yourself to get a *real* file-viewing program.

Many graphics viewers are available, but one of the best products in its class is IrfanView. It enables you to view just about any graphics file you throw at it and has features and options that will satisfy even hard-core graphics mavens. Best of all, it's free! To download a copy, visit www.irfanview.com.

You access the Clip Organizer by selecting the Insert ⇨ Picture ⇨ Clip Art command, which displays the Insert Clip Art task pane. You can search for clip art by using the controls at the top of the task pane. Figure 18-5 shows the task pane, along with the thumbnail images resulting from a search for "car". To insert an image into the active worksheet, just click the thumbnail. For additional options, right-click the thumbnail image.

Figure 18-5: Use the Excel task pane to search for clip art and other multimedia files.

You may prefer to use the Clip Organizer to access image files. To display the Clip Organizer, click the <u>Organize clips</u> hyperlink at the bottom of the task pane.

Tip   You can also add new files to the Clip Organizer. You might want to do this if you tend to insert a particular graphic file (such as your company logo) into your worksheets quite often. Use the File ➪ Add Clips to Organizer ➪ On My Own command to select the file. These images will be listed in the Unclassified Clips section. To place the image in a different category, just drag it to the category. You can also use the Edit ➪ Keywords command to associate words with your imported image. Doing this will enable you to locate the image when searching by keyword.

If you can't find a suitable image, you can go online and browse through the extensive clip art at Microsoft's Clip Gallery Live Web site. Click the <u>Clip Art on Office Online</u> hyperlink (at the bottom of the task pane), and your Web browser will be activated, at which point you can view the images (or listen to the sounds) and add those you want to your Clip Organizer.

Inserting graphics files

If the graphic image that you want to insert is available in a file, you can easily import the file into your worksheet. Choose the Insert ➪ Picture ➪ From File command. Excel displays its Insert Picture dialog box, which enables you to browse for the file.

Copying graphics by using the Clipboard

In some cases, you may want to use a graphic image that is not stored in a separate file or is in a file that Excel can't import. For example, you may have an obscure drawing program that uses a file format that Excel doesn't support. You may be able to export the file to a supported format, but it may be easier to load the file into the drawing program and copy the image to the Clipboard (using that program's Edit ➪ Copy command). Then you can activate Excel and paste the image to the drawing layer, using Edit ➪ Paste.

Suppose that you see a graphic displayed on-screen but you can't select it — it may be part of a program's logo, for example. In this case, you can copy the entire screen to the Clipboard and then paste it into Excel. To copy all or part of the screen, use the following keyboard commands:

  ✦ **PrintScreen:** Copies the entire screen to the Clipboard

  ✦ **Alt+PrintScreen:** Copies the active window to the Clipboard

Most of the time, you don't want the entire screen — just a portion of it. The solution is to crop the image by using the Excel Crop tool (in the Picture toolbar).

Importing from a digital camera or scanner

Another option lets you bring in an image directly from a digital camera or a scanner. To use this feature, make sure that your device is connected and set up properly.

Then choose Insert ➪ Picture ➪ From Scanner or Camera. The exact procedure will vary, depending on your camera or scanner. In most cases, the image will appear in Microsoft Photo Editor. You can adjust the image, if necessary, and then select File ➪ Exit and Return to Excel.

Note Many digital cameras use a USB port to transfer images. When that's the case, the digital camera's memory will be seen as a storage device located under My Computer and will be accessible with the normal Insert ➪ Picture ➪ From File command.

Displaying a worksheet background image

If you want to use a graphic image for a worksheet's background (similar to wallpaper on the Windows desktop), use the Format ➪ Sheet ➪ Background command and select a graphics file. The selected graphics file is tiled on the worksheet. Unfortunately, worksheet background images are for on-screen display only. These images do not appear when the worksheet is printed.

Modifying pictures

When you insert a picture on a worksheet, you can modify the picture in a number of ways by using the Picture toolbar, shown in Figure 18-6. This toolbar appears automatically when you select a picture object. For example, you can adjust the color, contrast, and brightness. In addition, you can add borders, crop the image, or rotate it.

Pasting Pictures of Cells and Charts

One of Excel's best-kept secrets is its ability to copy and paste pictures of cells. You can copy a cell or range and then paste a picture of the cell or range on any worksheet or chart. When pasting to a worksheet, the picture can be static or linked. With a linked picture, the link is to the cells. In other words, if you change the contents of a cell that's in a picture, the picture changes.

To create a picture of a cell or range, select a range and choose Edit ➪ Copy. Then press Shift and click the Edit menu. Choose Paste Picture to create a static picture, or choose Paste Picture Link to paste a linked picture of the selection. You can paste a picture of a range into a chart, but Excel does not allow you to paste a *linked* picture of a range into a chart.

Another useful technique is to copy an embedded chart and paste it as a picture. To do so, press Ctrl and click the chart. Then press the Shift key and choose Edit ➪ Copy Picture (this command is available only when you press Shift). Excel displays it's Copy Picture dialog box. Accept the default settings and click OK. Then, select a cell and choose Edit ➪ Paste. The result is a picture of the chart. It's not a "live" chart, so it will no longer be updated if the original chart's source data changes.

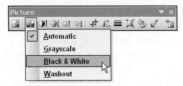

Figure 18-6: The Picture toolbar
lets you adjust a picture.

Using the Office Applets

Microsoft Office ships with a few graphics-related tools that, for lack of a better
term, I refer to as *applets*. The sections that follow discuss two of these applets:
Diagrams and Organization Charts and Word Art.

Creating diagrams and org charts

Excel also supports several types of diagrams. These diagrams are made up of
AutoShapes that are enclosed in a "shell" so that they work together as a group.
To insert a diagram, choose Insert ➪ Diagram, and you'll see the dialog box shown
in Figure 18-7.

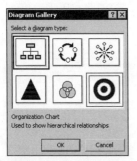

Figure 18-7: The Diagram
Gallery dialog box.

This dialog box offers the following diagram types:

✦ Organization Chart

✦ Cycle Diagram

✦ Radial Diagram

✦ Pyramid Diagram

✦ Venn Diagram

✦ Target Diagram

Choose a diagram type, click OK, and Excel inserts a diagram template, ready to be customized. Use the Diagrams toolbar to customize your diagram.

Caution Don't hide this toolbar! It's the only source for the tools you need to customize the diagrams. If you accidentally hide this toolbar, right-click on your diagram and select Show Diagram Toolbar.

With the exception of the organization chart, these diagrams are interchangeable. After a diagram is customized, you can convert it to a different type by using the Change To button on the Diagrams toolbar.

Perhaps the most useful diagram choice is the organization chart. You'll notice that an organization chart diagram displays its own toolbar (not the Diagram toolbar). Figure 18-8 shows an example of a simple org chart.

Noticeably absent is a diagram type for creating flow charts. You can, however, create flow charts by using the standard AutoShapes.

Figure 18-8: This org chart was created by using the Excel Diagram Gallery.

Working with these diagrams takes a bit of practice, but after you get the hang of it, you'll find that they can be customized in many ways. The best way to become familiar with diagrams is to experiment. However, you should be aware of these general tips:

✦ The Organization Chart and Diagram toolbars both have a button labeled Layout. When you click this button, you see an AutoLayout menu item. This is actually a toggle. When AutoLayout is turned on, you can't move the diagram elements around. For fine-tuning the position of the items in your diagram, you'll want to make sure that AutoLayout is turned off. But be careful. If you turn AutoLayout back on, the diagram will revert to its unedited state!

✦ You can change the AutoShape used by an element in a diagram. First, right-click the diagram and turn off the AutoFormat option. (By default, this option is turned on.) Then select the element, click the Draw item on the Drawing toolbar, and choose Change AutoShape. To revert to the original shapes, turn the AutoFormat option back on.

✦ To change the diagram background, right-click the background of the diagram and choose Format Diagram.

Creating WordArt

The WordArt applet enables you to create a graphic image from text. You can insert a WordArt image by using the WordArt tool on the Drawing toolbar or by selecting the Insert ➪ Picture ➪ WordArt command. Either method displays the WordArt Gallery dialog box. Select a style and then enter your text in the next dialog box. Click OK, and the image is inserted in the worksheet.

When you select a WordArt image, Excel displays the WordArt toolbar. Use these tools to modify the WordArt image. You'll find that you have *lots* of flexibility with this tool. In addition, you can use the Shadow and 3-D tools (located on the Drawing toolbar) to further manipulate the image. Figure 18-9 shows a few examples of WordArt images inserted on a worksheet.

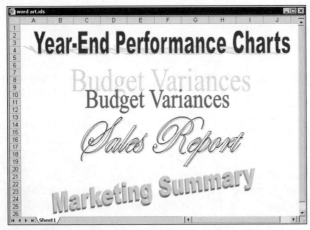

Figure 18-9: WordArt examples.

✦   ✦   ✦

Analyzing Data with Excel

Excel is a superb data analysis tool if you know how to extract the information you really need. In this part, you'll learn how to obtain and analyze data in Excel. As you'll see, many of the data analysis capabilities in Excel are both surprisingly powerful and easy to use.

◆ ◆ ◆ ◆

Working with Lists

One of the most common uses for Excel is to manage
lists, or *worksheet databases.* This chapter covers list
management and demonstrates useful techniques that involve
lists.

I also cover the new list-related features that were introduced
in Excel 2003.

What Is a List?

A list is essentially an organized collection of information.
More specifically, a list consists of a row of headers (descriptive text) followed by additional rows of data, which can be
values or text. You can also think of a list as a database table
that is stored in a worksheet.

**Cross-
Reference**   I cover external database files in Chapter 20.

Figure 19-1 shows an example of a list. This particular list has
its headers in row 2 and has 20 rows of data. The list occupies
six columns. Notice that the data consists of several different
types: text, values, dates, and logical values. Each cell in column D contains a formula that calculates the monthly salary
from the corresponding value in column C.

People often refer to the columns in a list as fields and to the
rows as records. Using this terminology, the list shown in the
figure has six fields (Name, Annual Salary, Monthly Salary,
Location, Date Hired, and Exempt) and 20 records.

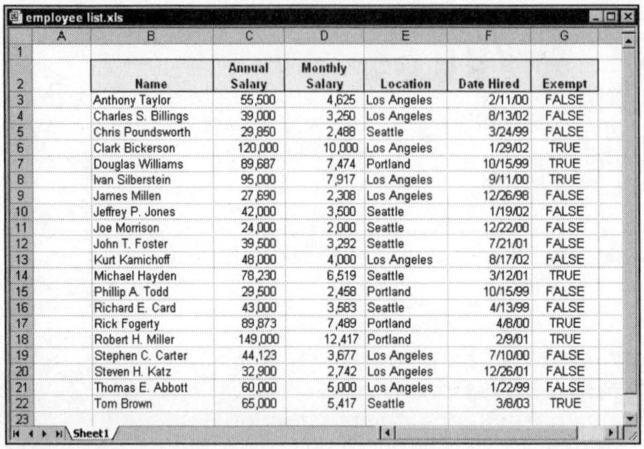

	A	B	C	D	E	F	G
1							
2		Name	Annual Salary	Monthly Salary	Location	Date Hired	Exempt
3		Anthony Taylor	55,500	4,625	Los Angeles	2/11/00	FALSE
4		Charles S. Billings	39,000	3,250	Los Angeles	8/13/02	FALSE
5		Chris Poundsworth	29,850	2,488	Seattle	3/24/99	FALSE
6		Clark Bickerson	120,000	10,000	Los Angeles	1/29/02	TRUE
7		Douglas Williams	89,687	7,474	Portland	10/15/99	TRUE
8		Ivan Silberstein	95,000	7,917	Los Angeles	9/11/00	TRUE
9		James Millen	27,690	2,308	Los Angeles	12/26/98	FALSE
10		Jeffrey P. Jones	42,000	3,500	Seattle	1/19/02	FALSE
11		Joe Morrison	24,000	2,000	Seattle	12/22/00	FALSE
12		John T. Foster	39,500	3,292	Seattle	7/21/01	FALSE
13		Kurt Kamichoff	48,000	4,000	Los Angeles	8/17/02	FALSE
14		Michael Hayden	78,230	6,519	Seattle	3/12/01	TRUE
15		Phillip A. Todd	29,500	2,458	Portland	10/15/99	FALSE
16		Richard E. Card	43,000	3,583	Seattle	4/13/99	FALSE
17		Rick Fogerty	89,873	7,489	Portland	4/8/00	TRUE
18		Robert H. Miller	149,000	12,417	Portland	2/9/01	TRUE
19		Stephen C. Carter	44,123	3,677	Los Angeles	7/10/00	FALSE
20		Steven H. Katz	32,900	2,742	Los Angeles	12/26/01	FALSE
21		Thomas E. Abbott	60,000	5,000	Los Angeles	1/22/99	FALSE
22		Tom Brown	65,000	5,417	Seattle	3/8/03	TRUE
23							

Figure 19-1: An example of a list.

The size of the lists that you develop in Excel is limited by the size of a single worksheet. In other words, a list can have no more than 256 fields and can consist of no more than 65,535 records. (One row contains the field names.) A list of this size would require a great deal of memory and even then may not be possible. At the other extreme, a list can consist of two cells (a field name, with a data cell below it). A two-cell list is not very useful, but it's still considered a list.

What Can You Do with a List?

Excel provides several tools to help you manage and manipulate lists. Consequently, people use lists for a wide variety of purposes. For some users, a list is simply a method to keep track of information (for example, customer lists); others use lists to store data that ultimately is to appear in a report. The following are common list operations:

✦ Enter data into the list.

✦ Filter the list to display only the rows that meet a certain criteria.

✦ Sort the list.

✦ Insert formulas to calculate subtotals.

✦ Create formulas to calculate results on the list filtered by certain criteria.

✦ Export the list to a SharePoint server so it can be shared with others.

✦ Create a summary table of the data in the list. (This is done by using a pivot table; see Chapter 21.)

With the exception of the last item, these operations are covered in this chapter.

Designing a List

Although Excel is quite accommodating when it comes to the information that is stored in a list, you should give some initial thought to how you want to organize your information. The following are some guidelines to keep in mind when creating lists:

✦ Insert descriptive labels (one for each column) in the first row of the list. This is the header row. If the labels are lengthy, consider using the word-wrap format so that you don't have to widen the columns.

✦ Each column should contain the same type of information. For example, don't mix dates and text in a single column.

✦ You can use formulas that perform calculations on other fields in the same record. If you use formulas that refer to cells outside the list, make these absolute references; otherwise, you get unexpected results when you sort the list.

✦ Don't use any empty rows within the list. For list operations, Excel determines the list boundaries automatically, and an empty row signals the end of the list.

✦ For best results, try to keep the list on a worksheet by itself. If this isn't possible, place other information above or below the list. In other words, don't use the cells to the left or the right of a list.

✦ Select the upper-left data cell and choose Window ➪ Freeze Panes to make sure that the headings are visible when the list is scrolled.

✦ You can preformat entire columns to ensure that the data has the same format. For example, if a column contains dates, format the entire column with the desired date format.

One of the most appealing aspects of spreadsheets is that you can change the layout relatively easily. This, of course, also applies to lists. For example, you may create a list and then decide that it needs another column (field). No problem. Just insert a new column, give it a field name, and your list is expanded. If you've ever used a database management program, you can appreciate how easy this is.

Entering Data into a List

Entering data into a list can be done in three ways:

✦ Manually, using all standard data entry techniques

✦ By importing it or copying it from another file

✦ By using a dialog box

There's really nothing special about entering data into a list. You just navigate through the worksheet and enter the data into the appropriate cells.

Excel has two features that assist with repetitive data entry:

✦ **AutoComplete:** When you begin to type in a cell, Excel scans up and down the column to see whether it recognizes what you're typing. If it finds a match, Excel fills in the rest of the text automatically. Press Enter to make the entry. You can turn this feature on or off in the Edit panel of the Options dialog box.

✦ **Pick Lists:** You can right-click on a cell and select Pick from List from the shortcut menu (see Figure 19-2). Excel displays a list box that shows all entries in the column. Click on the one that you want, and it is then entered into the cell. (No typing is required.)

If you prefer to use a dialog box for your data entry, Excel accommodates you. To bring up a data entry dialog box, move the cell pointer anywhere within the list and choose Data ➪ Form. Excel determines the extent of your list and displays a dialog box showing each field in the list. Figure 19-3 depicts an example of such a dialog box. Fields that have a formula don't have an edit box.

	A	B	C	D	E	F	G	H
12		John T. Foster	39,500	3,292	Seattle	7/21/01	FALSE	
13		Kurt Karnichoff	48,000	4,000	Los Angeles	8/17/02	FALSE	
14		Michael Hayden	78,230	6,519	Seattle	3/12/01	TRUE	
15		Phillip A. Todd	29,500	2,458	Portland	10/15/99	FALSE	
16		Richard E. Card	43,000	3,583	Seattle	4/13/99	FALSE	
17		Rick Fogerty	89,873	7,489	Portland	4/8/00	TRUE	
18		Robert H. Miller	149,000	12,417	Portland	2/9/01	TRUE	
19		Stephen C. Carter	44,123	3,677	Los Angeles	7/10/00	FALSE	
20		Steven H. Katz	32,900	2,742	Los Angeles	12/26/01	FALSE	
21		Thomas E. Abbott	60,000	5,000	Los Angeles	1/22/99	FALSE	
22		Tom Brown	65,000	5,417	Seattle	3/8/03	TRUE	
23		Mark Hampton	38,500	3,208				
24					Los Angeles			
25					Portland			
26					Seattle			
27								
28								
29								
30								

Figure 19-2: Choosing the Pick from List command on the shortcut menu gives you a list of all items in the current column.

Sheet1				
Name:	James Millen		7 of 20	
Annual☐Salary:	27690		New	
Monthly☐Salary:	2,308		Delete	
Location:	Los Angeles		Restore	
Date Hired:	12/26/1998		Find Prev	
Exempt:	FALSE		Find Next	
			Criteria	
			Close	

Figure 19-3: The Data ➪ Form command gives you a handy data entry dialog box.

Note   If the number of fields exceeds the limit of your display, the dialog box contains two columns of field names. If your list consists of more than 32 fields, however, the Data ➪ Form command doesn't work. You must forgo this method of data entry and enter the information directly into the cells.

On the CD-ROM   The companion CD-ROM contains a copy of the JWalk Enhanced Data Form. This free add-in eliminates the 32-field limit and offers many additional benefits over the Excel built-in data form.

Entering data with the Data Form dialog box

When the Data Form dialog box appears, the first record in the list is displayed. Notice the indicator in the upper-right corner of the dialog box; this indicator tells you which record is selected and the total number of records in the list.

To enter a new record, click the New button to clear the fields. Then you can enter the new information into the appropriate fields. Use Tab or Shift+Tab to move among the fields. When you click New (or Close), the data that you entered is appended to the bottom of the list. You also can press Enter, which is equivalent to clicking on the New button. If the list contains any formulas, these are also entered into the new record in the list for you automatically.

Tip   If your list is named Database, Excel automatically extends the range definition to include the new row(s) that you add to the list using the Data Form dialog box. Note that this works only if the list has the name Database; any other name doesn't work.

Other uses for the Data Form dialog box

You can use the Data Form dialog box for more than just data entry. You can edit existing data in the list, view data one record at a time, delete records, and display records that meet certain criteria.

The dialog box contains a number of additional buttons, which are described as follows:

✦ **Delete:** Deletes the displayed record.

✦ **Restore:** Restores any information that you edited. You must click this button before you click on the New button.

✦ **Find Prev:** Displays the previous record in the list. If you entered a criterion, this button displays the previous record that matches the criterion.

✦ **Find Next:** Displays the next record in the list. If you entered a criterion, this button displays the next record that matches the criterion.

✦ **Criteria:** Clears the fields and lets you enter a criterion upon which to search for records. For example, to locate records that have a salary greater than $50,000, enter **>50000** into the Salary field. Then you can use the Find Next and Find Prev buttons to display the qualifying records.

✦ **Close:** Closes the dialog box (and enters the data that you were entering, if any).

Filtering a List

Filtering a list is the process of hiding all rows in the list except those that meet some criteria that you specify. For example, if you have a list of customers, you can filter the list to show only those who live in Seattle. Filtering is a common (and very useful) technique. Excel provides two ways to filter a list:

✦ AutoFilter for simple filtering criteria

✦ Advance Filter for more-complex filtering

I discuss both of these options in the following sections.

Using autofiltering

To autofilter a list, start by moving the cell pointer anywhere within the list. Then choose Data ➪ Filter ➪ AutoFilter. Excel analyzes your list and adds drop-down arrows to the field names in the header row. When you click the arrow in one of these drop-down lists, the list expands to show the unique items in that column (as shown in Figure 19-4). Select an item, and Excel hides all rows except those that include the selected item. In other words, the list is filtered by the item that you selected.

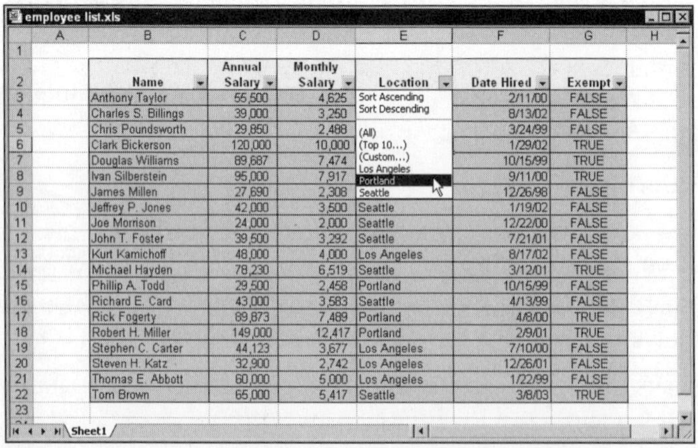

Figure 19-4: Using autofiltering to filter a list.

After you filter the list, the status bar displays a message that tells you how many rows qualified. In addition, the drop-down arrow changes color to remind you that the list is filtered by a value in that column.

Autofiltering has a limit. Only the first 1,000 unique items in the column appear in the drop-down list. If your list exceeds this limit, you can use advanced filtering, which I describe later.

Besides showing every item in the column, the drop-down list includes other items:

✦ **All:** Displays all items in the column. Use this to remove filtering for a column.

✦ **Top 10:** Filters to display the "top 10" items in the list; I discuss this later in this chapter.

✦ **Custom:** Lets you filter the list by multiple items; I discuss this in the "Custom autofiltering" section, later in this chapter.

✦ **Blanks:** Filters the list by showing rows that contain blanks in this column. This item appears at the bottom of the drop-down list and only if the column contains one or more blank cells..

✦ **NonBlanks:** Filters the list by showing rows that contain nonblanks in this column. This item appears at the bottom of the drop-down list and only if the column contains one or more blank cells.

To display the entire list again, click the arrow and choose All—the first item in the drop-down list. Or you can select Data ➪ Filter ➪ Show All.

To move out of AutoFilter mode and remove the drop-down arrows from the field names, choose Data ➪ Filter ➪ AutoFilter again. This removes the check mark from the AutoFilter menu item and restores the list to its normal state.

Caution   If you have any formulas that refer to data in a filtered list, be aware that the formulas don't adjust to use only the visible cells. For example, if a cell contains a formula that sums values in column C, the formula continues to show the sum for *all* the values in column C — not just those in the visible rows. The solution to this is to use the SUBTOTAL function, which I describe later in this chapter.

Multicolumn autofiltering

Sometimes you may need to filter a list by using values in more than one column. Figure 19-5 shows a list comprised of several fields. Assume that you want to see the records that show only the Exempt employees in Los Angeles. In other words, you want to filter out all records except those in which the Location field is *Los Angeles* and the Exempt field is *TRUE*.

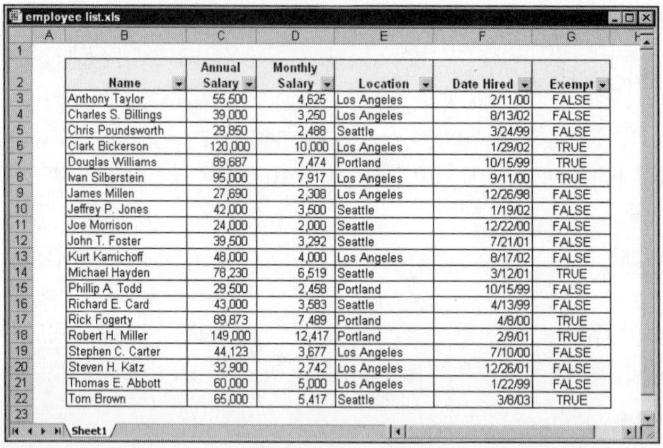

Name	Annual Salary	Monthly Salary	Location	Date Hired	Exempt
Anthony Taylor	55,500	4,625	Los Angeles	2/11/00	FALSE
Charles S. Billings	39,000	3,250	Los Angeles	8/13/02	FALSE
Chris Poundsworth	29,850	2,488	Seattle	3/24/99	FALSE
Clark Bickerson	120,000	10,000	Los Angeles	1/29/02	TRUE
Douglas Williams	89,687	7,474	Portland	10/15/99	TRUE
Ivan Silberstein	95,000	7,917	Los Angeles	9/11/00	TRUE
James Millen	27,690	2,308	Los Angeles	12/26/98	FALSE
Jeffrey P. Jones	42,000	3,500	Seattle	1/19/02	FALSE
Joe Morrison	24,000	2,000	Seattle	12/22/00	FALSE
John T. Foster	39,500	3,292	Seattle	7/21/01	FALSE
Kurt Kamichoff	48,000	4,000	Los Angeles	8/17/02	FALSE
Michael Hayden	78,230	6,519	Seattle	3/12/01	TRUE
Phillip A. Todd	29,500	2,458	Portland	10/15/99	FALSE
Richard E. Card	43,000	3,583	Seattle	4/13/99	FALSE
Rick Fogerty	89,873	7,489	Portland	4/8/00	TRUE
Robert H. Miller	149,000	12,417	Portland	2/9/01	TRUE
Stephen C. Carter	44,123	3,677	Los Angeles	7/10/00	FALSE
Steven H. Katz	32,900	2,742	Los Angeles	12/26/01	FALSE
Thomas E. Abbott	60,000	5,000	Los Angeles	1/22/99	FALSE
Tom Brown	65,000	5,417	Seattle	3/8/03	TRUE

Figure 19-5: This list is to be filtered by multiple columns.

On the CD-ROM The example shown in Figure 19-5 is demonstrated in a file on the companion CD-ROM.

First, select any cell in your list and then get into AutoFilter mode (choose Data ➪ Filter ➪ AutoFilter). Then click on the drop-down arrow in the Location field and select *Los Angeles*. This filters the list to show only records with *Los Angeles* in the Location field. Then click on the drop-down arrow in the Exempt field and select *TRUE*. This filters the filtered list. In other words, the list is filtered by values in two columns. As you can see in Figure 19-6, only two records meet both of the criteria.

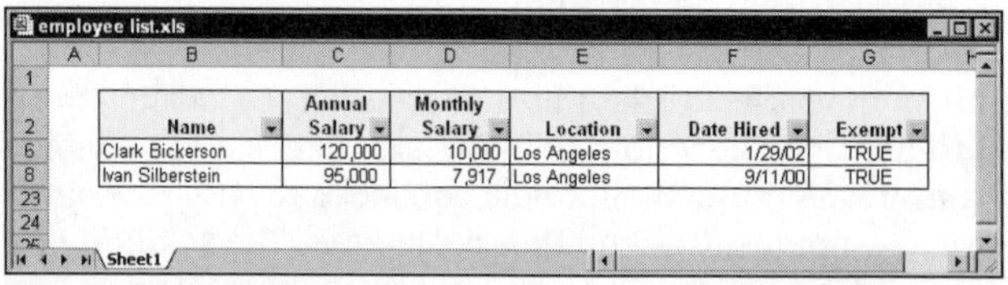

Name	Annual Salary	Monthly Salary	Location	Date Hired	Exempt
Clark Bickerson	120,000	10,000	Los Angeles	1/29/02	TRUE
Ivan Silberstein	95,000	7,917	Los Angeles	9/11/00	TRUE

Figure 19-6: This list is filtered by values in two columns.

You can filter a list by any number of columns. The drop-down arrows in the columns that have a filter applied are a different color.

Custom autofiltering

Usually, autofiltering involves selecting a single value for one or more columns. If you choose the Custom option in a drop-down list, you gain a bit more flexibility in filtering the list. Selecting the Custom option displays a dialog box like the one shown in Figure 19-7. The Custom AutoFilter dialog box lets you filter in several ways:

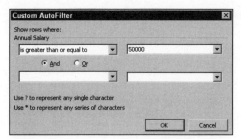

Figure 19-7: The Custom AutoFilter dialog box gives you more filtering options.

✦ **Values above or below a specified value:** For example, Annual Salary amounts greater than or equal to 50,000.

✦ **Values within a range:** For example, sales amounts greater than 10,000 AND sales amounts less than 50,000.

✦ **Two discrete values:** For example, state equal to New York OR state equal to New Jersey.

✦ **Approximate matches:** You can use the * and ? wildcards to filter in a number of other ways. The asterisk matches any number of characters, and the question mark matches any single character.

Custom autofiltering can be useful, but it definitely has limitations. For example, if you want to filter the list to show only three values in a field (such as New York or New Jersey or Connecticut), you can't do it by autofiltering. Such filtering tasks require the advanced filtering feature, which I discuss in "Using advanced filtering," later in this chapter.

Top 10 autofiltering

Sometimes, you may want to use a filter on numerical fields to show only the highest or lowest values in the list. For example, if you have a list of employees, you may want to identify the 12 employees with the longest tenure. You could use the custom autofilter option, but then you must supply a cutoff date (which you may not know). The solution is to use Top 10 autofiltering.

Top 10 autofiltering is a generic term; it doesn't limit you to the top *10* items. In fact, it doesn't even limit you to the *top* items. When you choose the Top 10 option in a drop-down list, you get the dialog box that is shown in Figure 19-8.

You can choose either Top or Bottom and specify any number. For example, if you want to see the 12 employees with the longest tenure, choose Bottom and 12. This filters the list and shows the 12 rows with the smallest values in the Date Hired field. You also can choose Percent or Value in this dialog box. For example, you can filter the list to show the Bottom 5 percent of the records.

Figure 19-8: The Top 10 AutoFilter gives you more autofilter options.

Copying and deleting filtered data

Some of the standard spreadsheet operations work differently with a filtered list. For example, you might use the Format ➪ Row ➪ Hide command to hide rows. If you then copy a range that includes those hidden rows, all of the data gets copied (even the hidden rows). But when you copy data in an autofiltered list, only the visible rows are copied.

Similarly, you can select and delete the visible rows in the table, and the rows hidden by autofiltering will not be affected.

Using advanced filtering

In many cases, autofiltering does the job. But if you run up against its limitations, you need to use advanced filtering. Advanced filtering is much more flexible than autofiltering, but it takes a bit of up-front work to use it. Advanced filtering provides you with the following capabilities:

✦ You can specify more-complex filtering criteria.

✦ You can specify computed filtering criteria.

✦ You can display unique (nonduplicated) records only.

✦ You can extract a copy of the rows that meet the criteria to another location.

Setting up a criteria range

Before you can use the advanced filtering feature, you must set up a *criteria range*. A criteria range is a designated range on a worksheet that conforms to certain requirements. The criteria range holds the information that Excel uses to filter the list. It must conform to the following specifications:

✦ It consists of at least two rows, and the first row must contain some or all field names from the list. An exception to this is when you use computed criteria. Computed criteria can use an empty header row. (See "Computed criteria," later in this chapter).

✦ The other rows consist of your filtering criteria.

Although you can put the criteria range anywhere in the worksheet, you should avoid putting the criteria range in rows that are used by the list. Because some of these rows are hidden when the list is filtered, you may find that your criteria range is no longer visible after the filtering takes place. Therefore, you should generally place the criteria range above or below the list.

Figure 19-9 shows a worksheet that contains real estate listings. The criteria range, located in A1:D2, is positioned above the list that it uses. Notice that not all field names appear in the criteria range. Fields that aren't used in the selection criteria need not appear in the criteria range.

	A	B	C	D	E	F	G	H
1	ListPrice	Area	Type	Pool				
2		Central	Single Family					
3								
4								
5								
6	ListPrice	Date Listed	Area	Bedrooms	Baths	SquareFt	Type	Pool
7	$350,000	January 12, 2003	N. County	3	2.5	1,991	Condo	FALSE
8	$215,000	January 14, 2003	Central	3	1.75	2,157	Single Family	TRUE
9	$315,000	January 16, 2003	S. County	2	2	1,552	Condo	FALSE
10	$379,000	January 20, 2003	N. County	4	3	3,000	Single Family	FALSE
11	$248,500	January 30, 2003	?	4	2.5	2,101	Single Family	TRUE
12	$297,500	February 1, 2003	S. County	4	3.5	2,170	Single Family	FALSE
13	$259,900	February 5, 2003	N. County	4	3	1,734	Condo	FALSE
14	$325,000	February 9, 2003	S. County	4	3	2,800	Condo	TRUE
15	$208,750	February 11, 2003	S. County	4	3	2,207	Single Family	TRUE
16	$227,500	February 11, 2003	S. County	4	3	1,905	Condo	FALSE
17	$259,900	February 11, 2003	N. County	3	2.5	2,122	Condo	FALSE
18	$405,000	February 14, 2003	N. County	2	3	2,444	Single Family	TRUE
19	$236,900	February 15, 2003	S. County	2	2	1,483	Condo	FALSE
20	$240,000	February 15, 2003	S. County	3	2.5	1,595	Condo	FALSE
21	$304,900	February 17, 2003	S. County	4	3	2,350	Single Family	FALSE
22	$349,900	February 21, 2003	N. County	4	3	2,290	Single Family	TRUE

Figure 19-9: A criteria range for a list.

The example shown in Figure 19-9 is demonstrated in a file on the companion CD-ROM.

In this example, the criteria range has only one row of criteria. The fields in each row of the criteria range (except for the header row) are joined with an AND operator. Therefore, the filtered list shows rows in which the Area column equals *Central* AND the Type field is *Single Family.* In other words, the filtering will display only single-family residences in the Central area.

To perform the filtering, choose Data ➪ Filter ➪ Advanced Filter. Excel displays the dialog box that is shown in Figure 19-10. Specify the List Range and the Criteria Range, and make sure that the option labeled Filter the List, In-Place is selected. Click OK, and the list is filtered by the criteria that you specified.

Figure 19-10: The Advanced
Filter dialog box.

Multiple criteria

If you use more than one row in the criteria range, the rows of criteria are joined
with an OR operator. Figure 19-11 shows a criteria range (A1:D3) with two rows of
criteria. In this example, the filtered list shows rows in either of the following:

✦ The ListPrice is less than 300,000 AND the Area field is Central.

✦ The ListPrice is less than 350,000, AND the Area field is S. County, AND the
Pool field is TRUE.

	A	B	C	D	E	F	G	H
1	ListPrice	Area	Type	Pool				
2	<300000	Central						
3	<350000	S. County		TRUE				
4								
5								
6	ListPrice	Date Listed	Area	Bedrooms	Baths	SquareFt	Type	Pool
7	$350,000	January 12, 2003	N. County	3	2.5	1,991	Condo	FALSE
8	$215,000	January 14, 2003	Central	3	1.75	2,157	Single Family	TRUE
9	$315,000	January 16, 2003	S. County	2	2	1,552	Condo	FALSE
10	$379,000	January 20, 2003	N. County	4	3	3,000	Single Family	FALSE
11	$248,500	January 30, 2003	?	4	2.5	2,101	Single Family	TRUE
12	$297,500	February 1, 2003	S. County	4	3.5	2,170	Single Family	FALSE
13	$259,900	February 5, 2003	N. County	4	3	1,734	Condo	FALSE
14	$325,000	February 9, 2003	S. County	4	3	2,800	Condo	TRUE
15	$208,750	February 11, 2003	S. County	4	3	2,207	Single Family	TRUE
16	$227,500	February 11, 2003	S. County	4	3	1,905	Condo	FALSE
17	$259,900	February 11, 2003	N. County	3	2.5	2,122	Condo	FALSE
18	$405,000	February 14, 2003	N. County	2	3	2,444	Single Family	TRUE

Figure 19-11: This criteria range has two sets of criteria.

This is an example of filtering that could not be done with autofiltering.

A criteria range can have any number of rows, each of which is joined to the others
with an OR operator.

Types of criteria

The entries that you make in a criteria range can be either of the following:

✦ **Text or value criteria:** The filtering involves comparisons to a value or string, using such operators as equal (=), greater than (>), not equal to (<>), and so on.

✦ **Computed criteria:** The filtering involves a computation of some sort.

Text or value criteria

Table 19-1 lists the comparison operators that you can use with text or value criteria.

Table 19-1 Comparison Operators	
Operator	**Comparison Type**
=	Equal to
>	Greater than
>=	Greater than or equal to
<	Less than
<=	Less than or equal to
<>	Not equal to

Using wildcard characters

Criteria that use text also can make use of two wildcard characters: An asterisk (*) matches any number of characters; a question mark (?) matches any single character. Table 19-2 shows examples of criteria that use text. Some of these are a bit counterintuitive. For example, to select records that match a single character, you must enter the criterion as a formula. (Refer to the last entry in the table.)

Table 19-2 Examples of Text Criteria	
Criteria	**Selects**
="=January"	Records that contain the text *January* (and nothing else). You enter this exactly as shown: as a formula, with an initial equal sign. Alternatively, you can use a leading apostrophe and omit the quotes:
'=January	

(continued)

	Table 19-2 *(continued)*
Criteria	**Selects**
January	Records that begin with the text *January*.
C	Records that contain text that begins with the letter *C*.
<>C*	Records that contain any text, except text that begins with the letter *C*.
>=L	Records that contain text that begins with the letters *L* through *Z*.
County	Records that contain text that includes the word *county*.
Sm*	Records that contain text that begins with the letters *SM*.
s*s	Records that contain text that begins with *S* and have a subsequent occurrence of the letter *S*.
s?s	Records that contain text that begins with *S* and has another *S* as its third character. Note that this does *not* select only three-character words.
="=s*s" '=s*s	Records that contain text that begins and ends with *S*. You must enter this exactly as shown: as a formula, with an initial equal sign. Alternatively, you can use a leading apostrophe and omit the quotes:
<>*c	Records that contain text that does not end with the letter *C*.
=????	Records that contain exactly four letters
<>?????	Records that don't contain exactly five letters.
<>*c*	Records that do not contain the letter *C*.
~?	Records that contain a single question mark character.
=	Records that contain a blank.
<>	Records that contain any nonblank entry.
="=c" '=c	Records that contain the single character *C*. You must enter this exactly as shown: as a formula, with an initial equal sign. Alternatively, you can use a leading apostrophe and omit the quotes:

Note The text comparisons are not case sensitive. For example, se* matches *Seligman*, *seller*, and *SEC*.

Computed criteria

Using computed criteria can make your filtering even more powerful. Computed criteria filter the list based on one or more calculations. Figure 19-12 shows an example that filters the real estate listings to determine the "good value" listings — homes with a below average List Price and an above average Square Footage.

Notice that this criteria range, in B1:C2, does not use field headers from the list. Rather, it uses new field headers. Using field headers for computed criteria is optional. A computed criteria essentially computes a new field for the list, so it's a good idea to add a descriptive header.

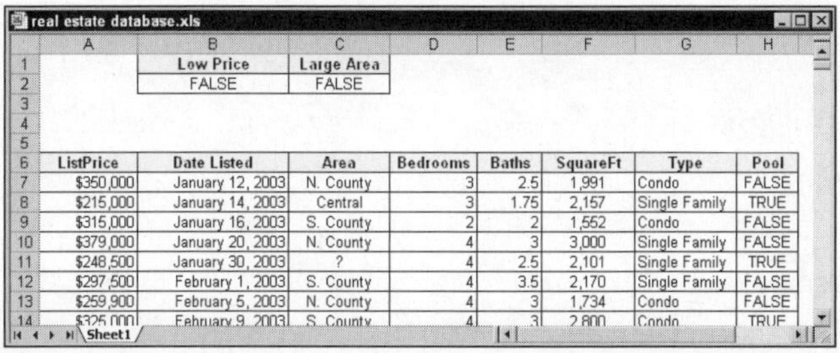

Figure 19-12: This list is to be filtered using computed criteria.

Cell B2 contains the following formula:

```
=A7<AVERAGE(A:A)
```

The formula computes the average List Price and compares it to the first data cell in the ListPrice field.

Cell C2 contains the following formula:

```
=F7>AVERAGE(F:F)
```

This formula computes the average Square Footage and compares it to the first data cell in the SquareFt field.

When the list is filtered by these criteria, it shows only rows that match both conditions: homes with a below average List Price and above average Square Footage.

Keep in mind the following items when using computed criteria:

✦ For the header of a column that contains a computed criteria, don't use a field name that appears in the list. Create a new field name or just leave the cell blank.

✦ You can use any number of computed criteria and mix and match them with noncomputed criteria.

✦ Don't pay attention to the values returned by formulas in the criteria range. These refer to the first row of the list.

✦ If your computed formula refers to a value outside the list, use an absolute reference rather than a relative reference. For example, use $C$1 rather than C1.

✦ Create your computed criteria formulas by using the first row of data in the list (not the field names). Make these references relative, not absolute. For example, use C5 rather than $C$5.

Other advanced filtering operations

The Advanced Filter dialog box gives you two other options, which I discuss in the following paragraphs:

✦ Copy to Another Location

✦ Unique Records Only

Copying qualifying rows

If you choose the Copy to Another Location option in the Advanced Filter dialog box, the qualifying rows are copied to another location in the worksheet or a different worksheet. You specify the location for the copied rows in the Copy to Edit box. Note that the list itself is not filtered when you use this option.

Displaying only unique rows

Selecting the check box labeled Unique Records Only hides all duplicate rows that meet the criteria that you specify. If you don't specify a criteria range, this option hides all duplicate rows in the list.

Using Database Functions with Lists

It's important to understand that Excel's worksheet functions don't ignore hidden cells. For example, if you have a Sum formula that calculates the total of the values in a column of a list, the formula returns the same value when the list is filtered.

To create formulas that return results based on filtering criteria, you have two choices:

✦ Use the SUBTOTAL function (see "Creating Subtotals," later in this chapter)

✦ Use Excel database worksheet functions.

This section focuses on the database functions. For example, you can create a formula that calculates the sum of values in a list that meets a certain criteria. Set up a criteria range as described in "Setting up a criteria range," earlier in this chapter. Then enter a formula, such as the following:

```
=DSUM(ListRange,FieldName,Criteria)
```

In this case, ListRange refers to the list, FieldName refers to the field name cell of the column that is being summed, and Criteria refers to the criteria range.

The Excel database functions are listed in Table 19-3.

Table 19-3 The Excel Database Worksheet Functions	
Function	**Description**
DAVERAGE	Returns the average of selected database entries
DCOUNT	Counts the cells containing numbers from a specified database and criteria
DCOUNTA	Counts nonblank cells from a specified database and criteria
DGET	Extracts from a database a single record that matches the specified criteria
DMAX	Returns the maximum value from selected database entries
DMIN	Returns the minimum value from selected database entries
DPRODUCT	Multiplies the values in a particular field of records that match the criteria in a database
DSTDEV	Estimates the standard deviation based on a sample of selected database entries
DSTDEVP	Calculates the standard deviation based on the entire population of selected database entries
DSUM	Adds the numbers in the field column of records in the database that match the criteria
DVAR	Estimates variance based on a sample from selected database entries
DVARP	Calculates variance based on the entire population of selected database entries

Note   You may find it cumbersome to set up a criteria range every time you need to use a database function. Fortunately, Excel provides some alternative ways to perform conditional sums and counts. Refer to Chapter 11 for examples that use SUMIF, COUNTIF, and various other techniques. Also, be aware that you can use the SUBTOTAL function for simple sums and counts. Unlike the other functions, SUBTOTAL ignores rows that are hidden by filtering. For more information about the SUBTOTAL function, see "Creating Subtotals," later in this chapter.

Sorting a List

In some cases, the order of the rows in your list doesn't matter. But in other cases, you want the rows to appear in a specific order. For example, in a price list, you may want the rows to appear in alphabetical order by product name. This makes the products easier to locate. Or if you have a list of accounts receivable information, you may want to sort the list so that the higher amounts appear at the top of the list (in descending order).

Rearranging the order of the rows in a list is called *sorting*. Excel is quite flexible when it comes to sorting lists, and you can often accomplish this task with the click of a mouse button.

Simple sorting

To quickly sort a list in ascending order, move the cell pointer to the column that you want to sort. Then click on the Sort Ascending button on the Standard toolbar. The Sort Descending button works the same way, but it sorts the list in descending order. In both cases, Excel determines the extent of your list and sorts all the rows in the list.

When you sort a filtered list, only the visible rows are sorted. When you remove the filtering from the list, the list is no longer sorted.

Excel's Sorting Rules

Because cells can contain different types of information, you may be curious about how this information is sorted. For an ascending sort, the information appears in the following order:

1. **Numerical values:** Numbers are sorted from smallest negative to largest positive. Dates and times are treated as values. In all cases, the sorting is done by using the actual values (not their formatted appearance).

2. **Text:** In alphabetical order, as follows: 0 1 2 3 4 5 6 7 8 9 (space) ! " # $ % & ' ( ) * + , – . / : ; < = > ? @ [\ ] ^ _ ` { ⇨ } ~ A B C D E F G H I J K L M N O P Q R S T U V W X Y Z.

   By default, sorting is not case sensitive. You can change this, however, in the Sort Options dialog box (described elsewhere in this chapter).

3. **Logical values:** False comes before True.

4. **Error values:** Error values (such as #VALUE! and #NA) appear in their original order and are not sorted by error type.

5. **Blank cells:** Blanks cells always appear last.

Sorting in descending order reverses this sequence — except that blank cells are *still* sorted last.

Be careful if you sort a list that contains formulas. If the formulas refer to cells in the list that are in the same row, you don't have any problems. But if the formulas refer to cells in other rows in the list or use relative references to cells outside the list, the formulas are not correct after the sorting. If formulas in your list refer to cells outside the list, make sure that the formulas use an absolute cell reference.

More-complex sorting

Sometimes, you may want to sort by two or more columns. This is relevant to break ties. A tie occurs when rows with duplicate data remain unsorted.

If you want to sort by two or three fields, choose Data ➪ Sort. Excel displays the Sort dialog box that is shown in Figure 19-13. Simply select the first sort field from the drop-down list labeled Sort By and specify Ascending or Descending order. Then, do the same for the second sort field. If you want to sort by a third field, specify the field in the third section. If the Header Row radio button is selected, the first row (field names) is not affected by the sort. Click on OK, and the list's rows rearrange in a flash.

Figure 19-13: The Sort dialog box lets you sort by up to three columns.

If the sorting didn't occur as you expected, select Edit ➪ Undo (or press Ctrl+Z) to undo the sorting.

What if you need to sort your list by more than three fields? It can be done, but it takes an additional step. For example, assume that you want to sort your list by five fields: Field1, Field2, Field3, Field4, and Field5. Start by sorting by Field3, Field4, and Field5. Then re-sort the list by Field1 and Field2. In other words, sort the three "least important" fields first; they remain in sequence when you do the second sort.

Tip
Often, you want to keep the records in their original order but perform a temporary sort just to see how it looks. The solution is to add an additional column to the list with sequential numbers in it. (Don't use formulas to generate these numbers.) Then, after you sort, you can return to the original order by re-sorting on the

field that has the sequential numbers. You can also use Excel's Undo feature to return the list to its original order. The advantage of using an additional column is that you can perform other operations while the list is temporarily sorted (and these operations won't be undone when you undo the sort operation).

When you click the Options button in the Sort dialog box, Excel displays the Sort Options dialog box, shown in Figure 19-14.

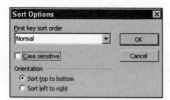

Figure 19-14: The Sort Options dialog box gives you some additional sorting options.

These options are described as follows:

✦ **First Key Sort Order:** Lets you specify a custom sort order for the sort (see the next section).

✦ **Case Sensitive:** Makes the sorting case sensitive so that uppercase letters appear before lowercase letters in an ascending sort. Normally, sorting ignores the case of letters.

✦ **Orientation:** Enables you to sort by columns rather than by rows (the default).

Using a custom sort order

Normal sorting is done either numerically or alphabetically, depending on the data being sorted. In some cases, however, you may want to sort your data in other ways. For example, if your data consists of month names, you usually want it to appear in month order rather than alphabetically. You can use the Sort Options dialog box to perform such a sort. Select the appropriate list from the drop-down list labled First Key Sort Order. Excel, by default, has four "custom lists," and you can define your own. Excel's custom lists are as follows:

✦ **Abbreviated days:** Sun, Mon, Tue, Wed, Thu, Fri, Sat

✦ **Days:** Sunday, Monday, Tuesday, Wednesday, Thursday, Friday, Saturday

✦ **Abbreviated months:** Jan, Feb, Mar, Apr, May, Jun, Jul, Aug, Sep, Oct, Nov, Dec

✦ **Months:** January, February, March, April, May, June, July, August, September, October, November, December

Note that the abbreviated days and months do not have periods after them. If you use periods for these abbreviations, they are not recognized (and are not sorted correctly).

You may want to create a custom list. For example, your company may have several stores, and you want the stores to be listed in a particular order (not alphabetically). If you create a custom list, sorting puts the items in the order that you specify in the list. You must use the Data ➪ Sort command to sort by a custom list. (Click on the Options button to specify the custom list.)

To create a custom list, use the Custom Lists panel of the Options dialog box, as shown in Figure 19-15. Select the NEW LIST option and make your entries (in order) in the List Entries box. Or you can import your custom list from a range of cells by using the Import button.

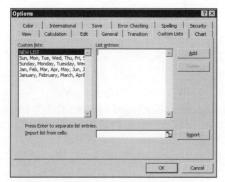

Figure 19-15: Excel lets you create custom sorting lists.

Custom lists also work with the autofill handle in cells. If you enter the first item of a custom list and then drag the cell's autofill handle, Excel fills in the remaining list items automatically.

Sorting nonlists

You can, of course, sort any range in a worksheet (it doesn't have to be a list). You need to be aware of a few things, however. The Sort Ascending and Sort Descending toolbar buttons may assume (erroneously) that the top row is a header row and not include these cells in the sort. Therefore, to avoid potential errors when sorting nonlists, don't use these toolbar buttons. Rather, select the entire range and select Data ➪ Sort (making sure that you choose the No Header Row option).

Creating Subtotals

Excel's ability to create automatic subtotals is a handy feature that can save you a great deal of time. To use this feature, your list must be sorted, because the subtotals are inserted whenever the value in a specified field changes.

To insert subtotal formulas into a list automatically, move the cell pointer anywhere in the list and choose Data ⇨ Subtotals. You see the dialog box shown in Figure 19-16. In this example, the list was sorted by Month.

Figure 19-16: The Sales list is a good candidate for subtotals, which are inserted at each change of the month.

A worksheet demonstrating the use of subtotals is included on the CD-ROM that accompanies this book.

This dialog box offers the following choices:

✦ **At Each Change In:** This drop-down list displays all fields in your list. The field that you choose must be sorted.

✦ **Use Function:** This gives you a choice of 11 functions. You should normally use Sum (the default).

✦ **Add Subtotal To:** This list box lists all the fields in your list. Place a check mark next to the field or fields that you want to subtotal.

✦ **Replace Current Subtotals:** If this box is checked, any existing subtotal formulas are removed and replaced with the new subtotals.

✦ **Page Break Between Groups:** If this box is checked, Excel inserts a manual page break after each subtotal.

✦ **Summary Below Data:** If this box is checked, the subtotals are placed below the data (the default). Otherwise, the subtotal formulas are placed above the totals.

✦ **Remove All:** This button removes all subtotal formulas in the list.

When you click OK, Excel analyzes the list and inserts formulas as specified — and creates an outline for you. The formulas all use the SUBTOTAL worksheet function. Figure 19-17 shows a worksheet after adding subtotals.

About the SUBTOTAL Function

The SUBTOTAL function is very versatile. It's unique in that it is the only Excel function that ignores cells in hidden rows. There is one caveat, however: The rows must be hidden as a result of autofiltering or an outline. Simply hiding rows manually will have no effect on the results calculated by the SUBTOTAL function.

The first argument for the SUBTOTAL function determines the actual function used. For example, when the first argument is 1, the SUBTOTAL function works like the AVERAGE function. The following table shows the possible values for the first argument for the SUBTOTAL function:

Value	Function
1	AVERAGE
2	COUNT
3	COUNTA
4	MAX
5	MIN
6	PRODUCT
7	STDEV
8	STDEVP
9	SUM
10	VAR
11	VARP

When the SUBTOTAL function is used within a List (designated by selecting Data ⇨ List ⇨ Create List), 100 is added to the first argument—for example, 109 instead of 9. When the first argument is greater than 100, the SUBTOTAL function behaves a bit differently. Specifically, it does not include data in rows that were hidden manually. When the first argument is less than 100, the SUBTOTAL function includes data in rows that were hidden manually but excludes data in rows that were hidden as a result of autofiltering.

List Ranges are discussed later in this chapter.

 Caution   When you add subtotals to a filtered list, the subtotals may no longer be accurate when the filter is removed.

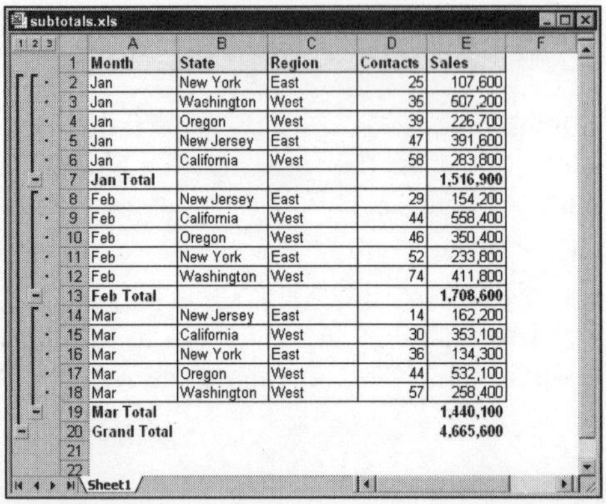

subtotals.xls

	A	B	C	D	E	F
1	Month	State	Region	Contacts	Sales	
2	Jan	New York	East	25	107,600	
3	Jan	Washington	West	35	507,200	
4	Jan	Oregon	West	39	226,700	
5	Jan	New Jersey	East	47	391,600	
6	Jan	California	West	58	283,800	
7	Jan Total				1,516,900	
8	Feb	New Jersey	East	29	154,200	
9	Feb	California	West	44	558,400	
10	Feb	Oregon	West	46	350,400	
11	Feb	New York	East	52	233,800	
12	Feb	Washington	West	74	411,800	
13	Feb Total				1,708,600	
14	Mar	New Jersey	East	14	162,200	
15	Mar	California	West	30	353,100	
16	Mar	New York	East	36	134,300	
17	Mar	Oregon	West	44	532,100	
18	Mar	Washington	West	57	258,400	
19	Mar Total				1,440,100	
20	Grand Total				4,665,600	
21						
22						

Sheet1

Figure 19-17: Excel added the subtotal formulas automatically — and even created an outline.

Working with a Designated List

Note This section discusses a feature that is available only in Excel 2003.

Excel has always had the ability to work with lists. But with Excel 2003, Microsoft introduced a new concept that lets you designate a range of cells to be an "official" list. Using this feature is optional. In fact, there is nothing that you can do with a designated list that you can't do with a normal list.

Note To avoid confusion with a normal list, I refer to the type of list described in this section as a "designated list."

A designated list is nothing more than a standard list. The only difference is that you specifically tell Excel that you're dealing with a list. After doing so, Excel displays an outline around the list and automatically expands the list as new data is added. A worksheet can contain any number of these designated lists.

Creating a designated list

To create a designated list, select any cell within your list and choose Data ➪ List ➪ Create List (or press Ctrl+L). Excel displays its Create List dialog box, which gives you an opportunity to verify the list's address and specify whether it contains headers. When you click OK, the list displays a colored border, and AutoFilter mode for the list will be enabled. In addition, Excel will display its List toolbar (as shown in Figure 19-18). This toolbar contains a menu and buttons relevant to working with a list.

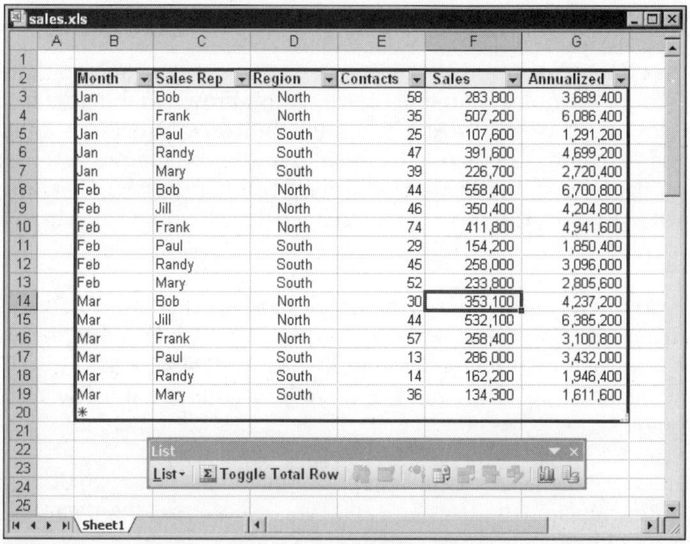

sales.xls						
	A	B	C	D	E	F	G

Figure 19-18: The data in range B2:G20 has been designated as a list.

An example of a worksheet using a designated list is included on the companion CD-ROM.

Notice that the designated list includes an additional empty row at the bottom. This row is reserved for new data that is entered into the list. The first cell in this empty row contains an asterisk.

To convert a designated list back to a standard range, choose Data ⇨ List ⇨ Convert to Range.

Adding rows or columns to a designated list

To add data to the end of a designated list, enter it into the empty row that contains the asterisk. To insert rows or columns, right-click and choose the appropriate command from the Insert menu (or use the List ⇨ Insert command on the List toolbar).

To delete rows or columns, right-click and choose the appropriate command from the Delete menu (or use the List ⇨ Delete command on the List toolbar).

Adding summary formulas to a designated list

A designated list can contain formulas that summarize the data in each column. Before you can add these formulas, you must insert a total row. Do this by using Data ➪ List ➪ Total Row. Or click the Toggle Total Row button on the List toolbar. Either of these actions appends a new row to the end of the designated list. Cells in the total row display drop-down list arrows, which resemble AutoFilter headings. Use these drop-downs to select the type of summary — for example, sum, average, count, and so on.

Note   Unfortunately, you cannot create your own formulas for the total row. You are limited to the functions displayed in the drop-down list. You will find that the only function that is used is the SUBTOTAL function. The first argument of the SUBTOTAL function determines the type of summary displayed. For example, if the first argument is 109, the function displays the sum.

Caution   Workbooks that use a designated list are not backwards compatible. If you distribute your workbook to someone who uses an earlier version of Excel, the data will be intact, but it will not function as a designated list. In addition, if you used summary formulas, they will display a #VALUE! error.

Advantage in using a designated list

Some users may find a few advantages in using a designated list. For example, you may like the idea that the list is clearly delineated with a dark border. Or, you may find that it's easier to insert summary formulas.

If your company happens to use Microsoft's SharePoint service, you'll see another advantage. You can easily publish a designated list to your SharePoint server. To do so, choose Data ➪ List ➪ Publish List. This command displays a dialog box in which you enter the address of your server and provide additional information.

✦   ✦   ✦

Using External Database Files

Worksheet-based lists, as described in the preceding chapter, are sufficient for many purposes. But in some cases, you may need to work with data stored in an external database file. External database files offer many advantages compared to data that is stored in an Excel workbook, and this chapter shows you how to use those files with Excel.

Understanding External Database Files

When you work with an Excel workbook, the entire workbook must be loaded into memory before you can begin working. Although this provides you with immediate access to the entire file and all the data it contains, it also means that you cannot work with extremely large amounts of data. Even if your system has plenty of memory, Excel has limits to the amount of data that it can handle in a worksheet database.

External database files work differently than Excel workbooks. When you access an external database file, you really load only a subset of the data into memory, so external database files can contain virtually unlimited amounts of data. In fact, external database files can be as large as your operating system allows and may contain many thousands of times as many records as an Excel list.

Understanding Some Database Terminology

People who spend their days working with databases seem to have their own special language. The following terms can help you hold your own among a group of database experts:

✦ **External database:** A collection of data that is stored in one or more files (not Excel files). A database contains one or more tables, and tables are composed of records and fields.

✦ **Field:** A component of a database table, that corresponds to a column in Excel.

✦ **ODBC:** An acronym for Open DataBase Connectivity, a standard developed by Microsoft that uses drivers to access database files in different formats. Microsoft Query comes with drivers for Access, dBASE, FoxPro, Paradox, SQL Server, Excel workbooks, and ASCII text files. ODBC drivers for other databases are available from Microsoft and from third-party providers.

✦ **OLAP Cube:** A multidimensional aggregate data source, often created from various other sources. OLAP is an acronym for OnLine Analytical Processing.

✦ **Query:** To search a database for records that meet specific criteria. This term is also used as a noun; you can write a query, for example.

✦ **Record:** In a database table, a single element that corresponds to a row.

✦ **Refresh:** To rerun a query to get the latest data. This is applicable when the database contains information that is subject to change, as in a multiuser environment.

✦ **Relational database:** A database that is stored in more than one table or file. At least one common field (sometimes called the *key field*) connects the tables.

✦ **Result set:** The data that is returned by a query, usually a subset of the original database. Query returns the result set to your Excel workbook or to a pivot table. (Pivot tables are discussed in Chapter 21.)

✦ **SQL:** An acronym for Structured Query Language (sometimes pronounced *sequel*). Query uses SQL to query data that is stored in ODBC databases.

✦ **Table:** A record- and field-oriented collection of data. A database consists of one or more tables.

Accessing external database files from Excel is useful in the following situations:

✦ You need to work with a very large database.

✦ You share the database with others; that is, other users have access to the database and may need to work with the data at the same time.

✦ You want to work with only a subset of the data—data that meets certain criteria that you specify.

✦ The database is in a format that Excel can't import.

✦ The database contains multiple tables with relationships between those tables.

If you need to work with external databases, you may prefer Excel to other database programs. The advantage? After you bring the data into Excel, you can manipulate and format it by using familiar tools. Of course, real database programs, such as Access, have advantages, too. For example, creating a complex database report in Access is much easier than creating it in Excel.

Note   Excel can open some database files directly. If the database table has fewer than 65,535 records and no more than 255 fields, you can load the entire file into a worksheet, memory permitting. Even if you have enough memory to load such a large file, however, Excel's performance is likely to be poor.

In many cases, you may not be interested in all the records or fields in the file. Instead, you may want to bring in just the data that meets certain criteria. In other words, you want to query the database and load into your worksheet a subset of the external database that meets the criteria. Excel makes this type of operation relatively easy.

Note   To perform queries using external databases, Microsoft Query must be installed on your system (this program is included with Excel). If Query is not installed, you will be prompted to install it when you first use the Data ➪ Import External Data ➪ New Database Query command.

Retrieving Data with Query: An Example

The best way to become familiar with Microsoft Query is to walk through an example. In the following sections, you learn how to use Query to open a database file and import a specified set of records.

On the CD-ROM   The database file used in this example is available on the companion CD-ROM.

The database file

The file that is used in this example is named `budget.mdb`. This is a single-table Access file that that consists of 15,840 records. This file contains the following fields:

✦ **Sort:** A numeric field that holds record sequence numbers.

✦ **Division:** A text field that specifies the company division. (This is either Asia, Europe, N. America, Pacific Rim, or S. America.)

✦ **Department:** A text field that specifies the department within the division. Each division is organized into the following departments: Accounting, Advertising, Data Processing, Human Resources, Operations, Public Relations, R&D, Sales, Security, Shipping, and Training.

✦ **Category:** A text field that specifies the budget category. The four categories are Compensation, Equipment, Facility, and Supplies & Services.

✦ **Item:** A text field that specifies the budget item. Each budget category has different budget items. For example, the Compensation category includes the following items: Benefits, Bonuses, Commissions, Conferences, Entertainment, Payroll Taxes, Salaries, and Training.

✦ **Month:** A text field that specifies the month (abbreviated as Jan, Feb, and so on).

✦ **Budget:** A numeric field that stores the budgeted amount.

✦ **Actual:** A numeric field that stores the actual amount spent.

✦ **Variance:** A numeric field that stores the difference between the Budget and Actual.

The task

The objective of this exercise is to develop a report that shows the first quarter (January through March) Compensation expenditures of the Training Department in the North American Division. In other words, the query will extract records that meet all of the following criteria:

✦ The Division is N. America.

✦ The Department is Training.

✦ The Category is Compensation.

✦ The Month is Jan, Feb, or Mar.

Using Query to get the data

One approach to this task would be to import the entire Access file into a worksheet and then choose Data ➪ Filter ➪ AutoFilter to filter the data as required. This approach would work because this particular file has fewer than 65,535 records. This isn't always the case. The advantage of using Query is that it imports only the data that's required.

Selecting a data source

Begin with an empty worksheet. Select Data ➪ Import External Data ➪ New Database Query, which displays the Choose Data Source dialog box, as shown in Figure 20-1. This dialog box contains three tabs:

✦ **Databases:** Lists the data sources that are known to Query—this tab may be empty, depending on which data sources are defined on your system.

✦ **Queries:** Contains a list of stored queries. Again, this may or may not be empty.

✦ **OLAP Cubes:** Lists OLAP databases that are available for query.

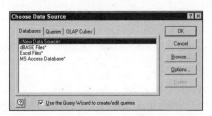

Figure 20-1: The Choose Data Source dialog box.

Your system may have some data sources already defined. If so, they appear in the list in the Databases tab. To set up a new data source, use the `<New Data Source>` option. For this example, choose `<New Data Source>` and click OK. This displays the Create New Data Source dialog box, which has four parts (see Figure 20-2):

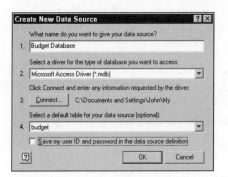

Figure 20-2: The Create New Data Source dialog box.

1. Enter a descriptive name for the data source. For this example, use the name **Budget Database**.

2. Select a driver for the data source by selecting from the list of installed drivers. For this example, choose `Microsoft Access Driver (*.mdb)`.

3. Click the Connect button to display another dialog box that asks for information specific to the driver that you selected in Step 2. In this example, you need to click the Select button and then locate the `budget.mdb` file. Click OK to return to the Create New Data Source dialog box.

4. Select the default data table that you want to use. For this example, the database file contains a single table named `budget`. If the database requires a password, you can also specify that the password be saved with the data source definition.

When you've supplied all the information in the Create New Data Source dialog box, click OK, and you are returned to the Choose Data Source dialog box — which now displays the data source that you created.

Note You only have to go through these steps once for each data source. The next time that you need to access this data source, the Budget Database (and any other database sources that you've defined) appears in the Choose Data Source dialog box.

Note The steps described above are general steps that will work with all supported database types. In some situations, you may prefer to open the database file directly and not create a named data source that will appear in the Choose Data Source dialog box. For example, if you won't be using the database again, you can open the file directly and not have to bother creating a new named data source. If you're using an Access file, you can select MS Access Database from the Databases tab in the Choose Data Source dialog box. Then, you can specify the file and you are taken directly to Microsoft Query.

Use the Query Wizard

The Choose Data Source dialog box has a check box at the bottom that lets you specify whether to use the Query Wizard to create your query. The Query Wizard walks you through the steps used to create your query, and if you use the Query Wizard, you don't have to deal directly with Query. I highly recommend using the Query Wizard, and the examples in this chapter use this tool.

In the Choose Data Source dialog box:

1. Select your data source (Budget Database, for this example).

2. Make sure that the Query Wizard check box is checked.

3. Click on OK to start the Query Wizard.

Query Wizard: Choosing the columns

In the first step of the Query Wizard, select the database columns that you want to appear in your query. Select one or more columns and click the > button to add them (see Figure 20-3).

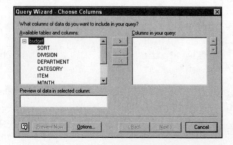

Figure 20-3: In the first step of Query Wizard, you select the columns to use in your query.

If you want to see the data for a particular column, select the column and click the Preview Now button. If you accidentally add a column that you don't need, select it in the right panel and click the < button to remove it.

For this example, add all of the fields and then click the Next button.

Query Wizard: Filtering data

In the second Query Wizard dialog box, you specify your record selection criteria—how you want to filter the data. This step is optional. If you want to retrieve all the data, just click the Next button to proceed.

Figure 20-4 shows the Filter Data dialog box of the Query Wizard.

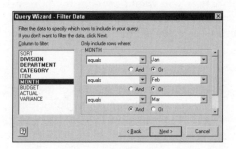

Figure 20-4: In the second step of the Query Wizard, you specify how you want to filter the data.

For the example, not all records are needed. Recall that you're interested only in the records in which one of the following applies:

✦ The Division is N. America.

✦ The Department is Training.

✦ The Category is Compensation.

✦ The Month is Jan, Feb, or Mar.

The criteria are entered by column. In this case, there are four criteria (one for each of four columns):

1. In the Column to Filter column, select *Division.* In the right panel, select *equals* from the first drop-down list, and select *N. America* from the second drop-down list.

2. In the Column to Filter column, select *Department.* In the right panel, select *equals* from the first drop-down list, and select *Training* from the second drop-down list.

3. In the Column to Filter column, select *Category.* In the right panel, select *equals* from the first drop-down list, and select *Compensation* from the second drop-down list.

4. In the Column to Filter column, select *Month*. In the right panel, select *equals* from the first drop-down list, and select *Jan* from the second drop-down list. Because this column is filtered by multiple values, click on the Or option, and then select *equals* and *Feb* from the drop-down lists in the second row. Finally, select *equals* and *Mar* from the drop-down lists in the second row.

To review the criteria that you've entered, just select the column from the Column to Filter list. The Query Wizard displays the criteria that you entered for the selected column.

When you've entered all the criteria, click Next.

Query Wizard: Sort order

The third step of the query lets you specify how you want the records to be sorted (see Figure 20-5). This step is optional, and you can click Next to move to the next step if you don't want the data sorted or if you prefer to sort it after it's returned to your worksheet.

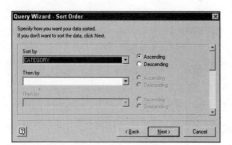

Figure 20-5: In the third step of the Query Wizard, you specify the sort order.

For this example, sort by *Category* in ascending order. You can specify as many sort fields as you like. Click on Next to move on to the next step.

Query Wizard: Finish

The final step of the Query Wizard, shown in Figure 20-6, lets you save the query so it can be reused. To save the query, click Save Query and then enter a filename.

Select an option that corresponds to what you want to do with the returned data. Normally, you want to return the data to Excel. If you know how to use the Microsoft Query application, you can return the data to Query and examine it or even modify the selection criteria. In addition, you can create an OLAP database from the query results.

Make your choices and click Finish.

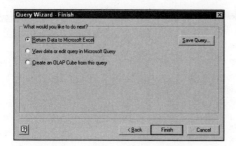

Figure 20-6: The final step of the Query Wizard.

Specifying a location for the data

Figure 20-7 shows the Import Data dialog box, which appears when you click the Finish button in the Query Wizard dialog box.

Figure 20-7: Specifying what to do with the data.

You can select from the following choices:

✦ **Existing Worksheet:** You can specify the upper-left cell.

✦ **New Worksheet:** Excel can insert a new worksheet and insert the data beginning in cell A1.

✦ **Create a Pivot Table Report:** Excel can display its Pivot Table Wizard so that you can specify the layout for a pivot table (see Chapter 21).

Figure 20-8 shows the data that is returned to a worksheet.

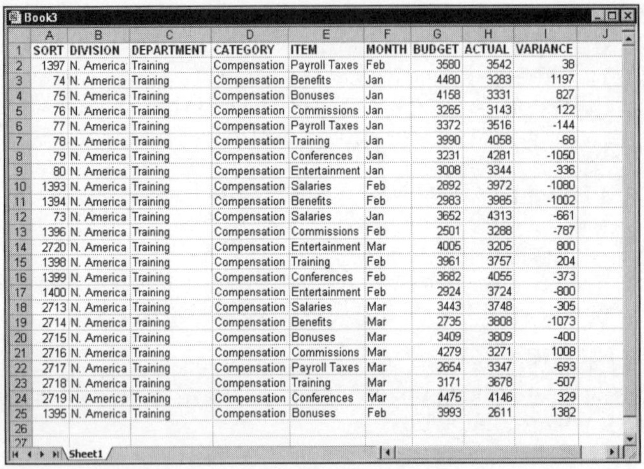

SORT	DIVISION	DEPARTMENT	CATEGORY	ITEM	MONTH	BUDGET	ACTUAL	VARIANCE
1397	N. America	Training	Compensation	Payroll Taxes	Feb	3580	3542	38
74	N. America	Training	Compensation	Benefits	Jan	4480	3283	1197
75	N. America	Training	Compensation	Bonuses	Jan	4158	3331	827
76	N. America	Training	Compensation	Commissions	Jan	3265	3143	122
77	N. America	Training	Compensation	Payroll Taxes	Jan	3372	3516	-144
78	N. America	Training	Compensation	Training	Jan	3990	4058	-68
79	N. America	Training	Compensation	Conferences	Jan	3231	4281	-1050
80	N. America	Training	Compensation	Entertainment	Jan	3008	3344	-336
1393	N. America	Training	Compensation	Salaries	Feb	2892	3972	-1080
1394	N. America	Training	Compensation	Benefits	Feb	2983	3985	-1002
73	N. America	Training	Compensation	Salaries	Jan	3652	4313	-661
1396	N. America	Training	Compensation	Commissions	Feb	2501	3288	-787
2720	N. America	Training	Compensation	Entertainment	Mar	4005	3205	800
1398	N. America	Training	Compensation	Training	Feb	3961	3757	204
1399	N. America	Training	Compensation	Conferences	Feb	3682	4055	-373
1400	N. America	Training	Compensation	Entertainment	Feb	2924	3724	-800
2713	N. America	Training	Compensation	Salaries	Mar	3443	3748	-305
2714	N. America	Training	Compensation	Benefits	Mar	2735	3808	-1073
2715	N. America	Training	Compensation	Bonuses	Mar	3409	3809	-400
2716	N. America	Training	Compensation	Commissions	Mar	4279	3271	1008
2717	N. America	Training	Compensation	Payroll Taxes	Mar	2654	3347	-693
2718	N. America	Training	Compensation	Training	Mar	3171	3678	-507
2719	N. America	Training	Compensation	Conferences	Mar	4475	4146	329
1395	N. America	Training	Compensation	Bonuses	Feb	3993	2611	1382

Figure 20-8: The results of the query.

Working with Data Returned by Query

Excel stores the data that Query returns in either a worksheet or a pivot table. When Excel stores data in a worksheet, it stores the data in a specially named range known as an *external data range;* Excel creates the name for this range automatically.

This section describes what you can do with the data that Excel receives from Query and stores in a worksheet.

Adjusting the external data range properties

You can adjust various properties of the external data range by using the External Data Range Properties dialog box (see Figure 20-9).

To display this dialog box, the cell pointer must be within the external data range. You can open this dialog box by using any of three methods:

- ✦ Right-click and select Data Range Properties from the shortcut menu.
- ✦ Select Data ➪ Import External Data ➪ Data Range Properties.
- ✦ Click the Data Range Properties tool on the External Data toolbar.

The following list describes the options in the External Data Range Properties dialog box:

- ✦ **Name:** The name of the external data range. You can change this name or use the default name that Excel creates. Excel substitutes, in the range name, the underscore character for any spaces that you see in the Name box of the External Data Range Properties box.

✦ **Query Definition:** If you check Save Query Definition, Excel stores the query definition with the external data range, enabling you to refresh the data or edit the query, if necessary. If the database requires a password, you can also store the password so that you don't need to enter it when you refresh the query.

✦ **Refresh Control:** Determines how and when Excel refreshes the data.

✦ **Data Formatting and Layout:** Determines the appearance of the external data range.

The External Data Range Properties dialog box has many options, and most of them are self-explanatory. For specific details, consult Excel's Help system.

You can manipulate data returned from a query just like any other worksheet range. For example, you can sort the data, format it, or create formulas that use the data.

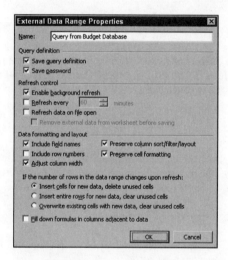

Figure 20-9: The External Data Range Properties dialog box enables you to specify various options for an external data range.

Refreshing a query

After performing a query, you can save the file and then retrieve it later. The file contains the data that you originally retrieved from the external database. The external database may have changed, however, in the interim.

If you checked the Save Query Definition option in the External Data Range Properties dialog box, Excel saves the query definition with the workbook. Simply move the cell pointer anywhere within the external data table in the worksheet and then use one of the following methods to refresh the query:

✦ Right-click and select Refresh Data from the shortcut menu.

✦ Select Data ➪ Refresh Data.

✦ Click the Refresh Data tool on the External Data toolbar.

Excel uses your original query to bring in the current data from the external database.

Tip   If you find that refreshing the query causes undesirable results, use Excel's Undo feature to "unrefresh" the data.

Note   A single workbook can hold as many external data ranges as you need. Excel gives each query a unique name, and you can work with each query independently. Excel automatically keeps track of the query that produces each external data range.

Caution   After performing a query, you may want to copy or move the external data range, which you can do by using the normal copy, cut, and paste techniques. However, make sure that you copy or cut the entire external data range — otherwise, the underlying query is not copied, and the copied data cannot be refreshed.

Deleting a query

If you decide that you no longer need the data that is returned by a query, you can delete it by selecting the entire external data range and pressing Delete. Excel will display a warning and ask you to verify your intentions.

Changing your query

If you bring the query results into your worksheet and discover that you don't have what you want, you can modify the query. Move the cell pointer anywhere within the external data table in the worksheet and then use one of the following methods:

✦ Right-click and select Edit Query from the shortcut menu.

✦ Select Data ➪ Import External Data ➪ Edit Query.

✦ Click the Edit Query tool on the External Data toolbar.

If you created your query by using the Query Wizard, Excel displays the Query Wizard again so you can make your changes. If you didn't use the Query Wizard to create your query, Excel launches Query, and you can make your changes there. See the next section to learn how to work with Query directly.

Using Query without the Wizard

When you select Data ➪ Import External Data ➪ New Database Query, the Choose Data Source dialog box gives you the option of whether to use Query Wizard. If you choose not to use Query Wizard, Microsoft Query is launched in a new window. You will also work directly with Query if you choose to edit a query that was created with the Query Wizard.

Creating a query manually

Before you can create a query, you must display the Criteria pane. In Query, open the View menu and confirm that a check appears next to the Criteria command. If you don't see a check, choose View ⇨ Criteria to display the Criteria pane in the middle of the window. Figure 20-10 shows Microsoft Query, after selecting the Budget Database from the Choose Data Source dialog box. The Criteria pane is also displayed.

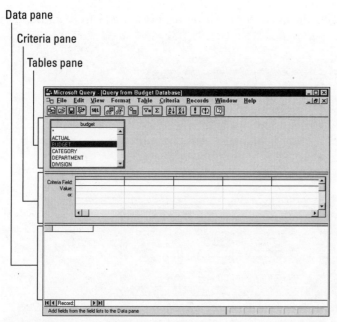

Figure 20-10: Display the Criteria pane as shown here so that you will be able to create your query.

The Query window has three panes, which are split horizontally:

✦ **Tables pane:** The top pane, which holds the selected data tables for the database. Each data table window has a list of the fields in the table.

✦ **Criteria pane:** The middle pane, which holds the criteria that determine the rows that the query returns.

✦ **Data pane:** The bottom pane, which holds the data that passes the criteria.

Creating a query consists of the following steps:

1. Drag fields from the Tables pane to the Data pane. You can drag as many fields as you want. These fields are the columns that the query will return. You can also double-click a field instead of dragging it.

2. Enter criteria in the Criteria pane. When you activate this pane, the first row (labeled Criteria Field) displays a drop-down list that contains all the field names. Select a field and enter the criteria below it. Query updates the Data pane automatically, treating each row like an OR operator.

3. Choose File ➪ Return Data to Microsoft Excel to execute the query and place the data in a worksheet or pivot table.

Figure 20-11 shows how the query for the example presented earlier in this chapter appears in Query.

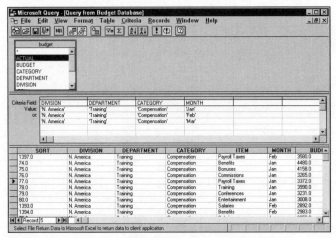

Figure 20-11: Add the fields and criteria to complete your query.

Tip   Double-click a criteria box to display the Edit Criteria dialog box. This enables you to select an operator and value.

Using multiple database tables

The example in this chapter uses only one database table. Some databases, however, use multiple tables. These databases are known as *relational databases* because a common field links the tables. Query lets you use any number of tables in your queries.

Note   When you add additional tables to a query, the Tables pane in Query connects the linked fields with a line between the tables. If no links exist, you can create a link yourself by dragging a field from one table to the corresponding field in the other table.

Adding and editing records in external database tables

To add, delete, and edit data when you are using Query, make sure that a check appears next to the Records ➪ Allow Editing command. Of course, you can't edit a database file that's set up as read-only.

Caution   You need to be careful with this feature because your changes are saved to disk as soon as you move the cell pointer out of the record that you're editing. (You do not need to choose File ➪ Save.)

Formatting data

If you don't like the data's appearance in the Data pane, you can change the font used by selecting Format ➪ Font. Be aware that selective formatting isn't allowed (unlike in Excel); changing the font affects all the data in the Data pane.

Tip   If you need to view the data in the Data pane in a different order, choose Records ➪ Sort (or click the Sort Ascending or Sort Descending toolbar icon).

Learning more about Query

This chapter isn't intended to cover every aspect of Microsoft Query; rather, it discusses the basic features that are used most often. In fact, if you use the Query Wizard, you may never need to interact with Query itself. But if you do need to use Query, you can experiment and consult the online Help to learn more. As with anything related to Excel, the best way to master Query is to use it — preferably with data that's meaningful to you.

✦   ✦   ✦

Analyzing Data with Pivot Tables

The pivot table feature is perhaps the most technologically sophisticated component in Excel. If you haven't yet discovered the power of pivot tables, this chapter demonstrates how easy it is to create powerful data summaries using pivot tables.

About Pivot Tables

A pivot table is essentially a dynamic summary report generated from a database. The database can reside in a worksheet or in an external data file. A pivot table can help transform endless rows and columns of numbers into a meaningful presentation of the data.

For example, a pivot table can create frequency distributions and cross-tabulations of several different data dimensions. In addition, you can display subtotals and any level of detail that you want. Perhaps the most innovative aspect of a pivot table lies in its interactivity. After you create a pivot table, you can rearrange the information in almost any way imaginable and even insert special formulas that perform new calculations. You even can create post hoc groupings of summary items (for example, combine Northern Region totals with Western Region totals).

One minor drawback to using a pivot table is that, unlike a formula-based summary report, a pivot table does not update automatically when you change the source data. This does not pose a serious problem, however, because a single click of the Refresh toolbar button forces a pivot table to use the latest data.

A pivot table example

The best way to understand the concept of a pivot table is to see one. Start with Figure 21-1, which shows a portion of the data used in creating the pivot table in this chapter.

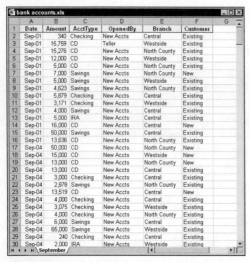

	A	B	C	D	E	F	G
1	Date	Amount	AcctType	OpenedBy	Branch	Customer	
2	Sep-01	340	Checking	New Accts	Central	Existing	
3	Sep-01	15,759	CD	Teller	Westside	Existing	
4	Sep-01	15,276	CD	New Accts	North County	Existing	
5	Sep-01	12,000	CD	New Accts	Westside	Existing	
6	Sep-01	5,000	CD	New Accts	North County	Existing	
7	Sep-01	7,000	Savings	New Accts	North County	New	
8	Sep-01	5,000	Savings	New Accts	Westside	Existing	
9	Sep-01	4,623	Savings	New Accts	North County	Existing	
10	Sep-01	5,879	Checking	New Accts	Central	Existing	
11	Sep-01	3,171	Checking	New Accts	Westside	Existing	
12	Sep-01	4,000	Savings	New Accts	Central	Existing	
13	Sep-01	5,000	IRA	New Accts	Central	Existing	
14	Sep-01	16,000	CD	New Accts	Central	New	
15	Sep-01	50,000	Savings	New Accts	Central	Existing	
16	Sep-01	13,636	CD	New Accts	North County	Existing	
17	Sep-04	50,000	CD	New Accts	North County	New	
18	Sep-04	15,000	CD	New Accts	Westside	New	
19	Sep-04	13,000	CD	New Accts	North County	New	
20	Sep-04	13,000	CD	New Accts	Central	Existing	
21	Sep-04	3,000	Checking	New Accts	Central	Existing	
22	Sep-04	2,878	Savings	New Accts	North County	Existing	
23	Sep-04	13,519	CD	New Accts	Central	New	
24	Sep-04	4,000	Checking	New Accts	Central	Existing	
25	Sep-04	3,075	Checking	New Accts	Westside	Existing	
26	Sep-04	4,000	Checking	New Accts	North County	Existing	
27	Sep-04	6,000	Savings	New Accts	Central	Existing	
28	Sep-04	65,000	Savings	New Accts	Westside	Existing	
29	Sep-04	240	Checking	New Accts	Central	Existing	
30	Sep-04	2,000	IRA	New Accts	Westside	Existing	

Figure 21-1: This database is used to create a pivot table.

This database consists of daily new-account information for a three-branch bank. The database contains 350 records and tracks the following:

✦ The date that each account was opened

✦ The opening amount

✦ The account type (CD, checking, savings, or IRA)

✦ Who opened the account (a teller or a new-account representative)

✦ The branch at which it was opened (Central, Westside, or North County)

✦ Whether a new customer or an existing customer opened the account

On the CD-ROM   The workbook shown in Figure 21-1 is available on the companion CD-ROM.

The bank accounts database contains a lot of information. But in its current form, the data does not reveal much. To make the data more useful, you need to summarize it. Summarizing a database is essentially the process of answering questions about the data. Following are a few questions that may be of interest to the bank's management:

- ✦ What is the total deposit amount for each branch, broken down by account type?
- ✦ How many accounts were opened at each branch, broken down by account type?
- ✦ What's the dollar distribution of the different account types?
- ✦ What types of accounts do tellers open most often?
- ✦ How does the Central branch compare to the other two branches?
- ✦ Which branch opens the most accounts for new customers?

You could, of course, write formulas to answer these questions. Often, however, a pivot table is a better choice. Creating a pivot table takes only a few seconds and doesn't require a single formula.

Figure 21-2 shows a pivot table created from the database displayed in Figure 21-1. This pivot table shows the amount of new deposits, broken down by branch and account type. This particular summary represents one of dozens of summaries that you can produce from this data.

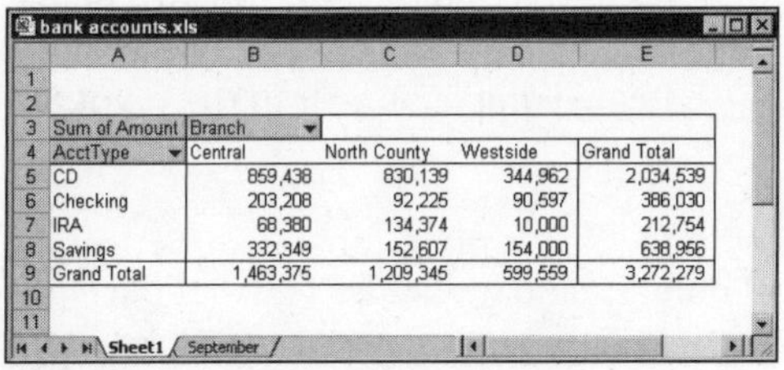
bank accounts.xls

Sum of Amount	Branch			
AcctType	Central	North County	Westside	Grand Total
CD	859,438	830,139	344,962	2,034,539
Checking	203,208	92,225	90,597	386,030
IRA	68,380	134,374	10,000	212,754
Savings	332,349	152,607	154,000	638,956
Grand Total	1,463,375	1,209,345	599,559	3,272,279

Sheet1 / September

Figure 21-2: A simple pivot table.

Figure 21-3 shows another pivot table generated from the bank data. This pivot table uses a page field for the Customer item (refer to Figure 21-1). In this case, the pivot table displays the data only for existing customers (the user could also select New or All from page field list). Notice the changes in the orientation of the table; branches appear in rows, and account types appear in columns. This is another example of the flexibility of a pivot table.

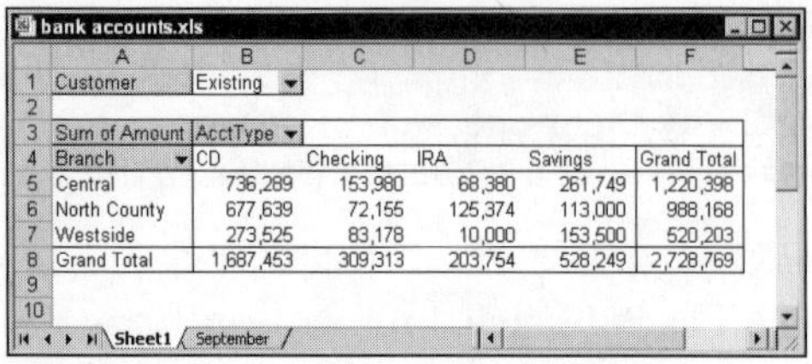

bank accounts.xls

	A	B	C	D	E	F
1	Customer	Existing				
2						
3	Sum of Amount	AcctType				
4	Branch	CD	Checking	IRA	Savings	Grand Total
5	Central	736,289	153,980	68,380	261,749	1,220,398
6	North County	677,639	72,155	125,374	113,000	988,168
7	Westside	273,525	83,178	10,000	153,500	520,203
8	Grand Total	1,687,453	309,313	203,754	528,249	2,728,769
9						
10						

Sheet1 / September

Figure 21-3: A pivot table that uses a page field.

Data appropriate for a pivot table

Not all data can be used to create a pivot table. The data that you summarize must be in the form of a database. You can store the database in either a worksheet (sometimes known as a *list*) or an external database file. Although Excel can generate a pivot table from any database, not all databases benefit.

Generally speaking, fields in a database table can consist of two types:

✦ **Data:** Contains a value or data to be summarized. In Figure 21-1, the Amount field is a data field.

✦ **Category:** Describes the data. In Figure 21-1, the Date, AcctType, OpenedBy, Branch, and Customer fields are category fields because they describe the data in the Amount field.

A single database table can have any number of data fields and category fields. When you create a pivot table, you usually want to summarize one or more of the data fields. Conversely, the values in the category fields appear in the pivot table as rows, columns, or pages.

Exceptions exist, however, and you may find Excel's pivot table feature useful even for databases that don't contain actual numerical data fields. The database columns A:C in Figure 21-4, for example, don't contain any numerical data, but you can create a useful pivot table that counts the items in fields rather than sums them. The pivot table cross-tabulates the Month Born field by the Sex field; the intersecting cells show the count for each combination of month and gender.

On the CD-ROM

A workbook demonstrating how to create a pivot table from non-numeric data is available on the companion CD-ROM.

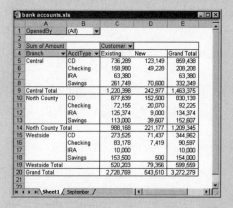

Figure 21-4: This database doesn't have any numerical fields, but you can use it to generate a pivot table.

Pivot Table Terminology

Understanding the terminology associated with pivot tables is the first step in mastering this feature. Refer to the accompanying figure to get your bearings.

✦ **Column field:** A field that has a column orientation in the pivot table. Each item in the field occupies a column. In the figure, Customer represents a column field that contains two items (Existing and New). You can have nested column fields.

✦ **Data area:** The cells in a pivot table that contain the summary data. Excel offers several ways to summarize the data (sum, average, count, and so on). In the figure, the Data area includes C5:E20.

Continued

Continued

✦ **Grand totals:** A row or column that displays totals for all cells in a row or column in a pivot table. You can specify that grand totals be calculated for rows, columns, or both (or neither). The pivot table in the figure shows grand totals for both rows and columns.

✦ **Group:** A collection of items treated as a single item. You can group items manually or automatically (group dates into months, for example). The pivot table in the figure does not have any defined groups.

✦ **Item:** An element in a field that appears as a row or column header in a pivot table. In the figure, Existing and New are items for the Customer field. The Branch field has three items: Central, North County, and Westside. AcctType has four items: CD, Checking, IRA (Investment Retirement Account), and Savings.

✦ **Page field:** A field that has a page orientation in the pivot table — similar to a slice of a three-dimensional cube. You can display only one item (or all items) in a page field at one time. In the figure, OpenedBy represents a page field that displays the New Accts item.

✦ **Refresh:** To recalculate the pivot table after making changes to the source data.

✦ **Row field:** A field that has a row orientation in the pivot table. Each item in the field occupies a row. You can have nested row fields. In the figure, Branch and AcctType both represent row fields.

✦ **Source data:** The data used to create a pivot table. It can reside in a worksheet or an external database.

✦ **Subtotals:** A row or column that displays subtotals for detail cells in a row or column in a pivot table. The pivot table in the figure displays subtotals for each branch.

Creating a Pivot Table

You create a pivot table by using a series of steps presented in the PivotTable and PivotChart Wizard. You access this wizard by choosing Data ➪ PivotTable and PivotChart Report. Then, carry out the steps outlined here.

Note   This discussion assumes that you use Excel 2000 or later. The procedure differs slightly in earlier versions of Excel.

Step1: Specifying the data location

After you choose Data ➪ PivotTable and PivotChart Report, you see the dialog box shown in Figure 21-5.

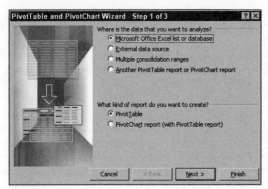

Figure 21-5: The first of three PivotTable and PivotChart Wizard dialog boxes.

In this step, you identify the data source. Excel is quite flexible in the data that you can use for a pivot table. (See the nearby sidebar "Pivot Table Data Sources.") This example uses a worksheet database.

Note   You see different dialog boxes while you work through the wizard, depending on the location of the data that you want to analyze. The following sections present the wizard's dialog boxes for data located in an Excel list or database.

Step 2: Specifying the data

To move on to the next step of the wizard, click the Next button. Step 2 of the PivotTable and PivotChart Wizard prompts you for the data. Remember that the dialog box varies depending on your choice in the first dialog box; Figure 21-6 shows the dialog box that appears when you select an Excel list or database in Step 1.

Figure 21-6: In Step 2, you specify the data range.

If you place the cell pointer anywhere within the worksheet database when you select Data ⇨ PivotTable Report, Excel identifies the database range automatically in Step 2 of the PivotTable and PivotChart Wizard.

You can use the Browse button to open a different worksheet and select a range. To move on to Step 3, click the Next button.

Pivot Table Data Sources

The data used in a pivot table can come from a variety of sources, including Excel databases or lists, data sources external to Excel, multiple tabled ranges, and other pivot tables. I describe these sources here.

Microsoft Excel List or Database

Usually, the data that you analyze is stored in a worksheet database (also known as a *list*). Databases stored in a worksheet have a limit of 65,535 records and 256 fields. Working with a database of this size isn't efficient, however (and memory may not even permit it). The first row in the database should contain field names. No other rules exist. The data can consist of values, text, or formulas.

External Data Source

If you use the data in an external database for a pivot table, use Query (a separate application) to retrieve the data. You can use dBASE files, SQL Server data, or other data that your system is set up to access. Step 2 of the PivotTable and PivotChart Wizard prompts you for the data source. Note that in Excel 2000 or later, you also can create a pivot table from an OLAP (OnLine Analytical Processing) database.

Multiple Consolidation Ranges

You also can create a pivot table from multiple tables. This procedure is equivalent to consolidating the information in tables. When you create a pivot table to consolidate information in tables, you have the added advantage of using all of the pivot table tools while working with the consolidated data.

Another Pivot Table Report or Pivot Chart Report

Excel enables you to create a pivot table from an existing pivot table or pivot chart. Actually, this is a bit of a misnomer. The pivot table that you create is based on the *data* that the first pivot table uses (not the pivot table itself). If the active workbook has no pivot tables, this option is grayed — meaning you can't choose it. If you need to create more than one pivot table from the same set of data, the procedure is more efficient (in terms of memory usage) if you create the first pivot table and then use that pivot table as the source for subsequent pivot tables.

Tip   If the source range for a pivot table is named *Database*, you can use Excel's built-in Data Form to add new data to the range. The named range will extend automatically to include the new records. In addition, if you create the pivot table from a list (designated by using the Data ➪ List ➪ Create List command), the pivot table will be linked to the list. Therefore, the pivot table will be accurate if the list shrinks or grows.

Step 3: Completing the pivot table

Figure 21-7 shows the dialog box for the final step of the PivotTable and PivotChart Wizard. In this step, you specify the location for the pivot table.

Figure 21-7: In Step 3, you specify the pivot table's location.

If you select the New Worksheet option, Excel inserts a new worksheet for the pivot table. If you select the Existing Worksheet option, the pivot table appears on the current worksheet. (You can specify the starting cell location.)

At this point, you can click the Options button to select some options that determine how the table appears. (Refer to the nearby sidebar "Pivot Table Options.") You can set these options at any time after you create the pivot table, so you do not need to do so before creating the pivot table.

You can set up the actual layout of the pivot table by using either of two techniques:

✦ By clicking the Layout button in Step 3 of the PivotTable and PivotChart Wizard. You then can use a dialog box to lay out the pivot table.

✦ By clicking the Finish button to create a blank pivot table. You then can use the PivotTable Field List toolbar to lay out the pivot table.

I describe both of these options in the following subsections.

Using a dialog box to lay out a pivot table

When you click the Layout button of the wizard's last dialog box, you get the dialog box shown in Figure 21-8. The fields in the database appear as buttons along the right side of the dialog box. Simply drag the buttons to the appropriate area of the pivot table diagram (which appears in the center of the dialog box).

The pivot table diagram has four areas:

✦ **Page:** Buttons in this area appear as page items in the pivot table.

✦ **Row:** Buttons in this area appear as row items in the pivot table.

✦ **Data:** Buttons in this area indicate the data that is summarized in the pivot table.

✦ **Column:** Buttons in this area appear as column items in the pivot table.

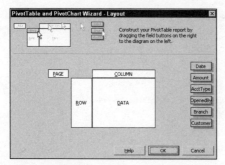

Figure 21-8: Specify the table layout.

You can drag as many field buttons as you want to any of these locations, and you don't have to use all the fields. Any fields that you don't use simply don't appear in the pivot table.

When you drag a field button to the Data area, the PivotTable and PivotChart Wizard applies the Sum function if the field contains numeric values; it applies the Count function if the field contains non-numeric values.

While you set up the pivot table, you can double-click a field button to customize it. You can specify, for example, to summarize a particular field as a Count or other function. You also can specify which items in a field to hide or omit. If you drag a field button to an incorrect location, just drag it off the table diagram to get rid of it. Note that you can customize fields at any time after you create the pivot table.

Figure 21-9 shows how the dialog box looks after dragging some field buttons to the pivot table diagram. This pivot table displays the sum of the Amount field, broken down by AcctType (as rows) and Customer (as columns). In addition, the Branch field appears as a page field. Click OK to redisplay the PivotTable and PivotChart Wizard — Step 3 of the dialog box.

Using the PivotTable Field List toolbar to lay out a pivot table

You may prefer to lay out your pivot table directly in the worksheet by using the PivotTable Field List toolbar. The technique closely resembles the one just described because you still drag and drop fields. But in this case, you drag fields from the toolbar into the worksheet.

Note   You cannot use this technique with versions prior to Excel 2000. Also, note that Excel 2000 doesn't have a PivotTable Field List toolbar. Rather, the fields are displayed as buttons on the PivotTable toolbar.

Complete the first two steps of the PivotTable and PivotChart Wizard. If you want, set options for the pivot table by using the Options button that appears in the third dialog box of the wizard. Don't bother with the Layout button, however. Select a location for the pivot table and choose Finish. Excel displays a pivot table template similar to the one you see in Figure 21-10. The template provides you with hints about where to drop various types of fields.

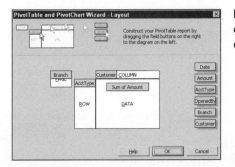

Figure 21-9: The table layout after dragging field buttons to the pivot table diagram.

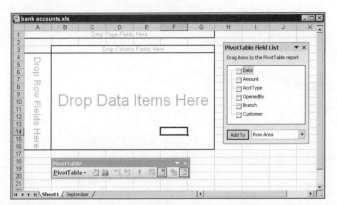

Figure 21-10: Use the PivotTable Field List toolbar to drag and drop fields onto the pivot table template that Excel displays.

Drag and drop fields from the PivotTable Field List toolbar onto the template. Or select the field name, choose the location from the drop-down list, and click the Add To button. Excel continues to update the pivot table as you add or remove fields. For this reason, you'll find this method easiest to use if you drag and drop *data* items last. In other words, set up the field items and then specify the data to summarize.

If you make a mistake, simply drag the field off the template and drop it on the worksheet — Excel removes it from the pivot table template. All fields remain on the PivotTable Field List toolbar, even if you use them.

The finished product

Figure 21-11 shows the result of this example. Notice that the page field displays as a drop-down box. You can choose which item in the page field to display by choosing it from the list. You also can choose an item called All, which displays all the data.

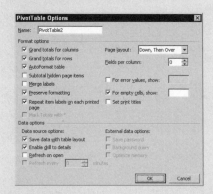

Figure 21-11: The pivot table created by the PivotTable and PivotChart Wizard.

Pivot Table Options

Excel provides plenty of options that determine how your pivot table looks and works. To access these options, click the Options button in the final step of the PivotTable and PivotChart Wizard to display the PivotTable Options dialog box. You also can access this dialog box after you create the pivot table. Right-click any cell in the pivot table and then select Table Options from the shortcut menu. The accompanying figure shows the PivotTable Options dialog box.

Here are its choices:

✦ **Name:** You can provide a name for the pivot table. Excel provides default names in the form of PivotTable1, PivotTable2, and so on.

✦ **Grand Totals for Columns:** Check this box if you want Excel to calculate grand totals for items displayed in columns.

✦ **Grand Totals for Rows:** Check this box if you want Excel to calculate grand totals for items displayed in rows.

✦ **AutoFormat Table:** Check this box if you want Excel to apply one of its AutoFormats to the pivot table. The selected AutoFormat sticks with the pivot table, even If you rearrange the table layout.

✦ **Subtotal Hidden Page Items:** Check this box if you want Excel to include hidden items in the page fields in the subtotals.

✦ **Merge Labels:** Check this box if you want Excel to merge the cells for outer row and column labels. Doing so may make the table more readable.

✦ **Preserve Formatting:** Check this box if you want Excel, when it updates the pivot table, to keep any of the formatting that you applied.

✦ **Repeat Item Labels on Each Printed Page:** Check this box to set row titles that appear on each page when you print a pivot table report.

✦ **Mark Totals with *:** Available only if you generated the pivot table from an OLAP data source. If checked, displays an asterisk after every subtotal and grand total to indicate that these values include any hidden items as well as displayed items.

✦ **Page Layout:** You can specify the order in which you want the page fields to appear.

✦ **Fields per Column:** You can specify the number of page fields to show before starting another row of page fields.

✦ **For Error Values, Show:** You can specify a value to show for pivot table cells that display an error.

✦ **For Empty Cells, Show:** You can specify a value to show for empty pivot table cells.

✦ **Set Print Titles:** Check this box to set column titles that appear at the top of each page when you print a PivotTable report.

✦ **Save Data with Table Layout:** If you check this option, Excel stores an additional copy of the data (called a *pivot table cache*), which is stored with the workbook. If this option is not enabled, then Excel must refresh the pivot table when the file is opened.

✦ **Enable Drill to Details:** If checked, you can double-click a cell in the data area of the pivot table to view the records that contributed to the summary value.

✦ **Refresh on Open:** If checked, the pivot table refreshes whenever you open the workbook.

✦ **Refresh Every *x* Minutes:** If you are connected to an external database, you can specify how often you want the pivot table refreshed while the workbook is open.

✦ **Save Password:** If you use an external database that requires a password, you can store the password as part of the query so that you don't have to re-enter it.

✦ **Background Query:** If checked, Excel runs the external database query in the background while you continue your work.

✦ **Optimize Memory:** This option reduces the amount of memory used when you refresh an external database query.

Grouping Pivot Table Items

One of the more useful features of a pivot table is the ability to combine items into groups. To group items, select them, right-click, and choose Group and Outline ⇨ Group from the shortcut menu that appears.

When a field contains dates, Excel can create groups automatically. Figure 21-12 shows a portion of a simple database table with two fields: Date and Sales. This table has 370 records and covers dates between June 1, 2001, and October 31, 2002. The goal is to summarize the sales information by month.

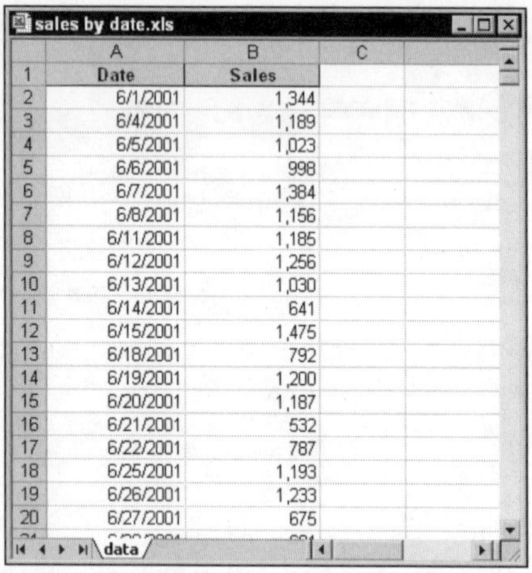

	A	B	C
1	Date	Sales	
2	6/1/2001	1,344	
3	6/4/2001	1,189	
4	6/5/2001	1,023	
5	6/6/2001	998	
6	6/7/2001	1,384	
7	6/8/2001	1,156	
8	6/11/2001	1,185	
9	6/12/2001	1,256	
10	6/13/2001	1,030	
11	6/14/2001	641	
12	6/15/2001	1,475	
13	6/18/2001	792	
14	6/19/2001	1,200	
15	6/20/2001	1,187	
16	6/21/2001	532	
17	6/22/2001	787	
18	6/25/2001	1,193	
19	6/26/2001	1,233	
20	6/27/2001	675	

Figure 21-12: You can use a pivot table to summarize the sales data by month.

A workbook demonstrating how to group pivot table items by date is available on the companion CD-ROM.

Figure 21-13 shows part of a pivot table created from the data. Not surprisingly, it looks exactly like the input data because the dates have not been grouped. To group the items by month, right-click the Data heading and select Group and Show Detail ⇨ Group. You'll see the Grouping dialog box shown in Figure 21-14.

In versions prior to Excel 2002, the shortcut menu command is Group and Outline ⇨ Group.

Figure 21-13: The pivot table, before grouping by month.

Figure 21-14: Use the Grouping dialog box to group items in a pivot table.

In the list box, select Months and Years, and verify that the starting and ending dates are correct. Click OK. The Date items in the pivot table are grouped by years and by months (as shown in Figure 21-15).

Note   If you select only Months in the Grouping list box, months in different years combine together. For example, the June item would display sales for both 2001 and 2002.

Copying a Pivot Table

A pivot table is a special type of *object,* and you cannot manipulate it as you may expect. For example, you can't insert a new row or enter formulas within the pivot table. If you want to manipulate a pivot table in ways not normally permitted, make a copy of it.

To copy a pivot table, select the table and choose Edit ➪ Copy. Then activate a new worksheet and choose Edit ➪ Paste Special. Select the Values option and click OK. The contents of the pivot table are copied to the new location so you can do whatever you like to them. You also may want to repeat the Edit ➪ Paste Special command and select Formats (to copy the formatting from the pivot table).

This technique is also useful when you want to create a standard chart. If you attempt to create a chart from a pivot table, Excel always creates a pivot chart that contains field buttons. Sometimes you may prefer a standard chart.

Note that the copied information is no longer linked to the source data. If the source data changes, your copied pivot table does not reflect these changes.

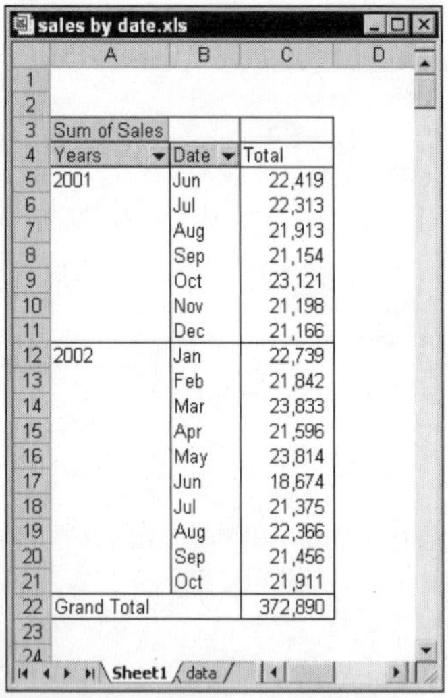

	A	B	C	D
1				
2				
3	Sum of Sales			
4	Years ▼	Date ▼	Total	
5	2001	Jun	22,419	
6		Jul	22,313	
7		Aug	21,913	
8		Sep	21,154	
9		Oct	23,121	
10		Nov	21,198	
11		Dec	21,166	
12	2002	Jan	22,739	
13		Feb	21,842	
14		Mar	23,833	
15		Apr	21,596	
16		May	23,814	
17		Jun	18,674	
18		Jul	21,375	
19		Aug	22,366	
20		Sep	21,456	
21		Oct	21,911	
22	Grand Total		372,890	
23				
24				

Figure 21-15: The pivot table, after grouping by month.

Creating a Calculated Field or Calculated Item

After you create a pivot table, you can create two types of calculations for further analysis:

✦ **A calculated field:** A new field created from other fields in the pivot table. A calculated field must reside in the Data area of the pivot table. (You can't use a calculated field in the Page, Row, or Column areas.)

✦ **A calculated item:** A calculated item uses the contents of other items within a field of the pivot table. A calculated item must reside in the Page, Row, or Column area of a pivot table. (You can't use a calculated item in the Data area.)

The formulas used to create calculated fields and calculated items are not standard Excel formulas. In other words, you do not enter the formulas into cells. Rather, you enter these formulas in a dialog box, and they are stored along with the pivot table data.

The examples in this section use the worksheet database table shown in Figure 21-16. The table consists of five fields and 48 records. Each record describes monthly sales information for a particular sales representative. For example, Amy is a sales rep for the North region, and she sold 239 units in January for total sales of $23,040.

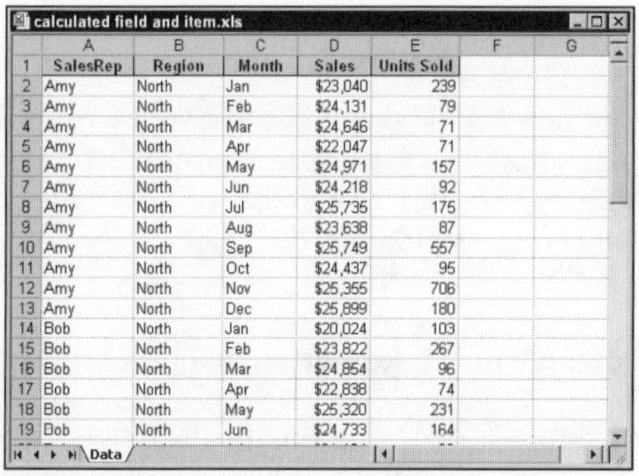

	A	B	C	D	E	F	G
1	SalesRep	Region	Month	Sales	Units Sold		
2	Amy	North	Jan	$23,040	239		
3	Amy	North	Feb	$24,131	79		
4	Amy	North	Mar	$24,646	71		
5	Amy	North	Apr	$22,047	71		
6	Amy	North	May	$24,971	157		
7	Amy	North	Jun	$24,218	92		
8	Amy	North	Jul	$25,735	175		
9	Amy	North	Aug	$23,638	87		
10	Amy	North	Sep	$25,749	557		
11	Amy	North	Oct	$24,437	95		
12	Amy	North	Nov	$25,355	706		
13	Amy	North	Dec	$25,899	180		
14	Bob	North	Jan	$20,024	103		
15	Bob	North	Feb	$23,822	267		
16	Bob	North	Mar	$24,854	96		
17	Bob	North	Apr	$22,838	74		
18	Bob	North	May	$25,320	231		
19	Bob	North	Jun	$24,733	164		

Figure 21-16: This data demonstrates calculated fields and calculated items.

A workbook demonstrating calculated fields and items is available on the companion CD-ROM.

Figure 21-17 shows the basic pivot table created from the data. This pivot table shows sales, broken down by month and sales rep.

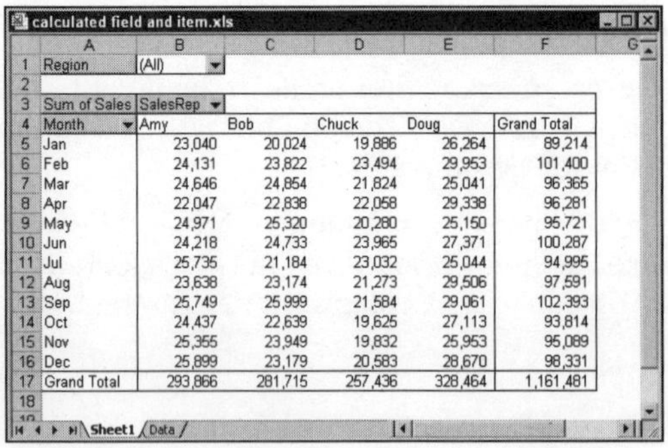
calculated field and item.xls

Region	(All)				
Sum of Sales	SalesRep				
Month	Amy	Bob	Chuck	Doug	Grand Total
Jan	23,040	20,024	19,886	26,264	89,214
Feb	24,131	23,822	23,494	29,953	101,400
Mar	24,646	24,854	21,824	25,041	96,365
Apr	22,047	22,838	22,058	29,338	96,281
May	24,971	25,320	20,280	25,150	95,721
Jun	24,218	24,733	23,965	27,371	100,287
Jul	25,735	21,184	23,032	25,044	94,995
Aug	23,638	23,174	21,273	29,506	97,591
Sep	25,749	25,999	21,584	29,061	102,393
Oct	24,437	22,639	19,625	27,113	93,814
Nov	25,355	23,949	19,832	25,953	95,089
Dec	25,899	23,179	20,583	28,670	98,331
Grand Total	293,866	281,715	257,436	328,464	1,161,481

Sheet1 / Data

Figure 21-17: This pivot table was created from the data in Figure 21-16.

The examples that follow will create

- ✦ A calculated field, to compute average sales per unit
- ✦ A calculated item, to summarize the data by quarters

Creating a calculated field in a pivot table

Because a pivot table is a special type of data range, you can't insert new rows or columns within the pivot table. This means that you can't insert formulas to perform calculations with the data in a pivot table. However, you can create calculated fields for a pivot table. A *calculated field* consists of a calculation that can involve other fields.

A calculated field is basically a way to display new information in a pivot table. It essentially presents an alternative to creating a new *Data* field in your source database. A calculated field cannot be used as a Row, Column, or Page field.

In the sales example, for instance, suppose you want to calculate the average sales amount per unit. You can compute this value by dividing the Sales field by the Units Sold field. The result shows a new field (a calculated field) for the pivot table.

Use the following procedure to create a calculated field that consists of the Sales field divided by the Units Sold field:

1. Move the cell pointer anywhere within the pivot table.
2. Using the PivotTable toolbar, choose PivotTable ➪ Formulas ➪ Calculated Field. Excel displays the Insert Calculated Field dialog box.

3. Enter a descriptive name in the Name field and specify the formula in the Formula field (see Figure 21-18). The formula can use other fields and worksheet functions. For this example, the calculated field name is Avg Unit Price, and the formula appears as the following:

```
=Sales/'Units Sold'
```

4. Click Add to add this new field.

5. Click OK to close the Insert Calculated Field dialog box.

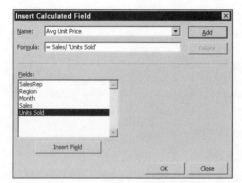

Figure 21-18: The Insert Calculated Field dialog box.

Note You can create the formula manually by typing it or by double-clicking items in the Fields list box. Double-clicking an item transfers it to the Formula field. Because the Units Sold field contains a space, Excel adds single quotes around the field name.

After you create the calculated field, Excel adds it to the Data area of the pivot table. You can treat it just like any other field, with one exception: You can't move it to the Page, Row, or Column area. (It must remain in the Data area.)

Figure 21-19 shows the pivot table after you've added the calculated field. The new field displays as Sum of Avg Unit Price. (You can change this text, if desired, by editing any of the cells in which that text appears.) The calculated field also appears on the PivotTable Field List toolbar, along with the other fields available for use in the pivot table.

Tip The formulas that you develop can also use worksheet functions, but the functions cannot refer to cells or named ranges.

Inserting a calculated item into a pivot table

The preceding section describes how to create a calculated field. Excel also enables you to create a *calculated item* for a pivot table field. Keep in mind that a calculated field can be an alternative to adding a new field to your data source. A calculated item, on the other hand, uses the contents of items within a single field.

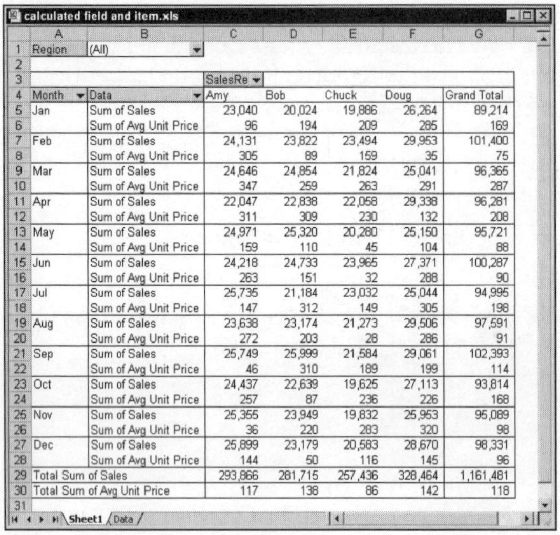

	A	B	C	D	E	F	G
1	Region	(All)					
2							
3			SalesRe				
4	Month	Data	Amy	Bob	Chuck	Doug	Grand Total
5	Jan	Sum of Sales	23,040	20,024	19,886	26,264	89,214
6		Sum of Avg Unit Price	96	194	209	285	169
7	Feb	Sum of Sales	24,131	23,822	23,494	29,953	101,400
8		Sum of Avg Unit Price	305	89	159	35	75
9	Mar	Sum of Sales	24,646	24,854	21,824	25,041	96,365
10		Sum of Avg Unit Price	347	259	263	291	287
11	Apr	Sum of Sales	22,047	22,838	22,058	29,338	96,281
12		Sum of Avg Unit Price	311	309	230	132	208
13	May	Sum of Sales	24,971	25,320	20,280	25,150	95,721
14		Sum of Avg Unit Price	159	110	45	104	88
15	Jun	Sum of Sales	24,218	24,733	23,965	27,371	100,287
16		Sum of Avg Unit Price	263	151	32	288	90
17	Jul	Sum of Sales	25,735	21,184	23,032	25,044	94,995
18		Sum of Avg Unit Price	147	312	149	305	198
19	Aug	Sum of Sales	23,638	23,174	21,273	29,506	97,591
20		Sum of Avg Unit Price	272	203	28	286	91
21	Sep	Sum of Sales	25,749	25,999	21,584	29,061	102,393
22		Sum of Avg Unit Price	46	310	189	199	114
23	Oct	Sum of Sales	24,437	22,639	19,625	27,113	93,814
24		Sum of Avg Unit Price	257	87	236	226	168
25	Nov	Sum of Sales	25,355	23,949	19,832	25,953	95,089
26		Sum of Avg Unit Price	36	220	283	320	98
27	Dec	Sum of Sales	25,899	23,179	20,583	28,670	98,331
28		Sum of Avg Unit Price	144	50	116	145	96
29	Total Sum of Sales		293,866	281,715	257,436	328,464	1,161,481
30	Total Sum of Avg Unit Price		117	138	86	142	118
31							

Figure 21-19: This pivot table uses a calculated field.

The sales example uses a field named Month, which consists of text strings. You can create a calculated item (called Qtr-1, for example) that displays the sum of Jan, Feb, and Mar.

You also can do this by grouping the items, but using grouping hides the individual months and shows only the total of the group. Creating a calculated item for quarterly totals is more flexible because it shows the total and the individual months.

To create a calculated item to sum the data for Jan, Feb, and Mar, follow these steps:

1. Move the cell pointer to the Row, Column, or Page area of the pivot table that contains the item that will be calculated. In this example, the cell pointer should be in the Month area.
2. Use the PivotTable toolbar, and choose PivotTable ➪ Formulas ➪ Calculated Item from the shortcut menu. Excel displays the Insert Calculated Item dialog box.
3. Enter a name for the new item in the Name field and specify the formula in the Formula field (see Figure 21-20). The formula can use items in other fields, but it can't use worksheet functions. For this example, the new item is named Qtr-1, and the formula appears as follows:

```
=Jan+Feb+Mar
```

4. Click Add.

5. Repeat Steps 3 and 4 to create additional calculated items for Qtr-2 (=Apr+May+Jun), Qtr-3 (=Jul+Aug+Sep), and Qtr-4 (=Oct+Nov+Dec).

6. Click OK to close the dialog box.

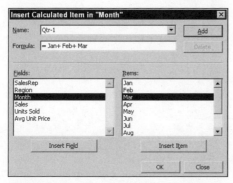

Figure 21-20: The Insert Calculated Item dialog box.

Caution   If you use a calculated item in your pivot table, you may need to turn off the Grand Total display to avoid double counting. In this example the Grand Total includes the calculated item, so each month is counted twice. To turn off Grand Totals, use the PivotTable Options dialog box (see the "Pivot Table Options" sidebar, earlier in this chapter).

After you create the items, they appear in the pivot table. Figure 21-21 shows the pivot table after you've added the four calculated items. Notice that the calculated items are added to the end of the Month items. You can rearrange the items by selecting and dragging. Figure 21-22 shows the pivot table after rearranging the items logically. (I also made the calculated items bold.)

Note   A calculated item appears in a pivot table only if the field on which it is based also appears. If you remove or pivot a field from either the Row or Column category into the Data category, the calculated item does not appear.

It's also possible to get quarterly summaries by grouping items. Because the month names are not actual dates, the grouping must be done manually. Figure 21-23 shows the pivot table after creating four groups. I created the first group by selecting the Jan, Feb, and Mar items. I then right-clicked and chose Group and Show Detail ➪ Group from the shortcut menu. Excel inserted the default name, Group 1 — which I changed to Qtr 1. Next, I right-clicked the group item and chose Field Settings to display the PivotTable Field dialog box. In this dialog box, I specified the SUM function to summarize the grouped data. I then repeated this process for the other three quarters.

calculated field and item.xls

	A	B	C	D	E	F
1	Region	(All)				
2						
3	Sum of Sales	SalesRep				
4	Month	Amy	Bob	Chuck	Doug	Grand Total
5	Jan	23,040	20,024	19,886	26,264	89,214
6	Feb	24,131	23,822	23,494	29,953	101,400
7	Mar	24,646	24,854	21,824	25,041	96,365
8	Apr	22,047	22,838	22,058	29,338	96,281
9	May	24,971	25,320	20,280	25,150	95,721
10	Jun	24,218	24,733	23,965	27,371	100,287
11	Jul	25,735	21,184	23,032	25,044	94,995
12	Aug	23,638	23,174	21,273	29,506	97,591
13	Sep	25,749	25,999	21,584	29,061	102,393
14	Oct	24,437	22,639	19,625	27,113	93,814
15	Nov	25,355	23,949	19,832	25,953	95,089
16	Dec	25,899	23,179	20,583	28,670	98,331
17	Qtr-1	71,817	68,700	65,204	81,258	286,979
18	Qtr-2	71,236	72,891	66,303	81,859	292,289
19	Qtr-3	75,122	70,357	65,889	83,611	294,979
20	Qtr-4	75,691	69,767	60,040	81,736	287,234
21						

Sheet1 / Data

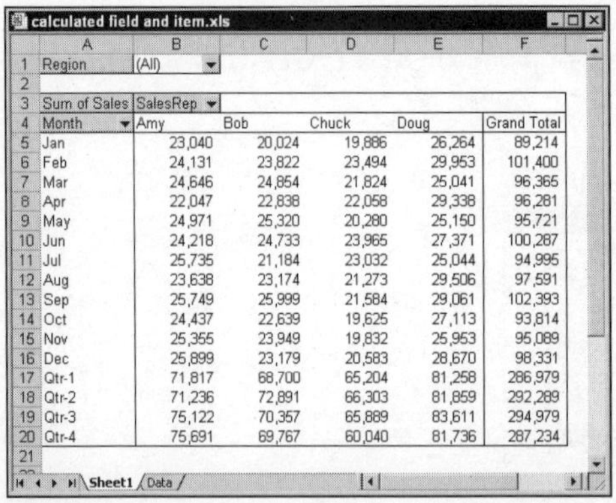

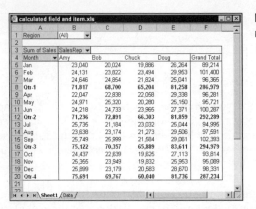

Figure 21-21: This pivot table uses calculated items for quarterly totals.

calculated field and item.xls

	A	B	C	D	E	F
1	Region	(All)				
2						
3	Sum of Sales	SalesRep				
4	Month	Amy	Bob	Chuck	Doug	Grand Total
5	Jan	23,040	20,024	19,886	26,264	89,214
6	Feb	24,131	23,822	23,494	29,953	101,400
7	Mar	24,646	24,854	21,824	25,041	96,365
8	**Qtr-1**	**71,817**	**68,700**	**65,204**	**81,258**	**286,979**
9	Apr	22,047	22,838	22,058	29,338	96,281
10	May	24,971	25,320	20,280	25,150	95,721
11	Jun	24,218	24,733	23,965	27,371	100,287
12	**Qtr-2**	**71,236**	**72,891**	**66,303**	**81,859**	**292,289**
13	Jul	25,735	21,184	23,032	25,044	94,995
14	Aug	23,638	23,174	21,273	29,506	97,591
15	Sep	25,749	25,999	21,584	29,061	102,393
16	**Qtr-3**	**75,122**	**70,357**	**65,889**	**83,611**	**294,979**
17	Oct	24,437	22,639	19,625	27,113	93,814
18	Nov	25,355	23,949	19,832	25,953	95,089
19	Dec	25,899	23,179	20,583	28,670	98,331
20	**Qtr-4**	**75,691**	**69,767**	**60,040**	**81,736**	**287,234**
21						

Sheet1 / Data

Figure 21-22: The pivot table, after rearranging the calculated items.

calculated field and item.xls

	A	B	C	D	E	F	G
1	Region	(All)					
2							
3	Sum of Sales		SalesRep				
4	Quarter	Month	Amy	Bob	Chuck	Doug	Grand Total
5	Qtr 1	Jan	23,040	20,024	19,886	26,264	89,214
6		Feb	24,131	23,822	23,494	29,953	101,400
7		Mar	24,646	24,854	21,824	25,041	96,365
8	Qtr 1 Sum		71,817	68,700	65,204	81,258	286,979
9	Qtr 2	Apr	22,047	22,838	22,058	29,338	96,281
10		May	24,971	25,320	20,280	25,150	95,721
11		Jun	24,218	24,733	23,965	27,371	100,287
12	Qtr 2 Sum		71,236	72,891	66,303	81,859	292,289
13	Qtr 3	Jul	25,735	21,184	23,032	25,044	94,995
14		Aug	23,638	23,174	21,273	29,506	97,591
15		Sep	25,749	25,999	21,584	29,061	102,393
16	Qtr 3 Sum		75,122	70,357	65,889	83,611	294,979
17	Qtr 4	Oct	24,437	22,639	19,625	27,113	93,814
18		Nov	25,355	23,949	19,832	25,953	95,089
19		Dec	25,899	23,179	20,583	28,670	98,331
20	Qtr 4 Sum		75,691	69,767	60,040	81,736	287,234
21	Grand Total		293,866	281,715	257,436	328,464	1,161,481
22							

Sheet1 / Data

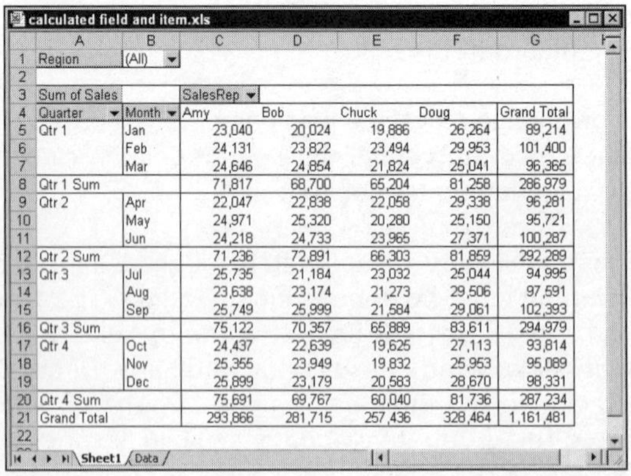

Figure 21-23: Grouping items to show quarterly summary information.

✦ ✦ ✦

Performing Spreadsheet What-If Analysis

One of the most appealing aspects of Excel is its ability to create dynamic models. A dynamic model uses formulas that instantly recalculate when you change values in cells to which the formulas refer. When you change values in cells in a systematic manner and observe the effects on specific formula cells, you're performing a type of *what-if* analysis. What-if analysis is the process of asking such questions as "What if the interest rate on the loan changes to 7.5 percent rather than 7.0 percent?" or "What if we raise our product prices by 5 percent?"

If you set up your spreadsheet properly, answering such questions is simply a matter of plugging in new values and observing the results of the recalculation. Excel provides useful tools to assist you in your what-if endeavors.

A What-If Example

Figure 22-1 shows a spreadsheet that calculates information pertaining to a mortgage loan. The worksheet is divided into two sections: the input cells and the result cells (which contain formulas).

On the CD-ROM The workbook shown in Figure 22-1 is available on the companion CD-ROM.

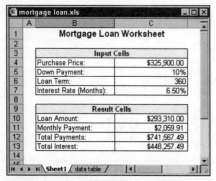

Figure 22-1: This worksheet model uses four input cells to produce the results.

With this worksheet, you can easily answer the following what-if questions:

✦ What if I can negotiate a lower purchase price on the property?

✦ What if the lender requires a 20-percent down payment?

✦ What if I can get a 40-year mortgage?

✦ What if the interest rate increases to 7.0 percent?

Avoid Hard-Coding Values in a Formula

The mortgage calculation example, simple as it is, demonstrates an important point about spreadsheet design: You should always set up your worksheet so that you have maximum flexibility to make changes. Perhaps the most fundamental rule of spreadsheet design is the following:

Do not hard-code values in a formula. Rather, store the values in separate cells and use cell references in the formula.

The term *hard-code* refers to the use of actual values, or *constants,* in a formula. In the mortgage loan example, all the formulas use references to cells, not actual values.

You *could* use the value 360, for example, for the loan term argument of the PMT function in cell C11. Using a cell reference has two advantages. First, you have no doubt about the values that the formula uses (they aren't buried in the formula). Second, you can easily change the value.

Using values in formulas may not seem like much of an issue when only one formula is involved, but just imagine what would happen if this value were hard-coded into several hundred formulas that were scattered throughout a worksheet.

You can answer these questions simply by changing the values in the cells in range C4:C7 and observing the effects in the dependent cells (C10:C13). You can, of course, vary any number of input cells simultaneously.

Types of What-If Analyses

As you may expect, Excel can handle much more sophisticated models than the preceding example. To perform a what-if analysis using Excel, you have three basic options:

✦ **Manual what-if analysis:** Plug in new values and observe the effects on formula cells.

✦ **Data tables:** Create a table that displays the results of selected formula cells as you systematically change one or two input cells.

✦ **Scenario Manager:** Create named scenarios and generate reports that use outlines or pivot tables.

Manual What-If Analysis

This method doesn't require too much explanation. In fact, the example that opens this chapter demonstrates how it's done. Manual what-if analysis is based on the idea that you have one or more input cells that affect one or more key formula cells. You change the value in the input cells and see what happens to the formula cells. You may want to print the results or save each scenario to a new workbook. The term *scenario* refers to a specific set of values in one or more input cells.

This is how most people perform what-if analysis. Manual what-if analysis certainly has nothing wrong with it, but you should be aware of some other techniques.

Creating Data Tables

When you're working with a what-if model, Excel displays only one scenario at a time. But you can compare the results of various scenarios by using any of the following techniques:

✦ Print multiple copies of the worksheet, each displaying a different scenario.

✦ Copy the model to other worksheets and set it up so that each worksheet displays a different scenario.

✦ Manually create a table that summarizes key formula cells for each scenario.

✦ Use Excel's Data ➪ Table command to create a summary table automatically.

This section discusses the last option — the Data ➪ Table command, which enables you to create a handy data table that summarizes formula cells for various values of either of the following:

✦ A single input cell

✦ Various combinations of two input cells

You can create a data table fairly easily, but data tables have some limitations. In particular, a data table can deal with only one or two input cells at a time. In other words, you can't create a data table that uses a combination of three or more input cells.

The Scenario Manager, discussed later in this chapter, can produce a report that summarizes any number of input cells and result cells.

Creating a one-input data table

A one-input data table displays the results of one or more formulas when you use multiple values in a single input cell. Figure 22-2 shows the general layout for a one-input data table. You can place the table anywhere in a worksheet. The left column contains various values for the single input cell. The top row contains formulas or, more often, references to formulas located elsewhere in the worksheet. You can use a single formula reference or any number of formula references. The upper-left cell of the table remains empty. Excel calculates the values that result from each level of the input cell and places them under each formula reference.

This example uses the mortgage loan worksheet from earlier in the chapter. The goal of this example is to create a table that shows the values of the four formula cells (loan amount, monthly payment, total payments, and total interest) for various interest rates ranging from 6 to 8 percent, in 0.25 percent increments.

Figure 22-3 shows the setup for the data table area. Row 3 consists of references to the formulas in the worksheet. For example, cell F3 contains the formula =C10, and cell G3 contains the formula =C11. Column E contains the values of the single input cell (interest rate) that Excel will use in the table.

To create the table, select the data table range (in this case, E3:I12) and then choose Data ➪ Table. Excel displays the Table dialog box, shown in Figure 22-4. You must specify the worksheet cell that contains the input value. Because variables for the input cell appear in a column in the data table rather than in a row, you place this cell reference in the text box called Column Input Cell. Enter **C7** or point to the cell in the worksheet. Leave the Row Input Cell field blank. Click OK, and Excel fills in the table with the appropriate results (see Figure 22-5).

Using this table, you can now quickly see the calculated loan values for varying interest rates. Examine the contents of the cells that Excel entered as a result of this command, and you'll see that the data is generated with a multicell array formula:

```
=TABLE(,C7).
```

Results of the one-input table (an array formula)

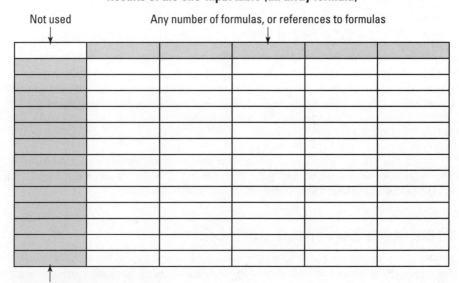

Not used   Any number of formulas, or references to formulas

Values of the single input cell

Figure 22-2: How a one-input data table is set up.

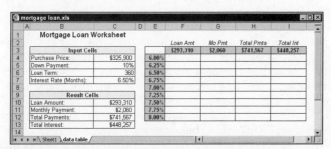

Figure 22-3: Preparing to create a one-input data table.

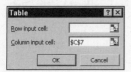

Figure 22-4: The Table dialog box.

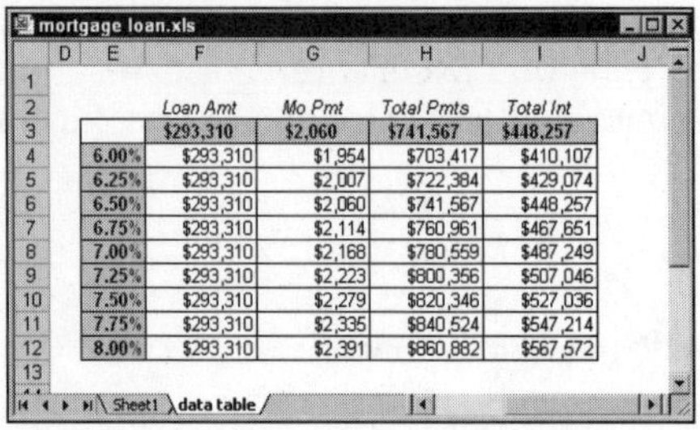

	Loan Amt	Mo Pmt	Total Pmts	Total Int
	$293,310	$2,060	$741,567	$448,257
6.00%	$293,310	$1,954	$703,417	$410,107
6.25%	$293,310	$2,007	$722,384	$429,074
6.50%	$293,310	$2,060	$741,567	$448,257
6.75%	$293,310	$2,114	$760,961	$467,651
7.00%	$293,310	$2,168	$780,559	$487,249
7.25%	$293,310	$2,223	$800,356	$507,046
7.50%	$293,310	$2,279	$820,346	$527,036
7.75%	$293,310	$2,335	$840,524	$547,214
8.00%	$293,310	$2,391	$860,882	$567,572

Figure 22-5: The result of the one-input data table.

As I discussed in Chapter 14, an *array formula* is a single formula that can produce results in multiple cells. Because the table uses formulas, Excel updates the table that you produce if you change the cell references in the first row or plug in different interest rates in the first column.

Note

You can arrange a one-input table vertically (as in this example) or horizontally. If you place the values of the input cell in a row, you enter the input cell reference in the text box labeled Row input cell in the Table dialog box.

Creating a two-input data table

As the name implies, a two-input data table lets you vary *two* input cells. You can see the setup for this type of table in Figure 22-6. Although it looks similar to a one-input table, the two-input table has one critical difference: It can show the results of only one formula at a time. With a one-input table, you can place any number of formulas, or references to formulas, across the top row of the table. In a two-input table, this top row holds the values for the second input cell. The upper-left cell of the table contains a reference to the single result formula.

In the preceding example, you could create a two-input data table that shows the results of a formula (say, monthly payment) for various combinations of two input cells (such as interest rate and down-payment percent). To see the effects on other formulas, you simply create multiple data tables — one for each formula cell that you want to summarize.

The worksheet that is shown in Figure 22-7 demonstrates a two-input data table. In this example, a company wants to conduct a direct-mail promotion to sell its product. The worksheet calculates the net profit from the promotion.

On the CD-ROM

The workbook shown in Figure 22-7 is available on the companion CD-ROM.

Results of the two-input table (an array formula)

A single formula, or a reference to a formula   Different values of input cell #2

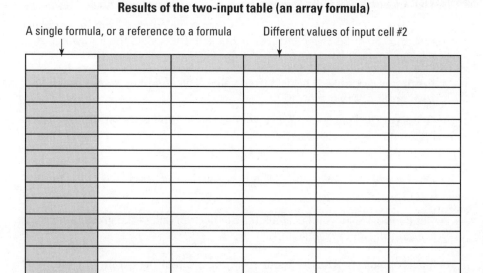

Different values of input cell #1

Figure 22-6: The setup for a two-input data table.

Figure 22-7: This worksheet calculates the net profit from a direct-mail promotion.

This model uses two input cells: the number of promotional pieces mailed and the anticipated response rate. The following items appear in the results area:

    ✦ **Printing costs per unit:** The cost to print a single mailer. The unit cost varies with the quantity: $0.20 each for quantities less than 200,000; $0.15 each for quantities of 200,001 through 300,000; and $0.10 each for quantities of more than 300,000. The following formula is used:

```
=IF(B4<200000,0.2,IF(B4<300000,0.15,0.1))
```

✦ **Mailing costs per unit:** This is a fixed cost, $0.28 per unit mailed.

✦ **Responses:** This is the number of responses, calculated from the response rate and the number mailed. The formula in this cell is the following:

```
=B5*B4
```

✦ **Profit per response:** This is a fixed value. The company knows that it will realize a profit of $19 per order.

✦ **Gross profit:** This is a simple formula that multiplies the profit per response by the number of responses:

```
=B11*B10
```

✦ **Print + mailing costs:** This formula calculates the total cost of the promotion:

```
=B4*(B8+B9)
```

✦ **Net Profit:** This formula calculates the bottom line—the gross profit minus the printing and mailing costs.

If you plug in values for the two input cells, you see that the net profit varies widely—often going negative to produce a net loss.

Figure 22-8 shows the setup of a two-input data table that summarizes the net profit at various combinations of quantity and response rate; the table appears in the range A18:I28. Cell A18 contains a formula that references the Net Profit cell:

```
=B15
```

To create the data table, select the range and choose Data ➪ Table. The Row input cell is B5 (the response rate), and the Column input cell is B4 (the number mailed). Figure 22-9 shows the result of this command.

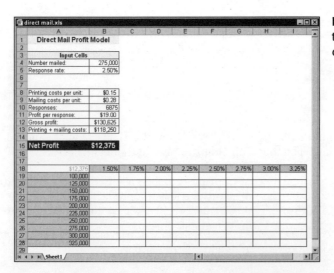

Figure 22-8: Preparing to create a two-input data table.

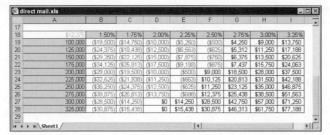

Figure 22-9: The result of the two-input data table.

As with the one-input data table, this data table is dynamic. You can change the formula in cell A1 to refer to other cells (such a gross profit).

Using Scenario Manager

Data tables are useful, but they have a few limitations:

✦ You can vary only one or two input cells at a time.

✦ The process of setting up a data table is not all that intuitive.

✦ A two-input table shows the results of only one formula cell (although you can create additional tables for more formulas).

✦ More often than not, you're interested in a few select combinations — not an entire table that shows all possible combinations of two input cells.

Excel's Scenario Manager feature makes it easy to automate your what-if models. You can store different sets of input values (called *changing cells* in the terminology of Scenario Manager) for any number of variables and give a name to each set. You can then select a set of values by name, and Excel displays the worksheet by using those values. You can also generate a summary report that shows the effect of various combinations of values on any number of result cells. These summary reports can be an outline or a pivot table.

Your sales forecast for the year, for example, may depend on several factors. Consequently, you can define three scenarios: best case, worst case, and most likely case. You then can switch to any of these scenarios by selecting the named scenario from a list. Excel substitutes the appropriate input values in your worksheet and recalculates the formulas.

Defining scenarios

To introduce you to the Scenario Manager, this section starts with an example that uses a simple production model, as shown in Figure 22-10.

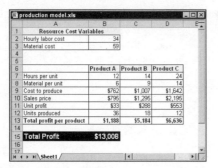

Figure 22-10: A simple production model to demonstrate Scenario Manager.

The workbook shown in Figure 22-10 is available on the companion CD-ROM.

This worksheet contains two input cells: the hourly labor cost (cell B2) and the unit cost for materials (cell B3). The company produces three products, and each product requires a different number of hours and a different amount of materials to produce. Formulas calculate the total profit per product (row 13), and the total combined profit (cell B15). Management is trying to predict the total profit but is uncertain what the hourly labor cost and material costs are going to be. They've identified three scenarios, as listed in Table 22-1.

Table 22-1
Three Scenarios for the Production Model

Scenario	Hourly Cost	Materials Cost
Best Case	30	57
Worst Case	38	62
Most Likely	34	59

The Best Case scenario has the lowest hourly cost and materials cost. The Worst Case scenario has high values for both the hourly cost and the materials cost. The third scenario, Most Likely Case, has intermediate values for both of these input cells. (This represents the management's best estimate.) The managers need to be prepared for the worst case, however, and they are interested in what would happen under the Best Case scenario.

Access the Scenario Manager by selecting Tools ⇨ Scenarios to display the Scenario Manager dialog box. When you first open this dialog box, it tells you that no scenarios are defined — which is not too surprising because you're just starting. As you add named scenarios, they appear in this dialog box.

Tip

I strongly suggest that you create names for the changing cells and all the result cells that you want to examine. Excel uses these names in the dialog boxes and in the reports that it generates. If you use names, you'll find that keeping track of what's going on is much easier; names also make your reports more readable.

To add a scenario, click the Add button in the Scenario Manager dialog box. Excel displays its Add Scenario dialog box, shown in Figure 22-11.

Figure 22-11: The Add Scenario dialog box lets you create a named scenario.

This dialog box consists of four parts:

✦ **Scenario Name:** The name for the scenario. You can give it any name that you like — preferably something meaningful.

✦ **Changing Cells:** The input cells for the scenario. You can enter the cell addresses directly or point to them. Multiple selections are allowed, so the input cells need not be adjacent. Each named scenario can use the same set of changing cells or different changing cells. The number of changing cells for a scenario is limited to 32.

✦ **Comment:** By default, Excel displays the name of the person who created the scenario and the date that it was created. You can change this text, add new text to it, or delete it.

✦ **Protection:** The two options (preventing changes and hiding a scenario) are in effect only when you protect the worksheet and choose the Scenario option in the Protect Sheet dialog box. Protecting a scenario prevents anyone from modifying it; a hidden scenario doesn't appear in the Scenario Manager dialog box.

In this example, define the three scenarios that are listed in Table 22-1. The changing cells are Hourly_Cost (B2) and Materials_Cost (B3).

After you enter the information in the Add Scenario dialog box, click OK. Excel then displays the Scenario Values dialog box, shown in Figure 22-12. This dialog box displays one field for each changing cell that you specified in the previous dialog box. Enter the values for each cell in the scenario. If you click OK, you return to the Scenario Manager dialog box, which then displays your named scenario in its list. If you have more scenarios to create, click the Add button to return to the Add Scenario dialog box.

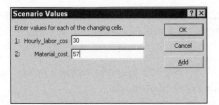

Figure 22-12: You enter the values for the scenario in the Scenario Values dialog box.

Displaying scenarios

After you define all the scenarios and return to the Scenario Manager dialog box, the dialog box displays the names of your defined scenarios. Select one of the scenarios and then click the Show button. Excel inserts the corresponding values into the changing cells and calculates the worksheet to show the results for that scenario.

Using the Scenarios Tool

Excel has a Scenarios tool, which is a drop-down list that shows all the defined scenarios and enables you to display a scenario or create a new scenario. Oddly, this useful tool doesn't appear on any of the prebuilt toolbars. But, if you use the Scenario Manager, you may want to add the Scenarios tool to one of your toolbars, using the following procedure:

1. Choose Tools ⇨ Customize.

2. In the Customize dialog box, click the Commands tab.

3. Select the Tools category.

4. In the Commands tab, locate the Scenarios tool and drag it to any toolbar.

5. Click the Close button.

Refer to Chapter 26 for additional details on customizing toolbars.

Using the Scenarios tool may be more efficient than bringing up the Scenario Manager dialog box to create or view a different scenario.

To create a scenario by using the Scenarios tool, enter the scenario's values, select the changing cells, and then enter the name for the scenario in the Scenario drop-down box. To view a named scenario, just choose it from the list. Scenarios that you define in this manner also appear in the Scenario Manager dialog box. So, if you want to perform any operations on your scenarios (add comments, edit values, or generate reports), you need to select Tools ⇨ Scenarios to display the Scenario Manager dialog box.

Modifying scenarios

The Edit button in the Scenario Manager dialog box lets you change one or more of the values for the changing cells of a scenario. From the Scenarios list, select the scenario that you want to change and click the Edit button. In the Edit Scenario dialog box, click OK to access the Scenario Values dialog box. Make your changes and click OK to return to the Scenario Manager dialog box. Notice that Excel automatically updates the Comments box with new text that indicates when the scenario was modified.

Merging scenarios

In workgroup situations, you may have several people working on a spreadsheet model, and several people may have defined various scenarios. The marketing department, for example, may have its opinion of what the input cells should be, the finance department may have another opinion, and your CEO may have yet another opinion.

Excel makes it easy to merge these various scenarios into a single workbook by using the Merge button in the Scenario Manager dialog box. Clicking this button displays the Merge Scenarios dialog box.

Before you merge scenarios, make sure that the workbook from which you're merging is open. Then, click the Merge button in the Scenario Manager dialog box. Excel displays its Merge Scenarios dialog box. Choose the workbook from which you're merging in the Book drop-down list. Then, choose the sheet that contains the scenarios you want to merge from the Sheet list box. (Notice that the dialog box displays the number of scenarios in each sheet as you scroll through the Sheet list box.) Click OK, and you return to the previous dialog box, which now displays the scenario names that you merged from the other workbook.

Generating a scenario report

You are ready to take the Scenario Manager through its final feat — generating a summary report. When you click the Summary button in the Scenario Manager dialog box, Excel displays the Scenario Summary dialog box.

You have a choice of report types:

✦ **Scenario Summary:** The summary report appears in the form of an outline.

✦ **Scenario PivotTable:** The summary report appears in the form of a pivot table (see Chapter 21).

For simple cases of scenario management, a standard Scenario Summary report is usually sufficient. If you have many scenarios defined with multiple result cells, however, you may find that a Scenario Pivot Table provides more flexibility.

The Scenario Summary dialog box also asks you to specify the result cells (the cells that contain the formulas in which you're interested). For this example, select B13:D13 and B15 (a multiple selection) to make the report show the profit for each product, plus the total profit (refer to Figure 22-10).

Note As you work with the Scenario Manager, you may discover its main limitation: A scenario can use no more than 32 changing cells. If you attempt to use more, you get an error message.

Excel creates a new worksheet to store the summary table. Figure 22-13 shows the Scenario Summary form of the report. If you gave names to the changing cells and result cells, the table uses these names. Otherwise, it lists the cell references.

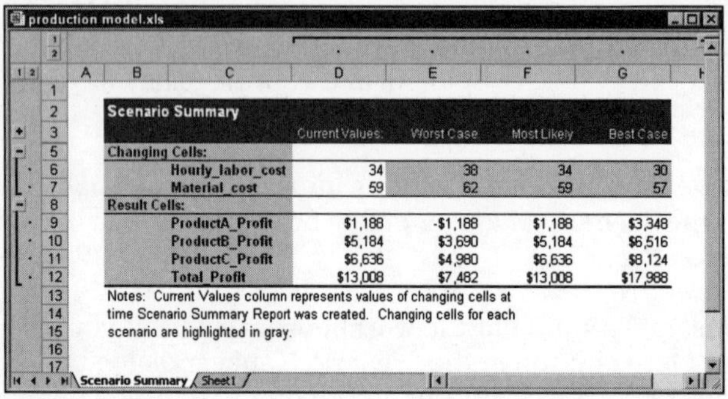

	Current Values:	Worst Case	Most Likely	Best Case
Scenario Summary				
Changing Cells:				
Hourly_labor_cost	34	38	34	30
Material_cost	59	62	59	57
Result Cells:				
ProductA_Profit	$1,188	-$1,188	$1,188	$3,348
ProductB_Profit	$5,184	$3,690	$5,184	$6,516
ProductC_Profit	$6,636	$4,980	$6,636	$8,124
Total_Profit	$13,008	$7,482	$13,008	$17,988

Notes: Current Values column represents values of changing cells at time Scenario Summary Report was created. Changing cells for each scenario are highlighted in gray.

Figure 22-13: A Scenario Summary report produced by the Scenario Manager.

✦　　✦　　✦

Analyzing Data Using Goal Seek and Solver

The preceding chapter discusses *what-if analysis* — the process of changing input cells to observe the results on other dependent cells. This chapter looks at that process from the opposite perspective: finding the value of one or more input cells that produces a desired result in a formula cell.

What-If Analysis — in Reverse

Consider the following what-if question: "What is the total profit if sales increase by 20 percent?" If you set up your worksheet properly, you can change the value in one cell to see what happens to the profit cell. Goal seeking takes the opposite approach. If you know what a formula result should be, Excel can tell you the values that you need to enter in one or more input cells to produce that result. In other words, you can ask a question such as "How much do sales need to increase to produce a profit of $1.2 million?" Excel provides two tools that are relevant:

✦ **Goal seeking:** Determines the value that you need to enter in a single input cell to produce a result that you want in a dependent (formula) cell.

✦ **Solver:** Determines the values that you need to enter in multiple input cells to produce a result that you want. Moreover, because you can specify certain constraints to the problem, you gain significant problem-solving ability.

Single-Cell Goal Seeking

Single-cell goal seeking is a rather simple concept. Excel determines what value in an input cell produces a desired result in a formula cell. Walk through the following example to understand how single-cell goal seeking works.

A goal-seeking example

Figure 23-1 shows the mortgage loan worksheet that was used in the preceding chapter. This worksheet has four input cells (C4:C7) and four formula cells (C10:C13). Originally, this worksheet was used for a what-if analysis example. This example demonstrates the opposite approach. Rather than supply different input cell values to look at the calculated formulas, this example lets Excel determine one of the input values that will produce the desired result.

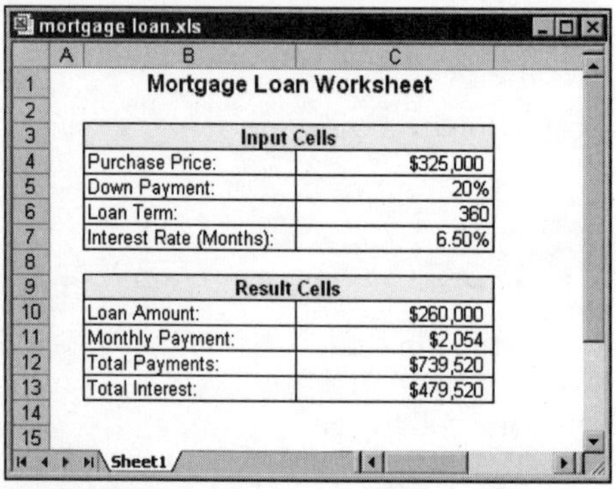
mortgage loan.xls

Mortgage Loan Worksheet

Input Cells	
Purchase Price:	$325,000
Down Payment:	20%
Loan Term:	360
Interest Rate (Months):	6.50%

Result Cells	
Loan Amount:	$260,000
Monthly Payment:	$2,054
Total Payments:	$739,520
Total Interest:	$479,520

Sheet1

Figure 23-1: This worksheet is a good demonstration of goal seeking.

Assume that you're in the market for a new home and you know that you can afford $1,800 per month in mortgage payments. You also know that a lender can issue a fixed-rate mortgage loan for 6.50 percent, based on an 80 percent *loan-to-value* (that is, a 20 percent *down payment*). The question is "What is the maximum purchase price I can handle?" In other words, what value in cell C4 causes the formula in cell C11 to result in $1,800? You could plug values into cell C4 until C11 displays $1,800; however, Excel can determine the answer much more efficiently.

To answer the question posed in the preceding paragraph, select Tools ⇨ Goal Seek. Excel displays the Goal Seek dialog box, shown in Figure 23-2. Completing this dialog box is similar to forming a sentence. You want to set cell C11 to 1800 by changing cell C4. Enter this information in the dialog box either by typing the cell references or by pointing with the mouse. Click OK to begin the goal-seeking process.

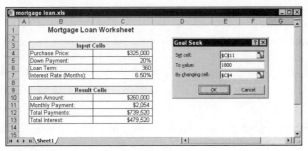

Figure 23-2: The Goal Seek dialog box.

In less than a second, Excel displays the Goal Seek Status box, which shows the target value and the value that Excel calculated. In this case, Excel found an exact value. The worksheet now displays the found value in cell C4 ($284,779). As a result of this value, the monthly payment amount is $1,800. At this point, you have two options:

✦ Click OK to replace the original value with the found value.

✦ Click Cancel to restore your worksheet to the form that it had before you chose Tools ➪ Goal Seek.

More about goal seeking

Excel can't always find a value that produces the result for which you're looking. Sometimes, a solution simply doesn't exist. In such a case, the Goal Seek Status box informs you of that fact (see Figure 23-3).

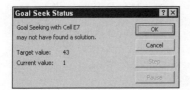

Figure 23-3: When Excel can't find a solution to your goal-seeking problem, it tells you so.

Other times, however, Excel may report that it can't find a solution, but you're pretty sure that one exists. If that's the case, you can try the following options:

✦ Change the current value of the By Changing Cell box in the Goal Seek dialog box to a value that is closer to the solution and then reissue the command.

✦ Adjust the Maximum iterations setting in the Options dialog box (select Tools ➪ Options, and choose the Calculation tab). Increasing the number of iterations (or calculations) makes Excel try more possible solutions.

✦ Double-check your logic and make sure that the formula cell does, indeed, depend on the specified changing cell.

Note   Like all computer programs, Excel has limited precision. To demonstrate this limitation, enter **=A1^2** into cell A2. Then, select Tools ➪ Goal Seek to find the value in cell A1 (which is empty) that makes the formula return 16. Excel comes up with a value of 4.0000915 (you may need to widen the column to see the complete value), which is close to the square root of 16, but certainly not exact. You can adjust the precision in the Calculation tab of the Options dialog box (make the Maximum change value smaller).

Note   In some cases, multiple values of the input cell produce the same desired result. For example, the formula =A1^2 returns 16 if cell A1 contains either –4 or +4. If you use goal seeking when multiple solutions are possible, Excel gives you the solution that is closest to the current value.

Introducing Solver

The Excel goal-seeking feature is a useful tool, but it clearly has limitations. It can solve for only one adjustable cell, and it returns only a single solution. Excel's powerful Solver tool extends this concept by enabling you to do the following:

✦ Specify multiple adjustable cells

✦ Specify constraints on the values that the adjustable cells can have

✦ Generate a solution that maximizes or minimizes a particular worksheet cell

✦ Generate multiple solutions to a problem

Although goal seeking is a relatively simple operation, using Solver can be much more complicated. In fact, Solver is probably one of the most difficult (and potentially frustrating) features in Excel. I'm the first to admit that Solver isn't for everyone. In fact, most Excel users have no use for this feature. However, many users find that having this much power is worth spending the extra time to learn about it.

Appropriate problems for Solver

Problems that are appropriate for Solver fall into a relatively narrow range. They typically involve situations that meet the following criteria:

✦ A target cell depends on other cells and formulas. Typically, you want to maximize or minimize this target cell or set it equal to some value.

✦ The target cell depends on a group of cells (called *changing cells*) that Solver can adjust to affect the target cell.

✦ The solution must adhere to certain limitations, or *constraints*.

No Tools ⇨ Solver Command?

Solver is an add-in, so it's available only when the add-in is installed. If the Tools menu doesn't show a Solver command, you need to install the add-in before you can use it.

Select Tools ⇨ Add-Ins. Excel displays its Add-Ins dialog box. Scroll down the list of add-ins and place a check mark next to the item named Solver Add-In. Click OK, and Excel installs the add-in and makes the Tools ⇨ Solver command available. If Solver isn't available on your computer, you'll be asked if you want to install it

After you set up your worksheet appropriately, you can use Solver to adjust the changing cells and produce the result that you want in your target cell—and simultaneously meet all the constraints that you have defined.

On the CD-ROM You can find all the Solver examples in this chapter on this book's CD-ROM.

A simple Solver example

I start with a simple example to introduce Solver and then present some increasingly complex examples to demonstrate what it can do.

Figure 23-4 shows a worksheet that is set up to calculate the profit for three products. Column B shows the number of units of each product, column C shows the profit per unit for each product, and column D contains formulas that calculate the profit for each product by multiplying the units by the profit per unit.

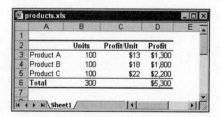

Figure 23-4: Use Solver to determine the number of units to maximize the total profit.

You don't need an MBA degree to realize that the greatest profit comes from Product C. Therefore, in order to maximize total profit, the logical solution is to produce only Product C. If things were really this simple, you wouldn't need tools such as Solver. As in most situations, this company has some constraints to which it must adhere:

✦ The combined production capacity is 300 total units per day.

✦ The company needs 50 units of Product A to fill an existing order.

✦ The company needs 40 units of Product B to fill an anticipated order.

✦ Because the market for Product C is relatively limited, the company doesn't want to produce more than 40 units of this product.

These four constraints make the problem more realistic and challenging. In fact, it's a perfect problem for Solver.

I go into more detail in a moment, but here is the basic procedure for using Solver:

1. Set up the worksheet with values and formulas. Make sure that you format cells logically; for example, if you cannot produce partial units of your products, format those cells to contain numbers with no decimal values.

2. Select Tools ⇨ Solver to bring up the Solver dialog box.

3. Specify the target cell.

4. Specify the changing cells.

5. Specify the constraints.

6. Change the Solver options, if necessary.

7. Let Solver solve the problem.

To start Solver, select Tools ⇨ Solver. Excel displays its Solver Parameters dialog box, shown in Figure 23-5.

Figure 23-5: The Solver Parameters dialog box.

In this example, the target cell is D6 — the cell that calculates the total profit for three products.

1. Enter (or point to) cell **D6** in the Set Target Cell field of the Solver Parameters dialog box.

2. Because the objective is to maximize this cell, click the Max option.

3. Next, specify the changing cells (which are in the range B3:B5) in the By Changing Cells box.

   The next step is to specify the constraints on the problem. The constraints are added one at a time and appear in the box labeled Subject to the Constraints.

4. To add a constraint, click the Add button. Excel displays the Add Constraint dialog box, shown in Figure 23-6. This dialog box has three parts: a Cell Reference, an operator, and a Constraint value.

5. To set the first constraint — that the total production capacity is 300 units — enter **B6** as the Cell Reference, choose equal (=) from the drop-down list of operators, and enter 300 as the Constraint value.

6. Click Add to add the remaining constraints. Table 23-1 summarizes the constraints for this problem.

Figure 23-6: The Add Constraint dialog box.

Table 23-1 Constraints Summary	
Constraint	**Expressed As**
Capacity is 300 units	B6=300
At least 50 units of Product A	B3>=50
At least 40 units of Product B	B4>=40
No more than 40 units of Product C	B5<=40

7. After you enter the last constraint, click OK to return to the Solver Parameters dialog box, which now lists the four constraints. At this point, Solver knows everything about the problem.

8. Click the Solve button to start the solution process. You can watch the progress onscreen, and Excel soon announces that it has found a solution. The Solver Results dialog box is shown in Figure 23-7.

Figure 23-7: Solver displays this dialog box when it finds a solution to the problem.

At this point, you have the following options:

✦ Replace the original changing cell values with the values that Solver found.

✦ Restore the original changing cell values.

✦ Create any or all three reports that describe what Solver did (press Shift to select multiple reports from this list).

✦ Click the Save Scenario button to save the solution as a scenario, so that the Scenario Manager can use it (see Chapter 22).

If you specify any report options, Excel creates each report on a new worksheet, with an appropriate name. Figure 23-8 shows an Answer Report. In the Constraints section of the report, two of the constraints are *binding,* which means that these constraints were satisfied at their limit with no more room to change.

This simple example illustrates how Solver works. The fact is, you could probably solve this particular problem manually just as quickly. That, of course, isn't always the case.

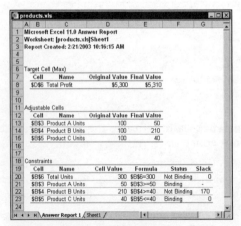

Figure 23-8: One of three reports that Solver can produce.

More about Solver

Before presenting complex examples, this section discusses the Solver Options dialog box—one of the more feature-packed dialog boxes in Excel. From this dialog box, you control many aspects of the solution process as well as load and save model specifications in a worksheet range.

Having Solver report to you that it can't find a solution isn't unusual, even when you know that one should exist. Often, you can change one or more of the Solver options and try again. When you choose the Options button in the Solver Parameters dialog box, Excel displays the Solver Options dialog box shown in Figure 23-9.

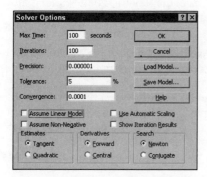

Figure 23-9: You can control many aspects of how Solver solves a problem.

This list describes Solver's options:

✦ **Max Time:** Specify the maximum amount of time (in seconds) that you want Solver to spend on a problem. If Solver reports that it exceeded the time limit, you can increase the amount of time that it spends searching for a solution.

✦ **Iterations:** Enter the maximum number of trial solutions that you want Solver to perform.

✦ **Precision:** Specify how close the Cell Reference and Constraint formulas must be to satisfy a constraint. Excel may solve the problem more quickly if you specify less precision.

✦ **Tolerance:** Designate the maximum percentage of error allowed for integer solutions (relevant only if an integer constraint is used).

✦ **Convergence:** Enter a value between 0 and 1 that specifies the amount of change to allow before Solver stops. This setting is relevant only for non-linear problems.

✦ **Assume Linear Model:** Choose this option to speed the solution process, but you can use it only if all the relationships in the model are linear. You can't use this option if the adjustable cells are multiplied or divided, or if the problem uses exponents.

✦ **Assume Non-Negative:** If checked, Solver assumes a lower limit of 0 for all adjustable cells that don't have a specified lower-limit constraint

✦ **Use Automatic Scaling:** Use when the problem involves large differences in magnitude — when you attempt to maximize a percentage, for example, by varying cells that are very large.

✦ **Show Iteration Results:** Instruct Solver to pause and display the results after each iteration by checking this box.

✦ **Estimates, Derivatives, and Search group boxes:** Use these options to control some technical aspects of the solution. In most cases, you don't need to change these settings.

✦ **Load Model:** Click this button to make Excel display the Load Model dialog box, in which you specify a range containing the set of Solver parameters that you want to load.

✦ **Save Model:** Click this button to make Excel display the Save Model dialog box, in which you specify a range where Excel should save the model parameters.

Usually, you want to save a model only when you're using more than one set of Solver parameters with your worksheet because Excel saves the first Solver model automatically with your worksheet (using hidden names). If you save additional models, Excel stores the information in the form of formulas that correspond to the specifications. (The last cell in the saved range is an array formula that holds the options settings.)

Solver Examples

The remainder of this chapter consists of examples of using Solver for various types of problems.

Minimizing shipping costs

This example involves finding alternative options for shipping materials, while keeping total shipping costs at a minimum (see Figure 23-10). A company has warehouses in Los Angeles, St. Louis, and Boston. Retail outlets throughout the United States place orders, which the company then ships from one of the warehouses. The company wants to meet the product needs of all six retail outlets from available inventory and keep total shipping charges as low as possible.

This workbook is rather complicated, so each part is explained individually:

✦ **Shipping Costs Table:** This table, at the top of the worksheet, contains per-unit shipping costs from each warehouse to each retail outlet. The cost to ship a unit from Los Angeles to Denver, for example, is $58.

✦ **Product needs of each retail store:** This information appears in C12:C17. For example, Denver needs 150 units, Houston needs 225, and so on. C18 holds the total needed.

✦ **Number to ship:** The range D12:F17 holds the adjustable cells that Solver varies. (They are all initialized with a value of 25 to give Solver a starting value.) Column G contains formulas that total the number of units the company needs to ship to each retail outlet.

✦ **Warehouse inventory:** Row 20 contains the amount of inventory at each warehouse, and row 21 contains formulas that subtract the amount shipped (row 18) from the inventory. For example, cell D21 contains the following formula: =D20–D18.

✦ **Calculated shipping costs:** Row 24 contains formulas that calculate the shipping costs. Cell D24 contains the following formula, which is copied to the two cells to the right of Cell D24:

```
=SUMPRODUCT(D3:D8,D12:D17)
```

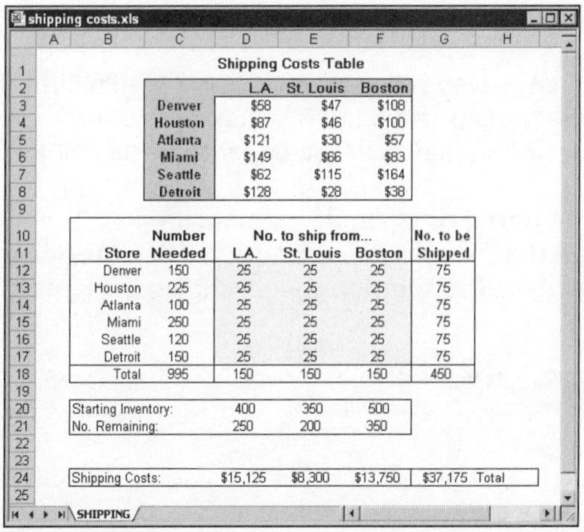

Figure 23-10: This worksheet determines the least expensive way to ship products from warehouses to retail outlets.

This formula calculates the total shipping cost from each warehouse. Cell G24 is the bottom line, the total shipping costs for all orders.

Solver fills in values in the range D12:F17 in a way that minimizes shipping costs while still supplying each retail outlet with the desired number of units. In other words, the solution minimizes the value in cell C24 by adjusting the cells in D12:F17, subject to the following constraints:

✦ The number of units needed by each retail outlet must equal the number shipped. (In other words, all the orders are filled.) These constraints are represented by the following specifications:

```
C12=G12    C14=G14    C16=G16
C13=G13    C15=G15    C17=G17
```

✦ The adjustable cells can't be negative because shipping a negative number of units makes no sense. These constraints are represented by the following specifications:

```
D12>=0    E12>=0    F12>=0
D13>=0    E13>=0    F13>=0
D14>=0    E14>=0    F14>=0
D15>=0    E15>=0    F15>=0
D16>=0    E16>=0    F16>=0
D17>=0    E17>=0    F17>=0
```

✦ The number of units remaining in each warehouse's inventory must not be negative (that is, they can't ship more than what is available). This is represented by the following constraint specifications:

```
D21>=0    E21>=0    F21>=0
```

Note   Before you solve this problem with Solver, you may want to try to minimize the shipping cost manually by entering values in D12:F17. Don't forget to make sure that all the constraints are met. Doing so may help you better appreciate Solver.

Setting up the problem is the difficult part. For example, you must enter 27 constraints. When you have specified all the necessary information, click the Solve button to put Solver to work. Solver displays the solution that is shown in Figure 23-11.

Figure 23-11: The solution that was created by Solver.

Learning More about Solver

Solver is a complex tool, and this chapter barely scratches the surface. If you'd like to learn more about Solver, I highly recommend the Web site for Frontline Systems:

```
www.solver.com
```

Frontline Systems is the company that developed Solver for Excel. Their Web site has several tutorials and lots of helpful information. They also sell additional Solver products for Excel that can handle much more complex problems.

The total shipping cost is $55,515, and all the constraints are met. Notice that shipments to Miami come from both St. Louis and Boston.

Allocating resources

The example in this section is a common type of problem that's ideal for Solver. Essentially, problems of this sort involve optimizing the volumes of individual production units that use varying amounts of fixed resources. Figure 23-12 shows an example for a toy company.

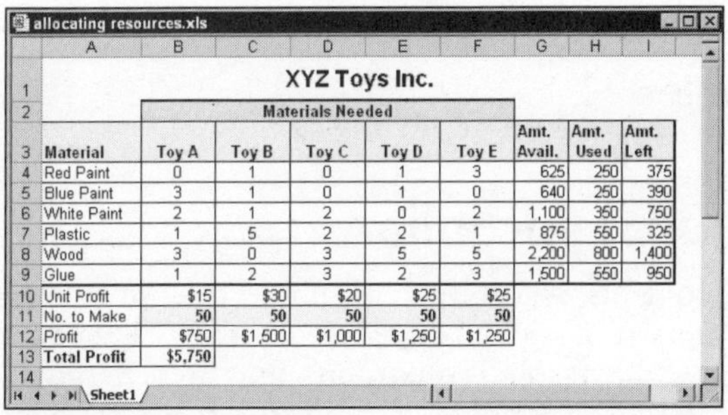
allocating resources.xls

XYZ Toys Inc.

Material	Toy A	Toy B	Toy C	Toy D	Toy E	Amt. Avail.	Amt. Used	Amt. Left
	Materials Needed							
Red Paint	0	1	0	1	3	625	250	375
Blue Paint	3	1	0	1	0	640	250	390
White Paint	2	1	2	0	2	1,100	350	750
Plastic	1	5	2	2	1	875	550	325
Wood	3	0	3	5	5	2,200	800	1,400
Glue	1	2	3	2	3	1,500	550	950
Unit Profit	$15	$30	$20	$25	$25			
No. to Make	50	50	50	50	50			
Profit	$750	$1,500	$1,000	$1,250	$1,250			
Total Profit	$5,750							

Figure 23-12: Using Solver to maximize profit when resources are limited.

This company makes five different toys, which use six different materials in varying amounts. For example, Toy A requires 3 units of blue paint, 2 units of white paint, 1 unit of plastic, 3 units of wood, and 1 unit of glue. Column G shows the current inventory of each type of material. Row 10 shows the unit profit for each toy. The number of toys to make is shown in the range B11:F11. These are the values that Solver determines. The goal of this example is to determine how to allocate the resources to maximize the total profit (B13). In other words, Solver determines how many units of each toy to make. The constraints in this example are relatively simple:

✦ Ensure that production doesn't use more resources than are available. This can be accomplished by specifying that each cell in column F is greater than or equal to zero.

✦ Ensure that the quantities produced aren't negative. This can be accomplished by specifying that each cell in row 11 be greater than or equal to zero.

Figure 23-13 shows the results that are produced by Solver. It shows the product mix that generates $12,365 in profit and uses all resources in their entirety, except for glue.

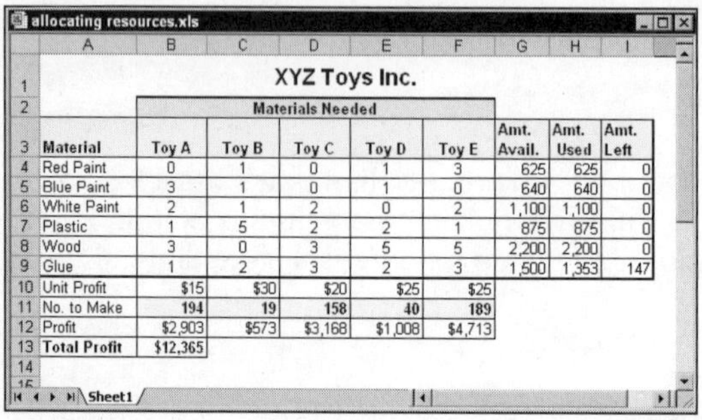

Material	Toy A	Toy B	Toy C	Toy D	Toy E	Amt. Avail.	Amt. Used	Amt. Left
Red Paint	0	1	0	1	3	625	625	0
Blue Paint	3	1	0	1	0	640	640	0
White Paint	2	1	2	0	2	1,100	1,100	0
Plastic	1	5	2	2	1	875	875	0
Wood	3	0	3	5	5	2,200	2,200	0
Glue	1	2	3	2	3	1,500	1,353	147
Unit Profit	$15	$30	$20	$25	$25			
No. to Make	194	19	158	40	189			
Profit	$2,903	$573	$3,168	$1,008	$4,713			
Total Profit	$12,365							

Figure 23-13: Solver determined how to use the resources to maximize the total profit.

Optimizing an investment portfolio

This example demonstrates how to use Solver to help maximize the return on an investment portfolio. Portfolios consist of several investments, each of which has different yields. In addition, you may have some constraints that involve reducing risk and diversification goals. Without such constraints, a portfolio problem becomes a no-brainer: Put all of your money in the investment with the highest yield.

This example involves a credit union, a financial institution that takes members' deposits and invests them in loans to other members, bank CDs, and other types of investments. The credit union distributes part of the return on these investments to the members in the form of *dividends,* or interest on their deposits. This hypothetical credit union must adhere to some regulations regarding its investments, and the board of directors has imposed some other restrictions. These regulations and restrictions comprise the problem's constraints. Figure 23-14 shows a workbook set up for this problem.

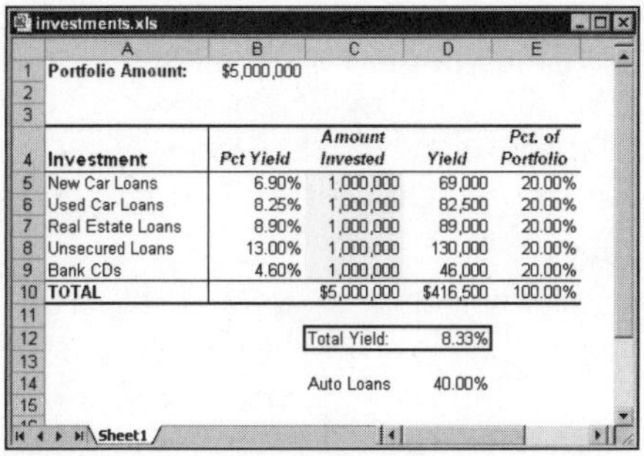

	A	B	C	D	E
1	Portfolio Amount:	$5,000,000			
2					
3					
4	Investment	Pct Yield	Amount Invested	Yield	Pct. of Portfolio
5	New Car Loans	6.90%	1,000,000	69,000	20.00%
6	Used Car Loans	8.25%	1,000,000	82,500	20.00%
7	Real Estate Loans	8.90%	1,000,000	89,000	20.00%
8	Unsecured Loans	13.00%	1,000,000	130,000	20.00%
9	Bank CDs	4.60%	1,000,000	46,000	20.00%
10	TOTAL		$5,000,000	$416,500	100.00%
11					
12			Total Yield:	8.33%	
13					
14			Auto Loans	40.00%	
15					

Figure 23-14: This worksheet is set up to maximize a credit union's investments, given some constraints.

The following constraints are the ones to which you must adhere in allocating the $5 million portfolio:

✦ The amount that the credit union invests in new-car loans must be at least three times the amount that the credit union invests in used-car loans. (Used-car loans are riskier investments.) This constraint is represented as C5>=C6*3.

✦ Car loans should make up at least 15 percent of the portfolio. This constraint is represented as D14>=.15.

✦ Unsecured loans should make up no more than 25 percent of the portfolio. This constraint is represented as E8<=.25.

✦ At least 10 percent of the portfolio should be in bank CDs. This constraint is represented as E9>=.10.

✦ The total amount invested is $5,000,000.

✦ All investments should be positive or zero. In other words, the problem requires five additional constraints to ensure that none of the changing cells go below zero.

The changing cells are C5:C9, and the goal is to maximize the total yield in cell D12. Starting values of 1,000,000 have been entered in the changing cells. When you run Solver with these parameters, it produces the solution that is shown in Figure 23-15, which has a total yield of 8.59 percent.

However, a total yield of 8.59 percent is *not* the optimal solution. If you select the Use Automatic Scaling option (refer to Figure 23-9), Solver will arrive at a solution that has a total yield of 9.25 percent.

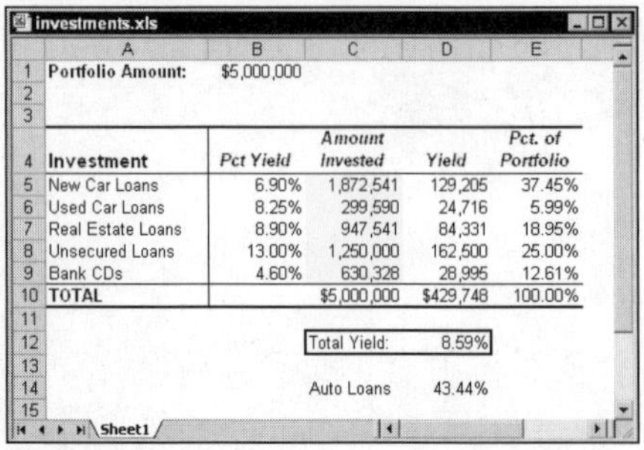

investments.xls

	A	B	C	D	E
1	Portfolio Amount:	$5,000,000			
2					
3					
4	Investment	Pct Yield	Amount Invested	Yield	Pct. of Portfolio
5	New Car Loans	6.90%	1,872,541	129,205	37.45%
6	Used Car Loans	8.25%	299,590	24,716	5.99%
7	Real Estate Loans	8.90%	947,541	84,331	18.95%
8	Unsecured Loans	13.00%	1,250,000	162,500	25.00%
9	Bank CDs	4.60%	630,328	28,995	12.61%
10	TOTAL		$5,000,000	$429,748	100.00%
11					
12			Total Yield:	8.59%	
13					
14			Auto Loans	43.44%	
15					

Sheet1

Figure 23-15: The results of the portfolio optimization.

This demonstrates that you can't always trust Solver to arrive at the optimal solution with one try, even when the Solver Results dialog box tells you that *All constraints and optimality conditions are satisfied.* The best advice? Make sure that you understand Solver well before you entrust it with helping you make major decisions. Try different starting values and adjust the options to see whether Solver can do better.

✦ ✦ ✦

Analyzing Data with the Analysis ToolPak

Although Excel was designed primarily for business users, it is often used in other disciplines, including education, research, statistics, and engineering. One way that Excel addresses these non-business users is with its Analysis ToolPak add-in. Many of the features and functions in the Analysis ToolPak are valuable for business applications as well.

The Analysis ToolPak: An Overview

The Analysis ToolPak is an add-in that provides analytical capability that normally is not available. The Analysis ToolPak consists of two parts:

✦ Analytical procedures

✦ Additional worksheet functions

These analysis tools offer many features that may be useful to those in the scientific, engineering, and educational communities — not to mention business users whose needs extend beyond the normal spreadsheet fare.

This section provides a quick overview of the types of analyses that you can perform with the Analysis ToolPak. Each of the following tools are discussed in detail in the course of this chapter:

✦ Analysis of variance (three types)

✦ Correlation

✦ Covariance

✦ Descriptive statistics

✦ Exponential smoothing

✦ F-test

✦ Fourier analysis

✦ Histogram

✦ Moving average

✦ Random number generation

✦ Rank and percentile

✦ Regression

✦ Sampling

✦ t-test (three types)

✦ z-test

As you can see, the Analysis ToolPak add-in brings a great deal of new functionality to Excel. These procedures have limitations, however, and in some cases, you may prefer to create your own formulas to do some calculations.

Besides the procedures just listed, the Analysis ToolPak provides many additional worksheet functions. These functions cover mathematics, engineering, unit conversions, financial analysis, and dates.

Using the Analysis ToolPak

This section discusses the two components of the Analysis ToolPak: its tools and its functions.

Installing the Analysis ToolPak add-in

The Analysis ToolPak is implemented as an add-in. Before you can use it, you need to make sure that the add-in is installed. Click the Tools menu. If you see a menu item labeled Data Analysis, the Analysis ToolPak is installed. If you don't see the Data Analysis menu item, install the add-in by following these steps:

1. Select Tools ➪ Add-Ins to display the Add-Ins dialog box.

2. Place a check mark next to Analysis ToolPak.

3. Click OK to close the Add-Ins dialog box.

Using the Analysis tools

The procedures in the Analysis ToolPak add-in are relatively straightforward. To use any of these tools, you select Tools ➪ Data Analysis, which displays the dialog box shown in Figure 24-1. Scroll through the list until you find the analysis tool that you want to use and then click OK. Excel displays a new dialog box that's specific to the procedure that you select.

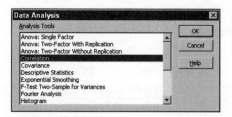

Figure 24-1: The Data Analysis dialog box enables you to select the tool in which you're interested.

Usually, you need to specify one or more input ranges, plus an output range (one cell is sufficient). Alternatively, you can choose to place the results on a new worksheet or in a new workbook. The procedures vary in the amount of additional information that is required. In many dialog boxes, you may be able to indicate whether your data range includes labels. If so, you can specify the entire range, including the labels, and indicate to Excel that the first column (or row) contains labels. Excel then uses these labels in the tables that it produces. Most tools also provide different output options that you can select, based on your needs.

Caution   The Analysis ToolPak is not consistent in how it generates its output. In some cases, the procedures use formulas, so you can change your data, and the results update automatically. In other procedures, Excel stores the results as values, so if you change your data, the results don't reflect your changes. Make sure that you understand what Excel is doing.

Using the Analysis ToolPak functions

After you install the Analysis ToolPak, you have access to all the additional functions (which are described fully in the online Help system). These functions appear in the Insert Function dialog box in the following categories:

✦ Date & Time

✦ Engineering (a new category that appears when you install the Analysis ToolPak)

✦ Financial

✦ Information

✦ Math & Trig

You access these functions just like any other functions, and they appear in the Function Wizard dialog box, intermixed with Excel's standard functions.

Note If you plan to share worksheets that use these functions, make sure that the other user has access to the add-in functions. If the other user doesn't install Analysis ToolPak add-in, formulas that use any of the Analysis ToolPak functions will return #VALUE.

The Analysis ToolPak Tools

This section describes each tool and provides an example. Space limitations prevent a discussion of every available option in these procedures. However, if you need to use some of these advanced analysis tools, you probably already know how to use most of the options not covered here.

On the CD-ROM The companion CD-ROM contains a workbook that shows output from all the tools discussed in this section.

The Analysis of Variance tool

Analysis of variance (sometimes abbreviated as Anova) is a statistical test that determines whether two or more samples were drawn from the same population. Using tools in the Analysis ToolPak, you can perform three types of analysis of variance:

✦ **Single-factor:** A one-way analysis of variance, with only one sample for each group of data.

✦ **Two-factor with replication:** A two-way analysis of variance, with multiple samples (or replications) for each group of data.

✦ **Two-factor without replication:** A two-way analysis of variance, with a single sample (or replication) for each group of data.

Figure 24-2 shows the dialog box for a single-factor analysis of variance. Alpha represents the statistical confidence level for the test.

The output for this test consists of the means and variances for each of the samples, the value of F, the critical value of F, and the significance of F (P-value).

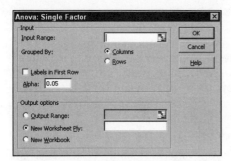

Figure 24-2: Specifying parameters for a single-factor analysis of variance.

The Correlation tool

Correlation is a widely used statistic that measures the degree to which two sets of data vary together. For example, if higher values in one data set are typically associated with higher values in the second data set, the two data sets have a positive correlation. The degree of correlation is expressed as a coefficient that ranges from –1.0 (a perfect negative correlation) to +1.0 (a perfect positive correlation). A correlation coefficient of 0 indicates that the two variables are not correlated.

Figure 24-3 shows the Correlation dialog box. Specify the input range, which can include any number of variables, arranged in rows or columns.

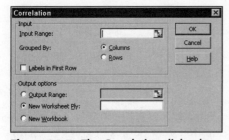

Figure 24-3: The Correlation dialog box.

The output consists of a correlation matrix that shows the correlation coefficient for each variable paired with every other variable.

Note   Notice that the resulting correlation matrix doesn't use formulas to calculate the results. Therefore, if any data changes, the correlation matrix isn't valid. You can use Excel's CORREL function to create a correlation matrix that changes automatically when you change data.

The Covariance tool

The Covariance tool produces a matrix that is similar to the one generated by the Correlation tool. *Covariance,* like correlation, measures the degree to which two variables vary together. Specifically, *covariance* is the average of the product of the deviations of each data point pair from their respective means.

The Descriptive Statistics tool

This tool produces a table that describes your data with some standard statistics. It uses the dialog box that is shown in Figure 24-4. The *K*th Largest option and *K*th Smallest option each displays the data value that corresponds to a rank that you specify. For example, if you check *K*th Largest and specify a value of 2, the output shows the second-largest value in the input range. (The standard output already includes the minimum and maximum values.)

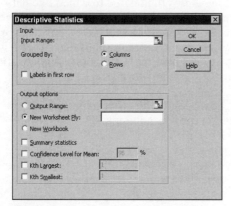

Figure 24-4: The Descriptive Statistics dialog box.

Because the output for this procedure consists of values (not formulas), you should use this procedure only when you're certain that your data isn't going to change; otherwise, you will need to re-execute the procedure. You can generate all of these statistics by using formulas.

The Exponential Smoothing tool

Exponential smoothing is a technique for predicting data that is based on the previous data point and the previously predicted data point. You can specify the *damping factor* (also known as a *smoothing constant*), which can range from 0 to 1. This determines the relative weighting of the previous data point and the previously predicted data point. You also can request standard errors and a chart.

The exponential smoothing procedure generates formulas that use the damping factor that you specify. Therefore, if the data changes, Excel updates the formulas.

The F-Test (Two-Sample Test for Variance) tool

The *F-Test* is a commonly used statistical test that enables you to compare two population variances. Figure 24-5 shows the dialog box for this tool.

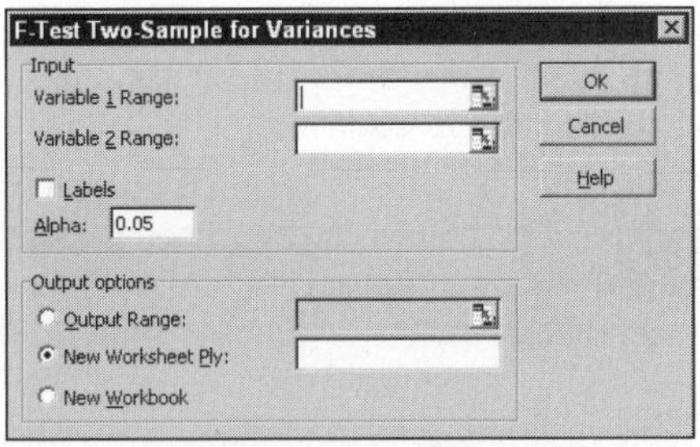

Figure 24-5: The F-Test dialog box.

The output for this test consists of the means and variances for each of the two samples, the value of F, the critical value of F, and the significance of F.

The Fourier Analysis tool

This tool performs a "fast Fourier" transformation of a range of data. Using the Fourier Analysis tool, you can transform a range limited to the following sizes: 1, 2, 4, 8, 16, 32, 64, 128, 256, 512, or 1,024 data points. This procedure accepts and generates complex numbers, which are represented as text string (not numerical values).

The Histogram tool

This procedure is useful for producing data distributions and histogram charts. It accepts an input range and a bin range. A *bin range* is a range of values that specifies the limits for each column of the histogram. If you omit the bin range, Excel creates 10 equal-interval bins for you. The size of each bin is determined by a formula of the following form:

```
=(MAX(input_range)-MIN(input_range))/10
```

The Histogram dialog box appears in Figure 24-6. As an option, you can specify that the resulting histogram be sorted by frequency of occurrence in each bin.

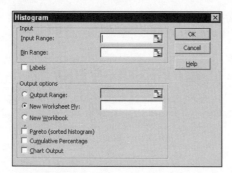

Figure 24-6: The Histogram tool enables you to generate distributions and graphical output.

If you specify the Pareto (Sorted Histogram) option, the bin range must contain values and can't contain formulas. If formulas appear in the bin range, Excel doesn't sort properly, and your worksheet displays error values. The Histogram tool doesn't use formulas, so if you change any of the input data, you need to repeat the histogram procedure to update the results.

Cross-Reference For other ways of generating frequency distributions, refer to "Creating a Frequency Distribution" in Chapter 11.

The Moving Average tool

The Moving Average tool helps you to smooth out a data series that has a lot of variability. This is best done in conjunction with a chart. Excel does the smoothing by computing a moving average of a specified number of values. In many cases, a moving average enables you to spot trends that otherwise would be obscured by noise in the data.

Figure 24-7 shows the Moving Average dialog box. You can, of course, specify the number of values that you want Excel to use for each average. If you place a check in the Standard Errors check box, Excel calculates standard errors and places formulas for these calculations next to the moving average formulas. The standard error values indicate the degree of variability between the actual values and the calculated moving averages. When you close this dialog box, Excel creates formulas that reference the input range that you specify.

You'll notice that the first few cells in the output are #N/A because not enough data points exist to calculate the average for these initial values.

The Random Number Generation tool

Although Excel contains a built-in function to calculate random numbers, the Random Number Generation tool is much more flexible, because you can specify what type of distribution you want the random numbers to have. Figure 24-8 shows the Random Number Generation dialog box. The Parameters box varies, depending on the type of distribution that you select.

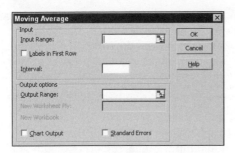

Figure 24-7: The Moving Average dialog box.

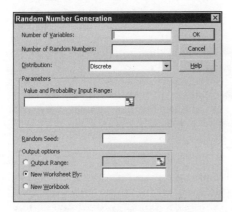

Figure 24-8: This dialog box enables you to generate a wide variety of random numbers.

The Number of Variables refers to the number of columns that you want, and the Number of Random Numbers refers to the number of rows that you want. For example, if you want 200 random numbers arranged in 10 columns of 20 rows, you specify 10 and 20, respectively, in these text boxes.

The Random Seed box enables you to specify a starting value that Excel uses in its random number-generating algorithm. Usually, you leave this blank. If you want to generate the same random number sequence, however, you can specify a seed between 1 and 32,767 (integer values only). You can create the following types of distributions by using the drop-down control in the Random Number Generation dialog box:

✦ **Uniform:** Every random number has an equal chance of being selected. You specify the upper and lower limits.

✦ **Normal:** The random numbers correspond to a normal distribution. You specify the mean and standard deviation of the distribution.

✦ **Bernoulli:** The random numbers are either 0 or 1, determined by the probability of success that you specify.

✦ **Binomial:** This returns random numbers based on a Bernoulli distribution over a specific number of trials, given a probability of success that you specify.

✦ **Poisson:** This option generates values in a Poisson distribution. This is characterized by discrete events that occur in an interval, where the probability of a single occurrence is proportional to the size of the interval. The lambda parameter is the expected number of occurrences in an interval. In a Poisson distribution, lambda is equal to the mean, which also is equal to the variance.

✦ **Patterned:** This option doesn't generate random numbers. Rather, it repeats a series of numbers in steps that you specify.

✦ **Discrete:** This option enables you to specify the probability that specific values are chosen. It requires a two-column input range; the first column holds the values, and the second column holds the probability of each value being chosen. The sum of the probabilities in the second column must equal 100 percent.

The Rank and Percentile tool

This tool creates a table that shows the ordinal and percentile ranking for each value in a range. You can also generate ranks and percentiles by using formulas.

The Regression tool

The Regression tool (see Figure 24-9) calculates a regression analysis from worksheet data. Use regression to analyze trends, forecast the future, build predictive models, and, often, to make sense out of a series of seemingly unrelated numbers.

Regression analysis enables you to determine the extent to which one range of data (the dependent variable) varies as a function of the values of one or more other ranges of data (the independent variables). This relationship is expressed mathematically, using values that Excel calculates. You can use these calculations to create a mathematical model of the data and predict the dependent variable by using different values of one or more independent variables. This tool can perform simple and multiple linear regressions and calculate and standardize residuals automatically.

As you can see, the Regression dialog box offers many options:

✦ **Input Y Range:** The range that contains the dependent variable.

✦ **Input X Range:** One or more ranges that contain independent variables.

✦ **Confidence Level:** The confidence level for the regression.

✦ **Constant Is Zero:** If checked, this forces the regression to have a constant of zero (which means that the regression line passes through the origin; when the X values are 0, the predicted Y value is 0).

✦ **Residuals:** These options specify whether to include residuals in the output. *Residuals* are the differences between observed and predicted values.

✦ **Normal Probability:** This generates a chart for normal probability plots.

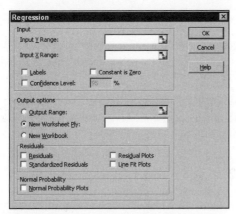

Figure 24-9: The Regression dialog box.

The Sampling tool

The Sampling tool generates a random sample from a range of input values. The Sampling tool can help you to work with a large database by creating a subset of it. The Sampling dialog box appears in Figure 24-10.

This procedure has two options: periodic and random. If you choose a periodic sample, Excel selects every *n*th value from the input range, where *n* equals the period that you specify. With a random sample, you simply specify the size of the sample you want Excel to select, and every value has an equal probability of being chosen.

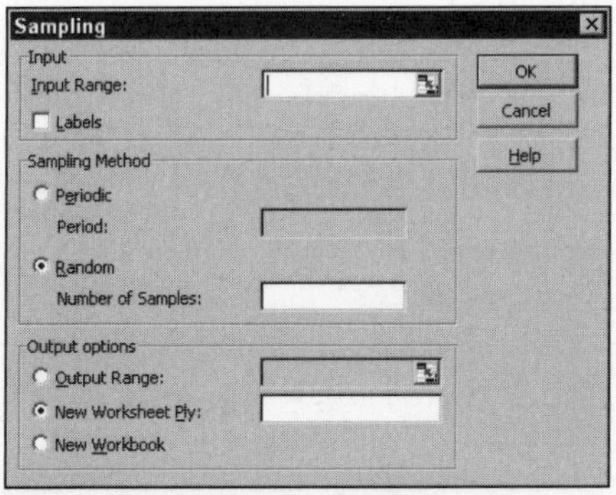

Figure 24-10: The Sampling dialog box is useful for selecting random samples.

The t-Test tool

Use the *t-test* to determine whether a statistically significant difference exists between two small samples. The Analysis ToolPak can perform three types of t-tests:

✦ **Paired two-sample for means:** For paired samples in which you have two observations on each subject (such as a pretest and a post-test). The samples must be the same size.

✦ **Two-sample assuming equal variances:** For independent, rather than paired, samples. Excel assumes equal variances for the two samples.

✦ **Two-sample assuming unequal variances:** For independent, rather than paired, samples. Excel assumes unequal variances for the two samples.

Figure 24-11 shows the dialog box for the Paired Two Sample for Means t-Test. You specify the significance level (alpha) and the hypothesized difference between the two means (that is, the *null hypothesis*).

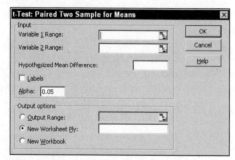

Figure 24-11: The paired t-Test dialog box.

The z-Test (Two-Sample Test for Means) tool

The t-test is used for small samples; the z-test is used for larger samples or populations. You must know the variances for both input ranges.

✦   ✦   ✦

Using Advanced Excel Features

A number of Excel's features can probably be fairly called advanced features if for no better reason than the ways in which they expand the definitions of what a spreadsheet program can do. The chapters in this part cover some useful features that you may not have used in the past but may find very useful.

Using Custom Number Formats

T he ability to create custom number formats is one of Excel's most powerful features. Although Excel provides a good variety of built-in number formats, you may find that none of these suit your needs. This chapter describes how to create custom number formats and provides many examples.

About Number Formatting

By default, all cells use the General number format. This is basically a "what you type is what you get" format. But if the cell is not wide enough to show the entire number, the General format rounds numbers with decimals and uses scientific notation for large numbers. In many cases, you may want to format a cell using something other than the General number format.

The key thing to remember about number formatting is that it affects only how a value is *displayed.* The actual number remains intact, and any formulas that use a formatted number use the actual number.

Note An exception to this rule occurs if you specify the Precision as Displayed option in the Calculation tab of the Options dialog box. If that option is in effect, formulas will use the values that are actually displayed in the cells.

Automatic number formatting

Excel is smart enough to perform some formatting for you automatically. For example, if you enter **12.3%** into a cell, Excel knows that you want to use a percentage format and applies it for you automatically. If you use commas to separate thousands (such as 123,456), Excel applies comma formatting for you. And if you precede your value with a currency symbol, Excel formats the cell for currency.

Note You have an option when it comes to entering values into cells formatted as a percentage. Select Tools ➪ Options and click the Edit tab in the Options dialog box. If the check box labeled Enable Automatic Percent Entry is checked, you can simply enter a normal value into a cell formatted to display as a percent (for example, enter **12.5** for 12.5%). If this check box is not checked, you must enter the value as a decimal (for example, **.125** for 12.5%).

Excel automatically applies a built-in number format to a cell based on the following criteria:

✦ If a number contains a slash (/), it may be converted to a date format or a fraction format.

✦ If a number contains a hyphen (-), it may be converted to a date format.

✦ If a number contains a colon (:) or is followed by a space and the letter *A* or *P*, it may be converted to a time format.

✦ If a number contains the letter *E* (in either uppercase or lowercase), it may be converted to scientific notation or exponential format.

Tip To avoid automatic number formatting when you enter a value, preformat the cell with the desired number format or precede your entry with an apostrophe. (The apostrophe makes the entry text.)

Formatting numbers by using toolbar buttons

The Formatting toolbar contains several buttons that enable you to apply common number formats quickly. When you click one of these buttons, the selected cells take on the specified number format. Table 25-1 summarizes the formats that these Formatting toolbar buttons perform in the U.S. English version of Excel.

Note These five toolbar buttons actually apply predefined styles to the selected cells. Access Excel's styles by using the Format ➪ Style command.

Table 25-1
Number-Formatting Buttons on the Formatting Toolbar

Button Name	Formatting Applied
Currency Style	Adds a dollar sign to the left, separates thousands with a comma, and displays the value with two digits to the right of the decimal point
Percent Style	Displays the value as a percentage, with no decimal places
Comma Style	Separates thousands with a comma and displays the value with two digits to the right of the decimal place
Increase Decimal	Increases the number of digits to the right of the decimal point by one
Decrease Decimal	Decreases the number of digits to the right of the decimal point by one

Using shortcut keys to format numbers

Another way to apply number formatting is to use shortcut keys. Table 25-2 summarizes the shortcut key combinations that you can use to apply common number formatting to the selected cells or range.

	Table 25-2
	Number-Formatting Keyboard Shortcuts
Key Combination	**Formatting Applied**
Ctrl+Shift+~	General number format (that is, unformatted values).
Ctrl+Shift+$	Currency format with two decimal places. (Negative numbers appear in parentheses.)
Ctrl+Shift+%	Percentage format with no decimal places.
Ctrl+Shift+^	Scientific notation number format with two decimal places.
Ctrl+Shift+#	Date format with the day, month, and year.
Ctrl+Shift+@	Time format with the hour, minute, and AM or PM.
Ctrl+Shift+!	Two decimal places, thousands separator, and a hyphen for negative values.

Using the format cells dialog box to format numbers

For maximum control of number formatting, use the Number tab of the Format Cells dialog box. Select the cells to format and then choose Format ➪ Cells. Select the Number tab of the Format Cells dialog box, and you'll see 12 categories of number formats from which to choose. When you select a category from the list box, the right side of the dialog box changes to display appropriate options.

Following is a list of the number-format categories along with some general comments:

- ✦ **General:** The default format; it displays numbers as integers, decimals, or in scientific notation if the value is too wide to fit into the cell.

- ✦ **Number:** Enables you to specify the number of decimal places, whether to use your system thousands separator (for example, a comma) to separate thousands, and how to display negative numbers.

- ✦ **Currency:** Enables you to specify the number of decimal places, to choose a currency symbol, and to display negative numbers. This format always uses the system thousands separator symbol (for example, a comma) to separate thousands.

✦ **Accounting:** Differs from the Currency format in that the currency symbols always line up vertically, regardless of the number of digits displayed in the value.

✦ **Date:** Enables you to choose from a variety of date formats and select the locale for your date formats.

✦ **Time:** Enables you to choose from a number of time formats and select the locale for your time formats.

✦ **Percentage:** Enables you to choose the number of decimal places; always displays a percent sign.

✦ **Fraction:** Enables you to choose from among nine fraction formats.

✦ **Scientific:** Displays numbers in exponential notation (with an E): 2.00E+05 = 200,000. 2.05E+05 = 205,000. You can choose the number of decimal places to display to the left of E.

✦ **Text:** When applied to a value, causes Excel to treat the value as text (even if it looks like a value). This feature is useful for such items as numerical part numbers and credit card numbers.

✦ **Special:** Contains additional number formats. The list varies, depending on the Locale you choose. For the English (United States) locale, the formatting options are Zip Code, Zip Code +4, Phone Number, and Social Security Number.

✦ **Custom:** Enables you to define custom number formats not included in any of the other categories.

Note If the cell displays a series of hash marks (such as ##########), it usually means that the column is not wide enough to display the value by using the number format that you selected. Either make the column wider (by dragging the right border of the column header) or change the number format. A series of hash marks also can mean that the cell contains an invalid date or time.

Creating a Custom Number Format

The Custom category on the Number tab of the Format Cells dialog box (see Figure 25-1) enables you to create number formats not included in any of the other categories. Excel gives you a great deal of flexibility in creating custom number formats.

Tip Custom number formats are stored with the worksheet. To make the custom format available in a different workbook, you can just copy a cell that uses the custom format to the other workbook.

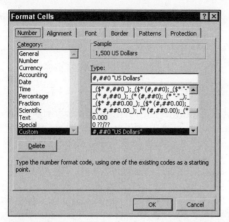

Figure 25-1: The Number tab of the Format
Cells dialog box.

About custom number formats

You construct a number format by specifying a series of codes as a *number format
string*. You enter this code sequence in the Type field after you select the Custom
category on the Number tab of the Format Cells dialog box. Here's an example of a
simple number format code:

```
0.000
```

This code consists of placeholders and a decimal point; it tells Excel to display the
value with three digits to the right of the decimal place. Here's another example:

```
00000
```

This custom number format has five placeholders and displays the value with five
digits (no decimal point). This is a good format to use when the cell holds a zip code.
(In fact, this is the code actually used by the Zip Code format in the Special category.)
When you format the cell with this number format and then enter a zip code, such
as 06604 (Bridgeport, CT), the value is displayed with the leading zero. If you enter
this number into a cell with the General number format, it displays 6604 (no leading
zero).

Scroll through the list of number formats in the Custom category in the Format
Cells dialog box to see many more examples. In many cases, you can use one of
these codes as a starting point, and you'll only need to customize it slightly.

On the CD-ROM   The companion CD-ROM contains a workbook with many custom number format examples.

Parts of a number format string

A custom format string enables you to specify different format codes for positive numbers, negative numbers, zero values, and text. You do so by separating the codes with a semicolon. The codes are arranged in the following structure:

```
Positive format; Negative format; Zero format; Text format
```

If you use only one section, the format string applies to all values. If you use two sections, the first section applies to positive values and zeros, and the second section applies to negative values. If you use three sections, the first section applies to positive values, the second section applies to negative values, and the third section applies to zeros. If you use all four sections, the last section applies to text stored in the cell.

The following is an example of a custom number format that specifies a different format for each of these types:

```
[Green]General;[Red]General;[Black]General;[Blue]General
```

This example takes advantage of the fact that colors have special codes. A cell formatted with this custom number format displays its contents in a different color, depending on the value. When a cell is formatted with this custom number format, a positive number is green, a negative number is red, a zero is black, and text is blue.

Cross-Reference   If you want to apply cell formatting automatically (such as text or background color) based on the cell's contents, a better solution is to use Excel's Conditional Formatting feature. Conditional formatting is discussed in Chapter 27.

Preformatting Cells

Usually, you'll apply number formats to cells that already contain values. You also can format cells with a specific number format *before* you make an entry. Then, when you enter information, it takes on the format that you specified. You can preformat specific cells, entire rows or columns, or even the entire worksheet.

Rather than preformat an entire worksheet, however, you can change the number format for the Normal style, (Unless you specify otherwise, all cells use the Normal style.) Change the Normal style by selecting Format ➪ Style. In the Style dialog box, click the Modify button and then choose the new number format that you want to use for the Normal style.

Custom number format codes

Table 25-3 lists the formatting codes available for custom formats, along with brief descriptions. I use most of these codes in examples later in this appendix.

Table 25-3
Codes Used to Create Custom Number Formats

Code	Comments
General	Displays the number in General format.
#	Digit placeholder. Displays only significant digits, and does not display insignificant zeros.
0 (zero)	Digit placeholder. Displays insignificant zeros if a number has fewer digits than there are zeros in the format.
?	Digit placeholder. Adds spaces for insignificant zeros on either side of the decimal point so that decimal points align when formatted with a fixed-width font. You can also use ? for fractions that have varying numbers of digits.
.	Decimal point.
%	Percentage.
,	Thousands separator.
E- E+ e- e+	Scientific notation.
$ - + / ( ) : space	Displays this character.
\	Displays the next character in the format.
*	Repeats the next character, to fill the column width.
_ (underscore)	Leaves a space equal to the width of the next character.
"text"	Displays the text inside the double quotation marks.
@	Text placeholder.
[color]	Displays the characters in the color specified. Can be any of the following text strings (not case sensitive): Black, Blue, Cyan, Green, Magenta, Red, White, or Yellow.
[Color n]	Displays the corresponding color in the color palette, where n is a number from 0 to 56.
[condition value]	Enables you to set your own criterion for each section of a number format.

Where Did Those Number Formats Come From?

Excel may create custom number formats without you realizing it. When you use the Increase Decimal or Decrease Decimal button on the Formatting toolbar, new number formats are created that appear on the Number tab of the Format Cells dialog box. (To access this dialog box, choose Format ➪ Cells.) For example, if you click the Increase Decimal button five times, the following custom number formats are created:

```
0.0
0.000
0.0000
0.000000
```

A format string for two decimal places is not created because that format string is built-in.

Table 25-4 lists the codes used to create custom formats for dates and times.

Table 25-4
Codes Used in Creating Custom Formats for Dates and Times

Code	Comments
m	Displays the month as a number without leading zeros (1–12).
mm	Displays the month as a number with leading zeros (01–12).
mmm	Displays the month as an abbreviation (Jan–Dec).
mmmm	Displays the month as a full name (January–December).
mmmmm	Displays the first letter of the month (J–D).
d	Displays the day as a number without leading zeros (1–31).
dd	Displays the day as a number with leading zeros (01–31).
ddd	Displays the day as an abbreviation (Sun–Sat).
dddd	Displays the day as a full name (Sunday–Saturday).
yy or yyyy	Displays the year as a two-digit number (00–99) or as a four-digit number (1900–9999).
h or hh	Displays the hour as a number without leading zeros (0–23) or as a number with leading zeros (00–23).
m or mm	Displays the minute as a number without leading zeros (0–59) or as a number with leading zeros (00–59).
s or ss	Displays the second as a number without leading zeros (0–59) or as a number with leading zeros (00–59).

Code	Comments
[]	Displays hours greater than 24 or minutes or seconds greater than 60.
AM/PM	Displays the hour using a 12-hour clock; if no AM/PM indicator is used, the hour uses a 24-hour clock.

Custom Number Format Examples

The remainder of this chapter consists of useful examples of custom number formats. You can use most of these format codes as-is. Others may require slight modification to meet your needs.

Scaling values

You can use a custom number format to scale a number. For example, if you work with very large numbers, you may want to display the numbers in thousands (that is, displaying 1,000,000 as 1,000). The actual number, of course, will be used in calculations that involve that cell. The formatting affects only how it is displayed.

Displaying values in thousands

The following format string displays values without the last three digits to the left of the decimal place and no decimal places. In other words, the value appears as if it's divided by 1,000 and rounded to no decimal places.

    #,###,

A variation of this format string follows. A value with this number format appears as if it's divided by 1,000 and rounded to two decimal places.

    #,###.00,

Table 25-5 shows examples of these number formats:

<table>
<tr><td colspan="3" align="center">Table 25-5
Examples of Displaying Values in Thousands</td></tr>
<tr><td>*Value*</td><td>*Number Format*</td><td>*Display*</td></tr>
<tr><td>123456</td><td>#,###,</td><td>123</td></tr>
<tr><td>1234565</td><td>#,###,</td><td>1,235</td></tr>
<tr><td>−323434</td><td>#,###,</td><td>−323</td></tr>
</table>

Continued

	Table 25-5 *(continued)*	
Value	*Number Format*	*Display*
123123.123	#,###,	123
499	#,###,	(blank)
500	#,###,	1
123456	#,###.00,	123.46
1234565	#,###.00,	1,234.57
−323434	#,###.00,	−323.43
123123.123	#,###.00,	123.12
499	#,###.00,	.50
500	#,###.00,	.50

Displaying values in hundreds

The following format string displays values in hundreds, with two decimal places. A value with this number format appears as if it's divided by 100 and rounded to two decimal places.

```
0"."00
```

Table 25-6 shows examples of these number formats:

	Table 25-6	
	Examples of Displaying Values in Hundreds	
Value	*Number Format*	*Display*
546	0"."00	5.46
100	0"."00	1.00
9890	0"."00	98.90
500	0"."00	5.00
−500	0"."00	−5.00
0	0"."00	0.00

Displaying values in millions

The following format string displays values in millions with no decimal places. A value with this number appears as if it's divided by 1,000,000 and rounded to no decimal places.

```
#,###,,
```

A variation of this format string follows. A value with this number appears as if it's divided by 1,000,000 and rounded to two decimal places.

```
#,###.00,,
```

Another variation follows. This adds the letter *M* to the end of the value.

```
#,###,,M
```

The following format string is a bit more complex. It adds the letter *M* to the end of the value — and also displays negative values in parentheses as well as displaying zeros.

```
#,###.0,,"M"_);(#,###.0,,"M)";0.0"M"_)
```

Table 25-7 shows examples of these format strings.

Table 25-7
Examples of Displaying Values in Millions

Value	Number Format	Display
123456789	#,###,,	123
1.23457E+11	#,###,,	123,457
1000000	#,###,,	1
5000000	#,###,,	5
−5000000	#,###,,	−5
0	#,###,,	(blank)
123456789	#,###.00,,	123.46
1.23457E+11	#,###.00,,	123,457.00
1000000	#,###.00,,	1.00
5000000	#,###.00,,	5.00
−5000000	#,###.00,,	−5.00
0	#,###.00,,	.00
123456789	#,###,,"M"	123M
1.23457E+11	#,###,,"M"	123,457M
1000000	#,###,,"M"	1M

Continued

Table 25-7 *(continued)*

Value	Number Format	Display
5000000	#,###,,"M"	5M
−5000000	#,###,,"M"	−5M
0	#,###,,"M"	M
123456789	#,###.0,,"M"_);(#,###.0,,"M)";0.0"M"_)	123.5M
1.23457E+11	#,###.0,,"M"_);(#,###.0,,"M)";0.0"M"_)	123,456.8M
1000000	#,###.0,,"M"_);(#,###.0,,"M)"";0.0"M"_)	1.0M
5000000	#,###.0,,"M"_);(#,###.0,,"M)";0.0"M"_)	5.0M
−5000000	#,###.0,,"M"_);(#,###.0,,"M)";0.0"M"_)	(5.0M)
0	#,###.0,,"M"_);(#,###.0,,"M)";0.0"M"_)	0.0M

Adding zeros to a value

The following format string displays a value with three additional zeros and no deci-mal places. A value with this number format appears as if it's rounded to no deci-mal places and then multiplied by 1,000.

```
#",000"
```

Examples of this format string, plus a variation that adds six zeros, are shown in Table 25-8.

Table 25-8
Examples of Displaying a Value with Extra Zeros

Value	Number Format	Display
1	#",000"	1,000
1.5	#",000"	2,000
43	#",000"	43,000
−54	#",000"	−54,000
5.5	#",000"	6,000
0.5	#",000,000"	1,000,000
0	#",000,000"	,000,000
1	#",000,000"	1,000,000
1.5	#",000,000"	2,000,000

Value	Number Format	Display
43	#",000,000"	43,000,000
−54	#",000,000"	−54,000,000
5.5	#",000,000"	6,000,000
0.5	#",000,000"	1,000,000

Displaying leading zeros

To display leading zeros, create a custom number format that uses the 0 character. For example, if you want all numbers to display with 10 digits, use the number format string that follows. Values with fewer than 10 digits will display with leading zeros.

```
0000000000
```

You also can force all numbers to display with a fixed number of leading zeros. The format string that follows, for instance, appends three zeros to the beginning of each number:

```
"000"#
```

In the following example, the format string uses the repeat character code (an asterisk) to apply leading zero to fill the entire width of the cell:

```
*00
```

Displaying fractions

Excel supports quite a few built-in fraction number formats (select the Fraction category from the Number tab of the Format Cells dialog box). For example, to display the value .125 as a fraction with 8 as the denominator, select As Eighths (4/8) from the Type list (see Figure 25-2).

You can use a custom format string to create other fractional formats. For example, the following format string displays a value in 50ths:

```
# ??/50
```

The following format string displays a value in terms of fractional dollars. For example, the value 154.87 is displayed as *154 and 87/100 Dollars*.

```
0 "and "??/100 "Dollars"
```

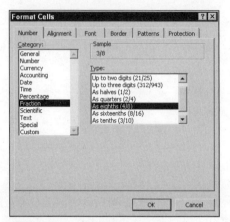

Figure 25-2: Selecting a number format
to display a value as a fraction.

The following example displays the value in sixteenths, with a quotation mark
appended to the right. This format string is useful when you deal with inches
(for example, 2/16").

```
# ??/16\"
```

Displaying a negative sign on the right

The following format string displays negative values with the negative sign to the
right of the number. Positive values have an additional space on the right, so both
positive and negative numbers align properly on the right.

```
0.00_-;0.00-
```

Testing Custom Number Formats

When you create a custom number format, don't overlook the Sample box in the Number
tab of the Format Cells dialog box. This box displays the value in the active cell using the format string in the Type box.

It's a good idea to test your custom number formats by using the following data: a positive
value, a negative value, a zero value, and text. Often, creating a custom number format
takes several attempts. Each time you edit a format string, it is added to the list. When you
finally get the correct format string, access the Format Cells dialog box one more time and
delete your previous attempts.

Formatting dates and times

When you enter a date into a cell, Excel formats the date using the system short date format. You can change this format by using the Windows Control Panel (Regional Settings).

Excel provides many useful built-in date and time formats. Table 25-9 shows some other date and time formats that you may find useful. The first column of the table shows the date/time serial number.

Table 25-9
Useful Built-In Date and Time Formats

Value	Number Format	Display
36676	mmmm d, yyyy (dddd)	May 30, 2000 (Tuesday)
36676	"It's" dddd!	It's Tuesday!
36676	dddd, mm/dd/yyyy	Tuesday, 05/30/2000
36676	"Month: "mmm	Month: May
36676	General (m/d/yyyy)	36676 (5/30/2000)
0.345	h "Hours"	8 Hours
0.345	h:mm o'clock	8:16 o'clock
0.345	h:mm a/p"m"	8:16 am
0.78	h:mm a/p".m."	6:43 p.m.

Cross-Reference See Chapter 10 for more information about Excel's date and time serial number system.

Displaying text with numbers

The ability to display text with a value is one of the most useful benefits of using a custom number format. To add text, just create the number format string as usual and put the text within quotation marks. The following number format string, for example, displays a value with the text *(US Dollars)* added to the end:

```
#,##0.00 "(US Dollars)"
```

Here's another example that displays text before the number:

```
"Average: "0.00
```

Formatting Numbers by Using the TEXT Function

Excel's TEXT function accepts a number format string as its second argument. For example, the following formula displays the contents of cell A1 using a custom number format that displays a fraction:

```
=TEXT(A1,"# ??/50")
```

Not all formatting codes function, however. For example, colors and repeating characters are ignored. The following formula does not display the contents of cell A1 in red:

```
=TEXT(A1,"[Red]General")
```

If you use the preceding number format, you'll find that the negative sign appears before the text for negative values. To display number signs properly, use this variation:

```
"Average: "0.00;"Average: "-0.00
```

The following format string displays a value with the words *Dollars and Cents*. For example, the number 123.45 displays as *123 Dollars and .45 Cents.*

```
0 "Dollars and" .00 "Cents"
```

Suppressing certain types of entries

You can use number formatting to hide certain types of entries. For example, the following format string displays text but not values:

```
;;
```

This format string displays values but not text or zeros:

```
0.0;-0.0;;
```

This format string displays everything except zeros:

```
0.0;-0.0;;@
```

You can use the following format string to completely hide the contents of a cell:

```
;;;
```

Note that when the cell is activated, however, the cell's contents are visible on the formula bar.

Caution   If the cell contains more than 1,024 characters, the ; ; ; format string does not hide the contents.

Filling a cell with a repeating character

The asterisk (*) symbol specifies a repeating character in a number format string. The repeating character completely fills the cell and adjusts if the column width changes. The following format string, for example, displays the contents of a cell padded on the right with dashes:

```
General*-;-General*-;General*-;General*-
```

Figure 25-3 shows several examples of number format strings that use an asterisk to repeat a character.

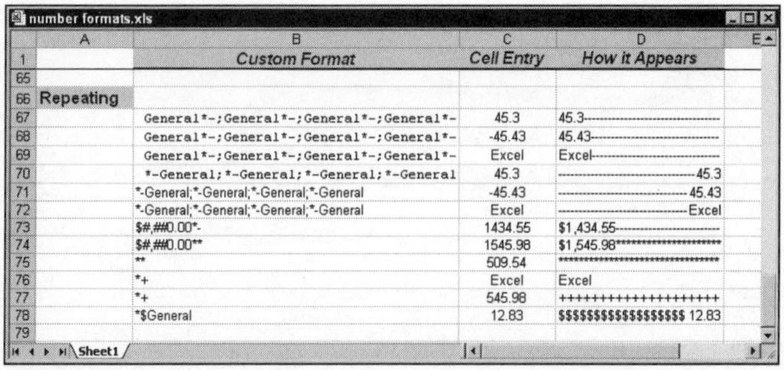

	A	B	C	D	E
		Custom Format	*Cell Entry*	*How it Appears*	
65					
66	**Repeating**				
67		General*-;General*-;General*-;General*-	45.3	45.3------------------------	
68		General*-;General*-;General*-;General*-	-45.43	45.43-----------------------	
69		General*-;General*-;General*-;General*-	Excel	Excel-----------------------	
70		*-General;*-General;*-General;*-General	45.3	-------------------------45.3	
71		*-General;*-General;*-General;*-General	-45.43	------------------------45.43	
72		*-General;*-General;*-General;*-General	Excel	------------------------Excel	
73		$#,##0.00*-	1434.55	$1,434.55-------------------	
74		$#,##0.00**	1545.98	$1,545.98*******************	
75		**	509.54	****************************	
76		*+	Excel	Excel	
77		*+	545.98	++++++++++++++++++++	
78		*$General	12.83	$$$$$$$$$$$$$$$$$$ 12.83	
79					

Figure 25-3: Examples of number formats that use a repeating character.

✦   ✦   ✦

Customizing Toolbars and Menus

You're probably familiar with many of Excel's built-in
toolbars, and you have most likely explored the menu
system. Excel lets you modify both toolbars and menus. This
chapter explains how to customize the built-in toolbars, create new toolbars, and change the menus that Excel displays.

Customizing Toolbars

All told, Excel comes with more than 100 built-in toolbars,
made up of the following:

- ♦ Two menu bars (one for worksheets and one for chart
  sheets).

- ♦ Traditional-style toolbars.

- ♦ Shortcut menus (the menus that appear when you right-
  click a selection).

Each toolbar consists of one or more "commands." A command
can take the form of an icon, text, or both. Some additional
commands don't appear on any of the prebuilt toolbars.

Note   There is virtually no distinction between a menu bar and a
toolbar. In fact, the menu bar that you see at the top of
Excel's window is actually a toolbar named Worksheet
Menu Bar. As with any toolbar, you can add new items to it
and even move it to a new location by dragging it (as
shown in Figure 26-1).

How Excel Keeps Track of Toolbars

When you start Excel, it displays the same toolbar configuration that was in effect the last time that you used it. Did you ever wonder how Excel keeps track of this information? When you exit Excel, it updates a file in your Windows folder. This file stores your custom toolbars, as well as information about which toolbars are visible and the on-screen location of each. The file is stored in your Windows directory and has an XLB extension (the actual filename will vary).

To restore the toolbars to their previous configuration, select File ⇨ Open to open this XLB file. This restores your toolbar configuration to the way that it was when you started Excel. You can also make a copy of the XLB file and give it a different name, which enables you to store multiple toolbar configurations that you can load at any time.

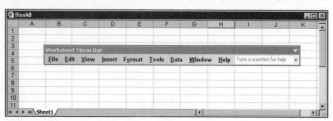

Figure 26-1: Excel's menu bar is actually a toolbar, and you can move it to any location that you want.

Types of customizations

The following list is a summary of the types of customizations that you can make when working with toolbars (which also include menu bars):

+ **Move toolbars:** Any toolbar can be moved to another location.

+ **Remove buttons from built-in toolbars:** You may want to do this to eliminate buttons that you never use.

+ **Add buttons to built-in toolbars:** You can add as many buttons as you want to any toolbar.

+ **Create new toolbars:** You can create as many new toolbars as you like, with as many buttons as you like.

+ **Change the functionality of a button:** You make such a change by attaching your own macro to a built-in toolbar button.

+ **Change the image that appears on any toolbar button:** A rudimentary but functional toolbar-button editor is included with Excel.

Shortcut menus

The casual user cannot modify Excel's shortcut menus (the menus that appear when you right-click an object). Doing so requires the use of VBA macros.

Moving Toolbars

A toolbar can be either floating or docked. A *docked* toolbar is fixed in place at the top, bottom, left, or right edge of Excel's workspace. *Floating* toolbars appear in an "always-on-top" window, and you can drag them wherever you like.

To move a toolbar, just click its border and drag it to its new position. If you drag it to one of the edges of Excel's window, it attaches itself to the edge and becomes docked. You can create several layers of docked toolbars. For example, the Standard and Formatting toolbars are (normally) both docked along the upper edge.

If a toolbar is floating, you can change its dimensions by dragging a border. For example, you can transform a horizontal toolbar to a vertical toolbar by dragging one of its corners.

Using the Customize Dialog Box

To make any changes to toolbars, you need to be in Customization mode. In Customization mode, the Customize dialog box is displayed, and you can manipulate the toolbars in a number of ways. To get into Customization mode, perform either of the following actions:

✦ Select View ➪ Toolbars ➪ Customize.

✦ Select Customize from the shortcut menu that appears when you right-click any toolbar.

Either of these methods displays the Customize dialog box that is shown in Figure 26-2. This dialog box lists all the available toolbars, including any custom toolbars that you have created.

The Customize dialog box has three tabs, each of which is described in the following sections.

The Toolbars tab

Figure 26-2 shows the Toolbars tab of the Customize dialog box. The following sections describe how to perform various procedures that involve toolbars.

Figure 26-2: The Customize dialog box.

Caution   Operations that you perform by using the Customize dialog box cannot be undone by clicking the Undo button. You can, however, go back and undo your changes manually.

Hiding or displaying a toolbar

The Toolbars tab displays every toolbar (built-in toolbars and custom toolbars). Add a check mark to display a toolbar; remove the check mark to hide it. The changes take effect immediately.

Tip   The names of some of the more popular toolbars are displayed in a list when you right-click a toolbar. To hide or display one of the toolbars in this list, just click its name to toggle the display. Not all toolbars are in this list, however, so you'll need to use the Toolbars tab of the Customize dialog box to access them all.

Creating a new toolbar

Click the New button and then enter a name in the New Toolbar dialog box. Excel creates and displays an empty toolbar. You can then add buttons to the new toolbar.

On the CD-ROM   The companion CD-ROM contains a workbook that has an attached custom toolbar that contains formatting tools. When you open the workbook, the toolbar is displayed. This custom toolbar contains a variety of formatting tools that you may find helpful.

Renaming a custom toolbar

Select a custom toolbar from the list on the Toolbars tab and click the Rename button. Enter a new name in the Rename Toolbar dialog box that appears. When you select a built-in toolbar, the Rename button is not available (you cannot rename a built-in toolbar).

Deleting a custom toolbar

Select a custom toolbar from the list in the Toolbars tab and click the Delete button. When you select a built-in toolbar, the Delete button is not available (you cannot delete a built-in toolbar).

Resetting a built-in toolbar

Select a built-in toolbar from the list and click the Reset button. The toolbar is restored to its default state. If you've added any custom tools to the toolbar, they are removed. If you've removed any of the default tools, they are restored.

The Reset button is not available when a custom toolbar is selected.

Be careful when resetting the menu bar. Many add-ins add one or more new menu items to Excel's menu bar. If you reset the menu bar, you may not be able to access the add-in. Usually, restarting Excel will solve this problem.

Attaching a toolbar to a workbook

If you create a custom toolbar that you want to share with someone else, you can "attach" it to a workbook. To attach a custom toolbar to a workbook, click the Attach button, which presents the Attach Toolbars dialog box. Select the toolbars that you want to attach to a workbook (as shown in Figure 26-3). You can attach any number of toolbars to a workbook.

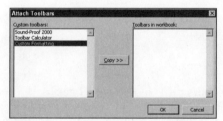

Figure 26-3: You can attach custom toolbars to a workbook in the Attach Toolbars menu.

A toolbar that's attached to a workbook appears automatically when the workbook is opened, unless the workspace already has a toolbar by the same name.

The toolbar that's stored in the workbook is an exact copy of the toolbar at the time that you attach it. If you modify the toolbar after attaching it, the changed version is not stored in the workbook automatically. You must manually remove the old toolbar and then add the edited toolbar.

The Commands tab

The Commands tab of the Customize dialog box contains a list of every tool that's available. Use this tab when you customize a toolbar. This feature is described later in the chapter (see "Adding or Removing Toolbar Buttons").

The Options tab

The Options tab of the Customize dialog box, shown in Figure 26-4, gives you several choices of ways to customize your menus, toolbars, icons, and the like. The following list explains these options.

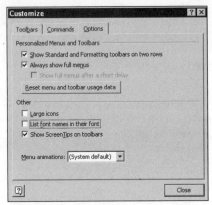

Figure 26-4: The Options tab of the Customize dialog box.

✦ **Show Standard and Formatting Toolbars on Two Rows:** If checked, the commonly used Standard and Formatting toolbars appear in two separate rows. Otherwise, these two toolbars appear next to each other. Depending on the screen resolution you use, displaying both toolbars in one row may cause some of the buttons to disappear.

✦ **Always Show Full Menus:** If checked, all menu items will be displayed when you click a menu. I can think of no reason to deselect this option.

✦ **Large Icons:** To change the size of the icons used in toolbars, select or deselect the Large Icons check box. This option only affects the images that are in buttons. Buttons that contain only text (such as buttons in a menu) don't change.

✦ **List Font Names in Their Font:** This feature displays the font names, using the actual font. The advantage is that you can preview the font before you select it. The disadvantage is that it's a bit slower.

Toolbar Autosensing

Normally, Excel displays a particular toolbar automatically when you change contexts; this is called *autosensing*. For example, when you activate a chart, the Chart toolbar appears. When you activate a sheet that contains a pivot table, the PivotTable toolbar appears.

You can easily defeat autosensing by hiding the toolbar. After you do so, Excel no longer displays that toolbar when you switch to its former context. You can restore this automatic behavior, however, by displaying the appropriate toolbar when you're in the appropriate context. Thereafter, Excel reverts to its normal automatic toolbar display when you switch to that context.

✦ **Show ScreenTips on Toolbars:** ScreenTips are the pop-up messages that display the button names when you pause the mouse pointer over a button. If you find the ScreenTips distracting, remove the check mark from the Show ScreenTips on Toolbars check box. The status bar still displays a description of the button when you move the mouse pointer over it.

✦ **Menu Animations:** When you select a menu, Excel animates the display of the menu as it is dropping down. You can select the type of animation that you want.

Adding or Removing Toolbar Buttons

As noted earlier in this chapter, you can put Excel into Customization mode by displaying the Customize dialog box. When Excel is in Customization mode, you have access to all the commands and options in the Customize dialog box. In addition, you can perform the following actions:

✦ Reposition a button on a toolbar.

✦ Move a button to a different toolbar.

✦ Copy a button from one toolbar to another.

✦ Add new buttons to a toolbar by using the Commands tab of the Customize dialog box.

Tip

Excel provides a simpler way to add or remove buttons from a toolbar. Just click the arrow at the right end of the toolbar and select Add or Remove Buttons. You'll see a list of all the buttons appropriate for the toolbar.

Buttons displayed with a check mark are visible in the toolbar; those without a check mark are not visible in the toolbar. Simply add or remove the check marks according to your preferences. For additional types of customization (for example, removing custom buttons), you need to use the Customize dialog box.

Moving and copying buttons

When the Customize dialog box is displayed, you can copy and move buttons freely among any visible toolbars. To move a button, drag it to its new location. (The new location can be within the current toolbar or on a different toolbar.)

To copy a button, press Ctrl while you drag the button to another toolbar. You can also copy a toolbar button within the same toolbar, but no reason exists to have multiple copies of a button on the same toolbar.

Inserting a new button

To add a new button to a toolbar, you use the Commands tab of the Customize dialog box (see Figure 26-5).

Figure 26-5: The Commands tab contains a list of every available button.

The buttons are arranged in 16 categories. When you select a category, the buttons in that category appear to the right in the Commands list box.

To add a button to a toolbar, locate it in the Commands tab and then click and drag it to the toolbar.

Other Toolbar Button Operations

When Excel is in Customization mode (that is, when the Customize dialog box is displayed), you can right-click a toolbar button to get a shortcut menu of additional actions for the tool. Figure 26-6 shows the shortcut menu that appears when you right-click a button in Customization mode.

Figure 26-6: In Customization mode, right-clicking a button displays this shortcut menu.

These commands are described in the following list (note that some of these commands are not available for certain toolbar tools):

✦ **Reset:** Resets the tool to its original state.

✦ **Delete:** Deletes the tool.

✦ **Name:** Lets you change the name of the tool.

✦ **Copy Button Image:** Makes a copy of the button's image and places it on the Clipboard.

✦ **Paste Button Image:** Pastes the image from the Clipboard to the button.

✦ **Reset Button Image:** Restores the button's original image.

✦ **Edit Button Image:** Lets you edit the button's image, using Excel's button editor (described later in this chapter).

✦ **Change Button Image:** Lets you change the image by selecting from a list of 42 button images.

✦ **Default Style:** Displays the tool with its default style (either text only or image and text).

✦ **Text Only (Always):** Always displays text (no image) for the tool.

✦ **Text Only (In Menus):** Displays text (no image) if the tool is in a menu bar.

✦ **Image and Text:** Displays the tool's image and text.

✦ **Begin a Group:** Inserts a divider in the toolbar. In a drop-down menu, a separator bar appears as a horizontal line between commands. In a toolbar, a separator bar appears as a vertical line.

✦ **Assign Hyperlink:** Lets you assign a hyperlink that will activate a Web page.

✦ **Assign Macro:** Lets you assign a macro that is executed when the button is clicked.

Changing a Toolbar Button's Image

To change the image that is displayed on a toolbar button, you have several options:

- ✦ Choose 1 of the 42 images that Excel provides.
- ✦ Modify or create the image by using Excel's Button Editor dialog box.
- ✦ Copy an image from another toolbar button.

Each of these methods is discussed in the following sections.

To make any changes to a button image, you must be in toolbar Customization mode. (The Customize dialog box must be visible.) Right-click any toolbar button and choose Customize from the shortcut menu that appears.

Using a built-in image

To change the image on a toolbar button, right-click the button and select Change Button Image from the shortcut menu. This menu expands to show 42 images from which you can choose. Just click the image that you want, and the selected button's image changes.

Editing a button image

If none of the 42 built-in images suits your tastes, you can edit an existing image or create a new image by using Excel's Button Editor.

First, make sure that you're in Customization mode. To begin editing, right-click the button that you want to edit and then choose Edit Button Image from the shortcut menu that appears. The image appears in the Button Editor dialog box (see Figure 26-7), in which you can change individual pixels and shift the entire image up, down, to the left, or to the right. If you've never worked with icons before, you may be surprised at how difficult it is to create attractive images in such a small area.

The Edit Button Image dialog box is straightforward. Just click one of the 16 colors, and then click a pixel (or drag across pixels) in the Picture area. To select a color that's not among the 16 colors, click the box labeled Color Picker. When the image looks good, click OK. Or if you don't like what you've done, click Cancel, and the button keeps its original image.

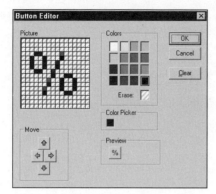

Figure 26-7: The Button Editor dialog box in which you can design your own button image or edit an existing one.

Copying another button image

Another way to get a button image on a custom toolbar is to copy it from another toolbar button. Make sure you're in Customization mode. Then right-click a toolbar button, and it displays a shortcut menu that enables you to copy a button image to the Clipboard or paste the Clipboard contents to the selected button.

✦   ✦   ✦

Using Conditional Formatting and Data Validation

This chapter explores two very useful Excel features: conditional formatting and data validation. These features enable you to add useful dynamic elements to your worksheet without using any macro programming.

Conditional Formatting

Conditional formatting enables you to apply cell formatting selectively and automatically, based on the contents of the cells. For example, you can set things up so that all negative values in a range have a light-yellow background color. When you enter or change a value in the range, Excel examines the value and evaluates the conditional formatting rules for the cell. If the value is negative, the background is shaded. If not, no formatting is applied.

Conditional formatting is very useful for quickly identifying erroneous cell entries or cells of a particular type. You can use a format (such as bright-red cell shading) to make particular cells easy to identify.

Is this a handy feature? No doubt. But dig a little deeper: You'll see that a lot more lurks in the shadows, and this feature can do things that you may not have thought possible. The key, as you'll see, is specifying your conditions by using formulas. In this section, I describe Excel's conditional formatting feature and point out some of its limitations — as well as a potentially serious design flaw.

Specifying conditional formatting

To apply conditional formatting to a cell or range

1. Select the cell or range.

2. Choose Format ⇨ Conditional Formatting. Excel displays its Conditional Formatting dialog box, as shown in Figure 27-1.

Figure 27-1: The Conditional Formatting dialog box.

3. In the first drop-down box, select either Cell Value Is (for simple conditional formatting) or Formula Is (for formatting based on a formula).

4. Specify the condition (or enter a formula).

5. Click the Format button and specify the formatting to apply if the condition is TRUE.

6. To add additional conditions (up to two more), click Add and then repeat Steps 3 through 5.

7. Click OK.

After you've performed these steps, the cell or range will be formatted based on the condition(s) you specify. This formatting, of course, is dynamic: If you change the contents of a cell, Excel re-evaluates the new contents and applies or removes the formatting accordingly.

Formatting types you can apply

When you click the Format button in the Conditional Formatting dialog box, you get the Format Cells dialog box, as shown in Figure 27-2. This is a modified version of the standard Format Cells dialog box. It does not have the Number, Alignment, and Protection tabs, and it includes a Clear button.

Note   The Find and Replace dialog box allows you to search your worksheet to locate cells that contain specific formatting. This feature does *not* locate cells that contain formatting resulting from conditional formatting.

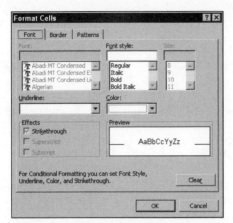

Figure 27-2: The Format Cells dialog box used in conditional formatting.

Specifying conditions

The leftmost drop-down list in the Conditional Formatting dialog box (refer to Figure 27-1) enables you to choose one of two options:

✦ **Cell Value Is:** For simple conditions

✦ **Formula Is:** For more-complex, formula-based conditions

I discuss these two types of conditions in the sections that follow.

Simple conditions

When you select Cell Value Is, you can specify conditions of the following types:

✦ Between (You specify two values.)

✦ Not Between (You specify two values.)

✦ Equal To (You specify one value.)

✦ Not Equal To (You specify one value.)

✦ Greater Than (You specify one value.)

✦ Less Than (You specify one value.)

✦ Greater Than or Equal To (You specify one value.)

✦ Less Than or Equal To (You specify one value.)

You can either enter the value(s) directly or specify a cell reference.

Formula-based conditions

When you select Formula Is, you can specify a formula. Do so by specifying a cell that contains a formula or by entering a formula directly into the Conditional Formatting dialog box. As with normal Excel formulas, the formula you enter here must begin with an equal sign (=).

Note   You must specify a logical formula that returns either TRUE or FALSE. If the formula evaluates to TRUE, the condition is satisfied, and the conditional formatting is applied. If the formula evaluates to FALSE, the conditional formatting is not applied.

As you'll see in the examples later in this chapter, the real power of conditional formatting is apparent when you enter a formula directly into the Conditional Formatting dialog box.

If the formula that you enter into the Conditional Formatting dialog box contains a cell reference, that reference is considered a *relative reference,* based on the upper-left cell in the selected range. For example, suppose you want to set up a conditional formatting condition that applies shading to empty cells in the range B2:B10. Follow these steps:

1. Select the range B2:B10 and ensure that cell B2 is the active cell.

2. Choose Format ➪ Conditional Formatting. The Conditional Formatting dialog box appears. (Refer to Figure 27-1.)

3. Select the Formula Is item from the drop-down list.

4. Enter the following formula in the Formula box:

   ```
   =B2=""
   ```

5. Click the Format button to display the Format Cells dialog box.

6. In the Format Cells dialog box, specify a pattern for the cell shading and click OK to return to the Conditional Formatting dialog box.

7. Click OK to close the Conditional Formatting dialog box.

Notice that the formula entered contains a reference to the upper-left cell in the selected range. To demonstrate that the reference is relative, select cell B5 and examine its conditional formatting formula. You'll see that the conditional formatting formula for this cell is

```
=B5=""
```

Generally, when entering a conditional formatting formula for a range of cells, you'll use a reference to the active cell — which is normally the upper-left cell in the selected range. One exception is when you need to refer to a specific cell.

For example, suppose that you select range A1:B20 and you want to apply formatting to all cells in the range that exceed the value in cell C1. Enter this conditional formatting formula:

```
=A1>$C$1
```

In this case, the reference to cell C1 is an *absolute reference;* it will not be adjusted for the cells in the selected range. In other words, the conditional formatting formula for cell A2 looks like this:

```
=A2>$C$1
```

The relative cell reference is adjusted, but the absolute cell reference is not.

Working with conditional formats

This section describes some additional information about conditional formatting that you may find useful.

Multiple conditions

You can specify as many as three conditions by clicking the Add button in the Conditional Formatting dialog box (refer to Figure 27-1). For example, you might enter the following three conditions (and specify different formatting for each):

```
Cell Value Is less than 0
Cell Value Is equal to 0
Cell Value Is greater than 0
```

In this case, the sign of the value (negative, 0, or positive) determines the applied formatting.

If none of the specified conditions is TRUE, the cells keep their existing formats. If you specify multiple conditions and more than one condition is TRUE for a particular cell, Excel applies only the formatting for the first TRUE condition. For example, you may specify the following two conditions:

```
Cell Value Is between 1 and 12
Cell Value Is less than 6
```

Entering a value of 4 satisfies both conditions. Therefore, the cell will be formatted using the format specified for the first condition.

Be careful when pasting

Keep in mind that it's very easy (too easy) to wipe out the conditional formatting in a cell or range by pasting copied data to the cell.

Caution   Copying a cell and pasting it to a cell or range that contains conditional formatting wipes out the conditional formatting in the destination range. You get no warning. This, of course, is a serious design flaw on the part of Microsoft—one that you should keep in mind if you use conditional formatting in your workbook. If you must paste copied data into a cell that contains conditional formatting, you can use the Paste Special dialog box and select the Values option. To display this dialog box, select Edit ⇨ Paste Special after you've copied your data.

Copying cells that contain conditional formatting

Conditional formatting information is stored with a cell much like standard formatting information is stored with a cell. This means that when you copy a cell that contains conditional formatting, the conditional formatting is also copied.

Tip   To copy only the conditional formats, use the Paste Special dialog box and select the Formats option.

Inserting rows or columns within a range that contains conditional formatting causes the new cells to have the same conditional formatting.

Deleting conditional formatting

When you press Delete to delete the contents of a cell, you do not delete the conditional formatting for the cell (if any). To remove all conditional formats (as well as all other cell formatting), select the cells and choose Edit ⇨ Clear ⇨ Formats. Or, use Edit ⇨ Clear ⇨ All to delete the cell contents and the conditional formatting.

To remove only conditional formatting (and leave the other formatting intact), you need to use the Conditional Formatting dialog box.

1. Select the cells; then choose Format ⇨ Conditional Formatting. The Conditional Formatting dialog box appears.

2. Click the Delete button in the Conditional Formatting dialog box. The Delete Conditional Format dialog box appears.

3. In the Delete Conditional Format dialog box, specify the conditions that you want to delete. This dialog box always displays check boxes for three conditions, even if you haven't defined that many.

4. Click OK to dismiss the Delete Conditional Format dialog box, and then click OK again to close the Conditional Formatting dialog box.

Locating cells that contain conditional formatting

You cannot tell, just by looking at a cell, whether it contains conditional formatting. You can, however, use Excel's Go To dialog box to select such cells.

1. Select Edit ⇨ Go To (or press F5) to display the Go To dialog box.

2. In the Go To dialog box, click the Special button. The Go To Special dialog box appears (as shown in Figure 27-3).

3. Select the Conditional Formats option (as shown in Figure 27-3).

4. To select all cells on the worksheet containing conditional formatting, select the All option. To select only the cells that contain the same conditional formatting as the active cell, select the Same option.

5. Click OK, and Excel selects the cells for you.

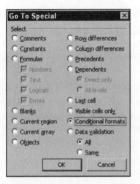

Figure 27-3: Use the Go To Special dialog box to locate cells that contain conditional formatting.

Using references to other sheets

If you enter a conditional formatting formula that uses one or more references to other sheets, Excel responds with an error message. If you need to refer to a cell on a different sheet, you must create a reference to that cell on the sheet that contains the conditional formatting. For example, if your conditional formatting formula needs to refer to cell A1 on Sheet3, you can insert the following formula into a cell on the active sheet:

```
=Sheet3!A1
```

Then, use a reference to that cell in your conditional formatting formula.

Tip   Another option is to create a name for the cell (by using Insert ⇨ Name ⇨ Define). After defining the name, you can use the name in place of the cell reference in the Conditional Formatting dialog box. If you use this technique, the named cell can be in any worksheet in the workbook.

Conditional formatting formula examples

This section contains a number of examples that demonstrate various uses for conditional formatting. Each of these examples uses a formula entered directly into the Conditional Formatting dialog box. You decide the type of formatting that you apply conditionally.

On the CD-ROM

The companion CD-ROM contains all of the examples in this section, plus additional examples.

Identifying non-numeric data

The following conditional formatting formula applies formatting to cell A1 only if the cell contains text:

```
=ISTEXT(A1)
```

To apply this conditional formatting formula to a range, select the range first. The argument for the ISTEXT function should be the active cell (usually the upper-left cell in the selected range).

Identifying above-average cells

I applied the following conditional formatting formula to range A1:D12. It applies formatting to all cells in the range A1:D12 that are above the average (as shown in Figure 27-4):

```
=A1>AVERAGE($A$1:$D$12)
```

	A	B	C	D	E	F	G	H
1	1	12	23	34		Conditional formatting:		
2	36	13	24	35		*Above average cells are formatted*		
3	3	14	25	2				
4	4	15	26	37				
5	5	16	27	38				
6	41	17	28	6				
7	7	18	12	40				
8	8	19	30	41				
9	9	20	31	42				
10	10	43	32	21				
11	11	22	33	44				
12	29	23	34	45				

Figure 27-4: Using conditional formatting to highlight all above-average cells.

Notice that the first cell reference (A1) is a relative reference, but the range argument for the Average formula is absolute.

Identifying dates in a particular month

Conditional formatting also works with dates. The conditional formatting formula that follows applies formatting only if the cell contains a date in the month of June:

```
=MONTH(A1)=6
```

This formula assumes that cell A1 is the active cell in the selected range. It works by using the MONTH function, which returns the month number for a date.

Note   The MONTH function does not distinguish between dates and non-dates. In other words, the MONTH function is applied to all cells, even if they don't contain a date.

Identifying today's date

Excel's TODAY function returns the current date. If you have a series of dates in a worksheet, you can use conditional formatting to make it easy to identify data for the current date. The conditional formatting formula that follows applies formatting only if the cell contains the current date. This assumes that you selected a range beginning with cell A1 when you entered the conditional formatting formula.

```
=A1=TODAY()
```

Identifying the maximum value in a range

Excel's MAX function returns the maximum value in a range. If you want to make this value stand out, you can use a conditional formatting formula such as this one:

```
=A1=MAX($A$1:$A$30)
```

In this case, the conditional formatting is applied to all cells in A1:A30, and the maximum value in that range will be formatted. You can, of course, modify this formula to use the MIN function (which returns the smallest value in a range).

Displaying alternate-row shading

The conditional formatting formula that follows was applied to the range A1:D18, as shown in Figure 27-5, to apply shading to alternate rows. This formula is quite useful for making your spreadsheets easier to read.

```
=MOD(ROW(),2)=0
```

This formula uses the ROW function (which returns the row number) and the MOD function (which returns the remainder of its first argument divided by its second argument). For cells in even-numbered rows, the MOD function returns 0, and cells in that row are formatted. For alternate shading of columns, use the COLUMN function instead of the ROW function.

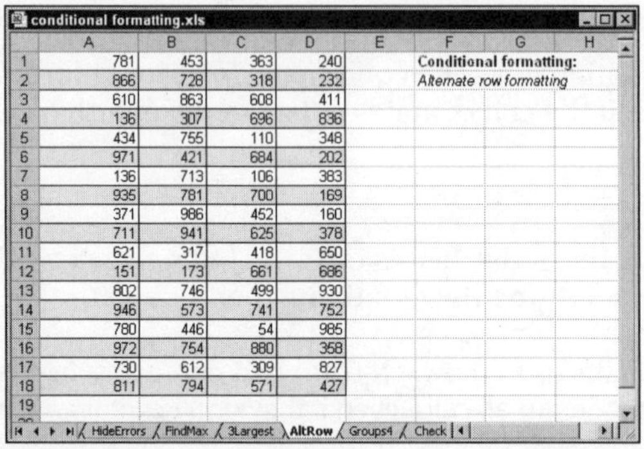

Figure 27-5: Using conditional formatting to apply formatting to alternate rows.

Identifying duplicate values in a range

You may find it helpful to identify duplicate values within a range (as shown in Figure 27-6). You can use a conditional formatting formula, such as the one that follows. In this case, formatting is applied to all cells that are not unique within the range A1:D12.

```
=COUNTIF($A$1:$D$12,A1)>1
```

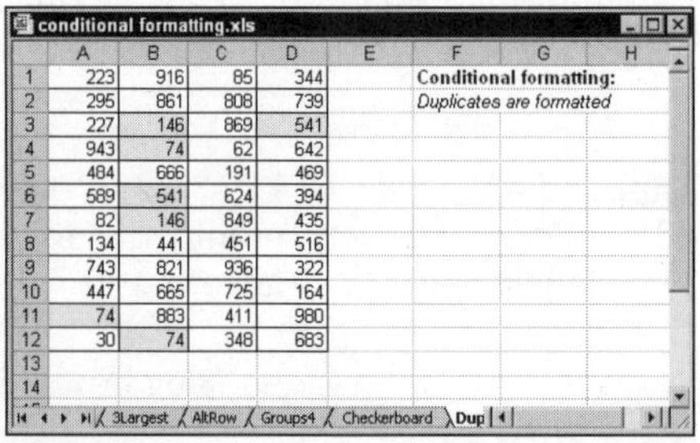

Figure 27-6: Using conditional formatting to identify duplicate values in a range.

To apply formatting only to non-duplicated values in a range, use a formula, such as this:

```
=COUNTIF($A$1:$D$12,A1)=1
```

Data Validation

Excel's data validation feature is similar in many respects to the conditional formatting feature. This feature enables you to set up certain rules that dictate what you can enter into a cell. For example, you may want to limit data entry to whole numbers between 1 and 12. If the user makes an invalid entry, you can display a custom message, such as the one shown in Figure 27-7.

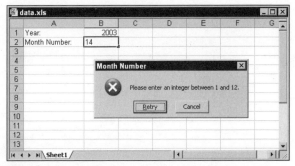

Figure 27-7: Displaying a message when the user makes an invalid entry.

As with the conditional formatting feature, you can use a formula to specify your data validation criteria.

Caution   The data validation feature suffers the same problem as conditional formatting: If the user copies a cell and pastes it to a cell that contains data validation, the data validation rules are deleted. Consequently, the cell then accepts any type of data.

Specifying validation criteria

To specify the type of data allowable in a cell or range, follow these steps:

1. Select the cell or range.

2. Choose Data ⇨ Validation. Excel displays its Data Validation dialog box.

3. Click the Settings tab (see Figure 27-8).

4. Choose an option from the drop-down box labeled Allow. To specify a formula, select Custom.

5. Specify the conditions by selecting from the drop-down box labeled Data. Your selection determines what other controls you can access.

6. (Optional) Click the Input Message tab and specify which message to display when a user selects the cell. You can use this optional step to tell the user what type of data is expected. If this step is omitted, no message will appear when the user selects the cell.

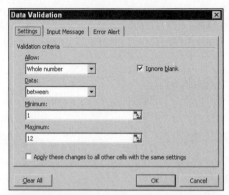

Figure 27-8: The Settings tab of the Data Validation dialog box.

7. (Optional.) Click the Error Alert tab and specify which error message to display when a user makes an invalid entry. The selection for Style determines what choices users have when they make invalid entries. To prevent an invalid entry, choose Stop. If this step is omitted, a standard message will appear if the user makes an invalid entry.

8. Click OK.

After you've performed these steps, the cell or range contains the validation criteria you specified.

Types of validation criteria you can apply

The Settings tab of the Data Validation dialog box enables you to specify a wide variety of data validation criteria. The following options are available in the Allow drop-down box (note that the other controls in the Settings tab vary, depending on your choice in the Allow drop-down box):

✦ **Any Value:** Selecting this option removes any existing data validation. Note, however, that the input message, if any, still displays if the check box is checked in the Input Message tab.

✦ **Whole Number:** The user must enter a whole number. You specify a valid range of whole numbers by using the Data drop-down list. For example, you can specify that the entry must be a whole number greater than or equal to 100.

✦ **Decimal:** The user must enter a number. You specify a valid range of numbers by using the Data drop-down list. For example, you can specify that the entry must be greater than or equal to 0 and less than or equal to 1.

✦ **List:** The user must choose from a list of entries you provide. See "Creating a drop-down list," later in this chapter.

✦ **Date:** The user must enter a date. You specify a valid date range by using the Data drop-down list. For example, you can specify that the entered data must be greater than or equal to January 1, 2003, and less than or equal to December 31, 2003.

✦ **Time:** The user must enter a time. You specify a valid time range by using the Data drop-down list. For example, you can specify that the entered data must be greater than 12:00 PM.

✦ **Text Length:** The length of the data (number of characters) is limited. You specify a valid length by using the Data drop-down list. For example, you can specify that the length of the entered data be 1 (a single alphanumeric character).

✦ **Custom:** A logical formula determines the validity of the user's entry. You can enter the formula directly into the Formula control (which appears when you select the Custom option), or you can specify a cell reference that contains a formula. This chapter contains examples of useful formulas.

The Settings tab of the Data Validation dialog box contains two other check boxes:

✦ **Ignore Blank:** If checked, blank entries are allowed.

✦ **Apply These Changes to All Other Cells with the Same Setting:** If checked, the changes you make apply to all other cells that contain the original data validation criteria.

It's important to understand that, even with data validation in effect, the user could enter invalid data. If the Style setting in the Error Alert tab of the Data Validation dialog box is set to anything except Stop, invalid data *can* be entered. Also, remember that data validation does not apply to the calculated results of formulas. In other words, if the cell contains a formula, applying conditional formatting to that cell will have no effect.

 Tip The Formula Auditing Toolbar contains a button named Circle Invalid Data. When you click this button, circles appear around cells that contain incorrect entries. If you correct an invalid entry, the circle disappears. In Figure 27-9, invalid entries are defined as values that are greater than 90. To display this toolbar, choose Tools ⇨ Formula Auditing ⇨ Show Formula Auditing Toolbar.

Creating a drop-down list

Perhaps one of the most common uses of data validation is to create a drop-down list of items. Figure 27-10 shows an example that uses the month names in A1:A12 as the list source.

First, enter the list items into a single-row or single-column range. (These are the items that appear in the drop-down list.) Then select the cell that will contain the drop-down list and access the Data Validation dialog box. In the Settings tab, select the List option and specify the range that contains the list using the Source control. Also, make sure that the In-Cell Dropdown check box is checked.

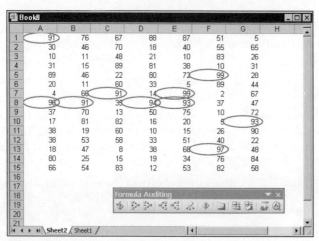

Figure 27-9: Circles are drawn around invalid entries (cells that contain a value greater than 90).

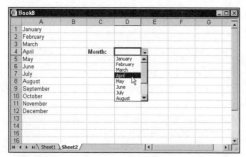

Figure 27-10: This drop-down list was created by using data validation.

Tip

If you have a short list, you can enter the items directly into the Source control in the Settings tab of the Data Validation dialog box (this control appears when you choose the List option in the Allow drop-down list). Just separate each item with list separator specified in your regional settings (a comma if you use the U.S. regional settings).

Tip

If you specify a range for a list, the range must be on the same sheet. If your list is in a range on a different worksheet, you can provide a name for the range and then use the name as your list source (preceded by an equal sign). For example, if the list is contained in a range named *MyList*, enter the following:

```
=MyList
```

After performing these steps, the cell displays a drop-down arrow when it is activated. Click the arrow and choose an item from the list that appears.

Using formulas for data validation rules

For simple data validation, the data validation feature is quite straightforward and easy to use. But the real power of this feature becomes apparent when you use data validation formulas.

 Note   The formula that you specify must be a logical formula that returns either TRUE or FALSE. If the formula evaluates to TRUE, the data is considered valid and remains in the cell. If the formula evaluates to FALSE, a message box appears that displays the message specified in the Error Alert tab of the Data Validation dialog box.

As noted earlier in this chapter, you specify a formula in the Data Validation dialog box by selecting the Custom option in the Allow drop-down list of the Settings tab. You can enter the formula directly into the Formula control or you can enter a reference to a cell that contains a formula. The Formula control appears in the Setting tab of the Data Validation dialog box when the Custom option is selected.

If the formula that you enter contains a cell reference, that reference will be considered to be a relative reference, based on the active cell in the selected range. This works exactly the same as using a formula for conditional formatting (see "Formula-based conditions," earlier in this chapter).

Using data validation formulas to accept only specific entries

This section contains a few data validation examples that use a formula entered directly into the Formula control on the Settings tab of the Data Validation dialog box.

 On the CD-ROM   All of the examples in this section are available on the companion CD-ROM.

Accepting text only

To force a range to accept only text (no values), use the following data validation formula:

```
=ISTEXT(A1)
```

This formula assumes that the active cell in the selected range is cell A1.

Accepting a larger value than the previous cell

The following data validation formula enables the user to enter a value only if it's greater than the value in the cell directly above it:

```
=A2>A1
```

This formula assumes that A2 is the active cell in the selected range. Note that you can't use this formula for a cell in row 1.

Accepting non-duplicate entries only

The following data validation formula does not permit the user to make a duplicate entry in the range A1:C20:

```
=COUNTIF($A$1:$C$20,A1)=1
```

This formula assumes that A1 is the active cell in the selected range. Note that the first argument for COUNTIF is an absolute reference. The second argument is a relative reference, and it adjusts for each cell in the validation range. Figure 27-11 shows this validation criterion in effect, using a custom error alert message.

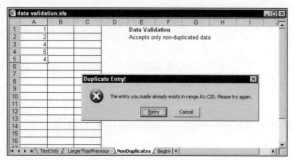

Figure 27-11: Using data validation to prevent duplicate entries in a range.

Accepting text that begins with *A*

The following data validation formula demonstrates how to check for a specific character. In this case, the formula ensures that the user's entry is a text string that begins with the letter *A* (either uppercase or lowercase).

```
=LEFT(A1)="a"
```

This formula assumes that the active cell in the selected range is cell A1.

The following formula is a variation of this validation formula. In this case, the formula ensures that the entry begins with the letter *A* and contains exactly five characters.

```
=COUNTIF(A1,"A????")=1
```

✦   ✦   ✦

Creating and Using Worksheet Outlines

If you use a word processor, you may be familiar with the concept of an outline. Most word processors (including Microsoft Word) have an outline mode that lets you view only the headings and subheadings in your document. You can easily expand a heading to show the detail (that is, the text) below it. Using an outline makes visualizing the structure of your document easy.

Excel also is capable of using outlines, and understanding this feature can make working with certain types of worksheets much easier for you.

Introducing Worksheet Outlines

You can use outlines to create summary reports in which you don't want to show all the details. You'll find that some worksheets are more suitable for outlines than others. If your worksheet uses hierarchical data with subtotals, it's probably a good candidate for an outline.

The best way to understand how worksheet outlining works is to look at an example. Figure 28-1 shows a simple budget model without an outline. Formulas are used to calculate subtotals by region and by quarter.

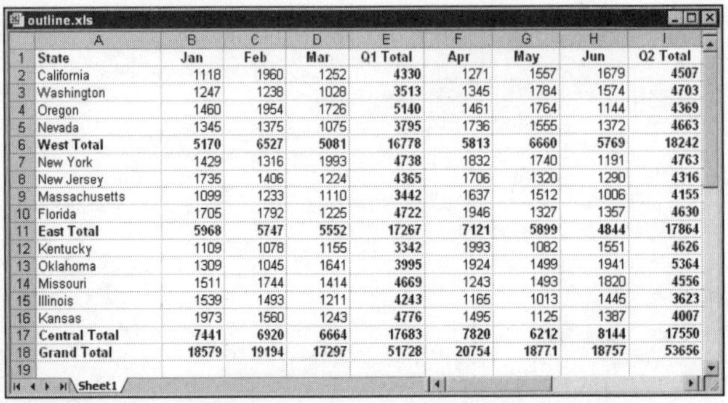

Figure 28-1: A typical budget model with subtotals.

Figure 28-2 shows the same worksheet after the outline was created. Notice that Excel adds a new border to the left of the screen. This border contains controls that enable you to determine which level to view. This particular outline has three levels: States, Regions (each region consists of states grouped into categories such as West, East, and Central), and Grand Total (the sum of each region's subtotal). In Figure 28-2, the outline is fully expanded so that you can see all the data.

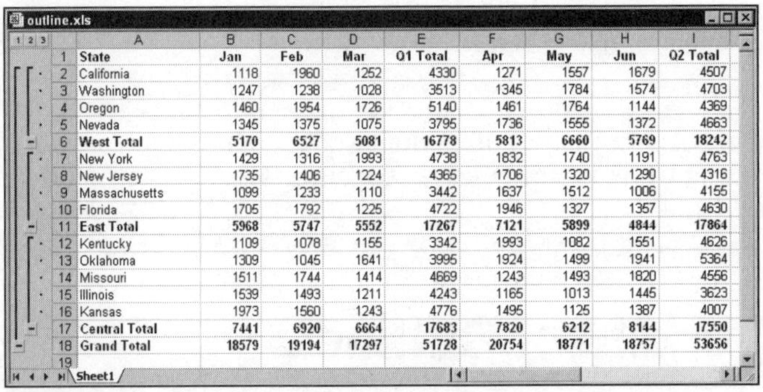

Figure 28-2: The budget model after creating an outline.

Figure 28-3 depicts the outline after clicking the 2 button, which displays the second level of details. Now, the outline shows only the totals for the regions (the detail rows are hidden). You can partially expand the outline to show the detail for a particular region by clicking one of the + buttons. Collapsing the outline to level 1 shows only the headers and the Grand Total row.

Excel can create outlines in both directions. In the preceding examples, the outline was a row (vertical) outline. Figure 28-4 shows the same model after a column (horizontal) outline was added. Now, Excel displays another border at the top.

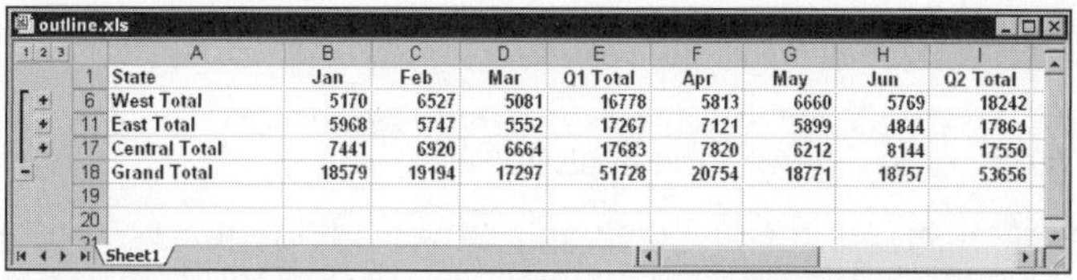

Figure 28-3: The budget model after collapsing the outline to the second level.

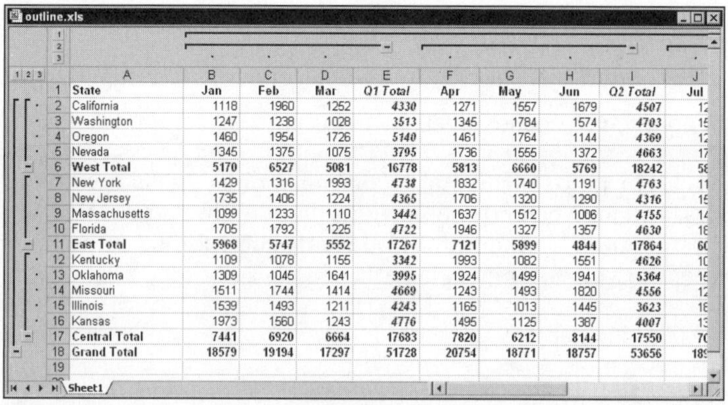

	A	B	C	D	E	F	G	H	I
1	State	Jan	Feb	Mar	Q1 Total	Apr	May	Jun	Q2 Total
6	West Total	5170	6527	5081	16778	5813	6660	5769	18242
11	East Total	5968	5747	5552	17267	7121	5899	4844	17864
17	Central Total	7441	6920	6664	17683	7820	6212	8144	17550
18	Grand Total	18579	19194	17297	51728	20754	18771	18757	53656
19									
20									

Figure 28-4: The budget model after adding a column outline.

	A	B	C	D	E	F	G	H	I	Jul
1	State	Jan	Feb	Mar	Q1 Total	Apr	May	Jun	Q2 Total	Jul
2	California	1118	1960	1252	4330	1271	1557	1679	4507	12
3	Washington	1247	1238	1028	3513	1345	1784	1574	4703	15
4	Oregon	1460	1954	1726	5140	1461	1764	1144	4369	12
5	Nevada	1345	1375	1075	3795	1736	1555	1372	4663	17
6	West Total	5170	6527	5081	16778	5813	6660	5769	18242	58
7	New York	1429	1316	1993	4738	1832	1740	1191	4763	11
8	New Jersey	1735	1406	1224	4365	1706	1320	1290	4316	15
9	Massachusetts	1099	1233	1110	3442	1637	1512	1006	4155	14
10	Florida	1705	1792	1225	4722	1946	1327	1357	4630	16
11	East Total	5968	5747	5552	17267	7121	5899	4844	17864	60
12	Kentucky	1109	1078	1155	3342	1993	1082	1551	4626	10
13	Oklahoma	1309	1045	1641	3995	1924	1499	1941	5364	15
14	Missouri	1511	1744	1414	4669	1243	1493	1820	4556	12
15	Illinois	1539	1493	1211	4243	1165	1013	1445	3623	18
16	Kansas	1973	1560	1243	4776	1495	1125	1387	4007	13
17	Central Total	7441	6920	6664	17683	7820	6212	8144	17550	70
18	Grand Total	18579	19194	17297	51728	20754	18771	18757	53656	189
19										

If you create both a row and a column outline in a worksheet, you can work with each outline independent of the other. For example, you can show the row outline at the second level and the column outline at the first level. Figure 28-5 shows the model with both outlines collapsed at the second level. The result is a nice summary table that gives regional totals by quarter.

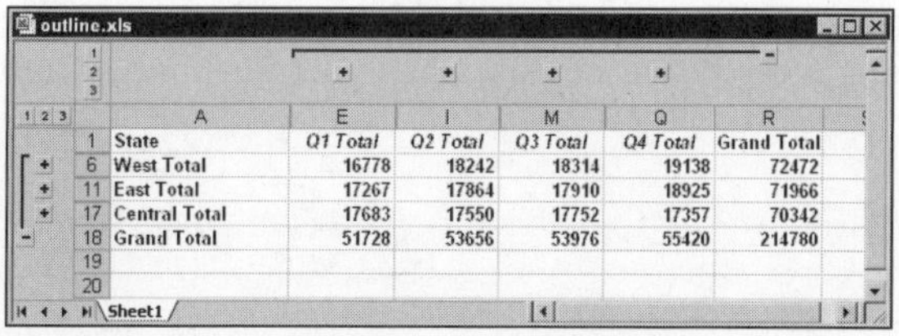

	A	E	I	M	Q	R	
1	State	Q1 Total	Q2 Total	Q3 Total	Q4 Total	Grand Total	
6	West Total	16778	18242	18314	19138	72472	
11	East Total	17267	17864	17910	18925	71966	
17	Central Total	17683	17550	17752	17357	70342	
18	Grand Total	51728	53656	53976	55420	214780	
19							
20							

Figure 28-5: The budget model with both outlines collapsed at the second level.

On the CD-ROM

You'll find the workbook used in the preceding examples on this book's CD-ROM.

The following are points to keep in mind about worksheet outlines:

✦ A worksheet can have only one outline. If you need to create more than one outline, move the data to a new worksheet.

✦ You can either create an outline manually or have Excel do it for you automatically. If you choose the latter option, you may need to do some preparation to get the worksheet in the proper format.

✦ You can create an outline for either all data on a worksheet or just a selected data range.

✦ You can remove an outline with a single command.

✦ You can hide the outline symbols (to free screen space) but retain the outline.

✦ You can have up to eight nested levels in an outline.

Worksheet outlines can be quite useful. But if your main objective is to summarize a large amount of data, you may be better off using a pivot table. A pivot table is much more flexible and doesn't require that you create the subtotal formulas; it does the summarizing for you automatically.

Cross-Reference   I discuss pivot tables in Chapter 21.

Creating an Outline

In this section, you learn the two ways to create an outline: automatically and manually. Before you create an outline, you need to ensure that data is appropriate for an outline and that the formulas are set up properly.

Preparing the data

What type of data is appropriate for an outline? Generally, the data should be arranged in a hierarchy, such as a budget that consists of an arrangement similar to the following:

Company

　　Division

　　　　Department

　　　　　　Budget Category

　　　　　　　　Budget Item

In this case, each budget item (for example, airfare and hotel expenses) is part of a budget category (for example, travel expenses). Each department has its own budget, and the departments are rolled up into divisions. The divisions make up the company. This type of arrangement is well suited for a row outline.

After you create such an outline, you can view the information at any level of detail that you want. When you need to create reports for different levels of management, consider using an outline. Upper management may want to see only the division totals. Division managers may want to see totals by department, and each department manager needs to see the full details for his or her department.

As demonstrated at the beginning of the chapter, you can include time-based information that is rolled up into larger units (such as months and quarters) in a column outline. Column outlines work just like row outlines, however, and the levels need not be time-based.

Before you create an outline, you need to make sure that all the summary formulas are entered correctly and consistently. *Consistently* means that the formulas are in the same relative location. Generally, formulas that compute summary formulas (such as subtotals) are entered below the data to which they refer. In some cases, however, the summary formulas are entered above the referenced cells. Excel can handle either method, but you must be consistent throughout the range that you outline. If the summary formulas aren't consistent, automatic outlining won't produce the results that you want.

Note   If your summary formulas aren't consistent (that is, some are above and some are below the data), you still can create an outline, but you must do it manually.

Creating an outline automatically

Excel can create an outline for you automatically in a few seconds, whereas it may take you 10 minutes or more to do the same thing manually.

To have Excel create an outline, move the cell pointer anywhere within the range of data that you're outlining. Then, choose Data ➪ Group and Outline ➪ Auto Outline. Excel analyzes the formulas in the range and creates the outline. Depending on the formulas that you have, Excel creates a row outline, a column outline, or both.

If the worksheet already has an outline, Excel asks whether you want to modify the existing outline. Click Yes to force Excel to remove the old outline and create a new one.

Note   Excel automatically creates an outline when you use the Data ➪ Subtotals command, which inserts subtotal formulas automatically if you set up your data as a list.

Cross-Reference   The Data ➪ Subtotals command is discussed in Chapter 19.

Creating an outline manually

Usually, letting Excel create the outline is the best approach. It's much faster and less error-prone. If the outline that Excel creates isn't what you have in mind, however, you can create an outline manually.

When Excel creates a row outline, the summary rows must all be above the data or all below the data. (They can't be mixed.) Similarly, for a column outline, the summary columns must all be to the right of the data or to the left of the data. If your worksheet doesn't meet these requirements, you have two choices:

✦ Rearrange the worksheet so that it does meet the requirements.

✦ Create the outline manually.

You also need to create an outline manually if the range doesn't contain any formulas. You may have imported a file and want to use an outline to display it better. Because Excel uses the formulas to determine how to create the outline, it is not able to make an outline without formulas.

Creating an outline manually consists of creating groups of rows (for row outlines) or groups of columns (for column outlines). To create a group of rows, click the row numbers for all the rows that you want to include in the group—but do not select the row that has the summary formulas. Then, choose Data ⇨ Group and Outline ⇨ Group. Excel displays outline symbols for the group. Repeat this for each group that you want to create. When you collapse the outline, Excel hides rows in the group, but the summary row, which is not in the group, remains in view.

Note   If you select a range of cells (rather than entire rows or columns) before you create a group, Excel displays a dialog box asking what you want to group. It then groups entire rows or columns based on the range that you select.

You can also select groups of groups to create multilevel outlines. When you create multilevel outlines, always start with the innermost groupings and then work your way out. If you realize that you grouped the wrong rows, you can ungroup the group by selecting Data ⇨ Group and Outline ⇨ Ungroup.

Excel has toolbar buttons that speed up the process of grouping and ungrouping. You also can use the following keyboard shortcuts:

✦ **Alt+Shift+right arrow:** Groups selected rows or columns

✦ **Alt+Shift+left arrow:** Ungroups selected rows or columns

Creating outlines manually can be confusing at first, but if you stick with it, you'll become a pro in no time.

Working with Outlines

This section discusses the basic operations that you can perform with a worksheet outline.

Displaying levels

To display various outline levels, click the appropriate outline symbol. These symbols consist of buttons with numbers on them (1, 2, and so on) and buttons with either a plus sign (+) or a minus sign (–). Refer to Figure 28-5, which shows these symbols for a row and column..

Clicking the 1 button collapses the outline so that it displays no detail, just the highest summary level of information, clicking the 2 button expands the outline to show one level, and so on. The number of numbered buttons depends on the number of outline levels. Choosing a level number displays the detail for that level, plus any lower levels. To display all levels (the most detail), click the highest-level number.

You can expand a particular section by clicking its + button, or you can collapse a particular section by clicking its – button. In short, you have complete control over the details that Excel exposes or hides in an outline.

If you prefer, you can use the Hide Detail and Show Detail commands on the Data ⇨ Group and Outline menu to hide and show details, respectively.

Tip   If you constantly adjust the outline to show different reports, consider using the Custom Views feature to save a particular view and give it a name. Then you can quickly switch among the named views. Use the View ⇨ Custom Views command for this.

Adding data to an outline

You may need to add additional rows or columns to an outline. In some cases, you may be able to insert new rows or columns without disturbing the outline, and the new rows or columns become part of the outline. In other cases, you'll find that the new row or column is not part of the outline. If you create the outline automatically, just select Data ⇨ Group and Outline ⇨ Auto Outline again. Excel makes you verify that you want to modify the existing outline. If you create the outline manually, you need to make the adjustments manually, as well.

Removing an outline

If you no longer need an outline, you can remove it by selecting Data ⇨ Group and Outline ⇨ Clear Outline. Excel fully expands the outline by displaying all hidden rows and columns, and the outline symbols disappear. Be careful before you do this, however: After you have removed an outline, you can't make it reappear using the Undo button. You must re-create the outline from scratch.

Hiding the outline symbols

The outline symbols Excel displays when an outline is present take up quite a bit of space. (The exact amount depends on the number levels.) If you want to see as much as possible on-screen, you can temporarily hide these symbols without removing the outline. The following are the two ways to do this:

✦ Use Tools ➪ Options to display the Options dialog box. Select the View tab, and remove the check from the Outline Symbols check box.

✦ Press Ctrl+8.

Note   When you hide the outline symbols, the outline still is in effect, and the worksheet displays the data at the current outline level. That is, some rows or columns may be hidden.

To redisplay the outline symbols, either place a check mark in the Outline Symbols check box in the Options dialog box or press Ctrl+8.

The Custom Views feature, which saves named views of your outline, also saves the status of the outline symbols as part of the view, enabling you to name some views with the outline symbols and other views without them.

✦   ✦   ✦

Linking and Consolidating Worksheets

In this chapter, I discuss two procedures that are common
in the world of spreadsheets: linking and consolidation.
Linking is the process of using references to cells in external
workbooks to get data into your worksheet. *Consolidation*
combines or summarizes information from two or more worksheets (which can be in multiple workbooks).

Linking Workbooks

When you link worksheets, you connect them together in such
a way that one depends on the other. The workbook that contains the link formulas (or external reference formulas) is called
the *dependent* workbook. The workbook that contains the information used in the external reference formula is called the
source workbook.

Why link workbooks?

When you consider linking workbooks, you may ask yourself
the following question: If Workbook A needs to access data in
another workbook (Workbook B), why not just enter the data
into Workbook A in the first place? In some cases, you can. But
the real value of linking becomes apparent when you continually update the source workbook. Creating a link in Workbook
A to Workbook B means that, in Workbook A, you always have
access to the most recent information in Workbook B because
Workbook A is updated whenever Workbook B changes.

Linking workbooks also can be helpful if you need to consolidate different files. For example, each regional sales manager may store data in a separate workbook. You can create a summary workbook that first uses link formulas to retrieve specific data from each manager's workbook and then calculates totals across all regions.

Linking also is useful as a way to break up a large model into smaller files. You can create smaller workbook modules that are linked together with a few key external references. Often, this approach makes your model easier to work with.

Linking has its downside, however. As you see later, external reference formulas are somewhat fragile, and accidentally severing the links that you create is relatively easy. You can prevent this from happening if you understand how linking works. Later in the chapter, some of the problems that may arise are discussed as well as how to avoid them (see "Potential problems with external reference formulas").

Creating external reference formulas

You can create an external reference formula by using several different techniques:

✦ **Type the cell references manually.** These references may be lengthy because they include workbook and sheet names (and, possibly, even drive and path information). The advantage of manually typing the cell references is that the source workbook doesn't have to be open.

✦ **Point to the cell references.** If the source workbook is open, you can use the standard pointing techniques to create formulas that use external references.

✦ **Use Paste Special.** Copy your data. Then, with the source workbook open, select Edit ⇨ Paste Special, to display the Paste Special dialog box. Choose the Paste Link option, and click OK.

✦ **Use Excel's Data ⇨ Consolidate command.** This method is discussed in "Consolidating worksheets by using the Consolidate command," later in this chapter.

Understanding the link formula syntax

The general syntax for an external reference formula is as follows:

```
=[WorkbookName]SheetName!CellAddress
```

Precede the cell address with the workbook name (in brackets), the worksheet name, and an exclamation point. Here's an example of a formula that uses cell A1 in the Sheet1 worksheet of a workbook named Budget:

```
=[Budget.xls]Sheet1!A1
```

If the workbook name or the sheet name in the reference includes one or more spaces, you must enclose the text in single quotation marks. For example, here's a formula that refers to cell A1 on Sheet1 in a workbook named Annual Budget:

```
='[Annual Budget]Sheet1'!A1
```

When a formula refers to cells in a different workbook, that other workbook doesn't need to be open. If the workbook is closed and not in the current folder, you must add the complete path to the reference; for example:

```
='C:\Data\Excel\Budget\[Annual Budget]Sheet1'!A1
```

Creating a link formula by pointing

Entering external reference formulas manually is usually not the best approach because it is easy to make an error. Instead, have Excel build the formula for you, as follows:

1. Open the source workbook.

2. Select the cell in the dependent workbook that will hold the formula.

3. Enter the formula. When you get to the part that requires the external reference, activate the source workbook and select the cell or range.

4. Back in the dependent workbook, finish the formula and press Enter.

When you point to the cell or range, Excel automatically takes care of the details and creates a syntactically correct external reference. When using this method, the cell reference is always an absolute reference (such as $A$1). If you plan to copy the formula to create additional link formulas, you can change the absolute reference to a relative reference by removing the dollar signs for the cell address.

As long as the source workbook remains open, the external reference doesn't include the path to the workbook. If you close the source workbook, however, the external reference formulas change to include the full path. If you use the File ➪ Save As command to save the source workbook with a different name, Excel changes the external references to use the new filename.

Pasting links

The Paste Special command provides another way to create external reference formulas. This method is applicable when you want to create formulas that simply reference other cells. Follow these steps:

1. Open the source workbook.

2. Select the cell or range that you want to link and then copy it to the Clipboard.

3. Activate the dependent workbook and select the cell in which you want the link formula to appear. If you're pasting a range, just select the upper-left cell.

4. Choose Edit ⇨ Paste Special and then click the Paste Link button.

Working with external reference formulas

This section discusses what you need to know about working with links.

Creating links to unsaved workbooks

Excel enables you to create link formulas to unsaved workbooks (and even to non-existent workbooks). Assume that you have two workbooks open and you haven't saved either of them. (They have the names Book1 and Book2.) If you create a link formula to Book1 in Book2 and then save Book2, Excel displays the dialog box shown in Figure 29-1. To avoid this prompt, simply save the source workbook first.

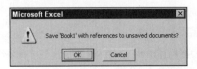

Figure 29-1: This message indicates that the workbook you're saving contains references to a workbook that you haven't yet saved.

You also can create links to documents that don't exist. You may want to do this if you'll be using a source workbook from a colleague but the file hasn't yet arrived. When you enter an external reference formula that refers to a nonexistent workbook, Excel displays its Update Values dialog box, which resembles the File Open dialog box. If you click Cancel, the formula retains the workbook name that you entered, but it returns a #REF! error. When the source workbook becomes available, you can use the Edit ⇨ Links command to update the link (see "Updating links," later in this chapter). After doing so, the error goes away, and the formula displays its proper value.

Opening a workbook with external reference formulas

When you open a workbook that contains one or more external reference formulas, Excel, by default, retrieves the current values from the source workbooks and calculates the formulas. However, you can change this behavior by using the Startup Prompt dialog box (see Figure 29-2). To display this dialog box, select Edit ⇨ Links. Then, in the Edit Links dialog box, click the Startup Prompt button. Select the option that corresponds with how you want to handle the links.

If Excel can't locate a source workbook that's referred to in a link formula, it displays a dialog box that asks you what to do (attempt to update the links, or don't update the links). If you click the Update button, Excel displays its Edit Links dialog box, shown in Figure 29-3. You can use the Change Source button to specify a different workbook, or click Break Link to destroy the link.

Figure 29-2: Use the Edit Links dialog box to specify how Excel handles links when the workbook is opened.

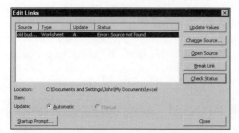

Figure 29-3: The Edit Links dialog box.

You can also access the Edit Links dialog box by using the Edit ➪ Links command. The dialog box that appears lists all source workbooks, plus other types of links to other documents.

Updating links

If you want to ensure that your link formulas have the latest values from their source workbooks, you can force an update. This step may be necessary if you just learned that someone made changes to the source workbook and saved the latest version to your network server.

To update linked formulas with their current value, open the Edit Links dialog box (choose Edit ➪ Links), choose the appropriate source workbook in the list, and then click the Update Values button. Excel updates the link formulas with the latest version of the source workbook.

Note

Excel always sets worksheet links to the Automatic Update option in the Links dialog box, and you can't change them to Manual. This means that Excel updates the links only when you open the workbook. Excel doesn't automatically update links when the source file changes (unless the source workbook is open).

Changing the link source

A time may come when you need to change the source workbook for your external references. For example, you may have a worksheet that has links to a workbook named Preliminary Budget, but you later receive a finalized version named Final Budget.

You *could* change all the cell links manually, or you could simply change the link source. Do this in the Edit Links dialog box, which you can reach by choosing Edit ⇨ Links. Select the source workbook that you want to change and click the Change Source button. Excel displays a dialog box that enables you to select a new source file. After you select the file, all external reference formulas are updated.

Severing links

If you have external references in a workbook and then decide that you no longer need the links, you can convert the external reference formulas to values, thereby severing the links. To do so, choose Edit ⇨ Links to access the Edit Links dialog box, select the linked file in the list and click Break Link. Be sure to verify your intentions because this operation cannot be undone.

Potential problems with external reference formulas

Using external reference formulas can be quite useful, but the links may be unintentionally severed. In almost every case, you'll be able to re-establish lost links. If you open the workbook and Excel can't locate the file, you're presented with a dialog box that enables you to specify the workbook and re-create the links. You also can change the source file by using the Change Source button in the Links dialog box. The following sections discuss some pointers that you must remember when you use external reference formulas.

Renaming or moving a source workbook

If you rename the source document or move it to a different folder, Excel won't be able to update the links. You need to use the Links dialog box and specify the new source document.

Note If the source and destination folder reside in the same folder, you can move both of the files to a different folder. In such a case, the links will remain intact.

Using the Save As command

If both the source workbook and the destination workbook are open, Excel doesn't display the full path in the external reference formulas. If you use the File ⇨ Save As command to give the source workbook a new name, Excel modifies the external references to use the new workbook name. In some cases, this may be what you want. But in other cases, it may not. Bottom line? Be careful when you use the File ⇨ Save As command with a workbook that is the source of a link in another open workbook.

Modifying a source workbook

If you open a workbook that is a source workbook for another workbook, be extremely careful if you don't open the destination workbook at the same time. For example, if you add a new row to the source workbook, the cells all move down one row. When you open the destination workbook, it continues to use the old cell references — which are now invalid.

You can avoid this problem in the following ways:

✦ **Open the destination workbook when you modify the source workbook.** If you do so, Excel adjusts the external references in the destination workbook when you make changes to the source workbook.

✦ **Use names rather than cell references in your link formula.** This is the safest approach.

The following link formula refers to cell C21 on Sheet1 in the budget.xls workbook:

```
=[budget.xls]Sheet1!$C$21
```

If cell C21 is named Total, the formula can be written using that name:

```
=budget.xls!total
```

Using a name ensures that the correct value will be retrieved by the link, even if row or columns are added or deleted from the source workbook.

Intermediary links

Excel doesn't place many limitations on the complexity of your network of external references. For example, Workbook A can contain external references that refer to Workbook B, which can contain an external reference that refers to Workbook C. In this case, a value in Workbook A can ultimately depend on a value in Workbook C. Workbook B is an *intermediary link.*

I don't recommend these types of links, but if you must use them, be aware that Excel doesn't update external reference formulas if the workbook isn't open. In the preceding example, assume that Workbooks A and C are open. If you change a value in Workbook C, Workbook A won't reflect the change because you didn't open Workbook B (the intermediary link).

Consolidating Worksheets

The term *consolidation,* in the context of worksheets, refers to several operations that involve multiple worksheets or multiple workbook files. In some cases, consolidation involves creating link formulas. Here are two common examples of consolidation:

✦ The budget for each department in your company is stored in a single workbook, with a separate worksheet for each department. You need to consolidate the data and create a company-wide budget.

✦ Each department head submits his or her budget to you in a separate workbook file. Your job is to consolidate these files into a company-wide budget.

These types of tasks can be very difficult or quite easy. The task is easy if the information is laid out exactly the same in each worksheet (as you'll see shortly). If the worksheets aren't laid out identically, they may be similar enough. In the second example, some budget files submitted to you may be missing categories that aren't used by a particular department. In this case, you can use a handy feature in Excel that matches data by using row and column titles. I discuss this feature in "Consolidating worksheets by using the Consolidate command," later in this chapter.

If the worksheets bear little or no resemblance to each other, your best bet may be to edit the sheets so that they correspond to one another. In some cases, simply re-entering the information in a standard format may be more efficient.

You can use any of the following techniques to consolidate information from multiple workbooks:

✦ Use external reference formulas.

✦ Copy the data and use the Paste Special command.

✦ Use Excel's Data ➪ Consolidate command.

✦ Use a pivot table with the Multiple Consolidation Ranges option (discussed in Chapter 21).

Consolidating worksheets by using formulas

Consolidating with formulas simply involves creating formulas that use references to other worksheets or other workbooks. The primary advantages to using this method of consolidation are

✦ Dynamic updating — if the values in the source worksheets change, the formulas are updated automatically.

✦ The source workbooks don't need to be open when you create the consolidation formulas.

If you are consolidating the worksheets in the same workbook and all the worksheets are laid out identically, the consolidation task is simple. You can just use standard formulas to create the consolidations. For example, to compute the total for cell A1 in worksheets named Sheet2 through Sheet10, enter the following formula:

```
=SUM(Sheet2:Sheet10!A1)
```

You can enter this formula manually or use the multisheet selection technique discussed in Chapter 4. You can then copy this formula to create summary formulas for other cells.

If the consolidation involves other workbooks, you can use external reference formulas to perform your consolidation. For example, if you want to add the values in cell A1 from Sheet1 in two workbooks (named Region1 and Region2), you can use the following formula:

```
=[Region1.xls]Sheet1!B2+[Region2.xls]Sheet1!B2
```

You can include any number of external references in this formula, up to the 1,024-character limit for a formula. However, if you use many external references, such a formula can be quite lengthy and confusing if you need to edit it.

Caution   Remember that Excel expands the references to include the full path, which can increase the length of the formula. Therefore, this expansion may cause the formula to exceed the limit, thus creating an invalid formula.

If the worksheets that you're consolidating aren't laid out the same, you can still use formulas, but you need to ensure that each formula refers to the correct cell.

Consolidating worksheets by using Paste Special

Another method of consolidating information is to use the Edit ➪ Paste Special command. This method is applicable only when all the worksheets that you're consolidating are open. The disadvantage is that the consolidation isn't dynamic. In other words, it doesn't generate formulas. So, if any data that was consolidated changes, the consolidation is no longer accurate.

This technique takes advantage of the fact that the Paste Special command can perform a mathematical operation when it pastes data from the Clipboard. For example, you can use the Add option to add the copied data to the selected range. Figure 29-4 shows the Paste Special dialog box.

Figure 29-4: The Paste Special dialog box.

Here's how to use this method:

1. Copy the data from the first source range.

2. Activate the destination workbook and select a location for the consolidated data.

3. Select Edit ➪ Paste Special. In the Paste Special dialog box, choose the Values option and the Add operation. Then click OK.

Repeat these steps for each source range that you want to consolidate. This method can be rather error-prone, and it isn't really the best method of consolidating data.

Consolidating worksheets by using the Consolidate command

For the ultimate in data consolidation, use Excel's Data ➪ Consolidate command. This method is very flexible, and in some cases, it even works if the source worksheets aren't laid out identically. This technique can create consolidations that are static (no link formulas) or dynamic (with link formulas). The Data ➪ Consolidate command supports the following methods of consolidation:

✦ **By position:** This method is accurate only if the worksheets are laid out identically.

✦ **By category:** Excel uses row and column labels to match data in the source worksheets. Use this option if the data is laid out differently in the source worksheets or if some source worksheets are missing rows or columns.

Figure 29-5 shows the Consolidate dialog box, which appears when you select Data ➪ Consolidate. Following is a description of the controls in this dialog box:

✦ **Function list box:** Specify the type of consolidation. Usually, you use Sum, but you also can select from 10 other options.

✦ **Reference text box:** Specify a range from a source file that you want to consolidate. You can enter the range reference manually or use any standard pointing technique (if the workbook is open). After you enter the range in this box, click the Add button to add it to the All References list. If you consolidate by position, don't include labels in the range. If you consolidate by category, *do* include labels in the range.

✦ **All References list box:** Contains the list of references that you have added with the Add button.

✦ **Use Labels In check boxes:** Use to instruct Excel to perform the consolidation by examining the labels in the top row, the left column, or both positions. Use these options when you consolidate by category.

✦ **Create Links to Source Data check box:** When you select this option, Excel adds summary formulas for each label and creates an outline. If you don't select this option, the consolidation doesn't use formulas.

✦ **Browse button:** Displays a dialog box that enables you to select a workbook to open. It inserts the filename in the Reference box, but you have to supply the range reference. You'll find that it's much easier if all of the workbooks to be consolidated are open.

✦ **Add button:** Adds the reference in the Reference box to the All References list.

✦ **Delete button:** Deletes the selected reference from the All References list.

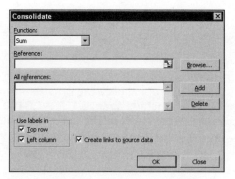

Figure 29-5: The Consolidate dialog box enables you to specify ranges to consolidate.

An example

The simple example in this section demonstrates the power of the Data ⇨ Consolidate command. Figure 29-6 shows three single-sheet workbooks that will be consolidated. These worksheets report product sales for three months. Notice, however, that they don't all report on the same products. In addition, the products aren't even listed in the same order. In other words, these worksheets aren't laid out identically. Creating consolidation formulas manually would be a very tedious task.

On the CD-ROM These workbooks are available on the companion CD-ROM.

To consolidate this information, start with a new workbook. The source workbooks can be open or not — it doesn't matter. Follow these steps to consolidate the workbooks:

1. Select Data ⇨ Consolidate. Excel displays its Consolidate dialog box.

2. Select the type of consolidation summary that you want to use. Use Sum for this example.

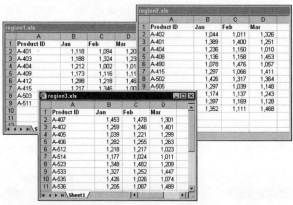

Figure 29-6: Three worksheets to be consolidated.

3. Enter the reference for the first worksheet to consolidate. If the workbook is open, you can point to the reference. If it's not open, click the Browse button to locate the file on disk. The reference must include a range. Use **A1:D100**. This range is larger than the actual range to consolidate, but using this range ensures that the consolidation still works if new rows are added to the source file. When the reference in the Reference box is correct, click Add to add it to the All References list.

4. Enter the reference for the second worksheet. You can simply edit the existing reference by changing Region1 to **Region2** and then clicking Add. This reference is added to the All References list.

5. Enter the reference for the third worksheet. Again, you can edit the existing reference by changing Region2 to **Region3** and then clicking Add. This final reference is added to the All References list.

6. Because the worksheets aren't laid out the same, select the Left column and Top row check boxes to force Excel to match the data by using the labels.

7. Select the Create Links to Source Data check box to make Excel create an outline with external references.

8. Click OK to begin the consolidation.

Excel creates the consolidation, beginning at the active cell. Figure 29-7 shows the result. Notice that Excel created an outline, which is collapsed to show only the subtotals for each product. If you expand the outline (by clicking the + symbols), you can see the details. Examine it further, and you discover that each detail cell is an external reference formula that uses the appropriate cell in the source file. Therefore, the destination range is updated automatically if any data is changed.

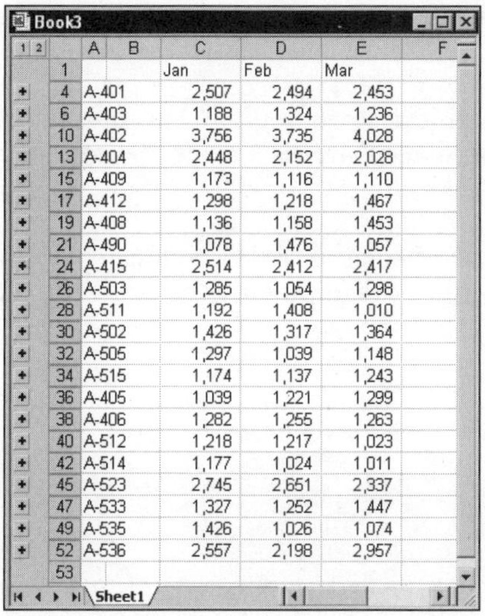

Figure 29-7: The result of the consolidation.

More about consolidation

Excel is very flexible regarding the sources that you can consolidate. You can consolidate data from the following:

✦ Workbooks that are open.

✦ Workbooks that are closed. (You need to enter the reference manually, but you can use the Browse button to get the filename part of the reference.)

✦ The same workbook in which you're creating the consolidation.

And, of course, you can mix and match any of the preceding choices in a single consolidation.

Excel remembers the references that you entered in the Consolidate dialog box and saves them with the workbook. Therefore, if you want to refresh a consolidation later, you won't have to re-enter the references.

If you perform the consolidation by matching labels, be aware that the matches must be exact. For example, *Jan* does not match *January*. The matching is not case-sensitive, however, so *April* does match *APRIL*. In addition, the labels can be in any order, and they need not be in the same order in all the source ranges.

If you don't choose the Create Links to Source Data check box, Excel generates a static consolidation. (It doesn't create formulas.) Therefore, if the data on any of the source worksheets changes, the consolidation doesn't update automatically.

To update the summary information, you need to select the destination range and repeat the Data ⇨ Consolidate command.

Tip   If you name the destination range **Consolidate_Area**, you don't need to select it before you update the consolidation. Consolidate_Area is a name that has special meaning to Excel.

If you choose the Create Links to Source Data check box, Excel creates an outline. This is a standard worksheet outline, and you can manipulate it by using the techniques described in Chapter 28.

✦   ✦   ✦

Excel and the Internet

◆ ◆ ◆ ◆

In This Chapter

Saving Excel files in HTML format

Saving interactive spreadsheets in HTML format

Using Excel's Internet tools

◆ ◆ ◆ ◆

These days, most people who use a computer are connected to the Internet. The Web has become an important way to share and gather information from a myriad of sources. To help you with these tasks, Excel has the capability to create files that can be used on the Internet, and also to gather and process data from the Web. This chapter covers topics related to Excel and the Internet.

Cross-Reference If you're looking for information about the new XML features in Excel 2003, refer to Chapter 31.

Understanding How Excel Uses HTML

HTML is the language of the World Wide Web. When you browse the Web, the documents that are retrieved and displayed by your browser are usually in HTML format. An HTML file consists of text information plus special tags that describe how the text is to be formatted. The browser interprets the tags, applies the formatting, and displays the information.

Excel 2000 and later versions can use HTML as a native file format. In other words, you can save a workbook in HTML format and then reopen that HTML file in Excel. Your work will look exactly as it did before you first saved it. All of the Excel-specific information (such as macros, charts, pivot tables, and worksheet settings) remains intact. The fact that an Excel workbook can survive the "round trip" is just short of amazing.

Caution Using HTML as a native file format may be amazing, but I think that Microsoft may have overemphasized the importance of this feature. In real life, this simply isn't very useful except in a small number of situations. The main problem is that the resulting HTML file is huge — much larger than you might expect.

How does it work?

The best way to understand how Excel workbooks can be saved as HTML files is to perform some simple experiments. Start with a new workbook and make sure that it has only one worksheet. Enter a few values and a formula, do some simple formatting, and then save the workbook in HTML format. Use the File ➪ Save As Web Page command. Make sure that you select the Entire Workbook option, and select Web Page (*.htm, *.html) as the Save As Type. Figure 30-1 shows a very simple workbook consisting of two values and a formula, with the formula cell formatted bold.

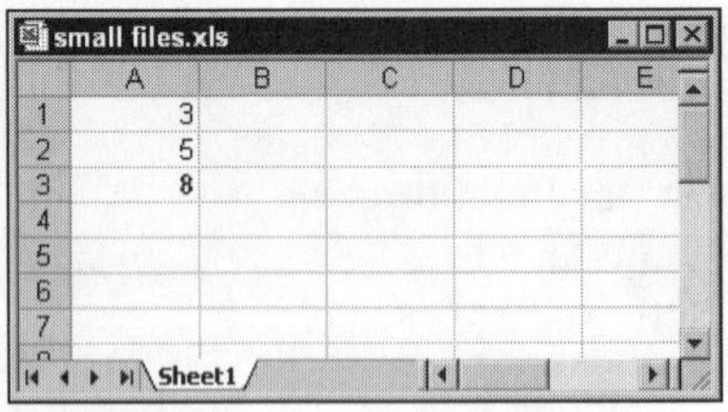

Figure 30-1: Try saving a simple workbook like this in HTML format.

Next, open the HTML file in your browser. It will look pretty much like the original workbook. However, it is a *dead* (noninteractive) document, meaning that you can't change any of the values. Use the browser's View ➪ Source command to view the HTML code. You may be surprised by what you see. Even HTML gurus may be overwhelmed by the complexity of this "simple" Web document.

Here are a few observations about the HTML file:

✦ The entire Excel workbook can be represented by a single HTML file. In other words, all the information needed to create an exact replica of the original workbook is usually contained in the HTML file. This isn't always the case, however. Keep reading to find out when a simple HTML file no longer suffices.

✦ Most of the document is contained within the <head> and </head> tags.

✦ A large portion consists of style definitions. This is the information between the <style> and </style> tags — which are embedded between the <head> and </head> tags.

✦ The actual text that's displayed in the browser is contained in a table (between the <table> and </table> tags).

✦ The formula is preserved by using a proprietary argument for the <td> tag. The proprietary argument is ignored by browsers, but Excel uses this information when the file is reopened.

The HTML file produced for the simple workbook is more than 4,000 bytes in size, which is quite large considering the simplicity of the displayed page. The extra information, of course, is what Excel uses to create a workbook when it reopens the HTML file.

Adding some complexity

The example workbook used in the preceding section is about as simple as it gets. Now, just add a small bit of complexity to the workbook and see what happens to the HTML file.

Using the simple example file, select A1:A3 and press F11 to create a new chart sheet. Save the file again, and then load it in your browser. You'll find that it still closely resembles the Excel workbook, even down to the sheet tabs and navigation arrows at the bottom.

The HTML file has more than doubled in size (it's now up to about 10,000 bytes). More importantly, you'll find that the directory in which you saved the file has a new subdirectory that contains additional files (six extra files using my simple workbook). The files in this subdirectory are necessary to display a replica of the workbook in a browser and to re-create the workbook when the HTML file is reopened in Excel.

If you examine the HTML file, you'll see that it's *much* more complicated than the original one and contains quite a bit of complex JavaScript code. (*JavaScript* is a scripting language supported by most browsers.) At this point, the HTML file has gotten well beyond the grasp of your average HTML author. And that's not even taking into account the other files dumped into the subdirectory.

Creating Smaller HTML Files

As I've noted, exporting your Excel data to an HTML file usually produces very large files. If you'd prefer to create smaller files, you have two options:

✦ Locate a third-party Excel add-in that creates HTML files. Several utilities are available. My Power Utility Pak, for example, enables you to create an HTML file from an entire worksheet or a specific range. The resulting file will be much smaller than if you use Excel's File ⇨ Save as Web Page command. A trial version is available on the companion CD-ROM.

✦ Download a copy of Microsoft's Office 2000 HTML Filter. This program will strip out the Office-specific tags in Excel workbooks (or Word documents). Search the Web for "Office 2000 HTML Filter," and you should find it at Microsoft's Web site. I don't provide the URL because Microsoft rearranges its content very frequently.

Note When saving a document as a Web page, the default file format is a Single File Web Page (*.mht; *.mhtml). If you use this option, the workbook is saved as a single file in the Web archive format. Also, be aware that Internet Explorer is probably the only Web browser that can read this file format.

What about interactivity?

Here I introduce yet another level of complexity. Excel can also save HTML files that include spreadsheet interactivity. In other words, when the HTML file is displayed in a browser, the user can actually interact with the document as a spreadsheet — enter data, change formulas, adjust cell formatting, see "live" charts, and even drag data around in pivot tables. This feature is limited in that you can only save one sheet (not an entire workbook).

Caution Microsoft Internet Explorer 5.0 or later is required to open a spreadsheet saved in this format.

To get a feel for how this works, activate a sheet that contains formulas. Use the File ➪ Save As Web Page command. In the Save As dialog box, choose the Selection: Sheet option and place a check mark next to Add Interactivity. Click the Publish button. You get another dialog box (Publish as Web Page). Accept the defaults and click Publish.

When you open the HTML file in Internet Explorer, you find that it displays a spreadsheet-like object that is, in fact, interactive. Figure 30-2 shows an example.

On the CD-ROM This file is available on the companion CD-ROM.

When you choose the Add Interactivity option, the HTML file contains an Office Web Component (an ActiveX control). This means that the user can perform standard Excel operations directly in the browser. For example, the user can change cells or manipulate data in a pivot table. Keep in mind that the interactivity is limited. For example, you can't execute macros when an interactive Excel file is displayed in a browser. In addition, it is not possible to save any changes made to the worksheet.

Everyone who accesses such a spreadsheet must have a license for Microsoft Office and have the Office Web Components installed on his or her system. If this is not the case, the information can be viewed, but without interactivity. Because of this, the end-user must have a license for the Microsoft Web Components ActiveX control in order to view an interactive Excel file in his or her browser. In other words, you would not want to post such a file on your Web site. These files are best used on a corporate intranet, in which everyone has the appropriate license.

Rebuilding Workbooks by Using HTML

As you work with Excel, you may notice that some workbooks become bloated — larger than they should be. These bloated files may eventually become corrupt to the point where they can no longer be opened.

One way to eliminate this bloat is to rebuild your workbook. And the easiest way to do that is to export the workbook as HTML. Then open the HTML version and save it to the standard XLS format.

For example I had an 8.8MB workbook file. I saved it to HTML, and the file (plus the corresponding directory) occupied 26.3MB. I reopened the HTML version and saved it back to XLS format. The new workbook then used only 5.2MB — a file size reduction of more than 40 percent.

You may expect that the HTML file generated for an interactive worksheet would be much more complex than the example in the previous section. In fact, the opposite is true. Such a worksheet occupies a single HTML file. The complexity is handled by an ActiveX control.

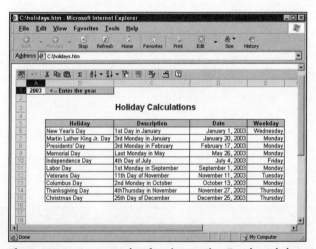

Figure 30-2: An example of an interactive Excel worksheet displayed in Internet Explorer.

Saving as an XML spreadsheet

Microsoft created an XML spreadsheet schema called XMLSS. The spreadsheet component of the Office Web Components can export data to this format, and you can also save your Excel workbook in XLMSS format.

Caution   When you save your file as an XML spreadsheet, you will lose quite a few elements, including charts, graphic objects, macros, and outlines. In other words, this is definitely not a "round-trip" file format for Excel.

When you view an XML spreadsheet file in a Web browser, you'll see the hierarchical data, as in Figure 30-3.

Figure 30-3: Viewing an XMLSS file in Microsoft Internet Explorer.

So what's the point? This file format may be useful if you need to create an Excel-readable file from a different application (without actually using Excel).

Web Options

If you save your work in HTML format, you should be aware of some additional options. Select Tools ⇨ Options, click the General tab, and then click the Web Options button. You'll see the Web Options dialog box. Most of the time, the default settings work just fine. However, familiarizing yourself with the options available is worthwhile. (These options are described in the online Help.) You can also access the Web Options dialog box from the Tools menu in the Save As dialog box.

Working with Hyperlinks

Hyperlinks are shortcuts that provide a quick way to jump to other workbooks and files. You can jump to files on your own computer, your network, and the Internet and Web. For example, you can create a series of hyperlinks to serve as a table of contents for a workbook.

Inserting a hyperlink

You can create hyperlinks from cell text or graphic objects, such as shapes and pictures. To create a text hyperlink, choose the Insert ⇨ Hyperlink command (or press Ctrl+K). Excel responds with the Insert Hyperlink dialog box, as shown in Figure 30-4.

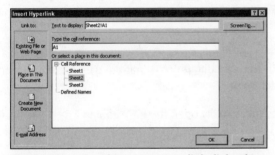

Figure 30-4: Use the Insert Hyperlink dialog box to add hyperlinks to your Excel worksheets.

Select an icon in the Link To column that represents the type of hyperlink you want to create. Then, specify the location for the file that you want to link to. The dialog box changes, depending on the icon selected. Click OK, and Excel creates the hyperlink in the active cell.

You can create hyperlinks to a file on your hard drive, a Web page on the Internet, a new document, or a location in your current workbook. In addition, you can create a hyperlink that consists of an e-mail address.

Adding a hyperlink to a graphic object works the same way. Add an object to your worksheet by using the Drawing toolbar. Select the object and then choose the Insert ⇨ Hyperlink command. Specify the required information as outlined in the previous paragraph.

Using hyperlinks

When working with hyperlinks, remember that Excel attempts to mimic a Web browser. For example, when you click a hyperlink, the hyperlinked document replaces the current document — it takes on the same window size and position. You can use the Back and Forward buttons on the Web toolbar to activate the documents.

If the hyperlink contains an e-mail address, your default e-mail program will be launched so you can send an e-mail.

Using Web Queries

Excel enables you to pull in data contained in an HTML file by performing a Web query. The data is transferred to a worksheet, where you can manipulate it any way you like.

This procedure is very similar to creating a query that uses an external database, which I discuss in Chapter 20. The only difference is that the data is coming from a Web page rather than a database file.

Performing a Web query does not actually open the HTML file in Excel — rather, it copies the information from the HTML file.

The best part about a Web query is that Excel remembers where the data came from. Therefore, after you create a Web query, you can *refresh* the query to pull in the most recent data.

To create a Web query, select Data ➪ Import External Data ➪ New Web Query. Excel displays the New Query dialog box, as shown in Figure 30-5. To begin, specify the address of the HTML file in the Address box. The HTML file can be on the Internet, on a corporate intranet, or on a local or network drive. Next, click to select the table you wish to import. Each table is indicated by an arrow in a yellow box (see Figure 30-5). Click Import, and you get the Import Data dialog box, asking where you want to place the data.

After you create your Web query, you have some options. Activate any cell in the data range and select Data ➪ Import External Data ➪ Data Range Properties. Or you can right-click any cell in the data range and select Data Range Properties from the shortcut menu. Either method displays the External Data Range Properties dialog box, shown in Figure 30-6. Adjust the settings to your liking.

Web queries are especially useful for data that is frequently updated — such as stock market quotes.

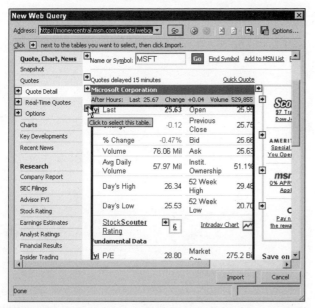

Figure 30-5: Use the New Web Query dialog box to specify the source of the data.

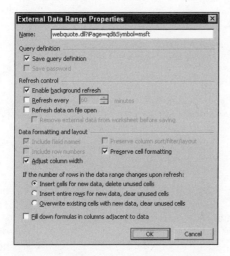

Figure 30-6: Use the External Data Range Properties dialog box to specify how Excel handles the imported data.

✦ ✦ ✦

Sharing Data with Other Applications

Some Windows applications are designed to work together. The applications in Microsoft Office are an excellent example of this. These programs have a common look and feel, and sharing data among these applications is quite easy. This chapter explores some ways in which you can make use of other applications while working with Excel as well as some ways in which you can use Excel while working with other applications.

In addition, the chapter provides an introduction to the new XML features introduced in Excel 2003. XML files offer another way to share data between applications.

Understanding Data Sharing

Besides importing and exporting files, you can transfer data to and from other Windows applications in several other ways:

✦ Copy and paste, using either the Windows Clipboard or the Office Clipboard. Copying and pasting information creates a static copy of the data.

✦ Create a link so that changes in the source data are reflected in the destination document.

✦ Embed an entire object from one application into another application's document.

✦ Use an XML file to store the data.

This chapter discusses these techniques and shows you how to use them.

Pasting and Linking Data

This section describes various ways to paste and link data.

Using the Clipboards

Whenever Windows is running, you have access to the Windows Clipboard—an area of your computer's memory that acts as a shared holding area for information that you have cut or copied from an application. The Windows Clipboard works behind the scenes, and you usually aren't aware of it. Whenever you select data and then choose either Edit ➪ Copy or Edit ➪ Cut, the application places the selected data on the Windows Clipboard. Excel can then access the Clipboard data when you choose the Edit ➪ Paste command (or the Edit ➪ Paste Special command).

 Note

If you copy or cut information while working in an Office application, the application places the copied information on both the Windows Clipboard and the Office Clipboard. After you copy information to the Windows Clipboard, it remains on the Windows Clipboard even after you paste it, so you can use it multiple times. However, because the Windows Clipboard can hold only one item at a time, when you copy or cut something else, the information previously stored on the Windows Clipboard is replaced. The Office Clipboard, unlike the Windows Clipboard, can hold up to 24 separate selections. The Office Clipboard operates in all Office applications; for example, you can copy two selections from Word and three from Excel and paste any or all of them in PowerPoint.

Copying information from one Windows application to another is quite easy. The application that contains the information that you're copying is called the *source* application, and the application to which you're copying the information is called the *destination* application.

The general steps that are required to copy from one application to another are

1. Activate the source document window that contains the information that you want to copy.

2. Select the information by using the mouse or the keyboard.

3. Select Edit ➪ Copy.

4. Activate the destination application. If the program isn't running, you can start it without affecting the contents of the Clipboards.

5. Move to the appropriate position in the destination application (where you want to paste the copied material).

6. Select Edit ➪ Paste from the menu in the destination application. If the Clipboard contents are not appropriate for pasting, the Paste command is grayed (not available). You can sometimes select the Edit ➪ Paste Special command, which displays a dialog box that presents different pasting options.

In Step 3 in the preceding steps, you also can select Edit ⇨ Cut from the source application menu. This step erases your selection from the source application after placing the selection on the Clipboard.

Note   If you repeat Step 3 in any Office application, the Office Clipboard task pane appears automatically. If it does not, select Edit ⇨ Office Clipboard.

To see an example of how this works, try copying an Excel chart into a Microsoft Word report. First, select the chart in Excel by clicking it once. Then copy it to the Clipboard by choosing Edit ⇨ Copy. Next, activate the Word document into which you want to paste the copy of the chart and move the insertion point to the place where you want the chart to appear. When you select Edit ⇨ Paste from the Word menu bar, the chart is pasted from the Clipboard and appears in your document (see Figure 31-1).

Note   Windows applications vary in the way that they respond to pasted data. If the Edit ⇨ Paste command is not available (is grayed on the menu) in the destination application, the application can't accept the information from the Clipboard. If you copy a range of data from Excel and paste it into Word, Word creates a table when you paste the data. Other applications may respond differently to Excel data.

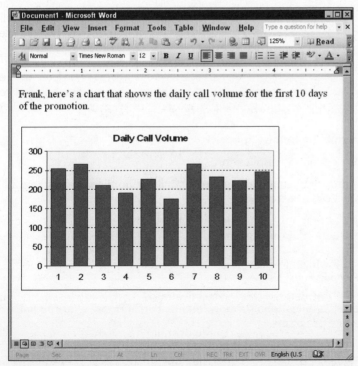

Figure 31-1: An Excel chart has been added to this Word document.

The copy-and-paste technique is static. In other words, no link exists between the information that you copy from the source application and the information that you paste into the destination application. If you're copying from Excel to a Word document, for example, the Word document *will not* reflect any subsequent changes that you make in your Excel worksheet or charts. Consequently, you have to repeat the copy-and-paste procedure to update the destination document with the source document changes. The next topic presents a way to get around this limitation.

Linking data

If you want to share data that may change, the static copy-and-paste procedure described in the preceding section isn't your best choice. Instead, you can create a dynamic link between the data that you copy from one Windows application to another. In this way, if you change the data in the source document, you don't *also* need to make the changes in the destination document because the link automatically updates the destination document.

> **Note**   Applications vary in how they handle linked data. In some situations, you may need to update the linked data manually.

When would you want to use this technique? If you generate proposals by using Word, for example, you may need to refer to pricing information that you store in an Excel worksheet. If you set up a link between your Word document and the Excel worksheet, you can be sure that your proposals always quote the latest prices. Not all Windows applications support dynamic linking, so you must make sure that the application to which you are copying is capable of handling such a link.

Setting up a link from one Windows application to another varies slightly from application to application. These are the general steps to take:

1. Copy the information to the Clipboard.

2. Switch to the destination application.

3. Select the appropriate command in the destination application to paste a link. This is usually Edit ⇨ Paste Special.

4. In the dialog box that appears, specify the type of link that you want to create. (See the next section, "Copying Excel data to Word," for an example.)

Keep in mind the following information when you're using links between two applications:

✦ Not all Windows applications support linking. Furthermore, you can link from, but not to, some programs.

✦ When you save an Excel file that has a link, you save the most-recent values with the document. When you reopen this document, Excel asks whether you want to update the links.

✦ Links can be broken rather easily. If you move the source document to another directory or save it under a different name, for example, the destination document's application won't be able to update the link. In such a case, you'll need to re-establish the link manually.

✦ You can use the Edit ⇨ Links command to break a link. After breaking a link, the data remains in the destination document, but it is no longer linked to the source document.

✦ In Excel, external links are sometimes stored in array formulas. If so, you can modify a link by editing the array formula.

Copying Excel data to Word

One of the most frequently used software combinations is a spreadsheet and a word processor. This section discusses the types of links that you can create by using Microsoft Word to create documents that include data from Excel.

Figure 31-2 shows the Paste Special dialog box from Microsoft Word after a range of data has been copied from Excel. The result that you get depends on whether you select the Paste or the Paste Link option and on your choice of the type of item to paste. If you select the Paste Link option, you can check the Display As Icon check box in order to have the information pasted as an icon. If you do so, you can double-click this icon to activate the source worksheet.

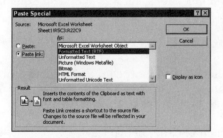

Figure 31-2: Use the Paste Special dialog box to specify the type of link to create.

Pasting without a link

Often, you don't need a link when you copy data. For example, if you're preparing a report in your word processor and you simply want to include a range of data from an Excel worksheet, you probably don't need to create a link.

If you select one of the choices in the Paste Special dialog box with the Paste option selected, the data is pasted without creating a link.

Tip

The pasted data looks the same regardless of whether the Paste or Paste Link option is selected.

Some Excel formatting does not transfer when pasted to Word as formatted text. For example, Word doesn't support vertical alignment for table cells (but you can use Word's paragraph formatting commands to apply vertical alignment).

Pasting with a link

If you think the data that you're copying will change, you may want to paste a link. If you paste the data by using the Paste Link option in the Paste Special dialog box, you can make changes to the source document, and the changes appear in the destination application (a few seconds of delay may occur). You can test these changes by displaying both applications on-screen, making changes to the source document, and watching for them to appear in the destination document.

Embedding Objects in Documents

Using *Object Linking and Embedding* (OLE), you can also embed an object to share information between Windows applications. This technique enables you to insert an object from another program and use that program's editing tools to manipulate it. The OLE objects can be such items as these:

✦ Text documents from other products, such as word processors

✦ Drawings or pictures from other products

✦ Information from special OLE server applications, such as Microsoft Equation

✦ Sound files

✦ Video or animation files

Many (but certainly not all) Windows applications support OLE. Embedding is often used for a document that you will distribute to others. It can eliminate the need to send multiple document files and help avoid broken link problems.

You can embed an object into your document in either of two ways:

✦ Choose Edit ➪ Paste Special and then select the "object" choice (if it's available). If you do this, select the Paste option rather than the Paste Link option.

✦ Select Insert ➪ Object.

Caution   Embedding an object can cause a dramatic increase in the size of your document.

Tip   Some applications—such as those in Microsoft Office—allow you to embed an object by dragging it from one application to another.

The following sections discuss these two methods and provide a few examples using Excel and Word.

Embedding an Excel range in a Word document

This example embeds in a Word document the Excel range shown in Figure 31-3.

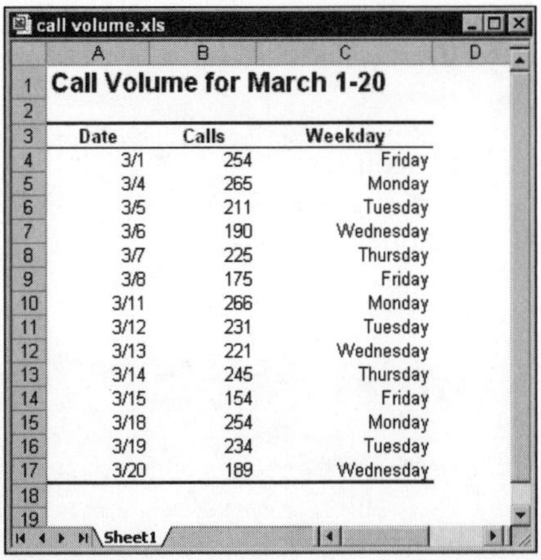

	A	B	C
1	Call Volume for March 1-20		
2			
3	Date	Calls	Weekday
4	3/1	254	Friday
5	3/4	265	Monday
6	3/5	211	Tuesday
7	3/6	190	Wednesday
8	3/7	225	Thursday
9	3/8	175	Friday
10	3/11	266	Monday
11	3/12	231	Tuesday
12	3/13	221	Wednesday
13	3/14	245	Thursday
14	3/15	154	Friday
15	3/18	254	Monday
16	3/19	234	Tuesday
17	3/20	189	Wednesday

Figure 31-3: This worksheet includes a range that will be embedded in a Word document.

To start, select A1:C17 and copy the range. Then activate (or start) Word, open the document in which you want to embed the range, and move the insertion point to the location in the document where you want the table to appear. Choose Word's Edit ⇨ Paste Special command. Select the Paste option (not the Paste Link option) and choose the Microsoft Excel Worksheet Object format. Click OK, and the range appears in the Word document.

The pasted object is not a standard Word table. For example, you can't select or format individual cells in the table. Furthermore, it's not linked to the Excel source range. If you change a value in the Excel worksheet, the change does not appear in the embedded object in the Word document.

If you double-click the object, however, you notice something unusual: Word's menus and toolbars change to those used by Excel. In addition, the embedded object appears with Excel's familiar row and column borders. In other words, you can edit this object *in place* by using Excel's commands. Figure 31-4 shows how this looks. To return to Word, just click anywhere in the Word document.

Caution

Remember that no link is involved here. If you make changes to the embedded object in Word, these changes do not appear in the original Excel worksheet. The embedded object is completely independent from the original source.

By using this technique, you have access to all of Excel's features while you are still in Word.

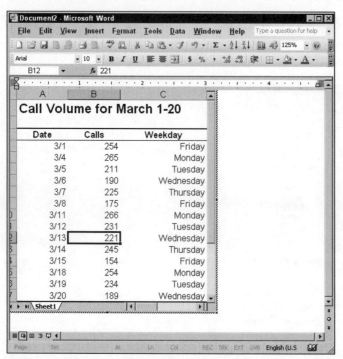

Figure 31-4: Double-clicking the embedded Excel object enables you to edit it in place. Note that Word now displays Excel's menus and toolbars.

Tip   You can accomplish the embedding previously described by selecting the range in Excel and then dragging it to your Word document. In fact, you can use the Windows desktop as an intermediary storage location. For example, you can drag a range from Excel to the desktop and create a scrap. Then you can drag this scrap into your Word document. The result is an embedded Excel object.

Creating a new Excel object in Word

The preceding example embeds a range from an existing Excel worksheet into a Word document. This section demonstrates how to create a new (empty) Excel object in Word. This may be useful if you're creating a report and need to insert a table of values that doesn't exist in a worksheet.

Tip   You could insert a normal Word table, but you can take advantage of Excel's formulas and functions in an embedded Excel worksheet.

To create a new Excel object in a Word document, choose Insert ⇨ Object in Word. Word responds with the Object dialog box. The Create New tab lists the types of objects that you can create. (The contents of the list depend on the applications that you have installed on your system.) Choose the Microsoft Excel Worksheet option and click OK.

Word inserts an empty Excel worksheet object into the document and activates it for you, as shown in Figure 31-5. You have full access to Excel commands, so you can enter whatever you want into the worksheet object. After you finish, click anywhere in the Word document. You can, of course, double-click this object at any time to make changes or additions.

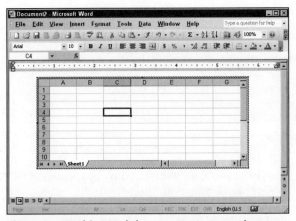

Figure 31-5: This Word document now contains an empty Excel worksheet object.

You can change the size of the object while it's activated by dragging any of the sizing handles (the little black squares and rectangles) that appear on the borders of the object. You also can crop the object so that when it isn't activated, the object displays only cells that contain information. To crop an object in Word, select the object so that you can see sizing handles. Then, display Word's Picture toolbar (right-click any toolbar button and choose Picture). Click the Cropping tool (it looks like a pair of plus signs), and then drag any sizing handle on the object.

Note   Even if you crop an Excel worksheet object in Word, double-clicking the object gives you access to all rows and columns in Excel. Cropping changes only the displayed area of the object.

Tip   When you click outside the Excel worksheet object, the worksheet's scroll bars, tabs, gridlines, and so on will disappear. Any data that you have added will remain visible, however.

Embedding objects in an Excel worksheet

The preceding examples involve embedding Excel objects in a Word document. The same procedures can be used to embed other objects into an Excel worksheet.

For example, if you have an Excel workbook that requires a great amount of explanatory text, you have several choices:

✦ You can enter the text into cells. This, however, is tedious and doesn't allow much formatting.

✦ You can use a text box. This is a good alternative, but it doesn't offer many formatting features.

✦ You can embed a Word document in your worksheet. This gives you full access to all of Word's formatting features.

To embed an empty Word document into an Excel worksheet, choose Excel's Insert ⇨ Object command. In the Object dialog box, click the Create New tab and select Microsoft Word Document from the Object type list.

The result is a blank Word document, activated and ready for you to enter text. Notice that Word's menus and toolbars replace Excel's menus and toolbars. You can resize the document as you like, and the words wrap accordingly.

You can embed many other types of objects, including audio clips, video clips, MIDI sequences, and even an entire Microsoft PowerPoint presentation.

Microsoft Office includes several additional applications that you may find useful. For example, you can embed a Microsoft Equation object in an Excel document to graphically illustrate a formula that you use in a worksheet.

Tip

Some of the object types listed in the Object dialog box can result in quite useful and interesting items when inserted into an Excel worksheet. If you're not sure what an object type is, try adding the object to a blank Excel workbook to see what is available.

Working with XML Data

This section introduces the new XML features found in Excel 2003. This feature provides another way to share data with other applications.

New Feature

This section is relevant only to those who use Excel 2003. If you're using Excel 2000 or Excel 2002, you'll find that you can open some XML files in Excel (using the File ⇨ Open command). But the features described here will not work.

What is XML?

XML is an accepted standard that enables exchange of data between different applications. XML is a markup language, just as HTML is a markup language.

XML uses tags to define elements within a document. XML tags define the document's structural elements and the meaning of those elements. Unlike HTML tags, which specify how a document looks or is formatted, XML can be used to define the document structure and content. Consequently, XML separates a document's content from its presentation.

Following is a very simple XML file that contains data from an e-mail message.

```
<?xml version="1.0" encoding="UTF-8"?>
<message>
<to>Bill Smith</to>
<from>Mark Jackson</from>
<subject>Meeting date</subject>
<body>The meeting will be at 8:00 a.m. on Tuesday</body>
</message>
```

When the file is viewed in Internet Explorer, the browser displays it as a structured document (as shown in Figure 31-6).

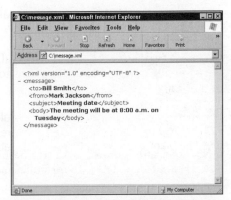

Figure 31-6: Internet Explorer displays XML files in a structured format.

Unlike HTML, the XML specification does not specify the tags themselves. Rather, it provides a standard way to define tags and relationships. Because there are no predefined tags, XML can be used to model virtually any type of document.

Note   This is an admittedly cursory overview of XML. Fact is, XML can be extremely complex. Many entire books are devoted to XML.

The two sections that follow consist of simplistic examples to give you a feel for how Excel handles XML.

Importing XML data by using a map

This example uses the worksheet shown in Figure 31-7. This worksheet uses data in column B to generate a loan amortization schedule. Assume that a back-end system generates XML files and each file contains data for a customer. An example of such a file is shown below:

```
<?xml version="1.0"?>
<Customer>
  <Name>Joe Smith</Name>
  <AcctNo>32374-94</AcctNo>
  <LoanAmt>$325,983</LoanAmt>
  <IntRate>6.25%</IntRate>
  <Term>30</Term>
</Customer>
```

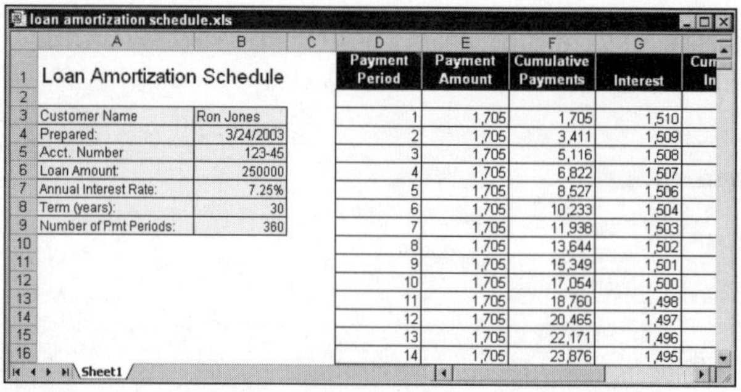

Figure 31-7: This worksheet uses imported XML data.

This file has five data elements: Name, AcctNo, LoanAmt, IntRate, and Term. Two of the fields (Prepared and Number of Pmt Periods) are calculated with formulas and are not considered data elements.

The trick here is to be able to import files, such as this, and have the data sent to the appropriate cells in the worksheet.

The first step is to add a Map to the workbook. Make sure that XML Source is displayed in the task pane (select Data ➪ XML ➪ XML Source).

To add the Map, follow these steps:

1. Click the Workbook Maps button at the bottom of the task pane. The XML Maps dialog box appears.

2. Click Add to display the XML Source dialog box.

3. Select one of the customer XML files. The exact file doesn't matter. This will be used only to infer the schema.

4. Click OK to dismiss the XML Maps dialog box.

   The task pane displays the data elements from the file (as shown in Figure 31-8).

Figure 31-8: The task pane shows the XML data elements.

The next step is to map the data elements to the appropriate worksheet cells.

1. In the task pane, click the Name element and drag it to cell B3.

2. Drag the AcctNo element to cell B5.

3. Drag the LoanAmt element to cell B6.

4. Drag the IntRate element to cell B7.

5. Drag the Term element to cell B8.

Finally, you can import an XML file. Choose Data ➪ XML ➪ Import, and select a customer XML file. You'll find that the data is fed into the appropriate cells. To calculate another amortization schedule, just import another XML file.

On the CD-ROM This workbook and two XML data files are available on the companion CD-ROM.

Importing XML data to a list

The example in the preceding section used XML files that contained only a single "record." XML files often contain multiple records, called *repeating elements*. Examples include a customer list or data for all employees in an organization.

You can use Excel's File ➪ Open command to open an XML file that contains repeating elements. After you specify the filename, Excel presents the Open XML dialog box, as shown in Figure 31-9. This dialog box has three options:

✦ **As an XML List:** The file opens, and Excel converts the data to a List Range (see Chapter 19).

✦ **As a Read-Only Workbook:** The data is imported into the worksheet, but the workbook is read-only. This is to prevent you from accidentally overwriting the original file.

✦ **Use the XML Source Task Pane:** Excel infers the schema for the XML data and displays it in the task pane. (The data is not actually imported.) You can then map the elements to cells and import the actual data.

Figure 31-9: The Open XML dialog box.

Figure 31-10 shows an XML file that has been imported to a worksheet.

Note   When displayed in the task pane, repeating elements use a different icon (a "double folder"). Nonrepeating elements display a single folder icon.

Exporting XML data from Excel

In order to export data to an XML file, you must add a map to the workbook, and the map must correspond to your data. Then you can use the Data ➪ XML ➪ Export command to create an XML file.

Contrary to what you may expect, it's not possible to export an arbitrary range of data in XML format. For example, if you create a List Range on your worksheet, you can't export that List Range to an XML file unless you add an appropriate map to your worksheet first. And it's not possible to create (or modify) a map using Excel.

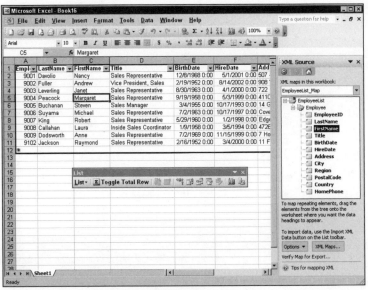

Figure 31-10: The imported XML data.

Note If you use Excel's File ➪ Save As command, you'll notice that one of the options is XML Spreadsheet. This produces an XML file that uses Microsoft's XMLSS schema. It will not export the data to a "normal" XML file.

✦   ✦   ✦

Using Excel in a Workgroup

Networks have become one of the most important pro-ductivity enhancements in the PC world. By enabling users to easily share data, networks have made it far easier for people to work together on projects. Excel has a number of features that facilitate this type of cooperation, and those features are the subject of this chapter.

Note   If you're working on a corporate network, you may need to consult with your network administrator before using any of the features described in this chapter.

Using Excel on a Network

A computer network consists of a group of PCs that are linked electronically. Users on a network can perform these tasks:

+ Access files on other systems

+ Share files with other users

+ Share resources, such as printers and fax modems

+ Communicate with each other electronically

Excel has tools that enable you to work cooperatively with other Excel users on a single project. For example, you can send an Excel workbook to other users for their review. In addition, you can allow others to add their own data before returning the workbook or sending it on to the next person in a routing list. After all the additions have returned to you, Excel can easily incorporate those additions into your master copy of the workbook. In this way, a whole team of Excel users can contribute to a project effectively.

Understanding File Reservations

Networks provide users with the ability to share information stored on other computer systems. Sharing files on a network has two major advantages:

✦ It eliminates the need to have multiple copies of the files stored locally on user PCs.

✦ It ensures that the file is always up-to-date; for example, if everyone makes changes to the same shared copy of a customer list, there's little likelihood that some portions of the list will be correct while other portions will be obsolete.

Note   Some networks—generally known as client-server networks—designate specific computers as file servers. On these types of networks, the shared data files are normally stored on the file server. Excel doesn't care whether you are working on a client-server or a peer-to-peer network (where all the PCs have essentially equal functions).

Some software applications are *multiuser applications*. Most database software applications, for example, enable multiple users to work simultaneously on the same database files. One user may be updating customer records in the database while another is extracting records. But what if a user is updating a customer record and another user wants to make a change to that same record? Multiuser database software contains record-locking safeguards that ensure that only one user at a time can modify a particular record.

Excel is *not* a multiuser application. When you open an Excel file, the entire file is loaded into memory. If the file is accessible to other users, you wouldn't want someone else to change the stored copy of a file that you've opened. If Excel allowed you to open and change a file that someone else on a network has already opened, the following scenario could happen.

Assume that your company keeps its sales information in an Excel file that is stored on a network server. Elaine wants to add this week's data to the file, so she loads it from the server and begins adding new information. A few minutes later, Albert loads the file to correct some errors that he noticed last week. Elaine finishes her work and saves the file. A while later, Albert finishes his corrections and saves the file. Albert's file overwrites the copy that Elaine saved, and her additions are gone.

This scenario *can't happen* because Excel uses a concept known as *file reservation*. When Elaine opens the sales file, she has the reservation for the file. When Albert tries to open the file, Excel informs him that Elaine is using the file. If he insists on opening it, Excel opens the file as *read-only*. In other words, Albert can open the file, but he can't save it under the same name. Figure 32-1 shows the message that Albert receives if he tries to open a file that is in use by someone else.

Figure 32-1: The File in Use dialog box appears if you try to open a file that someone else is using.

Albert has three choices:

✦ **Select Cancel, wait a while, and try again.** He may call Elaine and ask her when she expects to be finished.

✦ **Select Read Only.** This lets him open the file to read it, but it doesn't let him save changes to the same filename.

✦ **Select Notify, which opens the file as read-only.** Excel pops up a message that notifies Albert when Elaine is finished using the file.

Figure 32-2 shows the message that Albert receives when the file is available. If Albert opens the file as Read-Write, he will get another message if he has made any changes to his read-only version. He will have an opportunity to discard his changes or to save his file with a new name.

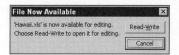

Figure 32-2: The File Now Available dialog box pops up with a new message when the file is available for editing.

Note   If you select Read Only, you can still save the file but only by using the File ➪ Save As command and specifying a different filename or a different location. You could, for example, save a local copy of the file instead of saving it back to the network drive where you opened the file.

Sharing Workbooks

Although Excel isn't a multiuser application, it does support a feature known as *shared workbooks,* which enables multiple users to work on the same workbook simultaneously. Excel keeps track of the changes and provides appropriate prompts to handle conflicts.

Caution   Although the ability to share workbooks sounds great in theory, it can be confusing if more than a few users are sharing a single workbook. Also, be warned that this feature has been known to cause problems, and it is certainly not 100 percent reliable. Therefore, use caution, and make frequent backup copies of your workbooks.

Understanding shared workbooks

Although you can share any Excel workbook, only certain workbooks contain information that is appropriate for sharing. The following are a few examples of workbooks that work well as shared workbooks:

✦ **Project tracking:** You may have a workbook that contains status information for projects. If multiple people are involved in the project, they can make changes and updates to the parts that are relevant.

✦ **Customer lists:** With a customer list, records are often added, deleted, and modified by multiple users.

✦ **Consolidations:** You may create a budget workbook in which each department manager is responsible for his or her department's budget. Usually, each department's budget appears on a separate sheet, with one sheet serving as the consolidation sheet.

If you plan to designate a workbook as shared, be aware that Excel imposes quite a few restrictions. For example, you cannot perform any of these actions while sharing the workbook:

✦ Delete worksheets or chart sheets.

✦ Insert or delete a blocks of cells. However, you can insert or delete entire rows and columns.

✦ Merge cells.

✦ Define or apply conditional formats.

✦ Set up or change data-validation restrictions and messages.

✦ Insert or change charts, pictures, drawings, objects, or hyperlinks.

✦ Assign or modify a password to protect individual worksheets or the entire workbook.

✦ Create or modify pivot tables, scenarios, outlines, or data tables.

✦ Insert automatic subtotals.

✦ Write, change, view, record, or assign macros. However, you can record a macro while a shared workbook is active as long as you store the macro in another unshared workbook.

Tip   You may want to use the Tools ⇨ Protection commands to further control what users can do while working in a shared workbook.

Designating a workbook as a shared workbook

To designate a workbook as a shared workbook, select Tools ⇨ Share Workbook. Excel displays the dialog box that is shown in Figure 32-3. This dialog box has two tabs: Editing and Advanced. In the Editing tab, select the check box to allow changes by multiple users and then click OK. Excel then prompts you to save the workbook.

Figure 32-3: Use the Share Workbook dialog box to control the sharing of your workbooks.

When you open a shared workbook, the window's title bar displays [Shared]. If you no longer want other users to be able to use the workbook, remove the check mark from the Share Workbook dialog box and save the workbook.

Tip   Whenever you're working with a shared workbook, you can find out whether any other users are working on the workbook. Choose Tools ➪ Share Workbook, and the Share Workbook dialog box lists the names of the other users who have the file open as well as the time that each user opened the workbook.

Controlling the advanced sharing settings

Excel enables you to set options for shared workbooks. Select Tools ➪ Share Workbook and click the Advanced tab to access these options (see Figure 32-4).

Tracking changes

Excel can keep track of the workbook's changes — which is known as *change history*. When you designate a workbook as a shared workbook, Excel automatically turns on the Change History option, enabling you to view information about previous (and perhaps conflicting) changes to the workbook. You can turn off change history by selecting the option labeled Don't Keep Change History. You can also specify the number of days for which Excel tracks change history.

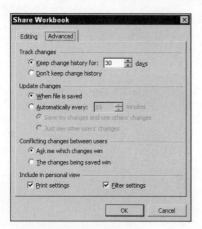

Figure 32-4: Use the Advanced tab of the Share Workbook dialog box to set the advanced sharing options for your workbook.

Updating changes

While you're working on a shared workbook, you can use the standard File ➪ Save command to update the workbook with your changes. The Update Changes settings (refer to Figure 32-4) determine what happens when you save a shared workbook:

✦ **When File Is Saved:** You receive updates from other users when you save your copy of the shared workbook.

✦ **Automatically Every:** Lets you specify a time period for receiving updates from other users of the workbook. You can also specify whether Excel should save your changes automatically, too, or just show you the changes made by other users.

Resolving conflicting changes between users

As you may expect, multiple users working on the same file can result in some conflicts. For example, assume that you're working on a shared customer database workbook and another user also has the workbook open. If you and the other user both make a change to the same cell, a conflict occurs. You can specify the manner in which Excel resolves the conflicts by selecting one of two options in the Advanced tab of the Share Workbook dialog box:

✦ **Ask Me Which Changes Win:** If you select this option, Excel displays a dialog box to let you determine how to settle the conflict.

✦ **The Changes Being Saved Win:** If you select this option, the most recently saved version always take precedence.

Caution

Notice that the second option, The Changes Being Saved Win, has slightly deceptive wording. Even if the other user saves his changes, any changes you make will automatically override his changes when you save the workbook. This could result in a loss of data because you won't have any warning that you've overwritten another user's changes.

About Document Workspaces and SharePoint Services

Excel 2003 supports another type of file sharing called Document Workspaces. A Document Workspace is a Web site that enables a group of users to share files, participate in discussions, and work together on documents. This feature requires that your organization use Windows SharePoint services. Access or create a Document Workspace by using the Tools ➪ Shared Workspace command. In addition, you can publish an Excel List Range to your SharePoint site so others can access it. Use the Data ➪ List ➪ Publish command for this.

A discussion of SharePoint is beyond the scope of this book. If your company uses SharePoint, consult your administrator for specific details on accessing this service.

Controlling the Include in Personal View settings

The final section of the Advanced tab of the Share Workbook dialog box enables you to specify settings that are specific to your view of the shared workbook. You can choose to use your own print settings and your own data-filtering settings. If you don't place check marks in these check boxes, you can't save your own print and filter settings.

Mailing and Routing Workbooks

Excel provides a few additional workgroup features. To use these features, your system must have one of these items installed:

✦ Microsoft Outlook.

✦ Microsoft Exchange.

✦ A mail system that is compatible with MAPI (Messaging Application Programming Interface). Examples include Outlook Express, Eudora, and Netscape Communicator.

✦ Lotus cc:Mail.

✦ A mail system that is compatible with VIM (Vendor Independent Messaging).

The procedures vary, depending on the mail system that you have installed; for this reason, discussions in the following sections are general in nature. You may need to experiment to see how these features work with your e-mail system.

E-mailing a worksheet or workbook

To send a copy of the active worksheet (not an entire workbook) to someone, select File ➪ Send To ➪ Mail Recipient. Or, you can click the E-Mail button of the Standard toolbar.

Excel displays the form shown in Figure 32-5. Enter the e-mail address for one or more recipients, and click Send this Sheet. The data is sent as an HTML-formatted e-mail message.

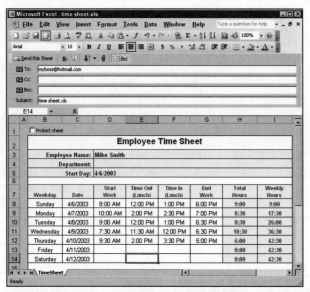

Figure 32-5: You can send a copy of a worksheet via e-mail.

Tip   Sending the current worksheet as the message body can be handy if the recipient just needs to do a quick review of some figures or if the recipient might not have Excel available.

To send the active workbook as an e-mail attachment, choose File ➪ Send To ➪ Mail Recipient (As Attachment). Your e-mail program then opens, so you can enter additional text into the e-mail body.

Routing a workbook to others

If you choose File ➪ Send To ➪ Routing Recipient, Excel enables you to attach a routing slip to a workbook. Routing a workbook is most useful when you want the first person in the group to review (and possibly edit) the workbook and then want that person to send it to the next person on the list.

For example, if you're responsible for your department's budget, you may need input from Alice, and her input may depend on Andy's input. You can set up the workbook and then route it to the others so that they can make their respective additions. When you set up the routing slip, you can tell Excel to return the workbook to you when the routing is finished.

When you route a workbook, you have these two options:

✦ **Sequential routing:** Enables you to route the workbook sequentially to workgroup members. When the first recipient is finished, the workbook goes to the second recipient. When the second recipient is finished, the workbook goes to the third, and so on. When all recipients have received the workbook, it can be returned to you. Choose One After Another at the bottom of the Routing Slip dialog box for this type of routing.

✦ **Simultaneous routing:** Enables you to route the workbook to all recipients at the same time. You receive a copy of the workbook from each recipient (not just one copy). This type of routing is useful if you want to solicit comments from a group of co-workers and you want the responses back quickly. (You don't want to wait until a single worksheet makes the circuit.) Choose All at Once at the bottom of the Routing Slip dialog box for this type of routing.

Click Route to route the workbook immediately. If you don't want to route immediately, click Add Slip. Later, when you're ready to route, choose File ➪ Send To ➪ Next Routing Recipient. Either choice places the workbook in the outgoing mail folder of your e-mail program. To actually route the workbook, open your e-mail program and send the message.

> **Note**   Whether you route or attach a workbook to an e-mail message, Excel uses your e-mail program. Because you can send a workbook to a number of people, either as an e-mail attachment or by using a routing slip, the distinction between the two methods lies in the distinction between sequential and simultaneous routing. If you choose simultaneous routing and you don't place a check mark in the Return When Done check box, routing and attaching are identical because you can't guarantee a reply to e-mail.

Tracking Workbook Changes

Excel has a feature that enables you to track changes made to a workbook. You might use this feature if you send a workbook to someone for reviewing. When the file is returned, you can then see what changes were made and then accept or reject them accordingly.

Turning Track Changes on and off

To turn on change tracking, select Tools ➪ Track Changes ➪ Highlight Changes. This displays the Highlight Changes dialog box, shown in Figure 32-6. Then place a check mark in the Track Changes While Editing check box.

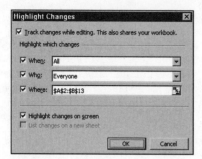

Figure 32-6: Use the Highlight Changes dialog box to track changes made to a workbook.

You can also specify the period to track (When), which users to track (Who), and specify a range of cells to track (Where). If you enable the Highlight Changes on Screen option, each changed cell will display a small triangle in its upper-left corner. And when a changed cell is selected, you'll see a note that describes what change was made (see Figure 32-7).

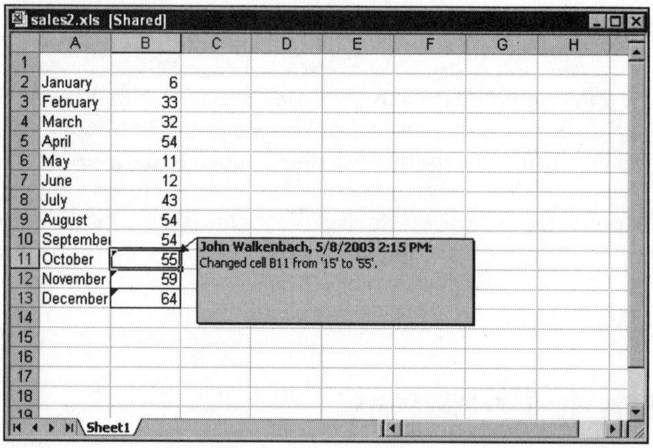

Figure 32-7: Excel displays a descriptive note when you select a cell that has been changed.

After you've selected the option(s) that you want, click OK. To stop tracking changes, choose Tools ➪ Track Changes ➪ Highlight Changes again, and then remove the check mark in the Track Changes While Editing check box.

Note   When tracking changes is enabled, the workbook always becomes a shared workbook. You will be prompted to save your workbook when you close the Highlight Changes dialog box.

Following are some points to keep in mind when using this feature.

✦ Changes made to cell contents are tracked, but other changes (such as formatting changes) are not tracked.

✦ The change history is kept only for a set interval. When you turn on Track Changes, the changes are kept for 30 days. You can increase or decrease the number of days of history to keep in the Highlight Changes dialog box (use the When setting).

✦ If you would like to generate a list of the changes made, choose Tools ➪ Track Changes ➪ Highlight Changes and then enable the List Changes on a New Sheet check box. Click OK, and Excel will insert a new worksheet named History. This sheet shows detailed information about each change made.

✦ Only one level of changes is maintained. Thus, if you change the value of a cell several times, only the most recent change is remembered.

Reviewing the changes

To review the changes made while using the Track Changes features, choose Tools ➪ Track Changes ➪ Accept or Reject Changes. This will display the Select Changes to Accept or Reject dialog box, which enables you to select the types of changes that you want to review. This dialog box is similar to the Highlight Changes dialog box. You can specify When, Who, and Where.

Click OK, and Excel will display each of the changes in a new dialog box, as shown in Figure 32-8. Click Accept to accept the change, or click Reject to reject the change. You can also click Accept All (to accept all changes) or Reject All (to reject all changes).

Figure 32-8: The Accept or Reject Changes dialog box displays information about each cell that was changed.

✦ ✦ ✦

Making Your Worksheets Error-Free

✦ ✦ ✦ ✦

In This Chapter

How to identify and correct common formula errors

Using Excel's auditing tools

Using formula AutoCorrect

Tracing cell relationships

Checking spelling and related features

✦ ✦ ✦ ✦

It goes without saying that you want your Excel worksheets to produce accurate results. Unfortunately, it's not always easy to be certain that the results are correct—especially if you deal with large, complex worksheets. This chapter introduces the tools and techniques available to help identify, correct, and prevent errors.

Finding and Correcting Formula Errors

Making a change in a worksheet—even a relatively minor change—may produce a ripple effect that introduces errors in other cells. For example, accidentally entering a value into a cell that previously held a formula is all too easy to do. This simple error can have a major impact on other formulas, and you may not discover the problem until long after you make the change, or you may never discover the problem.

Formula errors tend to fall into one of the following general categories:

✦ **Syntax errors:** You have a problem with the syntax of a formula. For example, a formula may have mismatched parentheses, or a function may not have the correct number of arguments.

✦ **Logical errors:** A formula doesn't return an error, but it contains a logical flaw that causes it to return an incorrect result.

✦ **Incorrect reference errors:** The logic of the formula is correct, but the formula uses an incorrect cell reference. As a simple example, the range reference in a Sum formula may not include all of the data that you want to sum.

✦ **Semantic errors:** An example is a function name that is spelled incorrectly. Excel will attempt to interpret it as a name, and will display the #NAME? error.

✦ **Circular references:** A circular reference occurs when a formula refers to its own cell, either directly or indirectly. Circular references are useful in a few cases, but most of the time a circular reference indicates a problem.

✦ **Array formula entry error:** When entering (or editing) an array formula, you must use Ctrl+Shift+Enter to enter the formula. If you fail to do so, Excel doesn't recognize the formula as an array formula.

✦ **Incomplete calculation errors:** The formulas simply aren't calculated fully. Microsoft has acknowledged some problems with Excel's calculation engine in some versions of Excel. To ensure that your formulas are fully calculated, use Ctrl+Alt+F9.

Syntax errors are usually the easiest to identify and correct. In most cases, you will know when your formula contains a syntax error. For example, Excel won't permit you to enter a formula with mismatched parentheses. Other syntax errors also usually result in an error display in the cell.

This remainder of this section describes some common formula problems and offers advice on identifying and correcting them.

Mismatched parentheses

In a formula, every left parenthesis must have a corresponding right parenthesis. If your formula has mismatched parentheses, Excel usually won't permit you to enter it. An exception to this rule involves a simple formula that uses a function. For example, if you enter the following formula (which is missing a closing parenthesis), Excel accepts the formula and provides the missing parenthesis.

```
=SUM(A1:A500
```

A formula may have an equal number of left and right parentheses, but the parentheses may not match properly. For example, consider the following formula, which converts a text string such that the first character is uppercase and the remaining characters are lowercase. This formula has five pairs of parentheses, and they match properly.

```
=UPPER(LEFT(A1))&RIGHT(LOWER(A1),LEN(A1)-1)
```

Using Formula AutoCorrect

When you enter a formula that has a syntax error, Excel attempts to determine the problem and offers a suggested correction. The accompanying figure shows an example of a proposed correction.

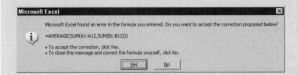

Exercise caution when accepting corrections for your formulas from Excel because it doesn't always guess correctly. For example, I entered the following formula (which has mismatched parentheses):

    =AVERAGE(SUM(A1:A12,SUM(B1:B12))

Excel then proposed the following correction to the formula:

    =AVERAGE(SUM(A1:A12,SUM(B1:B12)))

You may be tempted to accept the suggestion without even thinking. In this case, the proposed formula is syntactically correct — but not what I intended. The correct formula is

    =AVERAGE(SUM(A1:A12),SUM(B1:B12))

The following formula also has five pairs of parentheses, but they are mismatched. The result displays a syntactically correct formula that simply returns the wrong result.

    =UPPER(LEFT(A1)&RIGHT(LOWER(A1),LEN(A1)-1))

Often, parentheses that are in the wrong location will result in a syntax error — which is usually a message that tells you that you entered too many or too few arguments for a function.

 Tip Excel can help you out with mismatched parentheses. When you edit a formula, move the cursor to a parenthesis and pause. Excel displays it (and its matching parenthesis) in bold for about one second.

Cells are filled with hash marks

A cell is filled with a series of hash marks (#) for one of two reasons:

✦ The column is not wide enough to accommodate the formatted numeric value. To correct it, you can make the column wider or use a different number format.

✦ The cell contains a formula that returns an invalid date or time. For example, Excel doesn't support dates prior to 1900 or the use of negative time values. Attempting to display either of these results in a cell filled with hash marks. Widening the column won't fix it.

Blank cells are not blank

Some Excel users have discovered that by pressing the spacebar, the contents of a cell seem to erase. Actually, pressing the spacebar inserts an invisible space character, which isn't the same as erasing the cell.

For example, the following formula returns the number of nonempty cells in range A1:A10. If you "erase" any of these cells by using the spacebar, these cells are included in the count, and the formula returns an incorrect result.

```
=COUNTA(A1:A10)
```

If your formula doesn't ignore blank cells the way that it should, check to make sure that the blank cells are really blank cells. One way to do this is to choose Edit ➪ Go To, which displays the Go To dialog box. Click the Special button and then choose the Blanks option in the Go To Special dialog box. Excel will select all blank cells so that you can spot cells that appear to be empty but are not.

Formulas returning an error

A formula may return any of the following error values:

✦ #DIV/0!

✦ #N/A

✦ #NAME?

✦ #NULL!

✦ #NUM!

✦ #REF!

✦ #VALUE!

The following sections summarize possible problems that may cause these errors.

Tip   Excel allows you to choose how error values are printed. To access this feature, select File ➪ Page Setup and click the Sheet tab. You can choose to print error values as displayed (the default), or as blank cells, dashes, or #N/A.

Tracing Error Values

The Trace Error button on the Formula Auditing toolbar helps you to identify the cell that is causing an error value to appear. Often, an error in one cell is the result of an error in a precedent cell. Activate a cell containing an error and then click the Trace Error button. Excel draws arrows to indicate the error source.

#DIV/0! errors

Division by zero is not permitted. If you attempt to do so, Excel displays its familiar #DIV/0! error value.

Because Excel considers a blank cell to be zero, you also get this error if your formula divides by a missing value. This is a common problem when you create formulas for data that you haven't entered yet, as shown in Figure 33-1. The formula in cell D2, which was copied to the cells below it, is

```
=(C2-B2)/C2
```

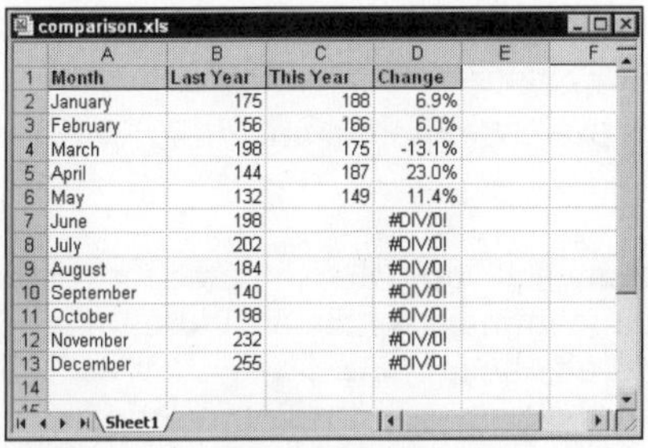
comparison.xls

Month	Last Year	This Year	Change
January	175	188	6.9%
February	156	166	6.0%
March	198	175	-13.1%
April	144	187	23.0%
May	132	149	11.4%
June	198		#DIV/0!
July	202		#DIV/0!
August	184		#DIV/0!
September	140		#DIV/0!
October	198		#DIV/0!
November	232		#DIV/0!
December	255		#DIV/0!

Figure 33-1: #DIV/0! errors occur when the data in column C is missing.

This formula calculates the percent change between the values in columns B and C. Data isn't available for months beyond May, so the formula returns a #DIV/0! error.

To avoid the error display, you can use an IF function to check for a blank cell in column C:

```
= IF(C2=0,"",(C2-B2)/C2)
```

This formula displays an empty string if cell C2 is blank or contains 0; otherwise, it displays the calculated value.

Another approach is to use an IF function to check for *any* error condition. The following formula, for example, displays an empty string if the formula results in any type of error.

```
=IF(ISERROR((C2-B2)/C2),"",(C2-B2)/C2)
```

#N/A errors

The #N/A error occurs if any cell referenced by a formula displays #N/A.

Note Some users like to enter =NA() or #N/A explicitly for missing data. This method makes it perfectly clear that the data is not available and hasn't been deleted accidentally.

The #N/A error also occurs when a lookup function (HLOOKUP, LOOKUP, MATCH, or VLOOKUP) can't find a match.

#NAME? errors

The #NAME? error occurs under these conditions:

✦ The formula contains an undefined range or cell name.

✦ The formula contains text that Excel *interprets* as an undefined name. A misspelled function name, for example, generates a #NAME? error.

✦ The formula uses a worksheet function that's defined in an add-in, and the add-in is not installed.

Note Excel has a bit of a problem with range names. If you delete a name for a cell or range and the name is used in a formula, the formula continues to use the name, even though it's no longer defined. As a result, the formula displays #NAME?. You may expect Excel to automatically convert the names to their corresponding cell references, but this doesn't happen.

#NULL! errors

The #NULL! error occurs when a formula attempts to use an intersection of two ranges that don't actually intersect. Excel's intersection operator is a space. The following formula, for example, returns #NULL! because the two ranges don't intersect.

```
=SUM(B5:B14 A16:F16)
```

The following formula doesn't return #NULL! but displays the contents of cell B9 — which represents the intersection of the two ranges.

```
=SUM(B5:B14 A9:F9)
```

#NUM! errors

A formula returns a #NUM! error if any of the following occurs:

✦ You pass a non-numerical argument to a function when a numerical argument is expected.

✦ You pass an invalid argument to a function. For example, this formula returns #NUM!:

=SQRT(-1)

✦ A function that uses iteration can't calculate a result. Examples of functions that use iteration are IRR and RATE.

✦ A formula returns a value that is too large or too small. Excel supports values between −1E-307 and 1E+307.

#REF! errors

The #REF! error occurs when a formula uses an invalid cell reference. This error can occur in the following situations:

✦ You delete a cell that is referenced by the formula. For example, the formula below displays a #REF! error if row 1, column A, or column B is deleted.

=A1/B1

✦ You copy a formula to a location that invalidates the relative cell references. For example, if you copy the following formula from cell A2 to cell A1, the formula returns #REF! because it attempts to refer to a nonexistent cell.

=A1-1

✦ You cut a cell (using Edit ➪ Cut) and then paste it to a cell that's referenced by a formula. The formula will display #REF!.

#VALUE! errors

The #VALUE! error is very common and can occur under the following conditions:

✦ An argument for a function is of an incorrect data type, or the formula attempts to perform an operation using incorrect data. For example, a formula that adds a value to a text string returns the #VALUE! error.

✦ A function's argument is a range when it should be a single value.

✦ A custom worksheet function is not calculated. With some versions of Excel, inserting or moving a sheet may cause this error. You can use Ctrl+Alt+F9 to force a recalculation.

✦ A custom worksheet function attempts to perform an operation that is not valid. For example, custom functions cannot modify the Excel environment or make changes to other cells.

✦ You forget to press Ctrl+Shift+Enter when entering an array formula.

Pay Attention to the Colors

When you edit a cell that contains a formula, Excel color-codes the cell and range references in the formula. Excel also outlines the cells and ranges used in the formula by using corresponding colors. Therefore, you can see at a glance the cells that are used in the formula.

You also can manipulate the colored outline to change the cell or range reference. To change the references that are used, drag the outline's border or fill handle (at the lower-right corner of the outline).

Absolute/relative reference problems

As described in Chapter 2, a cell reference can be relative (for example, A1), absolute (for example, $A$1), or mixed (for example, $A1 or A$1). The type of cell reference that you use in a formula is relevant only if the formula will be copied to other cells.

A common problem is using a relative reference when you should use an absolute reference. As shown in Figure 33-2, cell C1 contains a tax rate, which is used in the formulas in column C. The formula in cell C4 is

```
=B4+(B4*$C$1)
```

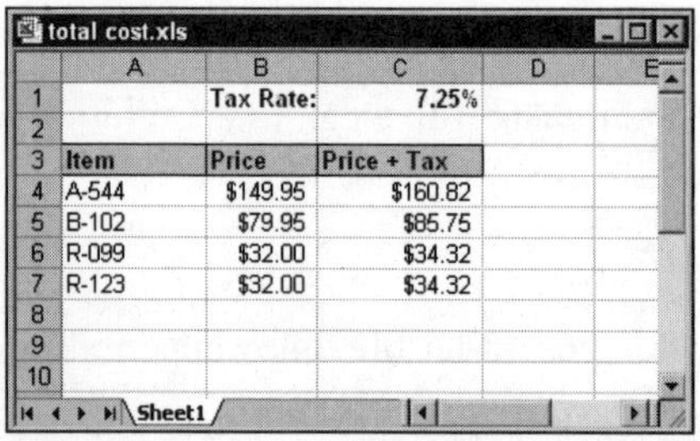

	A	B	C	D	E
1		Tax Rate:	7.25%		
2					
3	Item	Price	Price + Tax		
4	A-544	$149.95	$160.82		
5	B-102	$79.95	$85.75		
6	R-099	$32.00	$34.32		
7	R-123	$32.00	$34.32		
8					
9					
10					

Figure 33-2: Formulas in the range C4:C6 use an absolute reference to cell C1.

Notice that the reference to cell C1 is an absolute reference. When the formula is copied to other cells in column C, the formula continues to refer to cell C1. If the reference to cell C1 were a relative reference, the copied formulas would return an incorrect result.

Operator precedence problems

Excel has some straightforward rules about the order in which mathematical operations are performed (see Chapter 8). When in doubt (or when you simply need to clarify your intentions), you should use parentheses to ensure that operations are performed in the correct order. For example, the following formula multiplies A1 by A2 and then adds 1 to the result. The multiplication is performed first because it has a higher order of precedence.

```
= 1+A1*A2
```

The following is a clearer version of this formula. The parentheses aren't necessary; but in this case, the order of operations is perfectly obvious.

```
=1+(A1*A2)
```

Notice that the negation operator symbol is exactly the same as the subtraction operator symbol. This, as you may expect, can cause some confusion. Consider these two formulas:

```
=-3^2
=0-3^2
```

The first formula, as expected, returns 9. The second formula, however, returns –9. Squaring a number always produces a positive result, so how is it that Excel can return the –9 result?

In the first formula, the minus sign is a *negation* operator and has the highest precedence. However, in the second formula, the minus sign is a *subtraction* operator, which has a lower precedence than the exponentiation operator. Therefore, the value 3 is squared, and the result is subtracted from zero, which produces a negative result.

Using parentheses, as shown in the following formula, causes Excel to interpret the operator as a minus sign rather than a negation operator. This formula returns –9.

```
=-(3^2)
```

Formulas are not calculated

If you use custom worksheet functions written in VBA, you may find that formulas that use these functions fail to get recalculated and may display incorrect results. To force a recalculation of all formulas, press Ctrl+Alt+F9.

Actual versus displayed values

You may encounter a situation in which values in a range don't appear to add up properly. For example, Figure 33-3 shows a worksheet with the following formula entered into each cell in the range B3:B5:

    =1/3

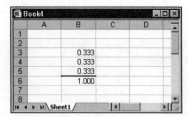

Figure 33-3: A simple demonstration of numbers that appear to add up incorrectly.

Cell B6 contains the following formula:

    =SUM(B3:B5)

All of the cells are formatted to display with three decimal places. As you can see, the formula in cell B6 appears to display an incorrect result. (You may expect it to display 0.999.) The formula, of course, *does* return the correct result. The formula uses the *actual* values in the range B3:B5, not the *displayed* values.

You can instruct Excel to use the displayed values by checking the Precision as Displayed check box on the Calculation tab of the Options dialog box. (Choose Tools ➪ Options to display this dialog box.)

Caution   Checking the Precision as Displayed check box also affects normal values (non-formulas) that have been entered into cells. For example, if a cell contains the value 4.68 and is displayed with no decimal places (that is, 5), checking the Precision as Displayed check box converts 4.68 to 5.00. This change is permanent, and you can't restore the original value if you later uncheck the Precision as Displayed check box. A better approach is to use Excel's ROUND function to round off the values to the desired number of decimal places.

Floating point number errors

Computers, by their very nature, don't have infinite precision. Excel stores numbers in binary format by using eight bytes, which can handle numbers with 15-digit accuracy. Some numbers can't be expressed precisely by using eight bytes, so the number stores as an approximation.

To demonstrate how this may cause problems, enter the following formula into cell A1:

```
=(5.1-5.2)+1
```

The result should be 0.9. However, if you format the cell to display 15 decimal places, you discover that Excel calculates the formula with a result of 0.899999999999999. This occurs because the operation in parentheses is performed first, and this intermediate result stores in binary format by using an approximation. The formula then adds 1 to this value, and the approximation error is propagated to the final result.

In many cases, this type of error doesn't present a problem. However, if you need to test the result of that formula by using a logical operator, it *may* present a problem. For example, the following formula (which assumes that the previous formula is in cell A1) returns FALSE:

```
=A1=.9
```

One solution to this type of error is to use Excel's ROUND function. The following formula, for example, returns TRUE because the comparison is made by using the value in A1 rounded to one decimal place.

```
=ROUND(A1,1)=0.9
```

Here's another example of a "precision" problem. Try entering the following formula:

```
=(1.333-1.233)-(1.334-1.234)
```

This formula should return 0, but it actually returns –2.220441E-16 (a number very close to zero).

If that formula were in cell A1, the following formula would return Not Zero.

```
=IF(A1=0,"Zero","Not Zero")
```

One way to handle these "very close to zero" rounding errors is to use a formula like this:

```
=IF(ABS(A1)<1E-6,"Zero","Not Zero")
```

This formula uses the less-than (<) operator to compare the absolute value of the number with a very small number. This formula would return Zero.

"Phantom link" errors

You may open a workbook and see a message like the one shown in Figure 33-4. This message sometimes appears even when a workbook contains no linked formulas. Often, these phantom links are created when you copy a worksheet that contains names.

Figure 33-4: Excel's way of asking you if you want to update links in a workbook.

First, try using Edit ⇨ Links to display the Edit Links dialog box. Then select each link and click Break Link. If that doesn't solve the problem, this phantom link may be caused by an erroneous name. Select Insert ⇨ Name ⇨ Define and scroll through the list of names. If you see a name that refers to #REF!, delete the name.

Using Excel's Auditing Tools

Excel includes a number of tools that can help you track down formula errors. This section describes the auditing tools built into Excel.

Identifying cells of a particular type

The Go To Special dialog box enables you to specify the type of cells that you want Excel to select. To display this dialog box, choose Edit ⇨ Go To (or press F5 or Ctrl+G). The Go To dialog box appears. Click the Special button, which displays the Go To Special dialog box, as shown in Figure 33-5.

Note   If you select a multicell range before choosing Edit ⇨ Go To, the command operates only within the selected cells. If a single cell is selected, the command operates on the entire worksheet.

You can use the Go To Special dialog box to select cells of a certain type, which can often help in identifying errors. For example, if you choose the Formulas option, Excel selects all of the cells that contain a formula. If you zoom the worksheet out to a small size, you can get a good idea of the worksheet's organization (see Figure 33-6).

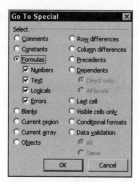

Figure 33-5: The Go To Special dialog box.

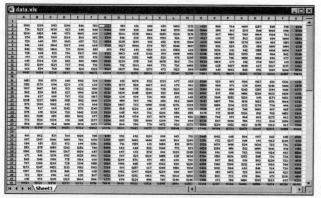

Figure 33-6: Zooming out and selecting all formula cells can give you a good overview of how the worksheet is designed.

Tip

Selecting the formula cells may also help you to spot a common error — a formula that has been replaced accidentally with a value. If you find a cell that's not selected amid a group of selected formula cells, chances are good that the cell previously contained a formula that has been replaced by a value.

Viewing formulas

You can become familiar with an unfamiliar workbook by displaying the formulas rather than the results of the formulas. Select Tools ➪ Options and then check the check box labeled Formulas on the View tab. You may want to create a new window for the workbook before issuing this command. This way, you can see the formulas in one window and the results of the formula in the other window. Use the Window ➪ New Window command to open a new window.

Tip   You can also use the Tools ➪ Formula Auditing ➪ Formula Auditing Mode command to toggle Formula view on and off. When Formula view is in effect, the Formula Auditing Toolbar is also displayed. You can also use Ctrl+` to toggle between Formula view and Normal view.

Figure 33-7 shows an example of a worksheet displayed in two windows. The window on the top shows Normal view (formula results), and the window on the bottom displays the formulas.

Comparing two windows

In some cases, you may want to compare data in two workbooks or worksheets. You can use Excel's Compare Side by Side feature to do this.

New Feature   This feature is available only in Excel 2003.

To use this feature, make sure that both windows are open. If you want to compare two sheets in the same workbook, use the Window ➪ New Window command to create a new window for the workbook. Then choose Window ➪ Compare Side by Side With. If more than two windows are open, you get a dialog box that lets you select the window to be compared with the active window.

The two windows will then be tiled horizontally (one on top of the other), and Excel displays its Compare Side by Side toolbar. Figure 33-8 shows an example. By default, the scrolling is synchronized. To turn off synchronized scrolling, use the toolbar.

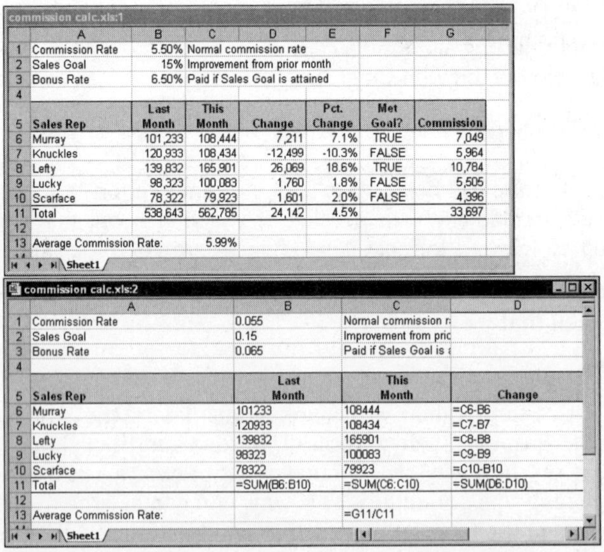

commission calc.xls:1

	A	B	C	D	E	F	G
1	Commission Rate	5.50%	Normal commission rate				
2	Sales Goal	15%	Improvement from prior month				
3	Bonus Rate	6.50%	Paid if Sales Goal is attained				
4							
5	Sales Rep	Last Month	This Month	Change	Pct. Change	Met Goal?	Commission
6	Murray	101,233	108,444	7,211	7.1%	TRUE	7,049
7	Knuckles	120,933	108,434	-12,499	-10.3%	FALSE	5,964
8	Lefty	139,832	165,901	26,069	18.6%	TRUE	10,784
9	Lucky	98,323	100,083	1,760	1.8%	FALSE	5,505
10	Scarface	78,322	79,923	1,601	2.0%	FALSE	4,396
11	Total	538,643	562,785	24,142	4.5%		33,697
12							
13	Average Commission Rate:	5.99%					

◄ ► ►∣ \ Sheet1 /

commission calc.xls:2

	A	B	C	D
1	Commission Rate	0.055	Normal commission r	
2	Sales Goal	0.15	Improvement from prio	
3	Bonus Rate	0.065	Paid if Sales Goal is a	
4				
5	Sales Rep	Last Month	This Month	Change
6	Murray	101233	108444	=C6-B6
7	Knuckles	120933	108434	=C7-B7
8	Lefty	139832	165901	=C8-B8
9	Lucky	98323	100083	=C9-B9
10	Scarface	78322	79923	=C10-B10
11	Total	=SUM(B6:B10)	=SUM(C6:C10)	=SUM(D6:D10)
12				
13	Average Commission Rate:		=G11/C11	

◄ ► ►∣ \ Sheet1 /

Figure 33-7: Displaying formulas (bottom window) and their results (top window).

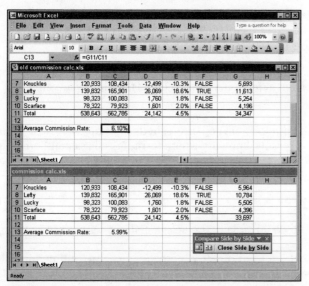

Figure 33-8: Using Excel's Compare Side by Side feature.

Note   If you would like to tile the windows vertically instead of horizontally, select Window ➪ Arrange and then select the Vertical option in the Arrange Windows dialog box. To restore the windows to the default positions, use the Reset Window Position button on the Compare Side by Side toolbar.

Unfortunately, that's all there is to this feature. It would be nice if Excel would actually compare the contents of the windows and report on the differences. But all comparisons must be done manually.

Tracing cell relationships

To understand how to trace cell relationships, you need to familiarize yourself with the following two concepts:

✦ **Cell precedents:** Applicable only to cells that contain a formula, a formula cell's precedents are all the cells that contribute to the formula's result. A *direct precedent* is a cell that you use directly in the formula. An *indirect precedent* is a cell that isn't used directly in the formula but is used by a cell that you refer to in the formula.

✦ **Cell dependents:** These are formula cells that depend on a particular cell. A cell's dependents consist of all formula cells that use the cell. Again, the formula cell can be a *direct dependent* or an *indirect dependent*.

For example, consider this simple formula entered into cell A4:

```
=SUM(A1:A3)
```

Cell A4 has three precedent cells (A1, A2, and A3). These are all direct precedents. Cells A1, A2, and A3 each have a dependent cell (cell A4), and they are all direct dependents.

Identifying cell precedents for a formula cell often sheds light on why the formula isn't working correctly. Conversely, knowing which formula cells depend on a particular cell is also helpful. For example, if you're about to delete a formula, you may want to check to see whether it has any dependents.

Identifying precedents

You can identify cells used by a formula in the active cell in a number of ways.

✦ Press F2. The cells that are used directly by the formula are outlined in color, and the color corresponds to the cell reference in the formula. This technique is limited to identifying cells on the same sheet as the formula.

✦ Select Edit ➪ Go To (or press F5) to display the Go To dialog box. Then click the Special button to display the Go To Special dialog box. Select the Precedents option, and then select either Direct Only (for direct precedents only) or All Levels (for direct and indirect precedents). Click OK, and Excel highlights the precedent cells for the formula. This technique is limited to identifying cells on the same sheet as the formula.

✦ Press Ctrl+[to select all direct precedent cells on the active sheet.

✦ Press Ctrl+Shift+{ to select all precedent cells (direct and indirect) on the active sheet.

✦ Display the Formula Auditing toolbar by selecting Tools ➪ Formula Auditing ➪ Show Formula Auditing Toolbar. Click the Trace Precedents button to draw arrows to indicate a cell's precedents. Click this button multiple times to see additional levels of precedents. Figure 33-9 shows a worksheet with precedent arrows drawn to indicate the precedents for the formula in cell C13.

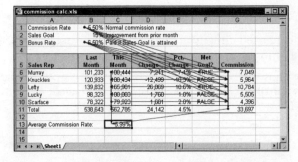

Figure 33-9: This worksheet displays lines that indicate cell precedents for the formula in cell C13.

Identifying dependents

You can identify formula cells that use a particular cell in a number of ways.

✦ Select Edit ➪ Go To (or press F5) to display the Go To dialog box. Then click the Special button to display the Go To Special dialog box. Select the Dependents option, and then select either Direct Only (for direct dependents only) or All Levels (for direct and indirect dependents). Click OK. Excel highlights the cells that depend on the active cell. This technique is limited to identifying cells on the active sheet only.

✦ Press Ctrl+] to select all direct dependent cells on the active sheet.

✦ Press Ctrl+Shift+} to select all dependent cells (direct and indirect) on the active sheet.

✦ Display the Formula Auditing toolbar by selecting Tools ➪ Formula Auditing ➪ Show Formula Auditing Toolbar. Click the Trace Dependents button to draw arrows to indicate a cell's dependents. Click this button multiple times to see additional levels of dependents.

Tracing error values

The Trace Error button on the Formula Auditing toolbar helps you to identify the cell that is causing an error value to appear. An error in one cell is often the result of an error in a precedent cell. Activate a cell that contains an error and click the Trace Error button. Excel draws arrows to indicate the error source.

Fixing circular reference errors

If you accidentally create a circular reference formula, Excel displays a warning message. If you click OK, Excel displays the Circular Reference toolbar. If you can't figure out the source of the problem, use the Navigate Circular Reference tool (a drop-down list control) on the toolbar to select a cell involved in the circular reference. Start by selecting the first cell listed, and then work your way down the list until you figure out the problem.

Using background error-checking feature

Some people may find it helpful to take advantage of Excel's automatic error-checking feature. This feature is enabled in the Error Checking tab in the Options dialog box (see Figure 33-10). Error checking is turned on or off by using the check box labeled Enable Background Error Checking. In addition, you can specify which types of errors to check for by using the check boxes in the Rules section.

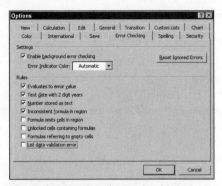

Figure 33-10: Excel can check your
formulas for potential errors.

When error checking is turned on, Excel continually evaluates your worksheet, including its formulas. If a potential error is identified, Excel places a small triangle in the upper-left corner of the cell. When the cell is activated, a Smart Tag appears. Clicking this Smart Tag provides you with some options. Figure 33-11 shows the options that appear when you click the Smart Tag in a cell that contains a #DIV/0 error. The options vary, depending on the type of error.

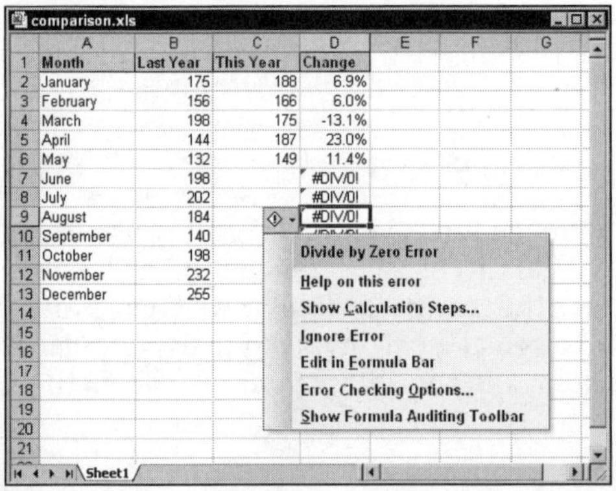

Figure 33-11: Clicking an error Smart Tag
gives you a list of options.

In many cases, you will choose to ignore an error by selecting the Ignore Error option. Selecting this option eliminates the cell from subsequent error checks. However, all previously ignored errors can be reset so that they appear again. (Use the Reset Ignored Errors button in the Error Checking tab of the Options dialog box.)

You can use the Tools ➪ Error Checking command to display a dialog box that displays each potential error cell in sequence, much like using a spell-checking program. Figure 33-12 shows the Error Checking dialog box. Note that this is a nonmodal dialog box, so you can still access your worksheet when the Error Checking dialog box is displayed.

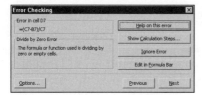

Figure 33-12: Using the Error Checking dialog box to cycle through potential errors identified by Excel.

Caution   It's important to understand that the error-checking feature isn't perfect. In fact, it's not even close to perfect. In other words, you can't assume that you have an error-free worksheet simply because Excel doesn't identify any potential errors! Also, be aware that this error-checking feature won't catch a very common type of error — that of overwriting a formula cell with a value.

Using Excel Formula Evaluator

Excel's Formula Evaluator lets you see the various parts of a nested formula evaluated in the order that the formula is calculated. To use the Formula Evaluator, select the cell that contains the formula and choose Tools ➪ Formula Auditing ➪ Evaluate Formula. Or click the Evaluate Formula button on the Formula Auditing toolbar. Either of these actions displays the Evaluate Formula dialog box, as shown in Figure 33-13.

Figure 33-13: Excel's Formula Evaluator shows a formula being calculated one step at a time.

Click the Evaluate button to show the result of calculating the expressions within the formula. Each click of the button performs another calculation. This feature may be useful in some situations, but overall, it leaves much to be desired.

Excel provides another way to evaluate a part of a formula:

1. Select the cell that contains the formula.

2. Press F2 to get into cell edit mode.

3. Use your mouse to highlight a portion of the formula. Or, press Shift and use the arrow keys.

4. Press F9.

The highlighted portion of the formula displays the calculated result. You can evaluate other parts of the formula or press Esc to cancel and return your formula to its previous state.

Searching and Replacing

Excel has a powerful search and replace feature that makes it easy to locate information in a worksheet or across multiple worksheets in a workbook. As an option, you can also search for text and replace it with other text.

To access the Find and Replace dialog box, choose Edit ➪ Find or Edit ➪ Replace. Either command displays the dialog box shown in Figure 33-14. If you're simply looking for information, click the Find tab. If you want to replace existing text with new text, use the Replace tab. Also note that you can use the Options button to display (or hide) additional options. (The dialog box shown in the figure displays these additional options.)

Searching for information

Enter the information to search for in the Find What text box. Use the Within drop-down list to specify where to search (the current sheet or the entire workbook). Use the Search drop-down list to specify the direction (by rows or by columns). Use the Look In drop-down list to specify what cell parts to search (formulas, values, or comments). Use the check boxes to specify whether the search should be case sensitive and whether the entire cell contents must be matched.

Click Find Next to locate the matching cells one at a time, or click Find All to locate all matches. If you use the Find All button, the Find and Replace dialog box expands to display the addresses of all matching cells in a list (see Figure 33-15). When you select an entry in this list, Excel scrolls the worksheet so that you can view it in context.

Note Unlike most Excel dialog boxes, the Find and Replace dialog box "stays on top." Therefore, you can access the worksheet and make changes without the need to dismiss the dialog box.

Figure 33-14: Use the Find and Replace dialog box to locate information in a worksheet or workbook.

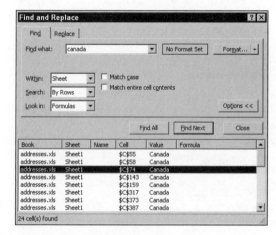

Figure 33-15: Displaying the result of a search in the Find and Replace dialog box.

Replacing information

To replace text with other text, use the Replace tab of the Find and Replace dialog box. Enter the text to be replaced in the Find What box and then enter the new text in the Replace With Box. Specify other options as described in the previous section. Click Find Next to locate the first matching item and then click Replace to do the replacement. When you click the Replace button, Excel then locates the next matching item. To override the replacement, click Find Next. To replace all items without verification, click Replace All.

Searching for formatting

The Find and Replace dialog box also enables you to locate cells that contain a particular type of formatting. As an option, you can replace that formatting with another type of formatting. For example, assume that you want to locate all cells that are formatted as bold and then change that formatting to bold and italic. Follow these steps:

1. Select Edit ➪ Replace to display the Find and Replace dialog box.

2. Make sure the Replace tab is displayed.

3. If the Find What and Replace With boxes are not empty, delete their contents.

4. Click the top Format button to display the Find Format dialog box. This dialog box resembles the standard Format Cells dialog box.

5. In the Find Format dialog box, select the Font tab.

6. Select Bold in the Font Style list and then click OK.

7. Click the bottom Format button to display the Replace Format dialog box.

8. In the Replace Format dialog box, select the Font tab.

9. Select Bold Italic in the Font Style list and then click OK. At this point, the Find and Replace dialog box resembles Figure 33-16. Notice that it displays previews of the formatting that will be found and replaced.

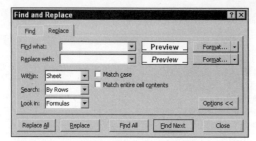

Figure 33-16: Using the Find and Replace dialog box to change formatting.

10. In the Find and Replace dialog box, click Replace All.

Excel locates all cells that have bold formatting and changes the formatting to bold italic.

Spell Checking Your Worksheets

If you use a word-processing program, you probably run its spell checker before printing an important document. Spelling mistakes can be just as embarrassing when they appear in a spreadsheet. Fortunately, Microsoft includes a spelling checker with Excel. You can access the spelling checker by using any of these methods:

✦ Selecting Tools ➪ Spelling

✦ Clicking the Spelling button on the Standard toolbar

✦ Pressing F7

Note When you activate the spelling checker, Excel may ask you whether you would like to begin at the beginning of the sheet. To avoid this prompt, you can select the range of cells you'd like to check before you activate the spelling checker.

If the spelling checker finds any words it does not recognize as correct, it displays the Spelling dialog box, as shown in Figure 33-17.

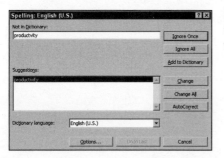

Figure 33-17: Use the Spelling dialog box to locate and correct spelling errors in your worksheets.

Note The spell checking checks cell contents, notes, text in graphic objects and charts, and page headers and footers. Even the contents of hidden rows and columns are checked.

The Spelling dialog box works similarly to other spelling checkers with which you may be familiar. If Excel encounters a word that isn't in the current dictionary or that is misspelled, it offers a list of suggestions. You can respond by clicking one of these buttons:

✦ **Ignore Once:** Ignores the word and continues the spell check.

✦ **Ignore All:** Ignores the word and all subsequent occurrences of it.

✦ **Add to Dictionary:** Adds the word to the dictionary.

✦ **Change:** Changes the word to the selected word in the Suggestions box.

✦ **Change All:** Changes the word to the selected word in the Suggestions list, and changes all subsequent occurrences of it without asking.

✦ **AutoCorrect:** Adds the misspelled word and its correct spelling to the AutoCorrect list.

Using AutoCorrect

AutoCorrect is a handy feature that automatically corrects common typing mistakes. You can also add to the list some words that Excel corrects auto-matically. The AutoCorrect dialog box appears in Figure 33-18. Choose Tools ⇨ AutoCorrect Options to access this feature.

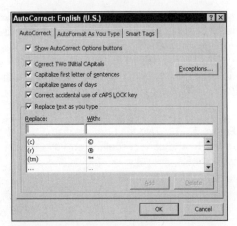

Figure 33-18: Use the AutoCorrect dialog box to control the spelling corrections Excel makes automatically.

This dialog box has several options:

✦ **Correct TWo INitial CApitals:** Automatically corrects words with two initial uppercase letters. For example, BUdget is converted to Budget. This is a common mistake among fast typists. You can click the Exceptions button to specify a list of exceptions to this rule.

✦ **Capitalize First Letter of Sentences:** Capitalizes the first letter in a sentence.

✦ **Capitalize Names of Days:** Capitalizes the days of the week. If you enter *monday*, Excel converts it to *Monday*.

✦ **Correct Accidental Use of cAPS LOCK key:** Corrects errors caused if you accidentally hit the CapsLock key while typing.

✦ **Replace Text as You Type:** AutoCorrect automatically changes incorrect words as you type them.

Excel includes a long list of AutoCorrect entries for commonly misspelled words. In addition, it has AutoCorrect entries for some symbols. For example, *(c)* is replaced with © and *(r)* is replaced with ®. You can also add your own AutoCorrect entries. For example, if you find that you frequently misspell the word *January* as *Janruary*, you can create an AutoCorrect entry so that it's changed automatically. To create a new AutoCorrect entry, enter the misspelled word in the Replace box and the correctly spelled word in the With box. You can also delete entries that you no longer need.

You also can use the AutoCorrect feature to create shortcuts for commonly used words or phrases. For example, if you work for a company named Consolidated Data Processing Corporation, you can create an AutoCorrect entry for an abbreviation, such as cdp. Then, whenever you type **cdp**, Excel automatically changes it to Consolidated Data Processing Corporation. Just make sure that you don't use a combination of characters that might normally appear in your text.

In some cases, you may want to override the AutoCorrect feature. For example, you may need to enter (c) rather than the copyright symbol. You can do this by selected Edit ➪ Undo or by pressing Ctrl+Z.

You can use the AutoFormat As You Type tab of the AutoCorrect dialog box to control how Excel treats Internet and network addresses. Use the Smart Tags tab to make Excel show Smart Tags — similar to hyperlinks — for certain types of data in your worksheets. The types of Smart Tags Excel recognizes vary depending on the types of software that are installed on your system.

Using AutoComplete

AutoComplete automatically finishes a word as soon as Excel recognizes it. For Excel to recognize the word, it must appear elsewhere in the same column. This feature is most useful when you're entering a list that contains repeated text in a column. For example, assume that you're entering customer data in a list and one of the fields is City. Whenever you start typing, Excel searches the other entries in the column. If it finds a match, it completes the entry for you. Press Enter to accept it. If Excel guesses incorrectly, keep typing to ignore the suggestion.

If AutoComplete isn't working, select Tools ➪ Options, click the Edit tab, and check the box labeled Enable AutoComplete for Cell Values.

You also can display a list of all items in a column by right-clicking and choosing Pick from List from the shortcut menu. Excel then displays a list box of all entries that are in the column. Click the one that you want, and Excel enters it into the cell for you.

✦ ✦ ✦

Programming Excel with VBA

If you've ever wanted to do a bit more, or to automate routine operations so you don't always have to perform boring, repetitious tasks manually, this part is for you. This part is also aimed at those Excel users who want to develop Excel-based applications for other users. VBA — Visual Basic for Applications — is the powerful programming language that you can use for these tasks as well as for more esoteric purposes, such as developing that specialized worksheet function that you simply can't find in Excel.

Introducing Visual Basic for Applications

This chapter is an introduction to the Visual Basic for Applications (VBA) macro language—a key component for users who want to customize Excel. This chapter teaches you how to record macros and create simple macro procedures. Subsequent chapters expand upon the topics in this chapter.

Introducing VBA Macros

In its broadest sense, a *macro* is a sequence of instructions that automates some aspect of Excel so that you can work more efficiently and with fewer errors. You may create a macro, for example, to format and print your month-end sales report. After the macro is developed, you can then execute the macro to perform many time-consuming procedures automatically.

You need not be a power user to create and use simple VBA macros. Casual users can simply turn on Excel's macro recorder: Excel records your actions and converts them into a VBA macro. When you execute this macro, Excel performs the actions again. More advanced users, though, can write code that tells Excel to perform tasks that can't be recorded. For example, you can write procedures that display custom dialog boxes, add new commands to Excel's menus, or process data in a series of workbooks.

What You Can Do with VBA

VBA is an extremely rich programming language with thousands of uses. The following list contains just a few things that you can do with VBA macros. (Not all of these are covered in this book.)

✦ **Insert a text string or formula:** If you need to enter your company name into worksheets frequently, you can create a macro to do the typing for you. The AutoCorrect feature can also do this.

✦ **Automate a procedure that you perform frequently:** For example, you may need to prepare a month-end summary. If the task is straightforward, you can develop a macro to do it for you.

✦ **Automate repetitive operations:** If you need to perform the same action in 12 different workbooks, you can record a macro while you perform the task once—and then let the macro repeat your action in the other workbooks.

✦ **Create a custom command:** For example, you can combine several of Excel's menu commands so that they are executed from a single keystroke or from a single mouse click.

✦ **Create a custom toolbar button:** You can customize Excel's toolbars with your own buttons to execute macros that you write.

✦ **Create a simplified "front end" for users who don't know much about Excel:** For example, you can set up a foolproof data entry template.

✦ **Develop a new worksheet function:** Although Excel includes a wide assortment of built-in functions, you can create custom functions that greatly simplify your formulas.

✦ **Create complete, turnkey, macro-driven applications:** Excel macros can display custom dialog boxes and add new commands to the menu bar.

✦ **Create custom add-ins for Excel:** Most of the add-ins that are shipped with Excel were created with Excel macros. I used VBA exclusively to create my Power Utility Pak.

Two Types of VBA Macros

Before getting into the details of creating macros, you need to understand a key distinction. A *VBA macro* (also known as a *procedure*) can be one of two types: a *Sub* or a *Function*. The next two sections discuss the difference.

VBA Sub procedures

You can think of a *Sub procedure* as a new command that can be executed by either the user or another macro. You can have any number of Sub procedures in an Excel workbook. Figure 34-1 shows a simple VBA Sub procedure. When this code is executed, VBA inserts the current date into the active cell, formats it, makes the cell bold, and then adjusts the column width.

Figure 34-1: A simple VBA procedure.

Sub procedures always start with the keyword Sub, the macro's name (every macro must have a unique name), and then a pair of parentheses. (The parentheses are required; they are empty unless the procedure uses one or more arguments.) The End Sub statement signals the end of the procedure. The lines in between comprise the procedure's code.

The macro shown in Figure 34-1 also includes a comment. *Comments* are simply notes to yourself, and they are ignored by VBA. A comment line begins with an apostrophe. You can also put a comment after a statement. In other words, when VBA encounters an apostrophe, it ignores the rest of the text in the line.

You execute a VBA Sub procedure in any of the following ways:

✦ Choose Tools ➪ Macro and then select the procedure's name from the list.

✦ Press the procedure's shortcut key combination (if it has one).

✦ If the Visual Basic Editor is active, move the cursor anywhere within the code and press F5.

✦ Refer to the procedure in another VBA procedure.

Sub procedures are covered in detail later in this chapter.

VBA functions

The second type of VBA procedure is a function. A *function* always returns a single value (just as a worksheet function always returns a single value). A VBA function can be executed by other VBA procedures or used in worksheet formulas, just as you would use Excel's built-in worksheet functions.

Figure 34-2 shows the listing of a custom worksheet function and shows the function in use in a worksheet. This function is named CubeRoot, and it requires a single argument. CubeRoot calculates the cube root of its argument. A Function procedure looks much like a Sub procedure. Notice, however, that function procedures begin with the keyword Function and end with an End Function statement.

```
Function CubeRoot (num)
    ' Returns the cube root of a number
    CubeRoot = num ^ (1 / 3)
End Function
```

Figure 34-2: This VBA function returns the cube root of its argument.

Cross-Reference   Creating VBA functions that you use in worksheet formulas can simplify your formulas and enable you to perform calculations that otherwise may be impossible. VBA functions are discussed in greater detail in Chapter 35.

Some Definitions

VBA newcomers are often overwhelmed by the terminology that is used in VBA. I've put together some key definitions to help you keep the terms straight. These terms cover VBA and UserForms (custom dialog boxes) — two important elements that are used to customize Excel:

✦ **Code:** VBA instructions that are produced in a module sheet when you record a macro. You also can enter VBA code manually.

✦ **Controls:** Objects on a UserForm (or in a worksheet) that you manipulate. Examples include buttons, check boxes, and list boxes.

✦ **Function:** One of two types of VBA macros that you can create. (The other is a Sub procedure.) A function returns a single value. You can use VBA functions in other VBA macros or in your worksheets.

✦ **Macro:** A set of VBA instructions that are performed automatically.

✦ **Method:** An action that is taken on an object. For example, applying the Clear method to a range object erases the contents and formatting of the cells.

✦ **Module:** A container for VBA code.

✦ **Object:** An element that you manipulate with VBA. Examples include ranges, charts, drawing objects, and so on.

✦ **Procedure:** Another name for a macro. A VBA procedure can be a Sub procedure or a Function procedure.

✦ **Property:** A particular aspect of an object. For example, a range object has properties, such as `Height`, `Style`, and `Name`.

✦ **Sub procedure:** One of two types of Visual Basic macros that you can create. The other is a function.

✦ **UserForm**: A container that holds controls for a custom dialog box and holds VBA code to manipulate the controls. (UserForms are explained in depth in Chapter 36.)

✦ **VBA:** Visual Basic for Applications. The macro language that is available in Excel as well as in the other applications in Microsoft Office.

✦ **VBE:** Visual Basic Editor. The window (separate from Excel) that you use to create VBA macros and UserForms.

Creating VBA Macros

Excel provides two ways to create macros:

✦ Turn on the macro recorder and record your actions.

✦ Enter the code directly into a VBA module.

The following sections describe both of these methods.

Recording VBA macros

The basic steps that you take to record a VBA macro are described in this section. In most cases, you can record your actions as a macro and then simply replay the macro; you needn't look at the code that's automatically generated. If this is as far as you go with VBA, you don't need to be concerned with the language itself (although a basic understanding of how things work doesn't do any harm).

Recording your actions to create VBA code: The basics

Excel's macro recorder translates your actions into VBA code. To start the macro recorder, choose Tools ➪ Macro ➪ Record New Macro. Excel displays the Record Macro dialog box, as shown in Figure 34-3.

The Record Macro dialog box presents several options:

✦ **Macro Name:** The name of the macro. By default, Excel proposes names, such as Macro1, Macro2, and so on.

✦ **Shortcut Key:** You can specify a key combination that executes the macro. The key combination always uses the Ctrl key. You can also press Shift when you enter a letter. For example, pressing Shift while you enter the letter *H* makes the shortcut key combination Ctrl+Shift+H.

✦ **Store Macro In:** The location for the macro. Your choices are the current workbook, your Personal Macro Workbook (described later in this chapter), or a new workbook.

✦ **Description:** A description of the macro. By default, Excel inserts the date and your name. You can add more information if you like.

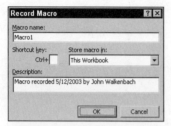

Figure 34-3: The Record Macro dialog box.

To begin recording your actions, click OK. Excel displays the Stop Recording toolbar, which contains two buttons: Stop Recording and Relative Reference. After you finish recording the macro, choose Tools ➪ Macro ➪ Stop Recording (or click the Stop Recording button on the toolbar).

Note   Recording your actions always results in a new Sub procedure. You can't create a Function procedure by using the macro recorder. Function procedures must be created manually.

Recording a macro: An example

This example demonstrates how to record a macro that changes the formatting for the current range selection. The macro makes the selected range use Arial 16-point type, boldface, and the color red. To create the macro, follow these steps:

1. Enter a value or text into a cell — anything is okay. This gives you something to start with.

2. Select the cell that contains the value or text that you entered in the preceding step.

3. Select Tools ➪ Macro ➪ Record New Macro. Excel displays the Record Macro dialog box.

4. Enter a new name for the macro, to replace the default `Macro1` name. A good name is **FormattingMacro**.

5. Assign this macro to the shortcut key Ctrl+Shift+F by entering **F** in the edit box labeled Shortcut Key.

6. Click OK. This closes the Record Macro dialog box. Excel displays a toolbar called Stop Recording.

7. Select Format ➪ Cells and then click the Font tab. Choose Arial font, Bold, and 16-point type, and make the color red. Click OK to close the Format Cells dialog box.

8. The macro is finished, so click the Stop Recording button on the Stop Recording toolbar (or select Tools ➪ Macro ➪ Stop Recording).

Examining the macro

The macro was recorded in a new module named Module1. To view the code in this module, you must activate the Visual Basic Editor (VBE). You can activate the VBE in either of two ways:

✦ Press Alt+F11.

✦ Choose Tools ➪ Macro ➪ Visual Basic Editor.

The Project window displays a list of all open workbooks and add-ins. This list is displayed as a tree diagram, which can be expanded or collapsed. The code that you recorded previously is stored in Module1 in the current workbook. When you double-click Module1, the code in the module is displayed in the Code window.

Figure 34-4 shows the recorded macro, as displayed in the Code window.

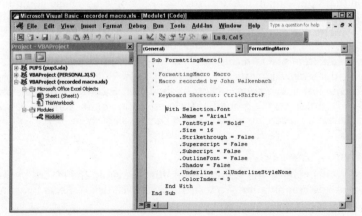

Figure 34-4: The FormattingMacro procedure was generated by Excel's macro recorder.

Activate the module and examine the macro. It should consist of the following code:

```
Sub FormattingMacro ()
'
' FormattingMacro Macro
' Macro recorded by John Walkenbach
'
' Keyboard Shortcut: Ctrl+Shift+F
'
    With Selection.Font
        .Name = "Arial"
        .FontStyle = "Bold"
        .Size = 16
        .Strikethrough = False
        .Superscript = False
        .Subscript = False
        .OutlineFont = False
        .Shadow = False
        .Underline = xlUnderlineStyleNone
        .ColorIndex = 3
    End With
End Sub
```

The macro recorded is a Sub procedure that is named FormattingMacro. The statements tell Excel what to do when the macro is executed.

Notice that Excel inserted some comments at the top of the procedure. This is some of the information that appeared in the Record Macro dialog box. These comment lines (which begin with an apostrophe) aren't really necessary, and deleting them has no effect on how the macro runs.

Note   You may notice that the macro recorded some actions that you didn't take. For example, it sets the `Strikethrough`, `Superscript`, and `Subscript` properties to `False`. This is just a byproduct of the method that Excel uses to translate actions into code. Excel sets the properties for every option in the Font tab of the Format Cells dialog box, even though you didn't change all of them.

Testing the macro

Before you recorded this macro, you set an option that assigned the macro to the Ctrl+Shift+F shortcut key combination. To test the macro, return to Excel by using either of the following methods:

   ✦ Press Alt+F11.

   ✦ Click the View Microsoft Excel button on the VBE toolbar.

When Excel is active, activate a worksheet. (It can be in the workbook that contains the VBA module or in any other workbook.) Select a cell or range and press Ctrl+Shift+F. The macro immediately changes the formatting of the selected cell(s).

Continue testing the macro with other selections consisting of one or more cells. You find that the macro always applies exactly the same formatting.

Note   In the preceding example, notice that you selected the cell to be formatted *before* you started recording your macro. This is important. If you select a cell while the macro recorder is turned on, the actual cell that you selected will be recorded into the macro. In such a case, the macro would always format that particular cell, and it would not be a "general-purpose" macro.

Editing the macro

After you record a macro, you can make some changes to it (although you must know what you're doing). Assume that you discover that you really want to make the text 14-point rather than 16-point. You could rerecord the macro, but this is a simple modification, so editing the code is more efficient. Just activate Module1, locate the statement that sets the font size, and change 16 to 14. You can also remove the following lines, which are not really necessary:

```
.Strikethrough = False
.Superscript = False
.Subscript = False
.OutlineFont = False
.Shadow = False
.Underline = xlUnderlineStyleNone
```

Removing these lines causes the macro to ignore the properties that are referred to in the statements. For example, if the cell has underlining, the underlining isn't affected by the macro.

The edited macro appears as follows:

```
Sub FormattingMacro()
    With Selection.Font
        .Name = "Arial"
        .FontStyle = "Bold"
        .Size = 14
        .ColorIndex = 3
    End With
End Sub
```

Test this new macro, and you see that it performs as it should. Also, notice that it doesn't remove a cell's underlining, which occurred in the original version of the macro.

Another example

This example shows you how to record a slightly more-complicated VBA macro that converts formulas into values. Converting formulas into values is usually a two-step process in Excel:

1. Copy the range to the Clipboard.

2. Choose Edit ⇨ Paste Special (with the Values option selected) to paste the values over the formulas.

This macro combines these steps into a single command.

Furthermore, you want to be able to access this command by pressing a shortcut key combination (Ctrl+Shift+V). Take the following steps to create this macro:

1. Enter a formula into a cell. Any formula will do.

2. Select the cell that contains the formula.

3. Choose Tools ⇨ Macro ⇨ Record New Macro. Excel displays the Record Macro dialog box.

4. In the Record Macro dialog box, enter **ConvertFormulas** for the macro name, and specify Ctrl+Shift+V as the shortcut key.

5. Click OK to begin recording.

6. With the range still selected, choose Edit ⇨ Copy to copy the range to the Clipboard.

7. Select Edit ⇨ Paste Special, click the Values option, and then click OK to close the dialog box.

8. Press Esc to cancel Paste mode. (Excel removes the moving border around the selected range.)

9. Click the Stop Recording button (or choose Tools ⇨ Macro ⇨ Stop Recording).

To test the macro, activate a worksheet, enter some formulas, and then select the formulas. You can execute the macro in two ways:

✦ Press Ctrl+Shift+V.

✦ Choose Tools ⇨ Macro ⇨ Macros command and double-click the macro name (ConvertFormulas).

Excel converts the formulas in the selected range to their values in a single step instead of two.

Caution   Be careful when you use this macro: You can't undo the conversion of formulas to values. You *can* edit the macro so that its results can be undone, but the procedure is beyond the scope of this discussion.

Note   The shortcut key combination (Ctrl+Shift+V) is valid only when the workbook is open. When you close the workbook, pressing Ctrl+Shift+V has no effect.

The recorded macro appears as follows:

```
Sub ConvertFormulas()
    Selection.Copy
    Selection.PasteSpecial Paste:=xlPasteValues, _
     Operation:=xlNone, SkipBlanks:=False, Transpose:=False
    Application.CutCopyMode = False
End Sub
```

The procedure has three statements. The first simply copies the selected range. The second statement, which is displayed on two lines (the underscore character means that the statement continues on the next line), pastes the Clipboard contents to the current selection. The second statement has several arguments, representing the options in the Paste Special dialog box. The third statement cancels the moving border around the selected range.

If you prefer, you can delete the underscore character in the second statement and combine the two lines into one. (A VBA statement can be any length.) This action may make the macro easier to read.

More about recording VBA macros

If you followed along with the preceding examples, you should have a better feel for how to record macros. If you find the VBA code confusing, don't worry. You don't really have to be concerned with it as long as the macro that you record works correctly. If the macro doesn't work, rerecording the macro rather than editing the code often is easier.

A good way to learn about what gets recorded is to set up your screen so that you can see the code that is being generated in the Visual Basic Editor windows. To do so, make sure that Excel's Window is not maximized; then arrange the Excel window and the VBE window so both are visible. While you're recording your actions, make sure that the VBE window is displaying the module in which the code is being recorded. (You may have to double-click the module name in the Project window.)

Absolute versus relative recording

If you're going to work with macros, you need to understand the concept of *relative* versus *absolute* recording. Normally, when you record a macro, Excel stores exact references to the cells that you select. (That is, it performs *absolute* recording.) If you select the range B1:B10 while you're recording a macro, for example, Excel records this selection as

```
Range("B1:B10").Select
```

This means exactly what it says: "Select the cells in the range B1:B10." When you invoke this macro, the same cells are always selected, regardless of where the active cell is located.

You may have noticed that the Stop Recording toolbar has a tool named Relative Recording. When you click this tool while recording a macro, Excel changes its recording mode from absolute (the default) to relative. When recording in relative mode, selecting a range of cells is translated differently, depending on where the active cell is located. For example, if you're recording in relative mode and cell A1 is active, selecting the range B1:B10 generates the following statement:

```
ActiveCell.Offset(0, 1).Range("A1:A10").Select
```

This statement can be translated as "From the active cell, move 0 rows down and 1 column right, and then treat this new cell as if it were cell A1. Now select what would be A1:A10." In other words, a macro that is recorded in relative mode starts out by using the active cell as its base and then stores relative references to this cell. As a result, you get different results, depending on the location of the active cell. When you replay this macro, the cells that are selected depend on the active cell. This macro selects a range that is 10 rows by 1 column, offset from the active cell by 0 rows and 1 column.

When Excel is recording in relative mode, the Relative Reference toolbar button appears depressed. To return to absolute recording, click the Relative Reference button again (and it displays its normal, undepressed state).

Note The recording mode (either absolute or relative) can make a *major* difference in how your macro performs. Therefore, understanding the distinction is important.

Storing macros in the Personal Macro Workbook

Most user-created macros are designed for use in a specific workbook, but you may want to use some macros in all of your work. You can store these general-purpose macros in the Personal Macro Workbook, so that they are always available to you. The Personal Macro Workbook is loaded whenever you start Excel. The file, personal.xls, is stored in the XlStart folder, which is in your Excel folder. This file doesn't exist until you record a macro, using Personal Macro Workbook as the destination.

Note The Personal Macro Workbook normally is in a hidden window (to keep it out of the way).

To record the macro in your Personal Macro Workbook, select the Personal Macro Workbook option in the Record Macro dialog box before you start recording. This is one of the options in the Store Macro In drop-down box.

If you store macros in the Personal Macro Workbook, you don't have to remember to open the Personal Macro Workbook when you load a workbook that uses macros. When you want to exit, Excel asks whether you want to save changes to the Personal Macro Workbook.

Assigning a macro to a toolbar button

When you record a macro, you can assign it to a shortcut key combination. After you record the macro and test it, you may want to assign the macro to a toolbar button. You can follow these steps to do so:

1. If the macro is a general-purpose macro that you plan to use in more than one workbook, make sure that the macro is stored in your Personal Macro Workbook.

2. Select View ⇨ Toolbars ⇨ Customize. Excel displays its Customize dialog box.

3. Click the Toolbars tab in the Customize dialog box and make sure that the toolbar that is to contain the new button is visible.

4. Click the Commands tab in the Customize dialog box.

5. Click the Macros category.

6. In the Commands list, drag the Custom Button icon to the toolbar.

7. Right-click the toolbar button and select Assign Macro from the shortcut menu. Excel displays its Assign Macro dialog box.

8. Select the macro name from the list and click OK.

9. At this point, you can right-click the button again if you want to change its name and button image.

10. Click Close to exit the Customize dialog box.

**Cross-
Reference**
See Chapter 26 for details about customizing toolbars.

Writing VBA code

As demonstrated in the preceding sections, the easiest way to create a simple macro is to record your actions. To develop more-complex macros, however, you have to enter the VBA code manually — in other words, write a program. To save time, you can often combine recording with manual code entry.

Before you can begin writing VBA code, you must have a good understanding of such topics as objects, properties, and methods. And it doesn't hurt to be familiar with common programming constructs, such as looping and If-Then statements.

This section is an introduction to VBA programming, which is essential if you want to write (rather than record) VBA macros. This is not intended to be a complete instructional guide. My book titled *Excel 2003 Power Programming with VBA* (Wiley Publishing, Inc.) covers all aspects of VBA and advanced spreadsheet application development.

The basics: Entering and editing code

Before you can enter code, you must insert a VBA module into the workbook. If the workbook already has a VBA module, you can use the existing module sheet for your new code.

Use the following steps to insert a new VBA module:

1. Press Alt+F11 to activate the Visual Basic Editor window. The Visual Basic Editor window is a separate application, although it works very closely with Excel.

2. The Project window displays a list of all open workbooks and add-ins. Locate the workbook that you are currently working in and select it.

3. Choose Insert ➪ Module. VBA inserts a new (empty) module into the workbook and displays it in the Code window.

VBA Coding Tips

When you enter code in a module sheet, you're free to use indenting and blank lines to make the code more readable. (In fact, this is an excellent habit.)

After you enter a line of code (by pressing Enter), it is evaluated for syntax errors. If none are found, the line of code is reformatted, and colors are added to keywords and identifiers. This automatic reformatting adds consistent spaces (before and after an equal sign, for example) and removes extra spaces that aren't needed. If a syntax error is found, you receive a pop-up message, and the line is displayed in a different color (red, by default). You need to correct your error before you can execute the macro.

A single statement can be as long as needed. However, you may want to break the statement into two or more lines. To do so, insert a space followed by an underscore(_). The following code, although written as two lines, is actually a single VBA statement:

```
Sheets("Sheet1").Range("B1").Value = _
    Sheets("Sheet1").Range("A1").Value
```

You can insert comments freely into your VBA code. The comment indicator is an apostrophe single quote character ('). Any text that follows a single quote is ignored. A comment can be a line by itself or can be inserted after a statement. The following examples show two comments:

```
' Assign the values to the variables
Rate = .085  'Rate as of November 16
```

A VBA module, which is displayed in a separate window, works like a text editor. You can move through the sheet, select text, insert, copy, cut, paste, and so on.

How VBA works

VBA is by far the most complex feature in Excel, and you can easily get overwhelmed. To set the stage for the details of VBA, here is a concise summary of how VBA works:

✦ You perform actions in VBA by writing (or recording) code in a VBA module sheet and then executing the macro in any one of various ways. VBA modules are stored in an Excel workbook, and a workbook can hold any number of VBA modules. To view or edit a VBA module, you must activate the Visual Basic Editor window (press Alt+F11 to toggle between Excel and the VBE window).

✦ A VBA module consists of procedures. A *procedure* is basically computer code that performs some action. The following is an example of a simple Sub procedure called ShowSum (it adds 1 + 1 and displays the result):

```
Sub ShowSum()
   Sum = 1 + 1
   MsgBox "The answer is " & Sum
End Sub
```

✦ A VBA module also can store function procedures. A *function procedure* performs some calculations and returns a single value. A function can be called from another VBA procedure or can even be used in a worksheet formula. Here's an example of a function named AddTwo. (It adds two values, which are supplied as arguments.)

```
Function AddTwo(arg1, arg2)
   AddTwo = arg1 + arg2
End Function
```

✦ VBA manipulates objects. Excel provides well over 100 classes of objects that you can manipulate. Examples of objects include a workbook, a worksheet, a range on a worksheet, a chart, and a drawn rectangle.

✦ Objects are arranged in a hierarchy and can act as containers for other objects. For example, Excel itself is an object called Application, and it contains other objects, such as Workbook objects. The Workbook object can contain other objects, such as Worksheet objects and Chart objects. A Worksheet object can contain objects such as Range objects, PivotTable objects, and so on. The arrangement of these objects is referred to as an *object model*. Excel's object model is depicted in the VBA Help system (a portion of which is shown in Figure 34-5).

✦ Objects that are alike form a *collection*. For example, the Worksheets collection consists of all worksheets in a particular workbook. The CommandBars collection consists of all CommandBar objects (that is, menu bars and toolbars). Collections are objects in themselves.

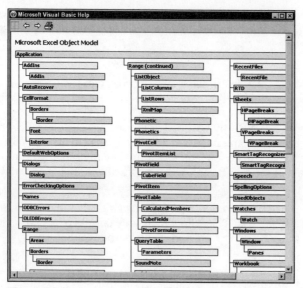

Figure 34-5: A portion of Excel's object model.

✦ You refer to an object in your VBA code by specifying its position in the object hierarchy, using a period as a separator.

For example, you can refer to a workbook named Book1.xls as

```
Application.Workbooks("Book1")
```

This refers to the Book1.xls workbook in the Workbooks collection. The Workbooks collection is contained in the Application object (that is, Excel). Extending this to another level, you can refer to Sheet1 in Book1 as follows:

```
Application.Workbooks("Book1").Worksheets("Sheet1")
```

You can take it to still another level and refer to a specific cell as follows:

```
Application.Workbooks("Book1").Worksheets("Sheet1").
Range("A1")
```

✦ If you omit specific references, Excel uses the *active* objects. If Book1 is the active workbook, the preceding reference can be simplified as follows:

```
Worksheets("Sheet1").Range("A1")
```

If you know that Sheet1 is the active sheet, you can simplify the reference even more:

```
Range("A1")
```

✦ Objects have properties. A *property* can be thought of as a setting for an object. For example, a Range object has properties, such as Value and Name. A Chart object has properties such as HasTitle and Type. You can use VBA both to determine object properties and to change them.

✦ You refer to properties by combining the object with the property, separated by a period. For example, you can refer to the value in cell A1 on Sheet1 as follows:

```
Worksheets("Sheet1").Range("A1").Value
```

✦ You can assign values to variables. To assign the value in cell A1 on Sheet1 to a variable called Interest, use the following VBA statement:

```
Interest = Worksheets("Sheet1").Range("A1").Value
```

✦ Objects have methods. A *method* is an action that is performed with the object. For example, one of the methods for a Range object is ClearContents. This method clears the contents of the range.

✦ You specify methods by combining the object with the method, separated by a period. For example, to clear the contents of cell A1, use the following statement:

```
Worksheets("Sheet1").Range("A1:C12").ClearContents
```

✦ VBA also includes all the constructs of modern programming languages, including arrays, looping, and so on.

The preceding describes VBA in a nutshell. Now you just have to learn the details, some of which are covered in the rest of this chapter.

Objects and collections

VBA is an *object-oriented language,* which means that it manipulates *objects,* such as Ranges, Charts, AutoShapes, and so on. These objects are arranged in a hierarchy. The Application object (which is Excel) contains other objects. For example, the Application object contains a number of objects, including the following:

✦ AddIns (a collection of AddIn objects)

✦ Windows (a collection of Window objects)

✦ Workbooks (a collection of Workbook objects)

Most of these objects can contain other objects. For example, a Workbook object can contain the following objects:

✦ Charts (a collection of Chart objects)

✦ Names (a collection of Name objects)

✦ Styles (a collection of Style objects)

✦ Windows (a collection of Window objects in the workbook)

✦ Worksheets (a collection of Worksheet objects)

Each of these objects, in turn, can contain other objects. A Worksheet object, for example, can contain the following objects:

✦ ChartObjects (a collection of all ChartObject objects)

✦ PageSetup (an object that stores printing information)

✦ PivotTables (a collection of all PivotTable objects)

A *collection* consists of all like objects. For example, the collection of all Workbook objects is known as the Workbooks collection. You can refer to an individual object in a collection by using an index number or a name. For example, if a workbook has three worksheets (named Sheet1, Sheet2, and Sheet3), you can refer to the first object in the Worksheets collection in either of these ways:

```
Worksheets(1)
Worksheets("Sheet1")
```

Properties

The objects that you work with have *properties,* which you can think of as attributes of the objects. For example, a Range object has properties, such as Column, Row, Width, and Value. A Chart object has properties, such as Legend, ChartTitle, and so on. ChartTitle is also an object, with properties such as Font, Orientation, and Text. Excel has many objects, and each has its own set of properties. You can write VBA code to do the following:

✦ Examine an object's current property setting and take some action based on it.

✦ Change an object's property setting.

You refer to a property in your VBA code by placing a period and the property name after the object's name. For example, the following VBA statement sets the Value property of a range named *Frequency* to 15. (That is, the statement causes the number *15* to appear in the range's cells.)

```
Range("frequency").Value = 15
```

Some properties are *read-only,* which means that you can examine the property, but you can't change the property. For a single-cell Range object, the Row and Column properties are read-only properties: You can determine where a cell is located (in which row and column), but you can't change the cell's location by changing these properties.

A Range object also has a Formula property, which is *not* read-only; that is, you can insert a formula into a cell by changing its Formula property. The following statement inserts a formula into cell A1 by changing the cell's Formula property:

```
Range("A1").Formula = "=SUM(A1:A10)"
```

Note Contrary to what you may think, Excel doesn't have a `Cell` object. When you want to manipulate a single cell, you use the `Range` object (with only one cell in it).

At the top of the object hierarchy is the `Application` object, which is actually Excel, the program. The `Application` object has several useful properties:

✦ `Application.ActiveWorkbook`: Returns the active workbook (a `Workbook` object) in Excel.

✦ `Application.ActiveSheet`: Returns the active sheet (a `Sheet` object) of the active workbook.

✦ `Application.ActiveCell`: Returns the active cell (a `Range` object) object of the active window.

✦ `Application.Selection`: Returns the object that is currently selected in the active window of the `Application` object. This can be a `Range`, a `Chart`, a `Shape`, or some other selectable object.

You also should understand that properties can return objects. In fact, that's exactly what the preceding examples do. The result of `Application.ActiveCell`, for example, is a `Range` object. Therefore, you can access properties by using a statement such as the following:

```
Application.ActiveCell.Font.Size = 15
```

In this case, `Application.ActiveCell.Font` is an object, and `Size` is a property of the object. The preceding statement sets the `Size` property to 15; that is, it causes the font in the currently selected cell to have a size of 15 points.

Tip Because `Application` properties are so commonly used, you can omit the object qualifier (`Application`). For example, to get the row of the active cell, you can use a statement such as the following:

```
ActiveCell.Row
```

In many cases, you can refer to the same object in a number of different ways. Assume that you have a workbook named Sales.xls and it's the only workbook open. Furthermore, assume that this workbook has one worksheet, named Summary. Your VBA code can refer to the Summary sheet in any of the following ways:

```
Workbooks("Sales.xls").Worksheets("Summary")
Workbooks(1).Worksheets(1)
Workbooks(1).Sheets(1)
Application.ActiveWorkbook.ActiveSheet
ActiveWorkbook.ActiveSheet
ActiveSheet
```

The method that you use is determined by how much you know about the workspace. For example, if more than one workbook is open, the second or third method is not reliable. If you want to work with the active sheet (whatever it may be), any of the last three methods would work. To be absolutely sure that you're referring to a specific sheet on a specific workbook, the first method is your best choice.

Methods

Objects also have *methods*. You can think of a method as an action taken with an object. For example, Range objects have a Clear method. The following VBA statement clears a Range, an action that is equivalent to selecting the Range and then choosing Edit ⇨ Clear ⇨ All:

```
Range("A1:C12").Clear
```

In VBA code, methods *look* like properties because they are connected to the object with a "dot." However, methods and properties are different concepts.

Variables

Like all programming languages, VBA enables you to work with variables. In VBA (unlike in some languages), you don't need to declare variables explicitly before you use them in your code (although doing so is definitely a good practice).

In the following example, the value in cell A1 on Sheet1 is assigned to a variable named Rate:

```
rate = Worksheets("Sheet1").Range("A1").Value
```

You then can work with the variable Rate in other parts of your VBA code. Note that the variable Rate is not a named range, which means that you can't use it as such in a worksheet formula.

Controlling execution

VBA uses many constructs that are found in most other programming languages. These constructs are used to control the flow of execution. This section introduces a few of the more common programming constructs.

The If-Then construct

One of the most important control structures in VBA is the If-Then construct. This common command gives your applications decision-making capability. The basic syntax of the If-Then structure is as follows:

```
If condition Then statements [Else elsestatements]
```

The following is an example (which doesn't use the optional `Else` clause). This procedure checks the active cell. If it contains a negative value, the cell's color is changed to red. Otherwise, nothing happens.

```
Sub CheckCell()
  If ActiveCell.Value < 0 Then ActiveCell.Font.ColorIndex = 3
End Sub
```

For-Next loops

You can use a `For-Next` loop to process a series of items. Here's an example of a `For-Next` loop:

```
Sub SumSquared()
  Total = 0
  For Num = 1 To 10
    Total = Total + (Num ^ 2)
  Next Num
  MsgBox Total
End Sub
```

This example has one statement between the `For` statement and the `Next` statement. This single statement is executed 10 times. The variable `Num` takes on successive values of 1, 2, 3, and so on, up to 10. The variable `Total` stores the sum of `Num` squared, added to the previous value of `Total`. The result is a value that represents the sum of the first 10 integers squared. This result is displayed in a message box.

The With-End With construct

Another construct that you encounter if you record macros is the `With-End With` construct. This is a shortcut way of dealing with several properties or methods of the same object. The following is an example:

```
Sub AlignCells()
  With Selection
    .HorizontalAlignment = xlCenter
    .VerticalAlignment = xlCenter
    .WrapText = False
    .Orientation = xlHorizontal
  End With
End Sub
```

The following macro performs exactly the same operations but doesn't use the `With-End With` construct:

```
Sub AlignCells()
  Selection.HorizontalAlignment = xlCenter
  Selection.VerticalAlignment = xlCenter
  Selection.WrapText = False
  Selection.Orientation = xlHorizontal
End Sub
```

The Select Case construct

The Select Case construct is useful for choosing among two or more options. The following example demonstrates the use of a Select Case construct. In this example, the active cell is checked. If its value is less than 0, it's colored red. If it's equal to 0, it's colored blue. If the value is greater than 0, it's colored black.

```
Sub CheckCell()
   Select Case ActiveCell.Value
      Case Is < 0
         ActiveCell.Font.ColorIndex = 3 'Red
      Case 0
         ActiveCell.Font.ColorIndex = 5 'Blue
      Case Is > 0
         ActiveCell.Font.ColorIndex = 1 'Black
   End Select
End Sub
```

Any number of statements can go below each Case statement, and they all get executed if the case is true.

A macro that can't be recorded

The following is a VBA macro that can't be recorded because it uses an If-Then structure. This macro enables you to quickly identify cells that exceed a certain value. When you run this macro, it prompts the user for a value and then evaluates every cell in the selection. If the cell's value is greater than the value that is entered by the user, the macro makes the cell bold and red.

```
Sub SelectiveFormat()
'This procedure selectively shades cells greater than
'a specified target value
'Get target value from user
  Message = "Change attributes of values greater than or
equal_to..."
  Target = InputBox(Message)
  Target=Val(Target)

'Evaluate each cell in the selection
  For Each Item In Selection
     If IsNumeric(Item) Then
        If Item.Value >= Target Then
           With Item
              .Font.Bold = True
              .Font.ColorIndex = 3 'Red
           End With
        End If
     End If
  Next Item
End Sub
```

Although this macro may look complicated, it's fairly simple when you break it down.

First, the macro assigns text to a variable named `Message`. It then uses the `InputBox` function to solicit a value from the user. The `InputBox` function has a single argument (which is the `Message` variable) and returns a string—which is assigned to the `Target` variable. Next, the `Val` function is used to convert this string to a value.

The `For-Next` loop checks every cell in the selected range. The first statement within the loop uses the `IsNumeric` function to determine whether the cell can be evaluated as a number. This is important, because a cell without a value would generate an error when the `Value` property is accessed in the next statement. If the cell is numeric, it is checked against the target value. If it's greater than or equal to the target value, the `Bold` and `ColorIndex` properties are changed. Otherwise, nothing happens, and the loop is incremented.

After entering this macro, named SelectiveFormat, into a module sheet, you can provide a shortcut key to access it. Choose Tools ➪ Macro ➪ Macros to display the Macros dialog box. Select the macro from the list and click Options. Excel displays a new dialog box that enables you to specify a shortcut key combination to execute the macro.

Figure 34-6 shows the macro in action. Note that you must select the range before you execute the macro.

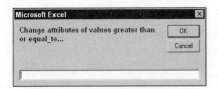

Figure 34-6: The macro uses the `InputBox` function to prompt the user for a value.

As macros go, this example is not very good. It's not very flexible and doesn't include any error handling. For example, if a nonrange object (such as a graphic object) is selected, the macro halts and displays an error message. To avoid this error message and abort the macro if anything except a range is selected, you can insert the following statement as the first statement in the procedure (directly below the `Sub` statement):

```
If TypeName(Selection) <> "Range" Then Exit Sub
```

This causes the macro to halt if the selection is not a `Range` object.

Notice also that the macro is executed even if you click Cancel in the input box. To avoid this problem, enter the following statement directly above the `Target=Val(Target)` statement:

```
If Target = "" then Exit Sub
```

This aborts the procedure if `Target` is empty.

Learning More

This chapter barely scratches the surface of what you can do with VBA. If this is your first exposure to VBA, you're probably a bit overwhelmed by objects, properties, and methods. I don't blame you. If you try to access a property that an object doesn't have, you get a run-time error, and your VBA code grinds to a screeching halt until you correct the problem. Fortunately, several good ways are available to learn about objects, properties, and methods.

Read the rest of the book

Chapters 35–40 of this book are devoted to VBA, and you'll find many more examples in those chapters.

Record your actions

The best way to become familiar with VBA is to turn on the macro recorder and record actions that you make in Excel. You can then examine the code to gain some insights regarding the objects, properties, and methods.

Use the online Help system

The main source of detailed information about Excel's objects, methods, and procedures is the online Help system. Help is very thorough and easy to access. When you're in a VBA module, just move the cursor to a property or method and press F1. You get help that describes the word that is under the cursor.

Get another book

Several books are devoted exclusively to using VBA with Excel. My book, *Excel 2003 Power Programming with VBA* (Wiley Publishing, Inc.), is one of them.

✦   ✦   ✦

Creating Custom Worksheet Functions

As mentioned in the preceding chapter, you can create two types of VBA procedures: Sub procedures and Function procedures. This chapter focuses on Function procedures.

Overview of VBA Functions

Function procedures that you write in VBA are quite versatile. You can use these functions in two situations:

✦ You can call the function from a different VBA procedure.

✦ You can use the function in formulas that you create in a worksheet.

This chapter focuses on creating functions for use in your formulas.

Excel contains hundreds of predefined worksheet functions. With so many from which to choose, you may be curious as to why anyone would need to develop additional functions. The main reason is that creating a custom function can greatly simplify your formulas by making them shorter, and shorter formulas are more readable and easier to work with. For example, you can often replace a complex formula with a single function. Another reason is that you can write functions to perform operations that would otherwise be impossible.

Note   This chapter assumes that you are familiar with entering and editing VBA code in the Visual Basic Editor (VBE). Refer to Chapter 34 for an overview of the VBE.

An Introductory Example

The process of creating custom functions is relatively easy, once you understand VBA. Without further ado, here's an example of a VBA function procedure. This function is stored in a VBA module, which is accessible from the VBE.

A custom function

This example function, named NumSign, uses one argument. The function returns a text string of Positive if its argument is greater than zero, Negative if the argument is less than zero, and Zero if the argument is equal to zero. The function is shown in Figure 35-1.

```
Function NumSign(InVal)
    Select Case InVal
        Case Is < 0
            NumSign = "Negative"
        Case 0
            NumSign = "Zero"
        Case Is > 0
            NumSign = "Positive"
    End Select
End Function
```

Figure 35-1: A custom function.

You could, of course, accomplish the same effect with the following worksheet formula, which uses a nested IF function:

```
=IF(A1=0,"Zero",IF(A1>0,"Positive","Negative"))
```

Many would agree that the custom function solution is easier to understand and to edit than the worksheet formula.

Using the function in a worksheet

When you enter a formula that uses the NumSign function, Excel executes the function to get the result. This custom function works just like any built-in worksheet function. You can insert it in a formula by using the Insert ⇨ Function command, which displays the Paste Function dialog box. Then you can use the Function Arguments dialog box to specify the arguments for the function (as shown in Figure 35-2). Custom functions are located in the User Defined category. You also can nest custom functions and combine them with other elements in your formulas.

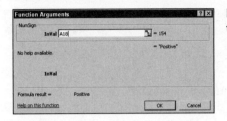

Figure 35-2: Creating a worksheet formula that uses a custom function.

Analyzing the custom function

This section describes the NumSign function. Here again is the code:

```
Function NumSign(InVal)
    Select Case InVal
        Case Is < 0
            NumSign = "Negative"
        Case 0
            NumSign = "Zero"
        Case Is > 0
            NumSign = "Positive"
    End Select
End Function
```

Notice that the procedure starts with the keyword Function rather than Sub, followed by the name of the function (NumSign). This custom function uses one argument (InVal); the argument's name is enclosed in parentheses. InVal is the cell or variable that is to be processed. When the function is used in a worksheet, the argument can be a cell reference (such as A1) or a literal value (such as -123). When the function is used in another procedure, the argument can be a numeric variable, a literal number, or a value that is obtained from a cell.

The NumSign function uses the Select Case construct (described in Chapter 34) to take a different action, depending on the value of InVal. If InVal is less than zero, NumSign is assigned the text "Negative". If InVal is equal to zero, NumSign is "Zero". If InVal is greater than zero, NumSign is "Positive". The value returned by a function is always assigned to the function's name.

About Function Procedures

A custom Function procedure has a lot in common with a Sub procedure, covered in the preceding chapter. Function procedures have some important differences, however. Perhaps the key difference is that a function returns a *value*. When writing a Function procedure, the value that's returned is the value that has been assigned to the function's name when a function is finished executing.

What a Function Can't Do

Almost everyone who starts creating custom worksheet functions using VBA makes a fatal mistake: They try to get the function to do more than is possible.

A worksheet function returns a value, and the function must be completely "passive." In other words, the function cannot change anything on the worksheet. For example, it's impossible to develop a worksheet function that changes the formatting of a cell. (Every VBA programmer has tried this, and not one of them has been successful!) If your function attempts to perform an action that is not allowed, the function simply returns an error.

VBA functions that are not used in worksheet formulas can do anything that a regular subroutine can do—including changing cell formatting.

To create a custom function, follow these steps:

1. Activate the Visual Basic Editor (or press Alt+F11).
2. Select the workbook in the Project window.
3. Choose Insert ⇨ Module to insert a VBA module. (Or you can use an existing module.)
4. Enter the keyword **Function** followed by the function's name and a list of the arguments (if any) in parentheses.
5. Insert the VBA code that performs the work—and make sure that the variable corresponding to the function's name has the appropriate value when the function ends. (This is the value that the function returns.)
6. End the function with an `End Function` statement.

Function names that are used in worksheet formulas must adhere to the same rules as variable names, and you can't use a name that looks like a worksheet cell (for example, a function named J21 isn't accepted).

Executing Function Procedures

There are many ways to execute a Sub procedure, but you can execute a Function procedure in just two ways:

✦ Call it from another procedure.

✦ Use it in a worksheet formula.

Calling custom functions from a procedure

You can call custom functions from a procedure just as you call built-in VBA functions. For example, after you define a function called `CalcTax`, you can enter a statement such as the following:

```
Tax = CalcTax(Amount, Rate)
```

This statement executes the `CalcTax` custom function with `Amount` and `Rate` as its arguments. The function's result is assigned to the `Tax` variable.

Using custom functions in a worksheet formula

Using a custom function in a worksheet formula is like using built-in functions. You must ensure that Excel can locate the function procedure, however. If the function procedure is in the same workbook, you don't have to do anything special. If the function is defined in a different workbook, you may have to tell Excel where to find the function. The following are the three ways in which you can do this:

✦ **Precede the function's name with a file reference.** For example, if you want to use a function called `CountNames` that's defined in a workbook named MyFunctions, you can use a reference such as the following:

```
=MyFunctions.xls!CountNames(A1:A1000)
```

If the workbook name contains a space, you need to add single quotes around the workbook name. For example:

```
='My Functions.xls'!CountNames(A1:A1000)
```

If you insert the function with the Paste Function dialog box, the workbook reference is inserted automatically.

✦ **Set up a reference to the workbook.** If the custom function is defined in a reference workbook, you don't need to precede the function name with the workbook name. You establish a reference to another workbook with the Tools ⇨ References command (in the Visual Basic Editor). You are presented with a list of references that includes all open workbooks. Place a check mark in the item that refers to the workbook that contains the custom function. (Use the Browse button if the workbook isn't open.)

✦ **Create an add-in.** When you create an add-in from a workbook that has function procedures, you don't need to use the file reference when you use one of the functions in a formula; the add-in must be installed, however. Chapter 40 discusses add-ins.

Note   Your function procedures don't appear in the Macros dialog box when you select Tools ⇨ Macro because you can't execute a function directly. As a result, you need to do extra, up-front work to test your functions as you're developing them. One approach is to set up a simple subroutine that calls the function. If the function is designed to be used in worksheet formulas, you can enter a simple formula to test it as you're developing the function.

Function Procedure Arguments

Keep in mind the following about function procedure arguments:

✦ Arguments can be variables (including arrays), constants, literals, or expressions.

✦ Some functions do not have arguments.

✦ Some functions have a fixed number of required arguments (from 1 to 60).

✦ Some functions have a combination of required and optional arguments.

The following section presents a series of examples that demonstrate how to use arguments effectively with functions. Coverage of optional arguments is beyond the scope of this book.

On the CD-ROM   The examples in this chapter are available on the companion CD-ROM.

A function with no argument

Like subroutines, functions don't necessarily have to use arguments. Excel, for example, has a few built-in worksheet functions that don't use arguments. These include RAND, TODAY, and NOW.

The following is a simple example of a function that has no arguments. This function returns the UserName property of the Application object, which is the name that appears in the Options dialog box (General tab). This example is simple, but it can be useful, because no other way is available to get the user's name to appear in a worksheet formula.

```
Function User()
' Returns the name of the current user
    User = Application.UserName
End Function
```

When you enter the following formula into a worksheet cell, the cell displays the name of the current user:

```
=User()
```

As with Excel's built-in functions, when you use a function with no arguments, you must include a set of empty parentheses.

A function with one argument

This section contains a more complex function that is designed for a sales manager who needs to calculate the commissions that are earned by the sales force. The commission rate is based on the amount sold — those who sell more earn a higher commission rate. The function returns the commission amount, based on the sales made (which is the function's only argument — a required argument). The calculations in this example are based on the following table:

Monthly Sales	Commission Rate
0–$9,999	8.0%
$10,000–$19,999	10.5%
$20,000–$39,999	12.0%
$40,000+	14.0%

You can use several ways to calculate commissions for various sales amounts that are entered into a worksheet. You could write a formula such as the following:

```
=IF(AND(A1>=0,A1<=9999.99),A1*0.08,IF(AND(A1>=10000,
A1<=19999.99), A1*0.105,IF(AND(A1>=20000,
A1<=39999.99),A1*0.12,IF(A1>=40000,A1*0.14,0))))
```

This is not the best approach for a couple of reasons. First, the formula is overly complex and difficult to understand. Second, the values are hard-coded into the formula, making the formula difficult to modify if the commission structure changes.

A better approach is to use a lookup table function to compute the commissions; for example:

```
=VLOOKUP(A1,Table,2)*A1
```

Using the VLOOKUP function requires that you have a table of commission rates set up in your worksheet.

Another approach is to create a custom function, such as the following:

```
Function Commission(Sales)
'    Calculates sales commissions
     Tier1 = 0.08
     Tier2 = 0.105
     Tier3 = 0.12
     Tier4 = 0.14
     Select Case Sales
          Case 0 To 9999.99
               Commission = Sales * Tier1
          Case 1000 To 19999.99
               Commission = Sales * Tier2
          Case 20000 To 39999.99
               Commission = Sales * Tier3
          Case Is >= 40000
               Commission = Sales * Tier4
     End Select
End Function
```

After you define the Commission function in a VBA module, you can use it in a worksheet formula. Entering the following formula into a cell produces a result of 3,000. (The amount, 25,000, qualifies for a commission rate of 12 percent.)

```
=Commission(25000)
```

A function with two arguments

This example builds on the previous one. Imagine that the sales manager implements a new policy: The total commission paid is increased by one percent for every year that the salesperson has been with the company. For this example, the custom Commission function (defined in the preceding section) has been modified so that it takes two arguments, both of which are required arguments. Call this new function Commission2:

```
Function Commission2(Sales, Years)
'    Calculates sales commissions based on years in service
     Tier1 = 0.08
     Tier2 = 0.105
     Tier3 = 0.12
     Tier4 = 0.14
     Select Case Sales
          Case 0 To 9999.99
               Commission2 = Sales * Tier1
          Case 1000 To 19999.99
               Commission2 = Sales * Tier2
          Case 20000 To 39999.99
               Commission2 = Sales * Tier3
          Case Is >= 40000
               Commission2 = Sales * Tier4
```

```
        End Select
        Commission2 = Commission2 + (Commission2 * Years / 100)
End Function
```

The modification was quite simple. The second argument (Years) was added to the Function statement, and an additional computation was included that adjusts the commission before exiting the function.

The following is an example of how you write a formula by using this function. It assumes that the sales amount is in cell A1, and that the number of years that the salesperson has worked is in cell B1.

```
=Commission2(A1,B1)
```

A function with a range argument

The example in this section demonstrates how to use a worksheet range as an argument. Actually, it's not at all tricky; Excel takes care of the details behind the scenes.

Assume that you want to calculate the average of the five largest values in a range named *Data*. Excel doesn't have a function that can do this, so you can write the following formula:

```
=(LARGE(Data,1)+LARGE(Data,2)+LARGE(Data,3)+
LARGE(Data,4)+LARGE(Data,5))/5
```

This formula uses Excel's LARGE function, which returns the *n*th largest value in a range. The preceding formula adds the five largest values in the range named *Data* and then divides the result by 5. The formula works fine, but it's rather unwieldy. And, what if you need to compute the average of the top *six* values? You would need to rewrite the formula and make sure that all copies of the formula also get updated.

Wouldn't it be easier if Excel had a function named TopAvg? For example, you could use the following (nonexistent) function to compute the average:

```
=TopAvg (Data,5)
```

This is an example of when a custom function can make things much easier for you. The following is a custom VBA function, named TopAvg, which returns the average of the top *n* values in a range:

```
Function TopAvg(InRange, Num)
' Returns the average of the highest Num values in InRange
  Sum = 0
  For i = 1 To Num
    Sum = Sum + WorksheetFunction.Large(InRange, i)
  Next i
  TopAvg = Sum / Num
End Function
```

This function takes two arguments: InRange (which is a worksheet range) and Num (the number of values to average). The code starts by initializing the Sum variable to 0. It then uses a For-Next loop to calculate the sum of the *n*th largest values in the range. Note that Excel's LARGE function is used within the loop. You can use an Excel worksheet function in VBA if you precede the function with WorksheetFunction and a period. Finally, TopAvg is assigned the value of Sum divided by Num.

You can use all of Excel's worksheet functions in your VBA procedures *except* those that have equivalents in VBA. For example, VBA has a Rnd function that returns a random number. Therefore, you can't use Excel's RAND function in a VBA procedure.

Debugging Custom Functions

Debugging a Function procedure can be a bit more challenging than debugging a Sub procedure. If you develop a function to use in worksheet formulas, an error in the function procedure simply results in an error display in the formula cell (usually #VALUE!). In other words, you don't receive the normal run-time error message that helps you to locate the offending statement.

When you are debugging a worksheet formula, using only one instance of the function in your worksheet is the best technique. The following are three methods that you may want to use in your debugging:

✦ **Place MsgBox functions at strategic locations to monitor the value of specific variables.** Fortunately, message boxes in function procedures pop up when the procedure is executed. But make sure that you have only one formula in the worksheet that uses your function; otherwise, the message boxes appear for each formula that's evaluated.

✦ **Test the procedure by calling it from a Sub procedure.** Run-time errors display normally, and you can either fix the problem (if you know what it is) or jump right into the debugger.

✦ **Set a breakpoint in the function and then use Excel's debugger to step through the function.** You then can access all the normal debugging tools.

Inserting Custom Functions

Excel's Insert Function dialog box is a handy tool that enables you to choose a worksheet function; you even can choose one of your custom worksheet functions. The Formula Palette prompts you for the function's arguments.

Function procedures that are defined with the Private keyword do not appear in the Paste Function dialog box.

You also can display a description of your custom function in the Paste Function dialog box. To do so, follow these steps:

1. Create the function in a module by using the VBE.

2. Activate Excel.

3. Choose the Tools ⇨ Macro ⇨ Macros command.

   Excel displays its Macro dialog box.

4. In the Macro dialog box, type the name of the function in the box labeled Macro Name. Notice that functions do not normally appear in this dialog box, so you must enter the function name yourself.

5. Click the Options button.

   Excel displays its Macro Options dialog box. (See Figure 35-3.)

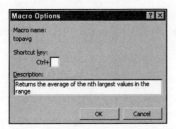

Figure 35-3: Entering a description for a custom function. This description appears in the Paste Function dialog box.

6. Enter a description of the function and then click OK. The Shortcut key field is irrelevant for functions.

   The description that you enter appears in the Paste Function dialog box.

Custom functions are listed under the User Defined category.

Figure 35-4 shows the Function Arguments dialog box, which prompts the user to enter arguments for a custom function.

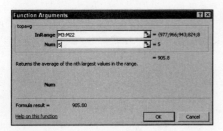

Figure 35-4: Using the Function Arguments dialog box to insert a custom function.

When you access a *built-in* function from the Insert Function dialog box, the Formula Palette displays a description of each argument. Unfortunately, you can't provide such descriptions for custom functions.

Learning More

The information in this chapter only scratches the surface when it comes to creating custom functions. It should be enough to get you started, however, if you're interested in this topic. Refer to Chapter 39 for more examples of useful VBA functions. You may be able to use the examples directly or adapt them for your needs.

✦   ✦   ✦

Creating UserForms

You can't use Excel very long without being exposed to dialog boxes. Excel, like most Windows programs, uses dialog boxes to obtain information, clarify commands, and display messages. If you develop VBA macros, you can create your own dialog boxes that work just like those that are built into Excel. These dialog boxes are known as UserForms.

Why Create UserForms?

Some macros that you create behave exactly the same every time that you execute them. For example, you may develop a macro that enters a list of your employees into a worksheet range. This macro always produces the same result and requires no additional user input. You may develop other macros, however, that you want to behave differently under different circumstances or that offer some options for the user. In such cases, the macro may benefit from a custom dialog box.

The following is an example of a simple macro that makes each cell in the selected range uppercase (but it skips cells that have a formula). The procedure uses VBA's built-in StrConv function.

```
Sub ChangeCase()
   For Each cell In Selection
     If Not cell.HasFormula Then
        cell.Value = StrConv(cell.Value,
vbUpperCase)
     End If
   Next cell
End Sub
```

This macro is useful, but it could be even more useful. For example, the macro would be more helpful if it could also change the cells to *lowercase* or *proper case* (only the first letter of each word is uppercase). This modification is not difficult to make, but if you make this change to the macro, you need some method of asking the user what type of change to make to the cells. The solution is to present a dialog box like the one shown in Figure 36-1. This dialog box is a UserForm that was created by using the Visual Basic Editor, and it is displayed by a VBA macro.

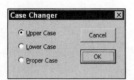

Figure 36-1: A UserForm that asks the user for an option.

Another solution would be to develop three macros, one for each type of text case change. Combining these three operations into a single macro and using a UserForm is a more efficient approach, however. This example, including how to create the UserForm, is discussed in "Another UserForm Example," later in the chapter.

UserForm Alternatives

Although developing UserForms isn't difficult, sometimes using the tools that are built into VBA is easier. For example, VBA includes two functions (InputBox and MsgBox) that enable you to display simple dialog boxes without having to create a UserForm in the VBE. These dialog boxes can be customized in some ways, but they certainly don't offer the options that are available in a UserForm.

The InputBox function

The InputBox function is useful for obtaining a single input from the user. A simplified version of the function's syntax follows:

```
InputBox(prompt[,title][,default])
```

The elements are defined as follows:

✦ prompt: Text that is displayed in the input box. (Required)

✦ title: Text that appears in the input box's title bar. (Optional)

✦ default: The default value. (Optional)

The following is an example of how you can use the InputBox function:

```
CName = InputBox("Customer name?","Customer Data")
```

When this VBA statement is executed, Excel displays the dialog box that is shown in Figure 36-2. Notice that this example uses only the first two arguments and does not supply a default value. When the user enters a value and clicks OK, the value is assigned to the variable `CName`.

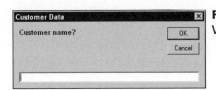

Figure 36-2: This dialog box is displayed by VBA's `InputBox` function.

The MsgBox function

VBA's `MsgBox` function is a handy way to display information and to solicit simple input from users. I use VBA's `MsgBox` function in many of this book's examples to display a variable's value. A simplified version of the `MsgBox` syntax is as follows:

```
MsgBox(prompt[,buttons][,title])
```

The elements are defined as follows:

✦ `prompt`: Text that is displayed in the message box. (Required)

✦ `buttons`: The code for the buttons that are to appear in the message box. (Optional)

✦ `title`: Text that appears in the message box's title bar. (Optional)

You can use the `MsgBox` function by itself or assign its result to a variable. If you use it by itself, don't include parentheses around the arguments. The following example displays a message and does not return a result:

```
Sub MsgBoxDemo()
  MsgBox "Click OK to continue"
End Sub
```

Figure 36-3 shows how this message box appears.

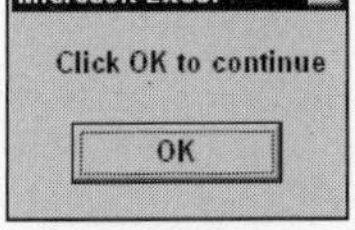

Figure 36-3: A simple message box, displayed with VBA's `MsgBox` function.

To get a response from a message box, you can assign the result of the `MsgBox` function to a variable. The following code uses some built-in constants (described in the

"Constants That Are Used in the MsgBox Function" table) to make it easier to work with the values that are returned by MsgBox:

```
Sub GetAnswer()
  Ans = MsgBox("Continue?", vbYesNo)
  Select Case Ans
   Case vbYes
'  ...[code if Ans is Yes]...
   Case vbNo
'  ...[code if Ans is No]...
  End Select
End Sub
```

When this procedure is executed, the Ans variable contains a value that corresponds to vbYes or vbNo. The Select Case statement determines the action to take based on the value of Ans.

You can easily customize your message boxes because of the flexibility of the button argument. Table 36-1 lists the built-in constants that you can use for the button argument. You can specify which buttons to display, whether an icon appears, and which button is the default.

Table 36-1
Constants That Are Used in the MsgBox Function

Constant	Value	Description
vbOKOnly	0	Display OK button.
vbOKCancel	1	Display OK and Cancel buttons.
vbAbortRetryIgnore	2	Display Abort, Retry, and Ignore buttons.
vbYesNoCancel	3	Display Yes, No, and Cancel buttons.
vbYesNo	4	Display Yes and No buttons.
vbRetryCancel	5	Display Retry and Cancel buttons.
vbCritical	16	Display Critical Message icon.
vbQuestion	32	Display Warning Query icon.
vbExclamation	48	Display Warning Message icon.
vbInformation	64	Display Information Message icon.
vbDefaultButton1	0	First button is default.
vbDefaultButton2	256	Second button is default.
vbDefaultButton3	512	Third button is default.
vbSystemModal	4096	System modal; all applications are suspended until the user responds to the message box.

The following example uses a combination of constants to display a message box with a Yes button, a No button (vbYesNo), and a question mark icon (vbQuestion); the second button is designated as the default button (vbDefaultButton2)— which is the button that is executed if the user presses Enter. For simplicity, these constants are assigned to the Config variable, and Config is then used as the second argument in the MsgBox function.

```
Sub GetAnswer()
   Config = vbYesNo + vbQuestion + vbDefaultButton2
   Ans = MsgBox("Process the monthly report?", Config)
   If Ans = vbYes Then RunReport
   If Ans = vbNo Then Exit Sub
End Sub
```

Figure 36-4 shows how this message box appears when the GetAnswer Sub is executed. If the user clicks the Yes button (or presses Enter), the routine executes the procedure named RunReport (which is not shown). If the user clicks the No button, the routine is ended with no action. Because the title argument was omitted in the MsgBox function, Excel uses the default title ("Microsoft Excel").

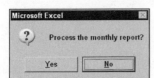

Figure 36-4: The second argument of the MsgBox function determines what appears in the message box.

The routine that follows is another example of using the MsgBox function:

```
Sub GetAnswer2()
  Msg = "Do you want to process the monthly report?"
  Msg = Msg & vbNewLine & vbNewLine
  Msg = Msg & "Processing the monthly report will take
approximately "
  Msg = Msg & "15 minutes. It will generate a 30-page report
for all "
  Msg = Msg & "sales offices for the current month."
  Title = "XYZ Marketing Company"
  Config = vbYesNo + vbQuestion
  Ans = MsgBox(Msg, Config, Title)
  If Ans = vbYes Then RunReport
  If Ans = vbNo Then Exit Sub
End Sub
```

This example demonstrates an efficient way to specify a longer message in a message box. A variable (Msg) and the concatenation operator (&) are used to build the message in a series of statements. In the second statement, vbNewLine is a constant that represents a line feed character. (Using two line feeds inserts a blank line.) The title argument is also used to display a different title in the message box. Figure 36-5 shows how this message box appears when the procedure is executed.

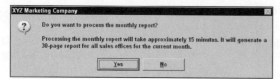

Figure 36-5: A message box with a longer
message and a title.

Creating UserForms: An Overview

The InputBox and MsgBox functions do just fine for many cases, but if you need to
obtain more information, you need to create a UserForm.

Following is a list of the general steps that you typically take to create a UserForm:

1. Determine exactly how the dialog box is going to be used and where it is to fit
   into your VBA macro.
2. Activate the Visual Basic Editor and insert a new UserForm.
3. Add the appropriate controls to the UserForm.
4. Create a VBA macro to display the UserForm.
5. Create event handler VBA procedures that are executed when the user manipulates the controls (for example, clicks the OK button).

The following sections provide more details on creating a UserForm.

Working with UserForms

To create a UserForm, you must first insert a new UserForm in the Visual Basic
Editor window. To activate the Visual Basic Editor, select Tools ➪ Macro ➪ Visual
Basic Editor (or press Alt+F11). Make sure that the correct workbook is selected in
the Project window and then select Insert ➪ UserForm. The Visual Basic Editor displays an empty UserForm, as shown in Figure 36-6. When you activate a UserForm,
the Visual Basic editor displays the Toolbox, which is used to add controls to the
UserForm.

Adding controls

The Toolbox, also shown in Figure 36-6, contains various ActiveX controls that you
can add to your UserForm.

When you move the mouse pointer over a control in the Toolbox, the control's
name is displayed. To add a control, click and drag it in the form. After adding a
control, you can move it or change its size.

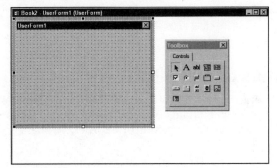

Figure 36-6: An empty UserForm.

Table 36-2 lists the Toolbox controls.

Table 36-2
Toolbox Controls

Control	Description
Select Objects	Lets you select other controls by dragging
Label	Adds a label (a container for text)
TextBox	Adds a text box (allows the user to type text)
ComboBox	Adds a combo box (a drop-down list)
ListBox	Adds a list box (to allow the user to select an item from a list)
CheckBox	Adds a check box (to control Boolean options)
OptionButton	Adds an option button (to allow a user to select from multiple options)
ToggleButton	Adds a toggle button (to control Boolean options)
Frame	Adds a frame (a container for other objects)
CommandButton	Adds a command button (a clickable button)
TabStrip	Adds a tab strip (a container for other objects)
MultiPage	Adds a multipage control (a container for other objects)
ScrollBar	Adds a scroll bar (to specify a value by dragging a bar)
SpinButton	Adds a spin button (to specify a value by clicking up or down)
Image	Adds a control that can contain an image
RefEdit	Adds a reference edit control (lets the user select a range)

Cross-Reference   You can also place some of these controls directly on your worksheet. Refer to Chapter 37 for details.

Changing the properties of a control

Every control that you add to a UserForm has several properties that determine how the control looks and behaves. You can change some of these properties (such as `Height` and `Width`) by clicking and dragging the control's border. To change other properties, use the Properties window.

To display the Properties window, select View ➪ Properties Window (or press F4). The Properties window displays a list of properties for the selected control. (Each control has a different set of properties.) If you click the form itself, the Properties window displays properties for the form. Figure 36-7 shows the Properties window for a CommandButton control.

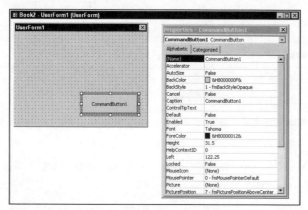

Figure 36-7: The Properties window for a CommandButton control.

To change a property, select the property in the Property window and then enter a new value. Some properties (such as `BackColor`) enable you to select a property from a list. The top of the Properties window contains a drop-down list that enables you to select a control to work with. You can also click a control to select it and display its properties.

When you set properties by using the Property window, you're setting properties at *design time*. You can also use VBA to change the properties of controls while the UserForm is displayed (that is, at *run time*).

A complete discussion of all the properties is well beyond the scope of this book. To find out about a particular property, select it in the Property window and press F1. The online Help for UserForm controls is extremely thorough.

Handling events

When you insert a UserForm, that form can also hold VBA Sub procedures to handle the events that are generated by the UserForm. An *event* is something that occurs when the user manipulates a control. For example, clicking a button causes an event. Selecting an item in a list box control also triggers an event. To make a UserForm useful, you must write VBA code to do something when an event occurs.

Event handler procedures have names that combine the control with the event. The general form is the control's name, followed by an underscore, and then the event name. For example, the procedure that is executed when the user clicks a button named MyButton is `MyButton_Click`.

Displaying a UserForm

You also need to write a procedure to display the UserForm. You use the `Show` method of the `UserForm` object. The following procedure displays the UserForm named UserForm1:

```
Sub ShowDialog()
    UserForm1.Show
End Sub
```

This procedure should be stored in a regular VBA module (not the code module for the UserForm).

When the `ShowDialog` procedure is executed, the UserForm is displayed. What happens next depends on the event handler procedures that you create.

A UserForm Example

The preceding section is, admittedly, rudimentary. This section demonstrates how to develop a UserForm. This example is rather simple. The UserForm displays a message to the user — something that could be accomplished more easily by using the `MsgBox` function. However, a UserForm gives you a lot more flexibility in terms of formatting and layout of the message.

On the CD-ROM   This workbook is available on the companion CD-ROM.

Creating the UserForm

If you're following along on your computer, start with a new workbook. Then follow these steps:

1. Choose Tools ➪ Macro ➪ Visual Basic Editor (or press Alt+F11) to activate the VBE window.

2. In the VBE Project window, double-click your workbook's name to activate it.

3. Choose Insert ➪ UserForm.

   The VBE adds an empty form named UserForm1 and displays the Toolbox.

4. Press F4 to display the Properties window and then change the following properties of the `UserForm` object:

Property	*Change To*
`Name`	AboutBox
`Caption`	About This Workbook

5. Use the Toolbox to add a `Label` object to the `UserForm`.

6. Select the `Label` object. In the Properties window, enter any text that you want for the label's `Caption`.

7. In the Properties window, click the `Font` property and adjust the font. You can change the typeface, size, and so on. The changes then appear in the form. Figure 36-8 shows an example of a formatted Label control.

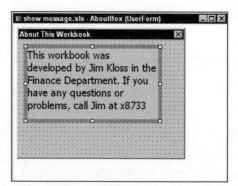

Figure 36-8: A Label control, after changing its `Font` properties.

8. Add a `CommandButton` object to the UserForm and change the following properties for the CommandButton:

Property	Change To
Name	OKButton
Caption	OK
Default	True

9. Make other adjustments so that the form looks good to you. You can change the size of the form or move or resize the controls.

Testing the UserForm

At this point, the UserForm has all the necessary controls. But what's missing is a way to display the UserForm. This section explains how to write a VBA Sub procedure to display the UserForm.

1. Insert a module by selecting Insert ⇨ Module.

2. In the empty module, enter the following code:

```
Sub ShowAboutBox()
 AboutBox.Show
End Sub
```

3. Activate Excel.

4. Choose Tools ⇨ Macro ⇨ Macros (or press Alt+F8).

5. In the Macros dialog box, select ShowAboutBox from the list of macros and click OK.

   The UserForm then appears.

If you click the OK button, notice that it doesn't close the UserForm as you may expect. This button needs to have an event handler procedure. To dismiss the UserForm, click the close button in its title box.

Cross-Reference You may prefer to display the UserForm by clicking a CommandButton on your worksheet. See Chapter 37 for details on attaching a macro to a Worksheet CommandButton.

Creating an event handler procedure

An event handler procedure is executed when an event occurs. In this case, you need a procedure to handle the Click event that's generated when the user clicks the OK button.

1. Activate the Visual Basic Editor. (Pressing Alt+F11 is the fastest way.)

2. Activate the AboutBox UserForm by double-clicking its name in the Project window.

3. Double-click the OKButton control.

4. VBE activates the module for the UserForm and inserts some code, as shown in Figure 36-9.

Figure 36-9: The module for the UserForm.

5. Insert the following statement before the `End Sub` statement:

```
Unload AboutBox
```

This statement simply dismisses the UserForm. The complete event handler procedure is listed below:

```
Private Sub OKButton_Click()
 Unload AboutBox
End Sub
```

Another UserForm Example

The example in this section is an enhanced version of the ChangeCase example presented at the beginning of the chapter. Recall that the original version of this macro changes the text in the selected cells to uppercase characters. This modified version asks the user what type of case change to make: uppercase, lowercase, or proper case (initial capitals).

On the CD-ROM   This workbook is available on the companion CD-ROM.

Creating the UserForm

This UserForm needs one piece of information from the user: the type of change to make to the text. Because only one option can be selected, OptionButton controls are appropriate. Start with an empty workbook and follow these steps to create the UserForm:

1. Choose Tools ⇨ Macro ⇨ Visual Basic Editor (or press Alt+F11) to activate the VBE window.

2. In the VBE window, choose Insert ⇨ UserForm.

   VBE adds an empty form named UserForm1 and displays the Toolbox.

3. Press F4 to display the Properties window and then change the following properties of the UserForm object:

Property	*Change To*
Name	CaseChangerDialog
Caption	Case Changer

4. Add a CommandButton object to the UserForm and then change the following properties for the CommandButton:

Property	*Change To*
Name	OKButton
Caption	OK
Default	True

5. Add another CommandButton object and then change the following properties:

Property	*Change To*
Name	CancelButton
Caption	Cancel
Cancel	True

6. Add an OptionButton control and then change the following properties. (This option is the default, so its Value property should be set to True.)

Property	*Change To*
Name	OptionUpper
Caption	Upper Case
Value	True

7. Add a second OptionButton control and then change the following properties:

Property	*Change To*
Name	OptionLower
Caption	Lower Case

8. Add a third OptionButton control and then change the following properties:

Property	Change To
Name	OptionProper
Caption	Proper Case

9. Adjust the size and position of the controls and the form until your UserForm resembles the UserForm shown in Figure 36-10. Make sure that the controls do not overlap.

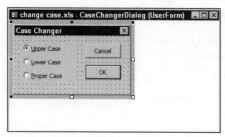

Figure 36-10: The UserForm after adding controls and adjusting some properties.

Tip   The Visual Basic Editor provides several useful commands to help you size and align the controls. Select the controls that you want to work with, and then choose a command from the Format menu. These commands are fairly self-explanatory, and the online Help has complete details.

Testing the UserForm

At this point, the UserForm has all the necessary controls. What's missing is a way to display the form. This section explains how to write a VBA procedure to display the UserForm.

1. Make sure that the VBE window is activated.

2. Insert a module by selecting Insert ➪ Module.

3. In the empty module, enter the following code:

```
Sub ChangeCase()
 CaseChangerDialog.Show
End Sub
```

4. Select Run ➪ Sub/UserForm (or press F5).

The Excel window is then activated, and the new UserForm is displayed, as shown in Figure 36-11. The OptionButtons work, but clicking the OK and Cancel buttons has no effect. These two buttons need to have event handler procedures. Click the Close button in the title bar to dismiss the UserForm.

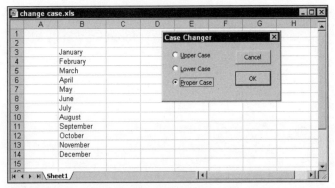

Figure 36-11: Displaying the UserForm.

Creating event handler procedures

This section explains how to create two event handler procedures: one to handle the `Click` event for the CancelButton CommandButton and the other to handle the `Click` event for the OKButton CommandButton. Event handlers for the OptionButtons are not necessary. The VBA code can determine which of the three OptionButtons is selected.

Event handler procedures are stored in the UserForm code module. To create the procedure to handle the `Click` event for the CancelButton, follow these steps:

1. Activate the CaseChangerDialog form by double-clicking its name in the Project window.

2. Double-click the CancelButton control.

3. VBE activates the module for the form and inserts an empty procedure.

4. Insert the following statement before the `End Sub` statement:

   ```
   Unload CaseChangerDialog
   ```

That's all there is to it. The following is a listing of the entire procedure:

```
Private Sub CancelButton_Click()
    Unload CaseChangerDialog
End Sub
```

This procedure is executed when the CancelButton is clicked. It consists of a single statement that unloads the CaseChangerDialog form.

The next step is to add the code to handle the Click event for the OKButton control. Follow these steps:

1. Select OKButton from the drop-down list at the top of the module.

VBE begins a new procedure called OKButton_Click.

2. Enter the following code.

The first and last statements have already been entered for you by VBE.

```
Private Sub OKButton_Click()
    Application.ScreenUpdating = False
'   Exit if a range is not selected
    If TypeName(Selection) <> "Range" Then Exit Sub
'     Upper case
    If OptionUpper Then
        For Each cell In Selection
        If Not cell.HasFormula Then
            cell.Value = StrConv(cell.Value, vbUpperCase)
        End If
        Next cell
    End If
'   Lower case
    If OptionLower Then
        For Each cell In Selection
        If Not cell.HasFormula Then
            cell.Value = StrConv(cell.Value, vbLowerCase)
        End If
        Next cell
    End If
'   Proper case
    If OptionProper Then
        For Each cell In Selection
        If Not cell.HasFormula Then
            cell.Value = StrConv(cell.Value, bProperCase)
        End If
        Next cell
    End If
    Unload CaseChangerDialog
End Sub
```

The macro starts by turning off screen updating. (This makes the macro run faster.) Next, the code checks the type of the selection. If a range is not selected, the procedure ends. The remainder of the procedure consists of three separate blocks. Only one block is executed, determined by which OptionButton is selected. The selected OptionButton has a value of True. Finally, the UserForm is unloaded (dismissed).

Testing the UserForm

To try out the UserForm, follow these steps:

1. Activate Excel.

2. Enter some text into some cells.

3. Select the range with the text.

4. Choose Tools ➪ Macro ➪ Macros (or press Alt+F8).

5. In the Macros dialog box, select ChangeCase from the list of macros and then click OK.

   The UserForm appears.

6. Make your choice and click OK.

Try it with a few more selections. Notice that if you click Cancel, the UserForm is dismissed, and no changes are made.

Making the macro available from a toolbar button

At this point, everything should be working properly. However, you have no quick and easy way to execute the macro. A good way to execute this macro would be from a toolbar button. You can use the following steps:

1. Right-click any toolbar and select Customize from the shortcut menu.

   Excel displays its Customize dialog box.

2. Click the Commands tab and then select Macros from the Categories list.

3. Click the Custom Button in the Commands list and drag it to a toolbar.

4. Right-click the new toolbar button and then select Assign Macro from the shortcut menu.

5. Choose ChangeCase from the list of macros and click OK.

   You can also change the button image and add a tool tip by using other commands that are on the shortcut menu.

6. Click Close to close the Customize dialog box.

After performing the preceding steps, clicking the toolbar button executes the macro and displays the UserForm.

Note If the workbook that contains the macro is not open already, it is opened when you click the toolbar button. You may want to hide the workbook window (select Window ➪ Hide) so that it isn't displayed. Another option is to create an add-in. See Chapter 40 for specifics.

More on Creating UserForms

Creating UserForms can make your macros much more versatile. You can create custom commands that display dialog boxes that look exactly like those that Excel uses. This section contains some additional information to help you develop custom dialog boxes that work like those that are built into Excel.

Adding accelerator keys

Dialog boxes should not discriminate against those who want to use the keyboard rather than a mouse. All of Excel's dialog boxes work equally well with a mouse and a keyboard because each control has an associated accelerator key. The user can press Alt plus the accelerator key to work with a specific dialog box control.

Adding accelerator keys to your UserForms is a good idea. You do this in the Properties window by entering a character for the Accelerator property.

The letter that you enter as the accelerator key must be a letter that is contained in the caption of the object. It can be any letter in the text (not necessarily the first letter). You should make sure that an accelerator key is not duplicated in a UserForm. If you have duplicate accelerator keys, the accelerator key acts on the first control in the tab order of the UserForm. Then, pressing the accelerator key again takes you to the next control.

Some controls (such as edit boxes) don't have a caption property. You can assign an accelerator key to a label that describes the control. Pressing the accelerator key then activates the next control in the tab order (which you should ensure is the edit box).

Controlling tab order

The previous section refers to a UserForm's *tab order*. When you're working with a UserForm, pressing Tab and Shift+Tab cycles through the dialog box's controls. When you create a UserForm, you should make sure that the tab order is correct. Usually, this means that tabbing should move through the controls in a logical sequence.

To view or change the tab order in a UserForm, select View ➪ Tab Order to display the Tab Order dialog box. You can then select a control from the list; use the Move Up and Move Down buttons to change the tab order for the selected control.

Learning More

Mastering UserForms takes practice. You should closely examine the dialog boxes that Excel uses to get a feeling for how dialog boxes are designed. You can duplicate nearly every dialog box that Excel uses.

The best way to learn more about creating dialog boxes is by using the VBA Help system.

✦   ✦   ✦

Using UserForm Controls in a Worksheet

◆ ◆ ◆ ◆

In This Chapter

Why use controls on
a worksheet?

Using controls

The Controls Toolbox
controls

◆ ◆ ◆ ◆

Chapter 36 presented an introduction to UserForms. If you like the idea of using dialog box controls—but don't like the idea of creating a dialog box—this chapter is for you. It explains how to enhance your worksheet with a variety of interactive controls, such as buttons, ListBoxes, and OptionButtons.

Why Use Controls on a Worksheet?

The main reason to use controls on a worksheet is to make it easier for the user to provide input. For example, if you create a model that uses one or more input cells, you can create controls to allow the user to select values for the input cells.

Adding controls to a worksheet requires much less effort than creating a dialog box. In addition, you may not have to create any macros because you can link a control to a worksheet cell. For example, if you insert a CheckBox control on a worksheet, you can link it to a particular cell. When the CheckBox is selected, the linked cell displays TRUE. When the CheckBox is not selected, the linked cell displays FALSE.

Figure 37-1 shows a simple example that uses OptionButtons, a ScrollBar, and a CommandButton control.

On the CD-ROM This workbook is available on the companion CD-ROM.

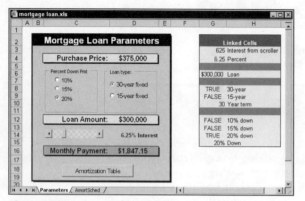

Figure 37-1: This worksheet uses UserForm controls.

Adding controls to a worksheet can be a bit confusing because these controls are available from two toolbars:

+ **Forms toolbar:** These controls are insertable objects.

+ **Control Toolbox toolbar:** These are ActiveX controls. These controls are a subset of those that are available for use on UserForms.

To add to the confusion, many controls are available on both toolbars. For example, the Forms toolbar and the Control Toolbox toolbar both have a control named ListBox. However, these are two entirely different controls. In general, the ActiveX controls (those on the Control Toolbox toolbar) provide more flexibility.

Note This chapter focuses exclusively on the controls that are available in the Control Toolbox toolbar, as shown in Figure 37-2.

Figure 37-2: The Control Toolbox toolbar.

A description of the buttons in the Control Toolbox appears in Table 37-1.

Table 37-1
Buttons on the Control Toolbox Toolbar

Button	What It Does
Design Mode	Toggles design mode
Properties	Displays the Properties window, where you make changes to the control's settings
View Code	Switches to the Visual Basic Editor so that you can write or edit VBA code for the selected control
CheckBox	Inserts a CheckBox control (to control Boolean options)
TextBox	Inserts a TextBox control (allows the user to type text)
CommandButton	Inserts a CommandButton control (a clickable button)
OptionButton	Inserts an OptionButton control (to allow a user to select from multiple options)
ListBox	Inserts a ListBox control (to allow the user to select an item from a list)
ComboBox	Inserts a ComboBox control (a drop-down list)
ToggleButton	Inserts a ToggleButton control (to control Boolean options)
SpinButton	Inserts a SpinButton control (to specify a value by clicking up or down)
ScrollBar	Inserts a ScrollBar control (to specify a value by dragging a bar)
Label	Inserts a Label control (a container for text)
Image	Inserts an Image control (to hold an image)
More Controls	Displays a list of other ActiveX controls that are installed on your system

Using Controls

Adding ActiveX controls in a worksheet is easy. After you add a control, you can adjust its properties to modify the way that the control looks and works.

Adding a control

To add a control to a worksheet, make sure that the Control Toolbox toolbar is displayed (and don't confuse it with the Forms toolbar). Then, click and drag the control that you want to use into the worksheet to create the control. You don't need to be too concerned about the exact size or position because you can modify these properties at any time.

About design mode

When you add a control to a worksheet, Excel goes into *design mode*. In this mode, you can adjust the properties of any controls on your worksheet, add or edit macros for the control, or change the control's size or position.

When Excel is in design mode, you can't try out the controls. To test the controls, you must exit design mode by clicking the Exit Design Mode button on the Control Toolbox toolbar. When you're working with controls, it's not uncommon to need to switch in and out of design mode frequently.

Adjusting properties

Every control that you add has various properties that determine how it looks and behaves. You can adjust these properties only when Excel is in design mode. When you add a control to a worksheet, Excel enters design mode automatically. If you need to change a control after you exit design mode, simply click the Design Mode button on the Control Toolbox toolbar.

To change the properties for a control, select the control and then click the Properties button on the Control Toolbox toolbar. Excel displays its Properties window, as shown in Figure 37-3. The Properties window has two tabs. The Alphabetic tab displays the properties in alphabetical order. The Categorized tab displays the properties by category. Both tabs show the same properties; only the order is different.

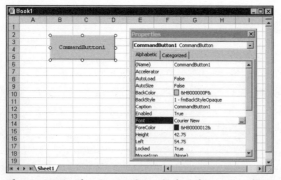

Figure 37-3: The Properties window lets you adjust the properties of a control.

To change a property, select it in the Properties window and then make the change. The manner in which you change a property depends on the property. Some properties display a drop-down list that enables you to select from a list of options. Others (such as Font) provide a button that, when clicked, displays a dialog box. Other properties require you to type the property value. When you change a property, the change takes effect immediately.

Tip   To learn about a particular property, select the property in the Properties window and press F1.

Common properties

Each control has its own unique set of properties. However, many controls share properties. This section describes some of the properties that are common to all or many controls, as set forth in Table 37-2.

Table 37-2
Properties Shared by Multiple Controls

Property	Description
AutoSize	If True, the control resizes itself automatically, based on the text in its caption.
BackColor	The background color of the control.
BackStyle	The style of the background (either transparent or opaque).
Caption	The text that appears on the control.
LinkedCell	A worksheet cell that contains the current value of a control.
ListFillRange	A worksheet range that contains items displayed in a ListBox or ComboBox control.
Value	The control's value.
Left **and** Top	Values that determine the control's position.
Width **and** Height	Values that determine the control's width and height.
Visible	If False, the control is hidden.
Name	The name of the control. By default, a control's name is based on the control type. You can change the name to any valid name. However, each control's name must be unique on the worksheet.
Picture	Enables you to specify a graphic image to display. The image must be contained in a file. (It can't be copied from the Clipboard.)

Linking controls to cells

Often, you can use ActiveX controls in a worksheet without using any macros. Many of the controls have a `LinkedCell` property, which specifies a worksheet cell that is "linked" to the control.

For example, you might add a SpinButton control and specify B1 as its `LinkedCell` property. After doing so, cell B1 contains the value of the SpinButton, and clicking the SpinButton changes the value in cell B1. You can, of course, use the value contained in the linked cell in your formulas.

Creating macros for controls

To create a macro for a control, you must use the Visual Basic Editor (VBE). The macros are stored in the code module for the sheet that contains the control. Each control can have a macro to handle any of its events. For example, a CommandButton control can have a macro for its `Click` event, its `DblClick` event, and various other events.

Tip   The easiest way to access the code module for a control is to double-click the control while in design mode. Excel displays the VBE and creates an empty macro for the control's default event. For example, the default event for a CommandButton control is the `Click` event. (See Figure 37-4.)

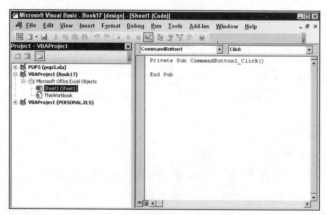

Figure 37-4: Double-clicking a control in design mode activates the Visual Basic Editor.

The control's name appears in the upper-left portion of the code window, and the event appears in the upper-right area. If you want to create a macro that executes when a different event occurs, select the event from the list in the upper-right area.

The following steps demonstrate how to insert a CommandButton and create a simple macro that displays a message when the button is clicked:

1. Make sure that the Control Toolbox toolbar is displayed.

2. Click the CommandButton tool in the Control Toolbox.

3. Click and drag in the worksheet to create the button.

4. Double-click the button.

    The VBE window is activated, and an empty subroutine is created.

5. Enter the following VBA statement before the End Sub statement:

    MsgBox "You clicked the command button."

6. Press Alt+F11 to return to Excel.

7. Adjust any other properties for the CommandButton.

8. Click the Exit Design Mode button in the Control Toolbox toolbar.

After performing the preceding steps, click the CommandButton to display the message box.

The Controls Toolbox Controls

The sections that follow describe the ActiveX controls that are available on the Controls Toolbox toolbar.

The companion CD-ROM contains a file that includes examples of all the ActiveX controls.

CheckBox control

A CheckBox control is useful for getting a binary choice: yes or no, true or false, on or off, and so on.

The following is a description of the most useful properties of a CheckBox control:

✦ **Accelerator:** A letter that enables the user to change the value of the control by using the keyboard. For example, if the accelerator is A, pressing Alt+A changes the value of the CheckBox control.

✦ **LinkedCell:** The worksheet cell that's linked to the CheckBox. The cell displays TRUE if the control is checked or FALSE if the control is not checked.

ComboBox control

A ComboBox control is similar to a ListBox control. A ComboBox, however, is a drop-down box, and it displays only one item at a time. Another difference is that the user may be allowed to enter a value that does not appear in the list of items.

Figure 37-5 shows a ComboBox control that uses the range D1:D12 for the ListFillRange and cell A1 for the LinkedCell.

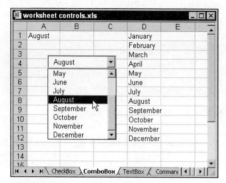

Figure 37-5: A ComboBox control.

The following is a description of the most useful properties of a ComboBox control:

✦ BoundColumn: If the list contains multiple columns, this property determines which column contains the returned value.

✦ ColumnCount: The number of columns in the list.

✦ LinkedCell: The worksheet cell that displays the selected item.

✦ ListFillRange: The worksheet range that contains the list items.

✦ ListRows: The number of items to display when the list drops down.

✦ ListStyle: Determines the appearance of the list items.

✦ Style: Determines whether the control acts like a drop-down list or a ComboBox. A drop-down list doesn't allow the user to enter a new value.

CommandButton control

A CommandButton is most commonly used to execute a macro. When a CommandButton is clicked, it executes a macro with a name that is made up of the CommandButton's name, an underscore, and the word *Click*. For example, if a CommandButton is named MyButton, clicking it executes the macro named MyButton_Click. This macro is stored in the code module for the sheet that contains the CommandButton.

Image control

An Image control is used to display an image that is contained in a file. For most situations, this control offers no significant advantages over using standard imported images (as described in Chapter 18).

Label control

A Label control simply displays text. This is not a useful control for use on worksheets, and a standard TextBox AutoShape gives you more versatility.

ListBox controls

The ListBox control presents a list of items, and the user can select an item (or multiple items). It's similar to a ComboBox. The main difference is that a ListBox displays more than one item at a time.

The following is a description of the most useful properties of a ListBox control:

✦ `BoundColumn`: If the list contains multiple columns, this property determines which column contains the returned value.

✦ `ColumnCount`: The number of columns in the list.

✦ `IntegralHeight`: This is `True` if the height of the ListBox adjusts automatically to display full lines of text when the list is scrolled vertically. If `False`, the ListBox may display partial lines of text when it is scrolled vertically.

✦ `LinkedCell`: The worksheet cell that displays the selected item.

✦ `ListFillRange`: The worksheet range that contains the list items.

✦ `ListStyle`: Determines the appearance of the list items.

✦ `MultiSelect`: Determines whether the user can select multiple items from the list.

 Note If you use a `MultiSelect` ListBox, you cannot specify a `LinkedCell`; you need to write a macro to determine which items are selected.

OptionButton controls

OptionButtons are useful when the user needs to select from a small number of items. OptionButtons are always used in groups of at least two.

The following is a description of the most useful properties of an OptionButton control:

✦ **Accelerator:** A letter that lets the user select the option by using the keyboard. For example, if the accelerator for an OptionButton is C, pressing Alt+C selects the control.

✦ **GroupName:** A name that identifies an OptionButton as being associated with other OptionButtons with the same `GroupName` property.

✦ **LinkedCell:** The worksheet cell that's linked to the OptionButton. The cell displays `TRUE` if the control is selected or `FALSE` if the control is not selected.

Note   If your worksheet contains more than one set of OptionButtons, you *must* ensure that each set of OptionButtons has a different `GroupName` property Otherwise, all OptionButtons become part of the same set.

ScrollBar control

The ScrollBar control is useful for specifying a cell value. Figure 37-6 shows a worksheet with three ScrollBar controls. These ScrollBars are used to change the color in the rectangle object. The value of the ScrollBars determines the red, green, or blue component of the rectangle's color. This example uses a few simple macros to change the colors.

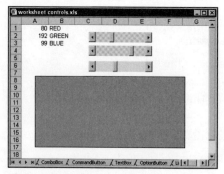

Figure 37-6: This worksheet has several ScrollBar controls.

The following is a description of the most useful properties of a ScrollBar control:

✦ `Value`: The current value of the control.

✦ `Min`: The minimum value for the control.

✦ `Max`: The maximum value for the control.

✦ `LinkedCell`: The worksheet cell that displays the value of the control.

✦ `SmallChange`: The amount that the control's value is changed by a click.

✦ `LargeChange`: The amount that the control's value is changed by clicking either side of the button.

The ScrollBar control is most useful for selecting a value that extends across a wide range of possible values.

SpinButton control

The SpinButton control lets the user select a value by clicking the control, which has two arrows (one to increase the value and the other to decrease the value). A SpinButton can display either horizontally or vertically.

The following is a description of the most useful properties of a SpinButton control:

✦ `Value`: The current value of the control.

✦ `Min`: The minimum value of the control.

✦ `Max`: The maximum value of the control.

✦ `LinkedCell`: The worksheet cell that displays the value of the control.

✦ `SmallChange`: The amount that the control's value is changed by a click. Usually, this property is set to 1, but you can make it any value.

TextBox controls

On the surface, a TextBox control may not seem useful. After all, it simply contains text—you can usually use worksheet cells to get text input. In fact, TextBox controls are useful not so much for input control but for output control. Because a TextBox can have ScrollBars, you can use a TextBox to display a great deal of information in a small area.

The following is a description of the most useful properties of a TextBox control:

✦ `AutoSize`: Determines whether the control adjusts its size automatically, depending on the amount of text.

✦ `IntegralHeight`: If `True`, the height of the TextBox adjusts automatically to display full lines of text when the list is scrolled vertically. If `False`, the ListBox may display partial lines of text when it is scrolled vertically.

✦ `MaxLength`: The maximum number of characters allowed in the TextBox. If 0, no limit exists on the number of characters.

✦ `MultiLine`: If `True`, the TextBox can display more than one line of text.

✦ `TextAlign`: Determines how the text is aligned in the TextBox.

✦ `WordWrap`: Determines whether the control allows word wrap.

✦ `ScrollBars`: Determines the type of ScrollBars for the control: horizontal, vertical, both, or none.

ToggleButton control

A ToggleButton control has two states: on or off. Clicking the button toggles between these two states, and the button changes its appearance. Its value is either `True` (pressed) or `False` (not pressed). You can often use a ToggleButton in place of a CheckBox control.

✦   ✦   ✦

Working with Excel Events

In the preceding chapters, you've seen examples of VBA event handler procedures. These procedures are the keys to making your Excel applications interactive. This chapter provides an introduction to the concept of Excel events and includes many examples that you can adapt to meet your own needs.

Understanding Events

Excel is capable of monitoring a wide variety of events and executing your VBA code when a particular event occurs. This chapter covers the following types of events.

+ **Workbook events:** These occur for a particular workbook. Examples include `Open` (the workbook is opened or created), `BeforeSave` (the workbook is aboutto be saved), and `NewSheet` (a new sheet is added). VBA code for workbook events must be stored in theThisWorkbook code module.

+ **Worksheet events:** These occur for a particular worksheet.Examples include `Change` (a cell on the sheet is changed), `SelectionChange` (the cell pointer is moved), and `Calculate` (the worksheet is recalculated). VBA code for worksheet events must be stored in the code module for the worksheet (for example, the module named Sheet1).

+ **Events not associated with objects:** The final category consists of two useful application-level events: `OnTime` and `OnKey`. These work differently from other events.

Entering event handler VBA code

Every event handler procedure must go into a specific type of code module. Code for workbook-level events goes into the ThisWorkbook code module. Code for worksheet-level events goes into the code module for the particular sheet (for example, the code module named Sheet1).

In addition, every event handler procedure has a predetermined name. You can declare the procedure by typing it, but a much better approach is to let the VBE do it for you. Figure 38-1 shows the code module for the ThisWorkbook object. To insert a procedure declaration, select Workbook from the objects list on the left. Then select the event from the procedures list on the right. When you do this, you get a procedure "shell" that contains the procedure declaration line and an End Sub statement.

Figure 38-1: The best way to create an event procedure is to let the VBE do it for you.

For example, if you select Workbook from the objects list and Open from the procedures list, the VBE inserts the following (empty) procedure:

```
Private Sub Workbook_Open()

End Sub
```

Your code goes between these two lines.

Some event handler procedures contain an argument list. For example, you may need to create an event handler procedure to monitor the SheetActivate event for a workbook. If you use the technique described in the previous section, the VBE creates the following procedure:

```
Private Sub Workbook_SheetActivate(ByVal Sh As Object)

End Sub
```

This procedure uses one argument (Sh), which represents the activated sheet. In this case, Sh is declared as an Object data type rather than a Worksheet data type because the activated sheet also can be a chart sheet.

Your code can, of course, make use of data passed as an argument. The following example displays the name of the activated sheet by accessing the argument's Name property. The argument becomes either a Worksheet object or a Chart object.

```
Private Sub Workbook_SheetActivate(ByVal Sh As Object)
    MsgBox Sh.Name & " was activated."
End Sub
```

Several event handler procedures use a `Boolean` argument named `Cancel`. For example, the declaration for a workbook's `BeforePrint` event is

```
Private Sub Workbook_BeforePrint(Cancel As Boolean)
```

The value of `Cancel` passed to the procedure is `False`. However, your code can set `Cancel` to `True`, which cancels the printing. The following example demonstrates this:

```
Private Sub Workbook_BeforePrint(Cancel As Boolean)
    Msg = "Have you loaded the 5164 label stock? "
    Ans = MsgBox(Msg, vbYesNo, "About to print... ")
    If Ans = vbNo Then Cancel = True
End Sub
```

The `Workbook_BeforePrint` procedure executes before the workbook prints. This procedure displays a message box asking the user to verify that the correct label stock is loaded. If the user clicks the No button, `Cancel` is set to `True`, and nothing prints.

Using Workbook-Level Events

Workbook-level events occur for a particular workbook. Table 38-1 lists the workbook events, along with a brief description of each. Keep in mind that workbook event handler procedures must be stored in the code module for the ThisWorkbook object.

Table 38-1 **Workbook Events**	
Event	**Action That Triggers the Event**
`Activate`	The workbook is activated.
`AddinInstall`	The workbook is installed as an add-in.
`AddinUninstall`	The workbook is uninstalled as an add-in.
`AfterXmlExport`	An XML file has been exported (Excel 2003 only).
`AfterXmlImport`	An XML file has been imported (Excel 2003 only).
`BeforeClose`	The workbook is about to be closed.
`BeforePrint`	The workbook (or anything in it) is about to be printed.

Continued

Table 38-1 *(continued)*

Event	Action That Triggers the Event
BeforeSave	The workbook is about to be saved.
BeforeXmlExport	An XML file is about to be exported (Excel 2003 only).
BeforeXmlImport	An XML file is about to be imported (Excel 2003 only).
Deactivate	The workbook is deactivated.
NewSheet	A new sheet is created in the workbook.
Open	The workbook is opened.
PivotTableCloseConnection	A PivotTable report closes its connection to its data source.
PivotTableOpenConnection	A PivotTable report opens its connection to its data source.
SheetActivate	Any sheet in the workbook is activated.
SheetBeforeDoubleClick	Any worksheet in the workbook is double-clicked. This event occurs before the default double-click action.
SheetBeforeRightClick	Any worksheet in the workbook is right-clicked. This event occurs before the default right-click action.
SheetCalculate	Any worksheet in the workbook is calculated (or recalculated).
SheetChange	Any worksheet in the workbook is changed by the user.
SheetDeactivate	Any sheet in the workbook is deactivated.
SheetFollowHyperlink	Any hyperlink in the workbook is clicked.
SheetPivotTableUpdate	A PivotTable report in the workbook has been updated.
SheetSelectionChange	The selection on any worksheet in the workbook is changed.
Sync	The worksheet that is part of a Document Workspace is synchronized with the copy on the server (Excel 2003 only).
WindowActivate	Any window of the workbook is activated.
WindowDeactivate	Any workbook window is deactivated.
WindowResize	Any workbook window is resized.

The remainder of this section presents examples of using workbook-level events. All the example procedures that follow must be located in the code module for the ThisWorkbook object. If you put them into any other type of code module, they will not work.

Using the Open event

One of the most common monitored events is a workbook's Open event. This event is triggered when the workbook (or add-in) opens and executes the Workbook_ Open procedure. A Workbook_Open procedure is very versatile and is often used for the following tasks:

✦ Displaying welcome messages.

✦ Opening other workbooks.

✦ Setting up custom menus or toolbars.

✦ Activating a particular sheet.

✦ Ensuring that certain conditions are met; for example, a workbook may require that a particular add-in is installed.

Caution

Be aware that there is no guarantee that your Workbook_Open procedure will be executed. For example, the user may choose to disable macros. And if the user holds down the Shift key while opening a workbook, the workbook's Workbook_Open procedure will not execute.

The following is a simple example of a Workbook_Open procedure. It uses VBA's Weekday function to determine the day of the week. If it's Friday, a message box appears to remind the user to perform a file backup. If it's not Friday, nothing happens.

```
Private Sub Workbook_Open()
    If Weekday(Now) = 6 Then
        Msg = "Make sure you do your weekly backup!"
        MsgBox Msg, vbInformation
    End If
End Sub
```

The following example performs a number of actions when the workbook is opened. It maximizes Excel's window, maximizes the workbook window, activates the sheet named DataEntry, and selects cell A1.

```
Private Sub Workbook_Open()
    Application.WindowState = xlMaximized
    ActiveWindow.WindowState = xlMaximized
    Worksheets("DataEntry").Activate
    Range("A1").Select
End Sub
```

Using the SheetActivate event

The following procedure executes whenever the user activates any sheet in the workbook. The code simply selects cell A1. Including the `On Error Resume Next` construct causes the procedure to ignore the error that occurs if the activated sheet is a chart sheet.

```
Private Sub Workbook_SheetActivate(ByVal Sh As Object)
    On Error Resume Next
    Range("A1").Select
End Sub
```

An alternative method to handle the case of a chart sheet is to check the sheet type. Use the `Sh` argument, which is passed to the procedure.

```
Private Sub Workbook_SheetActivate(ByVal Sh As Object)
    If TypeName(Sh) = "Worksheet" Then Range("A1").Select
End Sub
```

Using the NewSheet event

The following procedure executes whenever a new sheet is added to the workbook. The sheet is passed to the procedure as an argument. Because a new sheet can be either a worksheet or a chart sheet, this procedure determines the sheet type. If it's a worksheet, it inserts a date and time stamp in cell A1.

```
Private Sub Workbook_NewSheet(ByVal Sh As Object)
    If TypeName(Sh) = "Worksheet" Then _
        Range("A1") = "Sheet added " & Now()
End Sub
```

Using the BeforeSave event

The `BeforeSave` event occurs before the workbook is actually saved. As you know, using the File ⇨ Save command sometimes brings up the Save As dialog box. This happens if the file has never been saved or was opened in read-only mode.

When the `Workbook_BeforeSave` procedure executes, it receives an argument that enables you to identify whether the Save As dialog box will appear. The following example demonstrates this:

```
Private Sub Workbook_BeforeSave _
  (ByVal SaveAsUI As Boolean, Cancel As Boolean)
    If SaveAsUI Then
        MsgBox "Click OK to display the Save As dialog box."
    End If
End Sub
```

When the user attempts to save the workbook, the `Workbook_BeforeSave` procedure executes. If the save operation brings up the Save As dialog box, the `SaveAsUI` variable is `True`. The preceding procedure checks this variable and displays a message only if the Save As dialog box is displayed. If the procedure sets the `Cancel` argument to `True`, the file is not saved.

Using the BeforeClose event

The `BeforeClose` event occurs before a workbook is closed. This event often is used in conjunction with a `Workbook_Open` event handler. For example, use the `Workbook_Open` procedure to initialize items in your workbook, and use the `Workbook_BeforeClose` procedure to clean up or restore settings to normal before the workbook closes.

If you attempt to close a workbook that hasn't been saved, Excel displays a prompt that asks if you want to save the workbook before it closes.

Caution   A problem can arise from this event. By the time the user sees this message, the `BeforeClose` event has already occurred. This means that the `Workbook_BeforeClose` procedure has already executed.

Working with Worksheet Events

The events for a `Worksheet` object are some of the most useful. As you'll see, monitoring these events can make your applications perform feats that otherwise would be impossible.

Table 38-2 lists the worksheet events, with a brief description of each. Remember that these event procedures must be entered into the code module for the sheet.

Table 38-2 Worksheet Events	
Event	**Action That Triggers the Event**
`Activate`	The worksheet is activated.
`BeforeDoubleClick`	The worksheet is double-clicked.
`BeforeRightClick`	The worksheet is right-clicked.
`Calculate`	The worksheet is calculated (or recalculated).
`Change`	Cells on the worksheet are changed by the user.
`Deactivate`	The worksheet is deactivated.
`FollowHyperlink`	A hyperlink on the worksheet is clicked.
`PivotTableUpdate`	A PivotTable on the worksheet has been updated.
`SelectionChange`	The selection on the worksheet is changed.

Using the Change event

The Change event is triggered when any cell in the worksheet is changed by the user. The Change event is not triggered when a calculation generates a different value for a formula or when an object is added to the sheet.

When the Worksheet_Change procedure executes, it receives a Range object as its Target argument. This Range object represents the changed cell or range that triggered the event. The following example displays a message box that shows the address of the Target range:

```
Private Sub Worksheet_Change(ByVal Target As Excel.Range)
    MsgBox "Range " & Target.Address & " was changed."
End Sub
```

To get a feel for the types of actions that generate the Change event for a worksheet, enter the preceding procedure into the code module for a Worksheet object. After entering this procedure, activate Excel and, using various techniques, make changes to the worksheet. Every time that the Change event occurs, a message box displays the address of the range that changed.

Unfortunately, the Change event doesn't always work as expected. For example:

✦ Changing the formatting of a cell does not trigger the Change event (as expected), but using the Edit ➪ Clear Formats command *does*.

✦ Pressing Delete generates an event even if the cell is empty at the start.

✦ Cells changed via most Excel commands do not trigger the Change event. These commands include Data ➪ Form, Data ➪ Sort, Tools ➪ Spelling, and Edit ➪ Replace. However, using the AutoSum button *does* trigger the event.

✦ If your VBA procedure changes a cell, it *does* trigger the Change event.

Monitoring a specific range for changes

The Change event occurs when any cell on the worksheet changes. In most cases, you'll only be concerned with changes that are made to a specific cell or range. When the Worksheet_Change event handler procedure is called, it receives a Range object as its argument. This Range object represents the cell or cells that changed.

Assume that your worksheet has a range named InputRange and you want to monitor changes to this range only. No Change event exists for a Range object, but you can perform a quick check within the Worksheet_Change procedure. The following procedure demonstrates this:

```
Private Sub Worksheet_Change(ByVal Target As Excel.Range)
    Dim VRange As Range
    Set VRange = Range("InputRange")
```

```
    If Union(Target, VRange).Address = VRange.Address Then
        Msgbox "The changed cell is in the input range."
    End if
End Sub
```

This example creates a `Range` object named `VRange`, which represents the worksheet range that you want to monitor for changes. The procedure uses VBA's `Union` function to determine whether `VRange` contains the `Target` range (passed to the procedure in its argument). The `Union` function returns an object that consists of all the cells in both of its arguments. If the range address is the same as the `VRange` address, `Vrange` contains `Target`, and a message box appears. Otherwise, the procedure ends, and nothing happens.

The preceding procedure has a flaw. `Target` may consist of a cell or a range. For example, if the user changes more than one cell at a time, `Target` becomes a multi-cell range. Therefore, the procedure requires modification to loop through all the cells in `Target`. The following procedure checks each changed cell and displays a message box if the cell is within the desired range:

```
Private Sub Worksheet_Change(ByVal Target As Excel.Range)
    Set VRange = Range("InputRange")
    For Each cell In Target
        If Union(cell, VRange).Address = VRange.Address Then
            Msgbox "The changed cell is in the input range."
        End if
    Next cell
End Sub
```

Using the SelectionChange event

The following procedure demonstrates the `SelectionChange` event. It executes whenever the user makes a new selection on the worksheet.

```
Private Sub Worksheet_SelectionChange(ByVal Target
  As Excel.Range)
    Cells.Interior.ColorIndex = xlNone
    With ActiveCell
        .EntireRow.Interior.ColorIndex = 36
        .EntireColumn.Interior.ColorIndex = 36
    End With
End Sub
```

This procedure shades the row and column of an active cell, making it easy to identify. The first statement removes the background color of all cells. Next, the entire row and column of the active cell is shaded light yellow. Figure 38-2 shows the shading.

This workbook is available on the companion CD-ROM.

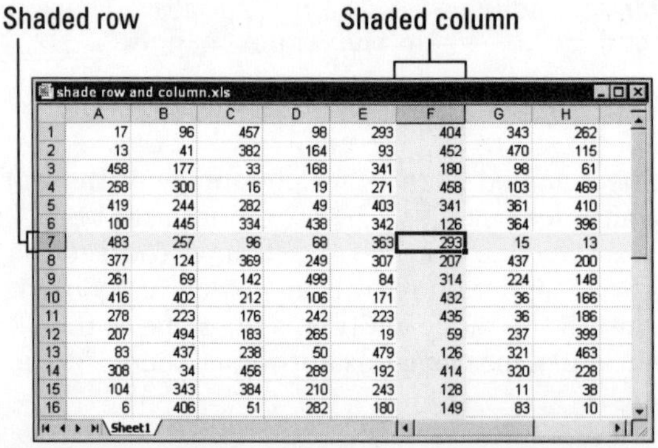

Shaded row   Shaded column

Figure 38-2: Moving the cell cursor causes the active cell's row and column to become shaded.

Caution
You won't want to use this procedure if your worksheet contains background shading because it will be wiped out.

Using the BeforeRightClick event

When the user right-clicks in a worksheet, a shortcut menu appears. If, for some reason, you want to prevent the shortcut menu from appearing, you can trap the RightClick event. The following procedure sets the Cancel argument to True, which cancels the RightClick event and, thus, the shortcut menu. Instead, a message box appears.

```
Private Sub Worksheet_BeforeRightClick _
  (ByVal Target As Excel.Range, Cancel As Boolean)
    Cancel = True
    MsgBox "The shortcut menu is not available."
End Sub
```

Using Non-Object Events

The events discussed in this chapter are associated with an object (Application, Workbook, Sheet, and so on). This section discusses two additional "rogue" events: OnTime and OnKey. These events are not associated with an object. Rather, they are accessed by using methods of the Application object.

Note
Unlike the other events discussed in this chapter, you use a general VBA module to program the "On" events in this section.

Using the OnTime event

The OnTime event occurs at a specified time. The following example demonstrates how to program Excel to beep and then display a message at 3 p.m.:

```
Sub SetAlarm()
    Application.OnTime 0.625, "DisplayAlarm"
End Sub

Sub DisplayAlarm()
    Beep
    MsgBox "Wake up. It's time for your afternoon break!"
End Sub
```

In this example, the SetAlarm procedure uses the OnTime method of the Application object to set up the OnTime event. This method takes two arguments: the time (0.625, or 3 p.m., in the example) and the procedure to execute when the time occurs (DisplayAlarm in the example). In the example, after SetAlarm executes, the DisplayAlarm procedure is called at 3 p.m., bringing up the message.

Most people find it difficult to think of time in terms of Excel's time numbering system. Therefore, you might want to use VBA's TimeValue function to represent the time. TimeValue converts a string that looks like a time into a value that Excel can handle. The following statement shows an easier way to program an event for 3 p.m.:

```
Application.OnTime TimeValue("3:00:00 pm"), "DisplayAlarm"
```

If you want to schedule an event that's relative to the current time—for example, 20 minutes from now—you can write an instruction like this:

```
Application.OnTime Now + TimeValue("00:20:00"), "DisplayAlarm"
```

You also can use the OnTime method to schedule a procedure on a particular day. Of course, you must keep your computer turned on, and Excel must be running.

Using the OnKey event

While you work, Excel constantly monitors what you type. Because of this, you can set up a keystroke or a key combination that when pressed, executes a particular procedure.

The following example uses the OnKey method to set up an OnKey event. This event essentially reassigns the PgDn and PgUp keys. After the Setup_OnKey procedure executes, pressing PgDn executes the PgDn_Sub procedure, and pressing PgUp executes the PgUp_Sub procedure. The next effect is that pressing PgDn moves down one row, and pressing PgUp moves up one row.

```
Sub Setup_OnKey()
    Application.OnKey "{PgDn}", "PgDn_Sub"
    Application.OnKey "{PgUp}", "PgUp_Sub"
End Sub

Sub PgDn_Sub()
    On Error Resume Next
    ActiveCell.Offset(1, 0).Activate
End Sub

Sub PgUp_Sub()
    On Error Resume Next
    ActiveCell.Offset(-1, 0).Activate
End Sub
```

Note Notice that the key codes are enclosed in brackets, not parentheses. For a complete list of the keyboard codes, consult the online Help. Search for OnKey.

Tip The preceding examples used `On Error Resume Next` to ignore any errors generated. For example, if the active cell is in the first row, trying to move up one row causes an error. Furthermore, if the active sheet is a chart sheet, an error occurs because no such thing as an active cell exists in a chart sheet.

By executing the following procedure, you cancel the `OnKey` events, and the keys return to their normal functions.

```
Sub Cancel_OnKey()
    Application.OnKey "{PgDn}"
    Application.OnKey "{PgUp}"
End Sub
```

Caution Contrary to what you might expect, using an empty string as the second argument for the `OnKey` method does *not* cancel the `OnKey` event. Rather, it causes Excel to ignore the keystroke and do nothing. For example, the following instruction tells Excel to ignore Alt+F4 (the percent sign represents the Alt key):

```
Application.OnKey "%{F4}", ""
```

✦　　✦　　✦

VBA Examples

✦ ✦ ✦ ✦

In This Chapter

Working with ranges

Changing Excel's settings

Working with charts

Modifying properties

VBA speed tips

✦ ✦ ✦ ✦

My philosophy about learning to write Excel macros places heavy emphasis on examples. I've found that a well-thought-out example often communicates a concept much better than a lengthy description of the underlying theory. In this book, space limitations don't allow describing every nuance of VBA, so I've prepared many examples. Don't overlook VBA's Help system for specific details. To get help while working in the VB Editor window, press F1 or type your search terms into the Type a Question for Help box in the menu bar.

This chapter consists of several examples that demonstrate common VBA techniques. You may be able to use some of the examples directly, but in most cases, you must adapt them to your own needs. These examples are organized into the following categories:

- ✦ Working with ranges
- ✦ Changing Excel's settings
- ✦ Working with charts
- ✦ Learning ways to speed your VBA code

On the CD-ROM Most of the examples in this chapter are available on the companion CD-ROM.

Working with Ranges

Most of what you do in VBA probably involves worksheet ranges. When you work with range objects, keep the following points in mind:

- ✦ Your VBA code doesn't need to select a range to do something with the range.
- ✦ If your code does select a range, its worksheet must be active.

✦ The macro recorder doesn't always generate the most efficient code. Often, you can use the recorder to create your macro and then edit the code to make it more efficient.

✦ I recommend that you use named ranges in your VBA code. For example, a reference such as Range ("Total") is better than Range ("D45"). In the latter case, you need to modify the macro if you add a row above row 45.

✦ When you record macros that select ranges, pay close attention to relative versus absolute recording mode (as described in Chapter 34). The recording mode that you choose can drastically affect the way the macro operates.

✦ If you create a macro that loops through each cell in the current range selection, be aware that the user can select entire columns or rows. In most cases, you don't want to loop through every cell in the selection. For example, you may want to eliminate empty cells. In such a case, you need to create a subset of the selection that consists only of nonblank cells. Or, you can work with cells in the worksheet's used range (by using the UsedRange property).

✦ Be aware that Excel allows multiple ranges to be selected in a worksheet. For example, you can select a range, press Ctrl, and then select another range. You can test for this in your macro and take appropriate actions.

The examples in the following sections demonstrate these points.

Copying a range

Copying a range is a frequent activity in macros. When you turn on the macro recorder (using absolute recording mode) and copy a range from A1:A5 to B1:B5, you get a VBA macro like this:

```
Sub CopyRange()
    Range("A1:A5").Select
    Selection.Copy
    Range("B1").Select
    ActiveSheet.Paste
    Application.CutCopyMode = False
End Sub
```

This macro works, but it's not the most efficient way to copy a range. You can accomplish exactly the same result with the following one-line macro:

```
Sub CopyRange2()
    Range("A1:A5").Copy Range("B1")
End Sub
```

This code takes advantage of the fact that the Copy method can use an argument that specifies the destination. Information such as this is available in the Help system.

The example demonstrates that the macro recorder doesn't always generate the most efficient code. As you see, you don't have to select an object to work with it. Note that `CopyRange2` doesn't select a range; therefore, the active cell doesn't change when this macro is executed.

Copying a variable-size range

Often, you want to copy a range of cells in which the exact row and column dimensions are unknown.

Figure 39-1 shows a range on a worksheet. This range contains data that is updated weekly. Therefore, the number of rows changes. Because the exact range address is unknown at any given time, writing a macro to copy the range can be challenging.

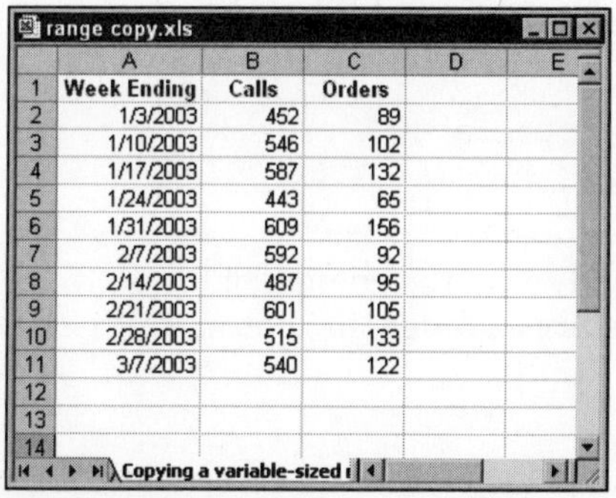

Figure 39-1: This range can consist of any number of rows.

The macro that follows demonstrates how to copy this range from Sheet1 to Sheet2 (beginning at cell A1). It uses the `CurrentRegion` property, which returns a `Range` object that corresponds to the block of used cells surrounding a particular cell. This is equivalent to choosing Edit ⇨ Go To, clicking the Special button, and then selecting the Current Region option.

```
Sub CopyCurrentRegion()
    Range("A1").CurrentRegion.Copy Sheets("Sheet2").Range("A1")
End Sub
```

Selecting to the end of a row or column

You probably are in the habit of using key combinations, such as pressing Ctrl+Shift+right-arrow key and Ctrl+Shift+down-arrow key, to select from the active cell to the end of a row or column. When you record these actions in Excel (using relative recording mode), you'll find that the resulting code works as you would expect it to.

The following VBA procedure selects the range that begins at the active cell and extends down to the last cell in the column (or to the first empty cell, whichever comes first). When the range is selected, you can do whatever you want with it — copy it, move it, format it, and so on.

```
Sub SelectDown()
   Range(ActiveCell, ActiveCell.End(xlDown)).Select
End Sub
```

Notice that the Range property has two arguments. These arguments represent the upper-left and lower-right cells in a range.

This example uses the End method of the Range object, which returns a Range object. The End method takes one argument, which can be any of the following constants: xlUp, xlDown, xlToLeft, or xlToRight.

Selecting a row or column

The macro that follows demonstrates how to select the column of the active cell. It uses the EntireColumn property, which returns a range that consists of a column.

```
Sub SelectColumn()
   ActiveCell.EntireColumn.Select
End Sub
```

As you may suspect, an EntireRow property also is available, which returns a range that consists of a row.

If you want to perform an operation on all cells in the selected column, you don't need to select the column. For example, the following procedure makes all cells bold in the row that contains the active cell:

```
Sub MakeRowBold()
   ActiveCell.EntireRow.Font.Bold = True
End Sub
```

Moving a range

Moving a range consists of cutting it to the Clipboard and then pasting it to another area. If you record your actions while performing a move operation, the macro recorder generates code as follows:

```
Sub MoveRange()
   Range("A1:C6").Select
```

```
      Selection.Cut
      Range("A10").Select
      ActiveSheet.Paste
   End Sub
```

As demonstrated with copying earlier in this chapter, this is not the most efficient way to move a range of cells. In fact, you can do it with a single VBA statement, as follows:

```
   Sub MoveRange2()
    Range("A1:C6").Cut Range("A10")
   End Sub
```

This statement takes advantage of the fact that the `Cut` method can use an argument that specifies the destination.

Looping through a range efficiently

Many macros perform an operation on each cell in a range, or they may perform selective actions based on the content of each cell. These operations usually involve a `For-Next` loop that processes each cell in the range.

The following example demonstrates how to loop through all the cells in a range. In this case, the range is the current selection. In this example, `Cell` is a variable name that refers to the cell being processed. (Notice that this variable is declared as a `Range` object.) Within the `For-Next` loop, the single statement evaluates the cell and changes its font color if the cell value is negative. (`vbRed` is a built-in constant that represents the color red.)

```
   Sub ProcessCells()
      Dim Cell As Range
      For Each Cell In Selection
      If Cell.Value < 0 Then Cell.Font.Color = vbRed
      Next Cell
   End Sub
```

The preceding example works, but what if the selection consists of an entire column or an entire range? This is not uncommon because Excel lets you perform operations on entire columns or rows. But in this case, the macro seems to take forever because it loops through each cell—even those that are blank. What's needed is a way to process only the nonblank cells.

This can be accomplished by using the `SelectSpecial` method. In the following example, the `SelectSpecial` method is used to create two new objects: the subset of the selection that consists of cells with constants, and the subset of the selection that consists of cells with formulas. Each of these subsets is processed, with the net effect of skipping all blank cells.

```
Sub SkipBlanks()
    Dim ConstantCells As Range
    Dim FormulaCells As Range
    Dim Cell As Range
'   Ignore errors
    On Error Resume Next

'   Process the constants
    Set ConstantCells = Selection.SpecialCells(xlConstants,
xlNumbers)
    For Each Cell In ConstantCells
        If Cell.Value < 0 Then Cell.Font.Color = vbRed
    Next Cell

'   Process the formulas
    Set FormulaCells = Selection.SpecialCells(xlFormulas,
xlNumbers)
    For Each Cell In FormulaCells
        If Cell.Value < 0 Then Cell.Font.Color = vbRed
    Next Cell
End Sub
```

The `SkipBlanks` procedure works fast, regardless of what is selected. For example, you can select the range, select all columns in the range, select all rows in the range, or even select the entire worksheet. In all these cases, only the cells that contain constants or values are processed. This is a vast improvement over the `ProcessCells` procedure presented earlier.

Notice that the following statement is used in the procedure:

```
On Error Resume Next
```

This statement causes Excel to ignore any errors that occur and simply to process the next statement. This is necessary because the `SpecialCells` method produces an error if no cells qualify and because the numerical comparison will fail if a cell contains an error value. Normal error checking is resumed when the procedure ends. To tell Excel explicitly to return to normal error-checking mode, use the following statement:

```
On Error GoTo 0
```

Prompting for a cell value

As discussed in Chapter 36, you can take advantage of VBA's `InputBox` function to solicit a value from the user. Figure 39-2 shows an example.

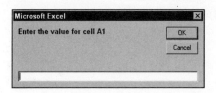

Figure 39-2: Using VBA's InputBox function to get a value from the user.

You can assign this value to a variable and use it in your procedure. Often, however, you want to place the value into a cell. The following procedure demonstrates how to ask the user for a value and place it into cell A1 of the active worksheet, using only one statement:

```
Sub GetValue()
    Range("A1").Value = InputBox("Enter the value for cell A1")
End Sub
```

Determining the type of selection

If your macro is designed to work with a range selection, you need to determine that a range is actually selected. Otherwise, the macro most likely fails. The following procedure identifies the type of object that is currently selected:

```
Sub SelectionType()
    MsgBox TypeName(Selection)
End Sub
```

If a Range object is selected, the MsgBox displays Range. If your macro is designed to work only with ranges, you can use an If statement to ensure that a range is actually selected. The following is an example that beeps, displays a message, and exits the procedure if the current selection is not a Range object:

```
Sub CheckSelection()
    If TypeName(Selection) <> "Range" Then
        Beep
        MsgBox "Select a range."
        Exit Sub
    End If
' ... [Other statements go here]
End Sub
```

Another way to approach this is to define a custom function that returns True if the selection is a Range object, and False otherwise. The following function does just that:

```
Function IsRange(sel) As Boolean
    IsRange = False
    If TypeName(sel) = "Range" Then IsRange = True
End Function
```

If you enter the `IsRange` function in your module, you can rewrite the `CheckSelection` procedure as follows:

```
Sub CheckSelection()
  If IsRange(Selection) Then
' ... [Other statements go here]
  Else
    Beep
    MsgBox "Select a range."
    Exit Sub
  End If
End Sub
```

Identifying a multiple selection

As you know, Excel enables you to make a multiple selection by pressing Ctrl while you select objects or ranges. This can cause problems with some macros; for example, you can't copy a multiple selection that consists of nonadjacent ranges. The following macro demonstrates how to determine whether the user has made a multiple selection:

```
Sub MultipleSelection()
  If Selection.Areas.Count > 1 Then
    MsgBox "Multiple selections not allowed."
    Exit Sub
  End If
' ... [Other statements go here]
End Sub
```

This example uses the `Areas` method, which returns a collection of all `Range` objects in the selection. The `Count` property returns the number of objects that are in the collection.

The following is a VBA function that returns `True` if the selection is a multiple selection:

```
Function IsMultiple(sel) As Boolean
  IsMultiple = Selection.Areas.Count > 1
End Function
```

Changing Excel's Settings

Some of the most useful macros are simple procedures that change one or more of Excel's settings. For example, it takes quite a few mouse clicks simply to change the Recalculation mode from automatic to manual.

This section contains two examples that demonstrate how to change settings in Excel. These examples can be generalized to other operations.

Changing Boolean settings

A *Boolean* setting is one that is either on or off. For example, you may want to create a macro that turns on and off the row and column headings. If you record your actions while you access the Options dialog box, you find that Excel generates the following code if you turn off the headings:

```
ActiveWindow.DisplayHeadings = False
```

It generates the following code if you turn on the headings:

```
ActiveWindow.DisplayHeadings = True
```

This may lead you to suspect that the heading display requires two macros: one to turn on the headings and one to turn them off. Actually, this isn't true. The following procedure uses the Not operator effectively to toggle the heading display from True to False and from False to True:

```
Sub ToggleHeadings()
  If TypeName(ActiveSheet) <> "Worksheet" Then Exit Sub
  ActiveWindow.DisplayHeadings = Not
ActiveWindow.DisplayHeadings
End Sub
```

The first statement ensures that the active sheet is a worksheet; otherwise, an error occurs. (Chart sheets don't have row and column headers.) This technique can be used with any other settings that take on Boolean (True or False) values. For example, you can create macros to toggle sheet tab display, gridlines, and so on. The best way to find out which properties control these items is to turn on the macro recorder while you change them. Then, examine the VBA code.

Changing non-Boolean settings

For non-Boolean settings, you can use the following Select Case structure. This example toggles the Calculation mode and displays a message indicating the current mode:

```
Sub ToggleCalcMode()
  Select Case Application.Calculation
    Case xlManual
      Application.Calculation = xlAutomatic
      MsgBox "Automatic Calculation Mode"
    Case xlAutomatic
      Application.Calculation = xlManual
      MsgBox "Manual Calculation Mode"
  End Select
End Sub
```

Working with Charts

Manipulating charts with VBA can be confusing, mainly because of the large number of objects involved. To get a feel for this, turn on the macro recorder, create a chart, and perform some routine chart editing. You may be surprised by the amount of code that's generated.

After you understand the objects in a chart, however, you can create some useful macros. This section presents a few macros that deal with charts. When you write macros that manipulate charts, you need to understand some terminology. An embedded chart on a worksheet is a `ChartObject` object, and the `ChartObject` contains the actual `Chart` object. A chart on a chart sheet, on the other hand, does not have a `ChartObject` container.

It's often useful to create an object reference to a chart (see "Simplifying object references," later in this chapter). For example, the following statement creates an object variable (`MyChart`) for the embedded chart named Chart 1 on the active sheet.

```
Dim MyChart As Chart
Set MyChart = ActiveSheet.ChartObjects("Chart 1")
```

Modifying the chart type

The following example changes the chart type of every embedded chart on the active sheet. It makes each chart an area chart by adjusting the `ChartType` property of the `Chart` object. A built-in constant, `xlArea`, represents an area chart.

```
Sub ChartType()
    Dim ChtObj As ChartObject
    For Each ChtObj In ActiveSheet.ChartObjects
        ChtObj.Chart.ChartType = xlArea
    Next ChtObj
End Sub
```

The preceding example uses a `For-Next` loop to cycle through all the `ChartObject` objects on the active sheet. Within the loop, the chart type is assigned a new value, making it an area chart.

The following macro performs the same function but works on all chart sheets in the active workbook:

```
Sub ChartType2()
    Dim Cht As Chart
    For Each Cht In ActiveWorkbook.Charts
        Cht.ChartType = xlAreaStacked
    Next Cht
End Sub
```

Modifying chart properties

The following example changes the legend font for all charts that are on the active sheet. It uses a `For-Next` loop to process all `ChartObject` objects and uses the `HasLegend` property to determine whether the chart has a legend. If so, it adjusts the properties of the `Font` object contained in the `Legend` object.

```
Sub LegendMod()
    Dim ChtObj As ChartObject
    For Each ChtObj In ActiveSheet.ChartObjects
        If ChtObj.Chart.HasLegend Then
            With ChtObj.Chart.Legend.Font
                .Name = "Arial"
                .FontStyle = "Bold"
                .Size = 8
            End With
        End If
    Next ChtObj
End Sub
```

Applying chart formatting

This example applies several different formatting types to the active chart. A chart must be activated before executing this macro. You activate an embedded chart by selecting it. Activate a chart on a chart sheet by activating the chart sheet.

```
Sub ChartMods()
    If ActiveChart Is Nothing Then
        MsgBox "Select a chart first"
        Exit Sub
    End If
    With ActiveChart
        .ChartType = xlArea
        .ChartArea.Font.Name = "Arial"
        .ChartArea.Font.FontStyle = "Regular"
        .ChartArea.Font.Size = 9
        .PlotArea.Interior.ColorIndex = 6
        .Axes(xlValue).TickLabels.Font.Bold = True
        .Axes(xlCategory).TickLabels.Font.Bold = True
        .Legend.Position = xlBottom
    End With
End Sub
```

The procedure starts by determining whether a chart is active. If a chart is not active, the `ActiveChart` is `Nothing`. Therefore, if a chart is not active, the user sees a message, and the procedure ends. Otherwise, the code adjusts various properties of the chart.

VBA Speed Tips

VBA is fast, but it's often not fast enough. This section presents some programming examples that you can use to help speed your macros.

Turning off screen updating

You've probably noticed that when you execute a macro, you can watch everything that occurs in the macro. Sometimes, this is instructive; but after you get the macro working properly, it can be annoying and slow things considerably.

Fortunately, a way exists to disable the normal screen updating that occurs when you execute a macro. Insert the following statement to turn off screen updating:

```
Application.ScreenUpdating = False
```

If, at any point during the macro, you want the user to see the results of the macro, use the following statement to turn screen updating back on:

```
Application.ScreenUpdating = True
```

Preventing alert messages

One of the benefits of using a macro is that you can perform a series of actions automatically. You can start a macro and then get a cup of coffee while Excel does its thing. Some operations cause Excel to display messages that must be attended to, however. For example, if your macro deletes a sheet, you see the message that is shown in the dialog box in Figure 39-3. These types of messages mean that you can't execute your macro unattended.

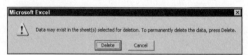

Figure 39-3: You can instruct Excel not to display these types of alerts while a macro is running.

To avoid these alert messages, insert the following VBA statement:

```
Application.DisplayAlerts = False
```

To turn alerts back on, use this statement:

```
Application.DisplayAlerts = True
```

Simplifying object references

As you may have discovered, references to objects can get very lengthy — especially if your code refers to an object that's not on the active sheet or in the active workbook. For example, a fully qualified reference to a Range object may look like this:

```
Workbooks("MyBook.xls").Worksheets("Sheet1").Range("IntRate")
```

If your macro uses this range frequently, you may want to use the Set command to create an object variable. For example, to assign this Range object to an object variable named Rate, use the following statement:

```
Set Rate= Workbooks("MyBook.xls").Worksheets("Sheet1"). _
Range("IntRate")
```

After this variable is defined, you can use the variable Rate instead of the lengthy reference. For example:

```
Rate.Value = .0725
```

Besides simplifying your coding, using object variables also speeds your macros quite a bit. I've seen some macros execute twice as fast after creating object variables.

Declaring variable types

Usually, you don't have to worry about the type of data that's assigned to a variable. Excel handles all these details behind the scenes. For example, if you have a variable named MyVar, you can assign a number or any type to it. You can even assign a text string to it later in the procedure.

But if you want your procedures to execute as fast as possible, you should tell Excel in advance what type of data is going be assigned to each of your variables. This is known as *declaring* a variables type.

Table 39-1 lists all the data types that are supported by VBA. This table also lists the number of bytes that each type uses and the approximate range of possible values.

	Table 39-1 **Data Types**	
Data Type	**Bytes Used**	**Approximate Range of Values**
Byte	1	0 to 255
Boolean	2	True or False
Integer	2	−32,768 to 32,767
Long (long integer)	4	−2,147,483,648 to 2,147,483,647
Single (single-precision floating-point)	4 3	−3.4E38 to −1.4E−45 for negative values 1.4E−45 to 4E38 for positive values
Double (double-precision floating-point)	8 1	−1.7E308 to −4.9E−324 for negative values 4.9E−324 to .7E308 for positive values
Currency (scaled integer)	8	−9.2E14 to 9.2E14
Decimal	14	+/−7.9E28 with no decimal point
Date	8	January 1, 100 to December 31, 9999
Object	4	Any object reference
String (variable-length)	10 + string length	0 to approximately 2 billion
String (fixed-length)	Length of string	1 to approximately 65,400
Variant (with numbers)	16	Any numeric value up to the range of a Double
Variant (with characters) String	22 + string length	Same range as for variable-length
User-defined (using Type)	Number required by elements	Range of each element is the same as the range of its data type

If you don't declare a variable, Excel uses the Variant data type. In general, the best technique is to use the data type that uses the smallest number of bytes yet can still handle all the data assigned to it. An exception is when you are performing floating-point calculations. In such a case, it is always best to use the Double data type (rather than the Single data type) to maintain maximum precision.

When VBA works with data, execution speed is a function of the number of bytes that VBA has at its disposal. In other words, the fewer bytes that are used by data, the faster VBA can access and manipulate the data.

To declare a variable, use the `Dim` statement before you use the variable for the first time. For example, to declare the variable `Units` as an integer, use the following statement:

```
Dim Units as Integer
```

To declare the variable `UserName` as a string, use the following statement:

```
Dim UserName as String
```

If you declare a variable within a procedure, the declaration is valid only within that procedure. If you declare a variable outside of any procedures (but before the first procedure), the variable is valid in all procedures in the module.

If you use an object variable (as described in "Simplifying object references," earlier in this chapter), you can declare the variable as the appropriate object data type. The following is an example:

```
Dim Rate as Range
Set Rate = Workbooks("MyBook").Worksheets("Sheet1").Range
("IntRate")
```

To force yourself to declare all the variables that you use, insert the following statement at the top of your module:

```
Option Explicit
```

If you use this statement, Excel displays an error message if it encounters a variable that hasn't been declared. After you get into the habit of correctly declaring all your variables, you will find that it helps eliminate errors and makes spotting errors easier.

✦　　✦　　✦

Creating Custom Excel Add-Ins

For developers, one of the most useful features in Excel is
the capability to create add-ins. This chapter discusses
this concept and provides a practical example of creating an
add-in.

What Is an Add-In?

Generally speaking, an *add-in* is something that's added to
software to give it additional functionality. Excel includes several add-ins, including the Analysis ToolPak and Solver. Some
add-ins (such as the Analysis ToolPak, discussed in Chapter
24) provide new worksheet functions that can be used in formulas. Ideally, the new features blend in well with the original
interface, so they appear to be part of the program.

Excel's approach to add-ins is quite powerful because any
knowledgeable Excel user can create add-ins from XLS workbooks. An Excel add-in is basically a different form of an XLS
workbook file. Any XLS file can be converted into an add-in,
but not every workbook is a good candidate for an add-in.
Add-ins are always hidden, so you can't display worksheets or
chart sheets that are contained in an add-in. But, you can
access its VBA procedures and display dialog boxes that are
contained on UserForms.

The following are some typical uses for Excel add-ins:

♦ **To store one or more custom worksheet functions.**
When the add-in is loaded, the functions can be used
like any built-in worksheet function.

♦ **To store Excel utilities.** VBA is ideal for creating general-
purpose utilities that extend the power of Excel. The
Power Utility Pak that I created is an example.

✦ **To store proprietary macros.** If you don't want end users to see (or modify) your macros, store the macros in an add-in and protect the VB project with a password. The macros can be used, but they can't be viewed or changed unless the user knows the password. An additional benefit is that the add-in does not display a workbook window, which can be distracting.

As previously noted, Excel ships with several useful add-ins (see the nearby sidebar "Add-Ins That Are Included with Excel"), and you can acquire other add-ins from third-party vendors or the Internet. In addition, Excel includes the tools that enable you to create your own add-ins. This process is explained later in the chapter, but first, some background is required.

Working with Add-Ins

The best way to work with add-ins is to use Excel's add-in manager, which you access by selecting Tools ➪ Add-Ins. This command displays the Add-Ins dialog box, as shown in Figure 40-1. The list box contains all the add-ins that Excel knows about. Those that are checked are currently open. You can open and close add-ins from this dialog box by selecting or deselecting the check boxes.

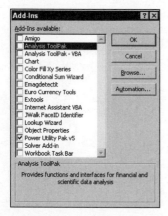

Figure 40-1: The Add-Ins dialog box.

 Note Most add-in files can also be opened by selecting File ➪ Open. You'll find that after an add-in is opened, however, you can't choose File ➪ Close to close it. The only way to remove the add-in is to exit and restart Excel or to write a macro to close the add-in.

When an add-in is opened, you may or may not notice anything different. In nearly every case, however, some change is made to the menu—either a new menu or one or more new menu items on an existing menu. For example, when you open the Analysis ToolPak add-in, a new menu item appears on the Tools menu: Data Analysis. When you open my Power Utility Pak add-in, you get a new Utilities menu, which is located between the Data and Window menus.

Add-Ins That Are Included with Excel

The following is a list of the add-ins that are included with Excel 2003. Some of these add-ins may not have been installed. If you try to use one of these add-ins and it's not installed, you receive a prompt asking whether you want to install it.

✦ **Analysis ToolPak:** Statistical and engineering tools, plus new worksheet functions.

✦ **Analysis ToolPak – VBA:** VBA functions for the Analysis ToolPak.

✦ **Conditional Sum Wizard:** Helps you to create formulas that add values based on a condition.

✦ **Euro Currency Tools:** Tools for converting and formatting the euro currency.

✦ **Lookup Wizard:** Helps you to create formulas that look up data in a list.

✦ **Solver Add-In:** A tool that helps you to use a variety of numeric methods for equation solving and optimization.

In addition, you can download additional Excel add-ins from `http://office.microsoft.com/`.

Why Create Add-Ins?

Most Excel users have no need to create add-ins. But if you develop spreadsheets for others — or if you simply want to get the most out of Excel — you may be interested in pursuing this topic further.

The following are several reasons why you may want to convert your XLS application to an add-in:

✦ **To avoid confusion.** If an end user-loads your application as an add-in, the file is not visible in the Excel window — and, therefore, is less likely to confuse novice users or get in the way. Unlike a hidden XLS workbook, an add-in can't be unhidden.

✦ **To simplify access to worksheet functions.** Custom worksheet functions that are stored in an add-in don't require the workbook name qualifier. For example, if you have a custom function named MOVAVG stored in a workbook named Newfuncs.xls, you would have to use a syntax such as the following to use this function in a different workbook:

```
=NEWFUNC.XLS!MOVAVG(A1:A50)
```

But if this function is stored in an add-in file that's open, the syntax is much simpler because you don't need to include the file reference:

```
=MOVAVG(A1:A50)
```

✦ **To provide easier access.** After you identify the location of your add-in, it appears in the Add-Ins dialog box and can display a friendly name and a description of what it does.

✦ **To permit better control over loading.** Add-ins can be opened automatically when Excel starts, regardless of the directory in which they are stored.

✦ **To omit prompts when unloading.** When an add-in is closed, the user never sees the `Save Change In` prompt because changes to add-ins are not saved unless you specifically do so from the Visual Basic Editor window.

Creating Add-Ins

Although any workbook can be converted to an add-in, not all workbooks benefit by this. In fact, workbooks that consist only of worksheets (that is, not macros or custom dialog boxes) become unusable because add-ins are hidden.

Workbooks that benefit from conversion to an add-in are those with macros. For example, you may have a workbook that consists of general-purpose macros and functions. This type of workbook makes an ideal add-in.

Creating an add-in is quite simple. These steps describe how to create an add-in from a normal workbook file:

1. Develop your application and make sure that everything works properly. Don't forget to include a means of executing the macro or macros. You may want to add a new menu item (described later in this chapter).

2. Test the application by executing it when a *different* workbook is active. This simulates its behavior when it's an add-in because an add-in is never the active workbook. You may find that some references no longer work. For example, the following statement works fine when the code resides in the active workbook, but fails when a different workbook is active:

```
x = Worksheets("Data").Range("A1")
```

You could qualify the reference with the name of the workbook object, like this:

```
x = Workbooks("MYBOOK.XLS").Worksheets("Data").Range("A1")
```

This method is not recommended because the name of the workbook changes when it's converted to an add-in. The solution is to use the `ThisWorkbook` qualifier, as follows

```
x = ThisWorkbook.Worksheets("Data").Range("A1")
```

3. Select File ➪ Summary Info, enter a brief descriptive title in the Title field, and then enter a longer description in the Comments field.

This step is not required, but it makes installing the add-in easier.

4. Lock the project.

This is an optional step that protects the VBA code and UserForms from being viewed. You do this in the Visual Basic Editor, using the Tools ➪ Properties command. Click the Protection tab and make the appropriate choices.

5. Save the workbook as an XLA file by selecting File ➪ Save As. Select Microsoft Excel Add-In from the Save As Type drop-down list.

By default, Excel will store your add-in in your AddIns directory. But you can override this and choose any directory you like.

After you create the add-in, you need to test it. Select Tools ➪ Add-Ins and use the Browse button in the Add-Ins dialog box to locate the XLA file that you created in Step 5. This installs the add-in. The Add-Ins dialog box uses the descriptive title that you provided in Step 3.

Note   You can continue to modify the macros and UserForms in the XLA version of your file and save your changes in the Visual Basic Editor.

An Add-In Example

This section discusses the steps that are used to create a useful add-in that displays a dialog box (as shown in Figure 40-2) in which the user can quickly change several Excel settings. Although these settings can be changed in the Options dialog box, the add-in makes these changes interactively. For example, if the Grid Lines check box is deselected, the gridlines are removed immediately.

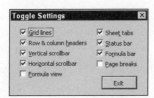

Figure 40-2: This dialog box enables the user to change various Excel settings interactively.

On the CD-ROM   This file is available on the companion CD-ROM. The file is not locked, so you have full access to the VBA code and UserForm.

Setting up the workbook

This workbook contains one worksheet, which is empty. Although the worksheet is not used, it must be present because every workbook must have at least one sheet.

Use the Visual Basic Editor to insert a VBA module (named Module1) and a UserForm (named UserForm1).

Module1

The following macro is contained in the Module1 code module. This procedure ensures that a worksheet is active. If the active sheet is not a worksheet, a message box is displayed, and nothing else happens. If a worksheet is active, the procedure displays the dialog box that is contained in UserForm1.

```
Sub ShowToggleSettingsDialog()
  If TypeName(ActiveSheet) <> "Worksheet" Then
    MsgBox "A worksheet must be active.", vbInformation
  Else
    UserForm1.Show
  End If
End Sub
```

ThisWorkbook

The ThisWorkbook code module contains a macro that adds a menu item to the Tools menu when the workbook (add-in) is opened. Another macro removes the menu item when the workbook (add-in) is closed. These two procedures, which appear in the following syntax, are explained next:

```
Private Sub Workbook_Open()
  Set NewMenuItem = Application.CommandBars _
    ("Worksheet Menu Bar").Controls("Tools").Controls.Add
  With NewMenuItem
    .Caption = "Toggle Settings..."
    .BeginGroup = True
    .OnAction = "ShowToggleSettingsDialog"
  End With
End Sub

Private Sub Workbook_BeforeClose(Cancel As Boolean)
  On Error Resume Next
  Application.CommandBars("Worksheet Menu Bar"). _
    Controls("Tools").Controls("Toggle Settings...").Delete
End Sub
```

The Workbook_Open procedure adds a menu item (Toggle Settings) to the bottom of the Tools menu on the worksheet menu bar. This procedure is executed when the workbook (or add-in) is opened.

The Workbook_BeforeClose procedure is executed when the add-in is closed. This procedure removes the Toggle Settings menu item from the Tools menu.

UserForm1

Figure 40-3 shows the UserForm1 form, which has 10 controls: nine check boxes and one command button. The controls have descriptive names, and the `Accelerator` property is set so that the controls display an accelerator key (for keyboard users).

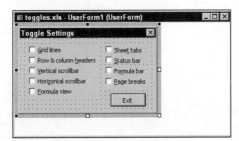

Figure 40-3: The custom dialog box.

The UserForm1 object contains the event handler procedures for the objects that are on the form. The following procedure is executed before the dialog box is displayed:

```
Private Sub UserForm_Initialize()
    cbGridlines = ActiveWindow.DisplayGridlines
    cbHeaders = ActiveWindow.DisplayHeadings
    cbVerticalScrollbar = ActiveWindow.DisplayVerticalScrollBar
    cbHorizontalScrollbar =
ActiveWindow.DisplayHorizontalScrollBar
    cbFormulaView = ActiveWindow.DisplayFormulas
    cbSheetTabs = ActiveWindow.DisplayWorkbookTabs
    cbStatusBar = Application.DisplayStatusBar
    cbFormulaBar = Application.DisplayFormulaBar
    cbPageBreaks = ActiveSheet.DisplayPageBreaks
End Sub
```

The `UserForm_Initialize` procedure adjusts the settings of the CheckBox controls in the dialog box to correspond to the current settings. For example, if the worksheet is displaying gridlines, `ActiveWindow.DisplayGridlines` returns `True`. This value is assigned to the `cbGridlines` CheckBox — which means that the CheckBox is displayed with a check mark.

Each CheckBox also has an event handler procedure, listed in the following code, that is executed when the control is clicked. Each procedure makes the appropriate changes. For example, if the Gridlines CheckBox is selected, the `DisplayGridlines` property is set to correspond to the CheckBox.

```
Private Sub cbGridlines_Click ()
  ActiveWindow.DisplayGridlines = cbGridlines
End Sub

Private Sub cbHeaders_Click ()
  ActiveWindow.DisplayHeadings = cbHeaders
End Sub

Private Sub cbVerticalScrollbar_Click ()
  ActiveWindow.DisplayVerticalScrollBar = cbVerticalScrollbar
End Sub

Private Sub cbHorizontalScrollbar_Click ()
  ActiveWindow.DisplayHorizontalScrollBar = cbHorizontalScrollbar
End Sub

Private Sub cbFormulaView_Click ()
  ActiveWindow.DisplayFormulas = cbFormulaView
End Sub

Private Sub cbSheetTabs_Click ()
  ActiveWindow.DisplayWorkbookTabs = cbSheetTabs
End Sub

Private Sub cbStatusBar_Click ()
  Application.DisplayStatusBar = cbStatusBar
End Sub

Private Sub cbFormulaBar_Click ()
  Application.DisplayFormulaBar = cbFormulaBar
End Sub

Private Sub cbPageBreaks_Click ()
  ActiveSheet.DisplayPageBreaks = cbPageBreaks
End Sub
```

The UserForm1 object has one additional event handler procedure for the Exit button. This procedure, listed as follows, simply closes the dialog box:

```
Private Sub ExitButton_Click ()
  Unload UserForm1
End Sub
```

Testing the workbook

Before you convert this workbook to an add-in, you need to test it. You should test it when a different workbook is active in order to simulate what happens when the workbook is an add-in. Remember that an add-in is never the active workbook, and it never displays any of its worksheets.

To test it, I saved the workbook, closed it, and then reopened it. When the workbook was opened, the `Workbook_Open` procedure was executed. This procedure added the new menu item to the Tools menu. Figure 40-4 shows how this looks.

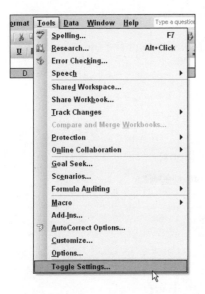

Figure 40-4: The Tools menu displays a new menu item, Toggle Settings.

Adding descriptive information

This step is recommended but not necessary. Choose File ➪ Properties to bring up the Properties dialog box. Then, click the Summary tab, as shown in Figure 40-5.

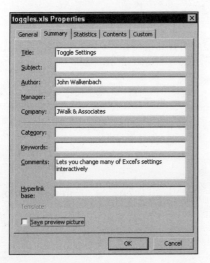

Figure 40-5: Use the Properties dialog box to enter descriptive information about your add-in.

Enter a title for the add-in in the Title field. This is the text that appears in the Add-Ins dialog box. In the Comments field, enter a description. This information appears at the bottom of the Add-Ins dialog box when the add-in is selected.

Protecting the project

You may want to protect your project so that others can't see the source code. To protect the project, follow these steps:

1. Activate the Visual Basic Editor.

2. In the Project window, click the project.

3. Select Tools ➪ *project name* Properties.

    VBE displays its Project Properties dialog box.

4. Click the Protection tab (as shown in Figure 40-6).

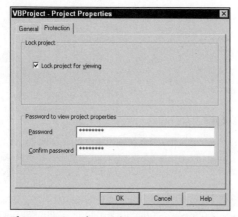

Figure 40-6: The Project Properties dialog box.

5. Select the Lock project for viewing check box.

6. Enter a password (twice) for the project.

7. Click OK.

Creating the add-in

To save the workbook as an add-in, activate Excel and then make sure that a worksheet (not a chart sheet) is active. Then choose File ➪ Save As. Select Microsoft Excel Add-In (*.xla) from the Save as Type drop-down list. Enter a name for the add-in file and then click OK. By default, Excel saves the add-in in your AddIns directory, but you can choose a different directory if you like.

Opening the add-in

To avoid confusion, close the XLS workbook before you open the add-in that was created from it. Then select Tools ➪ Add-Ins. Excel displays its Add-Ins dialog box. Click the Browse button and locate the add-in that you just created. After you do so, the Add-Ins dialog box displays the add-in in its list. Notice that the information that you provided in the Properties dialog box appears here (as shown in Figure 40-7). Click OK to close the dialog box and open the add-in.

Figure 40-7: The Add-Ins dialog box, with the new add-in selected.

When the add-in is open, the Tools menu displays a new menu item (Toggle Settings) that executes the `ShowToggleSettingsDialog` procedure in the add-in.

If you activate the VBE window, you find that the add-in is listed in the Project window. However, you can't make any modifications unless you provide the password.

✦   ✦   ✦

Appendixes

This part contains some very useful appendixes. Appendix A provides a complete reference of all the worksheet functions you're likely to use. Appendix B gives you the run-down on all the great sample files and software on the CD-ROM that accompanies this book. Look to Appendix C for games and fun animations using Excel. Appendix D contains some great additional Excel resources; discover Excel shortcut keys in Appendix E.

Worksheet Function Reference

T his appendix contains a complete listing of Excel's worksheet functions. The functions are arranged alphabetically by categories used by the Insert Function dialog box.

Note   Some of these functions are available only when the
Analysis ToolPak is installed.

For more information about a particular function, including its
arguments, select the function in the Insert Function dialog
box and click Help on This Function.

Table A-1
Database Category Functions

Function	What It Does
DAVERAGE	Averages the values in a column of a list or database that match conditions you specify
DCOUNT	Counts the cells that contain numbers in a column of a list or database that match conditions you specify
DCOUNTA	Counts the nonblank cells in a column of a list or database that match conditions you specify
DGET	Extracts a single value from a column of a list or database that matches conditions you specify
DMAX	Returns the largest number in a column of a list or database that matches conditions you specify
DMIN	Returns the smallest number in a column of a list or database that matches conditions you specify
DPRODUCT	Multiplies the values in a column of a list or database that match conditions you specify
DSTDEV	Estimates the standard deviation of a population based on a sample by using the numbers in a column of a list or database that match conditions you specify
DSTDEVP	Calculates the standard deviation of a population based on the entire population, using the numbers in a column of a list or database that match conditions you specify
DSUM	Adds the numbers in a column of a list or database that match conditions you specify
DVAR	Estimates the variance of a population based on a sample by using the numbers in a column of a list or database that match conditions you specify
DVARP	Calculates the variance of a population based on the entire population by using the numbers in a column of a list or database that match conditions you specify

Table A-2
Date and Time Category Functions

Function	What It Does
DATE	Returns the serial number of a particular date
DATEVALUE	Converts a date in the form of text to a serial number
DAY	Converts a serial number to a day of the month
DAYS360	Calculates the number of days between two dates, based on a 360-day year
EDATE	Returns the serial number of the date that is the indicated number of months before or after the start date
EOMONTH	Returns the serial number of the last day of the month before or after a specified number of months
HOUR	Converts a serial number to an hour
MINUTE	Converts a serial number to a minute
MONTH	Converts a serial number to a month
NETWORKDAYS	Returns the number of whole workdays between two dates
NOW	Returns the serial number of the current date and time
SECOND	Converts a serial number to a second
TIME	Returns the serial number of a particular time
TIMEVALUE	Converts a time in the form of text to a serial number
TODAY	Returns the serial number of today's date
WEEKDAY	Converts a serial number to a day of the week
WEEKNUM	Returns the week number in the year
WORKDAY	Returns the serial number of the date before or after a specified number of workdays
YEAR	Converts a serial number to a year
YEARFRAC	Returns the year fraction representing the number of whole days between *start_date* and *end_date*

Table A-3
Engineering Category Functions

Function	What It Does
BESSELI	Returns the modified Bessel function In(x)
BESSELJ	Returns the Bessel function Jn(x)
BESSELK	Returns the modified Bessel function Kn(x)
BESSELY	Returns the Bessel function Yn(x)
BIN2DEC	Converts a binary number to decimal
BIN2HEX	Converts a binary number to hexadecimal
BIN2OCT	Converts a binary number to octal
COMPLEX	Converts real and imaginary coefficients into a complex number
CONVERT	Converts a number from one measurement system to another
DEC2BIN	Converts a decimal number to binary
DEC2HEX	Converts a decimal number to hexadecimal
DEC2OCT	Converts a decimal number to octal
DELTA	Tests whether two values are equal
ERF	Returns the error function
ERFC	Returns the complementary error function
FACTDOUBLE	Returns the double factorial
GESTEP	Tests whether a number is greater than a threshold value
HEX2BIN	Converts a hexadecimal number to binary
HEX2DEC	Converts a hexadecimal number to decimal
HEX2OCT	Converts a hexadecimal number to octal
IMABS	Returns the absolute value (modulus) of a complex number
IMAGINARY	Returns the imaginary coefficient of a complex number
IMARGUMENT	Returns the argument *theta,* an angle expressed in radians
IMCONJUGATE	Returns the complex conjugate of a complex number
IMCOS	Returns the cosine of a complex number
IMDIV	Returns the quotient of two complex numbers
IMEXP	Returns the exponential of a complex number
IMLN	Returns the natural logarithm of a complex number
IMLOG10	Returns the base-10 logarithm of a complex number

Function	What It Does
IMLOG2	Returns the base-2 logarithm of a complex number
IMPOWER	Returns a complex number raised to an integer power
IMPRODUCT	Returns the product of complex numbers
IMREAL	Returns the real coefficient of a complex number
IMSIN	Returns the sine of a complex number
IMSQRT	Returns the square root of a complex number
IMSUB	Returns the difference of two complex numbers
IMSUM	Returns the sum of complex numbers
OCT2BIN	Converts an octal number to binary
OCT2DEC	Converts an octal number to decimal
OCT2HEX	Converts an octal number to hexadecimal

Table A-4
Financial Category Functions

Function	What It Does
ACCRINT	Returns the accrued interest for a security that pays periodic interest
ACCRINTM	Returns the accrued interest for a security that pays interest at maturity
AMORDEGRC	Returns the depreciation for each accounting period
AMORLINC	Returns the depreciation for each accounting period (the depreciation coefficient depends on the life of the assets)
COUPDAYBS	Returns the number of days from the beginning of the coupon period to the settlement date
COUPDAYS	Returns the number of days in the coupon period that contains the settlement date
COUPDAYSNC	Returns the number of days from the settlement date to the next coupon date
COUPNCD	Returns the next coupon date after the settlement date
COUPNUM	Returns the number of coupons payable between the settlement date and maturity date
COUPPCD	Returns the previous coupon date before the settlement date
CUMIPMT	Returns the cumulative interest paid between two periods

Continued

Table A-4 *(continued)*

Function	What It Does
CUMPRINC	Returns the cumulative principal paid on a loan between two periods
DB	Returns the depreciation of an asset for a specified period, using the fixed-declining-balance method
DDB	Returns the depreciation of an asset for a specified period, using the double-declining-balance method or some other method that you specify
DISC	Returns the discount rate for a security
DOLLARDE	Converts a dollar price, expressed as a fraction, into a dollar price, expressed as a decimal number
DOLLARFR	Converts a dollar price, expressed as a decimal number, into a dollar price, expressed as a fraction
DURATION	Returns the annual duration of a security with periodic interest payments
EFFECT	Returns the effective annual interest rate
FV	Returns the future value of an investment
FVSCHEDULE	Returns the future value of an initial principal after applying a series of compound interest rates
INTRATE	Returns the interest rate for a fully invested security
IPMT	Returns the interest payment for an investment for a given period
IRR	Returns the internal rate of return for a series of cash flows
ISPMT	Returns the interest associated with a specific loan payment
MDURATION	Returns the Macauley modified duration for a security with an assumed par value of $100
MIRR	Returns the internal rate of return where positive and negative cash flows are financed at different rates
NOMINAL	Returns the annual nominal interest rate
NPER	Returns the number of periods for an investment
NPV	Returns the net present value of an investment based on a series of periodic cash flows and a discount rate
ODDFPRICE	Returns the price per $100 face value of a security with an odd first period

Function	*What It Does*
ODDFYIELD	Returns the yield of a security with an odd first period
ODDLPRICE	Returns the price per $100 face value of a security with an odd last period
ODDLYIELD	Returns the yield of a security with an odd last period
PMT	Returns the periodic payment for an annuity
PPMT	Returns the payment on the principal for an investment for a given period
PRICE	Returns the price per $100 face value of a security that pays periodic interest
PRICEDISC	Returns the price per $100 face value of a discounted security
PRICEMAT	Returns the price per $100 face value of a security that pays interest at maturity
PV	Returns the present value of an investment
RATE	Returns the interest rate per period of an annuity
RECEIVED	Returns the amount received at maturity for a fully invested security
SLN	Returns the straight-line depreciation of an asset for one period
SYD	Returns the sum-of-years' digits depreciation of an asset for a specified period
TBILLEQ	Returns the bond-equivalent yield for a Treasury bill
TBILLPRICE	Returns the price per $100 face value for a Treasury bill
TBILLYIELD	Returns the yield for a Treasury bill
VDB	Returns the depreciation of an asset for a specified or partial period using a declining-balance method
XIRR	Returns the internal rate of return for a schedule of cash flows that is not necessarily periodic
XNPV	Returns the net present value for a schedule of cash flows that is not necessarily periodic
YIELD	Returns the yield on a security that pays periodic interest
YIELDDISC	Returns the annual yield for a discounted security, for example, a Treasury bill
YIELDMAT	Returns the annual yield of a security that pays interest at maturity

Table A-5
Information Category Functions

Function	What It Does
CELL	Returns information about the formatting, location, or contents of a cell
ERROR.TYPE	Returns a number corresponding to an error type
INFO	Returns information about the current operating environment
ISBLANK	Returns TRUE if the value is blank
ISERR	Returns TRUE if the value is any error value except #N/A
ISERROR	Returns TRUE if the value is any error value
ISEVEN	Returns TRUE if the number is even
ISLOGICAL	Returns TRUE if the value is a logical value
ISNA	Returns TRUE if the value is the #N/A error value
ISNONTEXT	Returns TRUE if the value is not text
ISNUMBER	Returns TRUE if the value is a number
ISODD	Returns TRUE if the number is odd
ISREF	Returns TRUE if the value is a reference
ISTEXT	Returns TRUE if the value is text
N	Returns a value converted to a number
NA	Returns the error value #N/A
TYPE	Returns a number indicating the data type of a value

Table A-6
Logical Category Functions

Function	What It Does
AND	Returns TRUE if all its arguments are TRUE
FALSE	Returns the logical value FALSE
IF	Specifies a logical test to perform
NOT	Reverses the logic of its argument
OR	Returns TRUE if any argument is TRUE
TRUE	Returns the logical value TRUE

Table A-7
Lookup and Reference Category Functions

Function	What It Does
ADDRESS	Returns a reference as text to a single cell in a worksheet
AREAS	Returns the number of areas in a reference
CHOOSE	Chooses a value from a list of values
COLUMN	Returns the column number of a reference
COLUMNS	Returns the number of columns in a reference
GETPIVOTDATA	Returns data stored in a PivotTable
HLOOKUP	Searches for a value in the top column of a table and then returns a value in the same column from a row you specify in the table
HYPERLINK	Creates a shortcut that opens a document on your hard drive, a server, or the Internet
INDEX	Uses an index to choose a value from a reference or array
INDIRECT	Returns a reference indicated by a text value
LOOKUP	Returns a value either from a one-row or one-column range or from an array
MATCH	Returns the relative position of an item in an array
OFFSET	Returns a reference offset from a given reference
ROW	Returns the row number of a reference
ROWS	Returns the number of rows in a reference
TRANSPOSE	Returns the transpose of an array
VLOOKUP	Searches for a value in the leftmost column of a table and then returns a value in the same row from a column you specify in the table

Table A-8
Math and Trig Category Functions

Function	What It Does
ABS	Returns the absolute value of a number
ACOS	Returns the arccosine of a number
ACOSH	Returns the inverse hyperbolic cosine of a number
ASIN	Returns the arcsine of a number

Continued

Table A-8 *(continued)*

Function	What It Does
ASINH	Returns the inverse hyperbolic sine of a number
ATAN	Returns the arctangent of a number
ATAN2	Returns the arctangent from x and y coordinates
ATANH	Returns the inverse hyperbolic tangent of a number
CEILING	Rounds a number to the nearest integer or to the nearest multiple of significance
COMBIN	Returns the number of combinations for a given number of objects
COS	Returns the cosine of a number
COSH	Returns the hyperbolic cosine of a number
DEGREES	Converts radians to degrees
EVEN	Rounds a number up to the nearest even integer
EXP	Returns e raised to the power of a given number
FACT	Returns the factorial of a number
FLOOR	Rounds a number down, toward 0
GCD	Returns the greatest common divisor
INT	Rounds a number down to the nearest integer
LCM	Returns the least common multiple
LN	Returns the natural logarithm of a number
LOG	Returns the logarithm of a number to a specified base
LOG10	Returns the base-10 logarithm of a number
MDETERM	Returns the matrix determinant of an array
MINVERSE	Returns the matrix inverse of an array
MMULT	Returns the matrix product of two arrays
MOD	Returns the remainder from division
MROUND	Returns a number rounded to the desired multiple
MULTINOMIAL	Returns the multinomial of a set of numbers
ODD	Rounds a number up to the nearest odd integer
PI	Returns the value of pi
POWER	Returns the result of a number raised to a power
PRODUCT	Multiplies its arguments

Function	What It Does
QUOTIENT	Returns the integer portion of a division
RADIANS	Converts degrees to radians
RAND	Returns a random number between 0 and 1
RANDBETWEEN	Returns a random number between the numbers that you specify
ROMAN	Converts an Arabic numeral to Roman, as text
ROUND	Rounds a number to a specified number of digits
ROUNDDOWN	Rounds a number down, toward 0
ROUNDUP	Rounds a number up, away from 0
SERIESSUM	Returns the sum of a power series based on the formula
SIGN	Returns the sign of a number
SIN	Returns the sine of the given angle
SINH	Returns the hyperbolic sine of a number
SQRT	Returns a positive square root
SQRTPI	Returns the square root of pi
SUBTOTAL	Returns a subtotal in a list or database
SUM	Adds its arguments
SUMIF	Adds the cells specified by a given criteria
SUMPRODUCT	Returns the sum of the products of corresponding array components
SUMSQ	Returns the sum of the squares of the arguments
SUMX2MY2	Returns the sum of the difference of squares of corresponding values in two arrays
SUMX2PY2	Returns the sum of the sum of squares of corresponding values in two arrays
SUMXMY2	Returns the sum of squares of differences of corresponding values in two arrays
TAN	Returns the tangent of a number
TANH	Returns the hyperbolic tangent of a number
TRUNC	Truncates a number (you specify the precision of the truncation)

Table A-9
Statistical Category Functions

Function	What It Does
AVEDEV	Returns the average of the absolute deviations of data points from their mean
AVERAGE	Returns the average of its arguments
AVERAGEA	Returns the average of its arguments and includes evaluation of text and logical values
BETADIST	Returns the cumulative beta probability density function
BETAINV	Returns the inverse of the cumulative beta probability density function
BINOMDIST	Returns the individual term binomial distribution probability
CHIDIST	Returns the one-tailed probability of the chi-squared distribution
CHIINV	Returns the inverse of the one-tailed probability of the chi-squared distribution
CHITEST	Returns the test for independence
CONFIDENCE	Returns the confidence interval for a population mean
CORREL	Returns the correlation coefficient between two data sets
COUNT	Counts how many numbers are in the list of arguments
COUNTA	Counts how many values are in the list of arguments
COUNTBLANK	Counts the number of blank cells in the argument range
COUNTIF	Counts the number of cells that meet the criteria you specify in the argument
COVAR	Returns covariance, the average of the products of paired deviations
CRITBINOM	Returns the smallest value for which the cumulative binomial distribution is less than or equal to a criterion value
DEVSQ	Returns the sum of squares of deviations
EXPONDIST	Returns the exponential distribution
FDIST	Returns the F probability distribution
FINV	Returns the inverse of the F probability distribution
FISHER	Returns the Fisher transformation
FISHERINV	Returns the inverse of the Fisher transformation
FORECAST	Returns a value along a linear trend
FREQUENCY	Returns a frequency distribution as a vertical array
FTEST	Returns the result of an F-Test
GAMMADIST	Returns the gamma distribution

Function	What It Does
GAMMAINV	Returns the inverse of the gamma cumulative distribution
GAMMALN	Returns the natural logarithm of the gamma function, G(x)
GEOMEAN	Returns the geometric mean
GROWTH	Returns values along an exponential trend
HARMEAN	Returns the harmonic mean
HYPGEOMDIST	Returns the hypergeometric distribution
INTERCEPT	Returns the intercept of the linear regression line
KURT	Returns the kurtosis of a data set
LARGE	Returns the kth largest value in a data set
LINEST	Returns the parameters of a linear trend
LOGEST	Returns the parameters of an exponential trend
LOGINV	Returns the inverse of the lognormal distribution
LOGNORMDIST	Returns the cumulative lognormal distribution
MAX	Returns the maximum value in a list of arguments, ignoring logical values and text
MAXA	Returns the maximum value in a list of arguments, including logical values and text
MEDIAN	Returns the median of the given numbers
MIN	Returns the minimum value in a list of arguments, ignoring logical values and text
MINA	Returns the minimum value in a list of arguments, including logical values and text
MODE	Returns the most common value in a data set
NEGBINOMDIST	Returns the negative binomial distribution
NORMDIST	Returns the normal cumulative distribution
NORMINV	Returns the inverse of the normal cumulative distribution
NORMSDIST	Returns the standard normal cumulative distribution
NORMSINV	Returns the inverse of the standard normal cumulative distribution
PEARSON	Returns the Pearson product moment correlation coefficient
PERCENTILE	Returns the kth percentile of values in a range
PERCENTRANK	Returns the percentage rank of a value in a data set
PERMUT	Returns the number of permutations for a given number of objects

Continued

Table A-9 (continued)

Function	What It Does
POISSON	Returns the Poisson distribution
PROB	Returns the probability that values in a range are between two limits
QUARTILE	Returns the quartile of a data set
RANK	Returns the rank of a number in a list of numbers
RSQ	Returns the square of the Pearson product moment correlation coefficient
SKEW	Returns the skewness of a distribution
SLOPE	Returns the slope of the linear regression line
SMALL	Returns the kth smallest value in a data set
STANDARDIZE	Returns a normalized value
STDEV	Estimates standard deviation based on a sample, ignoring text and logical values
STDEVA	Estimates standard deviation based on a sample, including text and logical values
STDEVP	Calculates standard deviation based on the entire population, ignoring text and logical values
STDEVPA	Calculates standard deviation based on the entire population, including text and logical values
STEYX	Returns the standard error of the predicted y-value for each x in the regression
TDIST	Returns the student's t-distribution
TINV	Returns the inverse of the student's t-distribution
TREND	Returns values along a linear trend
TRIMMEAN	Returns the mean of the interior of a data set
TTEST	Returns the probability associated with a student's t-Test
VAR	Estimates variance based on a sample, ignoring logical values and text
VARA	Estimates variance based on a sample, including logical values and text
VARP	Calculates variance based on the entire population, ignoring logical values and text
VARPA	Calculates variance based on the entire population, including logical values and text
WEIBULL	Returns the Weibull distribution
ZTEST	Returns the two-tailed P-value of a z-test

Table A-10
Text Category Functions

Function	What It Does
BAHTTEXT	Converts a number to Baht text
CHAR	Returns the character specified by the code number
CLEAN	Removes all nonprintable characters from text
CODE	Returns a numeric code for the first character in a text string
CONCATENATE	Joins several text items into one text item
DOLLAR	Converts a number to text, using currency format
EXACT	Checks to see whether two text values are identical
FIND	Finds one text value within another (case sensitive)
FIXED	Formats a number as text with a fixed number of decimals
LEFT	Returns the leftmost characters from a text value
LEN	Returns the number of characters in a text string
LOWER	Converts text to lowercase
MID	Returns a specific number of characters from a text string, starting at the position you specify
PROPER	Capitalizes the first letter in each word of a text value
REPLACE	Replaces characters within text
REPT	Repeats text a given number of times
RIGHT	Returns the rightmost characters from a text value
SEARCH	Finds one text value within another (not case sensitive)
SUBSTITUTE	Substitutes new text for old text in a text string
T	Returns the text referred to by value
TEXT	Formats a number and converts it to text
TRIM	Removes excess spaces from text
UPPER	Converts text to uppercase
VALUE	Converts a text argument to a number

✦ ✦ ✦

What's on the CD-ROM

This appendix provides you with information on the contents of the CD that accompanies this book. For the latest and greatest information, please refer to the ReadMe file located at the root of the CD.

This appendix provides information on the following topics:

✦ System Requirements

✦ Using the CD

✦ Files and software on the CD

✦ Troubleshooting

System Requirements

Make sure that your computer meets the minimum system requirements listed in this section. If your computer doesn't match up to most of these requirements, you may have a problem using the contents of the CD.

For Windows 9x, Me, XP, Windows 2000, Windows NT4 (with SP 4 or later):

✦ PC with a Pentium processor running at 120 MHz or faster.

✦ At least 32MB of total RAM installed on your computer; for best performance, we recommend at least 64MB.

✦ Ethernet network interface card (NIC) or modem with a speed of at least 28,800 bps.

✦ A CD-ROM drive.

Office 2003 Specific Requirements:

✦ PC with Pentium 133 MHz or higher processor; Pentium III recommended

✦ Microsoft Windows 2000 with Service Pack 3 or Windows XP or later operating system

Using the CD

To install the items from the CD to your hard drive, follow these steps:

1. Insert the CD into your computer's CD-ROM drive.

A window appears, displaying the License Agreement.

2. Click Accept to continue.

Another window appears with the following buttons (which are explained in greater detail in the next section of this chapter):

Excel 2003 Bible: Click this button to view an eBook version of the book as well as any author-created content specific to the book, such as templates and sample files.

Super Bible: Click this button to view an electronic version of the *Office 2003 Super Bible,* along with any author-created materials from the *Super Bible,* such as templates and sample files.

Bonus Software: Click this button to view the list and install the supplied third-party software.

Related Links: Click this button to open a hyperlinked page of Web sites.

Other Resources: Click this button to access other Office-related products that you may find useful.

Files and Software on the CD

The following sections provide more details about the software and other materials available on the CD.

eBook version of *Excel 2003 Bible*

The complete text of the book you hold in your hands is provided on the CD in Adobe's Portable Document Format (PDF). You can read and quickly search the content of this PDF file by using Adobe's Acrobat Reader, also included on the CD.

eBook version of the *Office 2003 Super Bible*

The *Super Bible* is an eBook PDF file made up of select chapters pulled from the individual Office 2003 *Bible* titles. This eBook also includes some original and exclusive content found only in this *Super Bible*. The products that make up the Microsoft Office 2003 suite have been created to work hand in hand. Consequently, Wiley has created this *Super Bible* to help you to master some of the most common features of each of the component products and to learn about some of their interoperability features as well. This *Super Bible* consists of more than 500 pages of content to showcase the way that Microsoft Office 2003 components work together.

Sample files from the *Excel 2003 Bible*

✦ **Chapter 1**

`monthly sales projection.xls`: The hands-on example workbook.

✦ **Chapter 2**

`loan payment calculator.xls`: Demonstrates text, values, and formulas.

`number formatting.xls`: Demonstrates some number formats.

✦ **Chapter 4**

`budget.xls`: Demonstrates a simple multisheet budget model.

✦ **Chapter 8**

`circular reference.xls`: Demonstrates an intentional circular reference.

`references.xls`: Demonstrates relative, absolute, and mixed references in formulas.

✦ **Chapter 9**

`character set.xls`: Displays the characters in any font.

`text formula examples.xls`: Contains the advanced text formula examples.

`text histogram.xls`: An example of a histogram created without using a chart.

✦ **Chapter 10**

`holidays.xls`: A workbook that calculates U.S. holidays for any year.

`jogging log.xls`: A workbook that stores jogging data.

`time sheet.xls`: A worksheet to keep a weekly time sheet.

`work days.xls`: Demonstrates the NETWORKDAYS function.

`xdate.exe`: Execute this file to install the Extended Date Functions add-in.

✦ **Chapter 11**

basic counting.xls: Demonstrates basic counting techniques.

conditional summing.xls: Contains examples of formulas that perform conditional summing.

count unique.xls: Demonstrates an array formula to count unique values in a range.

counting text in a range.xls: Demonstrates various ways to count characters in a range.

cumulative sum.xls: Demonstrates how to calculate a cumulative sum.

frequency distribution.xls: Demonstrates three ways to create a frequency distribution.

multiple criteria counting.xls: Demonstrates counting techniques using multiple criteria.

✦ **Chapter 12**

basic lookup examples.xls: Demonstrates basic lookup formulas.

case-sensitive lookups.xls: Demonstrates how to perform a case-sensitive lookup.

closest match.xls: Demonstrates how to look up a value by using the closest match.

gpa.xls: Demonstrates how to calculate a grade-point average.

grade lookup.xls: Demonstrates how to look up a letter grade for a score.

lookup cell address.xls: Demonstrates how to look up a cell address in a range.

lookup to the left.xls: Demonstrates two ways to look up a value to the left.

multiple lookup tables.xls: Demonstrates the use of multiple lookup tables.

two-column lookup.xls: Demonstrates how to perform a two-column lookup.

two-way lookup.xls: Demonstrates two ways to perform a two-way lookup.

✦ **Chapter 13**

annuity calculator.xls: Demonstrates various calculations for annuities.

credit card payments.xls: Calculates the number of payments required to pay off a credit card balance.

depreciation.xls: Demonstrations various types of depreciation calculations.

investment calculations.xls: Demonstrates various investment calculations.

`irregular payments.xls`: Demonstrates loan calculations with irregular payments.

`loan amortization schedule.xls`: Calculates a loan amortization schedule.

`loan data tables.xls`: Demonstrates the use of data tables to calculate loan information.

`loan payment.xls`: Calculates loan payments.

✦ Chapter 15

`calendar array.xls`: Demonstrates how to display a calendar month in a range, using a multi-cell array formula.

`logical array formulas.xls`: Examples of array formulas that use logical operations.

`multi-cell array formulas.xls`: Examples of multicell array formulas.

`single-cell array formulas.xls`: Examples of single-cell array formulas.

✦ Chapter 16

`3-d charts.xls`: 3-D chart examples.

`area charts.xls`: Area chart examples.

`bar charts.xls`: Bar chart examples.

`bubble charts.xls`: Bubble chart examples.

`column charts.xls`: Column chart examples.

`cylinder cone pyramid charts.xls`: Cylinder, cone, and pyramid chart examples.

`doughnut charts.xls`: Doughnut chart examples.

`hands-on example.xls`: The hands-on charting example.

`line charts.xls`: Line chart examples.

`pie charts.xls`: Pie chart examples.

`radar charts.xls`: Radar chart examples.

`six chart types.xls`: Displays the same data using six different chart types.

`stock charts.xls`: Stock market chart examples.

`surface charts.xls`: Surface chart examples.

`xy charts.xls`: XY chart examples.

✦ Chapter 17

`comparative histogram.xls`: Demonstrates a comparative histogram chart.

`daily.xls`: Demonstrates a chart that updates automatically when new data is added.

`function plot 2D.xls`: A general 2-D function plotting workbook.

`function plot 3D.xls`: A general 3-D function plotting workbook.

`function plots.xls`: Demonstrates 2-D and 3-D function plots.

`gantt.xls`: Demonstrates a Gantt chart.

`picture charts.xls`: Demonstrates using pictures in a chart series.

`single data point charts.xls`: Demonstrates various single-data-point examples, including a thermometer chart and a gauge chart.

`user-defined type.xls`: Contains an example of a user-defined chart type.

✦ **Chapter 19**

`dataform2.exe`: JWalk Enhanced DataForm. To install, execute the file and follow the instructions.

`employee list.xls`: Demonstrates autofiltering.

`real estate database.xls`: Demonstrates advanced filtering.

`sales.xls`: Demonstrates the designated list feature.

`subtotals.xls`: Demonstrates the use of subtotals.

✦ **Chapter 20**

`budget.mdb`: An Access database used for the examples in this chapter.

✦ **Chapter 21**

`bank accounts.xls`: The banking database used to create a pivot table.

`calculated field and item.xls`: Demonstrates creating a calculated field and a calculated item.

`employee list.xls`: Demonstrates creating a pivot table from non-numeric data.

`sales by date.xls`: Demonstrates grouping pivot-table items by date.

✦ **Chapter 22**

`direct mail.xls`: Contains the direct–mail two-way data table example.

`mortgage loan.xls`: Contains the mortgage–loan one-way data table example.

`production model.xls`: Contains an example used with the scenario manager.

✦ **Chapter 23**

`allocating resources.xls`: Contains a Solver demonstration.

`investments.xls`: Contains a Solver demonstration.

`mortgage loan.xls`: Contains a Solver demonstration.

`products.xls`: Contains a Solver demonstration.

`shipping costs.xls`: Contains a Solver demonstration.

✦ **Chapter 24**

`atp examples.xls`: Sample output from the Analysis Toolpak procedures.

✦ **Chapter 25**

`number formats.xls`: Contains examples of custom number formats.

✦ **Chapter 26**

`custom toolbar.xls`: Contains a custom toolbar with formatting tools.

✦ **Chapter 27**

`conditional formatting.xls`: Contains conditional formatting examples.

`data validation.xls`: Contains data validation examples.

✦ **Chapter 28**

`outline.xls`: Contains data suitable for an outline.

✦ **Chapter 29**

`region1.xls`: One of three workbooks used in the data consolidation example.

`region2.xls`: One of three workbooks used in the data consolidation example.

`region3.xls`: One of three workbooks used in the data consolidation example.

✦ **Chapter 30**

`holidays.htm`: An Excel workbook saved as an interactive HTML file.

`holidays.xls`: The original workbook that generated the `holidays.htm` file.

✦ **Chapter 31**

`amortization`: A directory that contains the file for the loan amortization XML example.

`employee list.xml`: A multielement XML file that can be imported into an Excel workbook.

`message.xml`: An example of a simple XML file.

✦ **Chapter 34**

`cube root.xls`: Contains a VBA function to calculate a cube root.

`current date.xls`: Contains a macro to insert a formatted date.

`recorded macro.xls`: Contains two examples of recorded macros.

`selective formatting.xls`: Contains a macro to format negative values in a range.

✦ **Chapter 35**

`vba functions.xls`: Contains the function examples.

✦ **Chapter 36**

    `change case.xls`: Contains the "change case" UserForm example.

    `show message.xls`: Contains the "show message" UserForm example.

✦ **Chapter 37**

    `mortgage loan.xls`: Contains an example of ActiveX controls on a worksheet.

    `worksheet controls.xls`: Contains examples of all ActiveX controls used on a worksheet.

✦ **Chapter 38**

    `shade row and column.xls`: Demonstrates the `SelectionChange` event.

✦ **Chapter 39**

    `chart macros.xls`: Contains the chart-related VBA macros.

    `loop.xls`: Demonstrates looping in VBA.

    `prompt.xls`: Demonstrates prompting for a cell value using VBA.

    `range copy.xls`: Demonstrates copying a range using VBA.

    `range move.xls`: Demonstrates moving a range using VBA.

    `select cells.xls`: Demonstrates various ways to select cells using VBA.

    `selection type.xls`: Contains a VBA procedure that determines the type of selection.

✦ **Chapter 40**

    `toggles.xla`: The add-in version of the toggles example.

    `toggles.xls`: The workbook version of the toggles example.

✦ **Appendix C**

    `analog clock chart.xls`: A functional clock in an Excel spreadsheet.

    `animated charts.xls`: Several examples of animated Excel charts.

    `animated shapes.xls`: Several examples of animated shapes in an Excel spreadsheet.

    `ascii art.xls`: Excel versions of several works of ASCII art.

    `bubble chart mouse.xls`: A bubble chart that looks like a cartoon mouse.

    `contour chart patterns.xls`: Change the parameters and colors in this Excel spreadsheet to view some awesome symmetrical patterns.

    `dice roller.xls`: This workbook simulates the roll of two dice.

    `doughnut chart wheel`: Round and round she goes, where she stops . . .

`guitar.xls`: This spreadsheet for guitar players displays the notes (and fret positions) of the selected scale or mode in any key.

`hypocycloid chart.xls` and hypocycloid - animated.xls: These spreadsheets will take you back to your childhood (assuming you played with the Hasbro Spirograph game as a child, that is).

`keno.xls`: An Excel version of the casino favorite.

`mountain ranges.xls`: Did you ever notice that area charts often look like mountain ranges?

`moving tile puzzle.xls`: Put all of the tiles in numerical order.

`radar chart designs.xls`: Play with the scroll bars to create some funky designs.

`symmetrical patterns.xls`: Draw a design with your keyboard arrow keys, and your design will be mirrored on the other three quadrants of the screen.

`tick tack toe.xls`: An Excel version of the classic children's game.

`trig function chart`: Change the values and watch the chart change accordingly.

`word search`: Enter whatever words you like, and Excel creates a word search.

`XY sketch`: This XY chart in disguise allows you to create simple sketches.

Bonus software

The CD contains software distributed in various forms: shareware, freeware, GNU software, trials, demos, and evaluation versions. The following list explains how these software versions differ:

✦ **Shareware programs:** Fully functional, trial versions of copyrighted programs. If you like particular programs, you can register with its authors for a nominal fee and receive licenses, enhanced versions, and technical support.

✦ **Freeware programs:** Copyrighted games, applications, and utilities that are free for personal use. Unlike shareware, these programs do not require a fee or provide technical support.

✦ **GNU software:** Software governed by its own license, which is included inside the folder of the GNU product. See the GNU license for more details.

✦ **Trial, demo, or evaluation versions:** Software usually limited either by time or functionality, such as not permitting you to save projects. Some trial versions are very sensitive to system date changes. If you alter your computer's date, the programs may *time out* and no longer be functional.

Software highlights

Here are descriptions of just a few of the programs available on the CD:

✦ **Power Utility Pak v5:** From J-Walk & Associates, PUP v5 is a unique collection of add-ins that brings significant new functionality to Excel. Requires Excel 2000 or later. This is a 30-day trial version. For more information, go to

    http://j-walk.com/ss

✦ **Convert Cell Reference Utility:** This handy-dandy utility helps you convert the cell reference of a formulas to any form of absolute reference.

✦ **Excel Tetris v1.1:** This spreadsheet contains a fully functional game. It doesn't compare to the real arcade version of Tetris, but it is a good way to have fun at the office while looking busy.

✦ **Gantt Chart Builder (Excel):** This product helps you create professional quality Gantt charts in Excel and then export them in either image or spreadsheet format.

Comprehensive list of software

Here is a list of all the products available on the CD. For more information and a description of each product, see the ReadMe or Bonus Software sections of the CD.

3D Charts for Excel	Acc Compact	Access Form Resizer
Access Image Albums Converter	Access Property Editor	Access to VB Object
AccessBooks	AccessViewer	Acrobat Reader
ActiveDocs 2002	Advanced Disk Catalog	Advanced Office Password Recovery
Analyse-It	Attach for Outlook	Attachment Options
BadBlue Prsnl Ed	Barcode ActiveX Control & DLL	c:JAM
Camtasia Studio	Capture Express	Charset Decoding
Classify for Outlook	Code 128 Fonts demo with VBA	Code Critter
Collage Complete	COM Explorer	CompareDataWiz 2002
CompareWiz 2002	Convert Cell Reference Utility	CSE HTML Validator
Database	Database Password Sniffer	Datahouse
DataWiz 2002	Document Management	Eliminate Spam!
Excel Import Assistant	Excel Link	Excel Tetris

Filter Builder	Fort Knox	Fundraising Mentor
Gantt Chart Builder (Excel)	Gif Movie Gear	GraphicsButton
GuruNet	HiddenFileDetector_addin	HtmlIndex
IntelligentApps 4excel Prem Ed	JustAddCommerce	Keyboard Express
Lark	LiveMath Maker and LiveMath Plug-in	Macro Express
Maillist Deluxe	MailWasher Pro	Math Easy for Excel
Mathematical Summary Utility	MathEQ Expression Editor	Mouse Over Effects
MultiNetwork Manager	Office Report Builder	OfficeBalloonX
OfficeRecovery Enterprise	OfficeSpy	Outcome XP
OutlookSpy	Passkeeper	PlanMagic Business
PlanMagic Finance Pro	PlanMagic Marketing	PlanMagic WebQuest
PocketKnife	Polar Spellchecker Component	Power Utility Pak
Recover My Files	Registry Crawler	ReplaceWiz 2002
Responsive Time Logger	RFFlow	RnR PPTools Starter Set
Scan to Outlook	Screen Capture	Secrets Keeper
ShrinkerStretcher	SimpleRegistry Control	Smart Login
Smart Online templates	SnagIt	Soft Graphics Buttons
Spreadsheet Assistant	StoreBot 2002 Stnd Ed	Summary Wizard
The Spreadsheet Detective	UltraPdf	VBAcodePrint
WebCompiler	WinACE	WinRAR
WinZIP	Word Link	Xbooks
XLSTAT-Pro	XlToHtml	Zip Express
Zip Repair		

Related links

Check out this page for links to all the third-party software vendors included on the CD, plus links to other vendors and resources that can help you work more productively with Office 2003.

Other resources

This page provides you with some additional handy Office-related products.

ReadMe file

The ReadMe file contains the complete descriptions of every piece of bonus software on the CD as well as other important information about the CD.

Troubleshooting

If you have difficulty installing or using any of the materials on the companion CD, try the following solutions:

✦ **Turn off any anti-virus software that you may have running.** Installers sometimes mimic virus activity and can make your computer incorrectly believe that it is being infected by a virus. (Be sure to turn the anti-virus software back on later.)

✦ **Close all running programs.** The more programs you're running, the less memory is available to other programs. Installers also typically update files and programs; if you keep other programs running, installation may not work properly.

✦ **Reference the ReadMe:** Please refer to the ReadMe file located at the root of the CD-ROM for the latest product information at the time of publication.

If you still have trouble with the CD, please call the Customer Care phone number: 1-800-762-2974. Outside the United States, call 1-317-572-3994. You can also contact Customer Service by e-mail at techsupdum@wiley.com. Wiley Publishing, Inc., will provide technical support only for installation and other general quality-control items; for technical support on the applications themselves, consult the program's vendor or author.

✦   ✦   ✦

Just for Fun

Although Excel is used primarily for serious applications, many users discover that this product has a lighter side. This appendix is devoted to the less-serious applications of Excel. Here, you find a variety of games and interesting diversions.

On the CD-ROM

All of the examples shown in this appendix are available on the companion CD-ROM. Many of these examples use macros. I don't discuss the programming aspects in this chapter, but the files are all unprotected, so you can view and experiment with the VBA code. Depending on your security setting, you may receive a macro virus warning when the workbook is opened. Be assured that these files are virus-free. If your security setting is High, the macros will be disabled.

In This Appendix

A variety of Excel games

Creative and non-serious chart examples

Other entertaining uses for Excel

Games and Amusements

Excel certainly wasn't designed as a platform for games. Nevertheless, I've developed a few games using Excel and have downloaded several others from various Web sites. I've found that the key ingredient in developing these games is creativity. In almost every case, I had to invent one or more workarounds to compensate for Excel's lack of game-making features. In this section, I show you a few of my own creations.

Tick-Tack-Toe

Tick-Tack-Toe is hardly the most mentally stimulating game, but everyone knows how to play it. Figure C-1 shows an Excel Tick-Tack-Toe game. In this implementation, the user plays against the computer. I wrote some formulas and VBA macros to determine the computer's moves, and it plays a reasonably good game — about on par with a three-year-old child. I'm embarrassed to admit that the program has even beaten me a few times. (Okay, so I was distracted!)

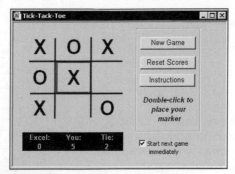

Figure C-1: Tick-Tack-Toe for Excel.

You can choose who makes the first move (you or the computer) and which marker you want to use (X or O). The winning games and ties are tallied in cells at the bottom of the window.

Note   I created the Tick-Tack-Toe game many years ago. As proof, you'll notice that it uses an "old school" dialog sheet rather than a UserForm. Excel still supports the old dialog sheets, so I never bothered to update it to use a UserForm.

Moving Tile Puzzle

At some time in your life, you've probably played one of those moving tile puzzles. They come in several variations, but the goal is always the same: rearrange the tiles so that they are in numerical order.

Figure C-2 shows a version of this game that I developed. It has a UserForm and makes heavy use of VBA. This version lets you choose the number of tiles (from a simple 3-x-3 matrix up to a challenging 6-x-6 matrix). The VBA code is relatively complex due to the option to choose a different number of tiles. The UserForm sizes itself to accommodate different tile configurations.

Figure C-2: A moving tile puzzle.

When you click the tile, it appears to move to the empty position. Actually, no movement is taking place. The program is simply changing the text on the buttons and making the button in the empty position invisible.

Keno

If you've ever spent any time in a casino, you may be familiar with Keno. The game is simple: You choose some numbers in a grid, and then 20 numbers are chosen at random. Your winnings are determined by how many numbers you chose and how many were selected at random (see Figure C-3).

If you're smart, you probably know to avoid this game like the plague because it has the lowest return of any casino game. With my Keno for Excel, however, you don't have to worry about losing any money: All the action takes place on a worksheet, no money changes hands, and it's a lot faster than the casino version.

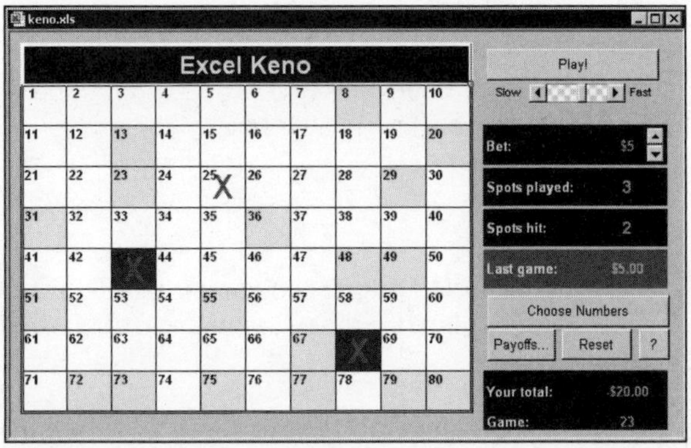

Figure C-3: Keno for Excel.

To select your numbers, click the Choose Numbers button. Then click in the cells to select (or deselect) a number. You can select from 1 to 10 *spots*.

Make your bet by using the spin button control. (The maximum bet is $100.) Then click the Play button, and the game begins. Use the scroll bar to control the speed of the game. (Slow it down to increase the drama.) Twenty numbers are chosen at random, and the corresponding square is colored yellow. The worksheet displays the number of spots hit, along with your winnings (if any) and cumulative winnings.

You can play another game using the same numbers or click the Choose Numbers button to select different numbers.

Click the Reset button to remove the yellow colors from the worksheet. Click the Payoffs button to see the payoffs and odds for the number of spots chosen.

Creating word-search puzzles

Many daily newspapers feature a word-search puzzle. These puzzles contain words that are hidden in a grid. The words can be vertical, diagonal, horizontal, forwards, or backwards. If you've ever had the urge to create your own word-search puzzle, this workbook can make your job a lot easier by doing it for you. You supply the words; the program places them in the grid and fills in the empty squares with random letters. You can then print the sheet if you like.

Figure C-4 shows the puzzle-creation sheet. (The word list is on the left.) Figure C-5 shows a puzzle that was created from those words.

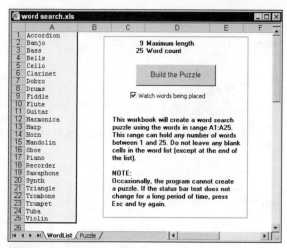

Figure C-4: Supply a list of words, and Excel creates a puzzle.

Creating the puzzle is done with VBA, and randomness plays a major role. Therefore, you can create multiple puzzles using the same words.

word search.xls

B	A	N	J	O	T	E	N	I	R	A	L	C	F
H	S	F	S	M	U	R	D	P	O	N	A	I	P
M	T	R	O	M	B	O	N	E	A	K	B	W	T
G	A	N	X	H	T	R	U	M	P	E	T	G	U
F	R	N	Y	B	R	A	T	I	U	G	Z	T	B
A	W	E	D	S	H	A	R	M	O	N	I	C	A
N	C	F	C	O	E	N	O	H	P	A	X	A	S
I	T	C	L	O	L	T	R	I	A	N	G	L	E
L	E	E	O	U	R	I	B	A	S	S	C	C	E
O	A	L	O	R	T	D	N	D	D	O	B	R	O
I	V	N	D	B	D	E	E	P	O	L	L	E	C
V	D	R	R	D	O	I	R	R	B	J	Q	E	U
O	Y	R	Z	O	I	F	A	T	J	A	T	F	T
S	L	L	E	B	H	F	P	N	B	P	R	A	H

Accordion
Banjo
Bass
Bells
Cello
Clarinet
Dobro
Drums
Fiddle
Flute
Guitar
Harmonica
Harp
Horn
Mandolin
Oboe
Piano
Recorder
Saxaphone
Synth
Triangle
Trombone
Trumpet
Tuba
Violin

WordList \ Puzzle

Figure C-5: A word-search puzzle, courtesy of Excel.

Dice Roller

The workbook shown in Figure C-6 simulates rolling two dice. The outcome of each roll is stored in a range, which is displayed in a chart. The chart shows the actual distribution of the dice rolls as well as the theoretical distribution of throwing two dice. This workbook may be useful for teaching elementary probability theory.

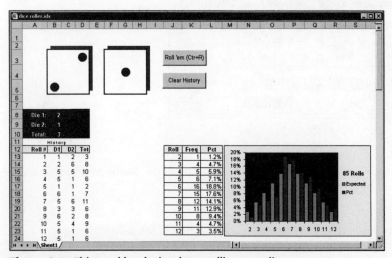

Figure C-6: This workbook simulates rolling two dice.

Following are a few points to keep in mind while you examine this workbook:

✦ A simple VBA macro, triggered by the Roll 'em button, is used to store the history of the dice rolls in column A:D. Another macro, which deletes the history, is attached to the Clear History button.

✦ The dice pictures use no graphic images. The graphics are generated by IF functions that determine whether a particular dot should be visible, based on the randomly generated dice value. The dot is actually a Wingdings font character.

✦ The chart series that displays the theoretical distribution uses an array, not a range. Because the series never changes, you don't need to store the values in a range.

✦ A text box in the chart displays the number of dice rolls. This text box is linked to a cell that determines the number of items in the History area of the worksheet.

Video Poker

Developing my Video Poker game for Excel (as shown in Figure C-7) was quite a challenge. I was forced to spend many hours performing research at a local casino to perfect this game so that it captures the excitement of a real poker machine. The only problem is that I haven't figured out a way to dispense the winnings. Oh well, maybe in the next version.

Figure C-7: Video Poker for Excel.

 This game is part of my Power Utility Pak (PUP v5). A 30-day trial version is available on the companion CD-ROM.

This version has two poker games. In Joker's Wild, a joker can be used for any card, and the minimum winning hand is a pair of aces. In Jacks or Better, a pair of jacks or better is required to win.

Click Deal to begin. You select which cards to discard by clicking the card face. The Deal button changes to the Get New Cards button. Click the Get New Cards button to replace the cards you discarded. You can change the game (or the bet) at any time while playing.

Click Payoffs to see the payoffs for various hands. If you'd like to change the amounts paid for each hand, open the file named `Video Poker Payoff.xls`. (This file is located in the directory where PUP v5 is installed.) Make the changes; then save and close the file. The change takes effect the next time you play the Video Poker game.

Click the Chart button to display a chart that shows your cumulative winnings (or, more typically, your cumulative losses).

Identifying the various poker hands is done using VBA procedures. The game also has a Hide button that temporarily hides the game. (Pressing Esc has the same effect.) You can then resume the game when your boss leaves.

Dice Game

The goal of the Dice Game (shown in Figure C-8) is to obtain a high score by assigning dice rolls to various categories. You get to roll the dice three times on each turn, and you can keep or discard the dice before rolling again. For a much higher-scoring game, select the Four Rolls check box.

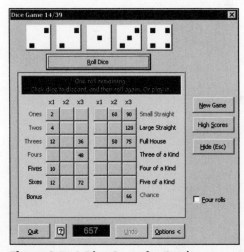

Figure C-8: A Dice Game for Excel.

After the third roll (or fourth roll if you use the Four Rolls option), click one of the unused buttons in the Scoring section. This section features 39 scoring buttons arranged in three columns (x1, x2, and x3). The scoring button you click corresponds to the dice that are showing. For example, if you have four of a kind, click a button in the Four of a Kind category. You may, however, prefer to assign it to a different category. As you gain experience playing the game, strategies will emerge.

In the later stages of the game, you may be forced to assign the dice to a button that results in a score of 0. After a scoring button is clicked, the value appears on the button, and you cannot assign any subsequent turns to that button.

Clicking a scoring button in the x1 column gives a normal score. Clicking a button in the x2 column gives double the normal score. Clicking a button in the x3 column gives triple the score. The Help file for Dice Game has complete rules and details on the scoring: Click the button with the question mark icon to access it.

Note   This game is part of my Power Utility Pak (PUP v5). A 30-day trial version is available on the companion CD-ROM.

Bomb Hunt

Windows comes with a game called Minesweeper. I developed a version of this game for Excel and named it Bomb Hunt (as shown in Figure C-9). The goal is to discover the hidden bombs in the grid. Double-clicking a cell reveals a bomb (you lose) or a number that indicates the number of bombs in the surrounding cells. You use logic to determine where the bombs are located.

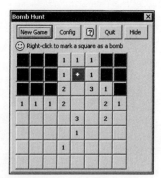

Figure C-9: Bomb Hunt for Excel.

Clicking a button exposes either a bomb or a number or a blank. If it's a bomb, the game is over. If clicking a button reveals a number, the number tells you how many bombs are in the surrounding cells. If clicking reveals a blank, that means that there are no bombs in the eight surrounding cells. In this case, the program automatically reveals the surrounding cells.

If you think that a location contains a bomb, right-click it to mark it. If you change your mind after marking a location as a bomb, right-click it again. The button then displays a question mark to remind you that you thought a bomb might be there. Right-clicking again returns the button to its normal state.

You win the game if you correctly identify each bomb by marking it and do not incorrectly mark any position as a bomb.

This game is highly customizable. Click the Config button, and you can select the number of rows, columns, and bombs.

Note   This game is part of my Power Utility Pak (PUP v5). A 30-day trial version is available on the companion CD-ROM.

Hangman

Hangman is another game that almost everyone has played. Figure C-10 shows a version that I developed for Excel. The objective is to identify a word by guessing letters. Correctly guessed letters appear in their proper position. Every incorrectly guessed letter adds a new body part to the person being hanged. (To reduce gratuitous violence, I substituted a skeleton for the hanged gentleman.) Ten incorrect guesses, and the skeleton is completed — that is, the game is over.

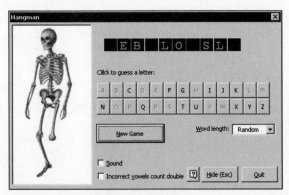

Figure C-10: Hangman for Excel.

The workbook includes 1,400 words, ranging in length from 6 to 12 letters. You can either choose how many letters you want in the word or have the number of letters determined randomly.

To make the game more challenging, choose the Incorrect Vowels Count Double option. Each incorrectly guessed vowel (that is, A, E, I, O, or U) adds two body parts. When the Sound option is in effect, end-of-game messages will be spoken (and also displayed in a message box).

By the way, the game has a cheat code that will reveal the current word. Hint: It uses the Ctrl and Shift keys.

Note   This game is part of my Power Utility Pak (PUP v5). A 30-day trial version is available on the companion CD-ROM.

Random Number Generator

This isn't really a game. It is simply a UserForm that generates a random number (as shown in Figure C-11).

Figure C-11: A random-number generator.

You specify the lower and upper limits. Click the Start button, and numbers start flashing. Click it again, and you see the randomly selected number. The Random Number Generator is perfect for office raffles and drawings (it's much easier than picking a number out of a hat), and it will keep a five-year-old child entertained for at least ten minutes.

Note   This application is part of my Power Utility Pak (PUP v5). A 30-day trial version is available on the companion CD-ROM.

Animated Shapes

If you've used the Excel AutoShapes, you may enjoy seeing them in action. Create an AutoShape, add a touch of 3-D formatting, and toss in a VBA macro. You've got a recipe for an animated AutoShape. The possibilities are, as they say, limited only by your imagination. The types of animations you can perform in the example on the CD include the following:

✦ Moving an AutoShape from one location to another

✦ Rotating an AutoShape

✦ Changing the colors of an AutoShape

✦ Changing the shape of an AutoShape

The practical applications are limited or maybe even nonexistent. But most people are amazed to discover that you can do this sort of thing in Excel, and it's a good way to take a break from number crunching.

Figure C-12 shows one of several examples that are available on the companion CD-ROM. Because we lack the technology to make moving images on a printed page, you'll need to open the actual file to experience the animation.

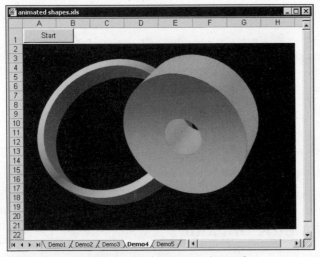

Figure C-12: These shapes become animated.

Symmetrical Pattern Drawing

I must admit, this program is rather addictive — especially for doodlers. It lets you create colorful symmetrical patterns by using the arrow keys on the keyboard. Figure C-13 shows an example. As you draw, the drawing is reproduced as mirror images in the other three quadrants. When you move the cursor to the edge of the drawing area, it wraps around and appears on the other side. This workbook is great for passing the time on the telephone when you've been put on hold.

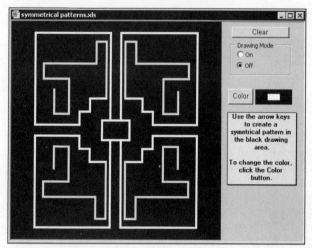

Figure C-13: Use the arrow keys to draw symmetrical patterns.

The drawing is all done with VBA macros. I used the `OnKey` method to trap the following key presses: left, right, up, and down. Each of these keystrokes executes a macro that shades a cell. The cells in the drawing area are very tiny, so the shading appears as lines.

Fun with Charts

Excel's charting feature has the potential to be a serious diversion. In this section, I provide examples of some interesting charting applications.

Plotting trigonometric functions

Although I don't know too much about trigonometry, I've always enjoyed plotting various trigonometric functions as XY charts. Sometimes, you can come up with attractive images.

Figure C-14 shows an example of a trigonometric plot. It uses formulas to generate the X and Y values, and these formulas make use of the values in column A. Cell A1 contains the increment value. Change the value in A1, and the chart changes dramatically.

Here's the formula in cell B3. (This formula was copied down for the X values.)

```
=SIN(A3)*COS(A3)*COS(TAN(A3))
```

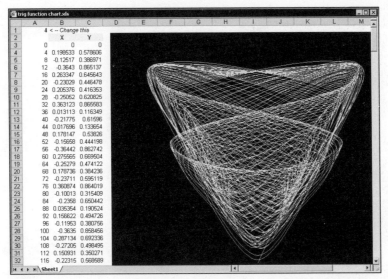

Figure C-14: An XY chart generated from trigonometric functions.

And here's the formula in cell C3 (for the Y values). This formula was also copied down the column.

```
=SIN(B3)*COS(B3)*SIN(A3+B3)*COS(A3-B3)+SQRT(ABS(B3))
```

Feel free to modify these formulas to create millions of other charts.

Hypocycloid charts

Figure C-15 shows an example of an XY chart that displays hypocycloid curves. A *hypocycloid curve* is defined as follows: The curve produced by fixed point P on the circumference of a small circle of radius b rolling around the inside of a large circle of radius a > b.

In other words, this type of curve is the same as that generated by Hasbro's popular Spirograph toy, which you may remember from your childhood.

The formulas that generate the data used in the series are rather complex, but they use three parameters, stored in B1:B3. Change any of these parameters and you get a completely different design. I guarantee that you will be amazed by the variety of charts that you can generate—some of them are simply stunning. Figure C-16 shows a few more examples.

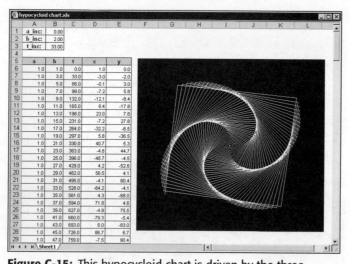

Figure C-15: This hypocycloid chart is driven by the three parameters in column B.

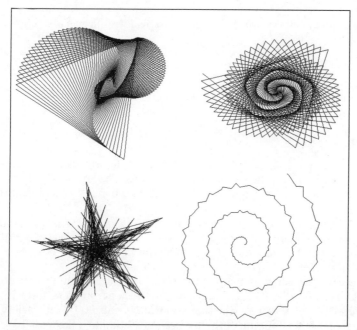

Figure C-16: More examples of hypocycloid charts.

Note The companion CD-ROM contains two versions of this file. The first, shown in the figure, enables you to change the parameters manually. A more sophisticated version uses macros to randomly generate parameter values, and it even has an animation option.

Animated charts

Excel doesn't support animated charts, but a relatively simple VBA procedure can convert a chart into an action-packed piece of entertainment. The macros in these examples increment the value in a cell. This cell is then used in formulas that are displayed in the chart.

Figure C-17 shows an example of an animated chart. This is a 3-D line chart. When animated, the effect is reminiscent of bird wings in flight.

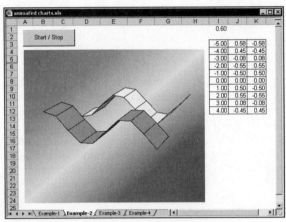

Figure C-17: These two 3-D line chart series get animated with the help of a macro.

The companion CD-ROM includes a few other animated charts, including a mind-boggling rotating surface chart.

Contour chart pattern generator

A contour chart is one of the chart subtypes of a surface chart. This chart type is basically a standard surface chart viewed from above. The contour chart in Figure C-18 uses only a 7-x-7 range of cells, but it can display some awesome (and very colorful) symmetrical patterns.

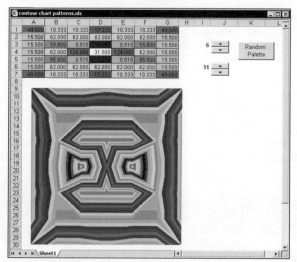

Figure C-18: Patterns displayed in this contour chart are controlled by the two spinner controls.

The number of colors used in a surface chart depends on the Major Unit setting on the Value axis. This example includes a spinner control (linked to cell I3) that enables you to easily change the Major Unit value for the chart. (This change is done with a simple macro.) Smaller Major Unit values produce more colors. Another spinner, linked to cell I6, feeds the formulas in the chart's source range (A1:G7). These formulas are color-coded to identify the cells that contain the same formula. Some of these formulas refer to a randomly generated value, which results in a wide variety of patterns.

Click the Random Palette button, and the workbook's colors change randomly. Not all random color choices look good, but a surprisingly high percentage of them do.

Radar chart designs

The chart in Figure C-19 is a radar chart that uses three series. The chart has 360 axes, which represent the degrees in a circle. The axes are hidden. If they were visible, they would completely overwhelm the chart.

Data for the three series is generated by formulas in columns B:D. These formulas use trigonometric functions and depend on the values in column A and the three adjustment parameters in B1:B3. These cells are linked to scroll-bar controls. Manipulating the scroll bars results in many variations on the design.

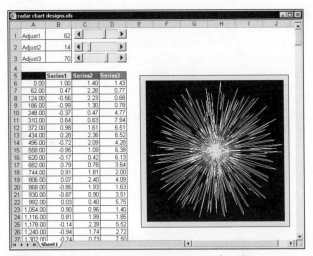

Figure C-19: Creating designs with a radar chart.

Analog clock chart

Figure C-20 shows an XY chart formatted to look like a clock. It not only *looks* like a clock but also functions like one. No one really needs to display a clock like this on a worksheet, but creating the workbook was challenging, and you may find it instructive.

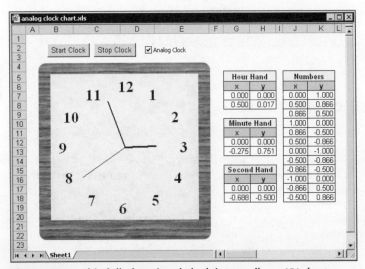

Figure C-20: This fully functional clock is actually an XY chart in disguise.

The chart uses three data series for the clock hands: one for the hour hand, one for the minute hand, and one for the second hand. These series contain formulas that use the Excel NOW function (which returns the current time). The formulas use trigonometric functions to determine the angle of the hands for the time of day. A simple macro is executed once each second. This macro simply calculates the sheet, which updates the formulas and the clock.

The chart uses another series to display the numbers. This data series draws a circle with 12 data points. The numbers consist of manually entered data labels.

Uncheck the Analog Clock check box to reveal a hidden digital clock (as shown in Figure C-21). This clock consists of 28 merged cells that contain a simple formula:

```
=NOW()
```

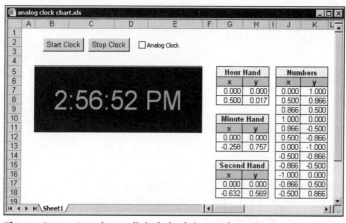

Figure C-21: Creating a digital clock is much easier.

A doughnut chart wheel of fortune

Round and round and round it goes. Where it stops, nobody knows.

Figure C-22 shows a doughnut chart with 12 data points, set up like a carnival wheel of fortune. The numbers are data labels, and the slices were formatted individually to get the alternating-color effect.

Click the button to kick off a macro that systematically changes the angle of the first slice, which results in a rotating chart. The difficult part was programming the macro so that the spinning gradually slows down before the wheel comes to a final stop.

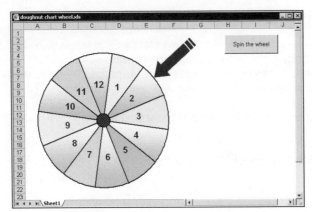

Figure C-22: Spin the wheel — uh, doughnut chart.

A mountain range chart

One day I was working with an area chart, and it occurred to me that the chart resembled a mountain range. I quickly abandoned my original task and set out to create the ultimate mountain range chart.

The result is shown in Figure C-23. (It looks better in color.) Okay, I cheated. The moon and stars are actually AutoShapes.

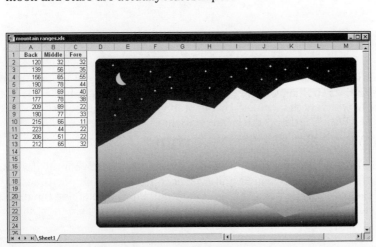

Figure C-23: A chart, or a mountain range?

A bubble chart mouse head

Work with bubble charts long enough, and you may start seeing faces take shape. Figure C-24 shows a cartoonlike mouse face made up of a data series with nine data points. The data in column C controls the size of the bubbles. Each bubble was formatted separately, of course, to control the color and gradient effects.

The folks at Pixar Animation Studios have nothing to worry about.

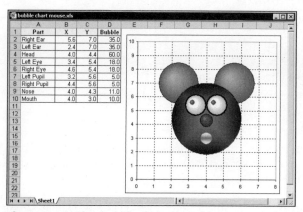

Figure C-24: This bubble chart resembles a mouse head.

XY-Sketch

The example in this section has absolutely no practical value — except, perhaps, to kill some time. The worksheet contains an XY chart along with a number of controls from the Excel Forms toolbar. Clicking one of the arrow buttons draws a line in the chart, the size of which is determined by the step value, which is set with one of the spinner controls. With a little practice (and patience), you can create simple sketches. Figure C-25 shows an example.

You'll appreciate the multilevel Undo button. Clicking this button simply erases the last set of values in the chart range. Additional accoutrements include the capability to change the color of the lines, display smoothed lines, and toggle the display of chart gridlines.

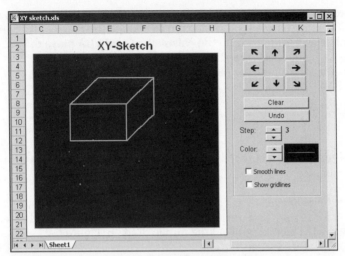

Figure C-25: This drawing is actually an XY chart.

For Guitar Players

If you play guitar, check out this workbook. As shown in Figure C-26, this workbook has a graphic depiction of a guitar's fret board. It displays the notes (and fret positions) of the selected scale or mode in any key. You can even change the tuning of the guitar, and the formulas automatically recalculate.

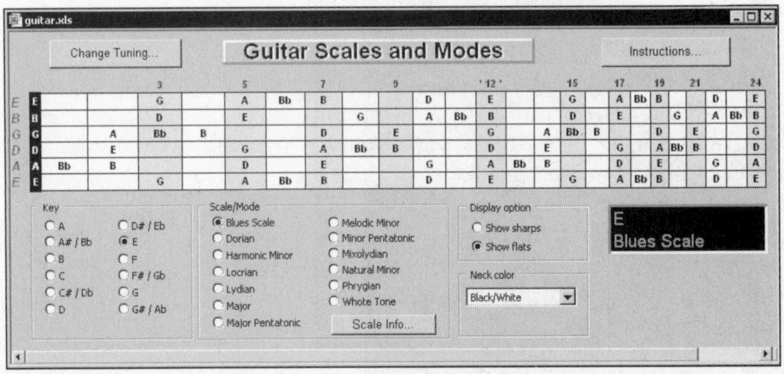

Figure C-26: This workbook displays various scales for a guitar fret board.

Other options include the choice to display half notes as sharps or flats, to pop up information about the selected scale or mode, and to change the color of the guitar neck. This workbook uses formulas to do the calculation, and VBA plays only a minor role. This file was once designated a *top pick* on America Online, and I've received positive feedback from fellow pickers all over the world.

ASCII Art

ASCII art consists of images made up of simple ASCII characters. You can find thousands of ASCII art examples on the Web.

It's possible to store these images in an Excel workbook. The trick is to ensure that you use a fixed-width font (such as Courier New). I created a workbook with a few examples of ASCII art that I picked up from the public domain. Figure C-27 shows an example.

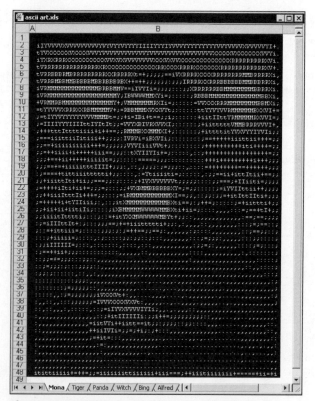

Figure C-27: ASCII art, stored in a workbook.

✦　　✦　　✦

APPENDIX

♦ ♦ ♦ ♦

In This Appendix

The Excel Help
system

Microsoft technical
support

Internet newsgroups

Internet Web sites

♦ ♦ ♦ ♦

Additional Excel Resources

If I've done my job, the information provided in this book will be very useful to you. The book, however, cannot cover every conceivable topic. Therefore, I've compiled a list of additional resources that you may find helpful. I classify these resources into four categories: Excel's Help System, Microsoft technical support, Internet newsgroups, and Internet Web sites.

The Excel Help System

Many users tend to forget about an excellent source of information: the Excel help system. This help information is available:

✦ By choosing Help ➪ Microsoft Excel Help.

✦ By pressing F1.

✦ By typing a question in the Type a Question Box. This box is located on the right side of the menu bar.

Any of these methods displays the task pane.

**New
Feature**

Excel 2003 can access updated help information from Microsoft's Web site. To control what is searched when you are seeking help, use the controls at the bottom of the task pane. For example, you may want to avoid searching on the Web. To do so, choose the Offline Help option.

The help system certainly isn't perfect — you'll find that it often provides only superficial help and ignores some topics altogether. But if you're stuck, it's worth a try.

Microsoft Technical Support

Technical support is the common term for assistance provided by a software vendor. In this case, I'm talking about assistance that comes directly from Microsoft.
Microsoft's technical support is available in several different forms.

Support options

To find out your support options, choose Help ➪ About Microsoft Excel to display
the About Microsoft Excel dialog box. Then click the Tech Support button. This
opens a help file that lists all the support options offered by Microsoft, including
both free and fee-based support.

Through my experience, I suggest you use vendor *standard telephone* support only
as a last resort. Chances are, you'll run up a big phone bill (assuming you can even
get through) and spend lots of time on hold, but you may or may not find an answer
to your question.

The truth is, the people who answer the phone are equipped to answer only the
most basic questions. And the answers to these basic questions are usually readily
available elsewhere.

Microsoft Knowledge Base

Your best bet for solving a problem may be the Microsoft Knowledge Base. This is
the primary Microsoft product information source — an extensive, searchable
database that consists of tens of thousands of detailed articles containing technical
information, bug lists, fix lists, and more.

You have free and unlimited access to the Knowledge Base via the Internet. To
access the Knowledge Base, use the URL below, and then click Search the
Knowledge Base.

```
http://support.microsoft.com
```

Microsoft Excel Home Page

The official home page of Excel is at

```
www.microsoft.com/office/excel
```

Microsoft Office Tools on the Web

For information about Office 2003 (including Excel), try this site:

```
http://office.microsoft.com
```

You'll find product updates, add-ins, examples, and lots of other useful information.

Note   As you know, the Internet is a dynamic entity that changes rapidly. Web sites are often reorganized, so a particular URL listed in this appendix may not be available when you try to access it.

Internet Newsgroups

Usenet is an Internet service that provides access to several thousand special interest groups that enable you to communicate with people who share common interests. A newsgroup works like a public bulletin board. You can post a message or questions, and (usually) others reply to your message.

Thousands of newsgroups cover virtually every topic you can think of (and many that you haven't thought of). Typically, questions posed on a newsgroup are answered within 24 hours — assuming, of course, that you ask the questions in a manner that makes others want to reply.

Note   Besides an Internet connection, you need special newsreader software to access newsgroups. Microsoft Outlook Express (free) is a good choice. This product is part of Internet Explorer.

Spreadsheet newsgroups

The primary Usenet newsgroup for general spreadsheet users is

```
comp.apps.spreadsheets
```

This newsgroup is intended for users of any spreadsheet brand, but about 90 percent of the postings deal with Excel.

Microsoft newsgroups

Microsoft maintains an extensive list of newsgroups, including quite a few devoted to Excel. If your Internet service provider doesn't carry the Microsoft newsgroups, you can access them directly from Microsoft's news server. (In fact, that's the preferred method.) You need to configure your newsreader software to access Microsoft's news server at this address:

```
msnews.microsoft.com
```

Or you can read and post to the Microsoft newsgroups directly from your Web browser. This option is significantly slower than using standard newsgroup software and is best suited for situations in which newsgroup access is prohibited by network policies. Access the Microsoft newsgroups from this URL:

```
http://communities.microsoft.com/newsgroups
```

Table D-1 lists the key English-language Excel newsgroups found on Microsoft's news server.

Table D-1
The Microsoft.com Excel-Related Newsgroups

Newsgroup	Topic
microsoft.public.excel.123quattro	Converting 1-2-3 or Quattro Pro sheets into Excel sheets
microsoft.public.excel.charting	Building charts with Excel
microsoft.public.excel.crashesGPFs	Help with General Protection Faults or system failures
microsoft.public.excel.interopoledde	OLE, DDE, and other cross-application issues
microsoft.public.excel.links	Using links in Excel
microsoft.public.excel.macintosh	Excel issues on the Macintosh operating system
microsoft.public.excel.misc	General topics that do not fit one of the other categories
microsoft.public.excel.newusers	Help for newcomers to Excel
microsoft.public.excel.printing	Printing with Excel
microsoft.public.excel.programming	Programming Excel with VBA or XLM macros
microsoft.public.excel.queryDAO	Using Microsoft Query and Data Access Objects (DAO) in Excel
microsoft.public.excel.sdk	Issues regarding the Excel Software Development Kit
microsoft.public.excel.setup	Setting up and installing Excel
microsoft.public.excel.templates	Spreadsheet Solutions templates and other XLT files
microsoft.public.excel.worksheet.functions	Worksheet functions

Searching newsgroups

Many people don't realize that you can perform a keyword search on past news-group postings. Often, this is an excellent alternative to posting a question to the newsgroup because you can get the answer immediately. The best source for searching newsgroup postings is Google.com at the following Web address:

```
http://groups.google.com
```

Note   Formerly, newsgroup searches were performed at the Deja.com Web site. That site has closed down, and Google purchased the newsgroup archives.

How does searching work? Suppose you have a problem identifying unique values in a range of cells. You can perform a search using the following keywords: **Excel**, **Range**, and **Unique**. The Google search engine probably will find dozens of news-group postings that deal with these topics.

Tips for Posting to a Newsgroup

1. Make sure that your question has not already been answered. Check the news-group's FAQ (if one exists) and also perform a Google.com search (see "Searching newsgroups" in this appendix).

2. Make the subject line descriptive. Postings with a subject line such as "Help me!" and "Another Question" are less likely to be answered than postings with a more specific subject, such as "Sizing a Chart's Plot Area."

3. Specify the spreadsheet product and version that you use. In many cases, the answer to your question depends on your version of Excel.

4. For best results, ask only one question per message.

5. Make your question as specific as possible.

6. Keep your question brief and to the point but provide enough information so that someone can answer it adequately.

7. Indicate what you've done to try to answer your own question.

8. Post in the appropriate newsgroup, and don't cross-post to other groups unless the question applies to multiple groups.

9. Don't type in all uppercase or all lowercase; check your grammar and spelling.

10. Don't include a file attachment unless it's absolutely necessary. And if it is necessary, make the file as small as possible by removing all extraneous information.

11. Avoid posting in HTML format. Plain text is the preferred format.

12. If you request an e-mail reply in addition to a newsgroup reply, don't use an "anti-spam" e-mail address that requires the responder to modify your address. Why cause extra work for someone doing you a favor?

If the number of results is too large, refine your search by adding search terms. It may take a while to sift through the messages, but you have an excellent chance of finding an answer to your question. In fact, I estimate that approximately 90 percent of the questions posted in the Excel newsgroups can be answered by searching Google.

Internet Web Sites

If you have access to the World Wide Web (WWW), you can find some very useful Web sites devoted to Excel. I list a few of my favorites here.

The Spreadsheet Page

This is my own Web site, which contains files to download, developer tips, instructions for accessing Excel Easter eggs, spreadsheet jokes, an extensive list of links to other Excel sites, and information about my books. The URL is

```
www.j-walk.com/ss
```

Pearson Software Consulting

This site, maintained by Chip Pearson, contains dozens of useful examples of VBA and clever formula techniques. The URL is

```
www.cpearson.com/excel.htm
```

Stephen Bullen's Excel Page

Stephen's Web site contains some fascinating examples of Excel code, including a section titled "They Said It Couldn't Be Done." The URL is

```
www.bmsltd.co.uk/excel
```

David McRitchie's Excel Pages

David's site is jam-packed with useful Excel information and is updated frequently. The URL is

```
www.mvps.org/dmcritchie/excel/excel.htm
```

Jon Peltier's Excel Page

Those who frequent the microsoft.public.excel.charting newsgroup are familiar with Jon Peltier. Jon has an uncanny ability to solve practically any chart-related problem. His Web site contains many Excel tips and an extensive collection of charting examples. The URL is

```
www.geocities.com/jonpeltier/Excel/
```

Spreadsheet FAQ

Many newsgroups have a FAQ—a list of frequently asked questions. The purpose of providing a list of FAQs is to prevent the same questions from being asked over and over. The FAQ for the comp.apps.spreadsheets newsgroup is available at

```
www.faqs.org/faqs/spreadsheets/faq
```

✦   ✦   ✦

Excel Shortcut Keys

T his appendix lists the most useful shortcut keys that are available in Excel. The shortcuts are arranged by context.

The keys listed assume that you are not using the Transition Navigation Keys, which are designed to emulate Lotus 1-2-3. You can select the Transition Navigation Keys option in the Transition tab of the Options dialog box.

Table E-1
Moving Through a Worksheet

Key(s)	What It Does
Arrow keys	Moves left, right, up, or down one cell
Home	Moves to the beginning of the row
Home*	Moves to the upper-left cell displayed in the window
End*	Moves to the lower-left cell displayed in the window
Arrow keys*	Scrolls left, right, up, or down one cell
PgUp	Moves up one screen
PgDn	Moves down one screen
Ctrl+PgUp	Moves to the previous sheet
Ctrl+PgDn	Moves to the next sheet
Alt+PgUp	Moves one screen to the left
Alt+PgDn	Moves one screen to the right
Ctrl+Home	Moves to the first cell in the worksheet (A1)
Ctrl+End	Moves to the last active cell of the worksheet
Ctrl+arrow key	Moves to the edge of a data block; if the cell is blank, moves to the first nonblank cell
Ctrl+Backspace	Scrolls to display the active cell
End, Home	Moves to the last nonempty cell on the worksheet
F5	Prompts for a cell address to go to
F6	Moves to the next pane of a window that has been split
Shift+F6	Moves to the previous pane of a window that has been split
Ctrl+Tab	Moves to the next window
Ctrl+Shift+Tab	Moves to the previous window

* With Scroll Lock on

Table E-2
Selecting Cells in the Worksheet

Key(s)	What It Does
Shift+arrow key	Expands the selection in the direction indicated
Shift+spacebar	Selects the entire row(s) in the selected range
Ctrl+spacebar	Selects the entire column(s) in the selected range
Ctrl+Shift+ spacebar	Selects the entire worksheet
Shift+Home	Expands the selection to the beginning of the current row
Ctrl+*	Selects the block of data surrounding the active cell
F8	Extends the selection as you use navigation keys. Press F8 again to return to normal selection mode.
Shift+F8	Adds other nonadjacent cells or ranges to the selection; pressing Shift+F8 again ends Add mode
F5	Prompts for a range or range name to select
Ctrl+G	Prompts for a range or range name to select
Ctrl+A	Selects the entire worksheet
Shift+Backspace	Selects the active cell in a range selection

Table E-3
Moving Within a Range Selection

Key(s)	What It Does
Enter	Moves the cell pointer. The direction depends on the setting in the Edit tab of the Options dialog box.
Shift+Enter	Moves the cell pointer up to the preceding cell in the selection
Tab	Moves the cell pointer right to the next cell in the selection
Shift+Tab	Moves the cell pointer left to the preceding cell in the selection
Ctrl+period (.)	Moves the cell pointer to the next corner of the current cell range
Shift+Backspace	Collapses the cell selection to just the active cell

Table E-4
Editing Keys in the Formula Bar

Key(s)	What It Does
F2	Begins editing the active cell
F3	Pastes a name into a formula
Arrow keys	Moves the cursor one character in the direction of the arrow
Home	Moves the cursor to the beginning of the line
Esc	Cancels the editing
End	Moves the cursor to the end of the line
Ctrl+right arrow	Moves the cursor one word to the right
Ctrl+left arrow	Moves the cursor one word to the left
Del	Deletes the character to the right of the cursor
Ctrl+Del	Deletes all characters from the cursor to the end of the line
Backspace	Deletes the character to the left of the cursor

Table E-5
Formatting Keys

Key(s)	What It Does
Ctrl+1	Format ➪ [Selected Object]
Ctrl+B	Sets or removes boldface
Ctrl+I	Sets or removes italic
Ctrl+U	Sets or removes underlining
Ctrl+5	Sets or removes strikethrough
Ctrl+Shift+~	Applies the general number format
Ctrl+Shift+!	Applies the comma format with two decimal places
Ctrl+Shift+#	Applies the date format (day, month, year)
Ctrl+Shift+@	Applies the time format (hour, minute, a.m./p.m.)
Ctrl+Shift+$	Applies the currency format with two decimal places
Ctrl+Shift+%	Applies the percent format with no decimal places
Ctrl+Shift+&	Applies border to outline
Ctrl+Shift+_	Removes all borders
Alt+'	Equivalent to Format ➪ Style

Table E-6
Other Shortcut Keys

Key(s)	What It Does
Alt+=	Inserts the AutoSum formula
Alt+Backspace	Equivalent to Edit ➪ Undo
Alt+Enter	Starts a new line in the current cell
Ctrl+;	Enters the current date
Ctrl+:	Enters the current time
Ctrl+0 (zero)	Hides columns
Ctrl+1	Displays the Format dialog box for the selected object
Ctrl+6	Cycles among various ways of displaying objects
Ctrl+7	Toggles the display of the standard toolbar
Ctrl+8	Toggles the display of outline symbols
Ctrl+9	Hides rows
Ctrl+A	After typing a function name in a formula, displays the Formula Palette
Ctrl+C	Equivalent to Edit ➪ Copy
Ctrl+D	Equivalent to Edit ➪ Fill Down
Ctrl+F	Equivalent to Edit ➪ Find
Ctrl+H	Equivalent to Edit ➪ Replace
Ctrl+Insert	Equivalent to Edit ➪ Copy
Ctrl+K	Equivalent to Insert ➪ Hyperlink
Ctrl+N	Equivalent to File ➪ New
Ctrl+O	Equivalent to File ➪ Open
Ctrl+P	Equivalent to File ➪ Print
Ctrl+R	Equivalent to Edit ➪ Fill Right
Ctrl+S	Equivalent to File ➪ Save
Ctrl+Shift+(	Unhides rows
Ctrl+Shift+)	Unhides columns
Ctrl+Shift+:	Enters the current time
Ctrl+Shift+A	After typing a valid function name in a formula, inserts the argument names and parentheses for the function

Continued

Table E-6 *(continued)*

Key(s)	What It Does
Ctrl+V	Equivalent to Edit ➪ Paste
Ctrl+X	Equivalent to Edit ➪ Cut
Ctrl+Z	Equivalent to Edit ➪ Undo
Delete	Equivalent to Edit ➪ Clear ➪ Contents
Shift+Insert	Equivalent to Edit ➪ Paste

Table E-7
Function Keys

Key(s)	What It Does
F1	Displays Help or the Office Assistant
Shift+F1	Displays the What's This cursor
Alt+F1	Inserts a chart sheet
Alt+Shift+ F1	Inserts a new worksheet
F2	Edits the active cell
Shift+F2	Edits a cell comment
Alt+F2	Issues Save As command
Alt+Shift+F2	Issues Save command
F3	Pastes a name into a formula
Shift+F3	Pastes a function into a formula
Ctrl+F3	Defines a name
Ctrl+Shift+F3	Displays the Creates Names dialog box, to create names using row and column labels
F4	Repeats the last action
Shift+F4	Repeats the last Find (Find Next)
Ctrl+F4	Closes the window
Alt+F4	Exits the program
F5	Displays the Go To dialog box
Shift+F5	Displays the Find dialog box
Ctrl+F5	Restores the window size

Key(s)	What It Does
F6	Moves to the next pane
Shift+F6	Moves to the previous pane
Ctrl+F6	Moves to the next window
Ctrl+Shift+F6	Moves to the previous workbook window
F7	Issues Spelling command
Ctrl+F7	Moves the window
F8	Extends a selection (toggle)
Shift+F8	Adds to the selection (toggle)
Ctrl+F8	Resizes the window
Alt+F8	Displays the Macro dialog box
F9	Calculates all sheets in all open workbooks
Shift+F9	Calculates the active worksheet
Ctrl+Alt+F9	Global calculation
Ctrl+F9	Minimizes the workbook
F10	Makes the menu bar active
Shift+F10	Displays a shortcut menu
Ctrl+F10	Maximizes or restores the workbook window
F11	Creates a chart
Shift+F11	Inserts a new worksheet
Ctrl+F11	Inserts an Excel 4.0 macro sheet
Alt+F11	Displays Visual Basic Editor
F12	Issues Save As command
Shift+F12	Issues Save command
Ctrl+F12	Issues Open command
Ctrl+Shift+F12	Issues Print command

✦   ✦   ✦

Index

Wiley Publishing, Inc.
End-User License Agreement

READ THIS. You should carefully read these terms and conditions before opening the software packet(s) included with this book "Book". This is a license agreement "Agreement" between you and Wiley Publishing, Inc. "WPI". By opening the accompanying software packet(s), you acknowledge that you have read and accept the following terms and conditions. If you do not agree and do not want to be bound by such terms and conditions, promptly return the Book and the unopened software packet(s) to the place you obtained them for a full refund.

1. **License Grant.** WPI grants to you (either an individual or entity) a nonexclusive license to use one copy of the enclosed software program(s) (collectively, the "Software," solely for your own personal or business purposes on a single computer (whether a standard computer or a workstation component of a multi-user network). The Software is in use on a computer when it is loaded into temporary memory (RAM) or installed into permanent memory (hard disk, CD-ROM, or other storage device). WPI reserves all rights not expressly granted herein.

2. **Ownership.** WPI is the owner of all right, title, and interest, including copyright, in and to the compilation of the Software recorded on the disk(s) or CD-ROM "Software Media". Copyright to the individual programs recorded on the Software Media is owned by the author or other authorized copyright owner of each program. Ownership of the Software and all proprietary rights relating thereto remain with WPI and its licensers.

3. **Restrictions On Use and Transfer.**

    (a) You may only (i) make one copy of the Software for backup or archival purposes, or (ii) transfer the Software to a single hard disk, provided that you keep the original for backup or archival purposes. You may not (i) rent or lease the Software, (ii) copy or reproduce the Software through a LAN or other network system or through any computer subscriber system or bulletin-board system, or (iii) modify, adapt, or create derivative works based on the Software.

    (b) You may not reverse engineer, decompile, or disassemble the Software. You may transfer the Software and user documentation on a permanent basis, provided that the transferee agrees to accept the terms and conditions of this Agreement and you retain no copies. If the Software is an update or has been updated, any transfer must include the most recent update and all prior versions.

4. **Restrictions on Use of Individual Programs.** You must follow the individual requirements and restrictions detailed for each individual program in the About the CD-ROM appendix of this Book. These limitations are also contained in the individual license agreements recorded on the Software Media. These limitations may include a requirement that after using the program for a specified period of time, the user must pay a registration fee or discontinue use. By opening the Software packet(s), you will be agreeing to abide by the licenses and restrictions for these individual programs that are detailed in the About the CD-ROM appendix and on the Software Media. None of the material on this Software Media or listed in this Book may ever be redistributed, in original or modified form, for commercial purposes.